The Houſe of Burgeſſes

of Virginia

Facsimile Reprint
Published 1996 By

HERITAGE BOOKS, INC.
1540E Pointer Ridge Place
Bowie, MD 20716
1-800-398-7709

ISBN 0-7884-0494-6

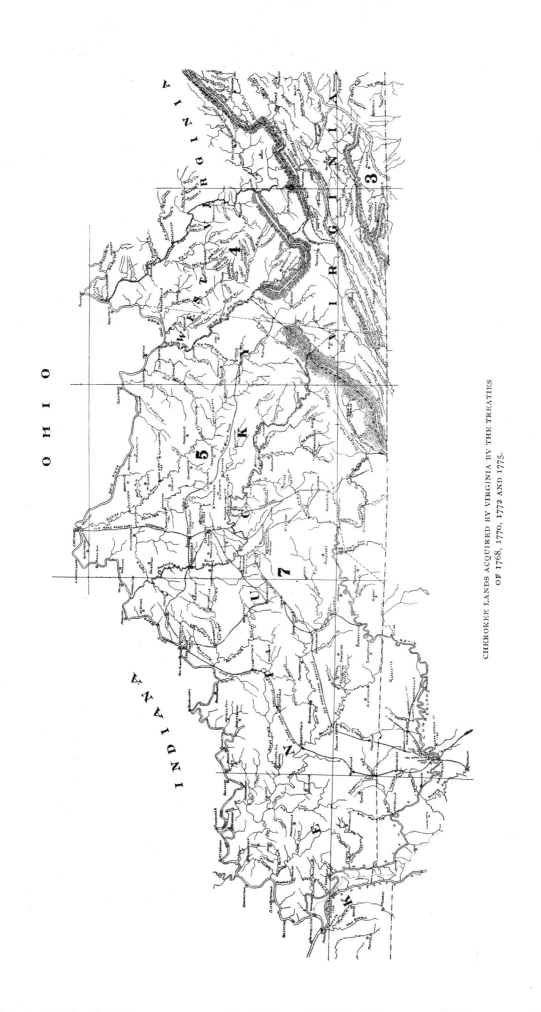

CHEROKEE LANDS ACQUIRED BY VIRGINIA BY THE TREATIES
OF 1768, 1770, 1772 AND 1775.

JOURNALS
of the
HOUSE *of* BURGESSES
of
VIRGINIA
1770-1772

Edited by
JOHN PENDLETON KENNEDY

RICHMOND, Virginia
MCMVI

CONTENTS

THE original Journal of the Houſe of Burgeſſes of *Virginia*, from *Monday* 21ſt *May* 1770, to *Thurſday* 28th of *June* of the ſame year, is bound with the *November* ſeſſion of 1769, and bears the following title; "Journal *November* 1769, *May* 1770." In printing this Journal the Public Printer continued the pagination of the 1769 ſeſſion, which contains one hundred and ſixty pages, the paging of the 1770 ſeſſion commencing with one hundred and ſixty-one and extending to two hundred and ſeventy-one. Three copies of this Journal are now in the *Virginia State Library*, one in the *Library of Congreſs*, and one in poſſeſſion of the *Philadelphia Library Company*.

The Journal of the ſeſſion beginning *Thurſday* the 11th of *July* 1771, and extending to *Saturday* the 20th of the ſame month, was originally bound with the printed "Journals 1769 to 1772." It contains twenty four pages incluſive of half title which heads page one. There is one copy of this Journal in the *Virginia State Library*.

The ſeſſion of 1772 met after ſeveral prorogations, on *Monday* the 12th day of *February*, and adjourned on *Saturday* the 11th of *April* following. This Journal is paged conſecutively from one to one hundred and ſixty-four, and, like the two preceding Journals, is bound under the following title "Journals 1769 to 1772." In addition to the two copies of this printed Journal in the *Virginia State Library*, another copy is to be found in the *Library of Congreſs*.

The large trade carried on by the Colonies with the *Indians* reached ſuch proportions in 1770, that *George* the Third determined to leave its future management to the ſeveral Aſſemblies. Prior to that time the trade had not been regulated, and the reſults were not ſatiſfactory to either of the Colonies. Acting upon inſtructions received from *Great Britain*, the various Legiſlatures proceeded to conform with the intentions of the Crown, and adopted reſolutions appointing commiſſioners to meet with thoſe of the neighboring Colonies, to perfect a ſyſtem by which the queſtion could be effectually ſettled.

John Penn, Governor of *Pennſylvania*, in his communication to Governor *Botetourt* upon this ſubject, called attention to the fact that commiſſioners had already been appointed in *New York* and *Pennſylvania*, and urged that no time be loſt in effecting ſimilar appointments in *Virginia:*

Philadelphia[1] 5th *March*, 1770.

My Lord,

> *His Majeſty having thought proper to commit the future management of the Indian Trade to the ſeveral Colonies, I beg leave to acquaint your Lordᵖ, that the Legiſlatures of* New York *and this Province have, in order to conform themſelves to His Majeſty's gracious intentions, reſpectively paſſed laws for appointing Commiſʳˢ to meet with thoſe who may be appointed by the neighbouring Colonies, to form and agree on a general plan for the Regulation of that Trade. But as the good purpoſes of this deſign cannot be effectually anſwered without the concurrence*

of

---

[1] Bancroft Tranſcripts—Library of Congreſs.

of all the Govern^{rs} concerned therein, I thought it neceffary to take the earlieft opportunity of requefting you will recommend it to your Affembly to adopt the fame
meafure, and to co-operate with the other Colonies in promoting the fuccefs of a
matter fo effential to the tranquility and profperity of the whole.

Governor Colden *informs me that he fhall lofe no time in communicating this
propofal to the Govr of* Quebec, *and I am now writing to Govr* Eden *on the fame
fubject. I have the honor to be*

Your Lord^{prs} moft obedient humble fervant,
JOHN PENN.

His Excell^{cy} the R^t Honble Lord Botetourt.

Replying to this communication, Governor *Botetourt* announced his intention of
laying the matter before the next Affembly, at which time he would communicate
their decifion:

Williamfburg[1], March, 1770.

*I have received your Excellcys letter dated March 5th together with an Act of
Affembly paffed by your Province, entitled: "An Act for appointing Commiff^{rs}
to meet with Commiffioners who are or may be appointed by the Legiflatures of
the Neighbouring Colonies, to form and agree on a general plan for the regulation
of the Indian Trade." I will lay them both before the Affembly of this Dominion, when they meet in May next, and will report their determinations as immediately as poffible. I have the honour to be*

Your Excellency's very obedient humble fervant
BOTETOURT.

John Penn, Governor of Pennfylvania

The matter of trade with the *Indians* was foon overfhadowed by the queftion of
extenfion of the Weftern boundary, which attracted fo much attention, both in *Virginia*
and *England*, as to prevent, for the time being, a difcuffion of the inter-colonial affairs.
The queftion of this particular purchafe was firft difcuffed in 1769, at which time a
memorial to the King, fetting forth the advantages to be derived by an acceffion of territory, was prefented to Governor *Botetourt*, and forwarded by his direction to Lord
Hillfborough.

In this extended Memorial of *Wednefday, December 13, 1769*, attention was called
to the fact that *John Stuart*, Superintendent of the *Indian* Affairs in the Southern Department, had propofed a fomewhat limited acquifition of Indian lands, which, in the
judgment of the Affembly, would not meet the requirements of the Colony. The bounds[2]
as propofed by this officer extended from the "interfection of *Holfton's* River, a Point,
which would terminate the Line dividing this Colony from *North Carolina* to the Mouth
of the Great *Kanhaway*."

The Burgeffes reprefented that this line, as propofed, would be about "Two Hundred
Miles in Length, and muft pafs through a Country abounding with high and rugged
Mountains, extremely difficult and Dangerous of Accefs, and interfected by many
water Courfes." They further reported that, in "eftablifhing this Line, the great Part of
the valuable Country lying on the *Ohio*, below the Mouth of the Great *Kanhaway*, which
had recently been ceded to the Crown by Northern *Indians* would be feparated from
other royal Poffeffions in that Section, and that it would be impoffible to eftablifh
fettlements in that fertile and extenfive country."

To his **Excellency** *the Right Honourable* **Norborne.** *Baron de* **Botetourt.**
*his Majefty's Lieutenant and Governor General, and Commander in Chief
of the Colony and Dominion of* **Virginia.** *and Vice Admiral of the fame.*

My Lord[3],

*We his Majefty's moft dutiful and loyal Subjects, the Burgeffes of Virginia,
having agreeable to our former Affurances, maturely and deliberately confidered
your Excellency's Speech beg Leave to renew our unfeigned Thanks for his Majefty's
kind*

[1] Bancroft Tranfcripts—Library of Congrefs.   [3] Journal Houfe of Burgeffes, December, 13, 1769.
[2] *See* Map, alfo Fifth Annual Report of the Bureau of Ethnology pp. 121-378.

kind Attention to the Interefts of this Colony, in fo readily approving the Report of the Right Honourable the Board of Trade and Plantations, in Favour of a more extended Boundary to the Weftward. We are perfuaded that his Majefty's fole Motive for fo doing arofe from his moft gracious Inclination to promote the Security and Happinefs of his dutiful Subjects; but permit us, my Lord, with all Humility and Deference to his Royal Wifdom, by an humble Memorial, to exprefs our Apprehenfions that his Majefty hath not yet been made properly and fully acquainted with the true Situation of our Frontiers; and fuffer us to intreat your Lordfhip, that you will be pleafed to lay before our Royal Sovereign a more perfect State of the Matter, and endeavor to procure for this Colony fuch farther Indulgencies, in enlarging its Boundary, as to his Majefty, in his great Wifdom, may feem juft and right. On our Parts, we do affure your Excellency, that we fhall, at all Times, be ready and willing chearfully to comply with every Requifition in our Power, that may tend to promote the Honour and Dignity of his Majefty's Crown, the Extenfion of his Dominions, and the true Interefts of this Colony.

But, if, unfortunately for this Colony, his Majefty hath already taken his ultimate Refolution to confine his Subjects to the Line propofed by your Excellency, we muft humbly acquiefce, and will furnifh the Two Thoufand Five Hundred Pounds Sterling, according to the Eftimate you have been pleafed to communicate to us. And the faid Memorial is as followeth, *viz.*

The MEMORIAL of the HOUSE of BURGESSES,

Humbly Reprefents,
That your Memorialifts having paid the earlieft Attention to your Lordfhip's Speech at the Opening of this Seffion, have taken under their moft ferious Confideration that very interefting Part of it which relates to the Report of the Right Honourable the Board of Trade and Plantations to his Majefty, refpecting the Extenfion of the Boundary of this Colony to the Weftward; and as your Memorialifts are extremely folicitous on all Occafions, to ftand fair in the Royal Opinion of their moft gracious Sovereign, they humbly prefume to lay before your Excellency their Reafons for not immediately complying with his Majefty's Requifition, communicated to them by your Lordfhip in fuch very polite and engaging Terms.

Senfible as your Memorialifts are of the many fignal Advantages which would redound as well to his Majefty as to feveral of his American Colonies, they fhould think themfelves blind to their Duty and Interefts if they did not receive, with all Thankfulnefs, your Lordfhip's Information of the Benefits intended to them by his Majefty's gracious Approval of a more extended Boundary, than had been propofed by the Superintendent of Indian Affairs in the Southern Department; but they flatter themfelves that a Revifion of the Subject, if his Majefty would once more be pleafed to condefcend to take it under his Princely Confideration, would convince his Majefty that his moft gracious Purpofe cannot be anfwered by eftablifhing the Line propofed.

Your Memorialifts beg Leave to obferve that the faid Line, if extended from the Interfection of Holfton's *River, the Point, which would terminate the Line dividing this Colony from* North Carolina *to the Mouth of the Great* Kanhaway, *would be near Two Hundred Miles in Length, and muft pafs through a Country abounding with high and rugged Mountains, extremely difficult and dangerous of Accefs, and interfected by many Water Courfes; that the prefent Pofture of Indian Affairs would make a ftrong Guard of armed Men neceffary for the Protection of thofe who might be commiffioned to run fuch a Line, as it muft neceffarily pafs through a Country uninhabited, and through which thofe Indians who feem at prefent moft inclined to Hoftilities, do frequently take their Routs;*

That by eftablifhing fuch Line, a great Part of that moft valuable Country, lying on the Ohio, *below the Mouth of the great* Kanhaway, *lately ceded to his Majefty by the Northern Indians, would be feparated and divided from the* Britifh *Territory, on the upper Part of* Holfton's *River, the great* Kanhaway, *and the* Ohio, *which your Memorialifts humbly conceive muft greatly impede, and may totally prevent the Settlement of that fertile and extenfive Country, which, from its*

Situation

Situation and many natural Advantages, would open the fairest Prospect of a very beneficial Commerce to our Mother Country, by securing to his Majesty's Subjects a new and extensive Trade with the several Tribes of Western Indians, which has hitherto been almost engroffed by the Subjects of France; *and by this Means many Indian Nations, heretofore living at Enmity with our most gracious Sovereign and his Subjects, might be made friendly and useful in extending the Trade and Navigation of* Great-Britain.

That your Memorialists have the greatest Reason to fear that the said Line, if confirmed, would constantly open to the Indians and others, Enemies to his Majesty, a free and easy Ingress to the Heart of the Country, on the Ohio, Holston's *River, and the great* Kanhaway, *whereby the Settlements, which may be attempted in those Quarters, will, in all Probability, be utterly destroyed, and that great Extent of Country, from the Mouth of the* Kanhaway *to the Mouth of the* Cherokee *River, extending Eastward as far as the* Laurel Hills, *so very lately ceded to his Majesty, and to which no Tribe of Indians, at present, sets up any Pretensions, will be entirely abandoned to the* Cherokees; *in Consequence of which Claims totally destructive of the true Interests of his Majesty, may, at some future Time arise, and Acquisitions justly ranked amongst the most valuable of the late war, be altogether lost.*

Your Memorialists further beg Leave to represent to your Lordship, that Lands, which have been granted by Patents regularly obtained, according to the known and fixed Rules of this Government, if the said Line were to take Place, would be entirely dismembered from this Colony, allotted to the Indians, and entirely lost to the Proprietors, who were authorized by Law, and encouraged by the Royal Instruction of his late Majesty to his Governor, to explore and settle this new Country at the Risque of their Lives, and at a great Expence.

Your Memorialists, from these weighty Considerations, have been induced to extend their Views, and do humbly offer, as their Opinions, that a Line beginning at the Western Termination of the North-Carolina *Line, and running thence in a due West Direction to the River* Ohio, *may be accomplished at a much less Expence than the other Line proposed; that the Extension of such a Line is necessary for the Safety and Advantage of his Majesty's Subjects, and that it would tend greatly to the Increase of his Majesty's Revenue, and to the Promotion of the Trade and Navigation of the Western Part of this Dominion, if a Purchase were made of the* Cherokee *Indians of all their Lands, which such due Western Line would include; especially if his Majesty would be graciously pleased, in his Royal Wisdom, to discourage all Monopolies of those Lands, and strengthen our Barrier, by granting them, in small or moderate Quantities, to such Adventurers as might incline to seat and settle the same.*

Your Memorialists, for the better Illustration of the foregoing Observations, beg Leave to lay before your Excellency as exact and perfect a Plan of that Part of the Country as they at present are able to procure, and humbly submit the whole Matter to your Excellency's Judgment.

From such Representation as your Excellency may think fit to make, we presume to flatter ourselves that his Majesty will be graciously pleased to order a Suspension of any other Line that may affect the very numerous Settlements of his Subjects to the Eastward of that now proposed, till the Matter is reconsidered, and fully and clearly understood.

On *December* 18th, 1769, Lord *Botetourt* enclosed a copy of the Memorial of the House of Burgesses concerning the boundary line, to *John Stuart,* then at *Charles Town, S. C.:*

Williamsburg[1] *Dec.* 18th 1769.

Sir

I have inclosed copies of an Address and Memorial from the House of Burgesses by which you will perceive that they have agreed to the Requisition I have had the honour

---

[1] Bancroft Transcripts, 1768—1776—Library of Congress.

honour to make to them by command from the King, but at the same time that they pray for a more extended Boundary than that you have recommended, and intreat that I will again implore His Majesty to reconsider the merits of their humble Petition. In consequence of that their desire I have wrote the Earl of Hillsborough and earnestly solicited that they may be indulged to the extent of their wishes. I have likewise acquainted him that I have intreated you not to take a step towards running any line until you shall have had fresh instructions from His Lordship. It remains that I beg your assistance towards compleating this great work, but should you deem giving that assistance inconsistent with your duty, shall be obliged to you for your reasons why this Colony may not be allowed to purchase from the Indians a most desirable country, which would in time add very greatly to the value of His Majesty's Quit-Rents. I have the honour to be Sir
Your very obedient humble Servant
BOTETOURT.

Mr Stuart Superintendent of Indian Affairs.

Replying to this communication, *Stuart* set forth his reasons in detail for his proposed line, and called attention to the Earl of *Hillsborough's* letter[1] of the 13th of *May* 1769, which alluded to the report of the Board of Trade, concerning boundaries, and had been approved by the Crown:

Charles Town[1], 13 *January*, 1770.

My Lord
I am honoured with your Excellencys letter of 18th December with the address and memorial of the House of Burgesses of the Colony of Virginia, praying for a greater extent of Boundary than that pointed out in the report of the Right Honourable the Board of Trade and directed by His Majesty to be ratified, and marked, as signified by the Earl of Hillsborough, in his letter of 13th May, 1769.

I must beg your Lordship will be perswaded that in negotiating a Boundary Line between the Indian Nations and the different Provinces, I have been solely actuated by principles of duty in conforming as nearly as possible to His Majesty's ideas and orders, so fully and clearly expressed in his additional instructions to all his Governors in 1761, by his Royal Proclamation of 7 October 1763, and by his orders relative to the report of his Board of Trade, contained in the Earl of Hillsborough's letter of 15 April 1768, which evince his most gracious purpose of protecting and rendering strict justice to the Indians, thereby to remove their jealousies and apprehensions, which our encroachments on their Hunting Grounds too well justified, and from which that dissatisfaction and hostile disposition which proved so expensive and destructive to His Majesty's subjects, principally arose. I am therefore extremely mortified, when from these considerations my reasoning on the subject of a more extended Boundary must differ from that of so respectable a body as the House of Burgesses of the Dominion of Virginia whose views and wishes I can have no motive to obstruct or oppose, except what arises from an earnest desire faithfully to discharge the trust reposed in me.

I beg your Lordship's permission to represent that from the knowledge of the disposition of the Indian tribes within the Southern District, which my office of Superintendent has enabled me to acquire, I am perswaded the Cherokees will never consent to give up the territory pointed at in your Assembly's memorial, because

First. A continuation of the Line dividing your Colony and North Carolina, from the point where it intersects Holsten's River, in a due Western course, can never touch the Ohio, but will run within less than sixty miles of the Cherokee towns, and fall upon the Cherokee River a little below Chuola or the Chickasaw landing.

Second. Said Line would cut off from the Cherokees and Chickasaws their only valuable Hunting Grounds, it being a fact well known, that they always hunt

at

1 Bancroft Transcripts 1768-8776—Library of Congress.

at the diftance of one or two hundred miles from their villages for an obvious reafon, the fcarcity of deer near the dwellings of a nation of Hunters.

Third. Befides the diftrefs which the Cherokees *and* Chickafaws *would certainly be fubjected to by the lofs of their Hunting Grounds, the fettlement of thefe lands by adventurers from your Colony, who are likewife hunters and in other refpects difagreeable to the Indians, would prove an infurmountable obftacle.*

Thefe difficultys, my Lord, would operate immediately with the Cherokees *and* Chickafaws; *but the jealoufies and apprehenfions of every Tribe on the Continent, efpecially of thofe within this Diftrict, would be again revived by fuch an extenfion of territory, altho' they are almoft effaced by His Majefty's having moft gracioufly directed to fettle and mark diftinct Boundaries; and in whatever manner the Ceffion pointed at in the Memorial might be obtained from the* Cherokees, *there is the greateft reafon to apprehend that it would be productive of a general rupture with, and coalition of, all the Tribes on the Continent; for however Indians may quarrel amongft themfelves, yet an encroachment on the lands of any Nation becomes a common caufe, and attracts the attention of the whole.*

The Creek Nation, *confifting of four thoufand gun men have lately complained to me of Settlement being made by emigrants from* Virginia *on the unceded lands on the* Miffiffipi, *the* Chickafaws *and* Choctaws *are more immediately affected by fuch fettlements, and alfo exprefs their uneafinefs. At this very time there are in the* Creek Nation, Deputies *from the* Shawnefe, Delawares *and other Northern Tribes, accompanied by fome* Cherokees, *endeavouring to form a general confederacy on the principle of defending their lands from our daily encroachments. The principal Chiefs of the* Cherokee Nation *fent me the enclofed meffage in* July laft, *and immediately afterwards* Ouconnaftotah *the principal leader fet out with 30 canoes of armed men, to reconnoitre the fettlements on* Holften's River, *and fee how far your inhabitants had extended beyond the line agreed upon by treaty in* November 1768. *Thefe circumftances appear to be worthy your Excellency's attention, and I hope will ferve to evince the propriety of my declining to recommend the propofed extenfion: and here permit me my Lord to exprefs my great forrow for being obliged to refufe my affiftance, of whatever weight it may be, in obtaining for the Colony of* Virginia *a Boundary to the extent of their wifhes. My fentiments on the propofal I fhall candidly fubmit to his Majefty's Minifters, and be extremely happy in carrying whatever orders they may think proper to give me relative to it, into execution.*

I hope your Lordfhip will think it for the good of His Majefty's fervice to reftrain adventurers from your Colony from fettling beyond the Line already agreed upon, untill His Majefty's ultimate orders can be received.

From the fuppofition in the Memorial that the Line therein propofed would fall upon the Ohio, *I muft conclude the plan referred to, to be erroneous, for the Divifion Line between* Virginia *and* North Carolina *appears by the Map to be in 36″ 30ᵐ. the* Cherokee Towns *are fituated between 35ᵈ and 35″ 40ᵐ.*

I inclofe your Lordfhip my bill on his Excellency Genˡ Gage *for the amount of the Bill of Expences contracted by direction of Mʳ* Cameron; *and I have the honour to be with the greateft refpect My Lord*

Your Excellency's moft obedient and moft humble fervant

JOHN STUART.

His Excellᶜʸ the Rᵗ Honᵇˡᵉ Lord Botetourt.

P. S. I have chofen rather to fend my bill upon my Agent at New York *for the amount of the Bill of expences above mentioned being £33* York *currency, which will certainly be paid duly. The abftract of the Additional Inftruction and Proclamation I fend merely to fave your Lordfhip the trouble of looking for the original.*

Replying to this communication, on *February* 8th[1] following Lord *Botetourt* ftated to Mʳ *Stuart* that he entirely agreed with the objections outlined by him, fo far as the acquifition of territory without the confent of the *Indians* was concerned. He flattered
himfelf

---

[1] Bancroft Tranfcripts, 1768-1776—Library of Congrefs.

himfelf, however, that his Majefty's fervants would be convinced of the neceffity of acquiring fuch territory, and he trufted that all officers of the colony would render their affiftance in bringing about a fatiffactory refult. The Affembly meeting on *May* 21ᶜᵗ, the Governor laid before them certain papers bearing upon *Indian* affairs, and on the 30ᵗʰ of *May* following prefented for their confideration other papers appertaining to the Weftern boundary, including letters from *John Stuart*, Superintendent of the Southern Department.

Thefe papers were referred to a Committee, and on *Friday* the 15ᵗʰ day of *June* following, a refolution concerning the boundary line was agreed upon. In reaching this conclufion it was neceffary for the Burgeffes to recede from their former pofition. This they determined to do, owing to the conftant menace to frontier interefts refulting from the difquietude of the *Indians*:

Refolved,[1] That it is the Opinion of this Committee, that it may be extremely Dangerous to the unhappy People who may Settle beyond the Lines fixed on by the Superintendent of *Indian* Affairs as Limits between the *Cherokees* and this Colony, to Delay any longer entering upon a Negotiation for a more extenfive Boundary, which his Majefty has approved of, and that an humble Addrefs be prefented to his Excellency the Governor, to defire that he would immediately take fuch Steps as were neceffary for entering upon a Treaty with the *Cherokees*, for the Lands lying within a Line to be run from a Place where the *North Carolina* Line terminates, in a due Weft direction, until it interfects *Holftein* River, and from thence to the Mouth of the Great *Kanhaway*, and that he will be Pleafed when a Ceffion of thefe Lands fhould be obtained, to proceed to Mark and to Eftablifh that Boundary.

Lord *Botetourt* immediately communicated a copy of the refolution of the Affembly to Mʳ *Stuart*, urging him to enter into an early treaty with the *Cherokees*, in order to fecure as foon as poffible a fixed boundary between their poffeffions and thofe of the Colony of *Virginia*:

Williamfburg[2], 21 *June*, 1770.

Sir

Being authorized by the inclofed Addrefs of the Houfe of Burgeffes, His Majefty's gracious permiffion and your letter of the third of Auguft 1769, *I earneftly intreat that you do immediately enter upon a treaty with the* Cherokees *in order to obtain, as foon as poffible, for this dominion, a ceffion of thofe lands to which His Majefty has been pleafed to confent, upon conditions which have been agreed to by the Legiflature of this Country.*

I muft likewife beg that you fend me an account of the feveral goods and fums of money which will be wanted for compleating this great work, fpecifying as near as may be the expence of each particular fervice; with the time and manner in which you would wifh to have them paid; as alfo what affiftance you will want from hence in running the Line, when it fhall have been agreed to, with the exact time when it will be wanted. You may depend upon the greateft punctuality in the courfe of this tranfaction. The whole expence muft come within the £2500 stirling, which have been granted by this Government in confequence of your own eftimate. The higher the favings the more we fhall be obliged to you.

I congratulate you on your being appointed a Counfellor Extraordinary of the Dominion and Colony of Virginia: *will fend by* 1ˡᵗ *opportunity a copy of this letter to the Earl of* Hillfborough, *and have the honour to be, Sir*
Your very obedient humble Servᵗ.

BOTETOURT.

Hon. Jⁿ Stuart Efq. Superintendent for Indian Affairs.

Acting

---
1 Journal Houfe of Burgeffes, June 15, 1770.
2 Bancroft Tranfcripts, 1768-1776—Library of Congrefs.

Acting under inftructions from Governor *Botetourt*, *Stuart*, who was then at *Charles Town*, replied[1] under date of *July* 12th that a convention of the *Cherokee* Chiefs would be held at *Lochabar* on the 5th of *October* following, and that the queftion of ceffion of lands would be taken up at that time. The Governor was apprifed at the fame time that the £2500 fet afide for the purchafe of *Cherokee* lands would not be fufficient to accomplifh the ends of the Colony, and that an additional of £400 fterling fhould be appropriated for this purpofe. Lord *Botetourt* at once communicated to the Earl of *Hillfborough* the contents of *Stuart's* letter, and notified him of his decifion to extract additional funds needed from his Majefty's Quit-Rents:

> Sir
>
> Mr Stuart *having in the inclofed anfwer to my exprefs acquainted me that near 400£ fterling, more than his original eftimate, would be wanting, in order to enable him to compleat the purchafe of thofe lands from the Indians, to which the King has been gracioufly pleafed to confent; I have prefumed to draw upon His Majefty's Quit Rents for that fum, as I could not otherwife have made good to the feveral branches of this Legiflature the promife I thought myfelf authorized to make. Shoud your Lordfhip be of a different opinion, I will immediately anfwer your draught for 400, out of my private fortune, as I wou'd rather forfeit the whole than be guilty of even the appearance of deceit.*
>
> *I have the honour to be*
> *Your Lordfhip's moft devoted humble Servant*
> BOTETOURT
>
> *Williamfburg*[1] *Aug.* 10th, 1770.
> *E. of Hillfborough.*

Replying, a month later, to *Stuart's* communication of *July* 12th, Governor *Botetourt* authorized him to draw upon Mefs. *Norton & Son* of *London* for £2900 fterling, the amount fet by him for the purchafe of *Cherokee* lands.

> *Williamfburg,*[1] *Aug.* 9th, 1770.
>
> Sir
>
> *I have inclofed to you an authority to draw upon Meffrs Norton and Son in London for £2900 Stirling by which you will perceive that the 384. 17. 6. which you have defired, together with £15. in order to enable you to purchafe gold by bills for 300 are both added to the eftimate of £2500 with which you originally engaged to procure for this dominion from the Indians thofe lands, to the purchafe of which His Majefty has been gracioufly pleafed to confent. I have likewife appointed Col. Donelfon a member of the Houfe of Burgeffes to meet you at Lochaber upon Friday the 5th of October that he may be able to report from view, to our General Affembly, the whole of that tranfaction, may fix with you a proper time for running the Line and may be inftructed in the knowledge of every thing which will be wanted for that material purpofe.*
>
> *I am extremely pleafed with the affurance you have given me that the ftricteft economy fhall be obferved; and as it has ever been the firft object of my life to be remarkable for good faith and punctuality, I fhall depend upon you in the prefent inftance for that credit with the Indians which my actions fhall deferve.*
>
> *I will be anfwerable that Meffrs. Norton and Son will pay due honour to your Bills for 2900 fterling.*
>
> *Extremely your obedient*
> BOTETOURT.
>
> *Hon. John Stuart Efqr.*

On the 18th day of *October* following, a congrefs of the leading Chiefs of the *Cherokee* Nation was held at *Lochaber* in the province of *South Carolina*, and the treaty negotiated

between

---

[1] Bancroft Tranfcripts, 1768-1776—Library of Congrefs.

between the *Cherokee* Nation and *Great Britain*. A copy of the deed of cession, refulting from this convention, was delivered to Colonel *Donelfon*[1], a reprefentative appointed by Lord *Botetourt* to be prefent upon that occafion, and forwarded by him to Governor *Nelfon* at *Williamfburg:*

𝕿𝖗𝖊𝖆𝖙𝖞 𝖂𝖎𝖙𝖍 𝖙𝖍𝖊 𝕮𝖍𝖊𝖗𝖔𝖐𝖊𝖊 𝕴𝖓𝖉𝖎𝖆𝖓𝖘[2]

SOUTH CAROLINA,

At a Congrefs of the Principal Chiefs of the *Cherokee* Nation held at *Lochaber* in the Province of *South Carolina* on the eighteenth day of *October* in the year of our Lord one thoufand feven hundred and feventy, by *John Stuart* Efq^r. agent for and Superintendant of the affairs of the *Indian* Nations in the Southern Diftrict of *North America.*

A Treaty for a ceffion to His Moft facred Majefty *George* the Third by the Grace of *God*, of *Great Britain, France* and *Ireland* King, Defender of the Faith &c. By the faid Nation of *Cherokee* Indians of certain lands lying within the limits of the Dominion of *Virginia.*

Whereas, by a treaty entered into and concluded at *Hard Labour* the fourteenth day of *October* in the Year one thoufand feven hundred and fixty eight by *John Stuart* Efq^r. His Majefty's Agent for and Superintendent of the affairs of the *Indian* Nations inhabiting the Southern Diftrict of *North America*, with the principal and ruling chiefs of the *Cherokee* Nation, all the Lands formerly claimed by and belonging to faid Nation of *Indians* lying in the Province of *Virginia* to the Eaftward of a Line beginning at the Boundary of the province of *North Carolina* and *Virginia*, running in a N. B. E. courfe to Col. *Chifwells* mine on the Eaftern Bank of the great *Conhoway* and from thence in a ftraight Line to the Mouth of the faid Great *Conhoway* River where it difcharged itfelf into the *Ohio* River were ceded to His Moft Sacred Majefty his heirs fucceffors; and *Whereas* by the above recited Treaty all the lands lying between *Holfton's* River and the line above fpecified were determined to belong to the *Cherokee* Nation to the great lofs and inconveniency of many of His Majefty's fubjects inhabiting the faid lands; and reprefentation of the fame having been made to His Majefty by His Excellency the Right Hon^bl. *Norborne* Baron de *Botetourt* His Majefty's Lieutenant and Governor General of the Dominion of *Virginia*, in confequence whereof His Majefty has been gracioufly pleafed to fignify His royal pleafure to *John Stuart* Efq^r. his agent for and Superintendant of *Indian* affairs in the Southern Diftrict of *North America*, by an injunction contained in a letter from the Right Hon^bl. the Earl of *Hillfborough* one of his Principal Secretaries of State dated the 13th *May* 1769 to enter into a Negotiation with the *Cherokees* for eftablifhing a New Boundary Line, Beginning at the Point where the *North Carolina* Line terminates and to run thence in a Weft Courfe to *Holfton's* River, where it is interfected by a continuation of the Line dividing the Provinces of *North Carolina* and *Virginia*, and thence a ftraight courfe to the confluence of the Great *Conhoway* and *Ohio* Rivers.

Article 1^ft Purfuant therefore to His Majefty's orders to and power and authority vefted in *John Stuart,* Efq^r agent for and Superintendant of the affairs of the *Indian* Tribes in the Southern Diftrict, It is agreed upon by the faid *John Stuart* Efquire, on behalf of His Moft Sacred Majefty *George* the Third, by the Grace of *God* of *Great Britain, France* and *Ireland*, King, Defender of the Faith &c. and by the fubfcribing *Cherokee* Chiefs and warriors on behalf of their faid Nation,in confideration of His Majefty's paternal goodnefs fo often demonftrated to them the faid *Cherokee Indians*, and from the affection and friendfhip for their Brethren the inhabitants of *Virginia*,as well as their earneft defire of removing as far as poffible all caufe of difpute between them and the faid inhabitants, on account of encroachment or lands referved by the faid *Indians* for themfelves, and alfo for a valuable confideration in various forts of goods paid to

them

---

[1] Member of the Houfe of Burgeffes from Pittfylvania County.   [2] Cherokee Mfs.—Virginia State Library.

them by the faid *John Stuart* Efq. on behalf of the Dominion of *Virginia*. That the hereafter recited Line be ratified and confirmed, and it is hereby ratified and confirmed accordingly, and it is by thefe prefents firmly ftipulated and agreed upon by the parties aforefaid, that a Line beginning where the Boundary Line between the Province of *North Carolina* and the *Cherokee* hunting grounds terminates, and running thence in a Weft Courfe to a point fix miles Eaft of *Long Ifland* in *Holften's* River, and thence to faid River fix miles above the faid *Long Ifland*, and thence in a direct courfe to the confluence of the Great *Conhoway* and *Ohio* Rivers, fhall remain and be deemed by all His Majefty's white Subjects as well as all the *Indians* of the *Cherokee* Nation, the true and juft limits and Boundaries of the lands referved by the faid Nation of *Indians* for their own proper ufe, and dividing the fame from the Lands ceded by them to His Majefty, within the limits of the Province of *Virginia*, and that His Majefty's white fubjects inhabiting the Province of *Virginia* fhall not, upon any pretence whatfoever fettle beyond the faid Line, nor fhall the faid *Indians* make any fettlements or encroachment on the Lands which by this Treaty they cede and confirm to His Majefty; and it is further agreed that as foon as His Majefty's Royall approbation of this Treaty fhall have been fignified to the Governor of *Virginia* or Superintendant, this Treaty fhall be carried into execution.

Article IInd. And it is further agreed upon and ftipulated by the contracting parties, that no alteration whatfoever fhall hence forward be made in the Boundary Line above recited and now folemnly agreed upon, except fuch as may hereafter be found expedient and neceffary for the material intereft of both parties, and which alteration fhall be made with the confent of the Superintendant, or fuch other perfon or perfons as fhall be authorized by His Majefty as well as with the Confent and approbation of the *Cherokee* Nation of *Indians*, at a congrefs or General meeting of faid Indians to be held for faid purpofe, and not in any other manner. In teftimony whereof the faid Superintendant on behalf of His Majefty, and the underwritten *Cherokee* Chiefs on behalf of their Nation, have figned and fealed this prefent Treaty at the time and place aforefaid.

(Signed)

JOHN STUART.

(Signed)

Anconaftotah's mark
Killagufta's mark
Attahkullakullah's mark
Kayaloy's mark
Kinnatitah's mark
Uka Youla's mark
Chukannuta's mark
Skyagufta Tuechkee's mark
Wolf of Kefwee's mark
Skyagufta Tefloy's mark
Turrapenis mark
Enry of Tugalo's mark
Scalelufky of Sugar Town's mark
Chiniftah of Sugar Town's mark
Chiniftah of Watoga's Mark
Otafite Keywaffee's Mark

Copy,

Tefte *JOHN BLAIR, JR.*

Early

Early in 1770 *Edward Montagu, London* Agent for the colony of *Virginia*, advifed the Committee of Correfpondence, that one of the Lords of the Treafury had reported to him that certain gentlemen were fecuring a grant of land in the fection recently ceded by the *Cherokees* to the Crown.

London¹ Janʳʸ. 18, 1770

Gent.

I have juft received Intelligence from one of the Lords of the Treafury that a Body of very refpectable and opulent Gentlemen have made a Propofal and offer'd a fatiffactory Sum for the Grant of Lands in your Colony which form the Frontier; from the beft Difcription I can get, "They are to the Southward Weftward of the Pennfylvania *Line, down the* Ohio *to the Mouth of the big* Canhaway *with the main Branches of the faid River to the Mountains—then with the Mountains to the Chief Waters of the River* Monongahela *and with them to the beginning.*

It is propofed to erect a feparate Government, and leaft it shoᵈ operate in any Degree to your Injuries, collectively or individually, I have enter'd a Caveat at the Board of Trade to whom, It will of Courfe be refer'd for Confideration. When it comes then I fhall devife a Sufpenfion of the Plan till you have Notice of it, and can tranfmit to me your Approbation or Objection. I find that one of the great Inducements to the Treafuryˢ Affent to the Propofition is that the Diftances of this Country is fo great from the prefent Seat of Government, that Juftice and Order can never take Place (shoᵈ. it be completely fettled,) without forming a new Government there.

I have the Honor to be
Gent.
Yʳ. moft obedient humble Servᵗ.

EDW. MONTAGU.

At the fame time *Montagu* addreffed¹ the Lords of Commerce and Trade upon this queftion of land ceffions, and called attention to the fact that he underftood that a grant had already been given of 1,350,000 acres of land to feveral gentlemen who termed themfelves the "*Ohio Company.*" This letter which bears no date, was moft likely written during the latter part of *January,* or about the fame time the communication was addreffed to the Committee of Correfpondence:

To the Rᵗ. Honᵇˡ. Lords Comⁱˢ. for Trade & Plantⁿ.
The humble Petitⁿ. of Edwᵈ. Montagu
Agent for Virgᵃ.

Sheweth

That your Petʳ. is informed "An Application has been made to the Rᵗ. Honᵇˡᵉ. Lords of Treafury for a Grant of certain Lands in part of his Majeftyˢ. Colony & Dominion of Virginia" That the Confideration tendr'd to their Lordᵖˢ. is fatiffactory and that fuch Propofition is refer'd to your Lordᵖˢ for your Deliberation as to the Policy & Expediency of fuch a Meafure, and whether it may not be neceffary to fever fuch Lands from the faid Colony and erect a new and diftinct Governmᵗ. thereof.

That Yʳ. Petʳ. is advifed no lefs than 1,350,000 Acres of fuch Land has been already granted, partly to a Society of Gentlemen called the Ohio Company, *and partly to Individuals of that Colony, who cauſe'd the fame to be furvey'd, and before the Comencemᵗ. of the late War had made fome Progrefs in the Setling and Cultivation thereof, but having been driven from their Poffeffions by the Indians and fince reftrain'd from returning by his Majeftyˢ. Proclamation they have not yet been reftor'd to their juft Rights.*

That your Petʳ. conceiving his Conftituents totally ignorant of fuch Application to the Lords Treafury, and that their Lordfhips are informed of the Circumftances above ftated, humbly fubmits it to your Lordfhips Wifdom & Juftice whether

before

¹ Montagu Correfpondence—Virginia State Library.

*before any farther Proceeding is had on the Subject refer'd to your Lordships to
the Colony of Virginia shoᵈ. not have Notice, and Time given to offer such Objections
as may occur agˡᵗ. the Completion of such Grant.*

*Yʳ. Petʳ. therefore humbly prays Yʳ. Lordᵖˢ. will represent to the Lords
of Treasury that it seems reasonable and just the Colʸ of Virginia Shoᵈ.
have Advice of an Application which if approved woᵈ. be attended with
a Severence of so large a part of its Dominion and affect the Rights of
many who under Grants already obtained conceive themselves entitled to
so large a Portion of the Lands apply'd for.*

E. M.

Again on *Feb.* 6ᵗʰ, 1770, *Montagu* forwarded a communication[1] to the Committee of
Correspondence, in which he referred to his previous letters concerning the grant of the
Ohio Company, and mentioned his protest to the Board of Trade upon the matter in
question:

London Febʸ. 6, 1770.

Gentlemen:

*My two last Letters to you were of the 10ᵗʰ and 18ᵗʰ of Janʳʸ. the first attended
with the Kings Speech on meeting his Parliamᵗ. the other relating to an Application
to the Treasury for a Grant of a very large Tract of your Lands that form your
Frontier. Very great and opulent Persons are combined in this Attempt, and it
has been conducted with so much Secrecy, that till this Treasury, had agreed on the
Consideration, no body knew of the Negotiation. The Instant I discovered it, I
enter'd my Caveat at the Board of Trade. The Proposition is now arrived there
for Consideration as to the Policy of the Design. I have presented my Petition of
which I send you a Copy, and as I have no Doubt of its Effect, you will be so good
to furnish me with your Objections in Case you think the Plan liable to any.*

*Not a Word yet has passed in Parliament about the American Grievances.
The only Object of Attention is the Middlesex Election. Our Merchants in London
have been extreme shy, and very unwilling to take the Lead in an Affair, as inter-
esting to them as America. We have prevailed on the Gentlemen of Bristol to begin.
They had a meeting, and have transmitted to one of their Representatives an Account
of conditional Orders from North America to the Amount of £200,000. The
Londoners have at last followed their Example and at a very numerous Meeting
last Week unanimously resolved to petition the House of Commons for a Repeal
of the Act that imposes Duties on Paper, Glass, Painters Colours and Tea. They
have likewise collected the several Amounts of the conditᴵ. Orders which when produced to the Publick must be alarming. Today, (if no other Business interferes)
Lord North intends to move for Repeal of so much of the Act as extends to the three
first Articles, retaining the odious Preeamble and the Duty on Tea. If the Debate
is carry'd on dispassionately, I have no Doubt about a total Repeal, but if Abuse
Invective shoᵈ start, the Metal of both sides of House is so violent, that I fear their
own true Interest will be forgot.*

*Two Events of Importance have happen'd in this Country since my Letter.
The Death of the new Chancellor Mʳ Yorke within three days after his appointment, and the sudden and unexpected Resignation of the Duke of Grafton.*

*I intend this by the New York to morrow, if your Business comes on in the
House to day I shall add what may occur.*

*The Parlᵗ. have passed a Bill to allow Ireland and America to continue their
Importation of Provision in England Duty free.*

I am

Gentˢ. with great Respect
Yʳ. very obedᵗ. faithfull Servᵗ.

EDWD. MONTAGU

P. S. Pontffract *Election came on to day, and nothing was done in America*
Business

Bufinefs, but preventing the merchants Petition, which is ordered for Confideration on Monday.

Concerning this grant of land, *Ford*, in his *Writings of Wafhington* notes the following:

"The treaty of Fort *Stanwix* (*September*, 1768) eftablifhed the bounds of *Englifh* territory effentially as they had been propofed at the *German* Flats. "Beginning at the mouth of the *Tenneffee* river, it followed the *Ohio* and *Alleghany* rivers to *Kittaning;* thence in a direct line to the neareft fork of the weft branch of the *Sufquehannah;* and thence following that ftream through the *Alleghanies*, it paffed by way of *Burnett's* Hills and the eaftern branch of the *Sufquehannah* and the *Delaware*, into *New York*, having its northern terminus at the confluence of *Canada* and *Wood* creeks. The line, thus propofed, was not in accordance with the inftruction of the Board of Trade. *Hillfborough*, who had fucceeded the liberal *Shelbourne* as Colonial Secretary, and was bitterly oppofed to any fettlements in ·the interior, wifhed to have the line extended no farther than the mouth of the great *Kenawha*, where it would then meet the line which *Stuart*, at a Council in *South Carolina*, had recently eftablifhed with the *Cherokees* as the weftern boundary of *Virginia*. The temper, however, of the Confederate deputies at this time rendered it impoffible for the Baronet to follow ftrictly his inftructions, without defeating the very object of congrefs." *Stone*, Life of Sir *Wm. Johnfon*, ii., 307. *Johnfon* claimed that the effect of this treaty, which was ratified in 1770, was to veft the claim of the northern *Indians* to the country fouth of the *Ohio* in the crown, leaving the Southern *Indians* only to be dealt with concerning it; "and fhould they refufe to give it up, it is in his majefty's power to prevent the colonies from availing themfelves of the late ceffion in that quarter, till it can be done with fafety and the common confent of all who have juft pretenfions to it." *Johnfon to Gage*, *16 December*, 1768.

"This plan reappears in *London* in 1770: 'A fociety of us, in which fome of the firft people in *England* are engaged, and in which you and Colonel *Crogan* are made original partakers, have concluded a bargain with the Treafury for a large tract of land lying and fronting on the *Ohio* (part of the lands lately ceded by the *Indians* to *Great Britain*), large enough for a government. Having it fuggefted to us by Lord *Hillfborough* that it would be right that we fhould have a charter of government, in confequence of this bargain fo concluded, we are next to apply to the Council Board, that the grant may iffue. We expect to meet with oppofition, and fome objections arifing from the impreffions made by fuch oppofition, yet have no doubt of carrying this point, as we have fettled the main point. As foon as the grant has iffued we are to apply to the Lords of Trade on the fubject of the charter.' *Thomas Pownall* to Sir *William Johnfon*, *April* 1770. The application for the grant was made in behalf of the company by *Thomas Walpole*, a *London* banker, *Benjamin Franklin*, *John Sargeant*, and *Samuel Wharton*, but was oppofed by Lord *Hillfborough* in a report that gave *Franklin* an opportunity to make such a crufhing reply as to lead to *Hillfborough's* refignation from the cabinet."

The grant of thefe lands to the *Ohio Company* created much concern in *Virginia*, fince a great many grants to foldiers for fervices in *Indian* wars had been made in that fection.

Wafhington writing to Lord *Botetourt*, from Mᵗ *Vernon*, on *October* 5ᵗʰ called attention to this attempt upon the part of the *Ohio Company* to acquire lands in the fection recently ceded by the *Indians* to *Virginia*, and urged that fome action be taken to protect the intereft of the foldiers, many of whom had already fettled on the difputed lands.

Mount

Mount Vernon,[1] *Oct.* 5 1770

My Lord,

    Being fully convinced of Your Lordship's inclination to render every juft and reafonable fervice to the people you govern, and to any fociety or body of them that fhall afk it, and being in a more particular manner encouraged by a letter which I have juft received from Mr *Blair (Clerk of the Council) to believe that Your Excellency is defirous of knowing how far the grant of land follicited by* Mr. *Walpole & others will effect the intereft of this country in general, or any fett of men in particular; I fhall take the liberty (being tolerably well acquainted with the fituation of the frontiers of this Dominion) to inform your Lordfhip that the bounds of that grant, if obtained upon the extenfive plan prayed for, will comprehend at leaft four fifths of the land for which this Colony hath lately voted £2500 fterling to the purchafe and furvey of, and muft deftroy the well grounded hopes of thofe (if no refervation is made in their favour) who have had the ftrongeft affurances which government could give them, of enjoying fome of thofe lands, the fecuring of which hath coft this country much blood and treafure.*

    By the extracts which your Excellency did me the honour to enclofe, I perceive that the Petitioners require to begin on the South fide of the Ohio *oppofite to the mouth of* Scioto, *which is at leaft* 70 *or* 75 *miles below the mouth of the Great* Kanhawa, *the place to which the Minifterial Line (as it is called) from* Holfton's *River is to run, and more than* 300 *from* Pittfburg, *and to extend from thence in a Southerly direction through the pafs of the* Onafioto *Mountain, which by* Evan's *Map,*[2] *the beft draughts of that country I have ever yet feen, and all the enquiries I have been able to make, from perfons who have explored thofe wilds, will bring them near the latitude of* North Carolina. *From thence they go North eafterly to the Fork of the Great* Kanhawa *(made by the junction of* Green Briar & New *River; on both of which waters we have many fettlers on lands actually patented) From hence they proceed up* Green Briar *to the Head of the North-Eafterly branch thereof, thence Eafterly to the* Alleghany *Mountains; thence along thofe mountains to the Line of the Lord* Fairfax, *thence with his line and the line of* Maryland *and* Pennfylvania *till the Weftern boundary of the latter fhall ftrike the* Ohio; *thence with the fame to the place of beginning.*

    Thefe my Lord, are the bounds of a grant under confideration, and if obtained, will, in my humble opinion give a fatal blow to the interefts of this country; but this I have prefumed to fay as the fum of my thoughts as a member of the community at large.

    I fhall beg leave now to offer myfelf to Your Excellency's notice, as an individual, in a more interefted point of view, and at the fame time as a perfon who confiders himfelf in fome degree the reprefentative of the Officers and Soldiers who claim a right to 200,000 *acres of this land petitioned for by* Mr *Walpole and others, under a folemn Act of Government, adopted at a very alarming and important crifis to His Majefty's affairs in* America. *To approach Your Lordfhip in thefe characters, it might feem neceffary to preface an apology, but I fhall rely on your ufual goodnefs and candour for the patient hearing of a few words in fupport of the equity of our pretentions; which cannot fail of being fhort, as I have taken the liberty of troubling your Lordfhip pretty fully on this head before.*

    The firft letter I ever did myfelf the honour of writing to your Excellency on the fubject of thefe lands, and to which I now beg leave to refer, contained a kind of hiftorical account of our claim, but as no embellifhment is requifite to illucidate a right, when fimple facts are fufficient to eftablifh the point, I fhall beg leave to give your Lordfhip the trouble of reading the inclofed order[3] *of Council of* 18 *of* Feby. 1754 *and Governor* Dinwiddie's *Proclamation in confequence thereof, and then add that thefe troops not only enlifted agreeable to the terms there ftipulated but behaved fo much to the fatiffaction of the country as to obtain the honour of its public thanks. Would it not be hard, my Lord, to deprive men under thefe circumftances (or their*

fucceffors

---

1 Bancroft Tranfcripts—Library of Congrefs.   2 Map Divifion—Library of Congrefs.
3 Page xxi.

fucceffors) of the juft reward of their toils? Could this act of the Governor and Council, offered to and accepted by the foldiery, be confidered in any other light than as an abfolute compact? An tho' the exigency of our affairs rendered it impracticable for us to fettle this country for fome years after the date of the proclamation, and the policy of government forbid it for a few years longer, yet the caufes being now removed and the land given to fome as a recompence for their loffes, and fought after by others for private emolument, have we not a title to be regarded among the firft? We fain would hope fo. We flatter ourfelves that in this point of view Your Excellency will alfo confider us, and by your kind interpofition and favourable reprefentation of our cafe His Majefty will be gracioufly pleafed to confirm the 200,000 acres of land to us, agreeable to the terms of the Proclamation. Or if it fhould be judged neceffary to be more particular in the location of it, and your Lordfhip will be pleafed to caufe the fame to be fignified to me, I will point out immediately thereupon, the particular fpots on which we would beg to have our furveys made; as part of the land prayed for in our petition of the 15th of December laft, to wit, that on Sandy creek, will not be comprehended within the line running from Holfton's river to the mouth of the Great Kanhawa.

Such an act of goodnefs as this, my Lord, would be conferring a fingular favour on men who do not know who elfe to apply to; on men, the moft of whom either in their perfons or fortunes have fuffered in the caufe of their country, and cannot fail of meeting with fuch acknowledgements as refult from grateful minds impreffed with the due fenfe of obligation. None will offer them with more fincere refpect than

> *Your Lordfhips moft obedient and moft*
> *humble Servt*
> GEO. WASHINGTON.

enclofure.

At a Council held 18 February 1754. The Governor was pleafed to fignify to the Board, that as it was determined a fort fhould be immediately built on the River Ohio, at the Fork of Monongahela, for the fecurity and protection of His Majefty's fubjects in this colony, and that a fufficient force fhould be raifed to erect and fupport the fame, he judged neceffary to give a reward of 200,000 acres of land on the Eaft fide of the river Ohio within this Dominion (clear of rights and free from the payment of Quit Rents for the term of fifteen years, 100,000 acres whereof to be contiguous to the faid fort, and the other 100,000 acres to be on or near the river Ohio) over and above their pay, to all who fhall voluntarily enter into the faid fervice; to be divided amongft them after the performance of the faid fervice, in a proportion due to their refpective merit: The Council, on due confideration of the great advantage which will accrue to His Majefty from the taking immediate poffeffion of thofe lands, & being fatiffied that there are other lands fufficient to anfwer the quantity granted to the Ohio Company, advifed His Honour to notify and publifh the faid encouragement by Proclamation.

[A Proclamation did accordingly iffue on 19 Feby, in the 27th year of the reign of His late Majefty, precifely to the above effect, wch Col. Wafhington has tranfcribed in his letter and a copy of which is lately delivered to his Honour the Prefident.]

It may not be amifs to add by way of remark that the complement of men judged neceffary [fufficient] for this fervice (tho' the event proved them otherwife) were actually raifed in confequence of this Proclamation; that they marched over the Alleghany Mountains thro' almoft inacceffible paffes, and built a fort on the waters of Monongahela which they were obliged afterwards to furrender to the fuperior force of the French and their Indian Allies;—that they conducted themfelves in that enterprize in fuch a manner as to receive the honour of their country's thanks,

as

as may appear by the Journals of the Houfe of Burgeffes in the Seffion following; and that many of them continued in the fervice till the total demolition of Fort Duquefne *and eftablifhment of an* Englifh *garrifon in its place.*

G. W.

Lord *Botetourt* having died on *October* 15th, *William Nelfon,* Prefident of the Council fucceeded him, pending the appointment of a new Governor. After having been in office three days, Governor *Nelfon,* in a letter to the Earl of *Hillfborough* fet forth practically the fame reafons advanced by *Wafhington* in the intereft of foldiers of the Colony, and urged that fome fteps be taken to protect them:

Virginia, Octr 18th 1770.[1]

My Lord,

On the 15th Inftant I did myfelf the honour of writing to your Lordfhip to acquaint you with the melancholly event of the death of Lord Botetourt, *which had thrown His Majefty's faithful fubjects of this Colony into the deepeft affliction. At the fame time I fent a copy of the proceedings in Council, to fhew your Lordfhip by what means the Adminiftration of the Government had fallen into my hands.*

On the evening of that day your Lordfhip's letter of the 20th of July to the Governor, was delivered to me; and as it contains matter of great variety and importance it hath been read in Council, and, together with the feveral papers inclofed in it, hath been maturely confidered; and I now trouble your Lordfhip with theirs as well as my own opinion upon the fubject of them. I muft firft acknowledge the propriety and juftice of your Lordfhip and my Lords Commiffioners of the Treafury in delaying to report in favour of Mr Walpole and his affociates, for fo large a grant of lands on the back of this Colony, until the Country fhould be made acquainted with it and their reafons, if they had any, in objection to it, fhould be heard; and our thanks are particularly due to your Lordfhip for affording the Governor and Council an opportunity of defending themfelves againft the indecent illiberal and unwarrantable charges contained in a letter of the 9th of July 1770 to Mr. Walpole, referring firft to your Lordfhip's confideration what degree of credibility an anonimous writer, who thus ftabs in the dark, is entitled to, tho' by the great commendation he gives of the generous Propofal of Mr Walpole and his affociates to Government for the purchafe of the lands they want, it is probable he is one of that refpectable body.

The charges in this letter are, that the Governor & Council of Virginia have made large and immoderate grants of the lands to the weftward of the Alleghany Mountains; that many fuch grants (of which a lift is annex'd to the letter) are made to the members of Council themfelves, who by felling thofe lands, to others make large profits, and that this practice hath been carried on and encouraged by them, notwithftanding His Majefty's Inftructions that no larger quantity fhall be granted to any one perfon than 1000 acres. The truth of this fact is that this inftruction was not given till 1763, and that all thefe grants fo loudly complained of, were made long before the exiftence of that inftruction, and in the æra when it was thought good policy to fettle thofe lands as faft as poffible, and that the granting them to men of the firft confequence who were likelieft and beft able to procure large bodies of people to fettle on them was the moft probable means of effecting the end propofed. As to the Grantees making large profits by the fale of them to others, I am confident the fact is otherwife, fince the ftated price for fuch lands (except in very few cafes) hath been £3 Virginia currency per 100 acres, a price very little higher than it would coft any man who fhould incline to take up fingly 3 4 or 500 acres. It is very fortunate for me that whilft I am writing upon this fubject, I do not find my name in any of thefe grants, tho' I have been 25 years a Member of the Board, and am therefore no otherwife concerned than to vindicate the honour of the Governor and the Gentlemen of the Council, efpecially of thofe whofe names are made ufe of in

fome

[1] Bancroft Tranfcripts—Library of Congrefs.

some of those grants. I claim no merit from this circumstance, as I do not think their conduct at all unwarrantable, which I hope to shew in the sequel of this letter. My reason for declining such engagements, proceeded from an opinion that little if any profit would arise from them, but some trouble, and the experience I have had now, shews that I was right in that opinion. For I have good cause to know that those gentlemen of the Council who did engage in those grants, have not received one shilling of advantage from them, nor do I believe they ever will. It is true that some of the Grantees residing on the frontiers, men of activity and strength of constitution, who have had all the trouble expence and fatigue of surveying the lands and of procuring others to purchase and settle on them, I presume have made some advantages by reserving some to themselves and by the sale of other parts; and this they seem to have deserved for their labour. In order to shew Your Lordship how groundless the charge is that the Governor and Council have acted unwarrantably in the making unreasonable grants of land, the inclosed Paper No. 1.[1] contains the proceedings relative to the grants to the Ohio Comp^y, by which it appears that by application to his late Majesty, He was pleased to order his then Governor and Council to grant them 200000 Acres upon the terms expressed in the said paper, and Your Lordship will observe, that tho' some of the grantees were of the Council yet many of them were also resident in Great Britain. The next grant in order of time, on or near the Ohio, was by Proclamation from Lieu^t Governor Dinwiddie, promising 200000 Acres of land to be given and divided among such as would voluntarily enter into His Majesty's service for the defence of the frontiers, at that time violently attacked by the French & Indians, and those lands the Officers and soldiers who served, are at this instant surveying in order to obtain Patents for them, and their right seems to be a good one, as many of them sealed the contract with their blood, whose shares will be apportioned among their surviving wives children and other legal representatives. Thus far the Governor and Council I hope have done right; indeed this last grant was so much approved of by his late Majesty, that he soon after adopted and enlarged the plan by offering by his royal proclamation large quantities of land to the Officers and Soldiers who should enter into his service on this Continent, the quantity not fix'd but 3000 acres to a Colonel and so less to the other Officers according to their rank, and even to the common soldiers. To satisfy the regiments rais'd in this Colony upon that promise, I presume 200000 acres will be required. Besides these, we have been told (tho' we have never had an authentick copy of the treaty at Fort Stanwix) that the Indians made it an express condition in the deed of Cession to his Majesty, that 100,000 acres of it should be granted to Col. Croghan, Deputy of Sir William Johnson, and a like quantity to the Pennsylvania traders, as a recompense to them for the injuries and damages they sustain'd from the Indians during the late war. All these amounting to 800,000 acres are to the northward, and I presume near the lands which these new Adventurers want, and I presume the Governor and Council to be blameless in all these. In all the other grants listed at the end of this anonimous letter N°. 9.[1] I do not find that any steps have been taken towards surveying and seating them; of course they are or will become lapsed, except in the two to John Lewis and others for 800,000 acres and to James Patton and others for 100,000 acres. On these lands which are located from Green Briar River to the branches of the Holston River and will be within the limits of the land now purchasing by His Majesty from the Cherokees, there are many hundred families settled. I ought here to observe that the Assembly of Virginia have given £2500 St. for the purchase of these lands: and these are the people My Lord who were so greatly distress'd by His Majesty's Proclamation of 1763, requiring them to abandon all the lands on the water courses running to the westward or into the Mississippi. This Proclamation they refus'd to comply with, nay they said they could not do it, for having expended their little all under the grants from this Government they had no other place to retire to, and have hitherto chose to rely on a kind providence, exposed as they have been to the resentment of the Indians: and this is the reason that I find that very

little

little if any Quit Rents have been received for His Majesty's use from that Quarter for some time past; for, they say, that as His Majesty hath been pleased to withdraw his protection from them since 1763, they think themselves bound not to pay Quit Rents. However as this Boundary with the Cherokees will be compleated in the Spring I have no doubt but regular government will take place there as it is in other parts of this Dominion, and that the Quit Rents will be there properly collected. I intreat Your Lordship to let me know His Majesty's pleasure with respect to those lands, whether he is pleased to permit them to be granted or not. For, notwithstanding the assertions in the Paper Nº. 9 we have not granted one acre in those parts since the Proclamation nor shall we until set at liberty to do it; tho' many applications have been made for that purpose without success. The people are still continuing to settle those lands under the equitable right they derive from the grant to John Lewis and others. James Patton's grant is also pretty full of inhabitants and his family receive some advantages from it, and truly I think they might, since the old man paid his scalp as the price of it, he being murdered by the Indians on the way as he was escorting amunition for the defence of the settlers on Green Briar. I can only say on the subject of those two grants and all the other large ones, that they were made at a time when the policy of the day was to make large grants to persons who were likeliest to procure people to inhabit and to cultivate the lands; which ends have been nearly attained in both these instances. The late war and the prohibition by proclamation have been the causes that those lands have not been more fully peopled, which I have reason to think will be effected soon after leave is given to grant Patents for such parts as are settled; those 1,700,000 acres which I have taken notice of in all, I suppose will take place of all new Adventurers. We do not presume to say to whom our gracious Sovereign shall grant his vacant lands nor do I set myself as an opponent to Mʳ Walpole and his associates. All that I can consistently with my duty, hope for is, that all prior rights, whether equitable or legal may be preferred and protected. By equitable, I mean all those who have had grants, but have been prevented from complying with the strict terms of them by the war or any other unavoidable impediment: by legal, I mean all those for which patents have been obtained.

If we take a comparative view of the merit of those new adventurers with that of the people who have run great hazards during the course of the war, many of whom lost their lives and fortunes in the prosecution of those settlements, others had their wives, children and other dearest relatives carried into a barbarous captivity, many of whom still languish in that distressful situation; it will not be difficult to determine on which side the weight prevails.

As to the Garbling the lands which the letter Nº. 9 twice mentions, I beg your Lordship to consider that the proposal of Mʳ. Walpole and his Associates of paying Quit Rents only for the cultivable lands, amounts to a great deal more in its consequences. For, under that description, who can suppose that they intend to include and pay Quit Rents for sterile mountains or rocky lands? Whereas we have a law of this country which the surveyors are obliged to conform to requiring that the breadth of every survey of land shall be at least one-third of the length: and this was enacted on purpose to prevent the practice of Garbling, as it is called, that is, that the Patentees shall be obliged to take some indifferent land with the good.

Permit me here to observe that the 20 years indulgence these gentlemen desire before they shall be obliged to pay Quit Rents, is more than ever hath been allowed, even by the law of 1754, which was passed by recommendation from his late Majesty, and the merit they make of purchasing these lands is not considerable, when we reflect that the price of 5 sterling for 50 acres, which every man pays before he can obtain a Patent (except in particular exemptions as above) amounts, on so great a quantity to as much or more. And as His Majesty and his late Royal Grandfather have been graciously pleased to permit the money arising from the sale of the rights to be applied to the fund for the support of Goverment and the Contingent

charges

charges thereof, that fund will fuſtain a heavy loſs if it ſhould be withdrawn at this time.

With reſpect to the eſtabliſhment of a new colony on the back of Virginia, *it is a ſubjeą of too great political importance for me to preſume to give an opinion upon. However permit me, my Lord, to obſerve that when that part of the country ſhall become ſufficiently populated it may be a wiſe and prudent meaſure; but the argument that the ſettlement of thoſe parts will be a good barrier and defence to the frontiers of* Virginia, *appears to me from experience to be rather ſpecious than ſolid; for the greateſt difficulty and expence of defending our frontiers in the laſt war proceeded from the vaſt diſtance and extent of them. If you increaſe that diſtance & extent the difficulty and expence of defending will be proportionably increaſed, and the people as ſettled there ſparſedly, were incapable of defending themſelves, and often called for aſſiſtance from the interior and more populous parts of the country.*

At all events I truſt that theſe gentlemen if they ſucceed in their ſcheme, will not be permitted to oppoſe their power and ſtrength to the feeble reſiſtance of the poor ſettlers, who have borne the heat and burden of the day, and that they will not ſhare the fate of the unfortunate Naboth *whoſe vineyard became a tempting objeą to a rich and powerful man.*

It will certainly be proper before any grant is made to M^r. Walpole *and his aſſociates, to have an exaą liſt taken of the people ſettled on thoſe lands, and under what rights, that they may be particularly reſerved, and not to leave a door open to future contention about them, which however I have at preſent no poſſible method of obtaining, nor do I think it can be done but by great length of time and at no ſmall expence.*

After I had wrote thus far, and was reading it to the Gentlemen of the Council for their approbation a letter from Col *George* Waſhington *to Lord* Botetourt *was delivered to me; which being read and appearing to be material on the preſent ſubjeą, they adviſed me to ſend a copy of it to Your Lordſhip, which is accordingly incloſed N°. 3. I ought to acquaint your Lordſhip that he is the Gentleman who had the honour to command the firſt raiſ'd troops, to whom the 200,000 acres promiſ'd by Lieut Governor* Dinwiddie's *Proclamation is due, and therefore he may be intereſted in the affair. However your Lordſhip will judge of the ſolidity of his reaſoning.*

I omitted to mention in its proper place that unleſs M^r. Walpole *and his Aſſociates ſhould ſett out the lands in ſmall parcels at reaſonable rates, they will remain long without much cultivation or ſettlement; ſince men in this quarter of the globe where it is ſo eaſy to become abſolute proprietors of lands, are not fond of farming them. It is a vaſt encouragement to the improvement and cultivation of the lands, when they can enjoy the pleaſure to refleą that their poſterity will receive the benefit of the labour they beſtow. If theſe gentlemen ſhould be left at liberty to exaą what terms they pleaſe for the lands, either by the ſale or letting them to farm; conſider, my Lord, how little ground will be left open to hope for a ſpeedy ſettlement or population. If they ſhould do neither of theſe but each individual ſhould keep poſſeſſion of his large ſhare, till lands ſhould become ſcarce and at a high price or they ſhould require a high rent, which may be raiſed from time to time, we may poſſibly have reaſon to apprehend ſuch convulſions and inſurreąions as happen'd in the colony of* New York *a very few years ſince between the great land-holders and their tenants on a ſubjeą of this nature.*

Thus my Lord have I endeavored to give the fulleſt and cleareſt anſwer I could to your letter, and the ſeveral papers referred to and incloſed in it. If I have done it to your Lordſhips ſatiſfaction I ſhall be happy.

I ougkt to beg pardon for being ſo prolix, which however I could not well avoid when I obſerved how very deſirous your Lordſhip is, of as full and particular information as poſſible, of every thing neceſſary to this great conſideration.

I have the honour to be with profound reſpeą My Lord,
> *Your Lordſhip's moſt obedt and very*
> *humble Servt*

WM. NELSON. P.

Succeeding

Succeeding Lord *Botetourt* as Governor of Virginia in the fall of 1770, Lord *Dunmore* at once condemned the project to eftablifh a colony on the *Ohio* River. He gave as his reafons for oppofing this grant, that a fettlement at fuch a great diftance from a colony would neither benefit the part fettled or the mother country. Thefe views he expreffed in a letter to the Earl of *Hillfborough*, dated *New York, November* 12, 1770:

New York[1], 12, *November*, 1770.

I have made it my bufinefs to enquire and to find out the opinion of the People here, on the fcheme in agitation of eftablifhing a Colony on the Ohio. *I find all who have any knowledge of fuch affairs concur in condemning the project; they allege among a variety of reafons, that a Colony at fuch an immenfe diftance from the fettled parts of* America *and from the Ocean, can neither benefit either thofe fettled parts, or the Mother Country, that they muft become immediately a loft people to both, and all communication of a commercial nature with them, be a vain attempt; from the difficulty and expence attending the tranfport of commodities to them, which would fo enhance the price thereof as to make it utterly impoffible for them to purchafe fuch commodities, for they could not raife a produce of any kind, that would anfwer fo difficult and expenfive tranfport back; fuch Colony therefore muft be their own Manufacturers; and the great expence of maintaining Troops there for their protection, be a dead weight on Govern^t without the hopes of reaping any advantage hereafter. The scheme alarms extremely all the fettled parts of* America, *the people of property being juftly apprehenfive of confequences that muft inevitably enfue, that fuch a Colony will only become a drain to them (now but thinly peopled) of an infinite number of their lower clafs of Inhabitants, who the defire of novelty alone will induce to change their fituation; and the withdrawing of thofe Inhabitants will reduce the value of lands in the provinces even to nothing, and make it impoffible for the Patentees to pay the Quit Rents; by which it is evident, his Maj^{ty:s} intereft muft be very much prejudiced. Add to this the great probability, I may venture to fay certainty, that the attempting a fettlement on* Ohio *will draw on an Indian war; it being well known, how ill affected the* Ohio *Indians have always been to our intereft, and their jealoufy of fuch a fettlement fo near them, must be eafily forefeen, therefore, as fuch a war would affect at leaft the neareft Provinces, as well as the New Colony your Lord^p muft expect thofe provinces, will not fail to make heavy complaints of the inattention of Govern^t to their intereft. I cannot therefore but think it my duty to recommend to your Lord^p not to fuffer this fcheme to have effect, at leaft, until your Lord^p fhall have from the moft fubftantial and clear proofs, been made thoroughly fenfible of its utility.*

DUNMORE.

The efforts upon the part of the Colony to protect the grants already made to the foldiers for fervices rendered in *Indian* wars, were accepted by the *Ohio Company* early in *December* 1770. *George Mercer*, the agent for this Company in *London*, writing to *Wafhington, Dec.* 18, 1770[2], advifed him that the 200,000 acres claimed by officers of the *Virginia* troops had been accepted by the Company as valid, and that their rights fhould be refpected. This conceffion being made, no further attempt upon the part of the Colony to prevent a ceffion to the *Ohio Company* was enacted. Inactivity, however, upon the part of thofe interefted caufed the matter to remain in an unfettled ftate until 1772, when a grant bearing that date was delivered. This grant was made out in the name of the *Grand Company*, and included much of the fertile lands acquired by the Colony at the *Cherokee* convention at *Lochaber* in 1770.

The Affembly of 1770 was prorogued on *June* 28th, after having difcuffed at fome length the queftions of commerce and taxation.

On *June* 22nd an *Affociation* was entered into by various members of the Houfe of Burgeffes and by a large number of merchants of *Williamfburg* and vicinity. Governor *Botetourt* writing to the Secretary of State[1] on *June* 30th following, called particular attention

tion to this *Affociation*, which had been prefented to him in the form of a petition. He ftated that the purpofe was to effect the repeal of the act which granted certain duties for the purpofe of raifing a revenue, and to be relieved from hardfhips refulting from the unlimited jurifdiction of the Courts of Admiralty.

In commenting upon this *Affociation*, Governor *Botetourt* was of the Opinion the merchants of *England* were largely refponfible for its adoption, and that various letters intended to promote diftrefs had emanated from *America* with this object in view.

A printed copy of the *Affociation* was forwarded at the time by Governor *Botetourt* to the Secretary of State. Numerous copies were likewife circulated throughout the colony and many received the fignatures of prominent refidents in their refpective counties. Several copies of this *Affociation*, fo endorfed, are on file in the *Library* of *Congrefs*.

The Association[1] Entered Into Last Friday, the 22d Instant, by the Gentlemen of the House of Burgesses, and the Body of Merchants, Assembled in this City.

We his Majefty's moft dutiful and loyal fubjects of *Virginia*, declaring our inviolable and unfhaken fidelity and attachment to our gracious fovereign, our affection for all our fellow fubjects of *Great Britain*, and our firm determination to fupport, at the hazard of our lives and fortunes, the laws, the peace, and good order of government in this colony; but at the fame time affected with great and juft apprehenfions of the fatal confequences certainly to follow from the arbitrary impofition of taxes on the people of *America*, for the purpofe of raifing a revenue from them, without the confent of their reprefentatives; and as we confider it to be the indifpenfible duty of every virtuous member of fociety to prevent the ruin, and promote the happinefs, of his country, by every lawful means, although in the profecution of fuch a laudable and neceffary defign fome unhappy confequences may be derived to many innocent fellow fubjects, whom we wifh not to injure, and who we hope will impute our conduct to the real neceffity of our affairs: Influenced by thefe reafons, we do moft earneftly recommend this our affociation to the ferious attention of all Gentlemen, merchants, traders, and other inhabitants of this colony, not doubting but they will readily and cordially accede thereto. And at the fame time we, and every of us, do moft folemnly oblige ourfelves, upon our word and honour, to promote the welfare and commercial interefts of all thofe truly worthy merchants, traders, and others, inhabitants of this colony, who fhall hereafter conform to the fpirit of this affociation; but that we will upon all occafions, and at all times hereafter, avoid purchafing any commodity or article of goods whatfoever from any importer or feller of *Britifh* merchandife or *European* goods whom we may know or believe, in violation of the effential interefts of this colony, to have preferred their own private emolument, by importing or felling articles prohibited by this affociation, to the deftruction of the deareft rights of the people of this colony. And for the more effectual difcovery of fuch defaulters, it is refolved,

That a committee of five be chofen in every county, by the majority of affociators in each county, who, or any three of them, are hereby authorized to publifh the names of fuch figners of the affociation as fhall violate their agreement; and when there fhall be an importation of goods into any county, fuch committee, or any three of them, are empowered to convene themfelves, and in a civil manner apply to the merchant or importers concerned and defire to fee the invoices and papers refpecting fuch importation, and if they find any goods there in contrary to the affociation to let the importers know that it is the opinion and requeft of the country that fuch goods fhall not be opened or ftored, but refhipped to the place from whence they came: And in cafe of refufal, without any manner of violence, inform them of the confequence, and proceed to publifh an account of their conduct.

Sesondly

---

1 Manufcript Divifion—Library of Congrefs.

Secondly. That we the subscribers, as well by our own example as all other legal ways and means in our power, will promote and encourage industry and frugality, and discourage a manner of luxury and extravagance.

Thirdly. That we will not hereafter, directly or indirectly, import, or cause to be imported, from *Great Britain*, any of the goods hereafter enumerated, either for sale or for our own use; to wit, spirits, cider, perry, beer, ale, porter, malt, pease, beef, fish, butter, cheese, tallow, candles, fruit, pickles, confectionary, chairs, tables, looking glasses, carriages, joiners work, and cabinet work of all sorts, riband, *India* goods of all sorts, except spices and calico of more than 3 *s.* sterling per yard, upholstery (by which is meant paper hangings, beds ready made, furniture for beds, and carpetting) watches, clocks, silversmiths work of all sorts, silks of all sorts (except womens bonnets and hats, sewing silk, and netting silk) cotton stuffs of more than 3 *s.* sterling per yard, linens of more than 2 *s.* sterling per yard (except *Irish* linens) gauze, lawns, cambrick of more than 6 *s.* sterling per yard, woollen and worsted stuffs of all sorts of more than 2 *s*, sterling per yard, broadcloths of more than 8 *s.* sterling per yard, narrow cloths of all kinds of more than 4 *s.* sterling per yard, not less than 7-8th yard wide, hats of greater value than 10 *s.* sterling, stockings of more than 36 *s.* sterling per dozen, shoes of more than 5 *s.* sterling per pair, boots, saddles, mens exceeding 25 *s.* and womens exceeding 40 *s.* sterling, exclusive of bridles, which are allowed, portmanteaus, saddle bags, and all other manufactured leather, neither oil or painters colours, if both, or either of them, be subject to any duty after the 1st of *December* next. And that we will not import, or cause to be imported, any horses, nor purchase those which may be imported by others after the 1st of *November* next.

Fourthly. That we will not import or bring into the colony or cause to be imported or brought into the colony, either by sea or land, any slaves, or make sale of any upon commission, or purchase any slave or slaves that may be imported by others after the 1st day of *November* next, unless the same have been twelve months upon the continent.

Fifthly. That we will not import any wines, on which a duty is laid by act of Parliament for the purpose of raising a revenue in *America*, or purchase such as may be imported by others, after the 1st day of *September* next.

Sixthly. That no wine be imported by any of the subscribers or other person, from any of the colonies on this continent, or any other place, from the time of signing this association, contrary to the terms thereof.

Seventhly. That all such goods as may or shall be imported into this colony, in consequence of their having been rejected by the association committees in any of our sister colonies, shall not be purchased by any associator; but that we will exert every lawful means in our power absolutely to prevent the sale of all such goods, and to cause the same to be exported as quickly as possible.

Eighthly. That we will not receive from *Great Britain*, or make sale of, upon commission, any of the articles above excepted to after the first day of *September* next, nor any of those articles which may have been really and *bona fide* ordered by us, after the 25th of *December* next.

Ninthly. That we will not receive into our custody, make sale of, or become chargeable with any of the articles aforementioned, that may be ordered after the 15th of *June* instant, nor give orders for any from this time; and that in all orders which any of us may hereafter send to *Great Britain* we will expressly direct and request our correspondents not to ship us any of the articles before excepted, and if any such goods are shipped contrary to the tenour of this agreement we will refuse to take the same or make ourselves chargeable therewith.

Provided nevertheless, that such goods as are already on hand, or may be imported according to the true intent and meaning of this *Association*, may be continued for sale.

Tenthly

Tenthly. That a committee of merchants, to be named by their own body, when called together by their chairman, be appointed to take under their confideration the general ftate of the trade in this colony, and report to the affociation, at their next meeting, a lift of fuch other manufactures of *Great Britain*, or commodities of any kind whatever, now imported, as may reafonably, and with benefit to the colony, be excepted to.

Eleventhly. That we do hereby engage ourfelves, by thofe moft facred ties of honour and love to our country, that we will not, either upon the goods which we have already upon hand or may hereafter import within the true meaning of this affociation, make any advance in price, with a view to profit by the reftrictions hereby laid on the trade of this colony.

Twelfthly. That we will not at any time hereafter, directly or indirectly, import, or caufe to be imported, or purchafe from any perfon who fhall import, any merchandife or manufactures exported from *Great Britain*, which are, or hereafter fhall be, taxed by act of Parliament for the purpofes of raifing a revenue in *America*.

Refolved, That a meeting of the affociators fhall be called at the difcretion of the Moderator, or at the requeft of twenty members of the affociation,fignified to him in writing; and in cafe of the death of the prefent Moderator, the next perfon fubfcribing hereto be confidered as Moderator, and act as fuch until the next general meeting.

Laftly. That thefe refolves fhall be binding on all and each of the fubfcribers, who do hereby, each and every perfon for himfelf, agree that he will ftrictly and firmly adhere to and abide by every article of this affociation from the time of this figning the fame until the act of Parliament which impofes a duty on tea, paper, glafs, and painters colours, be totally repealed, or until a general meeting of one hundred affociators, after one month's publick notice, fhall determine otherwife, the twelfth article of this agreement ftill and for ever continuing in force, until the contrary be declared by a general meeting of the members of this affociation.

Signed in *Williamfburg*, this 22ᵈ of *June*, 1770.

COLUMN NO. 1.

Peyton Randolph, *Moderator.*
Andrew Sprowle, *Chairman of the Trade.*
Ro. C. Nicholas.
Richard Bland.
Edmund Pendleton.
Archibald Cary.
Richard Henry Lee.
Henry Lee.
Charles Carter, *Corotoman.*
Thomas Jefferfon.
Severn Eyre.
Thomas Whiting.
Edward Hack Mofeley, jun.
George Wafhington.
Burwell Baffett.
Spencer M. Ball.
James Walker.
Edward Ofborn.
Southy Simpfon.
Richard Lee.

COLUMN NO. 2.

John Alexander.
John Burton.
William Clayton.
Richard Randolph.
Benjamin Harrifon.
P. Carrington.
James Pride.
William Acrill.
Peter Poythrefs.
James Mercer.
N. Edwards, jun.
Richard Adams.
Thomas Newton, jun.
Francis Peyton.
Thomas Barber.
Lewis Burwell.
James Cocke.
Richard Baker.
Benjamin Howard.
R. Rutherford.
Archibald Campbell.

COLUMN

COLUMN NO. 3.

James Balfour.
W. Cabell, jun.
Daniel Barraud.
James Mills.
David Jamefon.
Charles Duncan.
John Wayles.
John Bell.
Thomas Adams.
Henry Taylor.
Alexander Shaw.
John Banifter
Thomas Bailey.
William Robinfon.
James Wood.
Bolling Stark.
Thomas Pettus.
John Woodfon.
Henry Field, jun.
William Roane.
Wilfon Miles Cary.

COLUMN NO. 4.

John Blair.
James Wallace.
Richard Mitchell.
Cornelius Thomas.
James Denniftone.
William Snodgrafs.
Benjamin Baker.
Patrick Coutts.
Neill Campbell.
John Donelfon.
Neil M'Coull.
Thomas Jett.
Samuel Kerr.
James Robinfon.
Archibald Ritchie.
Samuel Efkridge.
Thomas Stith.
James Edmondfon.
Anthony Walke.
John Wilfon, of Augufta.
George Logan.

COLUMN NO. 5.

John Hutchings.
W. Lyne.
Edward Ker.
Alexander Trent.
John Talbott.
Jofeph Cabell.
Gardner Fleming.
Samuel Harwood.
Humphrey Roberts.
Thomas M. Randolph.
Robert Wormeley Carter.
Jerman Baker.
John Gilchrift
James Archdeacon.
Robert Donald.
James M'Dowall.
Alexander Baine.
John Smith.
Purdie & Dixon.
James Buchanan.
Thomas Scott.

COLUMN NO. 6.

Alexander Banks.
John Johnfon.
Archibald Govan.
Hugh M'Mekin.
Foufhee Tebbs.
Archibald M'Call.
Daniel Hutchings.
Henry Morfe.
Nathaniel Terry.
Ifaac Read.
William Rind.
Benjamin Harrifon, jun.
Jofiah Granbery.
James Robb.
Neil Jamiefon.
Walter Peter.
Robert Crooks.
John Winn.
John Efdale.
Nathaniel Lyttleton Savage.
Jacob Wray.

COLUMN NO. 7.

John Fifher.
Hartwell Cocke.
Edwin Gray.
Daniel M'Callum.
James Donald.
Thomas Nelfon, jun.
Robert Gilmour.

COLUMN NO. 8.

Archibald Buchanan.
Andrew Mackie.
Thomas Everard.
George Purdie.
Patrick Ramfay.
Walter Boyd.
John Tabb.

George

George Riddell.
John Bland.
Robert Miller.
Francis Lightfoot Lee.
Meriwether Smith.
Ro. Munford, *Mecklenburg.*
Roger Atkinſon.
J. H. Norton.
Lewis Burwell, *of Glouceſter*
Abraham Hite.
James Parker.
Edward Briſbane.
James Baird.
Neill Buchanan.

Richard Booker.
John Page, jun.
Robert Andrews.
John Tayloe Corbin.
John Tazewell.
John Prentis.
William Holt.
John Greenhow.
Haldenby Dixon.
William Ruſſell.
Thomas Hornſby.

This agreement entered into by the Burgeſſes and merchants of the colony was not as effective as deſired. Various committees appointed to operate in the reſpective counties, enforced for the time being the reſolutions of the *Aſſociation,* thereby hoping to promote induſtry throughout the colony. The plan however, was not ſatiſfactory, as is noted in Governor *Nelſon's* letter to Lord *Hillſborough,* Secretary of State, dated *Dec.* 19ᵗʰ, 1770.

Williamſburg, Decrˡ. 19, 1770.

My Lord,

Your Lordᵖ's diſpatch No. 37, *directed to Lord* Botetourt *is juſt come to my hands. I ſhall be happy to be informed of His Majeſtʸ's pleaſure upon the ſeveral Acts of Aſſembly which were paſſed in the laſt ſeſſion as ſoon as it is known.*

The Spirit of Aſſociation which hath prevailed in this Colony for ſome time paſt, ſeems to me from the defection of the Northern Provinces, to be cooling every day. There was a meeting appointed to be held the 14ᵗʰ *of this month upon this ſubject, but ſo few Aſſociators met, that they did nothing but adjourn till next ſummer, which diſcovers ſuch lukewarmneſs as convinces me that this Engagement will ſoon die away and come to nought.*

Having in a former letter acquainted your Lordſhip with the progreſs we are making towards completing the line between the Cherokee Indians *and this colony, I ſhall not now trouble your Lordᵉ on that ſubject.*

Lord Botetourt *I preſume adviſed your Lordᵉ of the preſſing neceſſity he was under of adopting ſo unuſual a meaſure as that of drawing upon His Majeſty's Quit rents for four hundred pounds. Permit me My Lord to expreſs my moſt grateful and humble acknowledgments of His Maj'tʸ's goodneſs in acquieſcing in this firſt attempt of the fort, and to aſſure you that we ſhall be far from endeavouring to draw this freſh inſtance of His Majeſty's favour into precedent.*

I obſerve what your Lordᵉ ſays about the appointment of Mʳ. Wormeley *or* Mʳ. Digges *to a ſeat at the Council Board. They are both well qualified for it, tho' one of them lives at a more convenient diſtance than the other from the ſeat of Government. Knowing that Lord* Botetourt *had wrote to your Lordᵉ on this ſubject, and conſidering that he was a much better judge of the fitneſs of Men to be preferred, I declined recommending any one to your Lordᵉ to ſupply the place of* Mʳ Blair *on his reſignation. I have the honour to be with the greateſt deference and reſpect, My Lord,*

Your Lordʸ's obedient humble ſervant,
WM. NELSON. P.

During the ſeſſion of the Aſſembly of July 1771 the queſtion of an American epiſcopate was agitated, and in ſome of the Northern colonies the preſs warmly advocated ſuch a meaſure. The co-operation of *Virginia* was ſought by *New York* and *New Jerſey* in
their

their effort to petition the King upon the subject, and Reverend Dr. *Cooper*, president of *King's College, New York* and Rev. Dr. *McKean* visited the Southern colonies with this object in view. As a result of the visit of these deputies a convocation of the clergy was held, though only a few attended; the Rev. *John Camm*, of *Virginia*, taking an active part in the proceedings, was one of those who joined in the petition to the crown urging its establishment. Four of the clergy in attendance, *Henley, Gwatkin, Hewitt,* and *Bland,* entered a protest against this scheme to introduce a bishopric, advancing as an argument that such an action would endanger the existence of the *British* Empire in *America.*

The Assembly having expressed its disapprobation of the project, all efforts soon relaxed, and the movement ended when a vote of thanks was extended by the House of Burgesses, through *Richard Henry Lee* and *Richard Bland,* to the protesting clergymen for their "wise and well-timed opposition:"

Resolved, Nemine Contradicente, [1] That the Thanks of this House be given to the Reverend Mr *Henley,* the Reverend Mr *Gwatkin,* the Reverend Mr *Hewitt,* and the Reverend Mr *Bland,* for the wise and well timed Opposition they have made to the pernicious Project of a few mistaken Clergymen, for introducing an *American* Bishop; a Measure by which much Disturbance, great Anxiety, and Apprehension, would certainly take Place among his Majesty's faithful *American* Subjects; and that Mr *Richard Henry Lee,* and Mr *Bland,* do acquaint them therewith.

Campbell, in commenting upon this attempt to establish an Episcopate in America, outlines the position of both sides in this controversy:

"Churchmen naturally sided with the English government, and the bench of bishops were arrayed in opposition to the rights of the Colonies. The protest of the four ministers gave rise to a controversy between them and the United Episcopal Conventions of *New York* and *New Jersey* and a war of pamphlets and newspapers ensued in the Northern and Middle States; and the stamp act itself, according to some writers, did not evoke more bitter denunciations, nor more violent threats, than the project of an episcopate: New England was in a flame against it. It was believed, that if bishops should be sent over they would unite with the Governors in opposition to the rights of *America.* The laity of the *Episcopal* Church in America were, excepting a small minority, opposed to the measure. Neither the people of *Virginia,* nor any of the *American* colonies, were at any time willing to receive a bishop appointed by the English government. Among the advocates of the scheme the Rev. *Jonathan Boucher* took a prominent part, and he sustained it ably from the pulpit. He held that the refusal of *Virginia* to consent to the appointment of a bishop, was 'to unchurch the church;' and his views on this subject were re-echoed by *Lowth,* Bishop of *Oxford,* in an anniversary sermon delivered before the Society for the Propagation of the Gospel in Foreign Parts. On this point of ecclesiastical government the members of the establishment in *Virginia* appear to have been looked upon as themselves dissenters. In one sense they were so; but their repugnance was to prelacy, not to the episcopate; a prelatic bishop was in their minds associated with the ideas of expense beyond their means, and of opposition to the principles of civil liberty. *Boucher,* in a sermon that he preached in this year at *St. Mary's* Church, in *Caroline* County, of which he was then rector, says of the dissenters in *Virginia:* 'I might almost as well pretend to count the gnats that buzz around us in a summer's evening."

"The scheme of sending over a bishop had been entertained more than a hundred years before; and *Dean Swift* at one time entertained hopes of being made Bishop of *Virginia,* with power, as is said, to ordain priests and deacons for all the colonies, and to parcel them out into deaneries, parishes, chapels, etc., and to recommend and present thereto. The favorite sermons of many of the *Virginia* clergy were *Sterne's.*" *Campbell-History of Virginia, pp.* 561-62.

The

---

[1] *See* page 122.

The Affembly of 1772 convened on *Monday* the 10th day of *February*, in the 12th year of the reign of George III. The death of *Botetourt* on *October* 15th, 1770; the temporary appointment of *Nelfon* to act as Governor, and the tranffer of Lord *Dunmore* from *New York* to *Virginia* refulted in the proclamation of *October* 12, 1771, for diffolving the General Affembly. This action upon the part of Lord *Dunmore* was taken fhortly after his arrival in *Virginia*, and was followed by prorogations of *November* 20th and *December* 12th of the fame year.

The firft announcement of *Dunmore*, of importance to the colony, was the difallowance by *George* III of an act of Affembly for appointing a commiffion to regulate the *Indian* trade. This action upon the part of the crown refulted in much diffatiffaction, and coming at a time when the boundary between the *Cherokees* and *Virginia* was being furveyed, gave rife to much fpeculation regarding the management of *Indian* trade in this new territory.

Additional territory was alfo in contemplation, in fact negotiations were then pending for large poffeffions owned by the *Indians* and adjoining *Virginia's* weftern boundary. This queftion was determined during the latter part of 1772, and eftablifhed a line running weftward from *White Top* Mountains in latitude 36° and 36'. By the conclufion of this treaty the fettlers on the *Watauga* River were left within the *Indian* limits, which neceffitated a leafe which extended for a term of eight years, for which the Indians were paid Six Thoufand Dollars.

On *March* 19, 1775, a deed in fee fimple for this tract of land was given upon further confideration of £2000. This deed was in the name of *Charles Robertfon*, a reprefentative of the *Watauga Settlers' Affociation*, and embraced all the territory within the following bounds:[1] "All that tract on the waters of the *Watauga, Holfton, Great Canaway* or *New* River, beginning on the fouth or fouthweft of *Holfton* River fix miles above *Long Ifland* in that river; thence a direct line in nearly a fouth courfe to the ridge dividing the waters of the *Watauga* from the waters of the *Nonachucky* and along the ridge in a foutheafterly direction to the *Blue Ridge* or line dividing *North Carolina* from the *Cherokee* lands; thence along the *Blue Ridge* to the *Virginia* line and weft along fuch line to the *Holfton* River; to the beginning, including all the waters of the *Watauga*, part of the waters of *Holfton*, and the head branches of *New* River or the *Great Canaway*, agreeable to the aforefaid boundaries."

In 1772 *Jacob Brown* leafed from the *Cherokees*, for a horfe load of goods, a tract on the *Watauga* and *Nonachucky* Rivers. On *March,* 25, 1775, he fecured for a further confideration of ten fhillings a deed in fee for the leafed tract, as well as an additional tract of confiderable extent.

The boundary of the firft of thefe bodies of land ran from the mouth of *Great Limeftone* Creek, thence up the fame to its main fork to the ridge dividing the *Watauga* and *Nonachucky* Rivers; thence to the head of *Indian* Creek, where it joins the *Great Iron* Mountains and along those mountains to the *Nonachucky* River; acrofs the *Nonachucky* River, including its creeks, and down the fide of the *Nonachucky* Mountain against the mouth of the *Great Limeftone* Creek, and from thence to the place of beginning.

The fecond purchafe comprifed a tract lying on the *Nonachucky* River below the mouth of *Big Limeftone* on both fides of the river and adjoining the tract juft defcribed. Its boundaries are defined as beginning on the fouth fide of the *Nonachucky* River below the old fields that lie below the *Limeftone* on the north fide of *Nonachucky* Mountain at a large rock, thence north 32° weft to the mouth of *Camp* Creek on the fouth fide of the river; thence acrofs the river; thence purfuing a northwefterly courfe to the dividing ridge between *Lick* Creek and the *Watauga* or *Holfton* Rivers, thence along the dividing ridge to the reft of *Brown's* lands; thence down the main fork of *Big Limeftone* to its mouth; thence croffing the *Nonachucky* River and purfuing a straight courfe to the *Nonachucky* Mountains, and along fuch mountains to the beginning.[2]

Henderfon's

---

[1] Ramfey's Annals of Tenneffee p. 109.   [2] Fifth Annual Report of Bureau of Ethnology, p. 109.

Henderfon's purchafe of *March* 17, 1775 was concluded at *Sycamore Shoals* on the *Watauga* River. By the terms of this treaty *Richard Henderfon* and eight other private citizens, purchafed for 10,000 lbs. in merchandife, all the land lying between the *Kentucky* and *Cumberland* Rivers. This purchafe was made under the name of the "*Colony of Tranfylvania in North America.*" The two deeds conveying this property were commonly known as the "Path Deed" and the "Great Grant;" the former beginning on the *Holfton*, "Where the courfe of *Powell's* Mountain ftrikes the fame; thence up the river to the croffing of the *Virginia* Line; thence wefterly along the line run by *Donelfon* *** to a point fix *Englifh* miles of *Long Ifland* in *Holfton* River; thence a direct courfe towards the mouth of the *Great Kanawha* until it reaches the top of the ridge of *Powell's* Mountain; thence wefterly along faid ridge to the beginning. This tract was located in northeaft *Tenneffee* and the extreme fouthweftern corner of *Virginia.*

The fecond deed known as the "Great Grant" comprifed the territory beginning on the *Ohio* River at the mouth of the *Kentucky, Cherokee*, or what, by the *Englifh*, is called *Louifa* river; thence up faid river and the moft northwardly fork of the fame to the head fpring thereof; thence a foutheaft courfe to the ridge of *Powell's* Mountain; thence weftwardly along the ridge of faid mountain to a point from which a north-weft courfe will ftrike the head fpring of the moft fouthwardly branch of *Cumberland* River; thence down faid river, including all its waters, to the *Ohio* River; thence up faid river as it meanders to the beginning.[1]

It will be feen from this ftatement of the boundary that this tract comprifed nearly the whole of central and weftern *Kentucky*, as well as part of northern central *Tenneffee.*

From the report of the treaty commiffioners of 1785 it is noted that *Henderfon's* purchafe did not extend fouth of the *Cumberland* River proper.[2] This ftatement is not upheld by literal reading of the boundaries given, as they include all the territory watered by the *Cumberland* River and its various branches.

A very thorough and comprehenfive map, outlining all *Cherokee* ceffions of territory, will be found in the excellent account of the "*Cherokee Nation of Indians, by Charles C. Royce.*" This account is contained in the Fifth Report of the *Bureau of Ethnology.*

Royce in commenting upon the various treaties of the *Cherokees* calls attention to the fact that all grants of private individuals were regarded as legally inoperative, though in fome inftances the beneficiaries were permitted to enjoy the benefits of their purchafes in a modified degree. All fuch purchafes had been inhibited by royal proclamation of King *George* III. under date of *October* 7, 1763,[3] wherein all provincial governors were forbidden to grant lands or iffue land warrants locatable upon any territory weft of the mountains of the fources of ftreams flowing into the *Atlantic.* All private perfons were enjoined from purchafing lands from the *Indians*, and purchafes of fuch lands could only be made for the crown by the governor or commander-in-chief of the colony, at fome general council or affembly of the *Indians* convened for that purpofe.

In the particular purchafe made by *Henderfon* and his coadjutors, the benefits thereof were afterwards claimed by the authorities of *Virginia* and *North Carolina* for thofe States, as the fucceffors of the royal prerogative within their refpective limits. In confideration, however, of *Henderfon's* valuable fervices on the frontier, and in compenfation for his large expenditures of money in negotiating the purchafe, the legiflature of *North Carolina* in 1783 granted to him and thofe interefted with him, a tract of 200,000 acres[4], conftituting a ftrip of land four miles in width from *Old Indian* Town on *Powell's* River to the mouth, and thence a ftrip, twelve miles in width, down the *Clinch* River. The legiflature of *Virginia* alfo granted them a tract of like extent upon the *Ohio* River, oppofite what is now *Evanfville, Ind.*[5]

A

---

[1] Fifth Annual Report of the Bureau of Ethnology pp. 148-149.
[2] American State Papers, Indian Affairs, Vol. 1, p. 38.   [3] Martin's North Carolina, Vol. II, p. 339.
[4] Haywood's Tenneffee, pp. 16, 17.   [5] Ramfey's Annals of Tenneffee, p. 204.

A thorough and comprehenſive map drawn from plate No. 8, of the Fifth Annual Report of the *Bureau of Ethnology*, appears as the frontiſpiece in this volume. The ſection deſignated by the numerals, 3, 4, 5, and 7, can be readily traced by dotted lines. Beginning near *Carrolton* on the *Ohio*, and following the *Kentucky* River to the mountains, thence a direct line to a point interſecting the boundary eſtabliſhed in 1770, clearly diſtinguiſhes the dividing line between ſections 5 and 7. The irregular boundary of Sections 4 begins at *Point Pleaſant*, and follows the *Kanawha* River to the *Alleghanies*, thence along *New River* to the mouth of *Cripple Creek*. Section 3, follows the mountain range from *Chiſwell's* Mine eaſt to the first interſecting range, thence ſouthweſt to *Virginia's* preſent Southern line.

Section 3 denotes the land acquired by the treaty of *October* 14, 1768, nearly the entire tract being in ſouthweſtern *Virginia*. Section 4 was acquired by the treaty of *October* 18, 1770, which was signed at *Lochabar, South Carolina*. This tract lay in *Virginia, Weſt Virginia*, Northeaſt *Tenneſſee* and the Eaſt end of *Kentucky*. Section 5 included the territory which now lies in *Virginia, Weſt Virginia*, and Eaſtern *Kentucky*, and was acquired by treaty of 1772. The treaty of *March* 17, 1775, ſhown on the map as ſection 7, included the territory now forming a part of *Kentucky, Virginia*, and *Tenneſſee*. This treaty was between *Richard Henderſon* and the various ſettlers who were intereſted with him in ſettling this particular ſection.

The treaty of 1772 being conſummated prior to the meeting of the Aſſembly, no legiſlation was neceſſary for its ratification. The Seſſion of this year however, was characterized by many important acts which were paſſed for the promotion of internal improvement. Such important matters as improving the navigation of the *Potomac;* the opening of a road from *Warm Springs* to *Jenning's Gap;* the determination to clear *Mattapony* River, and of circumventing the falls of *James* River, by a canal from *Weſtham* to a point below *Richmond*, and a canal from *Archer's Hope* Creek to *Queen's* Creek, through *Williamſburg*, to connect *James* River with the River *York*, were favorably acted upon. At no time in the hiſtory of the colony had ſuch ſtupendous undertakings been ſuggeſted, much leſs received ſerious conſideration, and the legiſlation of this Aſſembly marks an era in *Virginia's* development which is particularly noteworthy.

JOHN P. KENNEDY.

Richmond, July, 1906.

JOURNAL

of the

HOUSE OF BURGESSES

1770

Burgeffes.

Accomack	Thomas Parramore	Goochland	†*John Woodfon
	Southey Simpfon		Thomas Mann Randolph
Albemarle	Thomas Walker	Halifax	Nathaniel Terry
	Thomas Jefferfon		Walter Coles
Amelia	†*John Winn	Hampfhire	Abram Hite
	Robert Munford		James Mercer
Amherft	William Cabell, Jr.	Hanover	William Macon, Jr.
	†*Cornelius Thomas		Patrick Henry, Jr.
Augufta	Gabriel Jones	Henrico	Richard Randolph
	John Wilfon		Richard Adams
Bedford	†*John Talbot	Ifle of Wight	Richard Baker
	Charles Lynch		James Bridger
Botetourt	*William Prefton	James City	Lewis Burwell
	*John Bowyer		Robt. Carter Nicholas
Brunfwick	Nathaniel Edwards, Jr.	Jameftown	*Champion Travis
	Thomas Stith	King and Queen	William Lyne
Buckingham	Jofeph Cabell		John T. Corbin
	†*Benjamin Howard	King George	Charles Carter
Caroline	Edmund Pendleton		†*William Robinfon
	Walker Taliaferro	King William	Carter Braxton
Charles City	Benjamin Harrifon		Bernard Moore
	†*William Acrill	Lancafter	Richard Mitchell
Charlotte	Ifaac Read		Charles Carter
	Paul Carrington	Loudoun	Francis Peyton
Chefterfield	Archibald Cary		*James Hamilton
	Edward Ofborne	Louifa	Thomas Johnfon
The College	John Blair, Jr.		Richard Anderfon
Culpeper	Henry Pendleton	Lunenburg	†*Thomas Pettus
	†*Henry Field, Jr.		Lodowick Farmer
Cumberland	*John Mayo	Mecklenburg	*Matthew Marrable
	Alexander Trent		Robert Munford
Dinwiddie	Bolling Starke	Middlefex	Philip Ludwell Grymes
	John Banifter		Gawin Corbin
Elizabeth City	James Wallace	Nanfemond	Lemuel Riddick
	Wilfon Miles Cary		Benjamin Baker
Effex	William Roane	New Kent	Burwell Baffett
	James Edmondfon		William Clayton
Fairfax	George Wafhington	Norfolk	Thomas Newton, Jr.
	John Weft		John Wilfon
Fauquier	James Scott	Norfolk Borough	Jofeph Hutchings
	Thomas Marfhall	Northampton	John Burton
Frederick	Robert Rutherford		Severn Eyre
	James Wood	Northumberland	†*Spencer Mottrom Ball
Gloucefter	Lewis Burwell		Samuel Efkridge
	Thomas Whiting	Orange	James Walker
			†*Thomas Barbour

*Not fhown by the Journal to have been prefent during the Affembly.
†Signed the Affociation of June 22, 1770.

Pittſylvania	†*John Donelſon	Stafford	John Alexander
	Hugh Innes		*Thomſon Maſon
Prince Edward	Thomas Scott	Surry	Hartwell Cocke
	*Paſchall Greenhill		†*Thomas Bailey
Prince George	Richard Bland	Suſſex	David Maſon
	Peter Poythreſs		†*James Bell
Prince William	Henry Lee	Warwick	†*William Harwood
	Fouſhee Tebbs		William Digges
Princeſs Anne	Edward Hack Moſeley, Jr.	Weſtmoreland	Richard Henry Lee
	*John Ackiſs		Richard Lee
Richmond	Robert Wormeley Carter	Williamſburg	Peyton Randolph
	†*Francis Lightfoot Lee	York	Dudley Digges
Southampton	†*Edwin Gray		Thomas Nelſon, Jr.
	†*Henry Taylor		
Spotſylvania	Benjamin Grymes		
	Roger Dixon		

*Not ſhown by the Journal to have been preſent during the Aſſembly.
†Signed the Aſſociation of June 22, 1770.

Changes in the Perſonnel, 1770.

Amelia	Robert Munford ſucceeded Thomas Tabb
Loudoun	Joſias Clapham ſucceeded James Hamilton
Suſſex	James Bell ſucceeded John Edmunds

JOURNAL

of the

HOUSE OF BURGESSES

Monday, the 21st of May, 10 Geo. III. 1770.

MR *Speaker* acquainted the Houfe, that the Governor had delivered to him, and defired him to lay before the Houfe, an Extract of a Letter to his Excellency from the Earl of *Hillfborough*, dated *Whitehall, February* 17th, 1770, upon the Subject Matters of the Addreffes of this Houfe refpecting the Importation of Copper-money, the further Extenfion of the Boundary Line betwixt this Colony and the *Indians*,[1] and the Importation of Salt from foreign *European* Ports.

And he delivered the Extract in at the Clerk's Table.

Ordered, That the faid Extract do lie upon the Table, to be perufed by the Members of the Houfe.

Ordered, That an Addrefs be made to the Governor, to order a new Writ to be made out for the electing of a Burgefs to ferve in this prefent General Affembly for the County of *Suffex* in the Room of M[r] *John Edmunds*,[2] deceafed; and that M[r] *David Mafon* do wait upon his Excellency with the faid Addrefs.

Several *Petitions* of fundry Freeholders and Inhabitants of the Counties of *Prince George, Dinwiddie, Amelia, Brunfwick, Lunenburg, Mecklenburg, Charlotte* and *Suffex*, whofe Names are thereunto fubfcribed, were prefented to the Houfe, and read; fetting forth, that the very great quantities of Tobacco brought to the Ware-houfes for Infpection of that Commodity on *Appomattox* River, render it impoffible for the prefent Infpectors to give proper Difpatch; and therefore praying that another Infpection of Tobacco may be eftablifhed on the Lots of Col. *Robert Bolling*, which he lately purchafed of M[r] *Patrick Ramfay*, in the Town of *Blandford*, on the faid River.

Ordered, That the faid Petitions be referred to the Committee of propofitions and Grievances; and that they do examine the Matter thereof, and report the fame, with their Opinion thereupon, to the Houfe.

Several *Petitions* of fundry Perfons, Inhabitants of the County of *Dinwiddie*, whofe Names are thereunto fubfcribed, were prefented to the Houfe, and read; fetting forth, that the Quantities of Tobacco brought to the Warehoufes on *Appomattox* River are fo increafed, that the prefent Houfes are not fufficient to contain them, and the Infpectors cannot give the Planters reafonable Difpatch; and therefore praying that another Infpection of Tobacco may be eftablifhed on the Land of *Robert Bolling*, Gentleman, between *Bolling's* old Warehoufe and *Bollingbrook*, as a Place more proper and convenient for that Purpofe than *Blandford*.

Ordered, That the faid petition be referred to the Committee of propofitions and Grievances; and that they do examine the Matter thereof, and report the fame, with their Opinion thereupon, to the Houfe.

A *Petition* of the Rector and Veftry of the Parifh of *Briftol*, in the County of *Prince George*, whofe Names are thereunto fubfcribed, was prefented to the Houfe, and read; fetting forth, that the Glebe of the faid Parifh is inconveniently fituated, and con-

tains

---

[1] Cherokees.   [2] James Bell.

tains no more than One Hundred and Ninety-two Acres; and therefore praying that the said Glebe may be sold, and another, more convenient, purchased. 162

Ordered, That the said Petition be referred to the Committee for Religion; and that they do examine the Matter thereof, and report the same, with their Opinion thereupon, to the House.

A *Petition* of *Richard Eppes*, of the County of *Prince George*, was presented to the House, and read; setting forth, that the Ferry over *James* River from *City Point*, in the County aforesaid to *Shirley Hundred*, at the Ship Landing, in the County of *Charles City*, is a private Grievance, and not convenient to the Public, and hath been long disused; and therefore praying that so much of the Act¹ of General Assembly, made in the Sixth Year of the Reign of his late Majesty King *George* the Second, as established the said Ferry, may be repealed.

Ordered, That the said Petition be referred to the Committee of propositions and Grievances; and that they do examine the matter thereof, and report the same, with their Opinion thereupon, to the House.

A *Petition* of *John Ballantine*, of the County of *Westmoreland*, was presented to the House, and read; setting forth, that the petitioner, in the Year 1755, was employed by Lieutenant *John Hamilton*, of the *Virginia* Regiment, to transport, by Water, Forty-four Recruits, from *Mattox* to *Alexandria,* on *Potomack* River, and faithfully performed the Service, but had received no Satisfaction for it, not knowing to whom he should apply, the said *Hamilton* having been killed in the Campaign of that Year; and therefore praying that the House will make him a reasonable Satisfaction for his said Service.

Ordered, That the said Petition be referred to the Committee of Public Claims; and that they do examine the Matter thereof, and report the same, with their Opinion thereupon, to the House.

A *Message* from the *Governor*, by Mʳ *Walthoe:*

Mʳ *Speaker,*

His Excellency the Governor has commanded me to lay before your House, and to recommend to your immediate Notice, certain Letters and Papers, relative to Indian Affairs.

And he presented the said Letters and Papers at the Bar.

Ordered, That the said Letters and Papers do lie upon the Table, to be perused by the Members of the House.

The House being informed that Mʳ *Nathaniel Edwards*,² one of the Members for the County of *Brunswick*, had, since his Election for the said County, accepted a Commission from the Deputy Secretary of this Colony to execute the Office of Clerk of the Court of the said County of *Brunswick*, but had not qualified under his said Commission, the said County Court having refused to admit him to the said Office;

A *Motion* was made, and the Question being put, That the said Mʳ *Edwards* is capable to sit and vote as a Member of this House.

It was *resolved* in the Affirmative.

Ordered, That an Address be made to the *Governor*, to order a new Writ to be made out for the electing of a Burgess³ to serve in this present General Assembly for the County of *Essex*, in the Room of Mʳ *William Roane*, who, since his Election for the said County, hath accepted the Office of Deputy Attorney for the King in the said County; and that Mʳ *Edmondson* do wait upon his Excellency with the said Address.

A *Bill* to continue and amend the Act, intituled, *An Act⁴ for amending the Staple of Tobacco, and preventing Frauds in his Majesty's Customs*, was read a second Time. ¹⁶³

Resolved, That the Bill be committed.

Resolved, That the Bill be committed to a Committee of the whole House.

Resolved, That this House will, upon *Thursday* next, resolve itself into a Committee of the whole House upon the said Bill.

And then the House adjourned till Tomorrow Morning Eleven of the Clock.

𝕿uesday

---

¹ Hening, IV, p. 362.   ² Succeeded by John Jones in 1771.   ³ Roane was re-elected.
⁴ Hening, VIII, p. 69.

Tuesday, the 22d of May, 10 Geo. III. 1770.

ORDERED, That the Petition for feveral Merchants, Planters, and others, praying that a Tobacco Infpection may be eftablifhed at *Low Point*, on *Chipoake's* Creek, which, upon *Tuefday* the Twelfth Day of *December* laft, was ordered to lie upon the Table, be referred to the Committee of Propofitions and Grievances; and that they do examine the Matter thereof, and report the fame, with their Opinion thereupon, to the Houfe.

Several *Petitions* of fundry Inhabitants of the Counties of *Prince George* and *Brunfwick*, whofe Names are thereunto fubfcribed, was prefented to the Houfe, and read; taking Notice of the Petition prefented to this Houfe for removing the Warehoufes from *Cabin Point* to *Low Point*, and fetting forth that the latter is a much more inconvenient Place for an Infpection that the former; and therefore praying that the faid Petition, for a Removal, may be rejected.

Ordered, That the faid petitions be referred to the Committee of Propofitions and Grievances; and that they do examine the Matter thereof, and report the fame, with their Opinion thereupon, to the Houfe.

A *Petition* of fundry Freeholders and Houfekeepers, of the County of *Weftmoreland*, whofe Names are thereunto fubfcribed, was prefented to the Houfe, and read; taking Notice of the Application made to this Houfe, for new modelling the Counties in the *Northern Neck;* and fetting forth the Difficulties and Expenfes of executing, and the ill Confequences which will refult from the propofed Alteration; and therefore praying that the Boundaries of the faid Counties may remain as they are.

Ordered, That the faid petition be referred to the Committee of Propofitions and Grievances; and that they do examine the Matter thereof, and report the fame, with their Opinion thereupon, to the Houfe.

Ordered, That the Petition of feveral Freeholders, Merchants, and others, of the County of *Weftmoreland*, and the adjacent Counties, praying that the Infpection of Tobacco at *Stratford* Landing may be difcontinued, which, upon *Friday* the eighth Day of *December* laft, was ordered to lie upon the Table, be referred to the Committee of propofitions and Grievances; and that they do examine the Matter thereof, and report the fame, with their Opinion thereupon, to the Houfe.

164 A *Petition* of feveral Freeholders and Houfekeepers, Inhabitants of the County of *Weftmoreland*, whofe Names are thereunto fubfcribed, was prefented to the Houfe, and read, taking Notice of the Petition prefented to this House, for difcontinuing the Infpection at *Stratford* Landing; and fetting forth that the Reafons affigned for the fame are infufficient; and therefore praying that the faid Infpection may be continued.

Ordered, That the faid Petition be referred to the Committee of propofitions and Grievances; and that they do examine the Matter thereof, and report the fame, with their Opinion thereupon, to the Houfe.

A *Petition* of *Baylor Walker* and *William Fleet*, Executors of the laft Will and Teftament of *John Semple*, deceafed, was prefented to the Houfe, and read; fetting forth, that in the Year 1765, the faid *John Semple*, having become bound with *Philip Rootes*, who was appointed Sheriff of the County of *King and Queen*, as his Surety for the faithful Execution of that Office, and intending to take fome Meafures to be relieved from the faid Engagement, *John Robinfon*, Efquire, then Treafurer, obliged himfelf and his Reprefentatives to fave harmlefs the faid *John Semple*, who thereupon thought it unneceffary to provide further for his Indemnification; but after the Death of the faid *John Robinfon*, on a Motion of the fucceeding Treafurer, a Judgment was recovered againft the faid *John Semple* for 1271 *l.* 8 *s.* 7 *d.* for the Balance of Taxes collected by the faid *Philip Rootes*, and his Deputies, during the Time of his Sheriffalty, and Cofts, to fatiffy which Judgment the faid Decedent's Eftate hath been taken in Execution; and that the petitioners conceive it to be juft and equitable,

that

that the Money and Cofts recovered as aforefaid, fhould be confidered as fo much received by the faid *John Robinfon*, to whom, as Treafurer, the faid *Philip Rootes* was accountable for the fame, and be added to his public Account, and that the Eftate of the faid *John Semple* fhould be difcharged from the faid *Judgment;* and therefore humbly fubmitting the Cafe to the Wifdom and Juftice of the Houfe, and praying fuch Relief as to them fhall feem equitable.

Ordered, That the faid Petition be referred to the Committee of Public Claims; and that they do examine the Matter thereof, and report the fame, with their Opinion thereupon, to the Houfe.

M\u02b3 *Edmund Pendleton* reported, from the Committee to whom the Bill to veft certain Lands, whereof *John Robinfon*, Efquire, died feized, in Truft for *Philip Johnfon*, Gentleman, and his Children, in Truftees, for the Purpofes therein mentioned, was committed, that the Committee has examined the Allegations of the Bill, and found the fame to be true, and that the Committee had gone through the Bill, and made an Amendment thereunto, which they had directed him to report to the Houfe, and he read the Report in his Place, and afterwards delivered the Bill, with the Amendment, in at the Clerk's Table; where the Amendment was twice read, and, upon the Queftion put thereupon, was agreed to by the Houfe.

Ordered, That the Bill, with the Amendment, be ingroffed.

M\u02b3 *Bland* reported, from the Committee of Propofitions and Grievances, that the Committee had had under their Confideration the Petition of *Richard Eppes*, to them referred, praying that fo much of the Act of General Affembly paffed in the Sixth year of the Reign of his late Majefty King *George* the Second, intituled, *An Act[1] for fettling new Ferries over* James, Appomattox, Nottoway, Rappahannock, *and* Potomack *River*, as eftablifhes a Ferry from City Point, in the County of Prince George, to the Ship Landing at Shirley Hundred, in the County of Charles City, may be repealed, and had come to a Refolution thereupon, which the Committee had directed him to report to the Houfe, and he read the Report in his Place, and afterwards delivered it in at the Clerk's Table; where the Refolution of the Committee was read, and is as followeth, *viz.*

Refolved, That it is the Opinion of this Committee, that the faid petition is reafonable.

Ordered, That it be an Inftruction to the faid Committee, who are appointed to prepare and bring in a Bill, purfuant to the fourth Refolution of the faid Committee which was agreed to by the Houfe upon *Monday* the thirteenth Day of *November* laft, that they have Power to receive a Claufe or Claufes, purfuant to the faid Refolution of the faid Committee, which hath been this Day agreed to by the Houfe.

A *Petition* of *Henry Townfend*, late a Soldier in the *Virginia* Regiment, was prefented to the Houfe, and read; fetting forth that the Petitioner had ferved upwards of four Years in the faid Regiment, and on the twelfth Day of *November*, in the Year 1758, was fo wounded in his Breaft and Arm, that he is unable to labour; and therefore praying that this Houfe will take his Cafe into Confideration, and grant him fuch Relief as to them fhall feem reafonable.

Ordered, That the faid Petition be referred to the Committee of Public Claims; and that they do examine the Matter thereof, and report the fame, with their Opinion thereupon, to the Houfe.

The Houfe was moved, that the Extract of a Letter to his Excellency the Governor, from the Earl of *Hillfborough*, which was Yefterday ordered to lie upon the Table, might be read.

And the fame being read accordingly,

Refolved, That an humble Addrefs be prefented to his Excellency the Governor, returning him the Thanks of this Houfe for the very early Attention he hath been pleafed to give to their former Addreffes, refpecting the Copper Coin, the Extenfion of the Boundary Line, and the Importation of Salt into this Colony; and intreating his

Lordfhip

---

1 **Hening, IV.** p. 362.

Lordſhip to uſe his further good Offices in endeavoring to procure Succeſs to the earneſt Deſires of this Houſe in thoſe ſeveral important Articles.

Ordered, That a Committee be appointed to draw up an Addreſs to be preſented to the Governor, upon the ſaid Reſolution.

And a *Committee* was appointed of Mᵣ *Treaſurer,* Mᵣ *Bland,* Mᵣ *Richard Henry Lee,* and Mᵣ *Harriſon.*

Ordered, That the Letters¹ which have paſſed between the Committee of Correſpondence, and the Agent for this Colony, ſince the twenty-firſt Day of *December* laſt, be laid before the Houſe.

The Houſe was moved, that the Letters and papers relative to *Indian* Affairs, mentioned in his Excellency the Governor's Maſſage to this Houſe, which were Yeſterday ordered to lie upon the Table, might be read.

And the ſame being read accordingly,

Ordered, That the ſaid Meſſage, Letters, and Papers, be taken into Conſideration To-morrow.

166   *Reſolved,* That this Houſe will, To-morrow, reſolve itſelf into a Committee of the whole Houſe, to take into Conſideration the Governor's Meſſage, and the Letters and Papers relative to *Indian* Affairs, therein mentioned.

A *Petition* of the Juſtices of the County of *James City,* was preſented to the Houſe, and read; ſetting forth that the Petitioners and the Corporation of the City of *Williamſburg* had, for their mutual Convenience and Benefit, entered into a Contract to build a commodious Court-Houſe at their joint Expence; but that there is no Situation fit for the Purpoſe, within the Line of the ſaid County, as it is now eſtabliſhed; and therefore praying that an Act may paſs for adding to the ſaid County ſo much of the Market Square, in the ſaid City, as lies on the North Side of the Main Street, as far as *Nicholſon* Street, and between *Hugh Walker's* Lot and the Paling where Mᵣ *Haldenby Dixon's* Store ſtands, and for empowering the Petitioners to ſell a Lot of Land, whereon their preſent Court-Houſe ſtands, in the ſaid City, and applying the proceeds of ſuch Sale towards diſcharging their Proportion of the Expence of building a new Court-Houſe. *And also*

A *Petition* of the Mayor, Recorder, Alderman, and Common Council, of the City of *Williamſburg,* was preſented to the Houſe, and read; ſetting forth their Agreement with the Court of the County of *James City* to join in building a Court-Houſe on the Market Square of the ſaid City; and therefore praying that Part of the ſaid Market Square may be added to the ſaid County of *James City,* and that the Petitioners may be permitted to uſe the Guard-Houſe, in the ſaid City, the Guard being diſcontinued, as and for a Market-Houſe.

Ordered, That the ſaid ſeveral Petitions be ſeverally referred to the Committee of Propoſitions and Grievances; and that they do examine the Matter thereof, and report the ſame, with their Opinion thereupon, to the Houſe.

A *Petition* of *Nathaniel Littleton Savage,* of the County of *Northampton,* was preſented to the Houſe, and read; ſetting forth, that the Petitioner is ſeized in Fee Tail of Eighteen Hundred Acres of Land, in the County of *York,* and that it will be greatly to the Intereſt of the Petitioner, as well as thoſe claiming under him, to dock the Intail of the ſaid Land; and therefore praying that Leave may be given to bring in a Bill for that Purpoſe.

Ordered, That Leave be given to bring in a Bill, purſuant to the Prayer of the ſaid Petition; and that Mᵣ *Eyre* and Mᵣ *Edmund Pendleton* do prepare and bring in the ſame.

A *Petition* of the Juſtices of Peace of the County of *Culpeper,* and the Attornies practicing in the Court of the ſaid County, praying that the Court Day of the ſaid County may be altered from the third *Thurſday* to the third *Monday* in every Month.

Ordered, That Leave be given to bring in a Bill purſuant to the Prayer of the ſaid Petition; and that Mᵣ *Henry Pendleton* do prepare and bring in the ſame.

An ingroſſed *Bill* for eſtabliſhing a Town in the County of *Pittſylvania,* was read the third Time.

Reſolved

¹ Committee of Correſpondence Papers 1759-1774.

Refolved, That the Bill do pafs; and that the Title be, *An Act[1] for eftablifhing a Town in the County of* Pittfylvania.

Ordered, That Mr *Bland* do carry the Bill to the Council, and defire their Concurrance.

A *Bill* for fettling the Fees of the Clerk and Serjeant of the Court of *Huftings*, for the City of *Williamfburg*, was read a fecond Time. [167]

Ordered, That the Bill be ingroffed.

An engroffed *Bill* to oblige the Owners of Mills, Hedges, or Stops, on the Rivers therein mentioned, to make Openings or Slopes therein, for the Paffage of Fifh, was read the third Time.

Refolved, That the Bill do pafs; and that the Title be, *An Act[2] to oblige the Owners of Mills, Hedges, or Stops, on the Rivers therein mentioned, to make Openings or Slopes therein, for the Paffage of Fifh.*

Ordered, That Mr *Bland* do carry the Bill to the Council, and defire their Concurrence.

An Engroffed *Bill* to prevent Mafters or Skippers of Veffels from felling fpirituous Liquors, except to their own Crews, in fmall Quantities, was read the third Time.

And a *Motion* was made, and the Queftion being put, that the Bill do pafs;

It paffed in the Negative.

Refolved, That the Bill be rejected.

A *Bill* for the Relief of Parifhes from fuch Charges as may arife from Baftard Children born within the fame, was read a fecond Time.

Refolved, That the Bill be committed to the Committee for Religion.

A *Petition* of the Freeholders and Houfekeepers, of the Parifh of *Hungars*, in the County of *Northampton*, whofe Names are thereunto fubfcribed, was prefented to the Houfe, and read; complaining of the irregular Election, and inconvenient Refidence, and fome illegal Practices and unwarrantable Proceedings of the Veftry of the faid Parifh; and therefore praying that the faid Veftry may be diffolved.

Ordered, That the faid petition be referred to the Committee for Religion; and that they do examine the Matter thereof, and report the fame, with their Opinion thereupon, to the Houfe.

A *Petition* of fundry of the Inhabitants of this Colony, whofe Names are thereunto fufbcribed, was prefented to the Houfe and read; fetting forth, that a Ferry eftablifhed from the Land of *John Laidler*, in the Province of *Maryland*, over *Potomack* River, to this Colony, is very advantageous to the Inhabitants of both, and that the Brick-Houfe Landing, in the County of *Weftmoreland*, formerly belonging to *Henry Wafhington*, deceafed, is the moft convenient Place for Paffengers over the faid Ferry to be put on Shore at; and therefore praying that the faid Brick-Houfe Landing may be declared a Public Landing, and a road be opened from thence to the *Weftmoreland* main Road, as it now runs.

Ordered, That the faid Petition be referred to the Committee of Propofitions and Grievances; and that they do examine the Matter thereof, and report the fame, with their Opinion thereupon, to the Houfe.

Ordered, That an Addrefs be prefented to the Governor, to order a Writ to be made out for the electing of Burgeffes[3] to ferve in this prefent General Affembly for the County of *Botetourt*, no Writ having been iffued for that Purpofe; and that Mr *John Wilfon*, of *Augufta*, do wait upon his Excellency with the faid Addrefs.

And then the Houfe adjourned till Tomorrow Morning Eleven of the Clock.

𝖂𝖊𝖉𝖓𝖊𝖘𝖉𝖆𝖞

[1] Hening, VIII, p. 417 (Chatham.) [2] Ibid, VIII, p. 361.
[3] William Prefton and John Bowyer.

Wednesday, the 23d of May, 10 Geo. III. 1770.

A *Petition* of *Thomas Sumner*, Proprietor of the Public Warehouse, at *Conftance's* in the County of *Nanfemond*, was prefented to the Houfe, and read; fetting forth, that, at the Time the Rent of the faid Warehoufe was fettled to be paid out of the eight Pence *per* Hogfhead, great Quantities of Tobacco were brought there to be infpected which obliged the Petitioner to build large Houfes for their Reception; but that fince, the Hogfheads of Tobacco brought there are fo few that the Rents are not fufficient to defray the Expence of neceffary Repairs; and therefore praying that a certain yearly Rent for the faid Warehoufe, for the future, may be paid by the Public.

Ordered, That the faid petition be referred to the Committee of Propofitions and Grievances; and that they do examine the Matter thereof, and report the fame, with their Opinion thereupon, to the Houfe.

Mr *Bland* prefented to the Houfe, from the Committee of Correfpondence, according to Order, the Letters which have paffed between the faid Committee, and the Agent for this Colony, fince the 21ft Day of *December* laft.

And the faid Letters were read.

Ordered, That the faid Letters do lie upon the Table, to be perufed by the Members of the Houfe.

A *Bill* to continue and amend the *Act*[1] *for better regulating and difciplining the Militia*, was read a fecond Time.

Refolved, That the Bill be committed.

Refolved, That the Bill be committed to a Committee of the whole Houfe.

Refolved, That this Houfe will, upon *Tuefday* next, refolve itfelf into a Committee of the whole Houfe, upon the faid Bill.

A *Meffage* from the Council, by Mr *Hubard*.

Mr *Speaker*,

The Council have agreed to the Bill, *intituled*, An Act[2] to oblige the Owners of Mills, Hedges or Stops, on the Rivers therein mentioned, to make Openings or Slopes therein, for the Paffage of Fifh, *without any Amendment*. *And alfo*

The Council have agreed to the Bill, *intituled*, An Act[3] for eftablifhing a Town in the County of *Pittfylvania, with an Amendment; to which Amendment the Council defire the Concurrence of this Houfe.*

And then the Meffenger withdrew.

Several *petitions* of fundry of the Inhabitants of the County of *Spotfylvania*, whofe Names are thereunto fubfcribed, were prefented to the Houfe, and read; taking Notice of an Application made to this Houfe for appointing the General Mufters and Courts Martial in the faid County, to be in or near the Center thereof, and fetting forth that fuch a Regulation would be unreafonable and inconvenient, and therefore praying that the law relating to the Appointment of Mufters and Courts Martial in that Refpect may not be altered.

Ordered, That the faid Petitions do lie upon the Table.

A *Petition* of the Inhabitants of the County of *Augufta*, whofe Names are thereunto fubfcribed, was prefented to the Houfe, and read; fetting forth that the Time by Law appointed for General Mufters is very inconvenient, and therefore praying that the faid Law may be altered, by appointing General Mufters to be in the Month of *September* or *October*.

Ordered, That the faid Petition do lie upon the Table.

A *Petition* of *David Meade*, and *Sarah* his wife, was prefented to the Houfe, and read; fetting forth that the Petitioners are feized in Right of the Wife as Tenants in

Fee

---

1 Hening, VII, p. 93.   2 Ibid, VIII. p. 361.   3 Ibid, VIII, p. 417 (Chatham.)

Fee Tail of and in a Tract of Land, in the County of *Northampton*, situate on *King's* Creek, and the Bay of *Chesapeak*, containing Six Hundred Acres; and that it will be greatly for the Advantage of the petitioners and their Posterity, to dock the Intail of the said Land, and, in Lieu thereof, settle other Lands of equal or greater Value, in the County of *Nansemond*, whereof the said *David Meade* is seized in Fee Simple, to the same Uses; and therefore praying that an Act may pass for that Purpose.

Ordered, That Leave be given to bring in a Bill, pursuant to the Prayer of the said Petition; and that Mr *Blair* and Mr *Edmund Pendleton* do prepare and bring in the same.

A *Bill* to continue an Act, intituled, An Act¹ *for regulating the Practice of Attornies*, was read a second Time.

Ordered, That the Bill be ingrossed.

A *Petition* of *Martin Shearman*, and *Robert Mitchell*, Inspectors of Tobacco at *Deep Creek* Warehouse, in the County of *Lancaster*, was presented to the House, and read; setting forth that the said Warehouse was broke open in the Year 1759, and Three Thousand and Fifteen Pounds of Crop Tobacco were taken out of it, for which the petitioners were obliged to pay 60 *l.* 6 *s.* that the said Warehouse was again broke open in the year 1762, and One Thousand Nine Hundred Pounds of Crop Tobacco were taken out of it, for which the Petitioners were obliged to pay 19 *l.* and that since Five Thousand Nine Hundred Pounds of Transfer Tobacco were stolen out of the said Warehouse, for which the Petitioners were obliged to pay 59 *l.* and that this House had been pleased in this Session to reimburse the said last mentioned Sum of Money, and praying they may also be reimbursed the two former Sums of Money, amounting to 79 *l.* 6 *s.*

Ordered, That the said petition be referred to the Committee of Public Claims; and that they do examine the Matter thereof, and report the same, with their Opinion thereupon, to the House.

A *Petition* of *Samuel Meredith* was presented to the House, and read; setting forth that the Petitioner is seized as Tenant in Fee Tail of a Tract of Land, in the County of *Gloucester*, and hath no Slaves to work thereon, and that it would be greatly to his Interest to sell the said Land, and apply the Money arising from the Sale, to the Purchase of other Land and Slaves, to be settled to the same Uses as the said intailed Land; and therefore praying that an Act may pass for that Purpose.

Ordered, That Leave be given to bring in a Bill, pursuant to the Prayer of the said Petition; and that Mr *Edmund Pendleton* do prepare and bring in the same.

An engrossed *Bill* from the Council, intituled, An Act *to prevent selling Oysters at unseasonable Times*, was read a second Time.

Resolved, That the Bill be committed.

Resolved, That the Bill be committed to a Committee of the whole House. ¹⁷⁰

Resolved, That this House will now resolve itself into a Committee of the whole House upon the said Bill.

The House accordingly resolved itself into a Committee of the whole House upon the said Bill.

Mr *Speaker* left the Chair.

Mr *Bland* took the Chair of the Committee.

Mr *Speaker* resumed the Chair.

Mr *Bland* reported from the Committee, that they had directed him to report the Bill to the House, without any Amendment; and he delivered the Bill in at the Clerk's Table.

A *Motion* was made, and the Question being put, that the Bill be read a third Time; It passed in the Negative.

Resolved, That the Bill be rejected.

A *Bill* to impower the Inhabitants of *New-Kent* County, to retail Cyder and Brandy, the Produce of their own Orchards, was read a second Time.

A *Motion* was made, and the Question being put, that the Bill be committed; It passed in the Negative.

Resolved

¹ Hening, VI, p. 140.

Refolved, That the Bill be rejected.

A *Bill* to amend the Act, intituled, *An Act[1] to amend the Act for the better Government of Servants and Slaves*, was read a fecond Time.

Refolved, That the Bill be committed to the Committee of Propofitions and Grievances.

A *Bill* to repeal an Act made in the Twenty-fecond Year of his late Majefty's Reign, intituled *An Act[2] concerning Strays, and to eftablifh a more effectual Method to prevent Frauds committed by Perfons taking up Strays*, was read a fecond Time.

Refolved, That the Bill be committed to the Committee of propofitions and Grievances.

A *Bill* to dock the Intail of Two Thoufand Eight Hundred Acres of Land, in the County of *Brunfwick*, whereof *Armiftead Lightfoot* is feized in Fee Tail and vefting the fame in Truftees for certain Purpofes therein mentioned, was read a fecond Time.

Refolved, That the Bill be committed to all the Members who ferve for the Counties of *York, Brunfwick, Goochland, James City, Surry* and *Suffex*.

A *Bill* for encouraging the making of Hemp, was read a fecond Time.

Refolved, That the Bill be committed to the Committee of Trade.

A *Bill* to amend an Act, intituled *An Act againft ftealing Hogs*, was read a fecond Time.

Refolved, That the Bill be committed to the Committee of Propofitions and Grievances.

Ordered, That Leave be given to bring in a Bill to fufpend the Execution of an Act, intituled *An Act[3] to amend An Act, intituled An Act for the Infpection of Pork, Beef, Flour, Tar, Pitch and Turpentine;* and that Mr *Riddick* do prepare and bring in the fame.

The *Order* of the Day being read;

171 *Refolved*, That this Houfe will, upon *Friday* next, refolve itfelf into a Committee of the whole Houfe, to take into Confideration the Governor's Meffage, and the Letters and papers, relative to *Indian* Affairs, therein mentioned.

Mr *Riddick* prefented to the Houfe, according to Order, a Bill to fufpend the Execution of an Act, intituled *An Act to amend an Act, intituled An Act for the Infpection of Pork, Beef, Flour, Tar, Pitch and Turpentine;* and the fame was received, and read the firft time.

Refolved, That the Bill be read a fecond Time.

A *Bill* to impower certain Truftees to leafe the Lands of the *Pamunkey Indians* and for other Purpofes therein mentioned, was read a fecond Time.

Refolved, That the Bill be committed to all the Members who ferve for the Counties of *King William, Caroline, Hanover, New-Kent*, and *King & Queen*.

And then the Houfe adjourned till To-morrow Morning Eleven of the Clock.

Thursday, the 24th of May, 10 Geo. III. 1770.

A *Bill* to fufpend the Execution of an Act, intituled *An Act to amend an Act, intituled An Act for the Infpection of Pork, Beef, Flour, Tar, Pitch, and Turpentine*, was read a fecond Time.

Refolved, That the Bill be committed to Mr *Richard Baker*, Mr *Benjamin Baker*, Mr *Riddick*, Mr *Edmund Pendleton*, and Mr *Harrifon*.

Mr *Henry Pendleton* prefented to the Houfe according to Order, a Bill for altering the Court Day of the County of *Culpeper;* and the fame was received, and read the firft Time.

Refolved, That the Bill be read a fecond Time.

A *Petition* of *Bernard Moore*, Efq; was prefented to the Houfe, and read; fetting forth that the Petitioner is feized in Fee Tail, under the Will of his Father, *Auguftine Moore*, Gentleman, deceafed, of and in a valuable Tract of Land, containing about

Eighteen

---

[1] Hening, VIII, p. 135.   [2] Ibid. VI, p. 133.   [3] Ibid, VIII, p. 351.

Eighteen Hundred Acres, lying on *Mattapony* River, in the County of *King William*, and having a numerous Family, cannot make any Provifion for his younger Children, without diftributing his few Slaves among them, whereby his Heir will be left without any to work his intailed Lands; and that if the faid intailed Lands, which will produce a great Price, were vefted in Truftees to be fold, and the Money laid out in the Purchafe of frefh upper Lands, and fome Slaves, to be fettled to the fame Ufes, the Heir would have a much more profitable Eftate, when he fucceeds to the fame, and the Petitioner, in the mean Time, might be enabled, from the Profits, to make a better Provifion for his younger Children; and therefore praying that an Act may pafs for that Purpofe.

Ordered, That Leave be given to bring in a Bill, purfuant to the Prayer of the faid Petition; and that Mr *Richard Henry Lee* do prepare and bring in the fame.

A *Petition* of *Robert Burwell* was prefented to the Houfe, and read; fetting forth that the Petitioner, under the Will of his Father, *Nathaniel Burwell*, late of the County of *Gloucefter*, Efq; deceafed, is feized as Tenant in Fee Tail, of a Tract or Parcel of Land, at 172 *Warwickfqueak* Bay, in the Parifh of *Newport*, and County of *Ifle of Wight*; and that it will be advantageous to the Petitioner, as well as to his Iffue, and thofe claiming in Remainder or Reverfion, if he can fell the faid Lands, and, in Lieu thereof, fettle, to the fame Ufes, other Lands, of greater Value, lying at *Bull Run*, in the County of *Prince William*, whereof he is feized as Tenant in Fee Simple; and therefore praying that an Act may pafs to dock the Intail of the faid Lands in *Ifle of Wight*, and fettle an Equivalent for the fame out of his faid Lands in *Prince William* County.

Ordered, That Leave be given to bring in a Bill, purfuant to the Prayer of the faid Petition; and that Mr *Richard Baker* do prepare and bring in the fame.

A *Petition* of feveral Perfons, Inhabitants of the Counties of *Halifax* and *Charlotte*, whofe Names are thereunto fubfcribed, was prefented to the Houfe, and read; fetting forth, that a Ferry over *Staunton* River, at a Ford about Two Miles above *Fuqua's*, would be more convenient than the Ferry now kept at the latter Place; and therefore praying that the faid Ferry may be removed to the faid Ford.

Ordered, That the faid petition be referred to the Committee of Propofitions and Grievances; and that they do examine the Matter thereof, and report the fame, with their Opinion thereupon, to the Houfe.

A *Petition* of feveral Perfons, inhabiting on the South Side of *Dan* River, in the County of *Halifax*, whofe Names are thereunto fubfcribed, was prefented to the Houfe, and read; fetting forth that the Court of the faid County hath ordered a way to be viewed for a Road to be opened to the *Little Falls* of *Dan* River, below the Mouth of *Hyco*, which hath been reported to be convenient, and therefore praying that a Ferry may be eftablifhed at the faid Place, from the Land of *Richard Jones*, on the South Side, to the Land of the Reverend Mr *Miles Selden*, Clerk, on the North Side of the faid River.

Ordered, That the faid Petition be referred to the Committee of Propofitions and Grievances; and that they do examine the Matter thereof, and report the fame, with their Opinion thereupon, to the Houfe.

A *Petition* of *Charles Lewis*, Gentleman, and of *John Lewis*, Gentleman, his eldeft Son and Heir apparent, was prefented to the Houfe, and read; fetting forth that by Act of General Affembly paffed in the Thirty-fourth Year of the Reign of King *George* the Second, a Tract of Land, containing Eighteen Hundred and Fifty Acres, lying on *Tye* River, in that Part of the County of *Albemarle*, which is now the County of *Amherft*, was vefted in the faid *Charles Lewis*, and the male Heirs of his Body; that the faid *Charles Lewis* hath delivered Poffeffion of the faid Land to his faid eldeft Son, who hath the Ufe and Occupation thereof; that the faid *John Lewis* having lately obtained a Grant of Eleven Hundred and Forty-fix Acres of Land, lying on *Dan* River, in the County of *Pittfylvania*, to which he hath removed, is defirous that the faid Lands in *Amherft* may be fold, and the faid *Dan* River Lands, which are of greater Value, be fettled in Lieu thereof; and that the faid *Charles Lewis* confents to fuch fettlement, being fatis-fied the fame will be advantageous to his faid Son and Family; and therefore praying

that

that an Act may pafs to veft the faid *Tye* River Lands in the faid *John Lewis* in Fee Simple, and to fettle the other Lands in Lieu thereof.

173   *Ordered*, That Leave be given to bring in a Bill, purfuant to the Prayer of the faid Petition; and that Mr *Edmund Pendleton* do prepare and bring in the fame.

Ordered, That Leave be given to bring in a Bill to amend an Act paffed in the former Part of this Seffion of Affembly, for reimburfing the Counties of *Hanover* and *King William* the Expence of clearing *Pamunkey* River; and that Mr *Henry* and Mr *Johnfon* do prepare and bring in the fame.

Mr *Blair* prefented to the Houfe, according to Order, a Bill[1] to veft certain Lands in *David Meade* in Fee Simple, whereof the faid *David* and *Sarah* his wife are feized, in Right of the faid *Sarah*, in Fee Tail, and for fettling other Lands in Lieu thereof; and the fame was received, and read the firft Time.

Refolved, That the Bill be read a fecond Time.

A Petition of *George Brooke*, Gentleman, was prefented to the Houfe, and read; fetting forth, that the Petitioner is feized in Fee Tail, under the Will of his Grandfather, *George Braxton*, Efq; deceafed, and a Family Settlement, of a Tract of Land, containing Five Hundred and Seventy-eight Acres, lying on *Mattapony* River, in the County of *King William*; and that he is feized in Fee Simple of a more valuable Tract, called *Mantapike*, containing Seven Hundred and Eighty Acres, lying in the County of *King & Queen*, on which he has made confiderable Improvements, and is defirous to give the fame to his eldeft Son, but cannot do fo unlefs he is impowered to make Provifion for his younger Children out of the faid *King William* Lands; and therefore praying that an Act may pafs to veft the faid Lands, in the County of *King William*, in the Petitioner in Fee Simple, and to fettle the faid *Mantapike* Lands in Tail in Lieu thereof.

Ordered, That Leave be given to bring in a Bill perfuant to the Prayer of the faid petition; and that Mr *Edmund Pendleton* do prepare and bring in the fame.

The *Order* of the Day being read, for the Houfe to refolve itfelf into a Committee of the whole Houfe, upon the Bill to continue and amend the Act, intituled *An Act*[2] *for amending the Staple of Tobacco, and preventing Frauds in his Majefty's Cuftoms*;

Refolved, That this Houfe will, upon *Wednefday* next, refolve itfelf into the faid Committee.

A *Bill* to dock the Intail of Five Hundred and Fifty Acres of Land, in the County of *Gloucefter*, whereof *Sarah*, the Wife of *John Rootes*, Gentleman, is feized, and for vefting the fame in Truftees, for the Purpofes therein mentioned, was read a fecond Time.

Refolved, That the Bill be committed to Mr *Dixon* and all the Members who ferve for the Counties of *Gloucefter*, *King & Queen*, *Caroline*, and *York*.

A *Bill* to repeal an Act for increafing the Salary of the Minifter of the Parifh of *Frederick*, in the County of *Frederick*, was read a fecond Time.

Refolved, That the Bill be committed to Mr *Mercer*, Mr *Stark*, and Mr *Edmund Pendleton*.

A *Bill* to explain and amend the Act, intituled *An Act*[3] *to confirm the Charter of the Borough of* Norfolk, *and for enlarging the Jurifdiction of the Court of Huftings, in the City of* Williamfburg, was read a fecond Time.

174   *Refolved*, That the Bill be committed to the Committee of Propofitions and Grievances.

A *Bill* to dock the Intail of certain Lands and Slaves, whereof *John Page*, Efq; is feized, and for fettling other Lands, of greater Value, to the fame Ufes, was read a fecond Time.

Refolved, That the Bill be committed to Mr *Richard Lee*, and all the Members who ferve for the Counties of *Gloucefter*, *Caroline*, *King William* and *Hanover*.

And then the Houfe adjourned till Tomorrow Morning Eleven of the Clock.

𝕱𝖗𝖎𝖉𝖆𝖞

---

[1] Hening, VIII, 470.   [2] Ibid, VIII, 69.   [3] Ibid, IV, 541.

Friday, the 25th of May, 10 Geo. III. 1770.

A Claim of *Matthew Anderfon* for his Pay, as a Serjeant in the *Virginia* Regiment, in the Year 1759, was prefented to the Houfe, and read.

Ordered, That the faid Claim be referred to the Committee of Public Claims; and that they do examine the Matter thereof, and report the fame, with their Opinion thereupon, to the Houfe.

M*r Richard Henry Lee* prefented to the Houfe, according to Order, a Bill to veft certain Lands, whereof *Bernard Moore*, Efq; is feized in Fee Tail, in Truftees to be fold, and the Money laid out in the Purchafe of other Lands and Slaves, to be fettled to the fame Ufes; and the fame was received and read the firft Time.

Refolved, That the Bill be read a fecond Time.

Ordered, That Leave be given to bring in a Bill, for the more fpeedy Adminiftration of *Juftice* in this Colony; and that M*r Richard Henry Lee*, M*r Archibald Cary*, M*r Bland*, M*r Riddick*, M*r Edmund Pendleton*, M*r Treafurer*, M*r Blair*, M*r Mercer*, M*r Henry*, M*r Jones*, M*r Carrington*, and M*r Richard Baker*, do prepare and bring in the fame.

M*r Edmund Pendleton* prefented to the Houfe, according to Order, a Bill to veft certain intailed Lands, whereof *Charles Lewis*, Gentleman, is feized, in *John Lewis*, Gentleman, in Fee Simple, and fettle other Lands to the fame Ufes; and the fame was received, and read the firft Time.

Refolved, That the Bill be read a fecond Time.

M*r Eyre* prefented to the Houfe, according to Order, a Bill to veft certain intailed Lands and Slaves therein mentioned, in *Nathaniel Littleton Savage*, Gentleman, in Fee Simple, and to fettle other Lands, in Lieu thereof; and the fame was received, and read the firft Time.

Refolved, That the Bill be read a fecond Time.

M*r Bland* prefented to the Houfe, from the Committee of Correfpondence, according to Order, another Letter to the faid Committee from the Agent for this Colony, fince the 21ft Day of *December* laft.

And the faid Letter was read.

Ordered, That the faid Letter do lie upon the Table, to be perufed by the Members of the Houfe.

M*r Treafurer* reported from the Committee appointed, upon *Tuefday* laft, to draw up an Addrefs to be prefented to the Governor, that the Committee had drawn up an Addrefs accordingly, which they had directed him to report to the Houfe; and he read the same in his Place, and afterwards delivered it in at the Clerk's Table; where the fame was read, and is as followeth, *viz.*

175

My Lord,

We his Majefty's moft dutiful and loyal Subjects, the Burgeffes of Virginia, *beg Leave to prefent to your Excellency our fincere Thanks for the early Attention you have been pleafed to give our former Addreffes and Memorial refpecting the Extenfion of our Boundary to the Weftward, the Importation of Salt from foreign European Ports, and the future Currency of Copper Coin within this Colony.*

His Majefty's great Goodnefs in fo immediately referring the humble Petitions of his dutiful Subjects to his Board of Trade and Plantations cannot but afford us the higheft Satiffaction, and we acknowledge with Pleafure the great Candor of his Majefty's principal Secretary of State for this Department in having the Confideration of the feveral Matters, mentioned in your Lordfhip's Meffage, poftponed, till the Agent for this Colony fhould receive proper Inftructions from us; but, my Lord, having already through your Excellency, to us the moft agreeable Channel of conveying to the Throne our humble Requefts, fubmitted to his Majefty's Wifdom our Reafons for defiring a more extended Boundary, we have nothing farther to add on that head, except that, if the Truth of any of the Facts contained in our humble Memorial fhould be doubted, we are perfuaded it may be eftablifhed by unqueftionable Proofs.

The

*The Foundation of our Wishes respecting the free Importation of Salt we trust is
also fully explained and understood, and, as to the Copper Money, which we desire to have
circulating amongst us, our humble Request is that it may be current here as in* Great Britain,
*allowing for the Difference between Sterling Money and the Currency of this Colony at the
Rate of Twenty-five per Cent.*

*It only therefore remains for us to entreat your Lordship, in whom we have abundant
Reason to repose the greatest Confidence, to use your farther good Offices in endeavoring
to procure Success to the earnest Desires of this House in these several important Articles.*

The said *Address* being read a second Time;

Resolved, That the House doth agree with the Committee in the said Address, to
be presented to the *Governor*.

Ordered, That the said Address be presented to his Excellency by the whole House.

Ordered, That the Gentlemen who drew up the said Address, do wait upon the
Governor to know his Pleasure, when this House shall attend his Excellency, to present their Address.

The *Order* of the Day being read;

Resolved, That this House will, upon *Monday* next, resolve itself into a Committee
of the whole House, to take into Consideration the *Governor's* Message, and the Letters
and Papers, relative to *Indian* Affairs, therein mentioned.

Ordered, That Leave be given to bring in a Bill to explain an Act of this present
Session of Assembly, intituled *An Act¹ to divide the Parish of* Hamilton, *in the Counties
of* Fauquier *and* Prince William; and that Mʳ *Marshall* do prepare and bring in the same.

A *Petition* of *Andrew Estave* was presented to the House, and read; setting forth,
that the Petitioner, from his long Residence in *France*, hath attained a perfect Knowledge of the Culture of Vines, and the most approved Method of making Wine; that
having lived in this Colony about two Years, he hath, during that Time, made it his
particular Study to be acquainted with the Nature of the Soil, and Cultivation of the
wild Grape, which grows spontaneously through this Country, and is both larger and
better tasted than the wild Grape in *France*, and will, properly managed, produce very
fine Wine; but from the unsuccessful Attempts made here before by unskilful People,
such a Project might perhaps meet with Difficulties, not easily to be removed, without
the Assistance of the Legislature; and therefore praying this House to allot him One
176 Hundred Acres of Land, in the Neighbourhood of the City of *Williamsburg*, with an
House thereon for him to live in, and three Negro Men to assist him, which he would hold
on the following Terms, to wit; if he should not make good merchantable Wine in four
Years from the seating and planting the Vineyard, that he should pay the Rent of the
Land and Hire of the Slaves for that Term, but if he should succeed to the Satisfaction
of the Public, and this House, that then the Land and Slaves aforesaid should be and
remain his Property, as an Encouragement, for his Discovery.

Ordered, That the said Petition be referred to the Committee of Trade; and that
they do examine the matter thereof, and report the same, with their Opinion thereupon,
to the House.

Ordered, That Leave be given to bring in a Bill, for establishing a Town at *Rocky
Ridge*, in the County of *Chesterfield*, and for adding certain Lots to the Town of *Richmond*,
in the County of *Henrico*; and that Mʳ *Archibald Cary*, Mʳ *Adams*, Mʳ *Richard Randolph*,
and Mʳ *Trent*, do prepare and bring in the same.

Mʳ *Mercer* reported from the Committee, to whom the Bill to repeal the Act for
increasing the Salary of the Minister of the Parish of *Frederick*, in the County of *Frederick*,
was committed, that the Committee had gone through the Bill, and made several
Amendments thereunto, which they had directed him to report to the House; and he
read the report in his Place, and afterwards delivered the Bill, with the Amendments,
in at the Clerk's Table; where the Amendments were once read throughout, and then

a

¹ Hening, VIII, 403.

a fecond Time, one by one, and, upon the Queftion feverally put thereupon, were agreed to by the Houfe.

Ordered, That the Bill, with the Amendments, be ingroffed.

A *Petition* of *John Welch*, late a Soldier in the *Virginia* Regiment, was prefented to the Houfe, and read; fetting forth, that the Petitioner ferved in the faid Regiment feven Years, and was not difcharged until he was difbanded at Fort *Lewis* in *March* 1762; and that during that Time he fuffered much from Inclemency of Weather, which has brought on him a Rheumatifm and Weaknefs, and difabled him from getting his Livelihood; and therefore praying, that this Houfe will grant him fuch Relief as they fhall think meet.

Ordered, That the faid Petition be referred to the Committee of Public Claims; and that they do examine the Matter thereof, and report the fame, with their Opinion thereupon, to the Houfe.

A *Bill* to compel Ships infected with the Gaol Fever or Small-Pox to perform Quarantine, was read a fecond Time.

Refolved, That the Bill be committed to the Committee of Propofitions and Grievances.

M[r] *Archibald Cary* reported from the Committee of Public Claims, to whom the Petition of *Baylor Walker* and *William Fleet*, Executors of the laft Will and Teftament of *John Semple*, deceafed, was referred, that the Committee had examined the Matter of the faid Petition, and had directed him to report the fame, together with the Refolution of the Committee thereupon, to the Houfe; and he read the Report in his Place, and afterwards delivered it in at the Clerk's Table; where the fame was read, and is as followeth, *viz.*

It *appeared* to your Committee, that *John Robinfon*, Efq; then Treafurer, did, [177] by an Inftrument of Writing under his Hand, bearing Date the 9th Day of *July*, 1765, oblige himfelf, his Heirs, Executors, and Adminiftrators, to indemnify and fave harmlefs the faid *John Semple*, his Heirs, Executors, and Adminiftrators, of and from all Cofts, Charges, or Damages whatfoever, which fhould or might arife or accrue to him or them for or on Account of his having become Security for *Philip Rootes*, as High Sheriff of *King & Queen* County; that after the Death of the faid *John Robinfon*, which happened in *May* next following, a Judgment was recovered againft the faid *John Semple*, for 1271 *l.* 8 *s*, 7 *d.* for the Balance of Taxes collected by the faid *Philip Rootes*, and his Deputies, during the Time of his Sheriffalty, and Cofts; and that the faid Decedent's Eftate hath been taken in Execution to fatiffy the faid Judgment.

Whereupon the *Committee* came to the following Refolution;

Refolved, That it is the Opinion of this Committee, that the faid Petition be rejected.

The faid *Refolution* being read a fecond Time, was, upon the Queftion put thereupon, agreed to by the Houfe.

An ingroffed *Bill* to dock the Intail of Four Thoufand Acres of Land, in the County of *Ifle of Wight*, whereof *James Burwell* is feized in Fee Tail, and for vefting the fame in Truftees, in Fee Simple, and for other Purpofes therein mentioned, was read the third Time.

Refolved, That the Bill do pafs; and that the Title be, *An Act to dock the Intail of Four Thoufand Acres of Land, in the County of* Ifle of Wight, *whereof* James Burwell *is feized in Fee Tail, and for vefting the fame in Truftees, in Fee Simple, and for other Purpofes therein mentioned.*

Ordered, That M[r] *Lewis Burwell*, of *James City*, do carry the Bill to the Council and defire their Concurrence.

The Houfe proceeded to take into Confideration the Amendment made by the Council to the Bill, intituled *An Act for eftablifhing a Town in the County of* Pittfylvania.

And the faid *Amendment* was read, and is as followeth, *viz.*

Line 16, leave out "*And be it further enacted by the Authority aforefaid, That from*
and

---

1 Hening, VIII, p. 481

and after the 1st Day of October next enfuing, it fhall not be lawful for any Perfon or Perfons, inhabiting within the faid Town, to raife or keep any Swine, within the Limits thereof, and fuffer the fame to go and run at Large within the faid Town. And if any Swine fo raifed and kept fhall be found going or running at Large, within the Limits of the faid Town, it fhall and may be lawful for any Perfon whatfoever to kill and deftroy the fame."

The faid *Amendment* being read a fecond Time, was, upon the Queftion put thereupon, agreed to by the Houfe.

Ordered, That Mr *Bland* do carry the Bill to the Council, and acquaint them, that this Houfe hath agreed to the Amendment made by them.

A *Bill* to veft certain intailed Lands, whereof *Charles Lewis*, Gentleman, is feized, in *John Lewis*, Gentleman, in Fee Simple, and fettle other Lands to the fame Ufes, was read a fecond Time.

Refolved, That the Bill be committed to Mr *Edmund Pendleton*, and all the Members who ferve for the Counties of *Amherft, Pittfylvania, Charlotte,* and *Lunenburg.*

178 An ingroffed *Bill* for fettling the Fees of the Clerk and Serjeant of the Court of *Huftings* for the City of *Williamfburg*, was read the third Time.

Refolved, That the Bill do pafs; and that the Title be, *An Act¹ for fettling the Fees of the Clerk and Serjeant of the Court of* Huftings *for the City of* Williamfburg.

Ordered, That Mr *Bland* do carry the Bill to the Council, and defire their Concurrence.

And then the Houfe adjourned till To-morrow Morning Eleven of the Clock.

Saturday, the 26th of May, 10 Geo. III. 1770.

MR *Riddick* reported from the Committee of Trade, to whom the petition of *Andrew Eftave*, containing certain Propofals for the Culture of Vines, and making Wine, was referred, that the Committee had examined the Matter of the faid Petition, and had come to a Refolution thereupon, which they had directed him to report to the Houfe; and he read the Report in his Place, and afterwards delivered it in at the Clerk's Table; where the Refolution of the Committee was read, and is as followeth, *viz.*

Refolved, That it is the Opinion of this Committee, that the faid *Andrew Eftave* ought to be encouraged.

The faid *Refolution* being read a fecond Time, was, upon the Queftion put thereupon, agreed to by the Houfe.

Ordered, That a Bill be brought in purfuant to the faid Refolution; and that the Committee of Trade do prepare and bring in the fame.

Ordered, That Leave be given to bring in a Bill for the better regulating the Office of Sheriffs, and their Deputies; and that Mr *Bland* do prepare and bring in the fame.

A *Petition* of *Jofeph Williams* was prefented to the Houfe, and read; fetting forth, that the Petitioner had been robbed of One Hundred and Fifty Pounds of the public Money, collected by him, as Under Sheriff of the County of *Lunenburg*, in the Year 1764, for which *Matthew Marable*, Gentleman, High Sheriff of the faid County, had recovered a Judgment againft him; and praying the Confideration of the Houfe therein.

Ordered, That the faid Petition be referred to the Committee of Public Claims; and that they do examine the Matter thereof, and report the fame, with their Opinion thereupon, to the Houfe.

Ordered, That the Committee of Privileges and Elections, to whom the Information of Mr *Nathaniel Terry*, relating to the Accufation reflecting on his Character, was referred, do ftate an Account of the Expences of the Attendance, and taking the Examinations, of the Witneffes before the faid Committee, and before the Commiffioners in the Country, and report the fame to the Houfe.

A

---

1 Hening, VIII, p. 402.

A *Petition* of fundry Perfons, Inhabitants of the County of *Accomack*, whofe Names are thereunto fubfcribed, was prefented to the Houfe, and read; taking Notice of an Application intended to be made to this Houfe for removing the Infpection from *Guilford* to *Hunting Creek*, and praying that if a Removal fhall be thought neceffary, it [179] may be to *Tatham's* Landing, which is more convenient than *Hunting Creek*.

Ordered, That the faid Petition be referred to the Committee of propofitions and Grievances; and that they do examine the Matter thereof, and report the fame, with their Opinion thereupon, to the Houfe.

M[r] *Henry* prefented to the Houfe, according to Order, a Bill to amend an Act paffed in the former Part of this Seffion of Affembly, for reimburfing the Counties of *Hanover* and *King William* the Expence of clearing *Pamunkey* River; and the fame was received, and read the firft Time.

Refolved, That the Bill be read a fecond Time.

A *Petition* of feveral Perfons, being Proteftant Diffenters of the Baptift Perfuafion, whofe Names are thereunto fubfcribed, was prefented to the Houfe, and read; fetting forth the Inconveniences of compelling their licenced Preachers to bear Arms under the Militia Law, and to attend Mufters, by which they are unable to perform the Duties of their Function; and further fetting forth the Hardfhips they fuffer from the Prohibition to their Minifters to preach in Meeting Houfes, not particularly mentioned in their Licences; and therefore praying the Houfe to take their Grievances into Confideration, and to grant them Relief.

Ordered, That the faid *Petition* be referred to the Committee for Religion; and that they do examine the Matter thereof, and report the fame, with their Opinion thereupon, to the Houfe.

And then the Houfe adjourned till Monday Morning next Eleven of the Clock.

Monday, the 28th of May, 10 Geo. III. 1770.

A *Petition* of fundry Perfons, Inhabitants of the County of *Accomack*, whofe Names are thereunto fubfcribed, was prefented to the Houfe, and read; fetting forth that the white Tithables, in the faid County, are fo numerous, and the Bufinefs of the Court thereof, is fo multiplied, that the faid County ought to be divided; and therefore praying that the faid County may be divided into two Counties.

And alfo a *Petition* of fundry Perfons, Inhabitants of the County of *Accomack*, whofe Names are thereunto fubfcribed, was prefented to the Houfe, and read; taking Notice of a Petition intended to be prefented to this Houfe for dividing the faid County, and fetting forth that fuch a Divifion is unneceffary, and would be inconvenient; and therefore praying that the faid County may not be divided.

Ordered, That the faid feveral *Petitions* be feverally referred to the Committee of propofitions and Grievances; and that they do examine the Matter thereof, and report the fame, with their opinion thereupon, to the Houfe.

Several *Petitions* of fundry Freeholders, Inhabitants of the Counties of *Prince George, Dinwiddie, Amelia, Brunfwick, Lunenburg, Mecklenburg, Charlotte, Prince Edward*, and *Suffex*, whofe Names are thereunto fubfcribed, were prefented to the Houfe, and read; fetting forth that the very great Quantities of Tobacco brought to the Warehoufes for the Infpection of that Commodity on *Appomattox* River, render it [180] impoffible for the prefent Infpectors to give proper Difpatch; and therefore praying that another Infpection of Tobacco may be eftablifhed on the Lots of Colonel *Robert Bolling*, which he lately purchafed of M[r] *Patrick Ramfay*, in the Town of *Blandford*, on the faid River.

Ordered, That the faid *Petitions* be referred to the Committee of propofitions and Grievances; and that they do examine the Matter thereof, and report the fame, with their Opinion thereupon, to the Houfe.

M[r]

Mr *Edmund Pendleton* reported from the Committee of Privileges and Elections, to whom the Information of Mr *Nathaniel Terry*, relating to the Accusation reflecting on his Character, was recommitted, that the Committee had further examined the Matter of the said Information, and had directed him to report the same, as it appeared to them, to the House, together with the Resolutions of the Committee thereupon; and he read the Report in his Place, and afterwards delivered it in at the Clerk's Table; where the same was read, and is as followeth, *viz.*

It *appears* to your Committee by the Evidence of *James Bates*, that the said *Bates* meeting with Mr *Nathaniel Terry* at *Halifax* Court, the said *Terry* enquired of him what Part of his Dues he had paid, to which the said *Bates* replied he could not tell, without seeing his Receipts. The said *Terry* then asked, to whom he had paid them, whether to *Champnefs Terry?* To which the said *Bates* made Answer, that he had not paid them to the said *Champnefs*, but to *Mofes Terry* and *William Moone*. Whereupon the said *Terry* walked away, and in a little Time after the said *Bates* meeting *Champnefs Terry*, the said *Terry* asked him if he had paid him any Money for Dues, whilst he the said *Champnefs* was Under Sheriff to Mr *Nathaniel Terry?* To which the said *Bates* answered, he had not. Then the said *Champnefs* desired he would walk with him, and produced his Sheriff's Book, wherein the said *Bates* was credited for Thirty-five Shillings, observing at the same Time, that such Entry of Credit was made after the said *Champnefs* was gone to the Southward, or *Florida*, and that he would swear it was the said *Nathaniel's* writing. The said *Champnefs* moreover said, that the said *Nathaniel* had vilified him to Col. *John Lewis*, his particular Friend, for receiving Money which he had not accounted for with the said *Nathaniel*, and requested of the said *Bates*, to inform Col. *Lewis* of the Error; which the said Bates soon after did, in Presence of the said *Champnefs*. That some Time after, the said *Bates* being in a Conversation with the said *Nathaniel*, the said *Nathaniel* signified that the said *Bates* had taken great Freedoms with his Character, but being desired by the said *Bates* to mention in what Respect, the said *Terry* replied, in many, without taking Notice of any one, in particular.

The said *Bates* then observed to the said *Terry*, that he could recollect one Instance only of such Freedom, and that respected the Entry of Credit in the Book of *Champnefs Terry* made by the said *Nathaniel*, for Money, which the said *Bates* had not paid to the said *Champnefs*; on which the said *Nathaniel* confessed, that he had made such Entry, in the Books of the said *Champnefs*. That some Time in the same Day, a Dispute arising between Mr *Walter Coles* and the said *Nathaniel*, the said *Nathaniel* denied, that he had given such Credit, in the Book of *Champnefs Terry*, and threatened to sue the said *Coles* for saying he had done it; and the said *Bates* being informed, that the said *Terry* intended to Sue *Champnefs Terry* for Debt, and the said *Bates* for Slander, had Recourse to the said *Champnefs's* Book, wherein he took Notice that the Credit before mentioned had been given to him, the said *Champnefs* offering, at the same Time, to shew him many other Entries made by the said *Nathaniel*, but the said Bates declined looking into them, being in no Wife interested in them. That the said *Bates* being applied to by the said *Nathaniel*, to give him up the Receipts of the Deputy Sheriffs, and to accept the said *Nathaniel's* Receipt, in Lieu thereof, the said *Bates* thought it prudent to refuse to do so, being desired by *David Terry*, Brother to the said *Champnefs*, not to give them up, and being moreover apprehensive of some detriment to himself, from such compliance. That the said *Champnefs* informed the said *Bates*, that from the relation of the Wife of the said *Champnefs*, the said *Nathaniel* had often, in the absence of the said *Champnefs*, applied to her for the said *Champnefs's*, Book, but she denied any Knowledge of it unless it was put into a small Trunk; and by what Means the said *Nathaniel* got Possession of the Book, the said *Bates* has been informed, but does not now remember. The said *Bates* produced a Receipt for the said Thirty-five Shillings, from the said *William Moone*, bearing Date *September* 19, 1765.

It further *appears* to your Committee by the Evidence of *Thomas Yuille*, that the said

said *Yuille*, some Time in the Month of *July*, 1768, being in Company with *Champnefs Terry* and Mr *Walter Coles*, heard the said *Champnefs* exprefling himfelf very freely on the Character of Mr *Nathaniel Terry;* and among many other approbious Epithets, the said *Champnefs* alleged, that he believed his Coufin *Nathaniel* was as damned a Rogue as any in this Colony, but that it would take 100 honeft Men to find him out; which, together with a flying Report of fome Entries having been made in the said *Champnefs Terry's* Book, induced the said *Yuille* to ask the said *Champnefs* of the Truth of that Report; to which the said *Champnefs* anfwered, that the said *Nathaniel*, in the Time that he the said *Champnefs* was gone to the Southward, got at his Sheriff's Book and had made an Entry of Credit therein, of Money, which he the said *Champnefs* had never received; and that the said *Nathaniel* had brought a Suit againft him, and among other Articles had charged the Money, which the said *Nathaniel* had given Credit for, in the Book, as aforesaid. That fome Time after the Election of Burgeffes, for the County of *Halifax*, in the Year 1768, the said *Nathaniel* confeffed he had given credit in the Book of the said *Champnefs*, but that it was not done when the said *Champnefs* was gone to the Southward, but in the abfence of the said *Champnefs*, at *Williamfburg*. That the said *Yuille*, of his own Knowledge, can say nothing touching the Character or Reputation of the said *Nathaniel*.

It further *appears* to your Committee by the Evidence of *John Lewis*, Jun. that in the Year 1766 and 1767, *Champnefs Terry* lived with the said *Lewis*, and in the Month of *February* or *March*, of the laft mentioned Year, the said *Champnefs* informed him, that Mr *Nathaniel Terry* had made an Entry in the Book of the said *Champnefs*, and had given *James Bates's* Account Credit for Thirty-five Shillings, which the said *Champnefs* had never received; and which Entry had been made without the Privity or Confent of the said *Champnefs*. That foon after this information, the said *Champnefs* being about to make a Journey to *Weft Florida*, as the said *Lewis* believed, delivered his Books and Papers into the Care of the said *Lewis*, and that neither of them, with the Knowledge of the said *Lewis*, were infpected by the said *Nathaniel*, in the Abfence of the said *Champnefs*. That fome Time after the Return of the said *Champnefs*, in the Month of *September* or *October* following, the said *Nathaniel* being in Company with the said *Champnefs*, at the said *Lewis's* Houfe, the said *Champnefs* complained that the said *Nathaniel* had ufed him very ill, in Regard to the before mentioned Entry; whereupon the said *Nathaniel* confeffed, that he did make the Entry, and could not at that Time recollect for what Purpofe; but that he had no Intention of doing any Injuftice by that Entry. That fubfequent to this Converfation, both the said *Nathaniel* and *Champnefs* informed the said *Lewis*, that they had difcovered the Error of the said Entry and were mutually fatiffied.

It further *appears* to your Committee by the Evidence of *Robert Wooding*, that a Suit having been brought by Mr *Nathaniel Terry* againft *Champnefs Terry* to recover a balance due to the said *Nathaniel*, and referred out of Court to be fettled, as the said *Wooding* was told, the said *Wooding*, on Application made to him for that Purpofe, attended at the Time and Place of Meeting, in Order to fwear the Witneffes; but upon the Interceffion of the said *Wooding*, with fome others, the contending Parties agreed to give the Referees no further Trouble, and to fettle their Accounts themfelves. After which, the said *Champnefs* expreffed himfelf greatly pleafed, that they had fettled their Difpute in that Manner, as he would rather have given Forty Pounds, or even his Horfe, than that the fame fhould have been adjufted in a public Manner, as the said *Nathaniel* was his near Relation, and he fhould have been obliged to expofe him.

It further *appears* to your Committee by the Evidence of *Mofes Terry*, that he was prefent at the Time Mr *Nathaniel Terry* and *Champnefs Terry* were fettling their Accounts, and difputing who fhould pay the Cofts of the Suits brought by the said *Nathaniel* againft the said *Champnefs*, when the said *Mofes* propofed, in Order to put an End to the Difpute, to pay the Cofts himfelf, which they refufed to accept; and afterwards, as the said *Mofes* underftood, agreed it between themfelves.

It

It further *appears* to your Committee by the Evidence of *William Watkins*, that one *Alexander Troop* being chargeable on the Books of Mr *Nathaniel Terry*, as High Sheriff of *Halifax*, for his Dues, the said *Watkins* went with *Champnefs Terry*, the Under Sheriff and Collector, to the said *Troop's* House, and at the Instance of the said *Troop*, agreed to pay Fifty odd Shillings, as nearly as the said *Watkins* recollects, for the said *Troop*, the said *Champnefs's* whole Demand, as he understood at that Time; which Assumpsit the said *Champnefs* accepted, and the said *Watkins*, some Time after, paid the Money to the said *Champnefs*. That after the said *Champnefs* had left the Country to go to *Florida*, as was reported, the said *Troop* informed the said *Watkins*, that one *Lankford*, another Under Sheriff to the said *Nathaniel*, had applied to the said *Troop* for Part of his Dues, for the same Year; whereupon the said *Watkins* informed *Lankford*, of his having paid *Champnefs Terry* the said Fifty odd Shillings, as before mentioned, and was ready to make Affidavit to the Truth thereof. That the Matter rested until the Return of the said *Champnefs*, when the said *Watkins* meeting with him, for the first Time, at *Halifax* Court, asked the said *Champnefs*, in Presence of *Troop*, if he the said *Watkins* had not paid him, on Account of the said *Troop*, the said Fifty odd Shillings; to which the said *Champnefs* replied, if you say so, it is true. That the said *Champnefs*, then holding his Book in his Hand, said that the said *Nathaniel* had got it in his Absence and that it was not as he left it when he went away to *Florida*.

It further *appears* to your Committee by the Evidence of *George Boyd*, that in a Dispute between Mr *Nathaniel Terry* and Mr *Walter Coles*, the said *Terry* denied that he made the Entry, which the said *Boyd* understood to be an Entry in *Champnefs Terry's* Sheriff's Book.

It further *appears* to your Committee by the Evidence of *Thomas Tunstall*, that some Time in the latter End of the Year 1768, the said *Tunstall* being in Company with Mr *Nathaniel Terry*, Mr *Walter Coles*, and several other Persons, heard the said *Nathaniel Terry* complain of being ill used by Mr *Thomas Yuille*, who he said had reported, that he the said *Terry* had been guilty of Forgery: To which the said *Coles* answered, that if what the said *Yuille* and himself had been informed was true, that he looked upon it to be little short of Forgery, or Words to the same Purpose; upon which the said *Terry* demanded what that Information was, and the said *Walter Coles* answered, that he had been informed, that whilst one *Champnefs Terry* (who had collected some Time under the said *Nathaniel Terry* as Deputy Sheriff) was gone to the Southward, he the said *Terry* made an Entry, or Entries of Credits in the Books of the said *Champnefs Terry* for Money, which he had never received; which, according to the Best of the said *Tunstall's* Remembrance, the said *Terry* then denied, and said, that he had never seen the said *Champnefs Terry's* Books, while he was gone to the Southward, and demanded of the said *Coles* the Author of such Information; but the said *Coles* refused to give him his Author; upon which the said *Terry* declared, that unless the said *Coles* would do so, that he would bring a Suit against him to do Justice to his Character; to which the said *Coles* answered, that he might bring such Suit as soon as he pleased, and that it would be Time enough upon the Trial of that Suit, to produce his Author for the Information aforesaid.

It further *appears* to your Committee by the Evidence of *Champnefs Terry*, that he was not present at the making of the Entry in his Books by Mr *Nathaniel Terry*, whereby a Credit of Thirty five Shillings was placed to the Account of *James Bates*, but was gone on a Venire to *Williamsburg*: And that some Time before the said *Champnefs* went to the Southward, a Settlement of Accounts was proposed between the said *Champnefs* and the said *Nathaniel*, upon which the said *Champnefs* discovered the Entry in his Book as aforesaid, and told the said *Nathaniel* that he the said *Nathaniel* had made an Entry of Credit to *James Bates* of the aforesaid Sum, which the said *Champnefs* said he never had received, and asked the said *Nathaniel* if he had received it, who answered he had not; then the said *Champnefs* asked him why he had made such Entry, the said *Nathaniel* answered he did not know, and asked the said *Champnefs*, if he the said *Champnefs* did not direct him, which the said *Champnefs* denied; whereupon

whereupon a Difference arofe between the faid *Champnefs* and *Nathaniel*, that prevented their Settlement at that Time; and about a Year after, the faid *Champnefs*
went to *Florida*, and foon after his return, being at the Houfe of Mr *John Lewis*, with
the faid *Nathaniel*, a Difpute arofe between them, and among other Things the aforefaid Entry was mentioned by one or the other, but which the faid *Champnefs* does not
remember; however, the faid *Champnefs* then impeached the faid *Nathaniel* of Injuftice, in making fuch Entry; whereupon the faid *Nathaniel* faid, it did not appear fo
to him at that Time, and that he would clear up the Juftnefs of that Point, by applying
to Mr *James Bates*, and if Mr *Bates* would fay that the faid Thirty-five Shillings was
not paid, he the faid *Nathaniel* would give it up. That at the Time the faid *Champnefs* was Deputy Sheriff to the faid *Nathaniel*, he applied to the faid *Nathaniel* to re-
leafe him, and recommended one *William Moone*, whom the faid *Champnefs* had employed for the Month of *September*, 1765, as an Affiftant.

182

It further *appears* to your Committee by the Evidence of *Abraham Shelton*, who, on
a certain Day, was in Company with *James Bates*, at the Houfe of *Champnefs Terry*,
and in a very little Time after he got there the faid *Terry* and *Bates* engaged in a Converfation refpecting Mr *Nathaniel Terry*, when the faid *Champnefs* alleged, that the
faid *Nathaniel* had ufed him very ill, by applying to his the faid *Champnefs's* Wife, in
his Abfence, for his Sheriff's Book, and made fome Entries of Credit, particularly
mentioning the faid *James Bates's* Account, for which the faid *Champnefs* faid he
ftood charged to the faid *Nathaniel*. That he believes the faid *Champnefs* declared
he was down the Country when that, or thofe Entries were made.

It further *appears* to your Committee by the Evidence of *Benjamin Lankford*, that
in the Year 1765, *Champnefs Terry*, *Mofes Terry*, *Benjamin Terry* and the faid *Lankford*, ferved as Under Sheriffs to Mr *Nathaniel Terry*. That at the Court for *Halifax*
County, in the Month of *October*, the faid *Terry* informed the faid *Lankford*, that *Champnefs Terry* was gone to *Williamfburg*, and had declined acting any longer in the Office
of Under Sheriff; that he fhould be glad if the faid *Lankford* would ride up with him
to the faid *Champnefs Terry's*, and affift in making out a Book of the Balances, which
appeared on the faid *Champnefs's* Sheriff's Book, in order to put the fame into the Hands
of one *William Moone*, whom the faid *Nathaniel* had employed to collect them. That
the faid *Lankford* accordingly went up to the faid *Champnefs's* and the faid *Nathaniel*
afking for the faid *Champnefs's* Sheriff's Book, the faid *Champnefs's* Wife delivered
it to him, and the faid *Lankford* tranfcribed from it the Names and Balances of the
feveral Perfons, into another Book, for the faid *Moone* to collect by. That the faid
Moone being prefent, told the faid *Lankford* when he turned to Mr *James Bates's*
Account on the Book, that he the faid *Moone* had received of the faid *Bates* Thirty-
five Shillings. That after the Extracts were made as aforefaid, the faid *Nathaniel*
returned the Book again to the faid *Champnefs's* Wife, and fome Time after this Tranfaction, the faid *James Bates* told the faid *Lankford*, that he had paid *William Moone*
the faid Thirty-five Shillings.

The *Book* of the faid *Champnefs Terry* above mentioned, was produced to your
Committee, in which, Page 5, is ftated an Account againft the faid *James Bates* on
the Side, in which Debits are ufually entered, and appofite thereto, is ftated an Account
againft *Nathaniel Barkfdale*, both in the Hand Writing of the faid *Champnefs Terry*.
That at the Foot of the faid *Barkfdale's* Account, is entered in the Hand Writing of
the aforefaid *William Moone*, thefe Words and Figures, "*Sept.* 19, 1765, *by Cafh paid*
1 *l.* 15 *s.*" through which Entry a Line of Erafement appears now to be drawn, and under
it thefe Words, in the Hand Writing of Mr *Nathaniel Terry*; "*This ought to have been
James Bates.*" And at the Foot of *Bates's* Account, in the fame Hand Writing, is entered,
"*by* 35 *s.*"

It *appears* to your Committee by the Evidence of *Francis Cox*, that fome Time
about the laft of *November*, or firft of *December*, 1765, Mr *Nathaniel Terry* came to the
faid *Cox's* Houfe, in order to receive and pay for some Pork, which he had bought of
the faid *Cox*, when the faid *Terry* shewed the faid *Cox* a confiderable Quantity of Silver;
but

but the said *Cox* not thinking the Pork fat enough, put off the Delivery for a Week longer; at which Time the said *Terry* came again in the Evening, and enquiring whether *Benjamin Terry* had been there, and being told he had not, the said *Nathaniel* said to the said *Cox*, that he could not pay him all the Money for the Pork, unless the said *Benjamin* came. That in the Morning after, the said *Benjamin* came, and the said *Nathaniel* asking him if he had got any Money, the said *Benjamin* produced a Parcel, containing about 30 *l.* out of which he offered to pay the said *Cox* for the Pork, but *Cox* objecting to some of the Money, as bad, the said *Nathaniel* asked the said *Benjamin* of whom he received it; and he answered, of Mrs. *Perkins*. Then one or the other of the said *Terries* said to *Cox*, here is more Money, and produced another Parcel, which appeared to contain a 100 *l.* at least, out of which last Parcel the said *Cox* received the greatest Part of the Payment for his Pork in Bills, and the Residue in Specie of the said *Nathaniel*, amounting in the Whole to about 20 *l.* That some Time after, the said *Cox* went to Mrs. *Perkins*, and asking her how she came to pay the *Terries* bad Money, she answered if she had, she did not know it, but that her Name was written on the Back of the Money she paid to *Benjamin Terry*. That the said *Cox* afterwards discovered the said Mrs. *Perkins's* Name was written on some or all of the Bills he received of Mr *Nathaniel Terry* or the said *Benjamin* as aforesaid, which said Bills proved to be good.

It further *appears* to your Committee by the Evidence of *Bethenia Chadwell*, that the said *Bethenia* had been to *Orange* Court, in *North Carolina*, which was held on the second *Tuesday* in *November*, 1765, and upon her return Home, which, to the best of her Remembrance, was on the *Thursday* following, she was informed that one *Benjamin Terry*, who was Under Sheriff of the County of *Halifax*, had levied an Execution sued out upon a Judgment obtained in the Court of the said County, by *John Pleasants*, against the said *Bethenia*, as Executrix of her late Husband *Nicholas Perkins*, on a Negro Boy, which was carried away by the said *Benjamin* to the House of the said *Benjamin's* Father. That in two or three Days the Boy made his Escape, and returned Home alone to the said *Bethenia*, and in a short Time after the Return of the Boy, the said *Benjamin* came again to the House of the said *Bethenia*, when she paid him 22 *l.* 17 *s.* in Discharge of Part of the said Execution, and between 8 *l.* and 9 *l.* in Paper Currency, for her Dues, at the same Time. That in the succeeding Summer after this Transaction, the said *Benjamin*, with the said *Nathaniel*, came again, and asking to see the Receipt she had taken of the said *Benjamin*, for the Execution Money, the said *Bethenia* searched near an Hour for the same, to no Purpose; though she afterwards found it, and delivered it to Mr *Paul Carrington*, but never gave either of the said *Terries* Notice of her having found the said Receipt, which Receipt bears Date the 9th of *December*, 1764.

It further *appears* to your Committee by the Evidence of *Benjamin Lankford*, that *Benjamin Terry*, Father to the said *Benjamin*, to whose House the said Negro Boy was carried as aforesaid, lived at the Distance of 20 Miles from the said *Nathaniel Terry*.

It further *appears* to your Committee by the Evidence of *John Chadwell*, that some Time after the said *Benjamin Terry* had received the Money on *Pleasant's* Execution of *Bethenia Perkins*, now the Wife of the said *Chadwell*, he came in Company with Mr *Nathaniel Terry* to the said *Chadwell's* House, and was a considerable Time employed in searching for some Papers, but of what Kind, the said *Chadwell* does not remember.

It further *appears* to your Committee by the Evidence of *Thomas Tunstall*, that the Execution issued on *Pleasant's* Judgment against *Perkin's* Estate, was returnable to *December* Court, and that he does not remember the exact Time when the same was returned; but that it is not customary to return any Execution before the Return Day.

It further *appears* to your Committee by the Record of the Proceedings of *Halifax* Court, in the said *Pleasant's* Suit against the said *Bethenia Perkins*, that the Execution sued out against her, bears date the 25th Day of *September*, 1765, and is made returnable to the Court, on the third *Thursday* in *December* following. That the Return on the said Execution, in the Hand Writing of the said *Nathaniel Terry*, is in the following

lowing Words, "*Executed on a Negro Boy, who has made his Escape,*" and signed by the said *Benjamin Terry.*

It further *appears* to your Committee by the Evidence of Mr *Paul Carrington,* a Member of this House, that the said *Carrington* prosecuted a Suit in the Court of *Halifax,* for *John Pleasants,* against the Executors of *Nicholas Perkins;* that an Execution was ordered, which appears to have been issued in the Month of *September,* 1765, returnable to the *December* Court following, Mr *Nathaniel Terry,* being then High Sheriff of the County; that the said *Carrington* applied to the said *Terry* to be informed of the Circumstances of the said Execution, when the said *Terry* answered, it had been served on a Negro Boy, which had Escaped out of his Possession; that some Time after the said *Carrington* was informed by one *Peter Perkins,* that the Greatest Part of the Debt was paid; that the said *Carrington* then applied to Mr *Terry,* and told him of the Information he had received from *Perkins,* upon which Mr *Terry* said he believed some Part of the Money was paid, but how much he did not know; that the said *Carrington* then desired Mr *Terry* to make himself acquainted how much had really been paid, that Mr *Pleasants* might receive his Money; that the said *Carrington* attended the Court, as well as he remembers, in *November,* 1765, also *June, July, August,* and *October,* 1766, *February, March, May* and *July,* 1767, and made frequent Applications to Mr *Terry,* but had for Answer from him, that he was still unable to inform himself how much Money had been received on the said Execution; that in the last mentioned Month of *July,* 1767, the said *Carrington* went to Mrs. *Perkins's,* and desired she would inform him, why that Execution was not paid, or how much had been paid, when the said *Perkins* delivered to the said *Carrington* the Receipt bearing Date the 9th of *December,* 1764, signed by *Benjamin Terry,* Deputy Sheriff, for upwards of Twenty two Pounds, Part of the aforesaid Execution; that the said *Carrington* apprehends the said *Terry* was mistaken in the Date of the Receipt, as Mr *Nathaniel Terry* was not Sheriff of the County till the Year 1765; that the said *Carrington* took Possession of the said Receipt, gave Mr *Nathaniel Terry* Notice of an intended Motion, and in the Month of *August* obtained a Judgment against him for the Amount of the Money expressed in the said Receipt, the said *Terry* agreeing to pay Interest thereupon; that the said *Carrington* cannot recollect at what Court he made the first Application to Mr *Terry,* but thinks it might probably be in the Month of *November,* 1765; that in every other Instance, the said *Carrington* hath had no Reason to doubt the Veracity of the said *Terry;* and that the said *Terry* being an indifferent Accountant, his Transactions sometimes appear aukward and confused, till properly explained by himself.

Upon the whole Matter the Committee came to the following Resolutions, *viz.*

Resolved, That, with Respect to the first Article of Charge against the said *Nathaniel Terry,* 'that he had made, when he was Sheriff of *Halifax,* an Entry in the Book of *Champness Terry,* who was his Under Sheriff, in his Absence, without his Knowledge or Consent, that the Entry was a false one, and by that Entry he did endeavor to prejudice the Character of the said *Champness,* by accusing him of having received Money, as his Under Sheriff, which he had never paid to him;' It is the opinion of this Committee, that the said Mr *Nathaniel Terry* did make the Entry in the Book of *Champness Terry,* who was his Under Sheriff, in his Absence, without his Knowledge or Consent, but that the same was done to rectify a Mistake, and not with any fraudulent Intention.

Resolved, That, with Respect to the second Article of Charge, 'that one *Ralph Jackson,* of *Chesterfield* County, did publicly say, that he lost a Horse out of his Pasture, that he hired two Men to go after him, that they tracked the Horse to the Distance of Twenty odd Miles, and that, when they came up with him, Mr *Terry* was on the Back of the Horse: It is the Opinion of this Committee, that the said Mr *Nathaniel Terry* hath fully acquitted his Reputation upon the said Article of Charge.

Resolved, That, with Respect to the third Article of Charge, 'that Mr *Nathaniel Terry,* by a false Representation of Facts, did obtain an Order from the Court of *Halifax* to be paid Ten Pounds out of the County Levy, for maintaining a Bridge longer, as he affirmed, than by his Agreement he was obliged to do; but that some Time after, it was

further

further enquired into, and found that fo far from his having maintained it longer, near two Years of the Time was to expire; upon which the Order was reverfed: It is the Opinion of this Committee, that the faid Mʳ *Nathaniel Terry* hath fully acquitted his Reputation upon the faid Article of Charge.

Refolved, That, with Refpect to the fourth Article of Charge, 'that Mʳ *Nathaniel Terry*,when he was Sheriff of *Halifax*,had an Execution given him againft *Perkin's* Eftate, which Execution he returned ferved on a Negro, and the Negro run away; that it remained in that State for a Confiderable Time, and the faid *Terry* never gave the Gentleman, who was appointed to receive the Money, and who made Application for it, although he was in the County regularly every Month, any Reafon to believe he had got One Shilling of it: At Length it was difcovered, that near two Years before the greateft Part of it had been paid, and a Receipt given for it by a young Man, *Benjamin Terry*, who lived in the Houfe with Col. *Terry*, and was employed as his Deputy:' It is the Opinion of this Committee, that the faid Mʳ *Nathaniel Terry* hath not acquitted his Reputation upon the faid Article of Charge.

Refolved, That, with Refpect to the fifth Article of Charge, 'that a Suit was brought in the Court of *Halifax*, againft Mʳ *Nathaniel Terry*, on his Affumpfit for ufing a Stray Horfe; and that a Report ftrongly prevailed, that the faid *Terry* agreed to pay Two Piftoles to accommodate the Difpute touching the faid Horfe:' It is the Opinion of this Committee, that the faid Mʳ *Terry* hath fully acquitted his Reputation upon the faid Article of Charge.

Refolved, That, with Refpect to the fixth Article of Charge, 'that two Stray Horfes were feen tied at Mʳ *Nathaniel Terry's*, and a few days afterwards one of them was branded, either with the faid *Terry's* Brand, or the Brand of a young Man who lived with him, was his near Relation, and who, on many Occafions, was known to be the faid *Terry's* Agent:' It is the Opinion of this Committee, that the faid Mʳ *Nathaniel Terry* hath fully acquitted his Reputation upon the faid Article of Charge.

Refolved, That, with Refpect to the feventh Article of Charge, that in the Year 1756 or 1757, Mʳ *Nathaniel Terry* commanded a ranging Company in the Frontiers, and with his Company and others, built three Forts, and that he promifed he would fee them well paid; that he has been fince applied to for the Money, but gave for Anfwer he could not get any for them, although it appears from the Schedule referred to, by an Act paffed in the 32d Year of the Reign of *George* the Second, intituled *An Aᶜ¹ for the Defence of the Frontiers of this Colony, and for other Purpofes therein mentioned*, that the faid *Terry* had received Money for the faid *Services:*' It is the Opinion of this Committee, that the faid Mʳ *Nathaniel Terry* hath fully acquitted his Reputation upon the faid Article of Charge.

The *firft* Refolution of the Committee being read a fecond Time;

Mʳ *Terry* withdrew.

Then the faid *Refolution* was, upon the Queftion put thereupon, agreed to by the Houfe.

The *fecond* and *third* Refolutions of the Committee being feverally read a fecond Time, were, upon the Queftion feverally put thereupon, agreed to by the Houfe.

The *fourth* Refolution of the Committee being read a fecond Time;

The *Amendment* following was propofed to be made thereunto, *viz.*

To leave out, "*hath not acquitted his Reputation upon the faid Article of Charge,*' and infert "*was guilty of a Breach of Duty in his Office of Sheriff, in delaying to pay the Money fo received by his Under Sheriff, upon the faid Execution, for which he was liable to make Satiffaction to the Creditor, as he accordingly did, in allowing the Intereft of the faid Money; but that there was nothing criminal or corrupt in his faid Conduct, as it doth not appear he knew, at the Time of writing the Return upon the faid Execution for the faid* Benjamin, *that any Part of the Money was paid,*" inftead thereof.

And

---

¹ Hening, VII, p. 171.

And the *Queſtion* being put, that the Words '*hath not acquitted his Reputation upon the ſaid Article of Charge*' ſtand Part of the ſaid Reſolution;

It *paſſed* in the Negative.

And the *Queſtion* being put, that the Words '*was guilty of a Breach of Duty in his Office of Sheriff, in delaying to Pay the Money ſo received by his Under Sheriff, upon the ſaid Execution, for which he was liable to make Satiſſaction to the Creditor, as he accordingly did, in allowing the Intereſt of the ſaid Money; but that there was nothing criminal or corrupt in his ſaid Conduct, as it doth not appear he knew, at the Time of writing the Return upon the ſaid Execution for the ſaid Benjamin, that any Part of the Money was paid,*' be inſerted inſtead thereof;

It was *reſolved* in the Affirmative.

Reſolved, That the Houſe doth agree with the Committee in the ſaid Reſolution ſo amended, that, with Reſpect to the fourth Article of Charge, 'that Mr *Nathaniel Terry*, when he was Sheriff of *Halifax*, had an Execution given him againſt *Perkins's* Eſtate, which Execution he returned ſerved on a Negro and the Negro run away; that it remained in that State for a conſiderable Time, and the ſaid *Terry* never gave the Gentleman, who was appointed to receive the Money, and who made Application for it, although he was in the County regularly every Month, any Reaſon to believe he had got one Shilling of it; at length it was diſcovered that near two Years before the greateſt part of it had been paid, and a Receipt given for it by a young Man, *Benjamin Terry*, who lived in the Houſe with Colonel *Terry*, and was employed as his Deputy:' The ſaid *Nathaniel Terry* was guilty of a Breach of Duty in his Office of Sheriff, in delaying to pay the Money ſo received by his Under Sheriff, upon the ſaid Execution, for which he was liable to make Satiſſaction to the Creditor, as he accordingly did, in allowing the Intereſt of the ſaid Money; but that there was nothing criminal or corrupt in his ſaid Conduct, as it doth not appear he knew, at the Time of writing the Return upon the ſaid Execution for the ſaid *Benjamin*, that any Part of the Money was paid.

The ſubſequent *Reſolutions* of the Committee being ſeverally read a ſecond Time, were, upon the Queſtion ſeverally put thereupon, agreed to by the Houſe.

Mr *Bland* reported, from the Committee of Propoſitions and Grievances, that the Committee had had under their Conſideration the Petitions of the Juſtices of *James City* County, and of the Mayor, Recorder, Alderman, and Common Council of the City of *Williamſburg*, to them referred, and had come to ſeveral Reſolutions thereupon, which they had directed him to report to the Houſe; and he read the Report in his Place, and afterwards delivered it in at the Clerk's Table; where the Reſolutions of the Committee were read, and are as followeth, *viz.*

Reſolved, That it is the Opinion of this Committee, that ſo much of the ſaid Petitions as prays that an Act may paſs for adding to the ſaid County of *James City*, ſo much of the Market Square in the ſaid City of *Williamſburg* as lies on the North Side of the Main Street, as far as *Nicholſon* Street, and between the Line of *Hugh Walker's* Lot, and the Paling where Mr *Haldenby Dixon's* Store ſtands, and now in the County of *York*, is reaſonable.

Reſolved, That it is the Opinion of this Committee, that ſo much of the ſaid Petition of the Juſtices of *James City* County as prays that they may be impowered to ſell the Lot of Land whereon their preſent Court-Houſe ſtands, in the City of *Williamſburg*, and to apply the Proceeds of ſuch Sale towards diſcharging their Proportion of the Expence of building a new Court-Houſe, is reaſonable.

Reſolved, That it is the Opinion of this Committee, that ſo much of the ſaid Petition of the Mayor, Recorder, Aldermen, and Common Council of the City of *Williamſburg*, as prays that they may be permitted to uſe the Guard-Houſe in the ſaid City (the Guard being diſcontinued) as and for a Market-Houſe, be rejected.

The ſaid *Reſolutions* being ſeverally read a ſecond Time, were, upon the Queſtion ſeverally put thereupon, agreed to by the Houſe.

Ordered, That a Bill of Bills be brought in perſuant to the *firſt* and *ſecond* of the

ſaid

faid Refolutions; and that the Committee of Propofitions and Grievances do prepare and bring in the fame.

Mr *Edmund Pendleton* reported from the Committee of Privileges and Elections, to whom it was referred to ftate an Account of the Expences of the Attendance and taking the Examinations of the Witneffes, before the faid Committee, and before the Commiffioners in the Country, on the Information of Mr *Nathaniel Terry*, relating to the Accufation reflecting upon his Character, that the Committee had ftated an Account accordingly; and he read the Report in his Place, and afterwards delivered it in at the Clerk's Table; where the Account was read, and is as followeth, *viz.*

Upon the *fourth* Article of Charge.

For the Profecution	For Mr. *Terry*	Before Commif-fioners	Before the Committee	Diftance	Total Tobacco	Ferriages. l. s. d.		
Bethenia Chadwell,			3 Days	230	870	6		
Francis Cox,			3	230	870	5		
	John Chadwell		3	230	870	6		

Upon the other Articles of Charge.

Champnefs Terry,		1 Day	3	200	805	5		
Thomas Tunftall,		1	3	160	685	5		
William Wright,			3	160	660	5		
William Watkins,			3	168	684	5		
John Lewis,			3	200	780	5		
George Boyd,		1	3	175	730	5		
Abraham Skelton,		1	3	200	805	5		
Jofeph Mayes,		1	3	195	790	5		
Margaret Mayes,		1	3	195	790	5		
James Bates,		1	3	160	685	5		
Thomas Yuille,		1	3	160	685	5		
Jofeph Jackfon,		1	3	55	370	2		
Cain Jackfon,		1	3	55	370	2		
	Benajah Parker,		3	170	690	5		
	David Wall,		3	170	690	5		
	Daniel Wall,	1	3	170	715	5		
	Jeremiah Pate,		3	172	696	5		
	Jofhua Powell,		3	175	705	5		
	Benjamin Lankford,	1	3	200	805	5		
	Mofes Terry,		3	175	705	5		
	Robert Wooding,		3	175	705	2	6	
	Mary M'Kendre,		3	175	705	5		
	Clement Reade,		3	140	600	4		

To *William Wright*, for attending the Commiffioners as Clerk,   4

To *Abraham Skelton*, for fummoning 5 Witneffes,   35

To the Sheriff of *Halifax*, for fummoning 14 Witneffes,   98

To the Sheriff of *Charlotte*, for fummoning 3 Witneffes,   21

To the Sheriff of *Chefterfield*, for fummoning 2 Witneffes,   18

_____

18637£. 10 2 6

Ordered, That the faid Account be referred to the Confideration of the Committee of Public Claims; and that they do rate the Tobacco therein mentioned in Money, and allow all the faid Expences, amongft the Money Claims of this Seffion, to be paid by the Public.

Ordered, That Leave be given to bring in a Bill for reimburfing the Country the Expence incurred by the Profecution of Mr *Walter Coles's* Accufation againft Mr *Nathaniel Terry;* and that Mr *Mercer* and Mr *Henry Lee* do prepare, and bring in the fame.

A *Petition* of *Bowler Cocke* and *Charles Carter,* Efquires, was prefented to the Houfe, and

and read; fetting forth that in the Suppreffion of an Infurrection of Slaves, in the Month of *December* laft, two of the Infurgents were killed, and three fo wounded that one of them is fince dead, and the others are not yet recovered; of which five Slaves the faid *Bowler Cocke* was intitled to the Ufe for the Life of his Wife *Elizabeth*, and the faid *Charles Carter* had the property; and therefore praying the Confideration of the Houfe, and that the Petitioners may be allowed for the faid Slaves.

Ordered, That the faid Petition be referred to the Confideration of the Committee of Public Claims; and that they do examine the Matter thereof, and report the fame, with their Opinion thereupon, to the Houfe.

Several *Petitions* of fundry Perfons, of the Parifh of *Overwharton*, in the County of *Stafford*, whofe Names are thereunto fubfcribed, were prefented to the Houfe, and read; taking Notice of a Petition intended to be prefented to the Houfe, for continuing fix Members of the Veftry of the faid Parifh in Office; and fetting forth that the faid Veftry have neglected their Duty, and that fome of them have refigned, and others refufe to act; and that, as the Petitioners conceive, every Parifh hath a Right once to choofe a Veftry, which Right the faid Parifh never exercifed; and therefore praying that the faid Veftry be diffolved.

Ordered, That the faid *Petition* be referred to the Confideration of the Committee for Religion; and that they do examine the Matter thereof, and report the fame, with their Opinion thereupon, to the Houfe.

Ordered, That Mr *Terry* have Leave to be abfent from the Service of this Houfe, for the remainder of this Seffion.

Mr *Treafurer* reported from the Committee for Religion, to whom the Petition of the Rector and Veftry of the Parifh of *Briftol*, in the Counties of *Prince George* and *Dinwiddie*, was referred, that the Committee had examined the matter of the faid Petition, and come to a Refolution thereupon, which they had directed him to report to the Houfe; and he read the Report in his Place, and afterwards delivered it in at the Clerk's Table; where the Refolution of the Committee was read, and is as followeth, *viz.*

Refolved, That it is the Opinion of this Committee, that the Petition of the Rector and Veftry of the Parifh of *Briftol*, praying that the Glebe of the faid Parifh may be fold, and a more convenient Glebe purchafed, in Lieu thereof, is reafonable.

The faid *Refolution* being read a fecond Time, was, upon the Queftion put thereupon, agreed to by the Houfe.

Ordered, That a Bill be brought in purfuant to the faid Refolution; and that the Committee for Religion do prepare and bring in the fame.

The *Order* of the Day being read for the Houfe to refolve itfelf into a Committee of the whole Houfe, to confider of the prefent State of the Colony;

Refolved, That this Houfe will, upon *Wednefday* next, refolve itfelf into the faid Committee.

The other *Order* of the Day being read;

Refolved, That this Houfe will, To-morrow refolve itfelf into a Committee of the whole Houfe to take into Confideration the Governor's Meffage, and the Letters and papers, relative to *Indian* Affairs, therein mentioned.

And then the Houfe adjourned till Tomorrow Morning Eleven of the Clock.

Tuesday, the 29th of May, 10 Geo. III. 1770.

A Petition of feveral Perfons, Owners of Lands in *Gingoteague* Ifland, in the County of *Accomack*, whofe Names are thereunto fubfcribed, was prefented to the Houfe, and read; fetting forth, that the faid Ifland is very proper for raifing of neat Cattle and Sheep, though not plentifully fupplied with frefh Water; and that Hogs kept there are very detrimental, by rooting the Pafture, polluting the Water, and devouring the Lambs; and alfo that Dogs do great Mifchief there by

worrying

worrying and deftroying the grown Sheep; and therefore praying that an Act may pafs to prevent Hogs and Dogs going at Large on the faid Ifland.

Ordered, That the faid petition be referred to the Confideration of the Committee of propofitions and Grievances; and that they do examine the Matter thereof, and report the fame, with their opinion thereupon, to the Houfe.

Mr *Marfhall* prefented to the Houfe, according to Order, a Bill to explain and amend an Act of this prefent Seffion of Affembly, intituled, *An Act¹ to divide the Parifh of* Hamilton, *in the Counties of* Fauquier *and* Prince William; and the fame was received, and read the firft Time.

Refolved, That the Bill be read a fecond Time.

Mr *Archibald Cary* reported from the Committee of Public Claims, that the Committee had had under their Confideration feveral Petitions to them referred, and had come to feveral Refolutions thereupon, which they had directed him to report to the Houfe; and he read the Report in his Place, and afterwards delivered it in at the Clerk's Table; where the Refolutions of the Committee were read, and are as followeth, *viz*.

Refolved, That it is the Opinion of this Committee, that the Petition of *Henry Townfhend*, late a Soldier in the *Virginia* Regiment, is reafonable; and that he ought to be allowed the Sum of Ten Pounds for his prefent Relief, and the further Sum of Ten Pounds *per Annum*, during his Life, in Confideration of the Wound he received in the Service, and of his being thereby rendered incapable of getting a Livelihood.

Refolved, That it is the Opinion of this Committee, that the Petition of *John Welch*, late a Soldier in the *Virginia* Regiment, is reafonable; and that he ought to be allowed the Sum of Five Pounds for his prefent Relief, and the further Sum of Five Pounds *per Annum*, during his Life, in Confideration of the Hardfhips he fuffered in the Service, and of his being thereby rendered incapable of getting a Livelihood.

Refolved, That it is the Opinion of this Committee, that the Petition of *Jofeph Williams*, to be allowed the public Money ftolen out of his Houfe, as fet forth in the faid Petition, be rejected.

The faid *Refolutions* being feverally read a fecond Time, were, upon the Queftion feverally put thereupon, agreed to by the Houfe.

A *Petition* of *James Ford* was prefented to the Houfe, and read; fetting forth, that the Petitioner being in the Service of this Colony, at the Battle of the *Meadows*, in the Year 1754, received a Wound in his right Eye, by a Mufket Ball, which deprived him of the Sight thereof, and that he is now growing old, and become weak; and therefore praying the Houfe to take his condition into Confideration, and grant him Relief.

188 *Ordered*, That the faid Petition be referred to the Confideration of the Committee of Public Claims; and that they do examine the Matter thereof, and report the fame, with their Opinion thereupon, to the Houfe.

A *Petition* of *Enoch Fowler*, late a Soldier in the *Virginia* Regiment, was prefented to the Houfe, and read; fetting forth, that he is fo afflicted with a Rheumatifm, contracted whilft he ferved in the faid Regiment, as to be almoft helplefs, and unable, without extreme Difficulty, to provide Subfiftence for himfelf, with a Wife and fmall Children; and therefore imploring the Compaffion of the Houfe and praying Relief.

Ordered, That the faid *Petition* be referred to the Confideration of the Committee of Public Claims; and that they do examine the Matter thereof, and report the fame, with their Opinion thereupon, to the Houfe.

A *Petition* of *Thomas Davis*, late a Soldier in the *Virginia* Regiment, was prefented to the Houfe, and read; fetting forth, that the fuffered extraordinary Hardfhips, whilft he ferved in the faid Regiment, and after he was Difcharged from it was affected with a nervous Diforder, which is often a Confequence of repeated Colds and great Fatigue, fo that he is an Object of Compaffion; and therefore praying Relief.

Ordered

¹ Hening, VIII, p. 403.

Ordered, That the faid Petition be referred to the Confideration of the Committee of Public Claims; and that they do examine the Matter thereof, and report the fame, with their Opinion thereupon, to the Houfe.

A *Petition* of *John Knibb* and *Thomas Stratton*, Infpectors of Tobacco at *Bermuda Hundred*, in the County of *Chefterfield*, was prefented to the Houfe, and read; fetting forth, that feveral Parcels of Tobacco have been ftolen out of the Warehoufe at the Place aforefaid, for which the Petitioners were obliged to make Satiffaction to the Proprietors and therefore praying the Houfe to take the fame into Confideration, and to grant fuch Relief as fhall feem reasonable.

Ordered, That the faid Petition be referred to the Confideration of the Committee of Public Claims; and that they do examine the Matter thereof, and report the fame, with their Opinion thereupon, to the Houfe.

An engroffed *Bill* for clearing a Road from *Payne's Run*, in the County of *Augufta*, to *Thurman's*, in the County of *Albemarle*, was read the third Time.

Refolved, That the Bill do pafs; and that the Title be, *An Act[1] for clearing a Road from* Payne's Run, *in the County of* Augufta, *to* Thurman's, *in the County of* Albemarle.

Ordered, That Mr *Harrifon* do carry the Bill to the Council, and defire their Concurrence.

An engroffed *Bill* to continue an Act, intituled *An Act for regulating the Practice of Attornies*, was read the third Time.

Refolved, That the Bill do pafs; and that the Title be, *An Act[2] to continue an Act, intituled, An Act for regulating the Practice of Attornies.*

Ordered, That Mr *Eyre* do carry the Bill to the Council, and defire their Concurrence.

An engroffed *Bill* to repeal an Act for increafing the Salary of the Minifter of the Parifh of *Frederick*, in the County of *Frederick*, was read the third Time.

Refolved, That the Bill do pafs; and that the Title be, *An Act[3] to repeal an Act for increafing the Salary of the Minifter of the Parifh of* Frederick, *in the County of* Frederick.

Ordered, That Mr *Rutherford* do carry the Bill to the Council, and defire their Concurrence.

An engroffed *Bill* to veft certain Lands, whereof *John Robinfon*, Efq; died feized 189 in Truft for *Philip Johnfon*, Gentleman, and his Children, in Truftees, for the Purpofes therein mentioned, was read the third Time.

Refolved, That the Bill do pafs; and that the Title be, *An Act[4] to veft certain Lands, whereof* John Robinfon, *Efq; died feized in Truft for* Philip Johnfon, *Gentleman, and his Children, in Truftees, for the Purpofes therein mentioned.*

Ordered, That Mr *Edmund Pendleton* do carry the Bill to the Council, and defire their Concurrence.

Ordered, That Mr *William Digges* have Leave to be abfent from the Service of this Houfe till *Monday* next.

The *Order* of the Day being read for the Houfe to refolve itfelf into a Committee of the whole Houfe, upon the Bill to continue and amend the *Act for better regulating and difciplining the Militia*;

Refolved, That this Houfe will, upon *Thurfday* next, refolve itfelf into the faid Committee.

The other *Order* of the Day being read;

Refolved, That this Houfe will, To-morrow, refolve itfelf into a Committee of the whole Houfe, to take into Confideration the Governor's Meffage, and the Letters and Papers, relative to *Indian* Affairs, therein mentioned.

And then the Houfe adjourned till Tomorrow Morning Eleven of the Clock.

Wednesday

Wednesday, the 30th of May, 10 Geo. III. 1770.

A Petition of *John Wyatt*, *Francis Smith* and *Jofeph Fofter*, was prefented to the Houfe, and read; fetting forth, that a Gun of the faid *John Wyatt*, of the Value of Four Pounds, two Guns of the faid *Francis Smith* at the Value of Three Pounds, and one Gun of the faid *Jofeph Fofter*, of the Value of Two Pounds and Fifteen Shillings, were ufed in fuppreffing a late Infurrection of the Slaves of *Bowler Cocke*, Gentleman, and fpoiled in the Action; and therefore praying to be allowed for their faid feveral Loffes.

Ordered, That the faid Petition be referred to the Confideration of the Committee of Public Claims; and that they do examine the Matter thereof, and report the fame, with their Opinion thereupon, to the Houfe.

Ordered, That the Committee of Propofitions and Grievances, to whom the Petitions of feveral Perfons of the County of *Accomack*, praying that the faid County may be divided, and the *Petition of feveral* other Perfons of the faid County, in Oppofition to the faid Divifion, were feverally referred, be difcharged from proceeding upon the faid *Petition;* and that the Confideration of the faid feveral Petitions be deferred till the next Seffion of the General Affembly.

Ordered, That Mr *Treafurer* do lay his Accounts, fince the fixteenth Day of *November* laft before the Houfe.

Mr *Treafurer* reported to the Houfe, that the Governor having been waited upon, purfuant to the Order of *Friday* laft, to know his Pleafure when he would be attended by this Houfe, had been pleafed to appoint to be attended this Day, in the Council Chamber, and to fay he would acquaint the Houfe, by a Meffenger of his own, when he was ready to receive their Addrefs.

A *Bill* to veft certain Lands in *David Meade* in Fee Simple, whereof the faid *David* and *Sarah* his Wife are feized, in Right of the faid *Sarah*, in Fee Tail, and for fettling other Lands, in Lieu thereof, was read a fecond Time.

Refolved, That the Bill be committed to Mr *Blair*, and all the Members who ferve for the Counties of *Nanfemond*, *Northampton*, *Ifle of Wight*, and *Southampton*.

Mr *Treafurer*, according to Order, laid his Accounts, fince the fixteenth Day of *November* laft, before the Houfe.

Ordered, That the faid Accounts do lie upon the Table, to be perufed by the Members of the Houfe.

A *Bill* to veft certain intailed Lands and Slaves, therein mentioned, in *Nathaniel Littleton Savage*, Gentleman, in Fee Simple, and to fettle other Lands, in Lieu thereof, was read a fecond Time.

Refolved, That the Bill be committed to Mr *Eyre*, Mr *Burton*, and all the Members who ferve for the Counties of *York*, *Elizabeth City*, and *James City*.

A *Bill* to veft certain Lands, whereof *Bernard Moore*, Efq; is feized, in Fee Tail, in Truftees, to be fold, and the Money laid out in the Purchafe of other Lands and Slaves to be fettled to the fame Ufes, was read a fecond Time.

Refolved, That the Bill be committed to Mr *Richard Henry Lee*, Mr *Braxton*, Mr *Lyne*, Mr *John Tayloe Corbin*, Mr *Edmund Pendleton*, and Mr *Taliaforro*.

A *Bill* to amend an Act paffed in the former Part of this Seffion of Affembly, for reimburfing the Counties of *Hanover* and *King William*, the Expence of clearing *Pamunkey* River, was read a fecond Time.

Ordered, That the Bill be ingroffed.

A *Bill* to explain and amend an Act of this prefent Seffion of Affembly, intituled *An Act*[1] *to divide the Parifh of* Hamilton, *in the Counties of* Fauquier *and* Prince William, was read a fecond Time.

Ordered, That the Bill be engroffed.

Mr *Bland* reported from the Committee of propofitions and Grievances, that the

Committee

---

1   Hening, VIII, p. 403.

Committee had had under their Confideration feveral Petitions to them referred, and had come to feveral Refolutions thereupon, which the Committee had directed him to report to the Houfe; and he read the Report in his Place, and afterwards delivered it in at the Clerk's Table; where the Refolutions of the Committee were read, and are as followeth, *viz.*

Refolved, That it is the Opinion of this Committee, that the Petition of divers Inhabitants of the County of *Accomack*, praying that *Guilford* Warehoufe may be difcontinued, and new Warehoufes, eftablifhed at *Finley's* Point, on *Hunting* Creek, is reafonable.

Refolved, That it is the Opinion of this Committee, that the Petition of divers Inhabitants of the County of *Accomack*, in Oppofition thereto, and praying that new Warehoufes may be eftablifhed at *Tatham's* Landing, in the faid County of *Accomack*, be rejected.

A *Meffage* from the Governor, by Mr *Hubard*:

M^r. *Speaker*,
The Governor is now ready to receive the Addrefs of your Houfe in the Council Chamber.

Accordingly Mr *Speaker*, with the Houfe, went up; and being returned, he reported, that the Houfe had attended the Governor, with their Addrefs, to which his Excellency was pleafed to give this Anfwer:

Mr *Speaker, and Gentlemen of the Houfe of Burgeffes,*
I will report to the King the full contents of your very obliging Addrefs, and will again implore his Majefty, as immediately as poffible, to indulge his Houfe of Burgeffes in all their reafonable Defires.—To do lefs would be to neglect my Duty.
Having laft Night received certain material Papers from Mr Stuart, Superintendant of the Southern Diftrict, I muft beg Leave to fubmit them to your immediate Confideration.

Mr *Speaker* acquainted the Houfe, that the Governor had delivered to him the Papers mentioned in his Excellency's Anfwer to the Addrefs of this Houfe, to have been received from Mr *Stuart*, Superintendant of the Southern Diftrict.

And he delivered the faid Papers in at the Clerk's Table.

And the faid Papers were read.

Ordered, That the faid Papers do lie upon the Table, to be perufed by the Members of the Houfe.

Then the *Refolutions* of the Committee of Propofitions and Grievances upon the Petition of divers Inhabitants of the County of *Accomack*, praying that *Guilford* Warehoufe may be difcontinued, and new Warehoufes eftablifhed at *Finley's Point*, on *Hunting Creek*, and the Petition of divers Inhabitants of *Accomack*, in Oppofition thereto, and praying that new Warehoufes may be eftablifhed at *Tatham's* Landing, in the faid County of *Accomack*, being feverally read a fecond Time, were, upon the Queftion feverally put thereupon, agreed to by the Houfe.

Ordered, That the faid Report do lie upon the Table.

The *Order* of the Day being read, for the Houfe to refolve itfelf into a Committee of the whole Houfe, to take into Confideration the Governor's Meffage, and the Letters and Papers, relative to *Indian* Affairs, therein mentioned;

Ordered, That the faid Meffage, Letters, and Papers, be referred to the faid Committee.

Then the Houfe refolved itfelf into the faid Committee.

Mr *Speaker* left the Chair.

Mr *Bland* took the Chair of the Committee.

Mr *Speaker* refumed the Chair.

Mr *Bland* reported from the Committee, that they had come to a Refolution, which

he

he read in his Place, and afterwards delivered it in at the Clerk's Table; where the fame was read, and is as followeth, *viz.*

Refolved, That it is the Opinion of this Committee, that it may be of effential Service to the Intereft of this Colony, to appoint Commiffioners to join thofe of the Northern Provinces, in confidering a Plan for regulating the Trade of his Majefty's *American* Subjects with the *Indians*.

The faid *Refolution* being read a fecond Time, was, upon the Queftion put thereupon, agreed to by the Houfe.

Ordered, That a Bill be brought in purfuant to the faid Refolution; and that Mr *Bland*, Mr *Pendleton*, Mr *Henry* and Mr *Treafurer*, do prepare and bring in the fame.

192 The *Order* of the Day being read, for the Houfe to refolve itfelf into a Committee of the whole Houfe, to confider of the prefent State of the Colony;

Refolved, That this Houfe will, upon *Friday* next, refolve itfelf into the faid Committee.

The other *Order* of the Day being read, for the Houfe to refolve itfelf into a Committee of the whole Houfe, upon the Bill to continue and amend the Act, intituled *An Act[1] for amending the Staple of Tobacco, and preventing Frauds in his Majefty's Cuftoms;*

Refolved, That this Houfe will, upon *Monday* next, refolve itfelf into the faid Committee.

Mr *Archibald Cary* reported from the Committee of Public Claims, to whom the Petition of *Bowler Cocke* and *Charles Carter*, Efquires, was referred, that the Committee had examined the Matter of the faid Petition, and had directed him to report the fame, as it appeared to them, together with the Refolution of the Committee thereupon, to the Houfe; and he read the Report in his Place, and afterwards delivered it in at the Clerk's Table; where the fame was read.

And the Houfe being informed, that fome Alteration might be neceffary to be made in the faid Report;

Ordered, That the faid Report be re-committed.

Ordered, That the faid Report be re-committed to the fame Committee, to whom the faid Petition was referred.

And then the Houfe adjourned till Tomorrow Morning Eleven of the Clock.

Thursday, the 31st of May, 10 Geo. III. 1770.

MR *Bland* prefented to the Houfe, according to Order, a Bill for the better regulating the Office of Sheriffs, and their Deputies; and the fame was received, and read the firft Time.

Refolved, That the Bill be read a fecond Time.

Mr *Edmund Pendleton* reported from the Committee, to whom the Bill to veft certain intailed Lands, whereof *Charles Lewis*, Gentleman, is feized, in *John Lewis*, Gentleman, in Fee Simple, and fettle other Lands to the fame Ufes, was committed, that the Committee had examined the Allegations of the Bill, and found the fame to be true; and that the Committee had directed him to report the Bill to the Houfe, without any Amendment; and he delivered the Bill in at the Clerk's Table.

Ordered, That the Bill be ingroffed.

Ordered, That Leave be given to bring in a Bill to compel Perfons to find Security in certain Cafes; and that Mr *Edmund Pendleton* do prepare and bring in the fame.

A *Petition* of *Nicholas Alley* was prefented to the Houfe, and read; fetting forth, that in the Year 1757 the Petitioner fupplied the Militia of *Prince Edward* County with Three Hundred and Seventy-two Pounds of neat Pork, and Two Barrels of Corn, for which he hath never received any Satiffaction; and that the Petitioner's faid 193 Claim was prefented to the Houfe in 1764, and rejected, becaufe, as he was informed,

he

---

[1] Hening, VIII, p. 69.

he did not attend and fhew why he had not applied fooner, the Reafon whereof was, that having been wounded in an Engagement with the *Indians*, foon after he fupplied the faid Provifions, upon his Recovery he removed to *South Carolina*, where he remained till the faid Year 1764; and therefore praying the Houfe to make him a reafonable Allowance.

Ordered, That the faid Petition be referred to the Confideration of the Committee of Public Claims; and that they do examine the Matter thereof, and report the fame, with their Opinion thereupon, to the Houfe.

Mr *Bland* reported, from the Committee of Propofitions and Grievances, that the Committee had had under their Confideration feveral Petitions, to them referred, and had come to feveral Refolutions thereupon, which the Committee had directed him to report to the Houfe; and he read the Report in his Place, and afterwards delivered it in at the Clerk's Table; where the Refolutions of the Committee were read, and are as followeth; *viz.*

Refolved, That it is the Opinion of this Committee, that the Petition of fundry Freeholders and Inhabitants of the Counties of *Prince George, Dinwiddie, Amelia, Brunfwick, Lunenburg, Mecklenburg, Charlotte,* and *Suffex*, praying that another Infpection of Tobacco may be eftablifhed on the Lots of *Robert Bolling*, which he lately purchafed of *Patrick Ramfay*, in the Town of *Blandford*, is reafonable.

Refolved, That it is the Opinion of this Committee, that the Petition of fundry Inhabitants of *Dinwiddie* County, in Oppofition thereto, and praying that another Infpection of Tobacco may be eftablifhed on the Land of *Robert Bolling*, between *Bolling's* old Warehoufe and *Bollingbrook*, be rejected.

The faid Refolutions being feverally read a fecond Time, were, upon the Queftion feverally put thereupon, agreed to by the Houfe.

Ordered, That the faid Report do lie upon the Table.

A *Meffage from the Council by* Mr *Hubard:*

Mr *Speaker,*

The Council have agreed to the Bill, intituled, An Act[1], for fettling the Fees of the Clerk and serjeant of the Court of Huftings for the City of *Williamfburg, without any Amendment: And alfo*

The Council have agreed to the Bill, intituled An Act[2] to veft certain Lands, whereof *John Robinfon*, Efq; died feized, in Truft for *Philip Johnfon*, Gentleman, and his Children, in Truftees, for the Purpofes therein mentioned, *without any Amendment: And alfo*

The Council have agreed to the Bill, intituled An Act[3] for clearing a Road from *Payne's Run*, in the County of *Augufta*, to *Thurman's*, in the County of *Albemarle, with an Amendment, to which Amendment the Council defire the Concurrence of this Houfe.*

And then the Meffenger withdrew.

The Houfe proceeded to take the faid Amendment into Confideration;

And the faid *Amendment* was read, and is as followeth, *viz.*

Line 11, After '*required*' infert '*by Warrant from his Excellency the Governor.*'

The faid *Amendment* being read a fecond Time, was, upon the Queftion put thereupon, difagreed to by the Houfe.

Ordered, That a Meffage be fent to the Council to inform them, that this Houfe cannot agree to the Amendment by them propofed to the faid Bill, and defire that they will pafs the fame without the Amendment; and that Mr *Harrifon* do carry the faid Meffage.

Ordered, That Mr *Taliaferro* have leave to be abfent from the Service of this Houfe, till *Monday* Fortnight.

A *Petition* of fundry Perfons, Members of the Church of *England*, in the Parifh of *Frederick*, whofe Names are thereunto fubfcribed, was prefented to the Houfe, and read; fetting forth, that the faid Parifh being very extenfive, and there being not lefs

than

194

---

[1] Hening, VIII, p. 402.   [2] Ibid, VIII, p. 460.   [3] Not recorded as a law.

than feven Churches and Chapels therein, it is impoffible for the Minifter to perform the Duties of his Office in a proper Manner, and as the Law requires; neither can his Congregation attend Divine Service fo frequently and conveniently as they ought, nor can fome Perfons of them partake at all of the Benefits of his Miniftration; and therefore praying that the faid Parifh may be divided into three Parifhes by a Line, beginning at *William's Gap*, and running thence to the *Hampfhire* Boundary, in a direct Courfe fo as to pafs feven Miles to the North Eaftward of the Town of *Winchefter*, and by another Line, beginning at the Mouth of *Flint Run*, and running thence Eaft South Eaft to the *Culpeper* Line, and from the faid Mouth of the *Flint Run* to the Mouth of *Cedar Creek*, and from thence in a direct Weft North Weft Courfe to the Boundary of *Hampfhire* and *Frederick* Counties.

Ordered, That the faid *Petition* be referred to the Confideration of the Committee for Religion; and that they do examine the Matter thereof, and report the fame, with their Opinion thereupon, to the Houfe.

An engroffed *Bill* to explain and amend an Act of this prefent Seffion of Affembly, intituled *An Act*[1] *to divide the Parifh of* Hamilton, *in the Counties of* Fauquier *and* Prince William, was read the third Time.

Refolved, That the Bill do pafs; and that the Title be, *An Act*[2] *to explain and amend an Act of this prefent Seffion of Affembly*, intituled *An Act to divide the Parifh of* Hamilton, *in the Counties of* Fauquier *and* Prince William.

Ordered, That Mr *Marfhall* do carry the Bill to the Council, and defire their Concurrence.

A *Petition* of *Luke Luker* and *John Walton*, Infpectors of Tobacco at *Pungoteague*, was prefented to the Houfe and read; fetting forth, that the Warehoufe at that Place being damaged by the Guft in *September* laft, before the fame could be repaired, one Hogfhead of Tobacco was ftolen out of it, for which the Petitioners, not being able to recover it, have been obliged to made Satiffaction to the Owner thereof; and therefore praying that they may be reimburfed by the Public.

Ordered, That the faid petition be referred to the Confideration of the Committee of Public Claims; and that they do examine the Matter thereof, and report the fame, with their opinion thereupon, to the Houfe.

An engroffed *Bill* to amend an Act, paffed in the former Part of this Seffion of Affembly, for reimburfing the Counties of *Hanover* and *King William* the expence of clearing *Pamunkey* River, was read the third Time.

Refolved, That the Bill do pafs; and that the Title be, *An Act*[3] *to amend an Act paffed in the former Part of this Seffion of Affembly, for reimburfing the Counties of* Hanover *and* King William *the Expence of clearing* Pamunkey *River*.

Ordered, That Mr *Henry* do carry the Bill to the Council, and defire their Concurrence.

The *Order* of the Day being read, for the Houfe to refolve itfelf into a Committee of the whole Houfe, upon the Bill to continue and amend the Act for the better regulating and difciplining the Militia.

Refolved, That this Houfe will, To-morrow, refolve itfelf into the faid Committee. *And then the Houfe adjourned till To-Morrow Morning Eleven of the Clock.*

𝔉riday, the 1st of 𝔍une, 10 𝔊eo. III. 1770.

195

M R *Richard Henry Lee* reported, from the Committee to whom the Bill to veft certain Lands, whereof *Bernard Moore*, Efq; is feized in Fee Tail, in Truftees, to be fold and the Money laid out in the Purchafe of other Lands and Slaves, to be fettled to the fame Ufes, was committed, that the Committee had examined the Allegations of the Bill, and found the fame to be true; and that the Committee had directed him to report the Bill to the Houfe, without any Amendment: And he delivered the Bill in at the Clerk's Table.

Ordered

---

[1] Hening, VIII, p. 403.   [2] Ibid, VIII, p. 428.   [3] Ibid, VIII, p. 416.

Ordered, That the Bill be engroffed.

Refolved, That this Houfe will receive no Petitions or Public Claims after *Tuefday*, the Twelfth Day of this Inftant, *June*.

A *Petition* of *Benjamin Grymes*, in Behalf of himfelf and his Creditors, was prefented to the Houfe, and read; fetting forth, that a Negro Man Slave, Part of the Petitioner's Eftate, conveyed to Truftees for the Benefit of his Creditors, having been convicted of Hog-ftealing, and punifhed, was, by Order of the Court before whom he was tried, remanded to Gaol till the Petitioner fhould fend for him; and that the Petitioner, the next Day after he had Notice thereof, fent for the faid Slave, but he was fo froft-bitten during his faid Confinement, that he is thereby rendered of little Value; and therefore praying the Houfe to make fuch Satiffaction as they fhall think reafonable.

Ordered, That the faid Petition be referred to the Confideration of the Committee of Public Claims; and that they do examine the Matter thereof, and report the fame, with their Opinion thereupon, to the Houfe.

Mr *Richard Lee* reported, from the Committee to whom the Bill to dock the Intail of certain Lands and Slaves, whereof *John Page*, Efq; is feized, and for fetting other Lands, of greater Value, to the fame Ufes, was committed, that the Committee had examined the Allegations of the Bill, and found the fame to be true; and that the Committee had gone through the Bill, and made feveral Amendments thereunto, which they had directed him to report to the Houfe; and he read the Report in his Place, and afterwards delivered the Bill, with the Amendments, in at the Clerk's Table; where the Amendments were once read throughout, and then a fecond Time, one by one; and, upon the Queftion feverally put thereupon, were agreed to by the Houfe.

Ordered, That the Bill, with the Amendments, be ingroffed.

A *Petition* of fundry Perfons, Inhabitants of the County of *Spotfylvania*, whofe Names are thereunto fubfcribed, was prefented to the Houfe, and read; fetting forth, that the Act of General Affembly, made for Relief of infolvent Debtors, doth not fully anfwer the good Purpofes thereof, it being fometimes difficult for thofe unfortunate People to give Notice of their Intention to take the Benefit of the faid Act to the Creditors or their Agents, and the Courts being often prevented by unavoidable Accidents from fitting, to receive the Schedule of fuch Debtors Eftates; and that the Confinement of the faid Debtors in Gaol, Twenty Days before they can difcharge themfelves by the faid Act, is not only unprofitable to the Creditors, but is attended with unneceffary Expence to the Public; and therefore praying that the faid Act may be amended fo as to remedy the Evils complained of.

Ordered, That the faid Petition be referred to the Confideration of the Committee of Propofitions and Grievances; and that they do examine the matter thereof, and report the fame, with their Opinion thereupon, to the Houfe.

Mr *Eyre* reported, from the Committee to whom the Bill to veft certain intailed Lands and Slaves, therein mentioned, in *Nathaniel Littleton Savage*, Gentleman, in Fee Simple, and to fettle other Lands, in Lieu thereof, was committed, that the Committee had examined the Allegations of the Bill, and found the fame to be true; and that the Committee had gone through the Bill, and made an Amendment thereunto, which they had directed him to report to the Houfe; and he read the Report in his Place, and afterwards delivered the Bill, with the Amendment, in at the Clerk's Table; where the Amendment was twice read; and, upon the Queftion put thereupon, was agreed to by the Houfe.

Ordered, That the Bill, with the Amendment, be ingroffed.

A *Petition* of fundry Perfons, Inhabitants of the County of *Spotfylvania*, was prefented to the Houfe, and read; fetting forth, that the greater Number of People in the faid County, in Order to attend their Court, are obliged to go from Twenty to Six and Thirty Miles, to the Court-Houfe, in the Town of *Frederickfburg*, near one Corner of the County, which is not only a fingular Grievance, the Court-Houfes of other Counties being, for the moft part, in or not far from the Centers of them, but is a means of retarding the Bufinefs of the faid Court, and may be of pernicious Confequences, if, at the Time of an Election of Members, to reprefent the faid County in General Affembly,

the

the Weather fhould be fo bad as to hinder the Electors from going fo great Diftance; and that the Advantage the prefent Situation of the faid Court-Houfe is fuppofed to be of to the faid Town the Petitioners hope will not be put in Competition, with their Conveniency, contrary to the Policy of the Legiflature, which hath ever been, in forming Counties, to confult the Eafe of their refpective Inhabitants; and further fetting forth, that Suits of Law are, by the increafed Population of the Colony, exceedingly multiplied, the Profecution of them dilatory, and the Expences attending them enormous; and therefore praying, that this Houfe will addrefs the Governor that his Excellency will order the Court of the faid County of *Spotfylvania* to be held at the moft convenient Place, near the Center thereof; and alfo praying, that fome Mode may be adopted for the determining Law Suits with more Expedition and lefs Expence, agreeable to the Cuftom of the King's Courts in *Great-Britain*, and that Perfons, who have been brought up to the Law, and been refident in the Colony, at leaft five Years, may be appointed Judges, and be rewarded as they deferve, by the Houfe.

Ordered, That the faid petition be referred to the Confideration of the Committee of Propofitions and Grievances; and that they do examine the Matter thereof, and report the fame, with their Opinion thereupon, to the Houfe.

A *Petition* of *Benjamin Grymes,* in Behalf of himfelf and others, of the Parifh of *Saint George,* in the County of *Spotfylvania,* was prefented to the Houfe, and read; fetting forth, that the late Election of Veftrymen of the faid Parifh, made in Confequence of an Act of this prefent Seffion of General Affembly, was unfair, and unjuft, many perfons being permitted, who were not qualified, to vote therein; and that the Court of the faid County admitted only Eleven of the Veftrymen returned elected to be fworn into Office, upon a Prefumption that, inftead of the Twelfth Member returned, another Candidate would have been chofen, if the Sheriff had not acted partially; and therefore praying that the faid Election may be fet afide, and a new one appointed; and that no Perfon may be permitted to poll at fuch Election but thofe who pay their own Scot and Lot.

Ordered, That the faid Petition be referred to the Confideration of the Committee for Religion; and that they do examine the Matter thereof, and report the fame, with their Opinion thereupon, to the Houfe.

Mr *Bland* reported, from the Committee of Propofitions and Grievances, that the Committee had had under their Confideration two Petitions, to them referred, and had come to feveral Refolutions thereupon, which the Committee had directed him to Report to the Houfe; and he read the Report in his Place, and afterwards delivered it in at the Clerk's Table; where the Refolutions of the Committee were read, and are as followeth, *viz.*

Refolved, That it is the Opinion of this Committee, that the Petition of feveral Merchants, Planters, and others, praying that a Tobacco Infpection may be eftablifhed at *Low Point,* on *Chipoake's Creek,* be rejected.

Refolved, That it is the Opinion of this Committee, that the Petition of fundry Inhabitants of the Counties of *Prince George* and *Brunfwick,* in Oppofition thereto, are reafonable.

The faid *Refolutions* being feverally read a fecond Time, were, upon the Queftion feverally put thereupon, agreed to by the Houfe.

A *Petition* of *Thomas Shepherd* was prefented to the Houfe, and read; fetting forth that there was formerly a public Ferry eftablifhed from the Land of *Thomas Swearingen,* in the County of *Frederick,* acrofs *Potowmack* River, to the Province of *Maryland;* that a little below the faid Ferry, a Town called *Mecklenburg,* was eftablifhed on the Petitioner's Land, fome Diftance from the River, between which and the Town, but not adjoining either, the Petitioner agreed to fell the faid *Thomas* half an Acre of Land, which was laid off, but never conveyed or paid for during his Life; that it being found more convenient to have a Ferry from a Landing near the Town than at the former Place, fuch Ferry was eftablifhed from the Land of the Petitioner, by an Act paffed in the Year 1764, in Confequence of which Roads were laid out through the Petitioner's

Land

Land to the faid Ferry, and he provided Boats for keeping the fame; that the Widow and Sons of the faid *Thomas Swearingen* have been endeavoring to get the faid Ferry from the Petitioner, and the faid half Acre of Land being found not to extend to the River, and it being doubtful whether the Petitioner's Land did fo, the faid Land was entered for both by them and the Petitioner as wafte Land, and the Matter being heard upon a Caveat by Lord *Fairfax*, he granted the Land to the Petitioner; but whilft that Caveat was depending, and in the Abfence of the Petitioner, they applied to the Legiflature, and procured a Repeal of the Act for eftablifhing the Petitioner's Ferry, upon fuggeftion, that the fame was neceffary, as being but a fmall Diftance from *Swearingen's* old Ferry, although the latter hath been long fince difcontinued, and the Road thereto ftopped, and being poffeffed of Lands oppofite to the Petitioner's on the *Maryland* Side, they keep a Ferry to and from his Land, whereby he is fubject to the Inconvenience of Roads through his Land to the faid Ferry, while others are reaping the Advantages, which he conceives to be unjuft; and therefore praying that the Act for eftablifhing his faid Ferry may be revived.

Ordered, That the faid *Petition* be referred to the Confideration of the Committee of Propofitions and Grievances; and that they do examine the Matter thereof, and report the fame, with their Opinion thereupon, to the Houfe.

Mr *Treafurer* reported, from the Committee for Religion to whom the Petition of feveral Perfons, being Proteftant Diffenters, of the Baptift Perfuafion, was referred, that the Committee had partly examined the Matter of the faid Petition, and had come to a Refolution thereupon, which the Committee had directed him to report to the Houfe; and he read the Report in his Place, and afterwards delivered it in at the Clerk's Table; where the Refolution of the Committee was read, and is as followeth, *viz.*

Refolved, That it is the Opinion of this Committee, that fo much of the faid Petition as prays that the Minifters or Preachers of the Baptift Perfuafion may not be compelled to bear Arms or attend Mufters, be rejected.

The faid *Refolutions* being read a fecond Time, was, upon the Queftion put thereupon, agreed to by the Houfe.

Mr *Bland* prefented to the Houfe, according to Order, a Bill to amend the Act, intituled *An Act¹ for the better fecuring the Payment of Levies, and Reftraint of Vagrants, and for making Provifion for the Poor;* and the fame was received, and read the firft Time.

Refolved, That the Bill be read a fecond Time.

Mr *Edmund Pendleton* reported, from the Committee of Privileges and Elections, that the Committee had had under their further Confideration the Petition of Mr *Willis Riddick*, complaining of an undue Election and Return of Mr *Benjamin Baker* to ferve as a Burgefs in this prefent General Affembly for the County of *Nanfemond*, to them referred, and had come to a Refolution thereupon, which the Committee had directed him to report to the Houfe; and he read the Report in his Place, and afterwards delivered it in at the Clerk's Table; where the Refolution of the Committee was read, and is as followeth, *viz.*

Refolved, That it is the Opinion of this Committee, that the Confideration of the Subject-Matter of the faid Petition be put off until *Wednefday*, the 13th Inftant.

The faid *Refolution* being read a fecond Time, was, upon the Queftion put thereupon, agreed to by the Houfe.

Ordered, That Mr *Dixon* have Leave to be abfent from the Service of this Houfe until *Wednefday* next.

A *Bill* for altering the Court Day of the County of *Culpeper*, was read a fecond Time.

Refolved, That the Bill be committed to the Committee for Courts of Juftice.

Ordered, That it be an Inftruction to the Committee for Courts of Juftice, to whom the Bill for altering the Court Day of the County of *Culpeper* was committed, that they have Power to receive a Claufe or Claufes for altering the Court Day of the County of *Pittfylvania*, from the fourth *Friday* to the fourth *Thurfday* of every Month.

The *Order* of the Day being read, for the Houfe to refolve itfelf into a Committee of the whole Houfe, to confider of the prefent State of the Colony;

Ordered

---
¹ Hening, VI, p. 29.

199 *Ordered*, That the Papers mentioned in the Governor's Anſwer to the Addreſs of this Houſe to have been received from Mr *Stuart*, Superintendent of the Southern Diſtrict, which, upon *Wedneſday* laſt, were ordered to lie upon the Table; be referred to the ſaid Committee.

Ordered, That the Governor's Meſſage, and the Letters and Papers relative to *Indian* Affairs, therein mentioned, be referred to the ſaid Committee.

Then the Houſe reſolved itſelf into the ſaid Committee.

Mr *Speaker* left the Chair.

Mr *Bland* took the Chair of the Committee.

Mr *Speaker* reſumed the Chair.

Mr *Bland* reported from the Committee, that they had made ſome Progreſs in the Matters to them referred, and had directed him to move that they may have Leave to ſit again.

Reſolved, That this Houſe will, upon *Wedneſday* next, reſolve itſelf into a Committee of the whole Houſe, to conſider further of the preſent State of the Colony.

The *Order* of the Day being read, for the Houſe to reſolve itſelf into a Committee of the whole Houſe, to conſider further of the Bill to explain and amend one Act of Aſſembly made in the 4th Year of the Reign of Queen *Anne*, intituled *An Act[1] for regulating the Election of Burgeſſes, for ſettling their Privileges, and for aſcertaining their Allowances:* And alſo one other Act made in the 10th Year of the Reign of King *George* II. intituled *An Act[2] to declare who ſhall have a Right to vote in the Election of Burgeſſes to ſerve in the General Aſſembly for Counties, and for preventing fraudulent Conveyances in order to multiply Votes at ſuch Election;*

Reſolved, That this Houſe will, Tomorrow, reſolve itſelf into the ſaid Committee.

The other *Order* of the Day being read, for the Houſe to reſolve itſelf into a Committee of the whole Houſe, upon the Bill to continue and amend the Act for the better regulating and diſciplining the Militia;

Reſolved, That this Houſe will, upon *Thurſday* next, reſolve itſelf into the ſaid Committee.

And then the Houſe adjourned till Tomorrow Morning Eleven of the Clock.

Saturday, the 2d of June, 10 Geo. III. 1770.

ORDERED, That Mr *Henry* have Leave to be abſent from the Service of this Houſe till *Monday* ſevenight.

A *Petition* of *Francis Eppes* was preſented to the Houſe, and read; ſetting forth, that the Petitioner is ſeized of Four Hundred Acres of Land, in the County of *Henrico*, in Tail, adjoining to a larger Tract, which he holds in Fee Simple, and that it will be of great Advantage to him to dock the Intail of the ſaid Four Hundred Acres of Land, and, in Lieu thereof, to ſettle other Fee Simple Lands, of equal Value, adjoining ſome intailed Lands which he holds in *Bermuda Hundred*, in *Cheſterfield* County, as he is about ſelling his Lands in *Henrico* County, to pay off his Father's Legacies; and therefore praying that an Act may paſs for the Purpoſe aforeſaid.

200 *Ordered*, That Leave be given to bring in a Bill, purſuant to the Prayer of the ſaid Petition; and that Mr *Archibald Cary* do prepare and bring in the ſame.

Mr *Blair* reported, from the Committee, to whom the Bill to veſt certain Lands in *David Meade*, in Fee Simple, whereof the ſaid *David* and *Sarah* his Wife are ſeized in Right of the ſaid *Sarah*, in Fee Tail, and for ſettling other Lands, in Lieu thereof, was committed, that the Committee had examined the Allegations of the Bill, and found the ſame to be true; and that the Committee had gone through the Bill, and made ſeveral Amendments thereunto, which they had directed him to report to the Houſe; and he read the Report in his Place, and afterwards delivered the Bill, with the Amendments, in at the Clerk's Table; where the Amendments were once read throughout, and then

a

1 Hening, III, p. 236. 2 Ibid, IV, p. 475.

a fecond Time, one by one, and upon the Queftion feverally put thereupon, were agreed to by the Houfe.

Ordered, That the Bill, with the Amendments, be engroffed.

A *Petition* of feveral Freeholders and Inhabitants of the Parifh of *Dale*, in the County of *Chefterfield*, whofe Names are thereunto fubfcribed, fetting forth, that the faid Parifh is of equal Extent with the County, and hath four Churches in it, and that there are more than Three Thoufand Tithables in it; and therefore praying that the faid Parifh may be divided into two Parifhes, by a Line beginning at the Mouth of *Falling Creek*, and running thence up the faid Creek to Col. *Cary's* Mill Dam, thence along the Road leading from Col. *Cary's* Forge, to the Bridge over *Swift* Creek, near the Court-Houfe, and thence along the faid Road to the Mouth of *Winterpock* Creek, at its Confluence with *Appomattox* River; or by any other Line which the Houfe fhall think juft and equitable; *And Alfo*

Several *Petitions* of fundry Inhabitants of the Parifh of *Dale*, in the County of *Chefterfield*, whofe Names are thereunto fubfcribed, taking Notice of the Petition intended to be prefented to the Houfe for a Divifion of the faid Parifh; and fetting forth that it is yet unneceffary to divide the faid Parifh; that fuch a Divifion will be attended with very great Expence; and that by a Regulation intended by the Veftry of the faid Parifh, the Churches therein will be rendered convenient to the Congregations; and therefore praying that the faid Parifh may not be divided;

Were feverally prefented to the Houfe and read.

Ordered, That the faid feveral Petitions be feverally referred to the Confideration of the Committee for Religion; and that they do examine the Matter thereof, and report the fame, with their Opinion thereupon, to the Houfe.

Ordered, That Leave be given to bring in a Bill to continue and amend an Act intituled *An Act[1] for allowing Fairs to be kept in the Town of* Frederickfburg; and that Mr *Grymes* do prepare and bring in the fame.

A *Petition* of feveral Perfons, Inhabitants of the County of *Augufta*, living on the two Mill Creeks, *North* Fork, *South* Fork, and South Branch of *Potowmack*, whofe Names are thereunto fubfcribed, was prefented to the Houfe, and read; fetting forth, that the Petitioners refide much further from the Court-Houfe of their own County, than from that of *Hampfhire*, and in travelling to the former muft go through a more mountainous Country, and in a worfe Road than to the other, and crofs feveral Rivers; and therefore praying, that the aforefaid Part of the County of *Augufta*, may be added to the County of *Hampfhire*.

Ordered, That the faid *Petition* be referred to the Confideration of the Committee of Propofitions and Grievances; and that they do examine the Matter thereof, and report the fame, with their Opinion thereupon, to the Houfe.

Mr *Archibald Cary* reported, from the Committee of Public Claims, that the Committee had had under their Confideration feveral Petitions, to them referred, and had come to feveral Refolutions thereupon, which the Committee had directed him to report to the Houfe; and he read the Report in his Place, and afterwards delivered it in at the Clerk's Table; where the Refolutions of the Committee were read, and are as followeth, *viz.*

Refolved, That it is the Opinion of this Committee, that the Petition of *Enoch Fowler*, late a Soldier in the *Virginia* Regiment, is reafonable; and that he ought to be allowed the Sum of Ten Pounds, for his prefent Relief, and the further Sum of Six Pounds *per Annum*, during his Life, in Confideration of the Hardfhips he fuffered in the Service, and of his being thereby rendered incapable of getting a Subfiftence for himfelf and Family.

Refolved, That it is the Opinion of this Committee, that the Petition of *Thomas Davis* late a Soldier in the *Virginia* Regiment be rejected.

Refolved

201

---

[1] Hening, V, p. 82.

Refolved, That it is the Opinion of this Committee, that the Petition of *John Knibb* and *Thomas Stratton*, Infpectors of Tobacco at *Bermuda Hundred* Warehoufe, in *Chefterfield* County, to be reimburfed for Tobacco ftolen out of the faid Warehoufe, is reafonable; and that they ought to be allowed the Sum of Ten Pounds and Seventeen Shillings for the fame.

Refolved, That it is the Opinion of this Committee, that fo much of the Petition of *Martin Shearman* and *Robert Mitchell*, Infpectors of Tobacco, at *Deep Creek* Warehoufe, in *Lancafter* County, as relates to the Three Thoufand and Fifteen Pounds of Tobacco ftolen out of the faid Warehoufe, in the Year 1759, and for which they have paid at the Rate of Forty Shillings *per Cent.* is reafonable; and that they ought to be reimburfed the Sum of Sixty Pounds and Six Shillings for the fame.

Refolved, That it is the Opinion of this Committee, that fo much of the faid Petition as relates to the Nineteen Hundred Pounds of Tobacco ftolen out of the faid Warehoufe in the Year 1762, be rejected, for want of fufficient Proof.

Refolved, That it is the Opinion of this Committee, that the Petition of *Luke Luker* and *John Walton*, Infpectors of Tobacco, at *Pungoteague* Warehoufe, in *Accomack* County, to be reimburfed for a Hogfhead of Tobacco ftolen out of the faid Warehoufe, be rejected, for want of fufficient Proof.

The faid *Refolutions* being feverally read a fecond Time, were, upon the Queftion feverally put thereupon, agreed to by the Houfe.

Ordered, That a Committee be appointed to examine the Treafurer's Accounts.

And a *Committee* was appointed of Mr *Bland*, Mr *Richard Henry Lee*, Mr *Archibald Cary*, Mr *Harrifon*, Mr *Charles Carter*, of *Lancafter*, Mr *Eyre*, Mr *Henry*, Mr *Lewis Burwell*, of *James City*, and Mr *Blair*.

Ordered, That Mr *John Wilfon*, of *Norfolk*, have Leave to be abfent from the Service of this Houfe till this Day Fortnight.

Ordered, That Mr *Thomas Mann Randolph* have Leave to be abfent from the Service of this Houfe till this Day Sevenight.

Ordered, That Mr *Eyre* have Leave to be abfent from the Service of this Houfe till *Wednefday* next.

Mr *Treafurer* reported, from the Committee for Religion, to whom the Petition of fundry Freeholders and Inhabitants of the Parifh of *Overwharton*, in the County of *Stafford*, complaining of fundry illegal and unwarrantable Proceedings of the Veftry of the faid Parifh, and praying that the faid Veftry may be diffolved, was committed, that the Committee had examined the Matter of the faid Petition, and had come to feveral Refolutions thereupon, which the Committee had directed him to report to the Houfe; and he read the Report in his Place, and afterwards delivered it in at the Clerk's Table; where the Refolutions of the Committee were read, and are as followeth, *viz.*

Refolved, That it is the Opinion of this Committee, that the faid Veftry have, with Honour, fully acquitted themfelves of every Article of Charge contained in the faid Petition.

202 *Refolved*, Therefore, that it is the Opinion of this Committee, that the faid Petition be rejected.

The faid *Refolutions* being feverally read a fecond Time, were, upon the Queftion feverally put thereupon, agreed to by the Houfe.

Ordered, That the faid Committee do ftate an Account of the Expences of the Travelling and Attendance of the Witneffes, who were examined as well before the faid Committee touching the faid Petition, as before the Committee of Propofitions and Grievances, to whom a like Petition in the Year 1767, was referred, and report the fame, with their Opinion how the faid Expences ought to be defrayed, to the Houfe.

Ordered, That Leave be given to bring in a Bill for the better regulating the Election of Veftries; and that Mr *Mercer*, Mr *Bland*, Mr *Jones*, Mr *Richard Lee* and Mr *Stark*, do prepare and bring in the fame.

Mr

Mr *Treasurer* reported, from the Committee for Religion, to whom the Petitions of sundry Inhabitants of the Parish of *Overwharton*, in the County of *Stafford*, praying that the Vestry of the said Parish may be dissolved, was referred, that the Committee had come to several Resolutions thereupon, which the Committee had directed him to report to the House; and he read the Report in his Place, and afterwards delivered it in at the Clerk's Table; where the Resolutions of the Committee were read, and are as followeth, *viz.*

Resolved, That it is the Opinion of this Committee, that the said Petitions be heard before the Committee on *Saturday* the Sixteenth Instant.

Resolved, That it is the Opinion of this Committee, that the said Vestry be served with copies of the said Petitions, and have six Days previous Notice of the Time when the said Petitions are to be heard, before the Committee.

The said *Resolutions* being severally read a second Time, were, upon the Question severally put thereupon, agreed to by the House.

Mr *Archibald Cary* reported, from the Committee of Public Claims, to whom the certified Petition of *John Scott*, of *Lunenburg* County, was referred, that the Committee had examined the Matter of the said Petition, and had directed him to report the same, as it appeared to them, together with the Resolution of the Committee thereupon, to the House; and he read the Report in his Place, and afterwards delivered it in at the Clerk's Table; where the same was read, and is as followeth, *viz.*

It *appears* to your Committee, by the Depositions of sundry Witnesses, that some Time in the Month of *December* 1766, *Jack*, a Negro Man Slave, belonging to the Petitioner, was one day employed under one *William Chandler*, who was Surveyor of a Public Road, in cutting and levelling the Banks of *Meherrin* River; that the said Slave was seen some Time in the Night, in Company with other Negroes, at the Place where they had been at work that Day, in good Health; and that he was found the next Morning lying dead in the said River, and (as was supposed) was drowned.

Whereupon the *Committee* came to the following Resolution;

Resolved, that it is the Opinion of this Committee, that the said Petition be rejected.

The said *Resolution* being read a second Time, was, upon the Question put thereupon, agreed to by the House.

A *Petition* of *Daniel Cargill* was presented to the House, and read; setting forth, that *Wade's* Ferry, from the County of *Charlotte*, over *Roanoke* River, to the County of *Halifax*, is, by the Death of the Proprietor, become useless to the Public, and the Executors of the said Decedent are resolved not to keep up the said Ferry, and are willing that the same may be moved; and therefore praying that a Ferry may be established from the Petitioner's Land, in the said County of *Charlotte*, crossing the said River, to the Land of *John Foushee*, deceased, in the said County of Halifax.

Resolved, That the said Petition be referred to the Consideration of the Committee of Propositions and Grievances; and that they do examine the Matter thereof, and report the same, with their Opinion thereupon, to the House.

The *Order* of the Day being read;

Resolved, That this House will, upon *Tuesday* next, resolve itself into a Committee of the whole House to consider further of the Bill to explain and amend one Act of Assembly, made in the 4th Year of the Reign of Queen *Anne*, intituled *An Act*[1] *for regulating the Election of Burgesses, for settling their Privileges, and for ascertaining their Allowances:* And also one other Act made in the 10th Year of the Reign of King *George* II. intituled *An Act*[2] *to declare who shall have a Right to vote in the Election of Burgesses, to serve in the General Assembly for Counties and for preventing fraudulent Conveyances, in order to multiply votes at such Elections.*

And then the House adjourned until Monday Morning next Eleven of the Clock.

𝔐onday

---

[1] Hening, III, p. 236.   [2] Ibid, IV, p. 575.

Monday, the 4th of June, 10 Geo. III. 1770.

THE Houfe being informed by Mr *Bland*, that the Petition of fundry Perfons, Inhabitants of the County of *Spotfylvania*, praying that this Houfe will addrefs the *Governor*, that his Excellency will order the Court of the faid County of *Spotfylvania*, to be held at the moft convenient Place, near the Center thereof, and alfo praying that fome Mode may be adopted for determining Law Suits with more Expedition and lefs Expence, referred upon *Friday* laft to the Confideration of the Committee of Propofitions and Grievances, was not figned;

Ordered, That the faid Committee be difcharged from proceeding upon the faid Petition.

Ordered, That the faid Petition be withdrawn.

And the faid *Petition* was withdrawn accordingly.

Mr *Grymes* prefented to the Houfe, according to Order, a Bill to continue and amend an Act, intituled *An Act[1] for allowing Fairs to be kept in the Town of* Frederickfburg; and the fame was received, and read the firft Time.

Refolved, That the Bill be read a fecond Time.

A *Petition* of the Minifter, Veftry, and others, Inhabitants of the Parifh of *Cameron*, in the County of *Loudoun*, whofe Names are thereunto fubfcribed, was prefented to the Houfe, and read; fetting forth, that the faid Parifh is very extenfive, and inconvenient to the People who refide in the upper Parts thereof; and therefore praying that the faid Parifh may be divided in the Manner and upon the Terms mentioned in a Scheme to the faid Petition annexed.

Ordered, That the faid *Petition* be referred to the Confideration of the Committee for Religion; and that they do examine the Matter thereof, and report the fame with their Opinion thereupon, to the Houfe.

A *Petition* of *Nathan Chapman* was prefented to the Houfe, and read; fetting forth, that at the Battle of the *Meadows*, the Petitioner, then in the Service of this Country received a wound in his Hip, which has hindered him from labouring to maintain himfelf; and therefore praying the Houfe to take his Cafe into Confideration, and make him fuch Allowance as they fhall think proper.

Ordered, That the faid Petition be referred to the Confideration of the Committee of Public Claims; and that they do examine the Matter thereof, and report the fame, with their Opinion thereupon, to the Houfe.

Ordered, That it be an Inftruction to the Gentlemen who are appointed to prepare and bring in a Bill, for the better regulating the Election of Veftries, that they have Power to receive a Claufe or Claufes, for diffolving the Veftry of the Parifh of *Augufta*, in the County of *Augufta*.

Mr *Mercer* prefented to the Houfe, according to Order, a Bill declaring Slaves to be perfonal Eftate, and for other Purpofes therein mentioned; and the fame was received and read the firft Time.

Refolved, That the Bill be read a fecond Time.

Several Members, returned upon new Writs, having taken the Oaths appointed by Act of Parliament to be taken, inftead of the Oaths of Allegiance and Supremacy, and the Abjuration Oath, and repeated and fubfcribed the Teft, took their Seats in the Houfe.

Mr *Bland* reported, from the Committee of Propofitions and Grievances, that the Committee had had under their Confideration feveral Petitions, to them referred, and had come to feveral Refolutions thereupon, which the Committee had directed him to report to the Houfe; and he read the Report in his Place, and afterwards delivered it in at the Clerk's Table; where the Refolutions of the Committee were read, and are as followeth, *viz.*

Refolved

---

1 Hening, V, p. 82.

Refolved, That it is the Opinion of this Committee, that the Petition of feveral Free-holders, Merchants, and others, of the County of *Weftmoreland*, and the adjacent Counties, praying that the Infpection of Tobacco at *Stratford* Landing may be difcontinued, be rejected.

Refolved, That it is the Opinion of this Committee, that the Petition of feveral Freeholders, and Houfekeepers, Inhabitants of the County of *Weftmoreland*, praying that the faid Infpection may be continued, is reafonable, provided the Proprietor of the faid Warehoufes will rebuild the fame.

Refolved, That it is the Opinion of this Committee, that the Petition of *Thomas Sumner*, praying that a certain yearly Rent may hereafter be paid by the Public, for *Conftance's* Warehoufe in the County of *Nanfemond*, in Lieu of eight Pence *per* Hogfhead, be rejected.

Refolved, That it is the Opinion of this Committee, that the Petition of fundry Inhabitants of *Spotfylvania* County, praying that an Amendment be made to the Act declaring the Law concerning Executions, and for Relief of Infolvent Debtors, is reafonable.

The *firft* Refolution of the Committee being read a fecond Time;

And the Queftion being put, that the Houfe doth agree with the Committee in the faid Refolution;

It paffed in the Negative.

Refolved, That the Petition of feveral Freeholders, Merchants, and others of the County of *Weftmoreland*, and the adjacent Counties, praying that the Infpection of Tobacco at *Stratford* Landing may be difcontinued, is reafonable.

The *fecond* Refolution of the Committee being read a fecond Time;

And the *Queftion* being put, that the Houfe doth agree with the Committee in the faid Refolution;

It paffed in the Negative.

Refolved, That the Petition of feveral Freeholders, and Houfekeepers, Inhabitants, of the County of *Weftmoreland*, praying that the Infpection of Tobacco at *Stratford* Landing may be continued, be rejected.

The fubfequent *Refolutions* of the Committee being read a fecond Time, were, upon the Queftion feverally put thereupon, agreed to by the Houfe.

Ordered, That it be an Inftruction to the Committee of the whole Houfe, to whom the Bill to continue and amend the Act, intituled *An Act[1] for amending the Staple of Tobacco, and preventing Frauds in his Majefty's Cuftoms*, is committed, that they have Power to receive a Claufe or Claufes for difcontinuing the Infpection of Tobacco at *Stratford* Landing.

Ordered, That a Bill be brought in purfuant to the *fourth* Refolution of the Committee, and which hath been agreed to by the Houfe, and that the faid Committee do prepare and bring in the fame.

Ordered, That Mr *Grymes* have Leave to be abfent from the Service of this Houfe, until *Wednefday* Sevenight.

The *Order* of the Day being read;

Refolved, That this Houfe will, Tomorrow, refolve itfelf into a Committee of the whole Houfe, upon the Bill to continue and amend the Act, intituled *An Act for amending the Staple of Tobacco, and preventing frauds in his Majefty's Cuftoms*.

Mr *Bland* prefented to the Houfe according to Order, a Bill to make provifion for the Support and Maintenance of Ideots, Lunatics, and other Perfons of unfound Minds; and the fame was received and read the firft Time.

Refolved, That the Bill be read a fecond Time.

And then the Houfe adjourned till Tomorrow Morning Eleven of the Clock.

𝕿𝖚𝖊𝖘𝖉𝖆𝖞

---

[1] Hening, VIII, p. 69.

Tuesday, the 5th of June, 10 Geo. III. 1770.

A *Petition* of *John Henry* was prefented to the Houfe, and read; fetting forth, that the Petitioner hath, at great Expence and Trouble, perfected a Map of this Colony, wherein the Bounds of the feveral Counties, the Water-Courfes, Rivers, and other remarkable Places, are diftinguifhed, and marked out, by Means whereof he conceives that very confiderable Advantages may be derived to the Public; and therefore praying that the fame may be taken into Confideration by the Houfe, and that fo ufeful a Work may be encouraged, by allowing to him fuch a Sum of Money as may feem reafonable for reimburfing his Expence aforefaid.

And a *Motion* being made, and the Queftion being put, that the faid Petition be referred to the Confideration of a Committee;

It paffed in the Negative.

Refolved, That the faid Petition be rejected.

A *Petition* of fundry Inhabitants of the County of *King William*, whofe Names are thereunto fubfcribed, was prefented to the Houfe, and read; fetting forth, that the Infpection of Tobacco at *Walkerton* and *Waller's* is very convenient to the Petitioners, and not greatly expenfive to the Public; and therefore praying that the faid Infpection may be continued, and a Propofal, they are informed, will be made to the contrary, difagreed to.

Ordered, That the faid Petition do lie upon the Table.

Mr *Dudley Digges*, reported from the Committee to whom the Bill to dock the Intail of Two Thoufand Eight Hundred Acres of Land, in the County of *Brunfwick*, whereof *Armiftead Lightfoot* is feized in Fee Tail, and vefting the fame in Truftees, for certain Purpofes therein mentioned, was committed, that the Committee had examined the Allegations of the Bill, and found the fame to be true; and that the Committee had gone through the Bill, and made feveral Amendments thereunto, which they had directed him to report to the Houfe; and he read the Report in his Place, and afterwards delivered the Bill, with the Amendments, in at the Clerk's Table; where the Amendments were once read throughout, and then a fecond Time, one by one, and, upon the Queftion feverally put thereupon, were agreed to by the Houfe.

Ordered, That the Bill, with the Amendments, be engroffed.

A *Claim* of *Samuel Boufh*, Treafurer of *Norfolk* County, for fundry Sums of Money advanced, by Order of the Juftices of peace of the faid County, to *James Patrick*, *Robert Atken*, and *William Honeycomb*, Mariners, detained in the County as Witneffes for the Crown against *David Ferguson*, Mariner, late Mafter of the *Snow Betfey*, who is now in the Public Gaol, accufed of having murdered fome of the *Snow's* Crew upon the High Seas, was prefented to the Houfe, and read.

Ordered, That the faid Claim be referred to the Confideration of the Committee of Public Claims; and that they do examine the Matter thereof, and report the fame, with their Opinion thereupon, to the Houfe.

The Houfe being informed, that *Benjamin Grymes* defired Leave to withdraw the Petition on Behalf of himfelf and others, of the Parifh of *Saint George*, in the County of *Spotfylvania*, praying that an Election of Veftrymen of the faid Parifh, made in Confequence of an Act of this prefent General Affembly, may yet be fet afide, referred upon *Friday* laft to the Confideration of the Committee for Religion.

Ordered, That the faid Committee be difcharged from proceeding upon the faid Petition.

Ordered, That the faid *Benjamin Grymes* have Leave to withdraw the faid Petition.

And the faid *Petition* was withdrawn accordingly.

Ordered, That Leave be given to bring in a Bill to appoint Notaries Public; and that Mr *Bland* and Mr *Mercer* do prepare and bring in the fame.

Mr *Mercer* prefented to the Houfe, according to Order, a Bill for reimburfing the

Country

Country the Expence incurred by the Profecution of Mʳ Walter *Coles's* Accufation againft Mʳ *Nathaniel Terry;* the fame was received, and read the firft Time.

And a *Motion* was made, and the Queftion being put, that the Bill be read a fecond Time;

It paffed in the Negative.

Refolved, That the Bill be rejected.

A *Petition* of feveral Perfons, of the Parifh of *Suffolk,* in the County of *Nanfemond,* on the Eaft Side of the River, whofe Names are thereunto fubfcribed, was prefented to the Houfe, and read; fetting forth, that fome of the Petitioners were prevailed with by the Infinuations of the Minifter of the faid Parifh, and his Adherents, to fign a Petition formally prefented to this Houfe, and referred to the Confideration of the Committee for Religion, for dividing the faid Parifh, or diffolving the Veftry thereof, and repealing fo much of an Act of General Affembly, eftablifhing a free Ferry over *Nanfemond* River, as relates to all the Parifhioners, except the Minifter, and that the Petitioners have fince found moft of the Complaints againft the faid Veftry to be groundlefs, and the others of little Confequence, and believe the free Ferry over the faid River to be a Grievance to the People; and therefore praying that the Act of General Affembly, 207 eftablifhing the faid free Ferry, may be wholly repealed, and that the faid former Petition may be rejected.

Ordered, That the faid *Petition* be referred to the Confideration of the Committee for Religion; and that they do examine the Matter thereof, and report the fame, with their Opinion thereupon, to the Houfe.

The *Order* of the Day being read, for the Houfe to refolve itfelf into a Committee of the whole Houfe upon the Bill to continue and amend the Act, intituled *An Act*[1] *for amending the Staple of Tobacco, and preventing Frauds in his Majefty's Cuftoms;*

Ordered, That it be an Inftruction to the faid Committee, that they have Power to receive a Claufe or Claufes for difcontinuing the Infpection of Tobacco at *Guilford,* in the County of *Accomack,* and eftablifhing an Infpection at *Finley's Point,* on *Hunting Creek.*

Ordered, That it be an Inftruction to the faid Committee, that they have Power to receive a Claufe or Claufes for eftablifhing another Infpection of Tobacco on the Lots of *Robert Bolling,* which he lately purchafed of *Patrick Ramfay,* in the Town of *Blandford.*

Ordered, That the Petition of fundry Inhabitants of the County of *King William,* for continuing the Infpection of Tobacco at *Walkerton* and *Waller's,* this Day prefented to the Houfe, and ordered to lie upon the Table, be referred to the faid Committee.

Then the Houfe refolved itfelf into the faid Committee.

Mʳ *Speaker* left the Chair.

Mʳ *Bland* took the Chair of the Committee.

Mʳ *Speaker* refumed the Chair.

Mʳ *Bland* reported from the Committee, that they had made a Progrefs in the Bill; and that he was directed by the Committee to move, that they may have Leave to fit again.

Refolved, That this Houfe will, Tomorrow, refolve itfelf into a Committee of the whole Houfe, to confider further of the faid Bill.

The other *Order* of the Day being read;

Refolved, That this Houfe will, upon *Friday* next, refolve itfelf into a Committee of the whole Houfe, to confider further of the Bill to explain and amend one Act of Affembly, made in the fourth Year of the Reign of Queen *Anne,* intituled *An Act*[2] *for regulating the Election of Burgeffes, for fettling their Privileges, and for afcertaining their Allowances;* and alfo one other Act made in the tenth Year of the Reign of King *George* the Second, intituled *An Act*[3] *to declare who fhall have a Right to vote in the Election of Burgeffes to ferve in the General Affembly for Counties, and for preventing fraudulent Conveyances, in order to multiply Votes at fuch Elections.*

And then the Houfe adjourned till Tomorrow Morning Eleven of the Clock.

Wednesday

---

[1] Hening, VIII, p. 69   [2] Ibid, III, p. 236.   [3] Ibid, IV, p. 475.

Wednesday, the 6th of June, 10 Geo. III. 1770.

A *Petition* of the Hon. *John Tayloe*, Efq; was prefented to the Houfe, and read; fetting forth, that the Petitioner's Negro Man Slave named *Toby*, who, on the 19th Day of *January* laft, was convicted of Hog-ftealing by *King George* County Court, and whipped and pilloried, by the Inclemency of the Weather, whilft he remained in Gaol, before his Trial, was fo feverely Froft-bitten, that he died by Means thereof; and therefore praying the Houfe to make the Petitioner fuch Allowance for the faid Slave as may feem juft.

Ordered, That the faid Petition be referred to the Confideration of the Committee of Public Claims; and that they do examine the Matter thereof, and report the fame, with their Opinion thereupon, to the Houfe.

Mr *Archibald Cary* reported, from the Committee of Public Claims, that the Committee had had under their Confideration feveral Petitions, to them referred, and had come to feveral Refolutions thereupon, which the Committee had directed him to report to the Houfe; and he read the Report in his Place, and afterwards delivered it in at the Clerk's Table, where the Refolutions of the Committee were read, and are as followeth, *viz.*

Refolved, That it is the Opinion of this Committee, that the Petition of *James Ford*, late a Soldier in the Service of the Colony, under the Command of Col. *George Wafhington*, is reafonable; and that he ought to be allowed the Sum of Five Pounds for his prefent Relief, and the further Sum of Five Pounds *per Annum*, during his Life, in Confideration of the Wound he received at the Battle of the *Meadows*, and of his being thereby rendered incapable of getting a neceffary Subfiftence.

Refolved, That it is the Opinion of this Committee, that the Petition of *Nathan Chapman*, late A Soldier in the Service of the Colony, under the Command of Col. *George Wafhington*, is reafonable; and that he ought to be allowed the Sum of Five Pounds for his prefent Relief, and the further Sum of Five Pounds *per Annum*, during his Life, in Confideration of the Wound he received at the Battle of the *Meadows*, and of his being thereby rendered incapable of getting a neceffary Subfiftence.

Refolved, That it is the Opinion of this Committee, that the Petition of *John Ballantine*, to be paid for transporting Forty-four Recruits from *Mattox* to *Alexandria*, on *Potowmack* River, and furnifhing Provifions for them, is reafonable; and that he ought to be allowed the Sum of 18 *l.* 10 *s.* for the fame.

Refolved, That it is the Opinion of this Committee, that the Petition of *Nicholas Alley* to be paid for Provifions furnifhed the Militia of *Prince Edward* County, in the Year 1757, is reafonable; and that he ought to be allowed 3 *l.* 9 *s.* 9 *d½.*, for the fame.

The faid *Refolutions* being feverally read a fecond Time, were, upon the Queftion feverally put thereupon, agreed to by the Houfe.

Ordered, That Mr *Riddick* have Leave to be abfent from the Service of this Houfe until this Day Sevenight.

An engroffed *Bill* for altering the Court Day of *Middlefex* County, was read a third time.

And a *Motion* was made, and the Queftion being put, that the Bill do pafs; It paffed in the Negative.

Refolved, That the Bill be rejected.

Ordered, That it be an Inftruction to the Committee for Courts of Juftice to whom the Bill for altering the Court Day of the County of *Culpeper* is committed, that they have Power to receive a Claufe or Claufes for altering the Court Day of the County of *Middlefex* to the fourth *Monday* in every Month.

A *Petition* of *Jeffe Ewell*, Proprietor of the public Warehoufes for Infpection of Tobacco, at *Dumfries*, in the County of *Prince William*, was prefented to the Houfe, and read; fetting forth, that by Order of the faid County Court, at feveral Times, four Houfes have been directed to be built at the faid Infpection, the Expence whereof, and of keeping them in Repair, the Rents allowed by Law are not fufficient to defray, and

and make the Proprietor a reasonable Satisfaction for his Land; and therefore praying to be relieved, and that the Rents of the said warehouses may be raised to One Shilling *per* Hogshead.

Ordered, That the said petition be referred to the Consideration of the Committee of propositions and Grievances; and that they do examine the Matter thereof, and report the same, with their Opinion thereupon, to the House. 209

Ordered, That it be an Instruction to the Committee for Courts of Justice, to whom the Bill for altering the Court Day of the County of *Culpeper* is committed, that they have Power to receive a Clause or Clauses for altering the Court Day of the County of *Spotsylvania* to the third *Thursday* in every Month.

A *Bill* to continue and amend an Act, intituled *An Act¹ for allowing Fairs to be kept in the Town of* Fredericksburg, was read a second Time.

Resolved, That the Bill be committed to the Committee for Courts of Justice.

A *Claim* of *Joshua Powell*, for his Pay as an Ensign, under the Command of Capt. *John Dickerson*, at a Fort on *Smith's* River, and as a Carpenter, under the Command of Capt. *Joseph Terry*, at the Building of *Black Water* Fort, in the Year 1759, was presented to the House, and read.

Ordered, That the said Claim be referred to the Consideration of the Committee of Public Claims; and that they do examine the Matter thereof, and report the same, with their Opinion thereupon, to the House.

A *Claim* of *George Boyd*, for Work done on Fort *Mayo*, under the Command of Capt. *Samuel Harris*, was presented to the House, and read.

Ordered, That the said Claim be referred to the Consideration of the Committee of Public Claims; and that they do examine the Matter thereof, and report the same, with their Opinion thereupon, to the House.

Ordered, That the Gentlemen who are appointed to examine the Treasurer's Accounts do examine the Account of *Jacob Hite*, of public Tobacco levied in the County of *Frederick*, in the Year 1765, and report the same, as it shall appear to them, with their Opinion thereupon, to the House.

A *Claim* of *Joseph Kidd*, for gilding and painting the Weathercock, and Dial Plates and Hands of the *Capitol*, was presented to the House, and read.

Ordered, That the said Claim be referred to the Consideration of the Committee of Public Claims; and that they do examine the Matter thereof, and report the same, with their Opinion thereupon, to the House.

A *Petition* of *William Aylett*, Proprietor of the Tobacco Warehouses called *Aylett's*, on *Mattapony* River, in the County of *King William*, was presented to the House, and read; setting forth, that the Storage for Tobacco of Eight Pence per Hogshead is not sufficient to reimburse the Expences of building and repairing the Warehouses, with Interest; and therefore praying that the Rate of Storage may be increased, or else that the Petitioner may deliver up his said Warehouses to the Public, and that the Value thereof may be paid to him.

Ordered, That the said Petition be referred to the Committee of the whole House to whom the Bill to continue and amend the Act, intituled *An Act² for amending the Staple of Tobacco, and preventing Frauds in his Majesty's Customs*, is committed.

Mr *Dixon* reported, from the Committee, to whom the Bill to dock the Intail of Five Hundred and Fifty Acres of Land, in the County of *Gloucester*, whereof *Sarah*, the Wife of *John Rootes*, Gentlemen, is seized, and for vesting the same in Trustees for the Purposes therein mentioned, was committed, that the Committee had examined the Allegations of the Bill, and found the same to be true; and that the Committee had gone through the Bill, and made several Amendments thereunto, which they had directed him to report to the House; and he read the Report in his Place, and afterwards delivered the Bill, with the Amendments, in at the Clerk's Table; where the Amendments were once read throughout, and then a second Time, one by one, and upon the Question severally put thereupon, were agreed to by the House. 210

Ordered, That the Bill, with the Amendments, be ingrossed.

M^r

¹ Hening, V. p. 82. ² Ibid, VIII. p. 69.

Mr *Richard Baker* reported from the Committee, to whom the Bill to fufpend the Execution of an Act, intituled *An Act*[1] *to amend an Act, intituled an Act for the Infpection of Pork, Beef, Flour, Tar, Pitch, and Turpentine,* was committed, that the Committee had gone through the Bill, and made an Amendment thereunto, which they had directed him to report to the Houfe; and he read the Report in his Place, and afterwards delivered the Bill, with the Amendment, in at the Clerk's Table; where the Amendment was twice read, and, upon the Queftion put thereupon, was agreed to by the Houfe.

Ordered, That the Bill, with the Amendment, be ingroffed.

Ordered, That Leave be given to bring in a Bill for the better Adminiftration of Juftice in the County Courts; and that Mr *Richard Henry Lee,* Mr *Archibald Cary,* Mr *Bland,* Mr *Riddick,* Mr *Edmund Pendleton,* Mr *Treafurer,* Mr *Blair,* Mr *Mercer,* Mr *Henry,* Mr *Jones,* Mr *Carrington,* and Mr *Richard Baker,* do prepare and bring in the fame.

A *Petition* of feveral Perfons of the County of *Effex, King & Queen,* and *Caroline,* whofe Names are thereunto fubfcribed, was prefented to the Houfe, and read; fetting forth, that the Place called *Southern's* or *Layton's,* on *Rappahannock* River, in the faid County of *Effex,* is commodious for a Town, and convenient to Trade; and therefore praying that a Town may be eftablifhed at the Place aforefaid, on the Land of *Thomas Ley,* who is confenting thereto, under the fame Regulations, and with the like Immunities as other Towns.

Ordered, That the faid Petition be referred to the Confideration of the Committee of Propofitions and Grievances; and that they do examine the Matter thereof, and report the fame, with their Opinion thereupon, to the Houfe.

The *Order* of the Day being read, for the Houfe to refolve itfelf into a Committee of the whole Houfe to confider further of the prefent State of the Colony.

Refolved, That this Houfe will, upon this Day Sevenight, refolve itfelf into the faid Committee.

Ordered, That the Chaplain to this Houfe do attend to read Prayers in the Houfe, every Morning at Seven of the Clock.

Ordered, That a Meffage to fent to the Council, to acquaint them that the Chaplain will attend to read Prayers in the Houfe, every Morning at Seven of the Clock.

Ordered, That Mr *Robert Wormeley Carter* do carry the faid Meffage.

The other *Order* of the Day being read;

The Houfe refolved itfelf into a Committee of the whole Houfe, to confider further of the Bill, to continue and amend the Act for amending the Staple of Tobacco, and preventing Frauds in his Majefty's Cuftoms.

Mr *Speaker* left the Chair.

Mr *Bland* took the Chair of the Committee.

Mr *Speaker* refumed the Chair.

Mr *Bland* reported from the Committee, that they had made a further progrefs in the Bill; and that he was directed by the Committee to move that they may have leave to fit again.

Refolved, That this Houfe will, Tomorrow, refolve itfelf into a Committee of the whole Houfe, to confider further of the faid Bill.

Ordered, That Mr *Roane,* returned upon a new Writ, be added to the Committees of Propofitions and Grievances, and of Public Claims.

A *Petition* of *John Wormerly* was prefented to the Houfe, and read; fetting forth, that he is feized, in Fee Tail, of about Six Hundred Acres of Land, lying in the Parifh of *Yorkhampton,* in the County of *York,* under the Will of his Mother *Elizabeth Wormeley* deceafed, which it would be greatly for the Advantage of his Family if he was allowed to fell; and that *William Tayloe,* late of the County of *Lancafter,* Gentleman, deceafed, had devifed Eight Hundred Acres of Land, in the faid County of *Lancafter,* to *William Digges,* Gentleman, who had married the Petitioner's Daughter, for Payment of a Debt, and the Petitioner having undertaken to pay the faid Debt, the faid *William Digges,* for that Confideration, had agreed to convey the faid Land in *Lancafter* to the Petitioner and

211

---

[1] Hening, VIII. p. 351.

and therefore praying that an Act may pass to dock the Intail of the said Lands in the County of *York*, and to settle the said Land in the County of *Lancaster*, in Lieu thereof.

Ordered, That Leave be given to bring in a Bill, pursuant to the Prayer of the said Petition: And that Mr *Dudley Digges* do prepare and bring in the same.

Mr *Treasurer* reported from the Committee for Religion, that the Committee had had under their Consideration several Petitions to them referred, and had come to several Resolutions thereupon, which the Committee had directed him to report to the House; and he read the Report in his Place, and afterwards delivered it in at the Clerk's Table; where the Resolutions of the Committee were read, and are as followeth, *viz.*

Resolved, That it is the Opinion of this Committee, that so much of the petition of sundry Inhabitants of *Suffolk* Parish, in the County of *Nansemond*, on the East Side of the River, as prays that the said Parish may be divided, be rejected.

Resolved, That it is the Opinion of this Committee, that so much of the Petition of sundry Inhabitants of the said Parish, in Opposition thereto, as relates to the said Division, is reasonable.

Resolved, That it is the Opinion of this Committee, that so much of the said Petition, setting forth, that the Vestry and Churchwardens of the said Parish had mismanaged and misapplied certain charitable Donations given to the said Parish, and praying that the said Vestry may be dissolved, be rejected.

Resolved, That it is the Opinion of this Committee, that the said Vestry have with Honour fully acquitted themselves of every Article of Charge contained in the said Petition.

Resolved, therefore, That it is the Opinion of this Committee, that so much of the Petition, in Opposition thereto, as prays that the said Vestry may not be dissolved, is reasonable.

Resolved, That it is the Opinion of this Committee, that so much of the said Petition as prays that the Act of Assembly for establishing a free Ferry over *Nansemond* River, may be repealed, so far as it relates to all the Parishioners, except the Minister, is reasonable.

Resolved, That it is the Opinion of this Committee, that so much of the said Petition, in Opposition thereto, as prays that the said Act of Assembly may be wholly repealed, be rejected.

Resolved, That it is the Opinion of this Committee, that the Petition of sundry Inhabitants of *Hungars* Parish, in the County of *Northampton*, praying that the Vestry of the said Parish may be dissolved, is reasonable.

The said *Resolutions* being severally read a second Time, were, upon the Question severally put thereupon, agreed to by the House. 212

Ordered, That it be an Instruction to the Committee of Propositions and Grievances, who are appointed to prepare and bring in a Bill pursuant to the fourth Resolution of the said Committee, which was agreed to by the House, upon *Monday* the thirteenth Day of *November* last, that they have Power to receive a Clause or Clauses, pursuant to the sixth Resolution of the Committee for Religion, which hath been this day agreed to by the House.

Ordered, That it be an Instruction to the Gentlemen who are appointed to prepare and bring in a Bill for the better regulating the Election of Vestries, that they have Power to receive a Clause or Clauses, pursuant to the eighth Resolution of the Committee, for Religion, which hath been this Day agreed to by the House.

Ordered, That the Committee for Religion to state an Account of the Expences of traveling and Attendance of the Witnesses who were examined before the said Committee touching the Matters set forth and complained of in the Petition of sundry Inhabitants of *Suffolk* Parish, in the County of *Nansemond*, on the East Side of the River, and report the same, with the Opinion of the said Committee, who ought to be charged with the said Expences, to the House.

And then the House adjourned till To-morrow Morning Eleven of the Clock.

Thursday

Thursday, the 7th of June, 10 Geo. III. 1770.

A *Petition* of *Joseph Saunders* was presented to the House, and read; setting forth, that in the Year 1759, the Petitioner's Son, with several other young Men in the same Neighborhood, enlisted in the Service of the Country, and the petitioner let them have an Horse, worth Ten Pounds, to carry their Luggage, on being promised the said Horse should be sent back from *Winchester;* but that the said Horse was not returned, having been lost, as the Petitioner believes, with his said Son in the Service; and that the Petitioner would have applied before for Reparation of his Loss, but he was informed such Claims were not allowed, which Information he now understands not to have been true; and therefore praying the House to make him Satisfaction for his said Horse.

Ordered, That the said Petition be referred to the Consideration of the Committee of Public Claims; and that they do examine the Matter thereof, and report the same, with their Opinion thereupon, to the House.

An engroffed *Bill* to vest certain intailed Lands, whereof *Charles Lewis,* Gentleman, is seized, in *John Lewis,* Gentleman, in Fee Simple, and settle other Lands to the same Ufes, was read the third Time.

Resolved, That the Bill do pass; and that the Title be, *An Act¹ to vest certain intailed Lands, whereof* Charles Lewis, *Gentleman, is seized, in* John Lewis, *Gentleman, in Fee Simple, and settle other Lands to the same Ufes.*

Ordered, That Mʳ *Edmund Pendleton* do carry the Bill to the Council, and desire their Concurrence.

213 The *Order* of the Day being read, for the House to resolve itself into a Committee of the whole House to consider further of the Bill to continue and amend the Act, intituled *An Act² for amending the Staple of Tobacco, and preventing frauds in his Majesty's Customs;*

Resolved, That this House will, upon *Wednesday* next, resolve itself into a Committee of the whole House, to consider further of the said Bill.

A *Petition* of *John Armistead* and *William Armistead,* Gentlemen, was presented to the House, and read; setting forth, that their late Father *William Armistead,* Esq; by his Will devised all his Lands in the Counties of *Gloucester* and *Middlesex,* and Seventy Slaves to the said Petitioner *William,* and the Heirs of his Body, and Six Thousand Acres of Land in the County of *Prince William,* with several Slaves thereon, to the said Petitioner *John,* and the Heirs of his Body; that the Petitioners coming to full Age could not take Poffeffion of their Estates, before they engaged to pay about Seventeen Hundred Pounds each, for their Proportions of large Debts due from their said Father; that they have no Means to pay the said Money, without selling their Slaves, whereby their Lands would be unprofitable, and they would be unable to make Provision for their younger Children; and that they conceive it will be for the Advantage of their respective Families, by selling Part of their intailed Lands for Payment of their Proportions of the said Debts, to preserve their Slaves; and therefore praying that an Act may pass, to dock the Intail of Two Thousand Seven Hundred and Forty Acres of Land, whereof the Petitioner, *Willium,* is seized, in the County of *Middlesex,* and of Two Thousand Acres, Part of the said Land devised to the petitioner *John,* in the County of *Prince William.*

Ordered, That Leave be given to bring in a Bill, pursuant to the Prayer of the said Petition; and that Mʳ *Edmund Pendleton* do prepare and bring in the same.

Ordered, That this House be called over upon *Wednesday* next.

Several *Petitions* of sundry Inhabitants of the County of *Loudoun,* whose Names are thereunto subscribed, were presented to the House, and read; taking Notice of the Petition presented to the House for dividing the Parish of *Cameron,* in the said County; and setting forth, that such a Division is unnecessary and would be grevious, and burthenfome

---

¹ Hening, VIII, p. 478.   ² Ibid, VIII, p. 69.

enſome, and that the terms propoſed by the ſaid Petition are unequal and unjuſt; and therefore praying that the ſaid Diviſion may not take Place.

Ordered, That the ſaid petition be referred to the Conſideration of the Committee for Religion; and that they do examine the Matter thereof, and report the ſame, with their Opinion thereupon, to the Houſe.

Mr *Pendleton* preſented to the Houſe, according to Order, a Bill to veſt certain intailed Lands therein mentioned in *George Brooke*, Gentleman, in Fee Simple, and for ſettling other Lands, of greater Value, in Lieu thereof; and the ſame was received, and read the firſt Time.

Reſolved, That the Bill be read a ſecond Time.

Ordered, That Mr *Poythreſs* have Leave to be abſent from the Service of this Houſe till *Wedneſday* next.

A *Petition* of *David Barton*, was preſented to the Houſe, and read; ſetting forth, that the Petitioner having diſcovered a Remedy for Cancers is willing to Communicate it to the Public; and therefore praying the Houſe to grant him an adequate Reward.

Ordered, That the ſaid petition be referred to the Conſideration of the Committee of Propoſitions and Grievances; and that they do examine the Matter thereof, and report the ſame, with their Opinion thereupon, to the Houſe.

Ordered, That Mr *Richard Baker* have Leave to be abſent from the Service of this Houſe till *Saturday* Sevenight.

Mr *Edmund Pendleton* preſented to the Houſe, according to Order, a Bill to veſt certain intailed Lands, whereof *Samuel Meredith* is ſeized, in Truſtees, to be ſold for the Purpoſes therein mentioned; and the ſame was received, and read the firſt Time.

Reſolved, That the Bill be read a ſecond Time.

An engroſſed *Bill* to dock the intail of certain Lands and Slaves, whereof *John Page*, Eſq; is ſeized, and for ſettling other Lands, of greater Value, to the ſame Uſes, was read the third Time.

Reſolved, That the Bill do paſs; and that the Title be, *An Act[1] to dock the intail of certain Lands and Slaves, whereof* John Page, *Eſq; is ſeized, and for ſettling other Lands, of greater Value to the ſame Uſes.*

Ordered, That Mr *Edmund Pendleton* do carry the Bill to the Council, and deſire their Concurrence.

Ordered, That M^r *Eſkridge* have Leave to be abſent from the Service of this Houſe till *Thurſday* next.

The other *Order* of the Day being read;

Reſolved, That this Houſe will, upon this Day Sevenight, reſolve itſelf into a Committee of the whole Houſe upon the Bill to continue and amend the Act for better regulating and diſciplining the Militia.

A *Meſſage* from the Council by Mr *Hubard:*

Mr *Speaker,*

The Council do not inſiſt upon the Amendment made by them to the Bill, *intituled* An Act[2] for clearing a Road from *Payne's Run*, in the County of *Auguſta*, to *Thurmond's* in the County of *Albemarle; to which the Houſe have diſagreed: And alſo,*

The Council have agreed to the Bill, *intituled* An Act[3] to amend an Act paſſed in the former Part of this Seſſion of Aſſembly, for reimburſing the Counties of *Hanover* and *King William*, the Expence of clearing *Pamunkey* River: *And alſo,*

The Council have agreed to the Bill, *intituled,* An Act[4] to explain and amend an Act of this preſent Seſſion of Aſſembly, intituled An Act to divide the Pariſh of *Hamilton*, in the Counties of *Fauquier* and *Prince William: And alſo,*

The Council have agreed to the Bill, *intituled* An Act[5] to dock the intail of Four Thouſand Acres of Land, in the County of *Iſle of Wight*, whereof *James Burwell* is ſeized in

Fee

---

[1] Hening, VIII, p. 445.   [2] Not recorded as a law.   [3] Hening, VIII, p. 407.
[4] Ibid, VIII, p. 428.   [5] Ibid, VIII, p. 481.

Fee Tail, and for vefting the fame in Truftees in Fee Simple, *for certain purpofes therein mentioned.*

And then the Meffenger withdrew.

Mr *Edmund Pendleton* prefented to the Houfe, according to Order, a Bill to veft certain intailed Lands, whereof *William Armiftead* and *John Armiftead*, Gentlemen, are feized, in Truftees, to be fold for Payment of the Debts due from the Eftate of their Father; and the fame was received, and read the firft Time.

Refolved, That the Bill be read a fecond Time.

And engroffed *Bill* to veft certain intailed Lands and Slaves, therein mentioned, in *Nathaniel Littleton Savage*, Gentleman, in Fee Simple, and to settle other Lands in Lieu thereof, was read the third Time.

215 *Refolved*, That the Bill do pafs; and that the Title be, *An Act¹ to veft certain intailed Lands and Slaves therein mentioned, in* Nathaniel Littleton Savage, *Gentleman, in Fee Simple, and to fettle other Lands in Lieu thereof.*

Ordered, That Mr *Eyre* do carry the Bill to the Council, and defire their Concurrence.

Mr *Edmund Pendleton* reported from the Committee, to whom the Bill to impower certain Truftees to leafe the Lands of the *Pamunkey Indians*, and for other purpofes therein mentioned, was committed, that the Committee had gone through the Bill, and made an Amendment thereunto, which they had directed him to report to the Houfe; and he read the report in his Place, and afterwards delivered the Bill, with the Amendment, in at the Clerk's Table; where the Amendment was twice read, and, upon the Queftion put thereupon, was agreed to by the Houfe.

Ordered, That the Bill, with the Amendment, be ingroffed.

Ordered, That a Meffage be fent to the Council, to defire they will expedite the Paffage of a Bill, intituled *An Act² to dock the intail of certain Lands, whereof* Daniel M'Carty *is feized, and for fettling other Lands and Slaves to the fame Ufes.*

Ordered, That Mr *Edmund Pendleton* and Mr *Wafhington* do carry the faid Meffage.

Mr *Bland* prefented to the Houfe, according to Order, a Bill for adding Part of the City of *Williamfburg* to *James City* County, and for other Purpofes therein mentioned; and the fame was received, and read the firft Time.

Refolved, That the Bill be read a fecond Time.

Mr *Bland* reported, from the Committee of Propofitions and Grievances, to whom the Bill for better regulating the Collection of Public, County, and Parifh Levies, was committed, that the Committee had gone through the Bill, and made an Amendment thereunto, which they had directed him to report to the Houfe; and he read the Report in his Place, and afterwards delivered the Bill, with the Amendment, in at the Clerk's Table;

And the Houfe being informed, that fome other Amendments are neceffary to be made to the faid Bill,

Ordered, That the faid Bill be re-committed.

Ordered, That the faid Bill be re-committed to the Committee, to whom the fame was committed.

Mr *Richard Baker* prefented to the Houfe, according to Order, a Bill to dock the intail of certain Lands, whereof *Robert Burwell*, Efq, is feized in Tail Male, and for fettling other Lands, of greater Value, to the fame Ufes; and the fame was received, and read the firft Time.

Refolved, That the Bill be read a fecond Time.

An engroffed *Bill* to veft certain Lands, whereof *Bernard Moore*, Efq; is feized in Fee Tail, in Truftees to be fold, and the Money laid out in the Purchafe of other Lands and Slaves, to be fettled to the fame Ufes, was read the third Time.

Refolved, That the Bill do pafs; and that the Title be, *An Act³ to veft certain Lands whereof* Bernard Moore, *Efq; is feized in Fee Tail, in Truftees to be fold, and the Money laid out in the Purchafe of other Lands and Slaves, to be fettled to the fame Ufes.*

Ordered

¹ Hening, VIII, p. 468.　　² Not recorded as a law.　　³ Hening, VII, p. 476.

Ordered, That Mr *Richard Henry Lee* do carry the Bill to the Council, and defire 216 their Concurrence.

And then the Houfe adjourned till Tomorrow Morning Eleven of the Clock.

Friday, the 8th of June, 10 Geo. III. 1770.

MR *Bland* reported, from the Committee of Propofitions and Grievances, to whom the Bill for better regulating the Collection of Public, County, and Parifh Levies, was re-committed, that the Committee had made another Amendment to the Bill, which they had directed him to report to the Houfe; and he read the Report in his Place, and afterwards delivered the Bill, with the Amendments, in at the Clerk's Table; where the Amendments were read.

A *Meffage* from the Council by Mr *Hubard;*

Mr *Speaker,*

The Council's Anfwer to the Meffage of your Houfe to expedite the Paffage of a Bill, intituled An Act to dock the Intail of certain Lands, whereof *Daniel M'Carty* is feized, and for fettling other Lands and Slaves to the fame Ufes, *is (without taking Notice of the Novelty and unufual Terms of fuch a Meffage) that they have exercifed that Right which the Conftitution has vefted in them of rejecting the faid Bill, and it is accordingly rejected.*

And then the Meffenger withdrew.

Then the *Amendments* made by the Committee of Propofitions and Grievances to the Bill for better regulating the Collection of Public, County, and Parifh Levies, were feverally read a fecond Time, and, upon the Queftion feverally put thereupon, were, with Amendments to one of them, agreed to by the Houfe.

Ordered, That the Bill, with the Amendments, be ingroffed.

Ordered, That Mr *Wilfon Miles Cary* have Leave to be abfent from the Service of this Houfe till *Thurfday* next.

Mr *Richard Henry Lee* reported, from the Committee of Courts of Juftice, to whom the Bill for altering the Court Day of the County of *Culpeper* was committed, that the Committee had gone through the Bill, and made feveral Amendments thereunto, which they had directed him to report to the Houfe; and he read the Report in his Place, and afterwards delivered the Bill, with the Amendments, in at the Clerk's Table; where the Amendments were once read throughout, and then a fecond Time, one by one, and, Upon the Queftion feverally put thereupon, were agreed to by the Houfe.

Ordered, That the Bill, with the Amendments, be ingroffed.

Ordered, That Mr *Newton* have Leave to be abfent from the Service of this Houfe till *Friday* next.

A *Meffage* from the Council by Mr *Hubard;*

Mr *Speaker,*

The Council have agreed to the Bill, *intituled* An Act[1] to veft certain Lands, whereof *Bernard Moore*, Efq; is feized in Fee Tail, in Truftees, to be fold, and the Money laid out in the Purchafe of other Lands and Slaves, to be fettled to the fame Ufes, *without any Amendment; And alfo,*

The Council have agreed to the Bill, *intituled* An Act[2] to veft certain intailed Lands, 217 whereof *Charles Lewis*, Gentleman, is feized in *John Lewis*, Gentleman, in Fee Simple, and fettle other Lands to the fame Ufes, *without any Amendment; And alfo,*

The Council have agreed to the Bill, *intituled* An Act[3] to veft certain intailed Lands and

---

[1] Hening, VIII, p. 476.   [2] Ibid, VIII, p. 478.   [3] Ibid, VIII, p. 468.

and Slaves, therein mentioned, in *Nathaniel Littleton Savage*, Gentleman, in Fee Simple, and to fettle other Lands, in Lieu thereof, *without any Amendment*.

And then the Meffenger withdrew.

Mr *Edmund Pendleton* prefented to the Houfe, according to Order, a Bill to compel Perfons to find Security for Payment of Cofts in certain Cafes; and the fame was received, and read the firft Time.

Refolved, That the Bill be read a fecond Time.

The *Order* of the Day being read;

The Houfe refolved itfelf into a Committee of the whole Houfe, to confider further of the Bill to explain and amend one Act of Affembly, made in the 4th Year of the Reign of Queen *Anne*, intituled *An Act¹ for regulating the Election of Burgeffes, for fettling their Privileges, and for afcertaining their Allowances;* and alfo one other Act made in the 10th Year of the Reign of King *George II.* intituled *An Act² to declare who fhall have a Right to Vote in the Election of Burgeffes, to ferve in the General Affembly for Counties, and for preventing fraudulent Conveyances, in Order to multiply Votes at fuch Elections.*

Mr *Speaker* left the Chair.

Mr *Bland* took the Chair of the Committee.

Mr *Speaker* refumed the Chair.

Mr *Bland* reported, from the Committee, that they had gone through the Bill, and made feveral Amendments thereunto, which they had directed him to report to the Houfe; and he read the Report in his Place, and afterwards delivered the Bill, with the Amendments, in at the Clerk's Table; where the Amendments were once read throughout, and then a fecond Time, one by one, and, upon the Queftion feverally put thereupon, feveral of them were difagreed to, and the reft were agreed to by the Houfe.

Ordered, That the Bill, with the Amendments, be ingroffed.

And then the Houfe adjourned till Tomorrow Morning Eleven of the Clock.

Saturday, the 9th of June, 10 Geo. III. 1770.

AN ingroffed *Bill* to veft certain Lands in *David Meade*, in Fee Simple, whereof the faid *David* and *Sarah* his wife are feized, in Right of the faid *Sarah*, in Fee Tail, and for fettling other Lands, in Lieu thereof, was read the third Time.

Refolved, That the Bill do pafs; and that the Title be, *An Act³ to veft certain Lands in* David Meade, *in Fee Simple, whereof the faid* David *and* Sarah, *his Wife are feized, in Right of the faid* Sarah, *in Fee Tail, and for fettling other Lands, in Lieu thereof.*

Ordered, That Mr *Blair* do carry the Bill to the Council, and defire their Concurrence.

A Meffage from the Council by Mr *Hubard;*

218   Mr *Speaker,*

The Council have agreed to the Bill, *intituled* An Act⁴ to veft certain intailed Lands, therein mentioned, in *Charles Carter*, and for fettling other Lands to the fame Ufes, *with fome Amendments; to which Amendments the Council defire the Concurrence of this Houfe.*

And then the Meffenger withdrew.

The Houfe proceeded to take the faid Amendments into Confideration.

And the faid *Amendments* were read, and are as followeth, viz.

Line 7. Leave out '*containing Two Thoufand Acres, under the Defcription of*' and infert '*being*' inftead thereof.

Line 9. After '*Creek*' infert '*which Moiety or half Part is to be divided and laid off, according to the Direction of the Will of the faid* Robert Carter.''

Line 19. Leave out '*one fourth Part of.*'

Line

Line 20, 21. Leave out '*of Twenty Thoufand Acres, then in* Prince William, *but now in the Parifh of* Cameron, *and the County of* Loudoun, *commonly called and known by the Name of the Mine-Tract.*'

Line 30. Leave out '*Loudoun.*'

Line 51. Leave out '*Loudoun.*'

Line 61. Leave out '*Loudoun.*'

Line 70. Leave out '*Loudoun.*'

The faid *Amendments* being feverally read a fecond Time, were, upon the Queftion feverally put thereupon, agreed to by the Houfe.

Ordered, That M*r* *Richard Henry Lee* do carry the Bill to the Council, and acquaint them that this Houfe hath agreed to the Amendments made by them.

An engroffed *Bill* to dock the Intail of Two Thoufand Eight Hundred Acres of Land, in the County of *Brunfwick,* whereof *Armiftead Lightfoot* is feized in Fee Tail, and vefting the fame in Truftees, for certain Purpofes therein mentioned, was read the third Time.

Refolved, That the Bill do pafs; and that the Title be *An Act[1] to dock the Intail of Two Thoufand Eight Hundred Acres of Land, in the County of* Brunfwick, *whereof* Armiftead Lightfoot *is feized in Fee Tail, and vefting the fame in Truftees, to be fold, for certain Purpofes therein mentioned.*

Ordered, That M*r* *Nelfon* do carry the Bill to the Council, and defire their Concurrence.

Ordered, That M*r* *Stark* have Leave to be abfent from the Service of this Houfe till this Day Sevenight.

A *Petition* of *John Doncaftle* was prefented to the Houfe, and read; fetting forth, that the petitioner long fince paid Two Hundred and Fifty-nine Pounds and Eighteen Shillings, for the Hire of Two Waggons, employed 226 Days, in the Service of this Colony, for which he never received Satiffaction, having been prevented from an earlier Application to the Houfe; and therefore praying Relief.

Ordered, That the faid Petition be referred to the Confideration of the Committee of Public Claims; and that they do examine the Matter thereof, and report the fame, with their Opinion thereupon, to the Houfe.

An engroffed *Bill* to fufpend the Execution of an Act, intituled, *An Act[2] to amend an Act, intituled An Act for the Infpection of Pork, Beef, Flour, Tar, Pitch and Turpentine,* was read the third Time.

Refolved, That the Bill do pafs; and that the Title be, *An Act[3] to fufpend the Execution of an Act, intituled, an Act, to amend an Act, intituled an Act for the Infpection of Pork, Beef, Flour, Tar, Pitch and Turpentine.*

Ordered, That M*r* *Riddick* do carry the Bill to the Council, and defire their Concurrence. 219

An engroffed *Bill* to dock the Intail of Five Hundred and Fifty Acres of Land, in the County of *Gloucefter,* whereof *Sarah* the Wife of *John Rootes,* Gentleman, is feized, and for vefting the fame in Truftees, for the Purpofes therein mentioned was read the third Time.

Refolved, That the Bill do pafs; and that the Title be, *An Act[4] to dock the Intail of Five Hundred and Fifty Acres of Land, in the County of* Gloucefter, *whereof* Sarah *the Wife of* John Rootes, *Gentleman, is feized, and for vefting the fame in Truftees, for the Purpofes therein mentioned.*

Ordered, That M*r* *Dixon* do carry the Bill to the Council, and defire their Concurrence.

M*r* *Treafurer* reported, from the Committee for Religion, that the Committee had had under their Confideration feveral Petitions, to them referred, and had come to feveral Refolutions thereupon, which they had directed him to report to the Houfe; and he read the Report in his Place, and afterwards delivered it in at the Clerk's Table; where the Refolutions of the Committee were read, and are as followeth, *viz.*

Refolved, That it is the Opinion of this Committee, that the petition of fundry Inhabitants

---

[1] **Hening**, VIII. p. 457. [2] Ibid, VIII. p. 351. [3] Ibid, VIII. p. 366. [4] Ibid, VIII. p. 483

habitants of the Parifh of *Dale*, in the County of *Chefterfield*, praying a Divifion of the faid Parifh into two diftinct Parifhes, be rejected.

Refolved, That it is the Opinion of this Committee, that the Petitions of fundry Inhabitants of the faid Parifh, in Oppofition thereto, praying that the faid Parifh may not be divided, is reafonable.

Refolved, That it is the Opinion of this Committee, that the petition of fundry Inhabitants of the Parifh of *Frederick*, in the County of *Frederick*, praying a Divifion of the faid Parifh, into three feparate and diftinct Parifhes, is reafonable.

The faid *Refolutions* being feverally read a fecond Time, were, upon the Queftion feverally put thereupon, agreed to by the Houfe.

Ordered, That a Bill be brought in purfuant to the laft of the faid Refolutions; and that the Committee for Religion do prepare and bring in the fame.

Mr *Treafurer* prefented to the Houfe, according to Order, a Bill to impower the Veftry of *Briftol* Parifh, in the Counties of *Dinwiddie* and *Prince George*, to fell their Glebe: And the fame was received, and read the firft Time.

Refolved, That the Bill be read a fecond Time.

Mr *Treafurer* reported, from the Committee of Propofitions and Grievances, to whom the Petition of divers Inhabitants of *Augufta* County, praying that Part of the faid County of *Augufta* may be added to the County of *Hampfhire* was referred, that the Committee had examined the Matter of the faid petition, and come to a Refolution thereupon, which they had directed him to report to the Houfe; and he read the Report in his Place, and afterwards delivered it in at the Clerk's Table; where the Refolution of the Committee was read, and is as followeth, *viz.*

Refolved, That it is the Opinion of this Committee, that the faid Petition is reafonable.

Ordered, That a Bill be brought in purfuant to the faid Refolution; and that the Committee of Propofitions and Grievances do prepare and bring in the fame.

Mr *Eyre* reported from the Committee of Trade, to whom the Bill for encouraging the making of Hemp was committed, that the Committee had gone through the Bill, and made an Amendment thereunto, which they had directed him to report to the Houfe; and he read the Report in his Place, and afterwards delivered the Bill, with the Amendment, in at the Clerk's Table; where the Amendment was twice read, and, upon the Queftion put thereupon, was agreed to by the Houfe.

Ordered, That the Bill, with the Amendment, be ingroffed.

Mr *Eyre*, prefented to the Houfe, according to Order, a Bill for the Infpection of Hemp: And the fame was received, and read the firft Time.

Refolved, That the Bill be read a fecond Time.

Mr *Archibald Cary* prefented to the Houfe, according to Order, a Bill for eftablifhing a Town at *Rocky Ridge*, in the County of *Chefterfield*, and for adding certain Lots to the town of *Richmond*, in the County of *Henrico:* And the fame was received, and read the firft Time.

Refolved, That the Bill be read a fecond Time.

A *Petition* of fundry Inhabitants of the Town of *Tappahannock*, in the County of *Effex*, whofe Names are thereunto fubfcribed, was prefented to the Houfe and read; fetting forth, that Wooden Chimnies in the faid Town are dangerous; and therefore, praying that an Act may pafs for demolifhing Wooden Chimnies already built in the faid Town, and prohibiting the building of others therein for the future.

Ordered, That the faid petition be referred to the Confideration of the Committee of propofitions and Grievances; and that they do examine the matter thereof, and report the fame, with their Opinion thereupon, to the Houfe.

A *Petition* of *James Rofcow*, Gentleman, was prefented to the Houfe, and read; fetting forth, that the petitioner is feized in Fee Tail, under the Wills of his Anceftors, of about Two Thoufand and Two Hundred Acres of Land, in two Tracts, called *Blunt Point* and *Stanley Hundred*, and is feized of the Reverfion of the faid Lands in Fee, expectant upon his dying without Iffue; and that he is confiderably indebted, and now

under

under Confinement, from which he cannot difcharge himfelf without difpofing of his Intereft in the faid Lands (All the property he hath left) which muft be fold for lefs than the Value, by Reafon of the Poffibility of his having Iffue; and therefore praying that an Act may pafs to dock the Intail of the faid Lands.

Ordered, That Leave be given to bring in a Bill, purfuant to the Prayer of the faid Petition: And that Mr *Archibald Cary* do prepare and bring in the fame.

An engroffed *Bill* to impower certain Truftees to leafe the Lands of the *Pamunkey Indians*, and for other Purpofes therein mentioned, was read the third Time.

Refolved, That the Bill do pafs; and that the Title be, *An Act[1] to appoint Truftees in the Room of thofe who are dead, for the* Pamunkey *Indians, and with further Power to hear and determine Controverfies among them.*

Ordered, That Mr *Treafurer* do carry the Bill to the Council, and defire their Concurrence.

A *Petition* of *Richard Johnfon*, Gentleman, was prefented to the Houfe, and read; fetting forth, that the Petitioner formerly fold and conveyed One Thoufand Acres of Land or thereabouts, in the County of *King & Queen*, and One Hundred Acres of Land, in the County of *King William*, whereof he was feized, by the Will of his Father, in Fee Tail, to *John Robinfon*, Efq; deceafed, and is willing to confirm the Title of the faid Lands to the Perfons who afterwards purchafed the fame from the faid *John Robinfon;* and therefore praying that an Act may pafs to dock the Intail of the faid Lands, and to fettle to the fame Ufes Four Hundred Acres of Land in the County of *Louifa*, with Slaves thereunto annexed, which the Petitioner had conveyed to the faid *John Robinfon*, as a Counter Security for the Warranty of the Title of the other Lands fold to him.

Ordered, That Leave be given to bring in a Bill purfuant to the Prayer of the faid petition; and that Mr *Archibald Cary* do prepare and bring in the fame.

A *Bill* to amend the Act, intituled *An Act[2] for the better fecuring the Payment of Levies, and Reftraint of Vagrants, and for making Provifion for the Poor*, was read a fecond Time.

Refolved, That the Bill be committed.

Refolved, That the Bill be committed to a Committee of the whole Houfe.

Refolved, That this Houfe will, upon *Tuefday* next, refolve itfelf into a Committee of the whole Houfe, upon the faid Bill.

An ingroffed *Bill* to explain and amend one Act of Affembly, made in the 4th Year of the Reign of Queen *Anne*, intituled *An Act[3] for regulating the Election of Burgeffes, for fettling their Privileges, and for afcertaining their Allowances;* and alfo one other Act made in the 10th Year of the Reign of King *George* II. intituled *An Act[4] to declare who shall have a Right to Vote in the Election of Burgeffes to ferve in the General Affembly for Counties, and for preventing fraudulent Conveyances, in order to multiply Votes at fuch Elections*, was read the third Time.

The *Amendments* following were feverally propofed to be made to the Bill, viz.

Sheet 1, Line 76. To leave out '*may*' and infert '*shall*' inftead thereof.

Sheet 2, Line 70. After '*elected*' to leave out '*or for being elected.*'

Sheet 2, Line 85. After '*Day*' to infert '*befides Ferriages.*'

Sheet 2, Line 97. After '*returning*' to leave out '*and,*' and infert '*to*' inftead thereof.

And the faid *Amendments* were, upon the Queftion feverally put thereupon, agreed to by the Houfe; and the Bill was amended at the Table accordingly.

Refolved, That the Bill do pafs; and that the Title be, *An Act[5] for regulating the Election of Burgeffes, for declaring their Privileges and Allowances, and for fixing the Rights of Electors.*

Ordered, That Mr *Bland* do carry the Bill to the Council, and defire their Concurrence.

Ordered

---

[1] Hening, VIII, p. 433. [2] Ibid, VI. p. 29. [3] Ibid, III. p. 236. [4] Ibid, IV. p. 475.
[5] Ibid, VIII. p. 305.

Ordered, That Mr *Burton* have Leave to be abfent from the Service of this Houfe for a week.

Ordered, That Mr *Archibald Cary* have Leave to be abfent from the Service of this Houfe till *Wednefday* next.

A *Bill* to make Provifion for the Support and Maintenance of Ideots, Lunatics, and other Perfons of unfound Minds, was read a fecond Time.

Refolved, That the Bill be committed;

Refolved, That the Bill be committed to a Committee of the whole Houfe.

Refolved, That this Houfe will, upon *Thurfday* next, refolve itfelf into a Committee of the whole Houfe, upon the faid Bill.

222   The Houfe was moved, that the Order which was made upon *Wednefday* last, that it be an Inftruction to the Gentlemen, who are appointed to prepare and bring in a Bill for the better regulating the Election of Veftries, that they have Power to receive a Claufe or Claufes purfuant to the eighth Refolution of the Committee for Religion, which had been that Day agreed to by the Houfe, might be read.

And the fame being read accordingly;

Ordered, That the faid Order be difcharged.

Ordered, That a Bill be brought in purfuant to the faid Refolution; and that Mr *Eyre*, and Mr *Mercer*, do prepare and bring in the fame.

A *Bill* declaring Slaves to be perfonal Eftate, and for other Purpofes therein mentioned, was read a fecond Time.

Refolved, That the Bill be committed.

Refolved, That the Bill be committed to a Committee of the whole Houfe.

Refolved, That the Houfe will, upon *Friday* next, refolve itfelf into a Committee of the whole Houfe, upon the faid Bill.

And then the Houfe adjourned till Monday Morning next Eleven of the Clock.

Monday, the 11th of June, 10 Geo. III. 1770.

A Petition of *Rachel Spencer* was prefented to the Houfe, and read; fetting forth, that in the Years One Thoufand Seven Hundred and Sixty, and One Thoufand Seven Hundred and Sixty-Two, the petitioner furnifhed Diet, Liquors, and Lodging, for divers Recruits raifed for the Regiments in the Service of this Colony, for which she had not received any Satiffaction; and therefore praying that the Juftice of her Claim may be inquired into, and fuch Allowance made to her as the Houfe fhall think reafonable.

Ordered, That the faid Petition be referred to the Confideration of the Committee of Public Claims; and that they do examine the Matter thereof, and report the fame, with their Opinion thereupon, to the Houfe.

A *Petition* of the Inhabitants of the County of *Bedford*, whofe Names are thereunto fubfcribed, was prefented to the Houfe, and read; fetting forth, that the Petitioners are deprived of the Benefit they formerly enjoyed from a plentiful Supply of Fifh, the Paffage of them being obftructed by Mill Dams without Slopes, or with fuch as are infufficient; and therefore praying that an Act may pafs directing Slopes to be made in Mill Dams, and impowering certain Perfons to prefcribe the Manner of making the faid Slopes.

Ordered, That the faid Petition be referred to the Confideration of the Committee of Propofitions and Grievances; and that they do examine the Matter thereof, and report the fame, with their Opinion thereupon, to the Houfe.

A *Petition* of fundry Inhabitants on *Goofe* Creek, in the County of *Bedford*, whofe Names are thereunto fubfcribed, was prefented to the Houfe, and read; fetting forth, that one *Jeremiah Early* hath lately erected a Mill at the Mouth of the faid *Creek*, and
223   thereby interrupting the Paffage of Fifh, deprived the Petitioners of that Means of fupporting

porting their Families and therefore praying that the said *Early* may be compelled to open a Gate in his Mill Dam for admitting Fish to pass during the proper Season.

Ordered, That the said Petition be referred to the Consideration of the Committee of propositions and Grievances; and that they do examine the Matter thereof, and report the same, with their Opinion thereupon, to the House.

The House was moved, that the Order made upon *Monday* last, that it be an Instruction to the Gentlemen, who are appointed to prepare and bring in a Bill for the better regulating the Election of Vestries, that they have Power to receive a Clause or Clauses for dissolving the Vestry of the Parish of *Augusta*, in the County of *Augusta*, might be read.

And the same being read accordingly;

Ordered, That the said Order be discharged.

Ordered, That it be an Instruction to the Gentlemen who are appointed to prepare, and bring in a Bill pursuant to the eighth Resolution of the Committee for Religion, which upon *Wednesday* last, was agreed to by the House, that they have Power to receive a Clause or Clauses for dissolving the Vestry of the Parish of *Augusta*, in the County of *Augusta*.

Ordered, That Mr *Jones* have Leave to be absent from the Service of this House for the Remainder of this Session.

An engrossed *Bill*, for encouraging the making Hemp, was read the third Time.

Resolved, That the Bill do pass; and that the Title be, *An Act[1] for encouraging the making Hemp.*

Ordered, That Mr *Bland* do carry the Bill to the Council, and desire their Concurrence.

An engrossed *Bill*, for altering the Court Day of the County of *Culpeper*, was read the third Time.

Resolved, That the Bill do pass; and that the Title be, *An Act[2] for altering the Court Days of several Counties therein mentioned.*

Ordered, That Mr *Henry Pendleton* do carry the Bill to the Council, and desire their Concurrence.

A *Bill* to vest certain intailed Lands, whereof *William* and *John Armistead*, Gentlemen are seized, in Trustees, to be sold for Payment of the Debts due from the Estate of their Father, was read a second Time.

Resolved, That the Bill be committed to Mr *Edmund Pendleton*, Mr *Taliaferro*, Mr *Whiting*, Mr *Lewis Burwell*, of *Gloucester*, Mr *Henry Lee*, Mr *Tebbs*, Mr *Marshall*, and Mr *Scott*.

A *Bill* to dock the Intail of certain Lands, whereof *Robert Burwell*, Esq; is seized, in Tail Male, and for settling other Lands, of greater Value, to the same Uses, was read a second Time.

Resolved, That the Bill be committed to Mr *Richard Baker*, Mr *Bridger*, and all the Members who serve for the Counties of *Surry*, *Prince William*, *Loudoun* and *Fauquier*.

A *Bill* to vest certain intailed Lands, whereof *Samuel Meredith*, is seized, in Trustees, to be sold for the Purposes therein mentioned, was read a second Time.

Resolved, That the Bill be committed to Mr *Edmund Pendleton*, Mr *Whiting*, Mr *Lewis Burwell*, of *Gloucester*, Mr *Lyne*, Mr *John Tayloe Corbin*, Mr *Gawin Corbin*, and Mr *Philip Ludwell Grymes*.

A *Bill* for adding Part of the City of *Williamsburg* to *James City* County, and for other Purposes therein mentioned, was read a second Time.

Resolved, That the Bill be committed to Mr *Blair*, Mr *Treasurer*, and Mr *Lewis Burwell*, of *James City*.

A *Bill* to vest certain intailed Lands, therein mentioned, in *George Brooke*, Gentleman, in Fee Simple, and for settling other Lands, of greater Value, in Lieu thereof, was read a second Time.

Resolved, That the Bill be committed to Mr *Lyne*, Mr *John Tayloe Corbin*, Mr *Braxton*, Mr *Moore*, Mr *Edmund Pendleton*, and Mr *Taliaferro*.

A

[1] Hening, VIII. p. 363.   [2] Ibid, VIII. p, 400.

A *Bill* for the better regulating the Office of Sheriffs and their Deputies, was read a fecond Time.

Refolved, That the Bill be committed to Mr *Mercer*, Mr *Richard Lee*, Mr *Eyre*, Mr *Weft*, Mr *Blair*, Mr *Henry Lee*, Mr *Nelfon*, Mr *Bland*, Mr *Edmund Pendleton*, and Mr *Treafurer*.

A *Bill* to compel Perfons to find Security for Payment of Cofts in certain Cafes, was read a fecond Time.

Refolved, That the Bill be committed to Mr *Mercer*, Mr *Blair*, Mr *Edmund Pendleton*, Mr *Jefferfon*, and Mr *Thomas Walker*.

A *Bill* for the Infpection of Hemp, was read a fecond Time.

Refolved, That the Bill be committed.

Refolved, That the Bill be committed to a Committee of the whole Houfe.

Refolved, That this Houfe will, Tomorrow, refolve itfelf into a Committee of the whole Houfe, upon the faid Bill.

And then the Houfe adjourned till To-morrow Morning Eleven of the Clock.

Tuesday, the 12th of June, 10 Geo. III. 1770.

A Claim of *Thomas Claiborne* for the Ferriages of an Adjutant, and of feveral Sheriffs with Criminals, was prefented to the Houfe, and read.

Ordered, That the faid Claim be referred to the Confideration of the Committee of Public Claims; and that they do examine the Matter thereof, and report the fame, with their Opinion thereupon, to the Houfe.

A *Petition* of *John Earle*, late of the County of *Frederick*, but now of the Province of *South Carolina*, was prefented to the Houfe, and read; fetting forth, that upon its being fignified to the petitioner, that a Number of Volunteers from the Colony of *Virginia*, were defired to join Brigadier General *Bouquet*, in his Expedition againft the *Indian* Towns, in the Year 1764, the Petitioner did, at very confiderable Expence, and with much trouble, enlift Twenty-fix Men, who ferved under him during the Campaign, and until the Peace with the *Indians;* and that the Petitioner, foon after the Campaign, having removed to *Carolina*, was not included among the Volunteer Officers, whofe Petition was formerly preferred to the Houfe and confidered; and therefore praying the Houfe to take his Cafe into Confideration.

Ordered, That the faid *Petition* be referred to the Confideration of the Committee of Public Claims; and that they do examine the Matter thereof, and report the fame, with their Opinion thereupon, to the Houfe.

225 Mr *Eyre* prefented to the Houfe, according to Order, a Bill for diffolving the Veftry of the Parifh of *Hungars*, in the County of *Northampton:* And the fame was received, and read the firft Time.

Refolved, That the Bill be read a fecond Time.

A *Petition* of *William Edwards* and *James Price*, Infpectors at *Gray's* Creek Warehoufe, in the County of *Surry*, was prefented to the Houfe, and read; fetting forth, that in the Year 1763, the faid Warehoufe was broke open, and a Hogfhead of Tobacco, the Property of the faid *William Edwards*, ftolen thereout; and that in *May* laft, Four Hundred and Twenty-one Pounds of Tobacco were taken out of a prized Hogfhead and carried away; and therefore praying that fuch Allowance may be made to the Petitioners as fhall be thought reafonable.

Refolved, That the faid Petition be referred to the Confideration of the Committee of Public Claims; and that they do examine the Matter thereof, and report the fame, with their Opinion thereupon, to the Houfe.

A *Claim* of *Jofhua Kendall* for Services done in ornamenting the Capitol Gates, was prefented to the Houfe, and read.

Ordered, That the faid Claim be referred to the Confideration of the Committee of Public Claims; and that they report their Opinion thereupon, to the Houfe.

A

A *Petition* of *John Hancock*, and *Margaret* his Wife, was prefented to the Houfe, and read; fetting forth, that the faid *John* is feized, in Fee Tail, of Three Hundred Acres of Land, in the Parifh of *Dettingen*, and County of *Prince William*, called the *Deep Hole* Tract, and is feized in Fee Simple, in Right of his faid Wife, of Eight Hundred Acres of Land, in the County of *Amherft;* and that it will be greatly to the Advantage of their Iffue, and more to the Advantage of the Wife, who is confenting thereto, if the faid Eight Hundred Acres of Land, with Slaves, are fettled, in Lieu of the faid Three Hundred Acres; and therefore praying that an Act may pafs for that Purpofe.

Ordered, That Leave be given to bring in a Bill purfuant to the Prayer of the faid Petition; and that Mr *Henry Lee* do prepare and bring in the fame.

A *Claim* of *John Hickman* for the Ferriages of certain Criminals was prefented to the Houfe, and read.

Ordered, That the faid Claim be referred to the Confideration of the Committee of Public Claims; and that they do examine the Matter thereof, and report the fame, with their Opinion thereupon, to the Houfe.

A *Petition* of *John Corrie* and *Ewin Clements* was prefented to the Houfe, and read; fetting forth, that the Ferries over *Rappahannock* River, called *Ruft's* and *Lowry's*, are now little ufed, fince the Eftablifhment of a more convenient Ferry, in the Neighborhood of them, from the Town of *Tappahannock*, in the County of *Effex*, to the Land of *Moore Fauntleroy*, in the County of *Richmond*, and are detrimental to the Petitioners, who have intermarried with the Proprietors of the faid *Ruft's* and *Lowry's* Ferries; and therefore praying relief.

Ordered, That the faid petition be referred to the Confideration of the Committee of propofitions and Grievances; and that they do examine the Matter thereof, and report the fame, with their Opinion thereupon, to the Houfe.

A *Claim* of *William Rind*, Printer, for printing Paper Bills for Ten Thoufand Pounds and binding Fifty Books thereof, was prefented to the Houfe, and read.

Ordered, That the faid Claim be referred to the Confideration of the Committee of Public Claims; and that they do examine the Matter thereof, and report the fame, with their Opinion thereupon, to the Houfe. 226

A *Petition* of *Jofeph Mitchell*, of the Province of *Maryland*, was prefented to the Houfe, and read; fetting forth, that the petitioner having been robbed of Seventy Pounds current Money of *Pennfylvania*, by two Perfons in Difguife, with great Difficulty and Expence difcovered the Criminals, and caufed them to be apprehended, attempted to retake one of them who efcaped, and profecuted the other; and praying the Confideration of the Houfe whether the petitioner ought not to be indemnified for his Trouble and Expence in endeavoring to bring fuch daring Villians to condign Punifhment, and to receive Reparation for his Lofs from the Public.

Ordered, That the faid petition be referred to the Confideration of the Committee of Public Claims; and that they do examine the Matter thereof, and report the fame, with their Opinion thereupon, to the Houfe.

Ordered, That the Committee of Public Claims do ftate an Account of the Difburfements of *Thomas Walker*, *Thomas Rutherford*, *James Wood*, and *Abraham Hite*, Gentlemen, Commiffioners appointed by an Act of General Affembly, paffed in the 7th Year of his prefent Majefty's Reign, intituled *An Act for opening a Road through the Frontiers of this Colony, to Fort* Pitt *on the* Ohio, in Execution of the faid Act, and report the fame, with their Opinion thereupon, to the Houfe.

A *Petition* of *David Ker*, Clerk of the Court of the County of *Middlefex*, was prefented to the Houfe, and read; fetting forth, that Fifty-fix Pounds Fourteen Shillings and Four Pence Halfpenny, having been levied by an Execution and brought into the faid Court, the Petitioner was, by Order of the faid Court, directed to keep the fame till a certain Difpute between feveral Claimants thereof, fhould be determined; that the petitioner fealed up the faid Money, which, except the Pence, confifted of Treafury Notes, and delivered it to his Deputy *James Gregory*, living in *Urbanna*, near the Court-Houfe, and the Clerk's Office, that it might be ready to be diftributed as the faid Court

fhould

fhould appoint; and that before the faid Difpute was determined, or any other Order made for the Difpofition of the faid Money, the Houfe of the faid *James Gregory* was burned down, and the faid Notes therein confumed; and further fetting forth, that the Sum of Fourteen Pounds Five Shillings and Six Pence, confifting likewife of Treafury Notes, and received by the faid *James Gregory*, partly for the Petitioner's Fees, and partly for Fees on Marriage and Ordinary Licences, was, at the fame Time, and by the fame unfortunate Accident, deftroyed; and therefore praying the Confideration of the Houfe; and that the Treafurer may be directed and impowered to pay the faid feveral Sums of Money to the Petitioner.

Ordered, That the faid Petition be referred to the Confideration of the Committee of Public Claims; and that they do examine the Matter thereof, and report the fame, with their Opinion thereupon, to the Houfe.

A *Petition* of *Ezekiel Young* and *Jofeph Feddeman*, Infpectors of Tobacco at *Guilford*, was prefented to the Houfe, and read; fetting forth, that the Petitioners, befides their own Labour, were put to confiderable Expence, in picking and repacking the Tobacco damaged in the faid Warehoufe by the Storm in *September* laft, being obliged for that Purpofe to employ feveral Perfons on Wages, whereby they faved Forty-three Hogfheads of the faid Tobacco for the Public; and therefore praying that a reafonable Satiffaction may be made to the Petitioners for their faid Services and Expences.

Ordered, That the faid Petition be referred to the Confideration of the Committee of Public Claims; and that they do examine the Matter thereof, and report the fame, with their Opinion thereupon, to the Houfe.

A *Petition*, of *Charles Neilfon*, Naval Officer of Port *Rappahannock*, was prefented to the Houfe, and read; fetting forth, that the Sum of Nine Pounds, received by the Petitioner's Deputy, *James Gregory*, for the Duty on Liquors, imported into the Diftrict of *Rappahannock*, was by him depofited in a Defk to be paid into the Treafury at the Time appointed by Act of General Affembly; and that the faid *James Gregory's* Houfe was afterwards burned down, and the faid Money, confifting of Treafury Notes, therein confumed; and therefore praying that the Petitioner may be allowed to charge the faid Sum of Nine Pounds in his Account with the Treafurer.

Ordered, That the faid Petition be referred to the Confideration of the Committee of Public Claims; and that they do examine the Matter thereof, and report the fame, with their Opinion thereupon, to the Houfe.

The Houfe was moved that an Act made in the 32d Year of the Reign of King *Charles* II. intituled *An Act[1] of free and general Pardon, Indemnitie, and Oblivion*, might be read.

And the fame being read accordingly;

Ordered, That Leave be given to bring in a Bill to repeal Part of the faid Act; and that Mr *Eyre*, Mr *Treafurer*, and Mr *Bland*, do prepare and bring in the fame.

An ingroffed *Bill* for better regulating the Collection of Public, County, and Parifh Levies, was read the third Time.

The *Amendments* following were feverally propofed to be made to the Bill, *viz.*

Line 25.   To leave out '*immediately.*'

Line 26.   Leave out '*Twelve and Two*' and infert "*Two and Four,*" inftead thereof.

Line 60.   After '*Churchwardens*' to infert '*or Collector.*'

At the End of the Bill to add, '*and from thence to the End of the next Seffion of Affembly.*'

And the faid *Amendments* were, upon the Queftion feverally put thereupon, agreed to by the Houfe; and the Bill was amended at the Table accordingly.

Refolved, That the Bill do pafs; and that the Title be, *An Act[2] for better regulating the Collection of County and Parifh Levies.*

Ordered, That Mr *Bland* do carry the Bill to the Council, and defire their Concurrence.

A *Petition* of *William Rind* was prefented to the Houfe, and read; fetting forth, that the Bufinefs of his Department, as Printer to the Public, is greatly increafed in

many

---

1 Hening, II. p. 458.   2 Title varies--*See* Hening, VIII, p. 381.

many Particulars; and therefore praying the Confideration of the Houfe, and that fuch further Addition may be made to his Salary as they fhall think juft and reafonable.

Ordered, That the faid petition be referred to the Confideration of the Committee of Public Claims; and that they do examine the Matter thereof, and report the fame, with their Opinion thereupon, to the Houfe.

A *Bill* to impower the Veftry of *Briftol* Parifh, in the Counties of *Dinwiddie* and *Prince George*, to fell their Glebe, was read a fecond Time. ²²⁸

Ordered, That the Bill be ingroffed.

The Houfe, according to Order, refolved itfelf into a Committee of the whole Houfe, upon the Bill to amend the Act for the better fecuring the Payment of Levies, and Reftraint of Vagrants, and for making Provifion for the Poor.

Mr *Speaker* left the Chair.

Mr *Bland* took the Chair of the Committee.

Mr *Speaker* refumed the Chair.

Mr *Bland* reported from the Committee, that they had gone through the Bill, and made an Amendment thereunto, which they had directed him to report to the Houfe; and he read the Report in his Place, and afterwards delivered the Bill, with the Amendment, in at the Clerk's Table; where the Amendment was twice read, and, upon the Queftion put thereupon, was agreed to by the Houfe.

Ordered, That the Bill, with the Amendment, be ingroffed.

The other *Order* of the Day being read;

Refolved, That this Houfe will, upon this Day Sevenight, refolve itfelf into a Committee of the whole Houfe, upon the Bill for the Infpection of Hemp.

And then the Houfe adjourned till Tomorrow Morning Eleven of the Clock.

Wednesday, the 13th of June, 10 Geo. III. 1770.

MR *Bland* prefented to the Houfe, according to Order, a Bill for appointing Commiffioners to meet with Commiffioners, who are or may be appointed by the Legiflatures of the neighboring Colonies, to form and agree on a general Plan for the Regulation of the *Indian* Trade; and the fame was received, and read the firft Time.

Refolved, That the Bill be read a fecond Time.

Ordered, That Mr *Gawin Corbin*, and Mr *Philip Ludwell Grymes*, be added to the Gentlemen, to whom the Bill to veft certain intailed Lands, whereof *William* and *John Armiftead*, Gentlemen, are feized, in Truftees, to be fold for Payment of the Debts due from the Eftate of their Father, is committed.

Mr *Bland* prefented to the Houfe, according to Order, a Bill for adding Part of the County of *Augufta* to the County of *Hampfhire;* and the fame was received, and read the firft Time.

Refolved, That the Bill be read a fecond Time.

Mr *Bland* reported, from the Committee of propofitions and Grievances, that the Committee had had under their Confideration feveral Petitions, to them referred, and had come to feveral Refolutions thereupon, which they had directed him to report to the Houfe; and he read the Report in his Place, and afterwards delivered it in at the Clerk's Table; where the Refolutions of the Committee were read, and are as followeth, *viz.*

Refolved, That it is the Opinion of this Committee, that the petition of *Thomas Shepherd*, praying that the Act eftablifhing his Ferry, which was repealed, may be revived, be rejected.

Refolved, That it is the Opinion of this Committee, that the Petition of fundry Inhabitants of this Colony, praying that the Brick-Houfe Landing on *Wafhington's* Land, in the County of *Weftmoreland*, may be declared a Public Landing, and a Road opened from ²²⁹

from thence to the *Weftmoreland* main Road; be referred to the Confideration of the next Seffion of Affembly.

Refolved, That it is the Opinion of this Committee, that the petition of *Daniel Cargill*, praying that a Ferry may be eftablifhed from the faid *Cargill's* Land, in the County of *Charlotte*, over *Roanoke* River, to the Land of *John Foufhee*, deceafed, is reafonable.

Refolved, That it is the Opinion of this Committee, that the Petition of divers Inhabitants of the County of *Halifax*, praying that a Ferry may be eftablifhed on the Land of *Richard Jones*, on the South Side of *Dan* River, acrofs the faid River, to the Land of the Reverend *Miles Selden*, on the North Side, is reafonable.

Refolved, That it is the Opinion of this Committee, that the Petition of divers Inhabitants of the Counties of *Charlotte* and *Halifax*, praying that the Ferry over *Staunton* River, at *Fuqua's*, may be removed to a Ford two Miles above the faid *Fuqua's*, be referred to the Confideration of the next Seffion of Affembly.

Refolved, That it is the Opinion of this Committee, that the Petition of *John Corrie* and *Ewin Clements*, praying that the Ferries over *Rappahannock* River, eftablifhed at *Ruft's* and *Lowry's*, may be difcontinued, is reafonable.

Refolved, That it is the Opinion of this Committee, that the Petition of fundry Inhabitants of the Town of *Tappahannock*, in the County of *Effex*, praying that an Act may pafs, prohibiting the building of wooden Chimnies in the faid Town, and directing the Removal of fuch as are already built, is reafonable.

Refolved, That it is the Opinion of this Committee, that the Petition of the Inhabitants of the Counties of *Effex*, *King & Queen*, and *Caroline*, praying that a Town may be eftablifhed at a Place called *Southern's* or *Layton's*, on *Rappahannock* River, on the Land of *Thomas Ley*, is reafonable.

Refolved, That it is the Opinion of this Committee, that fo much of the Petition of *Jeffe Ewell*, Proprietor of the Warehoufes at *Dumfries*, in the County of *Prince William*, as prays that the Rents of the faid Warehoufe may be raifed to One Shilling *per* Hogfhead, is reafonable.

Refolved, That it is the Opinion of this Committee, that the Refidue of the faid Petition, be rejected.

The faid *Refolutions* being feverally read a fecond Time, were, upon the Queftion feverally put thereupon, agreed to by the Houfe.

Ordered, That it be an Inftruction to the faid Committee, who are appointed to prepare and bring in a Bill, purfuant to the fourth Refolution of the faid Committee, which, upon *Monday*, the thirteenth Day of *November* laft, was agreed to by the Houfe, that they have Power to receive a Claufe or Claufes, purfuant to the third, fourth, and fixth, of the faid Refolutions, this Day agreed to by the Houfe.

Ordered, That the feventh and eighth of the faid Refolutions, do lie upon the Table till the fecond reading of the Bill for eftablifhing a Town at *Rocky Ridge*, in the County of *Chefterfield*, and for adding certain Lots to the Town of *Richmond*, in the County of *Henrico*.

Ordered, That it be an Inftruction to the Committee of the whole Houfe, to whom the Bill to continue and amend the Act, intituled An Act[1] *for amending the Staple of Tobacco, and preventing Frauds in his Majefty's Cuftoms*, was committed, that they have Power to receive a Claufe or Claufes purfuant to the ninth of the faid Refolutions.

Ordered, That an Addrefs be made to the Governor, to Order a new Writ to be made out, for the electing of a Burgefs to ferve in this prefent General Affembly, for the County of *Loudoun*, in the Room of Mr *James Hamilton*, who, fince his Election, hath accepted the Office of one of his Majefty's Coroners of the faid County; and that Mr *Peyton* do wait upon his Excellency with the faid Addrefs.

Ordered, That it be an Inftruction to the Committee for Courts of Juftice, to whom the Bill to continue and amend an Act, intituled An Act[2] *for allowing Fairs to be kept*

in

---

[1] Hening, IV. p. 247.   [2] Ibid, V. p. 82.

in the Town of Frederickfburg, is committed, that they have Power to receive a Claufe or Claufes for enlarging the faid Town of *Frederickfburg.*

The Houfe was moved, that a Copy of a Letter from Mr *Thomas Walker*, a Member of this Houfe, to *Saluy*, the Great Warrior of *Eftatoe*, with an Affidavit thereunto annexed, might be read.

And the fame being read accordingly,

Ordered, That the faid Papers be referred to the Committee of the whole Houfe, to whom it is referred to confider further of the prefent State of the Colony.

Mr *Richard Henry Lee* reported, from the Committee for Courts of Juftice, to whom the Bill to continue and amend an Act, intituled *An Act[1] for allowing Fairs to be kept in the Town of* Frederickfburg, was committed, that the Committee had gone through the Bill, and made an Amendment thereunto, which they had directed him to report to the Houfe, and he read the Report in his Place; and afterwards delivered the Bill, with the Amendment, in at the Clerk's Table; where the Amendment was twice read, and, upon the Queftion put thereupon, was, with an Amendment thereto, agreed to by the Houfe.

Ordered, That the Bill, with the Amendment, be engroffed.

The Houfe, according to Order, refolved itfelf into a Committee of the whole Houfe, to confider further of the prefent State of the Colony.

Mr *Speaker* left the Chair.

Mr *Bland* took the Chair of the Committee.

Mr *Speaker* refumed the Chair.

Mr *Bland* reported from the Committee, that they had made a further Progrefs in the Matters referred to them; and that he was directed by the Committee to move, that they may have Leave to fit again.

Refolved, That this Houfe will, Tomorrow, refolve itfelf into a Committee of the whole Houfe, to confider further of the prefent State of the Colony.

Ordered, That Mr *Paramore* have Leave to be abfent from the Service of this Houfe till *Saturday* Sevenight.

Mr *Eyre* prefented to the Houfe, according to Order, a Bill to repeal Part of an Act, intituled *An Act[2] of free and general Pardon, Indemnity, and Oblivion;* and the fame was received, and read the firft Time.

Refolved, That the Bill be read a fecond Time.

Ordered, That Mr *Innes* have Leave to be abfent from the Service of this Houfe for the Remainder of this Seffion.

The *Order* of the Day being read, for the Houfe to refolve itfelf into a Committee of the whole Houfe, to confider further of the Bill to continue and amend the Act, intituled *An Act[3] for amending the Staple of Tobacco, and preventing Frauds in his Majefty's Cuftoms;*

Refolved, That this Houfe will, Tomorrow, refolve itfelf into the faid Committee.

Mr *Edmund Pendleton* reported from the Committee, to whom the Bill to veft certain intailed Lands, whereof *William* and *John Armiftead*, Gentlemen, are feized, in Truftees, to be fold for Payment of the Debts due from the Eftate of their father, was committed, that the Committee had examined the Allegations of the Bill, and found the fame to be true; and that the Committee had directed him to report the Bill to the Houfe, without any Amendment; and he delivered the Bill in at the Clerk's Table.

Ordered, That the Bill be engroffed.

The other *Order* of the Day being read;

Ordered, That the Call of the Houfe be adjourned till Tomorrow.

Mr *Edmund Pendleton* reported from the Committee, to whom the Bill to veft certain intailed Lands, therein mentioned, in *George Brooke*, Gentleman, in Fee Simple, and for fettling other Lands, of greater Value, in Lieu thereof, was committed, that the Committee had examined the Allegations of the Bill, and found the fame to be true;

and

---

[1] Hening, V. p. 82.   [2] Ibid, II. p. 458.   [3] Ibid, IV. p. 247.

and that the Committee had directed him to report the Bill to the Houfe, without any Amendment; and he delivered the Bill in at the Clerk's Table.

Ordered, That the Bill be engroffed.

Mr *Edmund Pendleton* reported from the Committee, to whom the Bill to veft certain intailed Lands, whereof *Samuel Meredith* is feized, in Truftees, to be fold for the Purpofes therein mentioned, was committed, that the Committee had examined the Allegations of the Bill, and found the fame to be true; and that the Committee had directed him to report the Bill to the Houfe, without any Amendment; and he delivered the Bill in at the Clerk's Table.

Ordered, That the Bill be engroffed.

And then the Houfe adjourned till Tomorrow Morning Eleven of the Clock.

Thursday, the 14th of June, 10 Geo. III. 1770.

MR *Bland* prefented to the Houfe, according to Order, A Bill for appointing feveral new Ferries, and for other Purpofes therein mentioned; and the fame was received, and read the firft Time.

Refolved, That the Bill be read a fecond Time.

A Member, returned upon a new Writ, having taken the Oaths appointed by Act of Parliament to be taken, and repeated and fubfcribed the Teft, took his Place in the Houfe.

The Houfe was moved, that the Order made upon *Monday*, the eighteenth Day of *December* laft, that a Bill be brought in purfuant to the Prayer of the Petition of *John Fox*, for laying off Sixty Acres of his Land in the County of *Gloucefter*, joining the Land whereon the Court-Houfe ftands, in a Town, and that Mr *Bland* and Mr *Alexander* do prepare and bring in the faid Bill, might be read.

And the fame being read accordingly;

Ordered, That the faid Order be difcharged.

A *Bill* for eftablifhing a Town at *Rocky Ridge*, in the County of *Chefterfield*, and for adding certain Lots to the Town of *Richmond*, in the County of *Henrico*, was read a fecond Time.

Refolved, That the Bill be committed to the Committee of Propofitions and Grievances.

Ordered, That it be an Inftruction to the faid Committee, that they have Power to receive a Claufe or Claufes for laying off Sixty Acres of the Land of *John Fox*, in the County of *Gloucefter*, joining the Land whereon the Court-Houfe ftands, in a Town.

Ordered, That it be an Inftruction to the faid Committee, that they have Power to receive a Claufe or Claufes, purfuant to the feventh and eighth Refolutions of the faid Committee, which were Yefterday agreed to by the Houfe, and ordered to lie upon the Table.

The *Order* of the Day being read for the Houfe to refolve itfelf into a Committee of the whole Houfe, to confider further of the prefent State of the Colony;

Refolved, That this Houfe will, Tomorrow, refolve itfelf into the faid Committee.

Ordered, That Mr *Hutchings* have Leave to be abfent from the Service of this Houfe till *Thurfday* next.

Mr *Bland* reported, from the Committee of Propofitions and Grievances, that the Committee had had under their Confideration feveral Petitions to them referred, and had come to feveral Refolutions thereupon, which they had directed him to report to the Houfe; and he read the Report in his Place, and afterwards delivered it in at the Clerk's Table; where the refolutions of the Committee were read, and are as followeth, *viz.*

Refolved, That it is the Opinion of this Committee, that the Petition of divers Inhabitants of the County of *Bedford*, praying that an Act may pafs directing Slopes to be made in Mill Dams, and empowering certain Perfons to prescribe the Method of making fuch Slopes, be referred to the Confideration of the next Seffion of Affembly.

Refolved

Refolved, That it is the Opinion of this Committee, that the Petition of divers Inhabitants on *Goofe Creek*, in the County of *Bedford*, praying that *Jeremiah Early* may be compelled to open a Gate in his Mill Dam, at the Mouth of the faid Creek, for the Admiffion of Fifh, be referred to the Confideration of the next Seffion of Affembly.

Refolved, That it is the Opinion of this Committee, that the Petition of the Proprietors of *Gingoteague* Ifland, in the County of *Accomack*, praying that an Act may pafs to reftrain Hogs and Dogs going at Large in the faid Ifland, is reafonable.

The faid *Refolutions* being feverally read a fecond Time, were, upon the Queftion feverally put thereupon, agreed to by the Houfe.

Ordered, That a Bill be brought in purfuant to the laft of the faid Refolutions; and that the faid Committee do prepare and bring in the fame.

Ordered, That Mr *Farmer* have Leave to be abfent from the Service of this Houfe for the Remainder of this Seffion.

The Houfe, according to Order, refolved itfelf into a Committee of the whole Houfe to confider further of the Bill to continue and amend the Act, intituled *An Act¹ for amending the Staple of Tobacco, and preventing Frauds in his Majefty's Cuftoms*.

Mr *Speaker* left the Chair.

Mr *Bland* took the Chair of the Committee.

Mr *Speaker* refumed the Chair.

Mr *Bland* reported from the Committee, that they had made a further progrefs in the Bill; and that he was directed by the Committee to move that they may have Leave to fit again.

Refolved, That this Houfe will, Tomorrow, refolve itfelf into a Committee of the whole Houfe, to confider further of the faid Bill.

An engroffed *Bill*, to amend the Act, intituled *An Act² for the better fecuring the Payment of Levies, and Reftraint of Vagrants, for making Provifion for the Poor*, was read the third Time.

Refolved, That the Bill do pafs; and that the Title be, *An Act³ to amend the Act, intituled An Act for the better fecuring the Payment of Levies, and Reftraint of Vagrants, and for making Provifion for the Poor*.

Ordered, That Mr *Bland* do carry the Bill to the Council, and defire their Concurrence.

The *Order* of the Day being read, for the Houfe to refolve itfelf into a Committee of the whole Houfe, upon the Bill to continue and amend the Act for the better regulating and difciplining the Militia;

Refolved, That this Houfe will, Tomorrow, refolve itfelf into a Committee of the whole Houfe upon the faid Bill.

An engroffed *Bill*, to continue and amend an Act, intituled *An Act for allowing Fairs to be kept in the Town of* Frederickfburg, was read the third Time.

Refolved, That the Bill do pafs; and that the Title be, *An Act⁵ for continuing and amending an Act, intituled An Act for reviving and amending the Acts for allowing Fairs to be kept in the Towns of* Frederickfburg *and* Richmond*; and for enlarging the Town of* Frederickfburg.

Ordered, That Mr *Dixon* do carry the Bill to the Council, and defire their Concurrence.

The *Order* of the Day being read, for the Houfe to refolve itfelf into a Committee of the whole Houfe, upon the Bill to make Provifion for the Support and Maintenance of Ideots, Lunatics, and other Perfons of unfound Mind;

Refolved, That this Houfe will, upon *Tuefday* next, refolve itfelf into a Committee of the whole Houfe, upon the faid Bill.

An engroffed *Bill*, to impower the Veftry of *Briftol* Parifh, in the Counties of *Dinwiddie* and *Prince George* to fell their Glebe, was read the third Time.

Refolved, That the Bill do pafs; and that the Title be, *An Act⁶ to impower the Veftry of* Briftol *Parifh, in the Counties of* Dinwiddie *and* Prince George*, to fell their Glebe*.

Ordered

233

---

¹ Hening, IV, p. 247.   ² Ibid, VI. p. 29.   ³ Not recorded as a law,   ⁴ Hening, V. p. 82.
⁵ Hening, VIII, p. 418.   ⁶ Ibid, VIII, p. 431.

Ordered, That Mr *Treasurer* do carry the Bill to the Council, and desire their Concurrance.

A *Bill* for appointing several new Ferries, and for other Purposes therein mentioned, was read a second Time.

Resolved, That the Bill be committed to the Committee of propositions and Grievances.

Mr *Mercer* reported from the Committee, to whom the Bill to compel Persons to find Security for Payment of Costs in certain Cases, was committed, that the Committee had gone through the Bill, and made several Amendments thereunto, which they had directed him to report to the House; and he read the Report in his Place, and afterwards delivered the Bill, with the Amendments, in at the Clerk's Table; where the Amendments were once read throughout, and then a second Time, one by one, and, upon the Question severally put thereupon, several of them were disagreed to, and the rest were agreed to, by the House.

Ordered, That the Bill, with the Amendments, be engrossed.

An engrossed *Bill* to vest certain intailed Lands, therein mentioned, in *George Brooke*, Gentleman, in Fee Simple, and for settling other Lands, of greater value, in Lieu thereof, was read the third Time.

Resolved, That the Bill do pass; and that the Title be, *An Act[1] to vest certain intailed Lands, therein mentioned, in* George Brooke, *Gentleman, in Fee Simple, and for settling other Lands, of greater Value, in Lieu thereof.*

Ordered, That Mr *Edmund Pendleton* do carry the Bill to the Council, and desire their Concurrence.

Ordered, That Mr Stith have Leave to be absent from the Service of this House for the Remainder of this Session.

An engrossed *Bill*, to vest certain intailed Lands, whereof *William* and *John Armistead*, Gentlemen, are seized, in Trustees; to be sold for Payment of the Debts due from the Estate of their Father, was read the third Time.

Resolved, That the Bill do pass; and that the Title be, *An Act[2] to vest certain intailed Lands, whereof* William *and* John Armistead, *Gentlemen, are seized, in Trustees, to be sold for the Payment of the Debts due the Estate of their Father.*

Ordered, That Mr *Edmund Pendleton* do carry the Bill to the Council, and desire their Concurrence.

The other *Order* of the Day being read;

Ordered, That the Call of the House be further adjourned till Tomorrow.

An engrossed *Bill*, to vest certain intailed Lands, whereof *Samuel Meredith* is seized, in Trustees, to be sold for the Purposes therein mentioned, was read the third Time.

Resolved, That the Bill do pass; and that the Title be, *An Act[3] to vest certain intailed Lands, whereof* Samuel Meredith *is seized, in Trustees, to be sold for the Purposes therein mentioned.*

Ordered, That Mr *Edmund Pendleton* do carry the Bill to the Council, and desire their Concurrance.

And then the House adjourned till To-morrow Morning Eleven of the Clock.

Friday, the 15th of June, 10 Geo. III. 1770.

A *Bill* for appointing Commissioners, to meet with Commissioners, who are or may be appointed by the Legislatures of the neighboring Colonies, to form and agree on a general Plan for the Regulation of the *Indian* Trade, was read a second Time.

Ordered, That the Bill be ingrossed.

Mr *Bland* reported from the Committee appointed to examine the Treasurer's Accounts, that the Committee had, according to Order, examined the Treasurer's

Accounts

---

[1] Hening, VIII, p. 474.   [2] Ibid, VIII, p. 487.   [3] Not recorded as a law.

Accounts of the feveral Sums of Money received into and iffued from the Treafury fince the laft Adjournment, and that the Committee had directed him to report the fame, as they appeared to them, to the Houfe; and he read the Report in his Place, and afterwards delivered it in at the Clerk's Table; where the fame was read, and is as followeth, *viz.*

The *Committee* having carefully compared the faid Accounts with the proper Vouchers, find them all fairly and juftly ftated.

It *appears* to your Committee, that the Balance in the Treafurer's Hands of Cafh received of the feveral Collectors for Taxes appropriated to the Redemption of the old Treafury Notes, amounted to Ten Thoufand Three Hundred and Twenty-fix Pounds Eleven Shillings, of which they have burnt and deftroyed Seven Thoufand Eight Hundred Pounds, and have left in the Treafury, on that Account, in Specie, a Balance of Two Thoufand Five Hundred and Twenty-fix Pounds Eleven Shillings to be exchanged for old Treafury Notes.

They likewife find, that there is in the Treafurer's Hands a Balance of Six Thoufand and Thirty-three Pounds Ten Shillings and Eleven pence due to the Account of the Public Treafury, which with the other Balance the Treafurer produced to them.

The faid *Report* being read a fecond Time, was, upon the Queftion put thereupon, agreed to by the Houfe.

Refolved, That the Treafurer's Accounts do pafs.

Ordered, That Mr *Bland* do carry the Treafurer's Accounts to the Council, and defire their Concurrence.

Refolved, That the feveral Sums of Forty Pounds Sterling, and Ten Pounds and Ten Shillings Sterling, be laid out by Mr *Treafurer*, in purchafing two Iron Chefts for fecuring the Public Money, in the Treafury.

Ordered, That Mr *Bland* do carry the Refolution to the Council, and defire their Concurrence.

235

Mr *Bland* prefented to the Houfe, according to Order, a Bill to prevent Hogs and Dogs running at Large on the Ifland of *Gingoteague:* And the fame was received, and read the firft Time.

Refolved, That the Bill be read a fecond Time.

Mr *Dudley Digges* prefented to the Houfe, according to Order, a Bill to dock the Intail of certain Lands, whereof *John Wormeley*, Gentleman, is feized, and for fettling other Lands and Slaves, to the fame Ufes: And the fame was received, and read the firft Time.

Refolved, That the Bill be read a fecond Time.

Mr *Richard Baker* reported, from the Committee, to whom the Bill to dock the Intail of certain Lands, whereof *Robert Burwell*, Efq; is feized in Tail Male, and for fettling other Lands, of greater Value, to the fame Ufes, was committed, that the Committee had examined the Allegations of the Bill, and found the fame to be true; and that the Committee had gone through the Bill, and made an Amendment thereunto, which they had directed him to report to the Houfe; and he read the Report in his Place, and afterwards delivered the Bill, with the Amendment, in at the Clerk's Table; where the Amendment was twice read, and, upon the Queftion put thereupon, was agreed to by the Houfe.

Ordered, That the Bill, with the Amendment, be ingroffed.

An ingroffed *Bill* to compel Perfons to find Security for Payment of Cofts in certain Cafes, was read the third Time.

Refolved, That the Bill do pafs; and that the Title be, An Act[1] *to compel Perfons to find Security for Payment of Cofts in certain Cafes.*

Ordered, That Mr *Edmund Pendleton* do carry the Bill to the Council, and defire their Concurrence.

Mr *Bland* reported, from the Committee of Propofitions and Grievances, to whom the Bill to amend the Act, intituled An Act[2] *to amend the Act for the better Government of Servants and Slaves*, was committed, that the Committee had gone through the Bill,

and

---

[1] Hening, VIII, p. 386.   [2] Ibid, VI, p. 356.

and made feveral Amendments thereunto, which they had directed him to report to the Houfe; and he read the Report in his Place, and afterwards delivered the Bill, with the Amendments, in at the Clerk's Table; where the Amendments were once read throughout, and then a fecond Time, one by one, and, upon the Queftion feverally put thereupon, were, with an Amendment to one of them, agreed to by the Houfe.

Ordered, That the Bill, with the Amendments, be ingroffed.

Mr *Bland* reported, from the Committee of Propofitions and Grievances, to whom the Bill for appointing feveral new Ferries, and for other Purpofes therein mentioned, was committed, that the Committee had gone through the Bill, and made feveral Amendments thereunto, which they had directed him to report to the Houfe; and he read the Report in his Place, and afterwards delivered the Bill, with the Amendments, in at the Clerk's Table; where the Amendments were once read throughout, and then a fecond Time, one by one, and, upon the Queftion feverally put thereupon, one of them was agreed to, and the reft were difagreed to, by the Houfe.

Ordered, That the Bill, with the Amendment, be ingroffed.

Mr *Bland* reported, from the Committee of Propofitions and Grievances, to whom the Bill to amend an Act, intituled *An Act[1] againft ftealing Hogs*, was committed, that the Committee had gone through the Bill, and made an Amendment thereunto, which they had directed him to report to the Houfe, and he read the Report in his Place; and afterwards delivered the Bill, with the Amendment, in at the Clerk's Table; where the Amendment was twice read, and, upon the Queftion put thereupon, was agreed to by the Houfe.

Ordered, That the Bill, with the Amendment, be ingroffed.

Mr *Harrifon* prefented to the Houfe, according to Order, a Bill for encouraging the making of Wine: And the fame was received, and read the firft Time.

Refolved, That the Bill be read a fecond Time.

The *Order* of the Day being read, for the Houfe to refolve itfelf into a Committee of the whole Houfe, upon the Bill declaring Slaves to be perfonal Eftate, and for other Purpofes therein mentioned;

Refolved, That this Houfe will, Tomorrow, refolve itfelf into a Committee of the whole Houfe, upon the faid Bill.

The *Order* of the Day being read, for the Houfe to refolve itfelf into a Committee of the whole Houfe, to confider further of the Bill to continue and amend the Act, intituled *An Act[2] for amending the Staple of Tobacco, and preventing Frauds in his Majefty's Cuftoms;*

Refolved, That this Houfe will, Tomorrow, refolve itfelf into a Committee of the whole Houfe, to confider further of the faid Bill.

Ordered, That Mr *Dixon* have Leave to be abfent from the Service of this Houfe for the Remainder of the Seffion.

Mr *Blair* reported, from the Committee, to whom the Bill for adding Part of the City of *Williamfburg* to *James City* County, and for other Purpofes therein mentioned, was committed, that the Committee had directed him to report the Bill to the Houfe, without any Amendment; and he delivered the Bill in at the Clerk's Table.

Ordered, That the Bill be ingroffed.

Ordered, That Mr *Lynch* have Leave to be abfent from the Service of this Houfe for the Remainder of this Seffion.

The *Order* of the Day being read for the Houfe to refolve itfelf into a Committee of the whole Houfe, to confider further of the prefent State of the Colony;

Ordered, That the fecond Refolution of the Committee for Courts of Juftice, which upon *Saturday* the Eleventh Day of *November* laft, was reported to the Houfe, and poftponed, be referred to the faid Committee.

Then the Houfe refolved itfelf into the faid Committee.

Mr *Speaker* left the Chair.

Mr *Bland* took the Chair of the Committee.

Mr

[1] Hening, VI, p. 121.   [2] Ibid, IV, p. 247.

Mr *Speaker* refumed the Chair.

Mr *Bland* reported, from the Committee, that they had come to a Refolution, which they had directed him to report to the Houfe; and he read the Report in his Place, and afterwards delivered it in at the Clerk's Table; where the Refolution of the Committee was read, and is as followeth, *viz.*

Refolved, That it is the Opinion of this Committee, that it may be extremely dangerous to the unhappy People who have fettled beyond the Lines fixed on by the Superintendant of *Indian* Affairs, as the Limits between the *Cherokees* and this Colony, to delay any longer entering on a Negotiation for that more extenfive Boundary which his Majefty has approved of; and that an humble Addrefs be prefented to his Excellency the Governor, to defire he would immediately take fuch Steps as are neceffary for entering upon a Treaty with the *Cherokees* for the Lands lying within a Line to be run from the Place where the *North Carolina* Line terminates, in a due Weftern Direction, till it interfects *Holftein* River, and from thence to the Mouth of the *Great Kanhawa;* and that he will be pleafed, when a Ceffion of thofe Lands fhall be obtained, to proceed to mark and eftablifh that Boundary.

The faid *Refolution* being read a fecond Time, was, upon the Queftion put thereupon, agreed to by the Houfe.

Refolved, That an humble addrefs be prefented to his Excellency the Governor, to defire that he will immediately take fuch Steps as are neceffary for entering upon a Treaty with the *Cherokees*, for the Lands lying within a Line, to be run from the Place where the *North Carolina* Line terminates, in a due Weftern Direction, till it interfects *Holftein* River, and from thence to the Mouth of the *Great Kanhawa;* and that he will be pleafed, when a Ceffion of thofe Lands fhall be obtained, to proceed to mark and eftablifh that Boundary.

Ordered, That the faid Addrefs be prefented to his Excellency, by Mr *Bland*, Mr *Richard Henry Lee*, Mr *Edmund Pendleton*, Mr *Treafurer*, and Mr *Henry*.

Mr *Bland* alfo acquainted the Houfe, that he was directed by the Committee to move, that they may have Leave to fit again.

Refolved, That this Houfe will, Tomorrow, refolve itfelf into a Committee of the whole Houfe, to confider further of the Prefent State of the Colony.

The *Order* of the Day being read, for the Houfe to refolve itfelf into a Committee of the whole Houfe, upon the Bill to continue and amend the Act for the better regulating and difciplining the Militia;

Refolved, That this Houfe will, Tomorrow, refolve itfelf into a Committee of the whole Houfe, upon the faid Bill.

The other *Order* of the Day being read;

Ordered, That the Call of the Houfe be further adjourned till Tomorrow.

And then the Houfe adjourned till Tomorrow Morning Eleven of the Clock.

Saturday, the 16th of June, 10 Geo. III. 1770.

MR *Bland* prefented to the Houfe, according to Order, a Bill to regulate the Inoculation of the Small-Pox within this Colony; and the fame was received, and read the firft Time.

Refolved, That the Bill be read a fecond Time.

Mr *Mercer* prefented to the Houfe, according to Order, a Bill for better regulating the Election of Veftries; and the fame was received, and read the firft Time.

Refolved, That the Bill be read a fecond Time.

The Houfe was moved, that the Order, made upon *Friday*, the Twenty-fifth Day of *May* laft, that Leave be given to bring in a Bill for the more fpeedy Adminiftration of Juftice in this Colony, might be read.

And the fame being read accordingly;

Ordered, That the faid Order be difcharged.

The

The Houfe was moved, that the Order, made upon *Wednefday*, the Sixth Day of this Inftant *June*, that Leave be given to bring in a Bill for the better Adminiftration of Juftice in the County Courts, might be read.

And the fame being read accordingly;

Ordered, That the faid Order be difcharged.

Mr *Bland* reported to the Houfe, that their Addrefs of Yefterday, that the Governor would immediately take fuch Steps as are neceffary for entering upon a Treaty with the *Cherokees*, for the Lands lying within a Line to be run from the Place, where the *North Carolina* Line Terminates, in a due Weftern Direction, till it interfects *Holftein* River, and from thence to the Mouth of the *Great Kanhawa;* and that he would be pleafed when a Ceffion of thofe Lands fhall be obtained, to proceed to mark and eftablifh that Boundary, had been prefented to his Excellency; and that his Excellency had directed him to acquaint this Houfe, that he would as immediately as poffible endeavor to do exactly what the Houfe defired.

Mr *Bland* reported from the Committee of Propofitions and Grievances, to whom the Bill to repeal an Act made in the 22nd Year of his late Majefty's Reign, intituled *An Act concerning Strays;* and to eftablifh a more effectual method to prevent Frauds committed by Perfons taking up Strays, was committed, that the Committee had gone through the Bill, and made feveral Amendments thereunto, which they had directed him to report to the Houfe; and he read the Report in his Place; and afterwards delivered the Bill, with the Amendments, in at the Clerk's Table; where the Amendments were once read throughout, and then a fecond Time, one by one, and, upon the Queftion feverally put thereupon, were agreed to by the Houfe.

Ordered, That the Bill, with the Amendments, be engroffed.

Mr *Archibald Cary* reported, from the Committee of Public Claims, that the Committee had had under their Confideration feveral Petitions to them referred, and had come to feveral Refolutions thereupon, which they had directed him to report to the Houfe; and he read the Report in his Place, and afterwards delivered it in at the Clerk's Table; where the Refolutions of the Committee were read, and are as followeth, *viz.*

Refolved, That it is the Opinion of this Committee, that the petition of *John Tayloe,* Efq; to be allowed for his Negro Man Slave *Toby,* who was Froft bitten in Gaol, and died, as fet forth in the faid Petition, is reafonable; and that he ought to be allowed the Sum of Seventy Pounds for the faid Slave.

Refolved, That it is the Opinion of this Committee, that the Petition of *Ezekiel Young* and *Jofeph Feddeman,* Infpectors at *Guilford* Warehoufe, to be allowed for Picking the Tobacco damaged in the faid Warehoufe by the late Guft, and reprizing Forty-four Hogfheads, and finding Nails, is reafonable; and that the faid *Ezekiel Young,* who did the Services and furnifhed the Nails, ought to be allowed the Sum of Nine Pounds and Fifteen Shillings for the fame.

Refolved, That it is the Opinion of this Committee, that the Petition of *John Earle* for an Allowance, as a Voluntier from this Colony, under Col. *Bouquet,* on an Expedition againft the *Indian* Towns is reafonable; and that he ought to be allowed by the Public, the Sum of Forty Pounds, as an acknowledgement of his Merit, and the extraordinary Service he rendered to this Colony, by his gallant Behaviour on the faid Expedition.

Refolved, That it is the Opinion of this Committee, that the Petition of *Jofeph Mitchell* to be allowed by the Public, for a Sum of Money of which he was robbed by fome Highwaymen, and for his Trouble and Expence in apprehending the Offenders, be rejected.

Refolved, That it is the Opinion of this Committee, that the Petition of *Rachel Spencer,* to be allowed for Diet, Liquors, and Lodging, furnifhed divers Recruits raifed for the *Virginia* Regiment, in the Years 1760 and 1762, be rejected; it appearing, that the Money for the Subfiftence of the Recruits has been received by *James Gun* and *Reuben Vafs,* the Officers who enlifted them.

The faid *Refolutions* being feverally read a fecond Time, were, upon the Queftion feverally put thereupon, agreed to by the Houfe.

M^r

Mr *Archibald Cary* prefented to the Houfe, according to Order, a Bill to dock the Intail of certain Lands whereof *Richard Johnfon*, Gentleman, is feized, and for fettling other Lands and Slaves to the fame Ufes; and the fame was received, and read the firft Time.

Refolved, That the Bill be read a fecond Time.

Mr *Bland* reported from the Committee of propofitions and Grievances, that the Committee had had under their Confideration feveral petitions to them referred, and had come to feveral Refolutions thereupon, which they had directed him to report to the Houfe; and he read the Report in his Place, and afterwards delivered it in at the Clerk's Table; where the Refolutions of the Committee were read, and are as followeth, *viz.* 289

Refolved, That it is the Opinion of this Committee, that the Petition of *David Barton*, praying an adequate Reward for difcovering a cure for Cancers, be rejected.

Refolved, That it is the Opinion of this Committee, that the Petition of divers Inhabitants of *Saint Anne's* Parifh, in the County of *Albemarle*, praying a Divifion of the faid Parifh, by a Line running with the Road from the old to the new Court-Houfe, is reafonable.

The firft *Refolution* of the Committee being read a fecond Time, was, upon the Queftion put thereupon, agreed to by the Houfe.

The fubfequent *Refolution* of the Committee being read a fecond Time;

A *Motion* was made, and the Queftion being put, that the Houfe do agree with the Committee in the faid Refolution;

It paffed in the Negative.

Refolved, That the Petition of divers Inhabitants of *Saint Anne's* Parifh, in the County of *Albemarle*, praying a Divifion of the faid Parifh, by a Line running with the Road, from the old to the new Court-Houfe, be rejected.

An engroffed *Bill* for appointing Commiffioners, to meet with Commiffioners, who are or may be appointed by the Legiflatures of the neighbouring Colonies, to form and agree upon a general Plan for the regulation of the *Indian* Trade, was read the third Time.

Refolved, That the Bill do pafs; and that the Title be, *An Act[1] for appointing Commiffioners, to meet with Commiffioners, who are or may be appointed by the Legiflatures of the neighbouring Colonies, to form and agree upon a general Plan for the regulation of the* Indian *Trade.*

Ordered, That Mr *Bland* do carry the Bill to the Council, and defire their Concurrence.

The Houfe, according to Order, refolved itfelf into a Committee of the whole Houfe, to confider further of the prefent State of the Colony.

Mr *Speaker* left the Chair.

Mr *Bland* took the Chair of the Committee.

Mr *Speaker* refumed the Chair.

Mr *Bland* reported from the Committee, that they had gone through the Matters to them referred, and had come to feveral Refolutions, which they had directed him to report to the Houfe; and he read the Report in his Place, and afterwards delivered it in at the Clerk's Table; where the Refolutions of the Committee were read, and are as followeth, *viz.*

Refolved, That it is the Opinion of this Committee, that the feveral Perfons who have fettled on Lands in this Colony, lying on the Waters of the *Miffiffippi* River, for which his Majefty's Patents have been obtained, and are Refident thereon, have not forfeited his Majefty's Protection, but are intitled to all fuch Privileges, Immunities, and Protection, as his Majefty's other good Subjects of this Colony do enjoy.

Refolved, That it is the Opinion of this Committee, that the Committee of Correfpondence ought to be directed to write to *Edward Montagu*, Efq; Agent for this Colony, in juftification of the Memorial prefented by this Houfe, in the former Part of this Seffion

---

[1] Hening, VIII. p. 367.

fion, to his Excellency Lord *Botetourt*, and therein to give a full Refutation of the Obfervations made on it by *John Stuart*, Efq; Superintendent of *Indian* Affairs.

The firft *Refolution* of the Committee being read a fecond Time, was, upon the Queftion put thereupon, agreed to by the Houfe.

The fubfequent *Refolution* of the Committee being read a fecond Time, the Amendment following was propofed to be made thereunto, *viz.* to add at the End thereof thefe Words, *viz.* '*And that they alfo take Notice of fome Parts of the faid Mr Stuart's Speeches to the* Indians, *at the Conferences on that Subject, which appear to be very exceptionable and unwarrantable.*'

240 And the faid *Amendment* was, upon the Queftion put thereupon, agreed to by the Houfe.

Refolved, That the Houfe doth agree with the Committee in the faid Refolution, fo amended, that the Committee of Correfpondence ought to be directed to write to *Edward Montagu*, Efq; Agent for this Colony, in juftification of the Memorial prefented by this Houfe, in the former Part of this Seffion, to his Excellency Lord *Botetourt*, and therein to give a full Refutation of the Obfervations made on it by *John Stuart*, Efq; Superintendant of *Indian* Affairs; and that they alfo take Notice of fome Parts of the faid Mr *Stuart's* Speeches to the *Indians* at the Conferences on that Subject, which appear to be very exceptionable and unwarrantable.

Ordered, That the Committee of Correfpondence do Write to *Edward Montagu*, Efq; Agent for this Colony, purfuant to the faid Refolution.

The *Order* of the Day being read for the Houfe to refolve itfelf into a Committee of the whole Houfe to confider further of the Bill to continue and amend the Act, intituled *An Act¹ for amending the Staple of Tobacco, and preventing Frauds in his Majefty's Cuftoms.*

Refolved, That this Houfe will, upon *Tuefday* next, refolve itfelf into a Committee of the whole Houfe to confider further of the faid Bill.

Ordered, That Mr *Jofeph Cabell* have Leave to be abfent from the Service of this Houfe for the Remainder of this Seffion.

The Houfe according to Order, refolved itfelf into a Committee of the whole Houfe, upon the Bill to continue and amend the Act for the better regulating and difciplining the Militia.

Mr *Speaker* left the Chair.

Mr *Bland* took the Chair of the Committee.

Mr *Speaker* refumed the Chair.

Mr *Bland* reported from the Committee, that they had gone through the Bill, and made feveral Amendments thereunto, which they had directed him to report to the Houfe, and he read the Report in his Place, and afterwards delivered the Bill, with the Amendments, in at the Clerk's Table; where the Amendments were once read throughout, and then a fecond Time, one by one, and, upon the Queftion feverally put thereupon, were, with Amendments, to fome of them, agreed to by the Houfe.

Ordered, That the Bill, with the Amendments, be ingroffed.

Ordered, That Mr *Read* have Leave to be abfent from the Service of this Houfe for the Remainder of this Seffion.

The *Order* of the Day being read, for the Houfe to refolve itfelf into a Committee of the whole Houfe, upon the Bill declaring Slaves to be perfonal Eftate, and for other Purpofes therein mentioned;

Refolved, That this Houfe will upon *Tuefday* next, refolve itfelf into a Committee of the whole Houfe upon the faid Bill.

The other *Order* of the Day being read;

Ordered, That the Call of the Houfe be further adjourned till *Tuefday* next.

And then the Houfe adjourned till Monday Morning next, Eleven of the Clock.

Monday

---

¹ Hening, IV. p. 247.

Monday, the 18th of June, 10 Geo. III. 1770.

MR *Treasurer* reported, from the Committee for Religion, to whom it was [241] referred to state an Account of the Expences of the traveling and Attendance of the Witnesses, who were examined, as well before the said Committee, touching the Petition of sundry Freeholders and Inhabitants of the Parish of *Overwharton*, in the County of *Stafford*, complaining of sundry illegal and unwarrantable Proceedings of the Vestry of the said Parish, and praying that the said Vestry may be dissolved, as before the Committee of propositions and Grievances, to whom a like Petition, in the Year 1767, was referred, that the Committee had stated an Account of the said Expences accordingly, which they had directed him to report, together with their Opinion thereupon, to the House; and he read the Report in his Place, and afterwards delivered it in at the Clerk's Table; where the Account and Resolution of the Committee were read, and are as followeth, *viz.*

	Witnesses.	Attendance.	Distance.	Total Tobacco.	Ferriage.		
1767	*William Garrett,*	2 Days	110 Miles	450	0	3	0
1770	The same,	2	110	450	0	3	0
	John Mauzy,	2	115	465	0	3	0
	Bailey Washington,	2	128	504	0	4	0
	Thomas Mountjoy,	2	115	465	0	3	3
	Yelverton Peyton,	2	122	486	0	3	0
	Humphrey Gaines,	2	115	465	0	3	0
	William Adie,	2	124	492	0	3	0
	Andrew Edwards,	2	110	450	0	3	0
	Joseph Thatcher,	2	113	459	0	3	0
				4686	1	11	3

Resolved, That it is the Opinion of this Committee, that the said Expences ought to be defrayed by the several Persons who subscribed the said Petitions.

The said *Resolution* being read a second Time, was, upon the Question put thereupon, agreed to by the House.

Ordered, That a Bill be brought in pursuant to the said Resolution; and that the said Committee do prepare and bring in the same.

Mr *Treasurer* reported, from the Committee for Religion, that the Committee had had under their Consideration several Petitions to them referred, and had come to several Resolutions thereupon, which they had directed him to report to the House; and he read the Report in his Place, and afterwards delivered it in at the Clerk's Table; where the Resolutions of the Committee were read, and are as followeth, *viz.*

Resolved, That it is the Opinion of this Committee, that the Petitions of sundry Inhabitants of the Parish of *Overwharton*, in the County of *Stafford*, praying that the Vestry of the said Parish may be dissolved, is reasonable.

Resolved, That it is the Opinion of this Committee, that the Petition of sundry Inhabitants of the parish of *Cameron* in the County of *Loudoun*, praying a Division of the said Parish, is reasonable.

Resolved, That it is the Opinion of this Committee, that the Petition of sundry Inhabitants of the said Parish, in Opposition thereto, be rejected.

The said *Resolutions* being severally read a second Time, were, upon the Question severally put thereupon, agreed to by the House.

Ordered, That the first of the said Resolutions do lie upon the Table, till the second Reading of the Bill for dissolving the Vestry of the Parish of *Hungars*, in the County of *Northampton.*

Mr *Treasurer* presented to the House, according to Order, a Bill for dividing the [242] Parish of *Frederick*, in the County of *Frederick*, into three distinct Parishes; and the same was received, and read the first Time.

Resolved

Resolved, That the Bill be read a second Time.

Resolved, That the Bill be now read a second Time.

The *Bill* was accordingly read a second Time.

Resolved, That the Bill be committed to Mr *Mercer*, Mr *Richard Henry Lee*, Mr. *Washington*, Mr *Wood*, Mr *Rutherford*, and Mr *Peyton*.

Ordered, That it be an Instruction to the said Committee, that they have Power to receive a Clause or Clauses, pursuant to the second Resolution of the Committee for Religion, which was this Day agreed to by the House, for dividing the Parish of *Cameron*, in the County of *Loudoun*.

Resolved, That the Treasurer pay One Hundred Pounds to each of the Commissioners appointed, in Behalf of this Colony, to meet with Commissioners, who are, or may be appointed by the Legislatures of the neighbouring Colonies, to form and agree upon a general Plan for the Regulation of the *Indian* Trade, towards defraying the Expences that may attend their Negotiation.

Ordered, That Mr *Archibald Cary* do carry the Resolution to the Council, and desire their Concurrence.

The House was moved, that the Order made upon *Saturday* the 11th Day of *November* last, that it be an Instruction to the Committee for Religion, that they prepare and bring in a Bill for granting Toleration to his Majesty's Subjects, being Protestant Dissenters, might be read.

And the same being read accordingly;

Ordered, That the said Order be discharged.

A *Bill* for better regulating the Election of Vestries was read a second Time.

Resolved, That the Bill be committed.

Resolved, That the Bill be committed to a Committee of the whole House.

Resolved, That this House will now resolve itself into a Committee of the whole House, upon the said Bill.

The House accordingly resolved itself into the said Committee.

Mr *Speaker* left the Chair.

Mr *Bland* took the Chair of the Committee.

Mr *Speaker*, resumed the Chair.

Mr *Bland* reported from the Committee, that they had gone through the Bill, and made an Amendment thereunto, which they had directed thereunto, which they had directed him to report to the House; and he read the Report in his Place, and afterwards delivered the Bill, with the Amendment, in at the Clerk's Table; where the Amendment was read.

Ordered, That the said Amendment be taken into Consideration Tomorrow.

The House was moved, that the second Resolution of the Committee for Courts of Justice, which upon *Saturday* the 11th Day of *November* last, was reported to the House, and postponed, might be read.

And the same was read Accordingly, and is as followeth, *viz.*

243 *Resolved*, That it is the Opinion of this Committee, that the Act of Assembly made in the 5th Year of his present Majesty's Reign, intituled *An Act[1] for continuing the Act for appointing an Agent, and two other Acts, therein mentioned*, which will expire on the 14th Day of *April*, 1771, ought to be further continued.

And a *Motion* was made, and the Question being put, that the House do agree with the Committee in the said Resolution;

It passed in the Negative.

Resolved, That the Act of Assembly, made in the 5th Year of his present Majesty's Reign, intituled *An Act for continuing the Act for appointing an Agent, and two other Acts, therein mentioned*, which will expire on the 14th Day of *April* 1771, ought not to be further continued.

And then the House adjourned till Tomorrow Morning Eleven of the Clock.

𝕿𝖚𝖊𝖘𝖉𝖆𝖞

---

1 Hening, VIII p. 113.

Tuesday, the 19th of June, 10 Geo. III. 1770.

A Bill for diffolving the Veftry of the Parifh of *Hungar's*, in the County of *North_ampton*, was read a fecond Time.

Refolved, That the Bill be committed to Mr *Eyre* and Mr *Alexander*.

Ordered, That it be an Inftruction to the faid Committee, that they have Power to receive a Claufe or Claufes purfuant to the firft Refolution of the Committee for Religion, which was Yefterday agreed to by the Houfe; and alfo to impower the Veftry to be elected for the Parifh of *Overwharton*, in the County of *Stafford*, to levy and affefs on the Tithable Perfons of the faid Parifh, all fuch Sums of Money, and Quantities of Tobacco, as the prefent Veftry of the faid Parifh, ought to have levied and affeffed in the two laft Years.

Mr *Bland* prefented to the Houfe, according to Order, a Bill to confirm an Agreement made by *Thomas Talbutt*, with the Court of *Norfolk* County; and the fame was received, and read the firft Time.

Refolved, That the Bill be read a fecond Time.

The Houfe, according to Order, refolved itfelf into a Committee of the whole Houfe, to confider further of the Bill to continue and amend the Act, intituled *An Act[1] for amending the Staple of Tobacco, and preventing Frauds in his Majefty's Cuftoms.*

Mr *Speaker* left the Chair.

Mr *Bland* took the Chair of the Committee.

Mr *Speaker* refumed the Chair.

Mr *Bland* reported from the Committee, that they had made a further Progrefs in the Bill; and that he was directed by the Committee to move that they may have Leave to fit again.

Refolved, That this Houfe will, Tomorrow, refolve itfelf into a Committee of the whole Houfe, to confider further of the faid Bill.

Mr *Bland* reported, from the Committee of Propofitions and Grievances, that the Committee had had under their Confideration feveral Petitions to them referred, and had come to feveral Refolutions thereupon, which they had directed him to report to the Houfe; and he read the Report in his Place, and afterwards delivered it in at the Clerk's Table; where the Refolutions of the Committee were read, and are as followeth, *viz.*

Refolved, That it is the Opinion of this Committee, that the petitions of divers Inhabitants of the Counties of *Stafford*, *King George*, and *Weftmoreland*, for reforming the Boundaries of the faid Counties refpectively, be referred to the Confideration of the next Seffion of Affembly.

Refolved, That it is the Opinion of this Committee, that the Petitions of divers In- 244 habitants of the Counties of *Richmond* and *Weftmoreland*, in Oppofition thereto, be referred to the Confideration of the next Seffion of Affembly.

The faid *Refolutions* being feverally read a fecond Time, were, upon the Queftion feverally put thereupon, agreed to by the Houfe.

Ordered, That Mr *Richard Henry Lee*, and Mr *Robert Munford*, of *Amelia*, have Leave to be abfent from the Service of this Houfe for the Remainder of this Seffion.

The *Order* of the Day being read, for the Houfe to refolve itfelf into a Committee of the whole Houfe, upon the Bill for the Infpection of Hemp;

Refolved, That this Houfe will, upon *Thurfday* next, refolve itfelf into a Committee of the whole Houfe, upon the faid Bill.

The *Order* of the Day being read, for the Houfe to refolve itfelf into a Committee of the whole Houfe, upon the Bill to make Provifion for the Support and Maintenance of Ideots, Lunatics, and other Perfons of unfound Minds;

Refolved, That this Houfe will, upon *Thurfday* next, refolve itfelf into a Committee of the whole Houfe upon the faid Bill.

The

---

[1] Hening, IV. p. 247.

The *Order* of the Day being read for the Houfe to refolve itfelf into a Committee of the whole Houfe, upon the Bill declaring Slaves to be perfonal Eftate; and for other Purpofes therein mentioned;

Refolved, That this Houfe will, upon *Thurfday* next, refolve itfelf into a Committee of the whole Houfe, upon the faid Bill.

The *Order* of the Day being read, for the Houfe to take into Confideration the Amendment made by the Committee of the whole Houfe, to the Bill for regulating the Election of Veftries;

Ordered, That the Confideration of the faid Amendment be adjourned till *Thurfday* next.

The other *Order* of the Day being read;

Ordered, That the Call of the Houfe be further adjourned till *Thurfday* next.

And then the Houfe adjourned till Tomorrow Morning Ten of the Clock.

Wednesday, the 20th of June, 10 Geo. III. 1770.

MR *Bland* reported, from the Committee of Propofitions and Grievances, to whom the Bill to explain and amend the Act, intituled *An Act[1] to confirm the Charter of the Borough of* Norfolk, *and for enlarging the Jurifdiction of the Court of Huftings, in the City of* Williamfburg, was committed, that the Committee had gone through the Bill, and made feveral Amendments thereunto, which they had directed him to report to the Houfe; and he read the Report in his Place, and afterwards delivered the Bill, with the Amendments, in at the Clerk's Table; where the Amendments were once read throughout, and then a fecond Time, one by one, and, upon the Queftion feverally put thereupon, were agreed to by the Houfe.

Ordered, That the Bill, with the Amendments, be ingroffed.

A *Meffage* from the Council by Mr *Hubard:*

245

Mr *Speaker*,

The Council have agreed to the Bill, *intituled* An Act[2] for regulating the Election of Burgeffes, for declaring their Privileges and Allowances, and for fixing the Rights of Electors, *without any Amendment: And alfo,*

The Council have agreed to the Bill, *intituled* An Act[3] to fufpend the Execution of an Act, intituled An Act to amend an Act, intituled an Act for the Infpection of Pork, Beef, Flour, Tar, Pitch, and Turpentine, *without any Amendment: And alfo,*

The Council have agreed to the Bill, *intituled* An Act[4] to continue an Act, intituled An Act for regulating the Practice of Attornies, *without any Amendment: And alfo,*

The Council have agreed to the Bill, *intituled* An Act[5] for appointing Commiffioners to meet with Commiffioners who are or may be appointed by the Legiflatures of the neighbouring Colonies, to form and agree upon a general Plan for the Regulation of the *Indian* Trade, *without any Amendment: And alfo,*

The Council have agreed to the Bill, *intituled* An Act[6] to compel Perfons to find Security for Payment of Cofts in certain Cafes, *without any Amendment: And alfo,*

The Council have agreed to the Bill, *intituled* An Act[7] to appoint Truftees, in the Room of thofe who are dead for the *Pamunkey* Indians, and with further Power to hear and determine Controverfies among them, *without any Amendment: And alfo,*

The Council have agreed to the Bill, *intituled* An Act[8] to impower the Veftry of *Briftol* Parifh, in the Counties of *Dinwiddie* and *Prince George*, to sell their Glebe, *without any Amendment: And alfo,*

The Council have agreed to the Bill, *intituled* An Act[9] to repeal an Act for increafing

1 Hening, IV, p. 541.   2 Ibid, VIII, p. 305.   3 Ibid, VIII, p. 366.   4 Ibid, VIII, p. 385.
5 Ibid, VIII, p. 367.   6 Ibid, VIII, p. 386.   7 Ibid, VIII, p. 433.   8 Ibid, VIII, p. 431.
9 Ibid, VIII' p. 430.

ing the Salary of the Minifter of the Parifh of *Frederick*, in the County of *Frederick*, *without any Amendment: And also,*

The Council have agreed to the Bill, *intituled* An Act[1] to dock the Intail of certain Lands and Slaves, whereof *John Page*, Efq; is feized, and for fettling other Lands of greater Value to the fame Ufes, *without any Amendment: And alfo,*

The Council have agreed to the Bill, *intituled* An Act[2] to dock the Intail of Two Thouf-and Eight Hundred Acres of Land, in the County of *Brunfwick*, whereof *Armiftead Lightfoot* is feized in Fee Tail, and vefting the fame in Truftees, to be fold, for certain Purpofes therein mentioned, *without any Amendment: And alfo,*

The Council have agreed to the Bill, *intituled* An Act[3] to veft certain Lands in *David Meade*, in Fee Simple, whereof the faid *David* and *Sarah* his wife are feized, in Right of the faid *Sarah*, in Fee Tail, and for fettling other Lands in Lieu thereof, *without any Amendment: And alfo,*

The Council have agreed to the Bill, *intituled* An Act[4] to veft certain intailed Lands whereof *William* and *John Armiftead*, Gentlemen, are feized, in Truftees, to be fold for Payment of the Debts due from the Eftate of their Father, *without any Amendment: And alfo,*

The Council have agreed to the Bill *intituled* An Act[5] to veft certain intailed Lands therein mentioned in *George Brooke*, Gentleman, in Fee Simple, and for fettling other Lands, of greater Value, in Lieu thereof, *without any Amendment: And alfo,*

The Council have agreed to the Refolve *for paying One Hundred Pounds to each of the Commiffioners for regulating the Indian Trade: And alfo,*

The Council have agreed to the Refolve *for paying Forty Pounds Sterling, and Ten Pounds and Ten Shillings Sterling, for purchafing two Iron Chefts for fecuring the Public Money in the Treafury: And alfo,*

The Council have agreed to the Bill, *intituled* An Act[6] for encouraging the making Hemp *with fome Amendments, to which Amendments the Council defire the Concurrence of this Houfe: And alfo,*

The Council have agreed to the Bill, *intituled* An Act[7] for altering the Court Days of feveral Counties therein mentioned, *with an Amendment, to which Amendment the Council defire the Concurrence of this Houfe: And alfo,*

The Council have agreed to the Bill, *intituled* An Act[8] for continuing and amending an Act, intituled An Act for reviving and amending the Acts for allowing Fairs to be kept in the Towns of *Frederickfburg* and *Richmond*, and for enlarging the Town of *Frederickfburg, with an Amendment, to which Amendment the Council defire the Concurrence of this Houfe: And alfo,*

The Council have agreed to the Bill, *intituled* An Act[9] to dock the Intail of Five Hundred and Fifty Acres of Land, in the County of *Gloucefter*, whereof *Sarah*, the Wife of *John Rootes*, Gentleman, is feized, and for vefting the fame in Truftees, for the Purpofes therein mentioned, *with fome Amendments, to which Amendments the Council defire the Concurrence of this Houfe.*

And then the Meffenger withdrew.

M[r] *Eyre* reported from the Committee, to whom the Bill for diffolving the Veftry of the Parifh of *Hungars*, in the County of *Northampton*, was committed, that the Committee had gone through the Bill, and made feveral Amendments thereunto, which they had directed him to report to the Houfe; and he read the Report in his Place, and afterwards delivered the Bill, with the Amendments, in at the Clerk's Table; where the Amendments were once read throughout, and then a fecond Time, one by one, and, upon the Queftion feverally put thereupon, were agreed to by the Houfe.

Ordered, That the Bill, with the Amendments, be ingroffed.

M[r] *Speaker* acquainted the Houfe, that the Governor had delivered to him, and
desired

[1] Hening, VIII, p. 445.   [2] Ibid, VIII, p. 457.   [3] Ibid, VIII, p. 470.   [4] Ibid. VIII, p. 487.
[5] Ibid, VIII, p. 474.   [6] Ibid, VIII, p. 363.   [7] Ibid, VIII, p. 400.   [8] Ibid, VIII, p. 418.
[9] Ibid, VIII, p. 483.

defired him to lay before the Houfe, an Act[1] of the Parliament of *Great-Britain*, made in this prefent Year of his Majefty's Reign, intituled *An Act[1] to repeal fo much of an Act made in the 7th Year of his prefent Majefty's Reign, intituled " An Act[2] for granting certain Duties in the* Britifh *Colonies and Plantations in* America; *for allowing a Drawback of the Duties of Cuftoms upon the Exportation, from this Kingdom, of Coffee and Cocoa Nuts of the Produce of the faid Colonies or Plantations; for difcontinuing the Drawbacks payable on China Earthen Ware exported to* America; *and for more effectually preventing the clandeftine running of Goods in the faid Colonies and Plantations,"* as relates *to the Duties upon Glafs, Red Lead, White Lead, Painters Colours, Paper, Pafte-Boards, Mill-Boards and Scale-Boards, of the Produce or Manufacture of* Great-Britain, *imported into any of his Majefty's Colonies in* America; *and alfo to the difcontinuing the Drawbacks payable on China Earthen-Ware exported to* America; *and for regulating the Exportation thereof;* and he delivered the Act in at the Clerk's Table.

Ordered, That the faid Act do lie upon the Table, to be perufed by the Members of the Houfe.

The Houfe proceeded to take into Confideration the Amendments made by the Council to the Bill, intituled, *An Act for encouraging the making Hemp.*

And the faid *Amendments* were read, and are as followeth, *viz.*

Line 9. After 'Peace' leave out '*or Conftable.*'

Line 12. After '*Juftice*' leave out '*or Conftable.*'

The faid *Amendments* being feverally read a fecond Time, were, upon the Queftion feverally put thereupon, difagreed to by the Houfe.

Ordered, That a Meffage be fent to the Council to inform them, that this Houfe cannot agree to the Amendments by them propofed to the faid Bill, and defire that they will pafs the fame without the Amendments; and that Mr *Harrifon* do carry the faid Meffage.

Ordered, That Mr *Wafhington*, Mr *Hite*, and Mr *Macon*, have Leave to be abfent from the Service of this Houfe for the Remainder of this Seffion.

The Houfe proceeded to take into Confideration the Amendment made by the Council to the Bill, intituled *An Act[3] for altering the Court Days of feveral Counties therein mentioned.*

And the faid *Amendment* was read, and is as followeth, *viz.*

Line 6. Leave out '*fourth*' and infert '*laft*' inftead thereof.

The faid *Amendment* being read a fecond Time, was, upon the Queftion put thereupon, agreed to by the Houfe.

Ordered, That Mr *Mercer* do carry the Bill to the Council, and acquaint them, that this Houfe hath agreed to the Amendment made by them.

The Houfe proceeded to take into Confideration the Amendment made by the Council to the Bill, intituled *An Act[4] for continuing and amending an Act, intituled An Act for reviving and amending the Acts for allowing Fairs to be kept in the Towns of* Frederickfburg *and* Richmond, *and for enlarging the Town of* Frederickfburg.

And the faid *Amendment* was read, and is as followeth, *viz.*

To the End of the Bill, add '*Provided always, that nothing herein contained fhall be conftrued, deemed or taken to derogate from, alter or infringe the Royal Power, and Prerogative of his Majefty, his Heirs and Succeffors, of granting to any Perfon or Perfons, Body Politic or Corporate, the Privilege of holding Fairs or Markets, in any fuch Manner as he or they, by his or their Royal Letters Patent, or by his or their Inftructions to the Governor or Commander in Chief of this Dominion, for the Time being, fhall think fit."*

The faid *Amendment* being read a fecond Time, was, upon the Queftion put thereupon, agreed to by the Houfe.

Ordered, That Mr *Mercer* do carry the Bill to the Council, and acquaint them, that this Houfe doth agree to the Amendment made by them.

The Houfe proceeded to take into Confideration the Amendments made by the
Council

---

1 Statutes at Large, *Great Britain*, Vol. VII, p. 62.   2 Ibid, Vol. VI, p. 768.   3 Hening, VIII, p. 400.   4 Ibid, VIII, p. 418.

Council to the Bill, intituled *An Act¹ to dock the Intail of Five Hundred and Fifty Acres of Land, in the County of* Gloucester, *whereof* Sarah, *the Wife of* John Rootes, Gentleman, *is seized, and for vesting the same in Trustees for the Purposes therein mentioned.*

And the said *Amendments* were read, and are as followeth, *viz.*

Page 2, Line 9. Leave out "*to the Use of the said John Rootes, during the joint Lives of him and the said Sarah his Wife, and to the longest Liver of the said John and Sarah, for his or her Life, and from and after the Death of the Survivor of them, then the said Slaves and their Increase,*" and insert "*to the sole and separate Use of the said Sarah, for and during her natural Life, and from and after the Death of the said Sarah to the Use of the said John Rootes, during his Life, and after the Death of the longest Liver of them, then the said Slaves and their Increase,*" instead thereof.

Line 16. Leave out "*Provided nevertheless, that the Slaves so annexed, and their future Increase, shall be liable to be taken in Execution, and sold for satisfying and paying the just Debts of the Tenant in Tail, for the Time being, in the same Manner as other intailed Slaves are liable; and shall moreover be subject to the Payment of the Debts of the said John Rootes, for and during his Life and Interest in the said Slaves, in the same Manner as the said Land would have been subject in Case this Act had never been made.*"

The said *Amendments* being severally read a second Time, were, upon the Question severally put thereupon, disagreed to by the House.

Ordered, That a Message be sent to the Council to inform them, that this House cannot agree to the Amendments by them proposed to the said Bill, and desire that they will pass the same without the Amendments; and that Mr *Edmund Pendleton* do carry the said Message.

The *Order* of the Day being read;

The House resolved itself into a Committee of the whole House, to consider further of the Bill to continue and amend the Act, intituled *An Act² for amending the Staple of Tobacco, and preventing Frauds in his Majesty's Customs.*

Mr *Speaker* left the Chair.

Mr *Bland* took the Chair of the Committee.

Mr *Speaker* resumed the Chair.

Mr *Bland* reported from the Committee, that they had made a further Progress in the Bill; and that he was directed by the Committee to move that they may have leave to sit again.

Resolved, That this House will, Tomorrow, resolve itself into a Committee of the whole House, to consider further of the said Bill.

And then the House adjourned till Tomorrow Morning Ten of the Clock.

Thursday, the 21st of June, 10 Geo. III. 1770.

MR *Archibald Cary* reported, from the Committee of Public Claims, that the Committee had had under their Consideration several Claims to them referred, and had come to several Resolutions thereupon, which they had directed him to report to the House; and he read the Report in his Place, and afterwards delivered it in at the Clerk's Table; where the Resolutions of the Committee were read, and are as followeth, *viz.* 248

Resolved, That it is the Opinion of this Committee, that the Claim of *Matthew Anderson*, to be allowed for 151 Days Pay, as a Serjeant in Captain *John Hickman's* Company, in 1759, be rejected, it appearing that it was the general Custom of the Officers to draw the whole Pay for their Men.

Resolved, That it is the Opinion of this Committee, that the Claim of *George Boyd*, to be allowed for Work done on *Mayo* Fort, be rejected, for want of Proof.

Resolved, That it is the Opinion of this Committee, that the Claim of *Joshua Powell*, to be allowed for 25 Days Pay as Ensign under Captain *John Dickinson*, and serving as a Carpenter at the building of *Black Water* Fort 105 Days, in the Year 1759, be rejected, for want of Proof.

Resolved

---

¹ Hening, VIII, p. 483.   ² Ibid, IV, p. 247.

Refolved, That it is the Opinion of this Committee, that the Claim of *John Hickman,* to be allowed for Ferriages of Criminals, in the Year 1767, be rejected.

The faid *Refolutions* being feverally read a fecond Time, were, upon the Queftion feverally put thereupon, agreed to by the Houfe.

The Houfe was moved that the Act of Parliament of *Great-Britain,* made in the 9th Year of the Reign of his prefent Majefty, intituled *An Act[1] to repeal fo much of an Act made in the 7th Year of his prefent Majefty's Reign, intituled An Act[2] for granting certain Duties in the Britifh Colonies and Plantations in America; for allowing a Draw-back of the Duties of Cuftoms upon the Exportation, from this Kingdom, of Coffee and Cocoa Nuts of the Produce of the faid Colonies or Plantations; for difcontinuing the Draw-backs payable on China Earthen-Ware exported to America; and for more effectually pre-venting the Clandeftine running of Goods in the faid Colonies and Plantations, as relates to the Duties upon Glafs, Red Lead, White Lead, Painters Colours, Paper, Pafte-Boards, Mill-Boards, and Scale Boards, of the Produce or Manufacture of Great-Britain, imported into any of his Majefty's Colonies in America; and alfo to the difcontinuing the Draw-backs payable on China Earthen-Ware exported to America; and for regulating the Ex-portation thereof;* might be read.

And the fame being read accordingly;

Refolved, Nemine Contradicente, That a moft humble and dutiful Petition be pre-fented to his Majefty, intreating that his Majefty will be gracioufly pleafed to take into his Royal Confideration the Grievances under which his faithful Subjects of *Virginia* still continue to labour, by having their Property taken from them by Laws to which they have never confented, either perfonally, or by their Reprefentatives; by being fubjected to the Decifion of diftant and arbitrary Courts of Admiralty, where Trial by Jury, the fureft Support of Property, is denied; both which Innovations in the Con-ftitution, tend immediately to deprive his Majefty's ever dutiful Subjects of thofe great and fundamental Rights, which, until lately, they have conftantly enjoyed, and which they and their Forefathers have ever claimed as their unalienable Rights as Men, their Conftitutional Rights as Subjects of the Britifh Empire, and their Right by Char-ters granted to the firft Settlers of this Diftant Country by his Majefty's Royal Ancef-tors, Kings of *England.* That to reftore the former Happinefs and Security of his faithful Subjects of this Colony, his Majefty will be pleafed, in his great Wifdom and Goodnefs, to recommend to his Parliament a total Repeal of certain Acts lately paffed for the purpofe of raifing a Revenue in *America,* and for fubjecting *American* Property to the Jurifdiction of diftant and arbitrary Courts of Admiralty, where Trial by Jury is not permitted, and where Diftance and Intereft may both confpire to ruin the In-nocent.

Ordered, That a Committee be appointed to draw up a Petition to be prefented to his Majefty upon the faid Refolution.

And a *Committee* was appointed of Mr *Richard Henry Lee,* Mr *Bland,* Mr *Henry Lee,* Mr *Treafurer,* Mr *Pendleton,* Mr *Archibald Cary,* and Mr *Harrifon.*

Mr *Archibald Cary* reported, from the Committee of Public Claims, that the Com-mittee had had under their Confideration feveral Petitions, to them referred, and had come to feveral Refolutions thereupon, which they had directed him to report to the Houfe; and he read the Report in his Place, and afterwards delivered it in at the Clerk's Table; where the Refolutions of the Committee were read, and are as followeth, *viz.*

Refolved, That it is the Opinion of this Committee, that fo much of the Petition of *David Ker,* Clerk of the County of *Middlefex,* as relates to the firft Sum of Paper Cur-rency, therein mentioned, which was depofited in his Hands by Order of Court, and burnt in the Houfe of *James Gregorie,* his Deputy, is reafonable; and that he ought to be allowed the fame, being 56 *l.* 14 *s.* by the Public.

Refolved, That it is the Opinion of this Committee, that fo much of the faid Peti-tion, as relates to the other Sum of 14 *l.* 5 *s.* 6 *d.* Paper Currency, therein mentioned, Part of which had been received by *James Gregorie,* his Deputy, for Clerks Fees, and Part for Fees on Marriage and Ordinary Licences, which was likewife burnt in the faid *Gregorie's* Houfe, be rejected; it being uncertain how much of that Sum was received for Fees on Licences.

Refolved

---

[1] Statutes at Large, *Great Britain,* Vol. VIII. p. 62.   [2] Ibid, Vol. VI. p. 768.

Refolved, That it is the Opinion of this Committee, that the Petition of *Charles Neilfon*, Naval Officer of Port *Rappahannock*, to be allowed the Sum of 9 *l.* which he had received in Paper Bills for Duties on Liquors, and was to have been paid into the Treafury, but was burnt in the Houfe of *James Gregorie*, his Deputy, as fet forth in the faid Petition, is reafonable; and that he ought to be allowed the fame in fettling his Accounts with the Treafury.

Refolved, That it is the Opinion of this Committee, that the Petition of *William Rind*, for an Addition to his Salary, as Public Printer, is reafonable; and that he ought to be allowed the further Sum of 75 *l. per annum*, as a Confideration for the Increafe of Public Bufinefs.

Refolved, That it is the Opinion of this Committee, that the Petition of *Jofeph Saunders*, to be allowed for the Horfe therein mentioned, be rejected.

Refolved, That it is the Opinion of this Committee, that fo much of the Petition of *William Edwards* and *James Price*, Infpectors of Tobacco, at *Grays Creek* Warehoufe, in *Surry* County, as relates to the Hogfhead of uninfpected Tobacco, ftole out of the faid Warehoufe in the Year 1763, is reafonable; and that the faid *William Edwards*, whofe Property the faid Tobacco was, ought to be allowed the Sum of 9 *l.* 18 *s.* for the fame.

Refolved, That it is the Opinion of this Committee, that fo much of the faid Petition, as relates to the 421 lb. of Tobacco, ftole out of the prized Hogfhead, in *May* laft, be rejected; it appearing that the Houfe, at that Time, was not properly fecured.

Refolved, That it is the Opinion of this Committee, that the Petition of *Benjamin Grymes*, in behalf of himfelf and his Creditors, to be allowed a reafonable Satiffaction for the Damage done their Slave, who was committed to Gaol for Hogftealing, and was Froft-bitten during his Confinement, ought to be referred to the Confideration of the next Seffion of Affembly.

Refolved, That it is the Opinion of this Committee, that the Petition of *John Doncaftle*, to be allowed for Waggonage in the Year 1759, be rejected.

The *eight* firft Refolutions being feverally read a fecond Time, were, upon the Queftion feverally put thereupon, agreed to by the Houfe.

The *ninth* Refolution of the Committee being read a fecond Time;

Ordered, That the faid Refolution be re-committed to the faid Committee of Public Claims.

Resolved, That the further Sum of Seventy-five Pounds *per Annum* be paid, as an additional Salary, to *William Rind*, Printer, to continue to the End of the next Seffion of General Affembly.

Ordered, That Mr *Archibald Cary* do carry the Refolution to the Council, and defire their Concurrence.

Ordered, That Mr *Mofeley*, Mr *Coles*, and Mr *Weft*, have Leave to be abfent from the Service of this Houfe for the Remainder of this Seffion.

Mr *Archibald Cary* prefented to the Houfe, according to Order, a Bill to dock the Intail of certain Lands whereof *James Rofcow* is feized, for the Purpofes therein mentioned; and the fame was received, and read the firft Time.

And a *Motion* was made, and the Queftion being put, that the Bill be read a fecond Time;

It paffed in the Negative.

Refolved, That the Bill be rejected.

Refolved, That an Addrefs be prefented to the Governor, praying his Excellency to ufe his earneft Intreaties with the Governor of *Maryland*, to recommend it to his Affembly to join this Colony in erecting and fupporting a Light-Houfe on *Cape Henry*, a Meafure we are convinced will conduce much to fecuring the extenfive Trade carried on by both Colonies up the Bay of *Chefapeak*.

Ordered, That the faid Addrefs be prefented to his Excellency, by Mr *Eyre* and Mr *Archibald Cary*.

Mr *Archibald Cary* prefented to the Houfe, according to Order, a Bill to dock the

Intail

250 Intail of certain Lands whereof *Francis Eppes* is feized, and for fettling other Lands in Lieu thereof; and the fame was received, and read the firft Time.

Refolved, That the Bill be read a fecond Time,

Refolved, That the Bill be now read a fecond Time.

The *Bill* was accordingly read a fecond Time.

Refolved, That the Bill be committed to Mr *Archibald Cary*, Mr *Ofborne*, Mr *Richard Randolph*, and Mr *Adams*.

Mr *Archibald Cary* reported, from the Committee of Public Claims, that the Committee had had under their further Confideration the petition of *Thomas* and *Bofwell Godwyne*, Infpectors of Tobacco, at *Bollingbrooke* Warehoufe, in *Dinwiddie* County, to them re-committed, and had come to a Refolution thereupon, which they had directed him to report to the Houfe; and he read the Report in his Place, and afterwards delivered it in at the Clerk's Table; where the Refolution of the Committee was read, and is as followeth, *viz.*

Refolved, That it is the Opinion of this Committee, that the faid Petition, praying that the faid Infpectors may be allowed for 13 Hogfheads of Tobacco, ftolen out of the faid Warehoufe laft Year, be rejected; it appearing that the faid Warehoufe was, at that Time, Infufficient.

The faid *Refolution* being read a fecond Time, was, upon the Queftion put thereupon, agreed to by the Houfe.

Mr *Archibald Cary* reported, from the Committee of Public Claims, to whom it was referred to ftate an Account of the Difburfements of *Thomas Walker*, *Thomas Rutherford*, *James Wood*, and *Abraham Hite*, Gentlemen, Commiffioners appointed by an Act of the General Affembly, made in the 7th Year of his prefent Majefty's Reign, intituled *An Act*[1] *for opening a Road through the Frontiers of this Colony to* Fort Pitt *on the* Ohio, in Execution of the faid Act, that the Committee had ftated an Account of the faid Difburfements accordingly, which they had directed him to report, together with the Refolution of the Committee thereupon, to the Houfe; and he read the Report in his Place, and afterwards delivered it in at the Clerk's Table; where the fame was read, and is as followeth, *viz.*

Dr.   The Commiffioners in Account with the Colony of *Virginia*.   Cr.

	l	s	d
To Cafh received of the Treafurer.	200	0	0
To Balance due to the Commiffioners,	66	14	0
	266	14	0
By Cafh paid *Abraham Kuykendall* and others, for opening, meafuring, and marking the faid Road,	200	0	0
By their Expences at two different Times on the Road, with two Pilots,	11	0	0
By their Affumption to *Richard Williams*, *Henry Hougland*, *John Hougland*, and *William Crawford*, who were employed as Pilots in finding out a nearer and more convenient Road, for 19 Days, each at 4s. *per* Day,	15	4	0
By *Abraham Hite*, for 25 Days Attendance on the faid Road, as a Commiffioner, at 15s. *per* Day,	18	15	0
By *Thomas Rutherford* for 12 Days, as ditto,	9	0	0
By *James Wood*, for 17 Days, as ditto,	12	15	0
	266	14	0

Refolved

---

1   Hening, VIII, p. 252.

Refolved, That it is the Opinion of this Committee, that *Abraham Hite, Thomas Rutherford* and *James Wood*, acting Commiffioners, ought to be allowed the Balance of the above Account, being 66 *l.* 14 *s.* as a Satiffaction for their extraordinary Expences and Attendance, as Commiffioners, on the faid Road.

The faid *Refolution* being read a fecond Time;

251

A *Motion* was made, and the Queftion being put, that the Houfe do agree with the Committee in the faid Refolution;

It paffed in the Negative.

The Houfe, according to Order, refolved itfelf into a Committee of the whole Houfe, to confider further of the Bill to continue and amend the Act, intituled *An Act[1] for amending the Staple of Tobacco, and preventing Frauds in his Majefty's Cuftoms.*

Mr *Speaker* left the Chair.

Mr *Bland* took the Chair of the Committee.

Mr *Speaker* refumed the Chair.

Mr *Bland* reported from the Committee, that they had gone through the Bill, and made feveral Amendments thereunto, which they had directed him to report to the Houfe; and he read the Report in his Place, and afterwards delivered the Bill, with the Amendments, in at the Clerk's Table; where the Report was read.

And the *firft* of the Amendments made by the Committee to the faid Bill being read a fecond Time, was, upon the Queftion put thereupon, agreed to by the Houfe.

A *Meffage* from the Council by Mr *Hubard;*

Mr *Speaker,*

The Council do infift upon the Amendments made by them to the Bill, intituled An Act[2] for encouraging the making Hemp, *difagreed to by this Houfe, and defire the Houfe will recede from their Difagreement thereunto: And alfo,*

The Council do infift upon the Amendments made by them to the Bill, *intituled* An Act[3] to dock the Intail of Five Hundred and Fifty Acres of Land, in the County of *Gloucefter,* whereof *Sarah,* the Wife of *John Rootes,* Gentleman, is feized, and for vefting the fame in Truftees for the Purpofes therein mentioned, *difagreed to by this Houfe, and defire the Houfe will recede from their Difagreement thereunto: And alfo,*

The Council have agreed to the Treafurer's Accounts.

And he prefented the faid Accounts at the Bar.

And then the Meffenger withdrew.

Ordered, That Mr *Archibald Cary* do carry the Treafurer's Accounts to the Governor, and defire his Excellency's Affent thereto.

The Houfe refumed the further Confideration of the Report from the Committee of the whole Houfe, to whom the bill to continue and amend the Act, intituled *An Act[4] for amending the Staple of Tobacco, and preventing Frauds in his Majefty's Cuftoms,* was committed.

And feveral other *Amendments,* made by the Committee to the faid Bill, being feverally read a fecond Time, were, upon the Queftion feverally put thereupon, with Amendments to fome of them, agreed to by the Houfe.

Ordered, That the further Confideration of the faid Report be adjourned till *Saturday* next.

The *Order* of the Day being read, for the Houfe to refolve itfelf into a Committee of the whole Houfe upon the Bill for the Infpection of Hemp;

Refolved, That this Houfe will, upon *Saturday* next, refolve itfelf into a Committee of the whole Houfe, upon the faid Bill.

The *Order* of the Day being read, for the Houfe to refolve itfelf into a Committee of the whole Houfe, upon the Bill to make Provifion for the Support and Maintenance of Ideots, Lunatics, and other Perfons of unfound Minds;

252

Refolved, That this Houfe will, upon *Saturday* next, refolve itfelf into a Committee of the whole Houfe, upon the faid Bill.

The

---

[1] Hening, IV, p. 247.   [2] Ibid, VIII, p. 363.   [3] Ibid, VIII, p. 483.   [4] Ibid, IV, p. 247.

The *Order* of the Day being read, for the Houfe to refolve itfelf into a Committee of the whole Houfe, upon the Bill declaring Slaves to be perfonal Eftate, and for other Purpofes therein mentioned;

Refolved, That this Houfe will, upon *Saturday* next, refolve itfelf into a Committee of the whole Houfe, upon the faid Bill.

The *Order* of the Day being read, for the Houfe to take into Confideration the Amendment made by the Committee of the whole Houfe, to the Bill for regulating the Election of Veftries;

Ordered, That the Confideration of the faid Amendment be further adjourned till *Saturday* next.

The other *Order* of the Day being read;

Ordered, That the Call of the Houfe be further adjourned till *Saturday* next.

And then the Houfe adjourned till Tomorrow Morning Ten of the Clock.

Friday, the 22d of June, 10 Geo. III. 1770.

*O*RDERED, That Leave be given to bring in a Bill to prevent the exorbitant Exactions of the Collectors of the County and Parifh Levies; and that Mr *Bland* do prepare and bring in the fame.

Mr *Treafurer* reported, from the Committee for Religion, to whom it was referred to ftate an Account of the Expences of travelling and Attendance of the Witneffes, who were examined before the faid Committee, touching the Matters fet forth and complained of in the petition of fundry Inhabitants of the Parifh of *Suffolk*, in the County of *Nanfemond*, on the Eaft Side of the River, that the Committee had ftated an Account of the faid Expences accordingly, which they had directed him to report, together with the Refolution of the Committee thereupon, to the Houfe; and he read the Report in his Place, and afterwards delivered it in at the Clerk's Table; where the fame was read, and is as followeth, *viz.*

Refolved, That it is the Opinion of this Committee, that the faid Expences ought to be defrayed by the feveral Perfons who fubfcribed the faid Petition, according to the Account below ftated.

Witneffes.	Attendance.	Diftance.	Total Tobacco.	Ferriage.		
Thomas Godwin,	3 Days	40 Miles twice	420	0	10	0
William Wife,	3	54	504	0	15	0
			924	1	5	0

It *appears* to your Committee, that *Jonathan Godwin, James Godwin, Miles King, Thomas Buxton,* and *John Drew*, five of the Members of the Veftry of the faid Parifh, did attend the Committee in Order to make their Defence, touching the Subject-Matter of the faid petition, an Account of whofe travelling and Attendance is likewife ftated; but whether the faid Veftrymen ought to be paid the faid Expences by the faid Petitioners, is fubmitted to the Confideration of the Houfe.

Veftrymen.	Attendance.	Diftance.	Total Tobacco.	Ferriage.		
Jonathan Godwin,	3 Days	40 Miles twice	420	0	10	0
James Godwin,	3	44	444	0	10	0
Miles King,	3	50	480	0	15	0
Thomas Buxton,	3	45	450	0	15	0
John Drew,	2	45	255		5	
			2049	2	15	0

The faid *Refolution* of the Committee being read a fecond Time, was, upon the Queftion put thereupon, agreed to by the Houfe.

Refolved, That the Expences of the Veftrymen, in the faid Report mentioned, be paid by the Subfcribers to the faid Petition, who did not retract the fame.

Ordered

Ordered, That it be an Inftruction to the faid Committee, who are appointed to prepare and bring in a Bill purfuant to the Refolution of the faid Committee, which, upon *Monday* laft, was agreed to by the Houfe, that they make Provifion in the faid Bill for paying the Expences of the faid Witneffes and Veftrymen, purfuant to the faid Refolutions of this Day.

Mr *Treafurer* reported, from the Committee for Religion, to whom the Bill for the Relief of Parifhes from fuch Charges as may arife from Baftard Children, born within the fame, was committed, that the Committee had gone through the Bill, and made feveral Amendments thereunto, which they had directed him to report to the Houfe; and he read the Report in his Place, and afterwards delivered the Bill, with the Amendments, in at the Clerk's Table; where the Amendments were once read throughout, and then a fecond Time, one by one; and, upon the Queftion feverally put thereupon, were agreed to by the Houfe, and feveral Amendments were made by the Houfe to the Bill.

Ordered, That the Bill, with the Amendments, be ingroffed.

Mr *Bland* prefented to the Houfe, according to Order, a Bill to prevent the exorbitant Exactions of the Collectors of the County and Parifh Levies; and the fame was received, and read the firft Time.

Refolved, That the Bill be read a fecond Time.

Refolved, That the Bill be now read a fecond Time.

The *Bill* was accordingly read a fecond Time.

Ordered, That the Bill be ingroffed.

A *Bill* to dock the Intail of certain Lands whereof *Richard Johnfon*, Gentleman, is feized, and for fettling other Lands and Slaves to the fame Ufes, was read a fecond Time.

Refolved, That the Bill be committed to Mr *Johnfon*, Mr *Anderfon*, Mr *Lyne*, Mr *John Tayloe Corbin*, Mr *Braxton*, Mr *Moore*, and Mr *Edmund Pendleton*.

A *Bill* to dock the Intail of certain Lands whereof *John Wormeley*, Gentleman, is feized, and for fettling other Lands and Slaves to the fame Ufes, was read a fecond Time.

Refolved, That the Bill be committed to Mr *Dudley Digges*, Mr *Nelfon*, Mr *Charles Carter*, of *Lancafter*, Mr *Mitchell*, Mr *Treafurer*, and Mr *Lewis Burwell*, of *James City*.

An ingroffed *Bill* to continue and amend the Act for the better regulating and difciplining the Militia, was read the third Time.

Refolved, That the Bill do pafs; and that the Title be, *An Act[1] to continue and amend the Act for the better regulating and difciplining the Militia.*

Ordered, That Mr *Bland* do carry the Bill to the Council, and defire their Concurrance.

Mr *Eyre* reported to the Houfe, that their Addrefs of Yefterday to the Governor, to ufe his earneft Intreaties with the Governor of *Maryland*, to recommend it to his Affembly to join this Colony in erecting and fupporting a Light-Houfe on *Cape Henry*, had been prefented to his Excellency, and that his Excellency had directed him to acquaint this Houfe, that the Subject-Matter of the Addrefs was extremely agreeable to him, and that he would take the earlieft Opportunity of writing to the Governor of *Maryland* on the Expediency of the Meafure propofed. 254

An ingroffed *Bill* to repeal an Act made in the 22d Year of his late Majefty's Reign, intituled *An Act[2] concerning Strays;* and to eftablifh a more effectual Method to prevent Frauds committed by Perfons taking up Strays, was read the third Time.

Refolved, That the Bill do pafs; and that the Title be, *An Act[3] to repeal an Act made in the 22d Year of his late Majefty's Reign, intituled An Act concerning Strays; and to eftablifh a more effectual Method to prevent Frauds committed by Perfons taking up Strays.*

Ordered, That Mr *Stark* do carry the Bill to the Council, and defire their Concurrence.

Mr *Archibald Cary* reported from the Committee of Public Claims, that the Committee had had under their Confideration feveral Claims for executed Slaves, and other Matters to them referred, and had ftated an Account thereof, which they had directed

him

---

[1] Hening, VIII. p. 241.   [2] Ibid. VI, p. 133.   [3] Ibid, VIII. p. 354.

him to report, together with the Refolution of the Committee thereupon, to the Houfe; and he read the Report in his Place, and afterwards delivered it in at the Clerk's Table; where the fame was read, and is as followeth, *viz.*

To *Carter Crafford*, jun. Orphan of *John Crafford*, deceafed, for his Negro Man Slave *Jeffery*, who was condemned and executed for Burglary, and by the Court of the County of *Warwick* valued at 65 *l.*

To *Catharine Hubard*, for her Negro Man Slave *Ifaac*, who was condemned and executed for Felony, and by the Court of the County of *York* valued at 70 *l.*

To the Eftate of *Ralph Piggot*, deceafed, for *Luke*, a Negro Man Slave belonging to the faid Eftate, who was condemned and executed for Felony, and by the Court of the County of *Norfolk* valued at 60 *l.*

To *John Hall*, for his Negro Man Slave *Cæfar*, who was condemned and executed for a Rape, and by the Court of the County of *Bedford* valued at 80 *l.*

To *Maximilian Robinfon*, for his Negro Man Slave *Bob*, who was condemned and executed for Murder, and by the Court of the County of *King George* valued at 60 *l.*

To *George Jamiefon*, for his Negro Man Slave *Lewis*, who was condemned and executed for Felony, and by the Court of the County of *Princefs Anne* valued at 50 *l.*

To *Thomas Thompfon*, for his Negro Man Slave *Glafgow*, who was condemned and executed for Felony, and by the Court of the County of *Norfolk* valued at 60 *l.*

To *John Lee*, for his Negro Man Slave *Frank*, who was condemned and executed for Felony, and by the Court of the County of *Essex* valued at 70 *l.*

To *Aaron Thorpe*, for his Negro Man Slave *Will*, who was condemned and executed for Felony, and by the Court of the County of *Southampton* valued at 60 *l.*

To *John Lewelling*, for his Negro Man Slave *Limus*, who was condemned and executed for Felony, and by the Court of the County of *Norfolk* valued at 75 *l.*

To *Meriwether Smith*, for his Negro Woman *Betty*, who was condemned and executed, and by the Court of the County of *Effex* valued at 80 *l.*

To *Carter Braxton*, for Provifions furnifhed the *Catawba Indians* on their March to join his Majefty's Forces on the *Ohio*, in 1759, 3 *l.* 8 *s.* 8 *d.*

To *Adam Wayland*, for a Gun, impreffed for the Ufe of the *Culpeper* Militia, in 1764, 1 *l.* 10 *s.*

To *Jofeph Pollard*, for ditto, in 1763, 1 *l.* 15 *s.*

To *Jofeph Worfhbourn*, for ditto, in ditto, 1 *l.* 7 *s.* 6 *d.*

To *Henry Field*, jun. for ditto, in ditto, 2 *l.* 5 *s.*

To *George Latham*, for ditto, for *Fauquier* Militia, 1 *l.*

To *Thomas Harrifon*, Affignee of *Charles Jones*, for ditto, in 1763, 15 *s.*

To *Burr Barton*, for ditto, in 1763 or 1764, 15 *s.*

To *Samuel Blackwell*, for ditto, for *Prince William* Militia, 2 *l.*

To *George Henry*, for ditto, 2 *l.*

To *William Courtney*, for ditto, 1 *l.* 17 *s.* 6 *d.*

To *Thomas Claiborne*, for Ferriage of Sheriffs with Criminals, in 1767 and 1768, 2 *l.* 13 *s.* 6 *d.*

To *William Rind*, for Printing, and Binding Books, the laft Emiffion of Paper Currency, 80 *l.*

To *Jofeph Kidd*, for Guilding and Painting the Dial-Plates and Arms of the Clock and Weather Cock of the Capitol, 35 *l.*

To *Jofhua Kendall*, for the Ornaments of the Capitol Gates, Leading the Balls, and Painting, 7 *l.* 10 *s.*

To *Samuel Boufh*, Treafurer of *Norfolk* County, to reimburfe the faid County for fundry Sums advanced by Order of the Juftices to *James Patrick*, *Robert Atkin*, and *William Honeycomb*, Mariners, detained in the County as Witneffes for the Crown, againft *David Fergufon*, a Criminal, now in the Public Gaol, for Murder, 36 *l.*

Refolved, That it is the Opinion of this Committee, that the faid Claims are reafonable, and that the refpective Claimants ought to be allowed for the fame by the Public

The

The faid *Refolution* being read a fecond Time, was, upon the Queftion put thereupon, agreed to by the Houfe.

Ordered, That Mr *James Walker* and Mr *Scott* have Leave to be abfent from the Service of this Houfe for the Remainder of this Seffion.

Mr *Archibald Cary* reported, from the Committee of Public Claims, to whom the Petition of *Bowler Cocke* and *Charles Carter*, Efquires, was re-committed, that the Committee had further examined the Matter of the faid petition, and come to a Refolution thereupon, which they had directed him to report to the Houfe; and he read the Report in his Place, and afterwards delivered it in at the Clerk's Table; where the Refolution of the Committee was read, and is as followeth, *viz.*

Refolved, That it is the Opinion of this Committee, that from the feveral Depofitions and Coroner's Inqueft hereto annexed, and to which your Committee begs Leave to refer the Houfe, the faid petition is reafonable; and that the petitioners ought to be allowed for the Slave *Tom* the Sum of Eighty five Pounds, for *Matt* One Hundred Pounds, and for *Phil* Eighty-five Pounds; and alfo the Sum of Twenty five Pounds for reimburfing them the Surgeon's Charge for attending and dreffing the Slaves concerned in the Infurrection, in the faid Petition mentioned.

The faid *Refolution* being read a fecond Time, was, upon the Queftion put thereupon, agreed to by the Houfe.

Mr *Archibald Cary* reported from the Committee, to whom the Bill to dock the Intail of certain Lands whereof *Francis Eppes* is feized, and for fettling other Lands in Lieu thereof, was committed, that the Committee had examined the Allegations of the Bill, and found the fame to be true; and that the Committee had gone through the Bill, and made feveral Amendments thereunto, which they had directed him to report to the Houfe; and he read the Report in his Place, and afterwards delivered the Bill, with the Amendments, in at the Clerk's Table; where the Amendments were once read throughout, and then a fecond Time, one by one; and, upon the Queftion feverally put thereupon, were agreed to by the Houfe.

Ordered, That the Bill, with the Amendments, be ingroffed.

Ordered, That it be an Inftruction to the Committee, to whom the Bill for dividing the Parifh of *Frederick*, in the County of *Frederick*, into three diftinct Parifhes, is committed, that they have Power to receive a Claufe or Claufes to impower the Veftry of the Parifh of *Cameron*, in the County of *Loudoun*, when elected, to fell their Glebe Lands, and purchafe a more convenient Glebe, in Lieu thereof.

An ingroffed *Bill* to dock the Intail of certain Lands whereof *Robert Burwell*, Efq; is feized, in Tail Male, and for fettling other Lands, of greater Value, in Lieu thereof, was read the third Time.

Refolved, That the Bill do pafs; and that the Title be, *An Act*[1] *to dock the Intail of certain Lands whereof* Robert Burwell, *Efq; is feized, in Tail Male, and for fettling other Lands, of equal Value, in Lieu thereof.*

Ordered, That Mr *Richard Baker* do carry the Bill to the Council, and defire their Concurrence.

And then the Houfe adjourned till To-morrow Morning Ten of the Clock.

Saturday, the 23d of June, 10 Geo. III. 1770.

AN ingroffed *Bill* to prevent the exorbitant Exactions of the Collectors of the County and Parifh Levies, was read the third Time.

Refolved, That the Bill do pafs; and that the Title be, *An Act*[2] *to prevent the exorbitant Exactions of the Collectors of the County and Parifh Levies.*

Ordered, That Mr *Carrington* do carry the Bill to the Council, and defire their Concurrence.

Ordered

---

[1] Hening, VIII. p. 448.   [2] Ibid, VIII, p. 381.

Ordered, That the Order of the Day for refuming the adjourned Confideration of the Report, which was made from the Committee of the whole Houfe, to whom the Bill to continue and amend the Act, intituled *An Act¹ for amending the Staple of Tobacco, and preventing Frauds in his Majefty's Cuftoms*, was committed, be now read.

And the faid *Order* being read accordingly;

The Houfe refumed the adjourned Confideration of the faid Report.

And the Refidue of the *Amendments* made by the Committee to the faid Bill, being feverally read a fecond Time, were, upon the Queftion feverally put thereupon, agreed to by the Houfe.

Ordered, That the Bill, with the Amendments, be ingroffed.

The Houfe proceeded to take into Confideration the Amendments infifted on by the Council to the Bill, intituled *An Act² for encouraging the making Hemp*, difagreed to by the Houfe.

And the fame being twice read;

Refolved, That this Houfe doth adhere to their Difagreement to the faid Amendments.

Ordered, That a Meffage be fent to the Council to inform them, that this Houfe doth adhere to their Difagreement to the Amendments by them infifted on to the faid Bill, and defire that they will pafs the Bill, without the Amendments; and that Mr *Harrifon* do carry the faid Meffage.

The *Order* of the Day being read for the Houfe to refolve itfelf into a Committee of the whole Houfe, upon the Bill declaring Slaves to be perfonal Eftate; and for other Purpofes therein mentioned;

Refolved, That this Houfe will, upon *Monday* next, refolve itfelf into a Committee of the whole Houfe, upon the faid Bill.

Ordered, That Mr *Edmund Pendleton*, Mr *Robert Munford*, of *Mecklenburg*, Mr *Gawin Corbin*, Mr *Wallace*, Mr *Eyre*, and Mr *Henry*, have Leave to be abfent from the Service of this Houfe for the Remainder of this Seffion.

The Houfe proceeded to take into Confideration the Amendments infifted on by the Council to the Bill, intituled *An Act³ to dock the Intail of Five Hundred and Fifty Acres of Land, in the County of* Gloucefter, *whereof* Sarah, *the Wife of* John Rootes, *Gentleman, is feized, and for vefting the fame in Truftees for the Purpofes therein mentioned*, difagreed to by the Houfe.

The faid *Amendments* were twice read;

And the *Queftion* being put, that this Houfe doth infift upon their Difagreement to the faid Amendments;

It paffed in the Negative.

Ordered, That Mr *Mercer* do carry the Bill to the Council, and acquaint them, that this Houfe hath agreed to the Amendments made by them.

Mr *Archibald Cary* reported from the Committee, to whom the Bill for eftablifhing a Town at *Rocky Ridge*, in the County of *Chefterfield*, and for adding certain Lots to the Town of *Richmond*, in the County of *Henrico*, was committed, that the Committee had gone through the Bill, and made feveral Amendments thereunto, which they had directed him to report to the Houfe, and he read the Report in his Place, and afterwards delivered the Bill, with the Amendments, in at the Clerk's Table; where the Amend-
257 ments were once read throughout, and then a fecond Time, one by one, and, upon the Queftion feverally put thereupon, were agreed to by the Houfe.

Ordered, That the Bill, with the Amendments, be ingroffed.

Ordered, That the Order of the Day for refuming the adjourned Confideration of the Report which was made from the Committee of the whole Houfe, to whom the Bill for regulating the Election of Veftries was committed, be now read.

And the faid *Order* being read accordingly;

The Houfe refumed the adjourned Confideration of the faid report.

And the *Amendment* made by the Committee, to the faid Bill being read a fecond
Time

---

¹ Hening, IV, p. 247.   ² Ibid, VIII, p. 363.   ³ Ibid, VIII, p. 483.

Time, was, upon the Queſtion put thereupon, with an Amendment, agreed to by the Houſe.

Ordered, That the Bill, with the Amendment, be ingroſſed.

Ordered, That Mr *Baniſter* have Leave to be abſent from the Service of this Houſe till *Friday* next.

An ingroſſed *Bill* for appointing ſeveral new Ferries, and for other Purpoſes therein mentioned, was read the third Time.

An ingroſſed *Clauſe* was offered to be added to the Bill, by Way of Rider, to repeal ſo much of an Act of General Aſſembly, exempting all the Inhabitants of the Pariſh of *Suffolk*, in the County of *Nanſemond*, from Payment of Ferriage for paſſing *Nanſemond* River, as relates to all the ſaid Inhabitants, except the Miniſter.

And the ſaid *Clauſe* was thrice read, and, upon the Queſtion put thereupon, was agreed to by the Houſe, to be made Part of the Bill, by Way of Rider.

Reſolved, That the Bill do paſs; and that the Title be, *An Act¹ for appointing ſeveral new Ferries; and for other Purpoſes therein mentioned.*

Ordered, That Mr *Treaſurer* do carry the Bill to the Council, and deſire their Concurrence.

The *Order* of the Day being read, for the Houſe to reſolve itſelf into a Committee of the whole Houſe, upon the Bill for the Inſpection of Hemp.

Reſolved, That this Houſe will, upon *Monday* next, reſolve itſelf into a Committee of the whole Houſe, upon the ſaid Bill.

Mr *Mercer* reported from the Committee, to whom the Bill for dividing the Pariſh of *Frederick*, in the County of *Frederick*, into three diſtinct Pariſhes, was committed, that the Committee had gone through the Bill, and made ſeveral Amendments thereunto, which they had directed him to report to the Houſe; and he read the Report in his Place, and afterwards delivered the Bill, with the Amendments, in at the Clerk's Table; where the Amendments were once read throughout, and then a ſecond Time, one by one, and, upon the Queſtion ſeverally put thereupon, were, with Amendments to ſome of them agreed to by the Houſe.

Ordered, That the Bill, with the Amendments, be ingroſſed.

An ingroſſed *Bill* for diſſolving the Veſtry of the Pariſh of *Hungar's*, in the County of *Northampton*, was read the third Time.

An ingroſſed *Clauſe* was offered to be added to the Bill, by Way of Rider, for enabling the Veſtries of the Pariſhes in the Bill mentioned, notwithſtanding their diſſolution, to proſecute and defend Suits already commenced by and againſt them.

And the ſaid *Clauſe* was thrice read, and, upon the Queſtion put thereupon, was agreed to by the Houſe, to be made a Part of the Bill, by Way of Rider.

Reſolved, That the Bill do paſs; and that the Title be, *An Act² for diſſolving the ſeveral Veſtries therein mentioned.* 258

Ordered, That Mr *Treaſurer* do carry the Bill to the Council, and deſire their Concurrence.

Mr *Edmund Pendleton* reported from the Committee, to whom the Bill, to dock the Intail of certain Lands whereof *Richard Johnſon*, Gentleman, is ſeized, and for ſettling other Lands and Slaves, to the ſame Uſes, was committed, that the Committee had examined the Allegations of the Bill, and found the ſame to be true; and that the Committee had gone through the Bill, and made ſeveral Amendments thereunto, which they had directed him to report to the Houſe; and he read the Report in his Place, and afterwards delivered the Bill, with the Amendments, in at the Clerk's Table; where the Amendments were once read throughout, and then a ſecond Time, one by one, and, upon the Queſtion ſeverally put thereupon, were agreed to by the Houſe.

Ordered, That the Bill, with the Amendments, be ingroſſed.

The *Order* of the Day being read, for the Houſe to reſolve itſelf into a Committee of the whole Houſe, upon the Bill to make Proviſion for the Support and Maintenance of Ideots, Lunatics and other Perſons of unſound Mind;

Reſolved

---

¹ **Hening**, VIII, p. 368.   ² Ibid, VIII, p. 432.

Refolved, That this Houfe will, upon *Monday* next, refolve itfelf into a Committee of the whole Houfe upon the faid Bill.

An ingroffed *Bill* to amend the Act, intituled *An Act to amend the Act for better Government of Servants and Slaves* was read the third Time.

Refolved, That the Bill do pafs; and that the Title be, *An Act¹ to amend the Act intituled An Act to amend the Act for the better Government of Servants and Slaves.*

Ordered, That Mr *Treafurer* do carry the Bill to the Council, and defire their Concurrence.

A *Bill* to repeal Part of an Act, intituled *An Act² of free and general Pardon, Indemnity and Oblivion*, was read a fecond Time.

Ordered, That the Bill be ingroffed.

An ingroffed *Bill* to amend an Act, intituled *An Act³ againft ftealing Hogs*, was read the third Time.

Refolved, That the Bill do pafs; and that the Title be *An Act⁴ to amend an Act, intituled An Act againft ftealing Hogs.*

Ordered, That Mr *Carrington* do carry the Bill to the Council, and defire their Concurrence.

The other *Order* of the Day being read;

Ordered, That the Call of the Houfe be further adjourned till *Monday* next.

A *Bill* for encouraging the making Wine, was read a fecond Time.

Ordered, That the Bill be ingroffed.

An ingroffed *Bill*, for adding Part of the City of *Williamfburg* to *James City* County and for other Purpofes therein mentioned, was read the third Time.

Refolved, That the Bill do pafs; and that the Title be, *An Act⁵ to annex Part of the County of* York *to the County of* James City, *and for other Purpofes therein mentioned*.

Ordered, That Mr *Treafurer* do carry the Bill to the Council, and defire their Concurrence.

259 A *Bill* to regulate the Inoculation of the Small-Pox, within this Colony, was read a fecond Time.

Refolved, That the Bill be committed to Mr *Treafurer*, Mr *Wilfon Miles Cary*, Mr *Henry Lee* and Mr *Edmund Pendleton*.

And then the Houfe adjourned till Monday Morning next, Ten of the Clock.

Monday, the 25th of June, 10 Geo. III. 1770.

AN ingroffed Bill to continue and amend the Act, intituled *An Act⁶ for amending the Staple of Tobacco*, and preventing Frauds in his Majefty's Cuftoms, was read the third Time.

Refolved, That the Bill do pafs; and that the Title be, *An Act⁷ to continue and amend the Act, intituled An Act for amending the Staple of Tobacco, and preventing Frauds in his Majefty's Cuftoms;*

Ordered, That Mr *Archibald Cary* do carry the Bill to the Council, and defire their Concurrence.

The Houfe, according to Order, refolved itfelf into a Committee of the whole Houfe, upon the Bill declaring Slaves to be perfonal Eftate, and for other Purpofes therein mentioned.

Mr *Speaker* left the Chair.

Mr *Treafurer* took the Chair of the Committee.

Mr *Speaker* refumed the Chair.

Mr *Treafurer* reported from the Committee, that they had gone through the Bill, and made feveral Amendments thereunto, which they had directed him to report, when the Houfe will pleafe to receive fame.

Ordered

---

1 Hening, VIII, p. 358.   2 Ibid, II. p. 458.   3 Ibid, VI, p. 121.   4 Ibid, VIII. p. 385.
5 Ibid, VIII. p. 419.   6 Ibid, IV. p. 247.   7 Ibid, VIII. p. 318.

Ordered, That the Report be received Tomorrow.

An ingroffed *Bill* to repeal Part of an Act, intituled *An Act¹ of free and general Pardon, Indemnity and Oblivion*, was read the third Time.

Refolved, That the Bill do pafs; and that the Title be, *An Act² to repeal Part of an Act, intituled An Act of free and general Pardon, Indemnity and Oblivion.*

Ordered, That Mr *Eyre* do carry the Bill to the Council, and defire their Concurrence.

The *Order* of the Day being read, for the Houfe to refolve itfelf into a Committee of the whole Houfe, upon the Bill for the Infpection of Hemp;

Refolved, That this Houfe will, Tomorrow, refolve itfelf into a Committee of the whole Houfe, upon the faid Bill.

An ingroffed *Bill* for better regulating the Election of Veftries, was read the third Time.

Refolved, That the Bill do pafs; and that the Title be, *An Act² for better regulating the Election of Veftries.*

Ordered, That Mr *Mercer* do carry the Bill to the Council, and defire their Concurrence.

The *Order* of the Day being read, for the Houfe to refolve itfelf into a Committee of the whole Houfe, upon the Bill to make Provifion for the Support and Maintenance of Ideots, Lunatics, and other Perfons of unfound Mind;

Refolved, That this Houfe will, Tomorrow, refolve itfelf into a Committee of the whole Houfe, upon the faid Bill.

An ingroffed *Bill* for encouraging the making Wine, was read the third Time.   260

Refolved, That the Bill do pafs; and that the Title be, *An Act³ for encouraging the making Wine.*

Ordered, That Mr *Harrifon* do carry the Bill to the Council, and defire their Concurrence.

Mr *Mercer* reported from the Committee, to whom the Bill for the better regulating the Office of Sheriffs and their Deputies, was committed, that the Committee had directed him to report the Bill, to the Houfe, without any Amendment; and he delivered the Bill in at the Clerk's Table.

A *Motion* was made, and the Queftion being put, that the Bill be ingroffed.

It paffed in the Negative.

Refolved, That the Bill be rejected.

An ingroffed *Bill* for dividing the Parifh of *Frederick*, in the County of *Frederick* into three diftinct Parifhes, was read the third Time.

Refolved, That the Bill do pafs; and that the Title be, *An Act⁴ for dividing the Parifhes of* Frederick, *in the County of* Frederick, *and* Cameron, *in the County of* Loudoun, *and for other Purpofes therein mentioned.*

Ordered, That Mr *Rutherford* do carry the Bill to the Council, and defire their Concurrence.

Ordered, That Mr *Carrington* have Leave to be abfent from the Service of this Houfe for the Remainder of this Seffion.

An ingroffed *Bill* for the Relief of Parifhes from fuch Charges as may arife from Baftard Children born within the fame, was read the third Time.

Refolved, That the Bill do pafs; and that the Title be, *An Act⁵ for the relief of Parifhes, from fuch Charges as may arife from Baftard Children born within the fame.*

An ingroffed *Bill* to explain and amend the Act, intituled *An Act⁶ to confirm the Charter of the Borough of* Norfolk, *and for enlarging the Jurifdiction of the Court of Huftings, in the City of* Williamfburg, *was read the third Time.*

Refolved, That the Bill do pafs; and that the Title be, *An Act⁷ to explain certain Doubts touching the Jurifdiction of the Court of Huftings, of the City of* Williamfburg.

Ordered, That Mr *Treafurer* do carry the Bill to the Council, and defire their Concurrence.

A

¹ Hening, II, p. 458.   ² Not recorded as a law.   ³ Hening, VIII. p. 364.   ⁴ Ibid, VIII. p. 425.
⁵ Ibid. VIII. 374.   ⁶ Ibid. IV, p. 541.   ⁷ Ibid, VIII. p. 401.

A *Bill* to prevent Hogs and Dogs running at Large, on the Iſland of *Gingoteague*, was read a ſecond Time.

Ordered, That the Bill be ingroſſed.

An ingroſſed *Bill* to dock the Intail of certain Lands whereof *Francis Eppes* is ſeized, and for ſettling other Lands in Lieu thereof, was read the third Time.

Reſolved, That the Bill do paſs; and that the Title be, *An Act[1] to dock the Intail of certain Lands whereof* Francis Eppes *is ſeized, and for ſettling other Lands, in Lieu thereof.*

Ordered, That Mr *Archibald Cary* do carry the Bill to the Council, and deſire their Concurrence.

The other *Order* of the Day being read;

Ordered, That the Call of the Houſe be further adjourned till Tomorrow.

An ingroſſed *Bill* to dock the Intail of certain Lands, whereof *Richard Johnſon*, Gentleman, is ſeized, and for ſettling other Lands and Slaves to the ſame Uſes, was read the third Time.

Reſolved, That the Bill do paſs; and that the Title be, *An Act[2] to dock the Intail of certain Lands whereof* Richard Johnſon, *Gentleman, is ſeized, and for ſettling other Lands and Slaves to the ſame Uſes.*

Ordered, That Mr *Archibald Cary* do carry the Bill to the Council, and deſire their Concurrence.

And then the Houſe adjourned till Tomorrow Morning Ten of the Clock.

Tuesday, the 26th of June, 10 Geo. III. 1770.

ORDERED, That the Adminiſtrators of *John Robinſon*, Eſq; do lay before this Houſe, at the next Seſſion, a Liſt of the Names of all thoſe who are indebted to the Eſtate of the ſaid *John Robinſon*, Eſq; with an exact Account of the Balances reſpectively due from ſuch Perſons.

Mr *Treaſurer*, according to Order, reported from the Committee of the whole Houſe, to whom the Bill declaring Slaves to be perſonal Eſtate, and for other Purpoſes therein mentioned, was committed, the Amendments which the Committee had made to the Bill, and which they had directed him to report to the Houſe; and he read the Report in his Place, and afterwards delivered the Bill, with the Amendments, in at the Clerk's Table; where the Amendments were once read throughout, and then a ſecond Time, one by one, and, upon the Queſtion ſeverally put thereupon, ſome of them were dif-agreed to, and the reſt were agreed to by the Houſe.

A *Motion* was made, and the Queſtion being put, that the Bill, with the Amendments, be ingroſſed;

It paſſed in the Negative.

Reſolved, That the Bill be rejected.

The Houſe according to Order, reſolved itſelf into a Committee of the whole Houſe, upon the Bill to make Proviſion for the Support and Maintenance of Ideots, Lunatics, and other Perſons of unſound Mind.

Mr *Speaker* left the Chair.

Mr *Treaſurer* took the Chair of the Committee.

Mr *Speaker* reſumed the Chair.

Mr *Treaſurer* reported from the Committee, that they had gone through the Bill, and made ſeveral Amendments thereunto, which they had directed him to report to the Houſe; and he read the Report in his Place, and afterwards delivered the Bill, with the Amendments, in at the Clerk's Table; where the Amendments were once read throughout, and then a ſecond Time, one by one, and, upon the Queſtion ſeverally put thereupon, were agreed to by the Houſe.

Ordered, That the Bill, with the Amendments, be ingroſſed.

A

[1] Hening, VIII. p. 450. [2] Ibid, VIII, p. 455.

A *Meffage* from the Council by Mr *Hubard;*

Mr *Speaker,*

The Council recede from the Amendment made by them to the Bill intituled An Act[1] for encouraging the making Hemp, *to which the Houfe have difagreed: And alfo,*

The Council have agreed to the Bill, *intituled* An Act[2] for encouraging the making Wine, *without any Amendment: And alfo,*

The Council have agreed to the Bill, *intituled* An Act[3] to amend the Act, intituled an Act to amend the Act for the better Government of Servants and Slaves, *without any Amendment: And alfo,*

The Council have agreed to the Bill, *intituled* An Act[4] for dividing the Parifhes of *Frederick,* in the County of *Frederick,* and *Cameron,* in the County of *Loudoun,* and for other Purpofes therein mentioned, *without any Amendment: And alfo,*

The Council have agreed to the Bill, *intituled* An Act[5] to explain certain Doubts touching the Jurifdiction of the Court of Huftings of the City of *Williamfburg, without any Amendment: And alfo,*

The Council have agreed to the Bill, *intituled* An Act[6] to amend an Act, intituled An Act againft ftealing Hogs, *without any Amendment: And alfo,*

The Council have agreed to the Bill, *intituled* An Act[7] to annex Part of the County of *York,* to the County of *James City,* and for other Purpofes therein mentioned, *without any Amendment: And alfo,*

The Council have agreed to the Bill, *intituled* An Act[8] for diffolving the feveral Veftries therein mentioned, *without any Amendment: And alfo,*

The Council have agreed to the Bill, *intituled* An Act[9] to dock the Intail of certain Lands whereof *Francis Eppes* is feized, and for fettling other Lands in Lieu thereof, *without any Amendment: And alfo,*

The Council have agreed to the Bill, *intituled* An Act[10] to dock the Intail of certain Lands whereof *Richard Johnfon,* Gentleman, is feized, and for fettling other Lands and Slaves to the fame Ufes, *without any Amendment: And alfo,*

The Council have agreed to the Refolve *for paying an additional Salary to the Printer: And alfo,*

The Council have agreed to the Bill, *intituled* An Act[11] for appointing feveral new Ferries, and for other Purpofes therein mentioned, *with an Amendment, to which Amendment the Council defire the Concurrence of this Houfe: And alfo,*

The Council have agreed to the Bill, *intituled* An Act[12] to dock the Intail of certain Lands whereof *Robert Burwell,* Efq; is feized, in Tail Male, and for fettling other Lands, of equal Value, in Lieu thereof, *with an Amendment, to which Amendment the Council defire the Concurrence of this Houfe:*

And then the Meffenger withdrew.

Mr *Treafurer* reported from the Committee, to whom the Bill to regulate the Inoculation of the Small-Pox within this Colony, was committed, that the Committee had directed him to report the Bill to the Houfe, without any Amendment; and he delivered the Bill in at the Clerk's Table.

Ordered, That the Bill be engroffed.

The Houfe proceeded to take into Confideration the Amendment made by the Council to the Bill, intituled *An Act for appointing feveral new Ferries, and for other Purpofes therein mentioned.*

And the faid *Amendment* was read, and is as followeth, *viz.*

At the End of the *Bill* add, 'And whereas *Doubts and Difputes have often arifen, to the great Delay and Hindrance of Paffengers, about the Right which a perfon appointed to keep a Ferry on one Side of a River or Creek hath to take in a Fare on the Oppofite Shore, and to receive the Pay for ferrying over':*

Be

[1] Hening, VIII, p. 363.   [2] Ibid, VIII, p. 364.   [3] Ibid, VIII, p. 358.   [4] Ibid, VIII, p. 425.
[5] Ibid, VIII, p. 401.   [6] Ibid, VIII. p. 385.   [7] Ibid, VIII, p. 419.   [8] Ibid, VIII, p. 432.
[9] Ibid, VIII, p. 450.   [10] Ibid, VIII, p. 455.   [11] Ibid, VIII, p. 368.   [12] Ibid, VIII, p. 448.

Be it therefore enacted by the Authority aforesaid, that it shall and may be lawful for any Keeper of a Ferry to take into his Boat or Boats any Passenger or Passengers, Carriage Horses, and Cattle of any Kind whatsoever, on either Side, to convey them over, and to receive the Ferriage for the same, any Law, Usage or Custom to the contrary in any Wise notwithstanding.'

The said *Amendment* being read a second Time, was, upon the Question put thereupon, agreed to by the House.

Ordered, That Mr *Archibald Cary* do carry the Bill to the Council, and acquaint them that this House hath agreed to the Amendment made by them.

Mr *Nelson* reported, from the Committee, to whom the Bill to dock the Intail of certain Lands, whereof *John Wormeley*, Gentleman, is seized, and for settling other Lands and Slaves to the same Uses was committed, that the Committee had examined the Allegations of the Bill, and found the same to be true; and that the Committee had gone through the Bill, and made an Amendment thereunto, which they had directed him to report to the House; and he read the Report in his Place, and afterwards delivered the Bill, with the Amendment, in at the Clerk's Table; where the Amendment was twice read, and upon the Question put thereupon, was agreed to by the House.

Ordered, That the Bill, with the Amendment, be ingrossed.

The House proceeded to take into consideration the Amendment made by the Council to the Bill, intituled *An Act[1] to dock the Intail of certain Lands, whereof* Robert Burwell, *Esq; is seized, in Tail Male, and for settling other Lands, of equal Value, in Lieu thereof.*

And the said *Amendment* was read, and is as followeth, *viz.*

Line 35. Leave out '*Four Thousand Three Hundred*,' and insert '*Three Thousand Four Hundred*,' instead thereof.

The said *Amendment* being read a second Time, was, upon the Question put thereupon, agreed to by the House.

Ordered, That Mr *Richard Baker* do carry the Bill to the Council, and acquaint them, that this House hath agreed to the Amendment made by them.

Mr *Archibald Cary* reported, from the Committee of Public Claims, to whom the Petition of *John Doncastle* was re-committed, that the Committee had come to a Resolution thereupon, which they had directed him to report to the House; and he read the Report in his Place, and afterwards delivered it in at the Clerk's Table; where the Resolution of the Committee was read, and is as followeth, *viz.*

Resolved, That it is the Opinion of this Committee, that the said petition be referred to the Consideration of the next Session of Assembly.

The said *Resolution* being read a second Time, was, upon the Question put thereupon, agreed to by the House.

The *Order* of the Day being read, for the House to resolve itself into a Committee of the whole House upon the Bill for the Inspection of Hemp;

Resolved, That this House will, upon this Day Fortnight, resolve itself into a Committee of the whole House, upon the said Bill.

A *Bill* for adding Part of the County of *Augusta*, to the County of *Hampshire*, was read a second Time.

A *Motion* was made, and the Question being put, that the Bill be ingrossed;

It passed in the Negative.

Resolved, That the Bill be rejected.

An ingrossed *Bill* for establishing a Town at *Rocky Ridge*, in the County of *Chesterfield*, and for adding certain Lots to the Town of *Richmond*, in the County of *Henrico*, was read the third Time.

Resolved, That the Bill do pass; and that the Title be, *An Act[2] for establishing Towns at* Rocky Ridge, Gloucester *Court-House, and* Layton's *Warehouse; and for other Purposes therein mentioned.*

Ordered

---

[1] Hening, VIII, p. 448.   [2] Ibid, VIII, p. 421.

Ordered, That Mr *Archibald Cary* do carry the Bill to the Council, and defire their Concurrence.

Ordered, That Mr *William Cabell* have Leave to be abfent from the Service of this Houfe for the Remainder of this Seffion.

Mr *Archibald Cary* reported, from the Committee of Public Claims, to whom the Petition of *John Wyatt, Francis Smith*, and *Jofeph Fofter*, was referred, that the Committee had examined the Matter of the faid Petition, and come to a Refolution thereupon, which they had directed him to report to the Houfe; and he read the Report in his Place, and afterwards delivered it in at the Clerk's Table; where the Refolution of the Committee was read, and is as followeth, *viz.* 264

Refolved, That it is the Opinion of this Committee, that the faid Petition praying an Allowance for the Guns which were ufed in fuppreffing a late Infurrection of the Slaves of *Bowler Cocke*, and fpoiled, as fet forth in the faid petition, is reafonable; and that the faid *John Wyatt* ought to be allowed the Sum of 1 *l.* and 10 *s. Francis Smith* 1 *l.* and 10 *s.* and *Jofeph Fofter* 1 *l.* for the damage done their Guns.

The faid *Refolution* being read a fecond Time, was, upon the Queftion put thereupon, agreed to by the Houfe.

An ingroffed *Bill* to prevent Hogs and Dogs running at Large on the Ifland of *Gingoteague*, was read the third Time.

Refolved, That the Bill do pafs; and that the Title be, *An Act^1 to prevent Hogs and Dogs running at Large on the Ifland of* Gingoteague.

Ordered, That Mr *Simpfon* do carry the Bill to the Council, and defire their Concurrence.

Ordered, That the Committee of Public Claims do ftate an Account of all Sums of Money, which have been agreed to by the Houfe, fince the 21ft Day of *December* laft, to be paid by the Public, and report the fame, in an ingroffed Schedule, to the Houfe.

A *Bill* to confirm an Agreement made by *Thomas Talbutt* with the Court of *Norfolk* County, was read a fecond Time.

Ordered, That the Bill be ingroffed.

The other *Order* of the Day being read;

Ordered, That the Call of the Houfe be further adjourned till Tomorrow.

And then the Houfe adjourned till Tomorrow Morning Ten of the Clock.

Wednesday, the 27th of June, 10 Geo. III. 1770.

A N ingroffed *Bill* to make Provifion for the Support and Maintenance of Ideots, Lunatics, and other Perfons of unfound Mind, was read the third Time.

Refolved, That the Bill do pafs; and that the Title be, *An Act^2 to make Provifion for the Support and Maintenance of Ideots, Lunatics, and other Perfons of unfound Minds.*

Ordered, That Mr *Treafurer* do carry the Bill to the Council, and defire their Concurrence.

An ingroffed *Bill* to regulate the Inoculation of the Small-Pox within this Colony, was read the third Time.

Refolved, That the Bill do pafs; and that the Title be, *An Act^3 to regulate the Inoculation of the Small-Pox, within this Colony.*

Ordered, That Mr *Treafurer* do carry the Bill to the Council, and defire their Concurrence.

An ingroffed *Bill* to dock the Intail of certain Lands whereof *John Wormeley*, Gentleman, is feized, and for fettling other Lands and Slaves to the fame Ufes, was read the third Time.

Refolved, That the Bill do pafs; and that the Title be, *An Act^4 to dock the Intail of certain*

---

1 Not recorded as a law.   2 Hening, VIII, p. 378.   3 Ibid, VIII, p. 371.   4 Ibid, VIII, p. 452.

certain Lands, whereof John Wormeley, *Gentleman, is feized, and for fettling other Lands and Slaves to the fame Ufes.*

Ordered, That M[r] *Nelfon* do carry the Bill to the Council, and defire their Concurrence.

265 An ingroffed *Bill* to confirm an Agreement made by *Thomas Talbutt*, with the Court of *Norfolk* County, was read the third Time.

Refolved, That the Bill do pafs; and that the Title be, *An Act[1] to confirm an Agreement made by* Thomas Talbutt, *with the Court of* Norfolk *County.*

Ordered, That M[r] *John Wilfon* of *Norfolk* do carry the Bill to the Council, and defire their Concurrence.

Refolved, That it be an Inftruction to the Committee of Public Claims, to whom it was referred to ftate an Account of all Sums of Money, which have been agreed by the Houfe, fince the Twenty-firft Day of *December* laft, to be paid by the Public, and Report the fame in an ingroffed Schedule to the Houfe, that they make the following Allowances to the Officers of the General Affembly, in the faid Schedule, *viz.*

To *George Wythe*, Clerk of the Houfe of Burgeffes,	£. 300 0 0
To *Nathaniel Walthoe*, Efq; Clerk of the General Affembly,	100 0 0
To the Reverend M[r] *Thomas Price*, Chaplain to the Houfe,	60 0 0
To M[r] *Francis Eppes*, Serjeant at Arms attending this Houfe,	85 0 0
To M[r] *Richard Starke*, Clerk of the Committees of Privileges and Elections, and Propofitions and Grievances,	100 0 0
To M[r] *Richard Cary*, Clerk of the Committees for Religion, and of Trade,	80 0 0
To M[r] *Hind Ruffell*, Clerk of the Committee of Public Claims,	100 0 0
To M[r] *Thomas Everard*, Clerk of the Committee for Courts of Juftice,	50 0 0
To *Robert Hyland, James Lavie, William Hicks,* and *John Creagh,* Doorkeepers 20 *l.* each,	80 0 0
To *Chriftopher Ayfcough*, Door-keeper to the Council,	20 0 0
To M[r] *Benjamin Powell*, for cleaning the Capitol,	5 0 0

M[r] *Treafurer* reported from the Committee appointed, upon *Thurfday* laft, to draw up a Petition to be prefented to his Majefty, that the Committee had drawn up a petition accordingly, which they had directed him to report to the Houfe; and he read the fame in his Place, and afterwards delivered it in at the Clerk's Table; where the fame was read, and is as followeth, *viz.*

MAY IT PLEASE YOUR MOST EXCELLENT MAJESTY,

Gracioufly to permit your ever dutiful and loyal Subjects, the Burgeffes of Virginia, *now met in General Affembly, to approach your Royal Prefence, and, with all humility, renew their moft earneft Entreaties, that your Majefty, in your great Goodnefs, would be pleafed to extend your fatherly Protection to them and all their fellow Subjects in* America.

Having, Sire, upon former and recent Occafions, humbly fubmitted to your Royal Wifdom, our juft Claims to be free and exempt from all Taxes impofed on us, without our own Confent, for the Purpofe of raifing and eftablifhing a Revenue in America, *we fhould not now prefume to recall your Majefty's gracious Attention to the fame Subject, had we not the moft convincing Teftimony that the Sentiments and Difpofitions of your Majefty's Miniftry, confirmed by the Voice of Parliament, ftill continue extremely unfavorable and alarming to your Majefty's* American *Subjects; a Reflection to us, at this Time, the more irkfome and grevious, as we had, from the late agreeable Profpect flattered ourfelves, that a broad and permanent Foundation would foon have been laid, for reftoring and perpetuating that pleafing Harmony, which once fo happily united the Interefts and Affections of all your Majefty's Subjects both* Britifh *and* American.

Words, moft gracious Sovereign, cannot fufficiently exprefs the exceeding great Concern and deep Affliction, with which our Minds have been agitated and tortur'd upon finding almoft a fix'd and determin'd Refolution in the Parliament of Great-Britain *to continue*

the

[1] Hening, VIII, p.454.

the several Acts impofing Duties for the fole Purpofe of raifing a Revenue in America; *expofing the perfons and Eftates of your Majefty's affectionate Subjects to the arbitrary Decifions of diftant Courts of Admiralty, and thereby depriving them of the ineftimable Right and Privilege of being tried by their Peers alone, according to the long eftablifh'd and well known Laws of the Land. From thefe baneful Sources have already been derived much Difquietude and Unhappinefs, which are not likely to abate under the Continuance of Meafures, apparently tending to deprive the Colonifts of every Thing dear and valuable to them.*

A partial Sufpenfion of Duties, and thefe fuch only, as were impofed on Britifh *Manufacturers, cannot, Great Sir, remove the two well grounded Fears and Apprehenfions of your Majefty's loyal Subjects, whilft Impofitions are continued on the fame Articles of foreign Fabrick, and entirely retain'd upon Tea, for the avow'd Purpofe of eftablifhing a Precedent againft us.*

We therefore judging it, at all Times, an indifpenfable Duty we owe to your Majefty, to our Country, ourfelves and Pofterity, humbly to lay our Grievances before the common Father of all his People, do now, imprefs'd with the higheft Senfe of Duty and Affection, proftrate ourfelves at the Foot of your Throne, moft humbly befeeching and imploring your Majefty gracioufly to interpofe your Royal Influence and Authority, to procure a total Repeal of thofe difagreeable Acts of Parliament, and to fecure to us the free and uninterrupted Enjoyment of all thofe Rights and Privileges, which from the Laws of Nature, of Community in general, and in a moft efpecial Manner, from the Principles of the Britifh *Conftitution, particularly recognized and confirm'd to this Colony by repeated and exprefs Stipulations, we prefume not to claim, but in common with all the reft of your Majefty's Subjects, under the fame or like Circumftances.*

That your Majefty and your Royal Defcendants may long and glorioufly reign in the Hearts of a free and happy People, is the conftant and fervent Prayer of
Yours Majefty's truly devoted, moft dutiful, loyal and affectionate Subjects.

The **Burgesses** *and* **Representatives.**

of the **People** *of* **Virginia.**

The faid *Petition* being read a fecond Time.

Refolved, Nemine Contradicente,

That the Houfe doth agree with the Committee in the faid Petition to be prefented to his Majefty.

Ordered, That the Committee of Correfpondence do fend the faid Petition to *Edward Montagu,* Efq; the Agent for this Colony, with Directions that he Caufe the fame to be prefented to his Majefty as foon as may be, and after it fhall be prefented, or offered to be prefented, that he procure it to be printed and publifhed in the *Englifh* Papers.

M⟨r⟩ *Treafurer* prefented to the Houfe, according to Order, a Bill to oblige fundry Inhabitants of the Parifhes of *Overwharton* and *Suffolk,* in the Counties of *Stafford* and *Nanfemond,* to Pay certain Expences therein mentioned; and the fame was received, and read the firft Time.

Refolved, That the Bill be read a fecond Time.

Refolved, That the Bill be now read a fecond Time.

The Bill was accordingly read a fecond Time.

Refolved, That the Bill be committed to M⟨r⟩ *Harrifon* and M⟨r⟩ *Henry Lee.*

A *Meffage* from the Council by M⟨r⟩ *Hubard;*

M⟨r⟩ *Speaker,*

The Council have agreed to the Bill, *intituled* An Act[1] to make Provifion for the Support and Maintenance of Ideots, Lunatics, and other Perfons of unfound Minds, *without any Amendment: And alfo,*

The Council have agreed to the Bill, *intituled* An Act[2] to repeal an Act made in the 22d Year of his late Majefty's Reign, intituled An Act concerning Strays; and

to

---

[1] Hening, VIII, p. 378.   [2] Ibid, VIII, p. 354.

to eftablifh a more effectual Method to prevent Frauds committed by Perfons taking up Strays, *without any Amendment: And alfo,*

The Council have agreed to the Bill, *intituled* An Act[1] for the Relief of Parifhes from fuch Charges as may arife from Baftard Children born within the fame, *without any Amendment: And alfo,*

The Council have agreed to the Bill, *intituled* An Act[2] for eftablifhing Towns at *Rocky Ridge, Gloucefter* Court Houfe, and *Layton's* Warehoufe; and for other Purpofes therein mentioned, *without any Amendment: And alfo,*

The Council have agreed to the Bill, *intituled* An Act[3] to confirm an Agreement made by *Thomas Talbutt* with the Court of *Norfolk* County, *without any Amendment: And alfo,*

The Council have agreed to the Bill, *intituled* An Act[4] to dock the Intail of certain Lands, whereof *John Wormeley,* Gentleman, is feized, and for fettling other Lands and Slaves, to the fame Ufes: *without any Amendment: And alfo,*

The Council have agreed to the Bill, *intituled* An Act[5] to regulate the Inoculation of the Small-Pox within this Colony, *with fome Amendments to which Amendments the Council defire the Concurrence of this Houfe: And alfo,*

The Council have agreed to the Bill, *intituled* An Act[6] to prevent the exorbitant Exactions of the Collectors of the County and Parifh Levies, *with fome Amendments, to which Amendments the Council defire the Concurrence of this Houfe.*

And then the Meffenger withdrew.

M[r] *Harrifon* reported from the Committee, to whom the Bill to oblige fundry Inhabitants of the Parifhes of *Overwharton* and *Suffolk,* in the Counties of *Stafford* and *Nanfemond,* to Pay certain Expences therein mentioned, was committed, that the Committee had gone through the Bill, and made feveral Amendments thereunto, which they had directed him to report to the Houfe; and he read the Report in his Place, and afterwards delivered the Bill, with the Amendments, in at the Clerk's Table; where the Amendments were once read throughout, and then a fecond Time, one by one, and, upon the Queftion feverally put thereupon, were agreed to by the Houfe.

Ordered, That the Bill, with the Amendments, be ingroffed.

The Houfe proceeded to take into Confideration the Amendments made by the Council to the Bill, intituled *An Act[7] to regulate the Inoculation of the Small-Pox within this Colony.*

And the faid *Amendments* were read, and are as followeth, *viz.*

287 Line 11. Leave out '*Hundred,*' and infert '*Thoufand*' inftead thereof.

Line 52. After '*Magiftrate*' infert '*fhall forfeit the Sum of One Hundred Pounds, upon his refufing or neglecting to give fuch Notice, without reafonable Excufe.*'

The faid *Amendments* being feverally read a fecond Time, were, upon the Queftion feverally put thereupon, agreed to by the Houfe.

Ordered, That M[r] *Archibald Cary* do carry the Bill to the Council, and acquaint them that this Houfe hath agreed to the Amendments made by them.

M[r] *Archibald Cary* prefented to the Houfe, according to Order, a Schedule containing an Account of all Sums of Money which have been agreed by the Houfe, fince the 21ft Day of *December* laft, to be paid by the Public.

And the *Schedule* was read.

Refolved, That the feveral Sums of Money mentioned in the faid Schedule be paid by the Treafurer out of the Public Money which may be in his Hands, on or before the 10th Day of *May* next.

Ordered, That M[r] *Archibald Cary* do carry the Schedule to the Council, and defire their Concurrence.

The Houfe proceeded to take into Confideration the Amendments made by the Council to the Bill, intituled *An Act[8] to prevent the exorbitant Exactions of the Collectors of the County and Parifh Levies.*

And

---

[1] Hening, VIII, p. 374.   [2] Ibid, VIII, p. 421.   [3] Ibid, VIII, p. 454.   [4] Ibid, VIII, p. 452.
[5] Ibid, VIII, p. 371.   [6] Ibid, VIII, p. 381.   [7] Ibid, VIII, p. 371.   [8] Ibid, VIII, p. 381.

And the faid *Amendments* were read, and are as followeth, *viz.*

Leave out from '*directed*' in Line 67, to the End of Line 86.

At the End of the Bill, add '*Provided always, that the Execution of this Act fhall be, and is hereby fufpended until his Majefty's Approbation thereof fhall be obtained.*'

The faid *Amendments* being feverally read a fecond Time, were, upon the Queftion feverally put thereupon, agreed to by the Houfe.

Ordered, That Mr *Archibald Cary* do carry the Bill to the Council, and acquaint them that this Houfe hath agreed to the Amendments made by them.

The *Order* of the Day being read;

Ordered, That the Call of the Houfe be further adjourned till to Tomorrow.

And then the Houfe adjourned till Tomorrow Morning Ten of the Clock.

Thursday, the 28th of June, 10 Geo. III. 1770.

AN ingroffed *Bill* to oblige fundry Inhabitants of the Parifhes of *Overwharton* and *Suffolk*, in the Counties of *Stafford* and *Nanfemond*, to pay certain Expences therein mentioned, was read the third Time.

A *Motion* was made, and the Queftion being put, that the Bill do pafs;

It paffed in the Negative.

A *Meffage* from the Council by Mr *Hubard;*

Mr *Speaker,*

The Council have agreed to the Schedule containing an Account of all Sums of Money which have been agreed by the Houfe, fince the 21ft Day of December laft, to be paid by the Public: And alfo,

The Council have agreed to the Bill *intituled* An Act[1] to continue and amend the Act, intituled An Act for amending the Staple of Tobacco, and for preventing Frauds in his Majefty's Cuftoms, *with fome Amendments, to which Amendments the Council defire the Concurrence of this Houfe.*

And then the Meffenger withdrew.

The Houfe proceeded to take the faid Amendments into Confideration.

And the faid *Amendments* were read, and are as followeth, *viz.*

Page 3, Line 18. After '*Record*' infert '*and upon every Profecution againft any* '*Infpector, for the faid Offence, the Proof of his Innocence fhall lie upon himfelf.*'

Line 21. After '*Norfolk,*' infert '*and.*'

Line 22. Leave out '*and at Totafkey, in the County of 'Richmond.*'

Line 43. Leave out '*at York and Rowe's, under one Infpection, Thirty Pounds.*'

Page 4, Line 29. After '*Office*' infert '*And be it further enacted, by the Authority afore-* '*faid, that all Tranffer Tobacco, to be delivered out of any Warehoufe hereafter, fhall* '*weigh at leaft One Thoufand Pounds Nett Tobacco; any Law, Cuftom or Ufage* '*to the contrary thereof in any Wife notwithftanding.*'

Line 29. After '*Act*' leave out to the End of the Bill, and infert '*fhall continue* '*and be in Force from and after the firft Day of October next; and that the faid* '*recited Act, as to fo much thereof as is not contrary to this Act, together with this* '*Act, fhall continue and be in Force from the faid firft Day of October, 1771, for* '*and during the Term of Two Years, and no longer.*'

The firft *Amendment* being read a fecond Time, was, upon the Queftion put thereupon, agreed to by the Houfe.

The two next *Amendments* being feverally read a fecond Time;

A *Motion* was made, and the Queftion being put, that the Houfe doth agree with the Council in the faid Amendments;

It paffed in the Negative.

The

263

---

[1] Hening, VIII, p. 318.

The next *Amendment* being read a fecond Time;

A *Motion* was made, and the Queftion being put, that the Houfe doth agree with the Council in the faid Amendment;

It paffed in the Negative.

The *two* laft of the faid *Amendments* being feverally read a fecond Time, were, upon the Queftion feverally put thereupon, agreed to by the Houfe.

Ordered, That a Meffage be fent to the Council to acquaint them, that this Houfe doth difagree to the fecond, third, and fourth of the faid Amendments by them propofed to the faid Bill, and doth defire that they will pafs the fame without the faid Amendments; and that Mr *Archibald Cary* do carry the faid Meffage.

A *Meffage* from the Council by Mr *Hubard;*

Mr *Speaker,*

The Council do not infift upon the fecond and third of the Amendments made by them to the Bill, *intituled* An Act[1] *to continue and amend the Act, intituled An Act for amending the Staple of Tobacco, and for preventing Frauds in his Majefty's Cuftoms, to which the Houfe have difagreed; but the Council do infift upon the fourth of the faid Amendments made by them to the faid Bill, difagreed to by this Houfe, and defire the Houfe will recede from their Difagreement thereunto.*

And then the Meffenger withdrew.

The faid *fourth Amendment* being twice read;

Refolved, That this Houfe doth infift upon their Difagreement to the faid Amendment.

Ordered, That a Meffage be fent to the Council to inform them, that this Houfe doth infift upon their Difagreement to the fourth Amendment by the Council infifted upon the faid Bill, and to defire that they will pafs the Bill, without the Amendment; and that Mr *Archibald Cary* do carry the faid Meffage.

A *Meffage* from the Council by Mr *Hubard;*

Mr *Speaker,*

I am commanded by the Council to acquaint this Houfe, that the Council do defire a prefent free Conference with this Houfe, in the Conference Chamber, upon the Subject-Matter of the fourth Amendment made by the Council to the Bill, intituled An Act[2] *to continue and amend the Act intituled an Act for amending the Staple of Tobacco, and for preventing Frauds in his Majefty's Cuftoms.*

And then the Meffenger withdrew.

Refolved, That this Houfe doth agree to a prefent free Conference with the Council as the Council do defire.

Ordered, That Mr *Treafurer* do go to the Council, and acquaint them that this Houfe doth agree to a prefent free Conference with the Council, as the Council do defire.

A *Meffage* from the Council by Mr *Hubard;*

Mr *Speaker,*

The Council have appointed three of their Members, who are now ready in the Conference Chamber, to meet the Managers appointed by this Houfe.

And then the Meffenger withdrew.

Refolved, That Mr *Treafurer*, Mr *Archibald Cary*, Mr *Wilfon Miles Cary*, Mr *Stark*, Mr *Jefferfon*, and Mr *Charles Carter*, of *King George*, do manage the Conference.

And they went up to the Conference accordingly; and being returned,

Mr *Treafurer* reported, from the Conference, that the Managers had attended the Council; that the Honourable *William Nelfon*, Efq; managed the Conference for the
Council

---

[1] Hening, VIII, p. 318.   [2] Ibid, VIII, p. 318.

Council, and faid that the Council infifted upon their Amendment, and gave their Reafons for the fame, as followeth, *viz.*

1. That the Quantities of Tranffer Tobacco brought to *York* and *Rowe's* Warehoufes being very confiderable, if thofe Infpections fo far afunder, fhould be united, the Infpectors could not faithfully difcharge their Duty at both.

2. That *York* being a Sea-Port, where Tobacco is frequently relanded from Ships in the Harbour there, and it being often neceffary to ftore Tobacco brought thither to be put on board Ships, which fometimes cannot take it in; the continual Prefence of the Infpectors, at that Place, in order to receive fuch Tobacco, is fo requifite, that the fame Perfons cannot properly attend *Rowe's* alfo.

And that the Council defired to be informed of the Reafons of this Houfe for difagreeing to the faid Amendment.

Ordered, That Mr *Treafurer* do go to the Council, to defire a free Conference upon the Subject-Matter of the laft free Conference.

A *Meffage* from the Council by Mr *Hubard;*

Mr *Speaker,*
The Council do agree to the free Conference defired by this Houfe, and do appoint the fame prefently in the Conference Chamber.

And then the Meffenger withdrew.

Refolved, That the Perfons who managed the laft free Conference, do manage this free Conference.

Ordered, That it be an Inftruction to the Managers that they inform the Council, of the Reafons of this Houfe for difagreeing to the faid Amendment.

The *Managers* went to the Conference accordingly.

A *Meffage* from the Council by Mr *Hubard;*

Mr *Speaker,*
The Council do adhere to the fourth of the Amendments made by them to the Bill, intituled An Act[1] to continue and amend the Act, intituled an Act for amending the Staple of Tobacco and for preventing Frauds in his Majefty's Cuftoms.

And then the Meffenger withdrew.

Refolved, That this Houfe doth recede from their Difagreement to the faid fourth Amendment.

Ordered, That Mr *Treafurer* do go to the Council, to defire a free Conference upon the Subject-Matter of the laft free Conference.

A *Meffage* from the Council by Mr *Hubard;*

Mr *Speaker,*
The Council do agree to the free Conference defired by this Houfe, and do appoint the fame prefently in the Conference Chamber.

And then the Meffenger withdrew.

Refolved, That the Perfons who managed the laft free Conference do Manage this free Conference.

Ordered, That it be an Inftruction to the Managers, that they acquaint the Council, that this Houfe is not fatiffied with their Reafons for the faid fourth Amendment to the faid Bill, but do recede from their Difagreement thereunto, becaufe otherwife, by the Council's Adherence, a Bill, in other Refpects, of very great Importance to this Colony, cannot pafs.

The *Managers* went to the Conference accordingly.

Mr *Dudley Digges* reported, from the Committee appointed to examine the enrolled
Bills

---

[1] Hening, VIII, p. 318.

Bills, that the Committee had examined the enrolled Bills, and rectified such Mistakes as were found therein, and that they are truly enrolled.

Ordered, That Mr *Dudley Digges* do carry the enrolled Bills to the Council, for their Inspection.

A *Message* from the Council by Mr *Hubard;*

Mr *Speaker,*
The Council have inspected the enrolled Bills, and are satisfied they are truly enrolled.

And then the Messenger withdrew.
A *Message* from the *Governor* by Mr *Hubard;*

Mr *Speaker,*
The Governor Commands this House to attend his Excellency immediately in the Council Chamber.

Accordingly Mr *Speaker,* with the House, went up to attend his Excellency in the Council Chamber, where his Excellency was pleased to give his Assent to the several Public and private Bills, and Resolves following, *viz.*

An Act[1] *for regulating the Election of Burgesses, for declaring their Privileges and Allowances, and for fixing the Rights of Electors.*

An Act[2] *to continue and amend the Act, intituled an Act for amending the Staple of Tobacco, and for preventing Frauds in his Majesty's Customs.*

An Act[3] *to repeal an Act, made in the 22d Year of his late Majesty's Reign, intituled an Act concerning Strays, and to establish a more effectual Method to prevent Frauds committed by Persons taking up Strays.*

An Act[4] *to amend the Act, intituled an Act to amend the Act for the better Government of Servants and Slaves.*

An Act[5] *to oblige the Owners of Mills, Hedges, or Stops, on the Rivers therein mentioned, to make Openings or Slopes therein for the Passage of Fish.*

An Act[6] *for encouraging the making Wine.*

An Act[7] *for encouraging the making Hemp.*

An Act[8] *to suspend the Execution of an Act, intituled an Act to amend an Act, intituled an Act for the Inspection of Pork, Beef, Flour, Tar, Pitch, and Turpentine.*

An Act[9] *for appointing Commissioners to meet with Commissioners, who are or may be appointed by the Legislatures of the neighbouring Colonies, to form and agree upon a general Plan for the Regulation of the Indian Trade.*

An Act[10] *for appointing several new Ferries, and for other Purposes therein mentioned.*

An Act[11] *to regulate the Inoculation of the Small-Pox within this Colony.*

An Act[12] *for the Relief of Parishes from such Charges as may arise from Bastard Children, born within the same.*

An Act[13] *to make Provision for the Support and Maintenance of Ideots, Lunatics, and other Persons of unsound Minds.*

An Act[14] *to prevent the exorbitant Exactions of the Collectors of the County and Parish Levies.*

An Act[15] *to amend an Act, intituled an Act against stealing Hogs.*

An Act[16] *to continue an Act, intituled an Act for regulating the Practice of Attornies.*

An Act[17] *to compel Persons to find Security for Payment of Costs in certain Cases.*

An Act[18] *for altering the Court Days of several Counties therein mentioned.*

An Act[19] *to explain certain Doubts, touching the Jurisdiction of the Court of Hustings of the City of Williamsburg.*

An Act[20] *for settling the Fees of the Clerk and Serjeant of the Court of Hustings for the City of Williamsburg.*

An

---

[1] Hening, VIII, p. 305. [2] Ibid, VIII, p. 318. [3] Ibid, VIII, p. 354. [4] Ibid, VIII, p. 358.
[5] Ibid, VIII, p. 361. [6] Ibid, VIII, p. 364. [7] Ibid, VIII, p. 363. [8] Ibid, VIII, p. 366
[9] Ibid, VIII, p. 367. [10] Ibid, VIII, p. 368. [11] Ibid, VIII, p. 371. [12] Ibid, VIII, p. 374.
[13] Ibid, VIII, p. 378. [14] Ibid, VIII, p. 381. [15] Ibid, VIII, p. 385. [16] Ibid, VIII, p. 385
[17] Ibid, VIII, p. 386. [18] Ibid, VIII, p. 400. [19] Ibid, VIII, p. 401. [20] Ibid, VIII, p. 402.

271

An Act[1] to amend an Act, paffed in the former Part of this Seffion of Affembly, for reimburfing the Counties of Hanover and King William the Expences of clearing Pamunkey River.

An Act[2] for eftablifhing a Town in the County of Pittfylvania.

An Act[3] for continuing and amending an Act, intituled an Act for reviving and amending the Acts for allowing Fairs to be kept in the Towns of Frederickfburg and Richmond, and for enlarging the Town of Frederickfburg.

An Act[4] to annex Part of the County of York to the County of James City, and for other Purpofes therein mentioned.

An Act[5] for eftablifhing Towns at Rocky Ridge, Gloucefter Court-Houfe, and Layton's Warehoufe, and for other Purpofes therein mentioned.

An Act[6] for dividing the Parifhes of Frederick, in the County of Frederick, and Cameron, in the County of Loudoun, and for other Purpofes therein mentioned.

An Act[7] to explain and amend an Act of this Seffion of Affembly, intituled an Act to divide the Parifh of Hamilton, in the Counties of Fauquier and Prince William.

An Act[8] to repeal an Act for increafing the Salary of the Minifter of the Parifh of Frederick, in the County of Frederick.

An Act[9] to impower the Veftry of Briftol Parifh, in the Counties of Dinwiddie and Prince George, to fell their Glebe.

An Act[10] for diffolving the feveral Veftries therein mentioned.

An Act[11] to appoint Truftees, in the room of thofe who are dead, for the Pamunkey Indians, and with further Power to hear and determine Controverfies among them.

An Act[12] to dock the Intail of certain Lands and Slaves, whereof John Page, Efq; is feized, and for fettling other Lands, of greater value, to the fame Ufes.

An Act[13] to dock the Intail of certain Lands, whereof Robert Burwell, Efq; is feized in Tail Male, and for fettling other Lands, of equal Value, in Lieu thereof.

An Act[14] to dock the Intail of certain Lands, whereof Francis Eppes is feized, and for fettling other Lands in Lieu thereof.

An Act[15] to dock the Intail of certain Lands, whereof John Wormeley, Gentleman, is feized, and for fettling other Lands and Slaves to the fame Ufes.

An Act[16] to confirm an Agreement made by Thomas Talbutt with the Court of Norfolk County.

An Act[17] to dock the Intail of certain Lands, whereof Richard Johnfon, Gentleman, is feized, and for fettling other Lands and Slaves to the fame Ufes.

An Act[18] to dock the Intail of Two Thoufand Eight Hundred Acres of Land, in the County of Brunfwick, whereof Armiftead Lightfoot is feized in Fee Tail, and vefting the fame in Truftees, to be fold for certain Purpofes therein mentioned.

An Act[19] to veft certain Lands, whereof John Robinfon, Efq; deceafed, is feized in Truft, for Philip Johnfon, Gentleman, and his Children, in Truftees, for the Purpofes therein mentioned.

An Act[20] to veft certain intailed Lands therein mentioned in Charles Carter, and for fettling other Lands to the fame Ufes.

An Act[21] to veft certain intailed Lands and Slaves therein mentioned in Nathaniel Lyttleton Savage, Gentleman, in Fee Simple, and to fettle other Lands in Lieu thereof.

An Act[22] to veft certain Lands in David Meade, in Fee Simple, whereof the faid David, and Sarah his Wife, are feized, in the Right of the faid Sarah, in Fee Tail, and for fettling other Lands in Lieu thereof.

An Act[23] to veft certain intailed Lands therein mentioned in George Brooke, Gentleman, in Fee fimple, and for fettling other Lands, of greater Value, in Lieu thereof.

An Act[24] to veft certain Lands, whereof Bernard Moore, Efq; is feized in Fee Tail, in

Truftees

[1] Hening, VIII, p. 407. [2] Ibid, VIII, p. 417. [3] Ibid, VIII, p. 418. [4] Ibid, VIII, p. 419.
[5] Ibid, VIII, p. 421. [6] Ibid, VIII, p. 425. [7] Ibid, VIII, p. 428. [8] Ibid, VIII, p. 430.
[9] Ibid, VIII, p. 431. [10] Ibid, VIII, p. 432. [11] Ibid, VIII, p. 433. [12] Ibid, VIII, p. 445.
[13] Ibid, VIII, p. 448. [14] Ibid, VIII, p. 450. [15] Ibid, VIII, p. 452. [16] Ibid, VIII, p. 454.
[17] Ibid, VIII, p. 455. [18] Ibid, VIII, p. 457. [19] Ibid, VIII, p. 460. [20] Ibid, VIII, p. 464.
[21] Ibid, VIII, p. 468. [22] Ibid, VIII, p. 470. [23] Ibid, VIII, p. 474. [24] Ibid, VIII, p. 476.

Truftees to be fold, and the Money laid out in the Purchafe of other Lands and Slaves, to be fettled to the fame Ufes.

An Act[1] to veft certain intailed Lands, whereof Charles Lewis, Gentleman, is feized, in John Lewis, Gentleman, in Fee Simple, and fettle other Lands to the fame Ufes.

An Act[2] to dock the Intail of Four Thoufand Acres of Land, in the County of Ifle of Wight, whereof James Burwell is feized in Fee Tail, and for vefting the fame in Truftees, in Fee Simple, for certain Purpofes therein mentioned.

An Act[3] to dock the Intail of Five Hundred and Fifty Acres of Land, in the County of Gloucefter, whereof Sarah, the Wife of John Rootes, Gentleman, is feized, and for vefting the fame in Truftees, for the Purpofes therein mentioned.

An Act[4] to veft certain intailed Lands, whereof William and John Armiftead, Gentlemen, are feized, in Truftees, to be fold for Payment of the Debts due from the Eftate of their Father.

A Refolve for paying One Hundred Pounds to each of the Commiffioners for regulating the Indian Trade.

A Refolve for purchafing two Iron Chefts for the Ufe of the Treafury.

A Refolve for paying an additional Salary to the Printer.

A Schedule, containing an Account of all Sums of Money which have been agreed fince the 21ft Day of December laft, to be paid by the Public.

After which his Excellency was pleafed to make a Speech to the Council, and this Houfe, as followeth, *viz.*

*Gentlemen of the Council, M*r *Speaker, and Gentlemen of the Houfe of Burgeffes,*

It is with the utmoft Gratitude I acknowledge the many Marks of Confidence with which I have been honoured by this Affembly. To what extent I may be able to ferve you, Time only can prove. Upon my Zeal you may depend, and that it will know no bounds, but what my Duty fhall impofe.

*As I underftand that you have gone through the Bufinefs of the Seffion, and wifh to return to your feveral Counties, I do prorogue you to Thurfday the 25*th *of October, and you are accordingly prorogued to Thurfday the 25*th *of October next.*

---

1 Hening, VIII, p. 478.   2 Ibid, VIII, p. 481.   3 Ibid, VIII. p. 483.   4 Ibid, VIII. p. 487.

JOURNAL

of the

HOUSE OF BURGESSES

1771

Burgeffes.

Accomack	*Southey Simpfon *Thomas Parramore	Hampfhire	*James Mercer *Abram Hite
Albemarle	Thomas Walker Thomas Jefferfon	Hanover	William Macon, Jr. Patrick Henry, Jr.
Amelia	*John Winn *Robert Munford	Henrico	*Richard Randolph Richard Adams
Amherft	*William Cabell, Jr. Cornelius Thomas	Ifle of Wight	*Richard Baker *James Bridger
Augufta	*Gabriel Jones John Wilfon	James City	Robt. Carter Nicholas Lewis Burwell
Bedford	*John Talbot *Charles Lynch	Jameftown	*Champion Travis
Botetourt	*William Prefton *John Bowyer	King and Queen	*William Lyne John Taylor Corbin
Brunfwick	Thomas Stith *John Jones	King George	*Charles Carter William Robinfon
Buckingham	*Jofeph Cabell Benjamin Howard	King William	*Carter Braxton *Bernard Moore
Caroline	Edmund Pendleton *Walker Taliaferro	Lancafter	*Richard Mitchell Charles Carter
Charles City	Benjamin Harrifon *William Acrill	Loudoun	Francis Peyton *Jofias Clapham
Charlotte	Paul Carrington *Ifaac Read	Louifa	*Thomas Johnfon *Richard Anderfon
Chefterfield	Archibald Cary Edward Ofborne	Lunenburg	*Thomas Pettus *Lodowick Farmer
The College	*John Page	Mecklenburg	*Robert Munford *Matthew Marrable
Culpeper	Henry Pendleton *Henry Field, Jr.	Middlefex	*Gawin Corbin Edmund Berkeley
Dinwiddie	*Bolling Starke John Banifter	Nanfemond	Lemuel Riddick *Willis Riddick
Elizabeth City	Wilfon Miles Cary *James Wallace	New Kent	Burwell Baffett *William Clayton
Effex	James Edmondfon *William Roane	Norfolk	*John Wilfon Thomas Newton, Jr.
Fairfax	George Wafhington *John Weft	Norfolk Borough	*Jofeph Hutchings
Fauquier	Thomas Marfhall *James Scott	Northampton	*Severn Eyre *John Burton
Frederick	Robert Rutherford James Wood	Northumberland	Spencer Mottrom Ball *Peter Prefley Thornton
Gloucefter	Thomas Whiting Lewis Burwell	Orange	*James Walker Thomas Barbour
Goochland	John Woodfon Thomas Mann Randolph	Pittfylvania	*John Donelfon *Hugh Innes
Halifax	*Nathaniel Terry Walter Coles	Prince Edward	*Thomas Scott Pafchall Greenhill

*Not fhown by the Journal to have been prefent during the Affembly.

Prince George	Richard Bland	Surry	Thomas Bailey
	Peter Poythrefs		Hartwell Cocke
Prince William	Henry Lee	Suffex	*David Mafon
	*Foufhee Tebbs		*James Bell
Princefs Anne	*Edward Hack Mofeley, Jr.	Warwick	William Harwood
	*John Ackifs		William Digges
Richmond	*Robert Wormeley Carter	Weftmoreland	Richard Henry Lee
	*Francis Lightfoot Lee		Richard Lee
Southampton	Edwin Gray	Williamfburg	Peyton Randolph
	Henry Taylor	York	Dudley Digges
Spotfylvania	*Roger Dixon		Thomas Nelfon, Jr.
	*Benjamin Grymes		
Stafford	John Alexander		
	*Thomfon Mafon		

*Not fhown by the Journal to have been prefent during the Affembly.

Changes in the Perfonnel, 1771.

Amelia	Robert Munford fucceeded Thomas Tabb
Brunfwick	John Jones fucceeded Nathaniel Edwards
Loudoun	James Hamilton fucceeded Jofias Clapham
Middlefex	Edmund Berkeley fucceeded Philip Ludwell Grymes
Nanfemond	Willis Riddick fucceeded Benjamin Baker
Northumberland	Peter Prefley Thornton fucceeded Samuel Efkridge
Princefs Anne	Chriftopher Wright fucceeded Edward Hack Mofeley
The College	John Page fucceeded John Blair, Jr.

By his **Excellency**, the Right Honourable **Norborne Berkeley**, Baron **Botetourt**, his Majefty's Lieutenant and Governor General of the Colony and Dominion of **Virginia**, and Vice Admiral of the fame:

A PROCLAMATION.

Virginia, to wit:

Whereas, the General Affembly ftands prorogued to the 25th day of next month, and *whereas* I find no urgent occafion for the faid Affembly's meeting at that time; I have therefore thought fit by and with the advice of his Majefty's Council, by this Proclamation, in his Majefty's name, farther to prorogue the faid Affembly to the 4th *Thurfday* in *Novem'*. next [If it was intended the Affembly fhould meet at the above mentioned time it would have been proper to add, at which time I require their attendance at the Capitol in Williamfburg for the difpatch of public bufinefs]

Given under my hand and the Seal of the Colony at *Williamfburg*, this 27th day of *Sep'*.
1770, and in the 10th year of his Majefty's Reign.

Botetourt.

GOD SAVE THE KING.

By the Honorable **Wm. Nelson, Esq.** Prefident of
the Council & Commander in Chief of the Colony
and Dominion of **Virginia:**

A PROCLAMATION.

Whereas, the Gen¹. Affembly ftands prorogued to the 4ᵗʰ *Thurfday* in this month
and I find no urgent occafion for the faid Affembly's meeting at that time; I have therefore thought fit, by and with the advice of his Majefty's Council, by this Proclamation
in his Majefty's Name further to prorogue the faid Affembly to the 3d *Thurfday* in *May*
next.

Given under my Hand and the Seal of the Colony at *Williamfburg*, this fixth Day of
November, 1770, and in the eleventh Year of his Majefty's Reign.

William Nelson.

GOD SAVE THE KING.

By the Honorable **Wm. Nelson Esq.** President
of the Council & Commander in Chief of the
Colony and Dominion of **Virginia:**

A PROCLAMATION.

Whereas, the General Affembly ftands prorogued to the third *Thurfday* in this Month, and I find no urgent Occafion for the faid Affembly meeting at that Time; I have therefore, thought fit, by and with the Advice of his Majefty's Council, by this Proclamation, in his Majefty's Name, further to prorogue the faid Affembly, to the third *Thurfday* in *October* next.

Given under my Hand and the Seal of the Colony, at *Williamfburg*, this firft Day of *May* 1771, and in the eleventh Year of his Majefty's Reign.

William Nelson.

GOD SAVE THE KING.

By the Honorable **Wm. Nelson, Esq.** President of
the Council & Commander in Chief of the Colony
and Dominion of **Virginia:**

A PROCLAMATION.

Whereas, the General Aſſembly ſtands prorogued to the third *Thurſday* in *October* next, and *whereas* it is judged expedient that the ſaid Aſſembly ſhould meet ſooner; I have therefore thought fit, by and with the advice and conſent of his Majeſty's Council, to appoint *Thurſday*, the eleventh Day of the next Month for that Purpoſe; at which Time their Attendance is accordingly required at the Capitol in *Williamſburg*.

Given under my Hand, and the Seal of the Colony this 13th Day of *June*, in the 11th Year of his Majeſty's Reign, and in the Year of our Lord 1771.

William Nelson.

GOD SAVE THE KING.

JOURNAL

of the

HOUSE OF BURGESSES

Thursday, the 11th of July, 11 Geo. III. 1771.

1   A Meffage from the Prefident by *John Blair*, the younger, Efq; Clerk of the Council.

Mʳ *Speaker*,
The Prefident commands this Houfe to attend his Honour immediately in the Council Chamber.

Accordingly the Houfe went up to attend his Honour in the Council Chamber.
And being returned;
Mʳ *Speaker* reported, That the Prefident was pleafed to make a Speech to the Council and this Houfe, of which, Mʳ *Speaker* faid, he had, to prevent Miftakes, obtained a Copy; which he read to the Houfe, and is as followeth, *viz.*

Gentlemen of the Council, Mʳ Speaker, and Gentlemen of the Houfe of Burgeffes,

The very great and heavy loffes which many refpectable Gentlemen, Merchants and other Inhabitants of this Colony, have fuftained by the late overflowing of the Rivers (as expreffed in their Memorial, a Copy of which fhall be delivered you) have inclined me, with the Advice of his Majefty's Council, to call you together at this unexpected Time, that you may have the earlieft Opportunity of confidering what ought to be done for the fpeedy Relief of the Sufferers by fo general and extenfive a Calamity.

The unfavorable Influence which this unhappy Event muft have on the credit of fome, in which many of the People might be deeply involved, if the Confideration of it fhould be long deferred, I hope will be a fufficient Apology for my convening you at this Seafon of the Year, when I know your own private Affairs require your more immediate Care and Attention.

Mʳ Speaker, and Gentlemen of the Houfe of Burgeffes,

I have defired the principal Sufferers to be prepared, against this Meeting, with a particular State of their feveral Loffes, to be immediately laid before you, that the Bufinefs may take up as little of your Time as poffible; and as the Relief which may be expected muft originate with you, I cannot but, in the warmeft Manner, recommend their Cafe to your ferious Confideration, not in the leaft doubting but that thofe Sentiments of Juftice, Honour, and Humanity, which have been your Guide in all fimilar Inftances, will, upon this Occafion alfo, form the Rule of your Conduct.

Gentlemen of the Council, Mʳ Speaker, and Gentlemen of the Houfe of Burgeffes,

Humbly to fubmit to the Hand of Providence in every Difpenfation, is the indifpenfable Duty of us all; but I confider it as equally incumbent on us, to endeavor to heal the Wounds which this Stroke hath given, as far as our Situation, and the Circumftances of the Country, will permit; for my own Part, I feel fo fenfibly for the Sharers in this melancholy Cataftrophe, that I fhall be happy, if, by my Affent to your Refolutions, I can be, in any Degree, inftrumental in alleviating their Diftreffes.

I fhould be wanting in the Duty I owe to his Majefty, and the affectionate Regard I bear

to

to this Country, if I did not embrace this firft Opportunity which hath offered fince the Adminiftration devolved upon me, of publicly condoling with you on the Death of our moft worthy Governor, the Right Honourable Lord Botetourt; a Lofs, the more to be lamented by us, as we were the frequent Witneffes of his Excellency's conftant and uniform Exertion of every public and private Virtue, and had abundant Reafon to be convinced that he made the real Happinefs of this Colony an Objeſt of his moft ardent Wifhes. But, though we may be defirous of paying a juft Tribute of Praife and Gratitude to fuch exalted Merit, let us be comforted, from this Perfuafion, that the fame favourable Attention and Regard to the true Interefts and Welfare of his Majefty's faithful Subjeſts of Virginia, which led to the appointment of this noble Lord to prefide over us, will ever incline our moft gracious Sovereign to fill the fame Department with a Succeffor, equally entitled to our dutiful and affeſtionate Efteem.

Refolved, That an humble Addrefs be prefented to his Honour the Prefident returning him the Thanks of this Houfe for his kind and affeſtionate Speech; earneftly to condole with him on the Death of our late excellent Governor, expreffing our firm Reliance on his Majefty's Goodnefs in repairing fo great a Lofs to his dutiful Subjeſts of *Virginia;* to congratulate his Honour on his Succeffion to the Adminiftration of this Government, a juft Reward of his long and faithful Services to his Majefty and this Country, affuring him of the Satiffaſtion and Happinefs we enjoy in having a Gentleman of his diftinguifhed Abilities and known Attachment to the true Interefts of this Colony to prefide over us, and that we will take the important Bufinefs, he hath been pleafed to recommend, under our immediate and moft ferious Confideration, and do therein whatever, by the Principles of Juftice, Honour and Humanity may be diſtated to us.

Ordered, That a Committee be appointed to draw up an Addrefs, to be prefented to the Prefident, upon the faid Refolution.

And a *Committee* was appointed of Mr *Bland* and Mr *Richard Henry Lee.*

Ordered, That the Prefident's Speech to the Council and this Houfe be referred to the faid Committee.

Mr *Speaker* acquainted the Houfe, that the Prefident had delivered to him the Memorial of the Merchants and other Inhabitants of this Colony, mentioned in his Honour's Speech, and defired him to lay it before the Houfe.

And he delivered the *Memorial* in at the Clerk's Table.

Ordered, That the faid Memorial do lie upon the Table, to be perufed by the Members of the Houfe.

A *Member* returned upon a new Writ, having taken the Oaths appointed to be taken by Aſt of Parliament, and repeated and fubfcribed the Teft, took his Place in the Houfe.

Refolved, That the Prefident's Speech be taken into Confideration Tomorrow.

Refolved, That this Houfe will, To-morrow, refolve itfelf into a Committee of the whole Houfe, to take into Confideration the Prefident's Speech.

Ordered, That an Addrefs be made to the Prefident, to order a new Writ to be made out for the eleſting of a Burgefs, to ferve in this prefent General Affembly, for the County of *Brunfwick,* in the Room of Mr *Nathaniel Edwards*[1], jun. deceafed; and that Mr *Bland* do wait upon his Honour with the faid Addrefs.

Ordered, That an Addrefs be made to the Prefident, to order a new Writ to be made out, for the eleſting of a Burgefs, to ferve in this prefent General Affembly, for the County of *Northumberland,* in the room of Mr *Samuel Efkridge*[2], deceafed; and that Mr *Richard Lee* do wait upon his Honour with the faid Addrefs.

Ordered, That an Addrefs be made to the Prefident, to order a new Writ to be made out for the eleſting of a Burgefs to ferve in this prefent General Affembly, for the County of *Princefs Anne,* in the Room of Mr *Edward Hack Mofeley*[3], jun. who, fince his Eleſtion for the faid County, hath accepted the Office of Clerk of the Court of the faid County; and that Mr *Newton* do wait upon his Honour with the faid Addrefs.

Ordered, That an Addrefs be made to the Prefident, to order a new Writ to be made

out

---

[1] John Jones.   [2] Peter Prefley Thornton.   [3] Chriftopher Wright.

out, for the electing of a Burgefs, to ferve in this prefent General Affembly, for the County of *Nanfemond*, in the Room of Mᷓ *Benjamin Baker*[1], who fince his Election for the faid County, hath accepted the Office of one of his Majefty's Coroners of the faid County; and that Mᷓ *Riddick* do wait upon his Honour with the faid Addrefs.

Ordered, That an Addrefs be made to the Prefident, to order a new Writ to be made out for the electing of a Burgefs, to ferve in this prefent General Affembly, for the College of *William and Mary*, in the Room of Mᷓ *John Blair*[2], jun. who, fince his Election for the faid College, hath accepted the Office of Clerk of his Majefty's Council; and that Mᷓ *Jefferfon* do wait upon his Honour with the faid Addrefs.

Ordered, That an Addrefs be made to the Prefident, to order a new Writ to be made out for the electing of a Burgefs to ferve in this prefent General Affembly, for the County of *Middlefex*, in the Room of Mᷓ *Philip Ludwell Grymes*[3], who, fince his Election for the faid County, hath accepted the Office of Sheriff of the faid County; and that Mᷓ *Nelfon* do wait upon his Honour with the faid Addrefs.

Ordered, That an Addrefs be made to the Prefident, to order a new Writ to be made out for the electing of a Burgefs, to ferve in this prefent General Affembly, for the County of *Charlotte*, in the Room of Mᷓ *Paul Carrington*[4], who, fince his Election for the faid County, hath accepted the Office of his Majefty's Deputy Attorney in the Court of the faid County; and that Mᷓ *Coles* do wait upon his Honour with the faid Addrefs.

Ordered, That the Reverend Mᷓ *Thomas Price* be continued Chaplain to this Houfe, and that he attend to read Prayers every Morning at Eight of the Clock.

Ordered, That Mᷓ *Bland* do go to the Council, and acquaint them that the Chaplain will attend to read Prayers at Eight of the Clock every Morning, in the Houfe.

Ordered, That *James Lavie, Robert Hyland, William Hicks*, and *John Creagh*, be continued Door-keepers to this Houfe, and that they give their Attendance accordingly.

And then the Houfe adjourned till To-morrow Morning nine of the Clock.

Friday, the 12th of July, 11 Geo. III. 1771.

SEVERAL *Petitions* of the Inhabitants of the County of *Spotfylvania*, whofe Names are thereunto fubfcribed, were prefented to the Houfe, and read; fetting forth, that the Petitioners, have long laboured under many Grievances from the inconvenient Situation of their County Court-Houfe; and therefore praying the Houfe to make Application to the commanding Officer of the Colony to iffue his Writ of Adjournment, and appoint the Court to be held at fome Place neareft to the Center of the County.

Ordered, That the Confideration of the faid feveral Petitions be deferred till the next Seffion of the General Affembly.

A *Petition* of feveral perfons, refiding in the Frontier Parts of this Colony, whofe Names are thereunto fubfcribed, was prefented to the Houfe, and read; fetting forth that the Times appointed by Law for General Mufters of the Militia are inconvenient; and therefore praying, that the General Mufters may be in the Months of *October* and *November* annually.

Ordered, That the faid Petition do lie upon the Table.

Ordered, That the Confideration of all fuch Propofitions and Petitions as were at the laft Seffion of the General Affembly deferred till the prefent Seffion, and all fuch Public Claims, Propofitions, and Petitions, as have come and fhall come certified to this Seffion, be deferred till the next Seffion of the General Affembly.

Several *Accounts* of the Tobacco damaged by the late Frefh in the public Ware-houfes at *Shockoe's, Rocky Ridge, Byrd's, Warwick, Falmouth*, and *Dixon's* were pre-fented to the Houfe.

And

---

[1] Willis Riddick.   [2] John Page.   [3] Edmund Berkeley.   [4] Carrington re-elected.

And the *Titles* of the faid Accounts were read.

Ordered, That the faid Accounts do lie upon the Table, to be perufed by the Members of the Houfe.

Refolved, Nemine Contradicente, That the Thanks of this Houfe be given to the Reverend Mr *Henley*, the Reverend Mr *Gwatkin*, the Reverend Mr *Hewitt*, and the Reverend Mr *Bland*, for the wife and well timed Oppofition they have made to the pernicious Project of a few miftaken Clergymen, for introducing an *American* Bifhop; a Meafure by which much Difturbance, great Anxiety, and Apprehenfion, would certainly take Place among his Majefty's faithful *American* Subjects; and that Mr *Richard Henry Lee*, and Mr *Bland*, do acquaint them therewith.

Mr *Bland* reported, from the Committee appointed to draw up an Addrefs to be prefented to the Prefident, that the Committee had drawn up an Addrefs accordingly, which they had directed him to report to the Houfe; and he read the fame in his Place, and afterwards delivered it in at the Clerk's Table, where the fame was read, and is as followeth, *viz.*

To the Honourable WILLIAM NELSON, Efq; Prefident of his Majefty's Council, and Commander in Chief of the Colony and Dominion of Virginia.

The humble ADDRESS of the HOUSE of BURGESSES.
SIR,

We his Majefty's moft dutiful and loyal Subjects, the Burgeffes of Virginia, *now met in General Affembly, beg Leave to return your Honour our unfeigned Thanks for your very affectionate Speech at the Opening of this Seffion.*

Our deep Senfe of the Lofs this Country fuftained by the Death of our late excellent and worthy Governor, the Right Honourable Lord Botetourt, *cannot but excite in us all the Warmth of the moft fincere Affection and Gratitude to his Memory, and we heartily lament, with your Honour, upon an Event fo unfortunate to this Country.*

When we reflect on his Lordfhip's unremitted Zeal in promoting the Caufe of Religion and Virtue; On that Dignity, tempered with fo becoming and proper a Degree of Affability, with which he filled his exalted Station; when we recall to our Remembrance his Excellency's unwearied Diligence and Activity in Bufinefs, and his uniform Exertion of every public and private Virtue, we have the ftrongeft Conviction that he made the real Happinefs of this Colony the Object of his moft ardent Wifhes: We fhould, therefore, think ourfelves wanting in Duty to his Majefty, and in the Regard we owe to our Country, did we not feize this firft Opportunity of publicly paying a juft Tribute to fo high a Character. Our chief Confolation arifes from a firm Perfuafion, that our Gracious Sovereign will, in his great Goodnefs, be pleafed to appoint a Governor, to prefide over us, equally worthy of the Royal Confidence, and of our dutiful and affectionate Efteem.

But, Sir, however we may defire to do Juftice to the Memory of one, who fo defervedly gained our Regard and Affection, we are very far from being unmindful of what is due to your Honour, and hope you will be perfuaded that we enjoy great Satiffaction and Happinefs in having a Gentleman of your Honour's diftinguifhed Abilities and known Attachment to the true Intereft of this Country, to prefide over us; we, therefore, moft fincerely congratulate your Honour on your Succeffion to the Adminiftration, which we confider as a juft Reward of your long and faithful Services to his Majefty and his dutiful Subjects of Virginia.

Moft earneftly concurring, with your Honour, in deploring the Calamities occafioned by the late dreadful overflowing of the Waters, and heartily commiferating the Diftreffes of the unhappy Sufferers, we will proceed to take their Cafe under our immediate and ferious Confideration; and we affure your Honour that we will, in the Courfe of our Deliberations, endeavor to follow, as our beft and fureft Guides, thofe Principles of Juftice, Honour and Humanity, which, we truft, in all similar Inftances, and upon every other Occafion, have formed the Rule of our Conduct.

The faid *Addrefs* being read a fecond Time;

Refolved, Nemine Contradicente, That the Houfe doth agree with the Committee in the faid Addrefs, to be prefented to the Prefident.

Refolved

Refolved, That the faid Addrefs be prefented to the Prefident by the whole Houfe.

Ordered, That the Gentlemen, who drew up the faid Addrefs, do wait upon the Prefident, to know his Pleafure when this Houfe fhall attend his Honour, to prefent their Addrefs.

The *Order* of the Day being read, for the Houfe to refolve itfelf into a Committee of the whole Houfe, to take into Confideration the Prefident's Speech;

Ordered, That the Memorial of the Merchants and other Inhabitants of this Colony, mentioned in the Prefident's Speech, and Yefterday ordered to lie upon the Table, be referred to the faid Committee.

Ordered, That the Accounts of the Tobacco damaged by the late Frefh in the public Warehoufes, at *Shockoe's*, *Rocky Ridge*, *Byrd's*, *Warwick*, *Falmouth*, and *Dixon's*, which were this Day ordered to lie upon the Table, be referred to the faid Committee.

Then the Houfe refolved itfelf into the faid Committee.

Mr *Speaker* left the Chair.

Mr *Bland* took the Chair of the Committee.

Mr *Speaker* refumed the Chair.

Mr *Bland* reported, from the Committee, that they had gone through the Matters to them referred, and had come to feveral Refolutions, which he read in his Place, and afterwards delivered in at the Clerk's Table, where the fame were read, and are as followeth, *viz.*

Refolved, That it is the Opinion of this Committee, that the Proprietors of Tobacco infpected, and damaged in the feveral Public Warehoufes, by the late Frefh, except fuch Tobacco as had remained in the Warehoufes above a Year, ought to be paid for their Loffes by the Public.

Refolved, That it is the Opinion of this Committee, that the Proprietors of Tobacco, delivered at the feveral Public Warehoufes, and not viewed for want of Leifure in the Infpectors to do the fame, and damaged, ought to be reimburfed for their faid Loffes by the Public.

The faid *Refolutions*, being feverally read a fecond Time, were, upon the Queftion feverally put thereupon, agreed to by the Houfe.

Ordered, That a Committee be appointed to examine and ftate Accounts of the Loffes fuftained, by means of the late Frefh, as well in the Tobacco infpected, as in fuch as was brought to be infpected, but not viewed, at the feveral Public Warehoufes, except fuch Tobacco as had remained in the faid Warehoufes above a Year.

And a *Committee* was appointed of Mr *Bland*, Mr *Edmund Pendleton*, Mr *Archibald Cary*, Mr *Richard Henry Lee*, Mr *Harrifon*, Mr *Lewis Burwell*, of *James City*, Mr *William Digges*, Mr *Dudley Digges*, Mr *Henry Lee*, Mr *Richard Lee*, Mr *Riddick*, Mr *Harwood*, Mr *Nelfon*, Mr *Alexander*, Mr *Adams*, Mr *Poythrefs*, Mr *Thomas Walker*, Mr *Cocke*, Mr *Whiting*, Mr *Baffett*, Mr *Rutherford*, Mr *Marfhall*, Mr *Robinfon*, Mr *Coles*, Mr *Ball*, and Mr *Wood;* and they are to meet and adjourn from Day to Day, and report their Proceedings to the Houfe; and the faid Committee are to have Power to fend for Perfons, Papers, and Records for their Information.

Refolved, That eleven of the faid Committee be a fufficient Number to proceed in the Bufinefs referred to them.

Ordered, That Mr *Hynd Ruffell* be appointed Clerk to the faid Committee.

And then the Houfe adjourned till To-morrow Morning nine of the Clock.

Saturday, the 13th of July, 11 Geo. III. 1771.

MR *Bland* reported to the Houfe, that the Prefident having been waited on, purfuant to the Order of Yefterday, to know his Pleafure when he would be attended by this Houfe, had been pleafed to appoint to be attended this Day in the Council Chamber, and to fay he would acquaint the Houfe, by a Meffenger of his own, when he was ready to receive their Addrefs.

Two *Members* returned upon new Writs, having taken the Oaths appointed to be taken

taken by Act of Parliament, and repeated and fubfcribed the Teft, took their Places in the Houfe.

Several *Petitions* of fundry Freeholders, of the County of *Henrico*, and others, whofe Names are thereunto fubfcribed, were prefented to the Houfe, and read; fetting forth, that the Warehoufes at *Shockoe's* and *Byrd's*, in the faid County, are inconveniently fituated, being on low Land, fubject to be overflowed by the River; that the late Frefh not only deftroyed and damaged large Quantities of Tobacco in the faid Warehoufes, but alfo, in great Meafure, filled up the Channel of the River leading thereto; and that it will be for the Advantage of the Public to difcontinue thofe Infpections, and to appoint others in their Room, about half a Mile below, on the upper End of the Land of Mr *Charles Lewis*, which is higher Ground, and near to a good Landing; and therefore praying that one or more Infpections of Tobacco may be eftablifhed on the Land of the faid *Charles Lewis*, at that Place.

Alfo feveral *Petitions* of fundry Inhabitants of the Counties of *Amherft, Buckingham, Goochland*, and *Henrico*, whofe Names are thereunto fubfcribed, in Oppofition to the faid Petitions for difcontinuing the Infpections at *Byrd's* and *Shockoe's*, and eftablifhing them on the Land of *Charles Lewis*, were feverally prefented to the Houfe, and read; fetting forth, that the moft convenient Places for eftablifhing thofe Infpections at, are the Lands diftinguifhed in the Plan of the Town of *Richmond* by the Names of *Bowyer's* and *Houfling's* Tenements; and that the Channel of the River from *Shockoe* Wharf, by Means of private Subfcriptions, will probably be foon opened, and made as fit for Navigation as ever, a Sum of Money, fufficient for that Purpofe, having been already raifed; and therefore praying, that Infpections, in the Room of *Byrd's* and *Shockoe's*, if they fhould be difcontinued, may be eftablifhed on the faid Tenements, called *Bowyer's* and *Houfling's*; or that this Honourable Houfe, until they can be fatiffied it is practicable to reftore the faid Channel, will fufpend their determination, as to the Situation of the faid Infpections.

Ordered, That the faid feveral Petitions do lie upon the Table.

A *Petition* of *John Sharp* and *William Lyon*, was prefented to the Houfe, and read; fetting forth, that, on the twenty-fixth Day of May laft, difcovering an extraordinary Rife of Water, the Petitioners, who were Tenders at *Dixon's* Warehoufes, with the Affiftance of fome Perfons by them hired, rolled out of the middle Warehoufe and faved one hundred and fifty-four Hogfheads of Tobacco ftored therein, which would otherwife have been deftroyed by the Frefh, and, after the Waters abated, returned the Tobacco into the Houfe again; and therefore praying, that this Honourable Houfe will allow them a reafonable Satiffaction for their Trouble.

Ordered, That the faid Petition be referred to the Confideration of the Committee appointed to examine and ftate Accounts of the Loffes fuftained by means of the late Frefh; and that they do examine the Matter thereof, and report the fame, with their Opinion thereupon, to the Houfe.

A *Meffage* from the Prefident by Mr *Blair*.

Mr *Speaker*,
The Prefident is now ready to receive the Addrefs of your Houfe in the Council Chamber.

Accordingly Mr *Speaker*, with the Houfe, went up; and being returned, he reported that the Houfe had attended the Prefident, with their Addrefs, to which his Honor was pleafed to give this Anfwer:

Mr *Speaker, and Gentlemen of the Houfe of Burgeffes, I return you my fincere Thanks for this kind Addrefs.*

It gives me particular Pleafure to find, that in doing Juftice to the Memory of the late Right Honourable Lord Botetourt, *your Ideas of his Excellency's great Merit appear fo conformable to thofe I had conceived of him.*

The Approbation with which you are pleafed to honour my poor Endeavors for his Majefty's

Majefty's Service, and the Happinefs of his Subjects of Virginia, *affords me the highest satiffaction; for which you will be pleafed to accept my moft grateful Acknowledgements.*

Ordered, That a Committee be appointed to enquire what Laws will expire at the End of this Seffion, and to report their Opinion to the Houfe which of them are fit to be continued.

And a *Committee* was appointed of Mr *Richard Henry Lee,* Mr *Bailey,* Mr *Thomas,* Mr *Lewis Burwell,* of *Gloucefter,* Mr *Stith,* Mr *Howard,* Mr *Barbour,* Mr *Henry Pendleton,* Mr *Macon,* Mr *Woodfon,* Mr *John Tayloe Corbin,* Mr *Gray,* Mr *Taylor,* Mr *Peyton,* Mr *Thomas Mann Randolph,* Mr *Greenhill,* and Mr *Edmondfon;* and they are to meet and adjourn from Day to Day.

Ordered, That Leave be given to bring in a Bill, to impower the Inhabitants of the Parifh of *Augufta,* in the County of *Augufta,* to elect a Veftry; and that Mr *Bland,* and Mr *John Wilfon,* of *Augufta,* do prepare and bring in the fame.

Several *Petitions* of the Inhabitants in the Fork of *Rapidan* and *Robinfon* Rivers, in the County of *Culpeper,* whofe Names are thereunto fubfcribed, were prefented to the Houfe, and read; fetting forth, that the petitioners live much further from the Court-Houfe in their own County, than they do from the Court-Houfe in the County of *Orange;* and therefore praying that fo much of the County of *Culpeper* as lies between the *Rapidan* and *Robinfon* Rivers, may be added to the County of *Orange.*

Ordered, That the Confideration of the faid feveral Petitions be deferred till the next Seffion of the General Affembly.

And then the Houfe adjourned till Monday Morning next nine of the Clock.

Monday, the 15th of July, 11 Geo. III. 1771.

A *Petition* of the Veftrymen of the Parifh of *Hamilton,* in the County of *Fauquier,* whofe Names are thereunto fubfcribed, in Behalf of the Inhabitants of the faid Parifh, was prefented to the Houfe, and read; fetting forth, that before the late Divifion of the faid Parifh, made by Act of General Affembly, a Majority of one hundred Tithables, by Agreement, was to be left therein, but that by the Line eftablifhed the faid Parifh hath, inftead of a Majority, fixty Tithables fewer than the other Parifh of *Leeds;* and therefore praying that an Act may pafs for dividing the faid Parifhes by a Line beginning at the Place mentioned in the faid Act of Affembly, and running from thence in a direct Courfe to the Mouth of *Carter's* Run, which will include fuch a Number of Tithables as the Petitioners think themfelves entitled to by the faid Agreement.

Ordered, That the Confideration of the faid Petition be deferred till the next Seffion of General Affembly.

Ordered, That a Committee be appointed to enquire into the Funds for the Redemption of the Paper Currency iffued during the late War, and that they ftate an Account thereof, and report the fame to the Houfe.

And a *Committee* was appointed of Mr *Bland,* Mr *Richard Henry Lee,* Mr *Edmund Pendleton,* Mr *Harrifon,* Mr *Archibald Cary,* Mr *Wafhington,* Mr *Charles Carter,* of *Lancafter,* Mr *Henry,* and Mr *Banifter.*

Mr *Richard Henry Lee* reported, from the Committee who were appointed to enquire what Laws would expire at the End of this Seffion, and to report their Opinion to the Houfe which of them are fit to be continued, that the Committee had enquired accordingly, and had come to a Refolution, which they had directed him to report to the Houfe, which he read in his Place, and afterwards delivered it in at the Clerk's Table, where the fame was read, and is as followeth, *viz.*

Refolved, That it is the Opinion of this Committee, that the Act, made in the thirtieth Year of the Reign of his late Majefty, intituled *An Act[1] for the better regulating and difciplining*

---

[1] Hening, VII, p. 93.

difciplining the Militia, which was continued by an Act made in the thirty-fecond Year of his faid late Majefty's Reign, and was continued and amended by two Acts, made in the third and feventh Years of his prefent Majefty's Reign, will expire at the end of this feffion of General Affembly, and ought to be further continued, with Amendments.

The faid *Refolution* being read a fecond Time, was, upon the Queftion put thereupon, agreed to by the Houfe.

Ordered, That a Bill be brought in purfuant to the faid Refolution; and that Mr *Richard Henry Lee*, and Mr *Henry Lee*, do prepare and bring in the fame.

A *Petition* of *Robert Donald* was prefented to the Houfe, and read; fetting forth, that, the Day before the late Frefh, the Infpectors of Tobacco at *Warwick*, upon *James* River, by Direction of the Petitioner, had turned out from the Public Warehoufes, at that Place, fixty-one Hogfheads of Tobacco, in order to be forthwith fhipped for Exportation, twenty-nine of which Hogfheads had been infpected at *Warwick*, and the Remainder, having been infpected at *Milner's* Warehoufes, was re-landed at *Warwick*, for which the Petitioner had paid the Rent of re-landed Tobacco; that, before the Tobacco could be taken off, the Waters rofe between the Warehoufes and the Place where the re-landed Tobacco was; that the faid re-landed Tobacco was put into Houfes belonging to the Petitioner, near the Public Wharf, in order to preferve it, but was foon carried off, with the faid Houfes; that the Tobacco Infpected at Warwick was returned into the Warehoufes, which were alfo carried away; that the Infpectors had not delivered out the fhipping Manifefts for the faid Tobacco; that the Petitioner, as foon as it was in his Power, procured the faid Tobacco to be overhauled, and that it is now drying, and properly attended to; but the Petitioner apprehends there will be a Lofs of one hundred Pounds, on the Tobacco infpected at *Warwick*, and of one hundred and fifty Pounds, on that re-landed from *Milner's;* and therefore praying fuch Relief as this Honourable Houfe fhall think juft and reafonable.

Ordered, That the faid Petition be referred to the Confideration of the Committee appointed to examine and ftate Accounts of the Loffes fuftained by Means of the late Frefh; and that they do examine the Matter thereof, and report the fame, with their Opinion thereupon, to the Houfe.

A *Petition* of feveral Perfons of the Counties of *Augufta, Botetourt, Hanover*, and *Albemarle*, whofe Names are thereunto fubfcribed, was prefented to the Houfe, and read; fetting forth, that the warm Springs, in the Counties of *Augufta* and *Botetourt*, had been found to be very falutary to the difeafed and infirm, who had drank of their Waters, but that it is very difficult for the Perfons who moft want that Relief, to procure it, there being no good Roads to thofe Places; and that great Advantages would be derived to the Country, by opening and clearing fuch Roads thither; and therefore propofing, that a Sum of Money, fufficient for the Purpofe, may be allowed by the Public, to open a fafe and good Road from the warm Springs to *Jenning's* Gap; that a Turnpike be eftablifhed, at the Pafs of the warm Springs Mountains, with a reafonable Toll, for keeping the Road in Repair; and that Truftees be appointed to receive Subfcriptions, as well for keeping the Road in Repair, as for building Houfes for the Reception and Security of the poor Sick who refort to the Springs, and to fee the public and private Money, appropriated for the Purpofes aforefaid, faithfully applied.

Ordered, That the Confideration of the faid Petition be deferred till the next Seffion of General Affembly.

A *Petition* of *Littleton Dennis* was prefented to the Houfe, and read; fetting forth, that twenty-eight Hogfheads of Tobacco, containing twenty-eight thoufand two hundred and feventy-three Pounds Weight, belonging to the Petitioner, had been lately confumed by Fire, in the Public Warehoufe at *Naffwaddox;* and therefore praying that the Value thereof may be paid to him by the Public, according to the Directions of the Act of General Affembly.

Ordered, That the faid petition be referred to the Confideration of the Committee appointed

appointed to examine and ftate Accounts of the Loffes fuftained by Means of the late Frefh; and that they do examine the Matter thereof, and report the fame, with their Opinion thereupon, to the Houfe.

Ordered, That a Committee be appointed to prepare a Table of the Fees to be paid to the Clerk of this Houfe, for Copies of private Acts, and of other Papers; and report the fame to the Houfe.

And a *Committee* was appointed of Mʳ *Edmund Pendleton*, Mʳ *Bland*, Mʳ *Treafurer*, Mʳ *Henry*, and Mʳ *Banifter*.

And then the Houfe adjourned till To-morrow Morning nine of the Clock.

Tuesday, the 16th of July, 11 Geo. III. 1771.

ORDERED, That the feveral Petitions of fundry Freeholders of the County of *Henrico*, and others, for difcontinuing the Infpections of Tobacco at *Shockoe's* and *Byrd's*, in the faid County, and for eftablifhing in their Room, Infpections on the Land of *Charles Lewis*, and alfo the feveral Petitions of fundry Inhabitants of the Counties of *Amherft*, *Buckingham*, *Goochland*, and *Henrico*, in Oppofition thereto, which, upon *Saturday* laft, were ordered to lie upon the Table, be referred to the Confideration of the Committee appointed to examine and ftate Accounts of the Loffes fuftained by Means of the late Frefh; and that they do examine the Matter thereof, and report the fame, with their Opinion thereupon, to the Houfe.

A *Memorial* of *Luke Luker* and *John Walter* was prefented to the Houfe, and read; fetting forth, that the Warehoufes eftablifhed at *Naffwaddox*, in the County of *Northampton*, at which they Act as Infpectors, were lately burnt by Accident, and forty-two Hogfheads of infpected Tobacco, weighing forty-two thoufand five hundred and ninety-four Pounds nett, confumed therein; and therefore referring it to the Confideration of the Houfe, to provide for repairing the Lofs of the Sufferers, in fuch Manner as to them fhall feem juft.

Ordered, That the faid Memorial be referred to the Confideration of the Committee appointed to examine and ftate Accounts of the Loffes fuftained by Means of the late Frefh; and that they do examine the Matter thereof, and report the fame, with their Opinion thereupon, to the Houfe.

A *Member* returned upon a new Writ, having taken the Oaths appointed to be taken by Act of Parliament, and repeated and fubfcribed the Teft, took his Place in the Houfe.

Mʳ *Bland* reported from the Committee, appointed to examine and ftate Accounts of the Loffes fuftained by Means of the late Frefh, as well in the Tobacco infpected, as in fuch as was brought to be infpected, but not viewed, at the feveral Public Warehoufes, except fuch Tobacco as had remained in the faid Warehoufes above a Year, that the Committee had examined and ftated Accounts of the Loffes accordingly, and had directed him to report the fame, as it appeared to them, to the Houfe; and he read the Report in his Place, and afterwards delivered it in at the Clerk's Table; where the fame was read, and is as followeth, *viz.*

Your *Committee* beg Leave to inform the Houfe, that upon examining the Accounts of all the Infpectors of the feveral Warehoufes at *Shockoe's*, *Byrd's*, *Rocky Ridge*, and *Warwick*, they find the total Lofs of the Tobacco, at the faid Warehoufes, to amount to 2,375,541 Pounds of Tobacco; and that the Expences attending the examining, forting, and reprizing the faid Tobacco amount to 244*l.* 8 *s.* 6 *d.* a particular Account of which is ftated in a Schedule annexed to this Report.

Your *Committee* beg Leave further to inform the Houfe, that at the Time of the Frefh 107 Hogfheads of uninfpected Tobacco were lying at *Byrd's* Warehoufe, which the Infpectors have fince viewed, 87 Hogfheads of which were paffed, and carried to the Credit of the Proprietors, after cutting off 9266 Pounds damaged, which ought to be allowed to the feveral Proprietors; the other 20 Hogfheads were refufed, and put by to be picked.

That

That 131 Hogfheads of uninfpected Tobacco, fuppofed to be carried away from *Shockoe's*, have been found, and perfons have been employed by the Infpectors to pick and reprize them, but no Account is yet returned of the Quantity faved.

It further *appears* to your Committee, that the Infpectors at *Shockoe's*, *Byrd's* and the *Rocky Ridge*, not having proper Houfes to hold the Tobacco, and not being able to hire Hands fufficient to examine all the damaged Tobacco under their own immediate View, did, by the Advice of feveral Gentlemen of the Houfe of Burgeffes, contract with fundry Perfons to take feveral Hogfheads of damaged Tobacco to their Houfes, to be forted and reprized, and to allow them one third or one half of the Tobacco (as it was more or lefs damaged) that fhould be faved; under which Agreement feveral Hogfheads were by the Infpectors delivered out, of which none have yet been accounted for, except 8 Hogfheads returned to *Rocky Ridge;* fo that the Savings upon this Tobacco cannot, at this Time, be afcertained, but it appears that it will probably amount, in the Whole, to about 400 Hogfheads, after paying the Salvage agreed for, including the Tobacco the Infpectors have faved themfelves, of which they cannot, at this Time, render a particular Account.

It further *appears* that at *Shockoe's* were 79 Hogfheads, and at *Byrd's* 24 Hogfheads of Tobacco refufed, and put by to be picked, and which were damaged.

Your *Committee* are informed that a confiderable Number of Hogfheads of Tobacco have been taken up by feveral Perfons, living upon *James* River, below the faid Warehoufes, great Part of which have been faved. And your Committee beg Leave to give it as their Opinion, that the Tobacco fo faved fhould be inquired into, and if it fhould appear it was carried from any of the Public Warehoufes, that it ought to be accounted for to the Public, after allowing a reafonable Salvage.

It further *appears* that about 800 Hogfheads of Tobacco were loft in *Dixon's* and *Falmouth* Warehoufes, on *Rappahannock* River, but as the Infpectors are not attending, and their Accounts are not upon Oath, the Committee have fent for them, and cannot adjuft that Lofs until they fhall attend.

Dr.   The Public for Tobacco deftroyed by the late Frefh at the feveral Warehoufes
      upon *James* River.   Cr.

To *Shockoe's* Infpectors,.........	1,480,028	By old Tobacco at *Shockoe's*			
To Col. *William Cabell*,........	1,768	infpected above a Year,....			17,614
To Mr *John Woodfon*,.............	1,307	Balance to be paid for at			
To Col. *Wilfon Miles Cary*,.....	1,849	*Shockoe's*..............			1,467,338
	1,484,952				1,484,952
To Mr *Field Trent* for eight Hogfheads of Tobacco, the Weights not afcertained.......		By eight Hogfheads of old Tobacco at *Byrd's* infpected above a Year,..............			8,436
To *Byrd's* Infpectors on Crop Tobacco,....·..............	766,145	Balance to be paid for at *Byrd's* ..			773,336
To ditto on Tranffer Tobacco ...	15,627				781,772
To *Warwick* Infpectors, to be paid for, ...	781,772 41,165	By Tobacco faved at *Rocky Ridge*, ...			235,720
		By ditto,.................			4,058
To *Rocky Ridge*	341,450	By old Tobacco infpected			
Cafh Account	Dr.	above a Year, ...			7,970
	l. *s.* *d.*	Balance to be paid for,......			93,702
To *Shockoe's* Infpectors,.......49 10 6					341,450
To Col. *William Cabell*,....... 2 12 6					
To Mr *John Woodfon*,........ 15					
To *Byrd's* Infpectors.........33 15 6					
To *Rocky Ridge* Infpectors 157 15					
244 8 6					

Ordered

Ordered, That the faid Report do lie upon the Table.

Refolved, That this Houfe will now refolve itfelf into a Committee of the whole Houfe to confider of Ways and Means for raifing Money to repair the Loffes of Tobacco fuftained by Means of the late Frefh.

Ordered, That the faid Report be referred to the faid Committee.

The Houfe accordingly refolved itfelf into the faid Committee.

Mr *Speaker* left the Chair.

Mr *Bland* took the Chair of the Committee.

Mr *Speaker* refumed the Chair.

Mr *Bland* reported, from the Committee, that they had come to feveral Refolutions, which they had directed him to report to the Houfe, and he read the Report in his Place, and afterwards delivered it in at the Clerk's Table; where the Refolutions of the Committee were read, and are as followeth, *viz.*

Refolved, That it is the Opinion of this Committee, that for repairing the Loffes of Tobacco fuftained by Means of the late Frefh, a Sum of Paper Money, fufficient for the Purpofe, be emitted.

Refolved, That it is the Opinion of this Committee, that for finking the Paper Money, to be emitted for repairing the Loffes of Tobacco fuftained by Means of the late Frefh, Taxes be impofed upon Tobacco exported, and upon Wheel Carriages, Ordinary Licences, and Writs.

The faid *Refolutions* being feverally read a fecond Time, were, upon the Queftion feverally put thereupon, agreed to by the Houfe.

Ordered, That a Bill be brought in, purfuant to the faid Refolutions; and that Mr *Bland*, Mr *Treafurer*, Mr *Edmund Pendleton*, Mr *Richard Henry Lee*, Mr *Harrifon*, and Mr *Riddick*, do prepare and bring in the fame.

And then the Houfe adjourned till To-morrow Morning Nine of the Clock.

Wednesday, the 17th of July, 11 Geo. III. 1771.

A *Petition* of the Infpectors at *Shockoe's*, *Byrd's*, and *Rocky Ridge* Warehoufes, was prefented to the Houfe, and read; fetting forth that the Petitioners had undergone great Labour, in looking after and fecuring the Tobacco damaged by Means of the Frefh, in the Month of *May* laft, and tranfcribing their Books, and preparing fair Copies of their Accounts, to be laid before this Honourable Houfe, and had been put to confiderable Expence in attending at *Williamfburg* ever fince the meeting of this General Affembly; and therefore praying that they may be allowed a reafonable Satiffaction.

Ordered, That the faid Petition be referred to the Confideration of the Committee appointed to examine and ftate Accounts of the Loffes fuftained by Means of the late Frefh; and that they do examine the Matter thereof, and report the fame, with their Opinion thereupon, to the Houfe.

Mr *Bland* reported, from the Committee to whom the Petition of *Robert Donald* was referred, that the Committee had confidered the fame, and had come to feveral Refolutions, which they had directed him to report to the Houfe, and he read the Report in his Place, and afterwards delivered it in at the Clerk's Table, where the Refolutions of the Committee were read, and are as followeth, *viz.*

Refolved, That it is the Opinion of this Committee, that fo much of the faid Petition, as prays to be allowed by the Public, for the Lofs the Petitioner fuftained upon the Tobacco infpected at *Warwick* Warehoufe, and damaged by the late Flood, be rejected.

Refolved, That it is the Opinion of this Committee, that the Refidue of the faid Petition, praying to be allowed by the Public for the Lofs fuftained upon the Tobacco infpected at *Milner's* Warehoufe, and relanded at *Warwick* Warehoufe, be rejected.

The faid *Refolutions* being feverally read a fecond Time, were, upon the Queftion feverally put thereupon, agreed to by the Houfe.

A

A *Petition* of *Peter Pelham*, Keeper of the Public Gaol, was prefented to the Houfe, [18] and read; praying that the ufual Salary of forty Pounds per Annum may be continued.

Refolved, That the Sum of forty Pounds, per Annum, be allowed to *Peter Pelham*, as Public Gaoler, to continue to the End of the next Seffion of General Affembly.

Ordered, That M[r] *Nelfon* do carry the faid Refolution to the Council, and defire their Concurrence.

A *Petition* of the Reverend *Alexander Gordon*, Clerk, Rector of the Parifh of *Antrim*, was prefented to the Houfe, and read; fetting forth, that the Law, which was propofed laft Seffion of General Affembly, for raifing the price of his Tobacco, or paying it in Kind, but did not receive the Affent of the *Governor*, was founded in Juftice and Equity; That the Petitioner fuffers more Toil and Fatigue in attending his Cure, than moft other Clergymen in the Colony; and that his Salary, as it is now paid, is not adequate to his Expence and Trouble; and therefore praying that this Houfe will grant him fuch Re-drefs as fhall appear juft and reafonable.

Ordered, That the Confideration of the faid Petition be deferred till the next Seffion of General Affembly.

A *Petition* of *William Wilkinfon* and *John Pinchback*, Infpectors of Tobacco at *Waddy's* Warehoufes, in the County of *New Kent*, was prefented to the Houfe, and read; fetting forth that the faid Warehoufes were broken open the eighth Day of *July* laft, and five hundred and thirty-fix Pounds of Tobacco ftolen out of the fame, for which the Petitioners had been obliged to pay; and therefore praying that they may be repaid for the faid Tobacco.

Ordered, That the Confideration of the faid Petition be deferred till the next Seffion of General Affembly.

M[r] *Bland* prefented to the Houfe, according to Order, a Bill to impower the Inhabit-ants of the Parifh of *Augufta*, in the County of *Augufta*, to elect a Veftry; and the fame was received, and read the firft Time.

Refolved, That the Bill be read a fecond Time.

A *Petition* of *William Rind*, Printer, was prefented to the Houfe, and read; fetting forth that his Salary, as Printer to the Public, will expire at the End of this Seffion of Affembly; and therefore praying that the fame may be further continued.

Refolved, That the Sum of four hundred and fifty Pounds per Annum, be allowed to *William Rind*, Printer, to continue to the End of the next Seffion of Affembly, as a full Confideration for printing the Journal of the Houfe of Burgeffes, and the Laws of each Seffion, and fending as many Copies of the Laws to the County Court Clerks as there are acting Juftices in the Commiffion, in each refpective County, and one other, which is to be Half Bound, for the Ufe of the Court, and ten to the Clerks of the Courts of Huftings, in the City of *Williamfburg*, and Borough of *Norfolk*, and printing Infpectors Receipts and Books, Proclamations, and Public Advertifements.

Ordered, That M[r] *Archibald Cary* do carry the faid Refolution to the Council, and defire their Concurrence.

A *Petition* of the Freeholders and Inhabitants of the County of *Lunenburg*, whofe Names are thereunto fubfcribed, was prefented to the Houfe, and read; fetting forth, that large Quantities of Tobacco are annually brought from *North-Carolina* to this Colony, and infpected, and fold here moftly for Gold and Silver, which is carried out from hence, and paffed at higher Rates than it is here; and that the Owners of fuch [14] Tobacco do not contribute any Thing towards building and fupporting Bridges, and clearing and repairing Roads; and therefore praying that a Duty be laid upon Tobacco, imported from *North-Carolina*, and that the Value of Gold and Silver Coin in this Colony be made equal to Sterling, or to what it paffeth for in the neighbouring Colonies.

Ordered, That the Confideration of the faid Petition be deferred till the next Seffion of General Affembly.

A *Petition* of *William Tebbs* and *Thomas Attwell*, Infpectors of Tobacco at *Quantico* Warehoufes, in the County of *Prince William*, was prefented to the Houfe, and read; fetting forth, that the faid Warehoufes have long been, and yet are, in a ruinous Condi-

tion

tion, notwithstanding the petitioners have done all in their Power to get them repaired; and that by Means of their Infufficiency, and of the driving Rains this Summer, large Quantities of the Tobacco ftored in the faid Houfes, have been fo damaged, that the Owners refufe to receive them; and therefore praying that the Houfe will take the Matter into Confideration, and fo provide that the Petitioners may be indemnified for the Lofs they are likely to fuftain, without any Default in them.

Ordered, That the faid Petition be referred to the Confideration of the Committee appointed to examine and ftate Accounts of the Loffes fuftained by Means of the late Frefh; and that they do examine the Matter thereof, and report the fame, with their Opinion thereupon, to the Houfe.

Mr *Pendleton* reported, from the Committee appointed to prepare a Table of Fees, to be paid to the Clerk of this Houfe, for Copies of private Acts, and of other Papers, that the Committee had prepared a Table accordingly, which the Committee had directed him to report to the Houfe; and he read the Report in his Place, and afterwards delivered it in at the Clerk's Table, where the faid Table of Fees was read, and is as followeth, *viz.*

	l.	s.	d.
For a Copy of an Act of General Affembly	0	15	0
For a Copy of any other Paper, for every twenty Words,	0	0	2

Refolved, That the Clerk of this Houfe be governed by the faid Table, in receiving his Fees.

Mr *Richard Henry Lee* prefented to the Houfe, according to Order, a Bill for further continuing and amending the Act intituled *An Act[1] for the better regulating and difciplining the Militia;* and the fame was received and read the firft Time.

Refolved, That the Bill be read a fecond Time.

Ordered, That it be an Inftruction to the Gentlemen appointed to prepare and bring in a Bill purfuant to the Refolutions of the Committee of the whole Houfe, which were Yefterday reported, and agreed to by the Houfe, that they have Power to receive a Claufe or Claufes, for enabling the Infpectors at *Byrd's*, *Shockoe's*, and *Rocky Ridge* Warehoufes, to pay fuch Tobacco as they have faved, out of what was damaged in the faid Houfes, by Means of the late Frefh, in Difcharge of their Tranffer Notes, refpectively.

A *Petition* of *John Heath* was prefented to the Houfe, and read; fetting forth that a Negro Man Slave, named *Jacob*, belonging to *George Parker*, and hired by the Petitioner, was drowned in endeavoring to fave fome of the Tobacco, carried out of *Falmouth* Warehoufe, and floating down the River, in the late Frefh; and therefore praying that the Value of the faid Negro may be paid by the Public.

A *Motion* was made, and the Queftion being put, that the faid Petition be referred to the Confideration of the Committee;

It paffed in the Negative.

Ordered, That the faid Petition be rejected.

A *Petition* of *William Rind* was prefented to the Houfe, and read; fetting forth, that, in Obedience to an Order of this Honourable Houfe, he has Half-Bound twelve hundred Copies of the Acts of the laft Seffion of Affembly, and delivered them to the refpective County Court Clerks; and paying a reafonable Allowance for the fame.

Ordered, That the faid Petition be referred to the Confideration of the Committee; and that they do examine the Matter thereof, and report the fame, with their Opinion thereupon, to the Houfe.

And it is *referred* to Mr *Archibald Cary*, Mr *Richard Henry Lee*, Mr *Bland*, Mr *Richard Lee*, and Mr *Henry Lee*.

Mr *Bland* reported, from the Committee to whom the Petitions of the Inhabitants of the feveral Counties of *Amherft*, *Buckingham*, *Goochland*, and *Henrico*, were referred, that the Committee had examined the Matter of the faid Petitions, and had come to

feveral

---

[1] Hening, VII, p. 93.

several Resolutions, which they had directed him to report to the House; and he read the Report in his Place, and afterwards delivered it in at the Clerk's Table, where the Resolutions of the Committee were read, and are as followeth, *viz.*

Resolved, That it is the Opinion of this Committee, that so much of the said Petitions as prays that the Public Warehouses, at *Shockoe's*, and *Byrd's*, may be removed to a Place not subjected to be overflowed by the Waters, is reasonable.

Resolved, That it is the Opinion of this Committee, that the petitions, which pray that the said Warehouses may be removed to *Bowyer's* and *Housling's* Tenements, in the Town of *Richmond*, is reasonable.

Resolved, That it is the Opinion of this Committee, that the Petitions which pray that the said Warehouses may be removed to *Lewis's* Land, below the Town of *Richmond*, be rejected.

The said *Resolutions* being severally read a second Time, were, upon the Question severally put thereupon, agreed to by the House.

Ordered, That it be an Instruction to the Gentlemen appointed to prepare and bring in a Bill, pursuant to the Resolutions of the Committee of the whole House, which were Yesterday reported, and agreed to by the House, that they make Provision, in the said Bill, for discontinuing the Inspections at *Shockoe's* and *Byrd's*, and establishing them on *Bowyer's* and *Housling's* Tenements, in the Town of *Richmond*.

A *Petition* of Edward Brisbane, of the Town of *Petersburg*, Merchant, was presented to the House, and read; setting forth, that the Petitioner had, at the Time of the late great rising of the Waters, in *James River*, twenty seven Hogsheads of Tobacco, in the Public Warehouses, at Bermuda Hundred, which Tobacco was brought from the Falls of *James* River, and put under their Care, according to Law, being intended for Exportation, but came too late to be taken on board the Ship, towards whose Load it was designed; and that the said Tobacco, in the said Warehouses, was very much damaged, but that, by the Care and Vigilance of the Inspectors at *Petersburg*, to which Place, by Direction of the Petitioner, the same, after it was damaged, had been brought, fifteen Hogsheads, and a Parcel of about five hundred Pounds Weight, are saved; and therefore praying, as to the Residue of the said Tobacco, that this House will grant him such Relief as shall seem meet.

Ordered, That the said Petition be referred to the Consideration of the Committee appointed to examine and state Accounts of the Losses sustained by Means of the late Fresh; and that they do examine the Matter thereof, and report the same, with their Opinion thereupon, to the House.

A *Petition* of John Young, of the County of *Dinwiddie*, was presented to the House, and read; setting forth that a Slave called *Moses*, belonging to the Petitioner, having been some time absent from his Master's Service, and having committed Thefts and Outrages in the Neighbourhood, and being outlawed, in due Form, was apprehended and brought before a Magistrate, and charged with Felony, and there being strong Proofs of his Guilt, was ordered by the Magistrate to be carried to Prison, but that the said Slave, before he could be committed, died, through some Mismanagement, as is suspected, in the Persons who apprehended and were conveying him to the Court-House; and therefore praying that this Honourable House will grant such Relief to the Petitioner as shall seem just.

Ordered, That the Consideration of the said Petition be deferred till the next Session of General Assembly.

A *Bill* for further continuing and amending the Act intituled An Act[1] *for the better regulating and disciplining the Militia*, was read a second Time.

Resolved, That the Bill be committed to Mr *Archibald Cary*, and Mr *Bland*.

A *Bill* to empower the Inhabitants of the Parish of *Augusta*, in the County of *Augusta* to elect a Vestry, was read a second Time.

Resolved

---

[1] Hening, VII, p. 93.

Refolved, That the Bill be committed to Mr *Edmund Pendleton*, and Mr *John Wilfon*, of *Augufta*.

And then the Houfe adjourned till To-morrow Morning nine of the Clock.

Thursday, the 18th of July, 11 Geo. III. 1771.

A *Petition* of the Freeholders and Inhabitants of the County of *Lunenburg*, whofe Names are thereunto fubfcribed, was prefented to the Houfe, and read; fetting forth, that Part of the Act of General Affembly, intituled *an Act[1] for amending the Staple of Tobacco, and for preventing Frauds in his Majefty's Cuftoms*, allowing the Purchafers of Tobacco to have the fame reviewed, is unreafonable; and therefore praying that that Part of the faid Act may be repealed, or that the Owner of Tobacco, unjuftly refufed, may have a Review as well as the Purchafer.

Ordered, That the Confideration of the faid Petition be deferred till the next Seffion of General Affembly.

Mr *Archibald Cary* reported, from the Committee to whom the Bill for further continuing and amending the Act intituled *An Act[2] for the better regulating and difciplining the Militia*, was committed, that the Committee had gone through the Bill, and made feveral Amendments thereunto, which they had directed him to report to the Houfe; and he read the Report in his Place; and afterwards delivered the Bill, with the Amendments, in at the Clerk's Table: Where the Amendments were once read throughout, and then a fecond Time, one by one, and upon the Queftion feverally put thereupon, were agreed to by the Houfe.

Ordered, That the Bill, with the Amendments, be ingroffed.

A *Petition* of the Infpectors at *Dixon's* and *Falmouth* Warehoufes, was prefented to the Houfe, and read; fetting forth that the petitioners had undergone great Labour and Fatigue, in looking after and fecuring the Tobacco damaged in the faid Warehoufes, by the late Frefh, tranfcribing their Books, and preparing fair Copies of their Accounts and Proceedings, to be laid before this Honourable Houfe, and have been put to confiderable Expence in traveling to, and attending at *Williamfburg;* and therefore praying that they may be allowed a reafonable Satiffaction.

Ordered, That the faid Petition be referred to the Confideration of the Committee appointed to examine and ftate Accounts of the Loffes fuftained by Means of the late Frefh; and that they do examine the Matter thereof, and report the fame, with their Opinion thereupon, to the Houfe.

A *Member* returned upon a new Writ, having taken the Oaths appointed to be taken by Act of Parliament, and repeated and fubfcribed the Teft, took his Place in the Houfe.

Ordered, That it be an Inftruction to the Gentlemen appointed to prepare and bring in a Bill, purfuant to the Refolutions of the Committee of the whole Houfe, which were, upon *Tuefday* laft, reported, and agreed to by the Houfe, that they make provifion in the faid Bill for removing the Warehoufes at *Falmouth* Infpection.

A *Meffage* from the Council by Mr *Blair:*

Mr *Speaker*,
The Council have agreed to the Refolve for paying the Public Printer his Salary.

And then the Meffenger withdrew.

Mr *Archibald Cary* reported from the Committee to whom the Petition of *William Rind* was referred, that the Committee had examined the Matter of the faid Petition, and had come to a Refolution, which they had directed him to report to the Houfe, and he read the Report in his Place, and afterwards delivered it in at the Clerk's Table; where the Refolution of the Committee was read, and is as followeth, *viz.*

Refolved

---

[1] Hening, VIII, p. 69.   [2] Ibid, VIII, p. 93.

Refolved, That it is the Opinion of this Committee, that the faid Petitioner be allowed three Shillings for every Book of the Laws of laft Seffion, which he fhall prove, before the Treafurer, to have been delivered for the Ufe of the Public.

The faid *Refolution* being read a fecond Time, was, upon the Queftion put thereupon, agreed to by the Houfe.

Refolved, That there be paid to *William Rind*, Printer to the Public, three Shillings for every Book of the Laws of laft Seffion, that he fhall prove, before the Treafurer, to have been delivered for the Ufe of the Public.

Ordered, That Mr *Archibald Cary* do carry the faid Refolution to the Council, and defire their Concurrence.

A *Petition* of *Rowland Ward* was prefented to the Houfe, and read; fetting forth that his Negro Man Slave, named *Cæfar*, having been duly outlawed, was killed in an Attempt to apprehend him; and that the faid Slave was valued, by the Court of *Amelia* County, to the Sum of one hundred Pounds; and therefore praying that the Value of the faid Slave may be paid to him by the Public.

Ordered, That the Confideration of the faid Petition be deferred till the next Seffion of General Affembly.

Mr *Pendleton* reported, from the Committee to whom the Bill to impower the Inhabitants of the Parifh of *Augufta*, in the County of *Augufta*, to elect a Veftry, was committed, that the Committee had gone through the Bill, and made an Amendment thereunto, which they had directed him to report to the Houfe; and he read the Report in his Place, and afterwards delivered the Bill, with the Amendment, in at the Clerk's Table, where the Amendment was twice read, and upon the Queftion put thereupon, was agreed to by the Houfe.

Ordered, That the Bill, with the Amendment, be ingroffed.

A *Petition* of fundry Inhabitants of the County of *Mecklenburg*, whofe Names are thereunto fubfcribed, was prefented to the Houfe, and read; fetting forth that the Importation of Tobacco from *North-Carolina* to this Colony is very detrimental to the Trade of the latter; and therefore praying that fuch Importation may be prohibited or reftrained.

Ordered, That the Confideration of the faid Petition be deferred till the next Seffion of General Affembly.

Mr *Bland* reported, from the Committee appointed to examine and ftate Accounts of the Loffes fuftained by Means of the late Frefh, as well in the Tobacco infpected, as in fuch as was brought to be infpected, but not viewed, at the feveral Public Warehoufes, except fuch Tobacco as had remained in the faid Warehoufes above a Year, that the Committee had examined and ftated Accounts of the Loffes of the Tobaccoes of *Dixon's* and *Falmouth* Warehoufes, and had directed him to report the fame, as it appeared to them, to the Houfe; and he read the Report in his Place, and afterwards delivered it in at the Clerk's Table; where the fame was read, and is as followeth, *viz.*

It *appears* to your Committee that the total Lofs of Tobacco at the faid Warehoufes amounts to feven hundred and eighty-five thoufand fix hundred and fifty Pounds of Tobacco; and that the Expences attending the forting and reprizing the faid Tobacco amount to one hundred and eleven Pounds fix Shillings and fix Pence; that forty-eight thoufand nine hundred and two Pounds were faved out of the damaged Tobacco, and fold by the Infpectors, by the Advice of *King George* County Court, for four hundred and fifty-nine Pounds eighteen Shillings and four Pence, a particular Account whereof is ftated in a Schedule annexed to this Report.

It further *appears* to the Committee, that about fifty Hogfheads of uninfpected Tobacco, and thirty Hogfheads that had been refufed and not picked, were carried from *Falmouth* Warehoufe by the Frefh.

The

The Public	Dr.	Contra	Cr.
	lbs. Nett.		*lbs. Nett.*

To the Infpectors at *Dixon's* Warehoufe for 152 Hogf-heads of Crop Tobacco dam-aged..................... 156,584

By 10 Hogfheads of old Tobacco which have been infpected above a Year,................ 9,284

Balance to be paid by the Pub-lic,..................... 147,300

———

156,584

To the Infpectors at *Falmouth* Warehoufe for 630 Hogf-heads of Crop Tobacco dam-aged 651,916

By 14 Hogfheads of old Tobac-co which have been infpected above a Year, ... 13,566

Balance to be paid by the Public, 638,350

———

651,916

Cafh   Dr.

l.   s.   d.

Contra   Cr.

l.   s.   d

To fundry Expences for fort-ing and prizing damaged To-bacco,.......................111   6   6

By Cafh for 48,902 lbs. of To-bacco fold by the Infpectors, by Advice of the Court of the County of *King George*,.... 372   2   4

By Cafh for wet Tobacco fold,.. 87 16

———

459 18 4

Ordered, That it be an Inftruction to the Gentlemen, appointed to prepare and bring in a Bill, purfuant to the Refolutions of the Committee of the whole Houfe, which were, upon *Tuefday* laft, reported and agreed to by the Houfe, that they make provifion, in the faid Bill, for paying the Owners of the Tobacco loft and damaged in *Dixon's* and *Falmouth* Warehoufes by the late Frefh.

Mʳ *Bland* reported, from the Committee to whom the feveral Petitions of the Infpectors at *Shockoe's*, *Byrd's*, and *Rocky Ridge* Warehoufes, *Edward Brifbane*, and *William Tebbs*, and *Thomas Attwell*, were referred, that the Committee had examined the Matter of the faid Petitions, and come to feveral Refolutions, which they directed him to report to the Houfe, and he read the Report in his Place, and afterwards delivered it in at the Clerk's Table; where the Refolutions of the Committee were read, and are as followeth, *viz*.

Refolved, That it is the Opinion of this Committee, that the petition of the Infpectors at *Shockoe's*, *Byrd's*, and *Rocky Ridge* Warehoufes, praying to be allowed by the Public for their extraordinary Trouble in forting and reprizing the damaged Tobacco, is reafon-able; and that they ought to be allowed fifteen Pounds each, for their Trouble in the faid Service; and that *Turner Southall*, *Daniel Price*, and *Matthew Branch*, ought to be allowed five Pounds each, for their Expences in attending the faid Committee, with their Accounts.

Refolved, That it is the Opinion of this Committee, that the Petition of *Edward Brifbane*, praying to be allowed by the Public for the Loffes fuftained upon the Tobacco, damaged by the late Flood, as fet forth in the faid Petition, be rejected.

Refolved, That it is the Opinion of this Committee, that the Petition of *William Tebbs* and *Thomas Attwell*, Infpectors at *Quantico* Warehoufe, praying to be allowed for the Tobacco damaged therein, by Rain, is reafonable; and that Commiffioners ought to be appointed to examine, ftate, and fettle an Account thereof.

The *two firft Refolutions* of the Committee being feverally read a fecond Time, were, upon the Queftion feverally put thereupon, agreed to by the Houfe.

The fubfequent *Refolution* of the Committee being read a fecond Time, and the

Queftion

Queftion being put, that the Houfe doth agree with the Committee in the faid Refolution;

It paffed in the Negative.

Refolved, That the Petition of *William Tebbs* and *Thomas Attwell*, Infpectors at *Quantico* Warehoufe, praying to be allowed for the Tobacco damaged therein, by Rain, be rejected.

Ordered, That it be an Inftruction to the Gentlemen appointed to prepare and bring in a Bill, purfuant to the Refolutions of the Committee of the whole Houfe, which were, upon *Tuefday* laft, reported and agreed to by the Houfe, that they have Power to receive a Claufe or Claufes, for appointing Commiffioners to examine the Condition of the Warehoufes at *Quantico*, at the Time the Tobacco mentioned in the Petition of *William Tebbs* and *Thomas Attwell* was damaged, and by what Accidents, or by whofe Neglect, fuch Damage, if any, happened; and to ftate an Account of the faid damaged Tobacco; and to report their Proceedings to the next Seffion of General Affembly.

A *Petition* of *William Hackney* and *Rowland Sutton*, Infpectors at *Kemp's* Warehoufe, in the County of *Middlefex*, was prefented to the Houfe, and read; fetting forth that in the Night of the ninth Day of this Inftant *July*, the Doors of the faid Warehoufe were broke open, and a Hogfhead of Tobacco, belonging to *Philip Ludwell Grymes*, Efq; weighing nine hundred and ninety-five Pounds Nett, was taken out of the faid Warehoufe, and all the Tobacco, except a few Bundles, carried away; and that the faid Lofs did not happen by any Neglect of the Petitioners, who are neverthelefs liable to make the faid *Grymes* Satiffaction for the fame; and therefore praying that this Honourable Houfe will afford them fuch Relief as they fhall think juft and reafonable.

Ordered, That the Confideration of the faid Petition be deferred till the next Seffion of General Affembly.

And then the Houfe adjourned till To-morrow Morning nine of the Clock.

Friday, the 19th of July, 11 Geo. III. 1771.

MR *Bland* reported, from the Committee to whom the feveral Petitions of the Infpectors at *Dixon's* and *Falmouth* Warehoufes, and *John Sharpe* and *William Lyon* were referred, that the Committee had examined the Matter of the faid Petitions, and had come to feveral Refolutions, which they had directed him to report to the Houfe, and he read the Report in his Place, and afterwards delivered it in at the Clerk's Table; where the Refolutions of the Committee were read, and are as followeth, *viz.*

Refolved, That it is the Opinion of this Committee, that the Petition of *William Newton* and *John Pollard*, Infpectors at *Dixon's* and *Falmouth* Warehoufes, is reafonable; and that they ought to be allowed ten Pounds each for their Trouble and Expence in travelling to *Williamfburg*, and attending the Committee.

Refolved, That it is the Opinion of this Committee, that the Petition of *John Sharpe* and *William Lyon*, praying to be allowed a reafonable Satiffaction for their Affiftance in faving from the late Flood one hundred and fifty four Hogfheads of Tobacco at *Falmouth* Warehoufe, be rejected.

The faid *Refolutions* being feverally read a fecond Time, were, upon the Queftion feverally put thereupon, agreed to by the Houfe.

An ingroffed *Bill* for further continuing and amending the Act intituled An Act[1] *for the better regulating and difciplining the Militia*, was read the third Time.

Refolved, That the Bill do pafs; and that the Title be An Act[2] *for further continuing the Act intituled An Act for the better regulating and difciplining the Militia.*

Ordered, That Mr *Archibald Cary* do carry the Bill to the Council, and defire their Concurrence.

Ordered

---

[1] Hening, VII, p. 93.　　[2] Ibid, VIII, p. 503.

Ordered, That the Treafurer be directed to pay the additional Sum of feventy-five Pounds to *Richard Bland* and *Patrick Henry,* Efquires, for their Trouble and Expences in going as Commiffioners to *New-York,* to meet with Commiffioners appointed by the Legiflatures of the neighbouring Colonies, to form and agree upon a general Plan for the Regulation of the *Indian* Trade.

An engroffed *Bill* to empower the Inhabitants of the Parifh of *Augufta,* in the County of *Augufta,* to elect a Veftry, was read the third Time.

21 *Refolved,* That the Bill do pafs; and that the Title be *An Act¹ to empower the Inhabitants of the Parifh of* Augufta, *in the County of* Augufta, *to elect a Veftry.*

Ordered, That Mr *Bland* do carry the Bill to the Council, and defire their Concurrence.

Ordered, That Leave be given to bring in a Bill for the Eafe and Relief of the People, by paying the Burgeffes Wages in Money, for this prefent Seffion of Affembly; and that Mr *Henry Lee* and Mr *Baffett* do prepare and bring in the fame.

A *Meffage* from the Council by Mr *Blair:*

Mr *Speaker,*

The Council have agreed to the Bill, *intituled* An Act to empower the Inhabitants of the Parifh of *Augufta,* in the County of *Augufta,* to elect a Veftry, *without any Amendment: And also,*

The Council have agreed to the Bill, *intituled* An Act² for further continuing the Act, intituled An Act for the better regulating and difciplining the Militia, *without any Amendment, to which Amendment the Council defire the Concurrence of this Houfe: And alfo,*

The Council have agreed to the Refolve *for paying to the Keeper of the Public Gaol his Salary.*

And then the Meffenger withdrew.

The Houfe proceeded to take into Confideration the Amendment made by the Council to the Bill, intituled *An Act for further continuing the Act,* intituled An Act for the better regulating and difciplining the Militia.

And the faid *Amendment* was read, and is as followeth, *viz.*

Line the laft, leave out '*one Year*', and infert '*two Years,*' inftead thereof.

The faid *Amendment* being read a fecond Time, was, upon the Queftion put thereupon, agreed to by the Houfe.

Ordered, That Mr *Archibald Cary* do carry the Bill to the Council, and acquaint them that this Houfe hath agreed to the Amendment made by them.

Mr *Bland* prefented to the Houfe, according to Order, a Bill for the Relief of the Sufferers by the Lofs of Tobacco damaged or burnt in feveral Warehoufes; and the fame was received and read the firft Time.

Refolved, That the Bill be read a fecond Time.

Refolved, That the Bill be now read a fecond Time.

The *Bill* was accordingly read a fecond Time.

Refolved, That the Bill be committed.

Refolved, That the Bill be committed to a Committee of the whole Houfe.

Refolved, That this Houfe will now refolve itfelf into a Committee of the whole Houfe, upon the faid Bill.

The Houfe accordingly refolved itfelf into the faid Committee.

Mr *Speaker* left the Chair.

Mr *Bland* took the Chair of the Committee.

Mr *Speaker* refumed the Chair.

Mr *Bland* reported from the Committee, that they had gone through the Bill, and made feveral Amendments thereunto, which they had directed him to report to the Houfe; and he read the Report in his Place, and afterwards delivered the Bill, with the

22 Amendments in at the Clerk's Table; where the Amendments were once read
throughout

¹ Hening, VIII, p. 504. ² Ibid, VIII, p. 503.

throughout, and then, a fecond Time, one by one; and upon the Queftion feverally put thereupon, were agreed to by the Houfe.

Ordered, That the Bill, with the Amendments, be ingroffed.

Mr *Henry Lee* prefented to the Houfe, according to Order, a Bill for the Eafe and Relief of the People, by paying the Burgeffes Wages in Money, for this prefent Seffion of Affembly; and the fame was received, and read the firft Time.

Refolved, That the Bill be read a fecond Time.

Refolved, That the Bill be now read a fecond Time.

The *Bill* was accordingly read a fecond Time.

Ordered, That the Bill be ingroffed.

And then the Houfe adjourned till To-morrow Morning nine of the Clock.

Saturday, the 20th of July, 11 Geo. III. 1771.

AN ingroffed *Bill* for the Relief of the Sufferers by the Lofs of Tobacco damaged or burnt in feveral Warehoufes, was read the third Time.

Refolved, That the Bill do pafs; and that the Title be *An Act*[1] *for the Relief of the Sufferers by the Lofs of Tobacco damaged or burnt in feveral Warehoufes.*

Ordered, That Mr *Bland* do carry the Bill to the Council and defire their Concurrence.

An engroffed *Bill* for the Eafe and Relief of the People, by paying the Burgeffes Wages in Money for this prefent Seffion of Affembly, was read the third Time.

Refolved, That the Bill do pafs; and that the Title be *An Act*[2] *for the Eafe and Relief of the People, by paying the Burgeffes Wages in Money, for this prefent Seffion of Affembly.*

Ordered, That Mr *Henry Lee* do carry the Bill to the Council, and defire their Concurrence.

Refolved, Nemine Contradicente, That an elegant Statue of his late Excellency the Right Honourable *Norborne*, Baron de *Botetourt* be erected in Marble at the Public Expence, with proper Infcriptions, expreffing the grateful Senfe this Houfe entertains of his Lordfhip's prudent and wife Adminiftration, and their great Solicitude to perpetuate, as far as they are able, the Remembrance of thofe many public and focial Virtues which adorned his illuftrious Character. That the fame be fent for to *Great-Britain* under the Direction of the Honourable *William Nelfon*, *Thomas Nelfon*, and *Peyton Randolph*, Efquires, *Robert Carter Nicholas*, *Lewis Burwell*, and *Dudley Digges*, Efquires.

Refolved, That the Treafurer pay for the Statue to be erected to the Memory of Lord *Botetourt* out of the public Money in the Treafury.

Ordered, Mr *Bland* do carry the Refolution to the Council, and defire their Concurrence.

Refolved, That the Sum of fifteen Pounds be paid to each of the Infpectors at *Shockoe*, *Byrd's* and *Rocky Ridge* Warehoufes; the Sum of five Pounds to *Turner Southall*, *Daniel Price*, and *Matthew Branch*, each; ten Pounds to *Lufby Turpin*, and five Pounds to *Thomas Cheatham*, Infpectors at *Warwick;* and the Sum of ten Pounds to *William Newton* and *John Pollard*, each, for their Services in faving the Tobacco damaged in the Public Warehoufes, and their Trouble and Expences in travelling to *Williamfburg*, and attending the Houfe of Burgeffes, with their Books and Accounts of the faid Tobacco.

Ordered, That Mr *Archibald Cary* do carry the Refolution to the Council and defire their Concurrence.

Refolved, That the feveral Sums of Money following be paid to the feveral Officers of the General Affembly, *viz.*

To

---

[1] Hening, VIII, p. 493.   [2] Ibid, VIII, p. 505.

To *George Wythe*, Efq; Clerk of the Houfe of Burgeffes, £75 0 0
To *John Blair*, jun. Efq; Clerk of the General Affembly, 40 0 0
To the Reverend Mr *Thomas Price*, Chaplain, 20 0 0
To Mr *Francis Eppes*, Serjeant at Arms, 30 0 0
To Mr *Hind Ruffell*, 10 0 0
To *Jafper Mauduit Gidley*, 10 0 0
To the Door Keeper of the Council, 8 0 0

To *James Lavie*,
To *Robert Hyland*,
To *William Hicks*,   Door Keepers to the Houfe, each 8*l*.   32 0 0
To *John Creagh*,

Ordered, That Mr *Archibald Cary* do carry the Refolution to the Council, and defire their Concurrence.

Ordered, That a Committee be appointed to examine the enrolled Bills and Refolves.

And a *Committee* was appointed of Mr *Dudley Digges*, Mr *Lewis Burwell*, of *James City*, Mr *Wilfon Miles Cary*, and Mr *Jefferfon*.

A *Meffage* from the Council by Mr *Blair*:

Mr *Speaker*,
The Council have agreed to the Bill, *intituled* An Act[1] for the Relief of the Sufferers by the Lofs of Tobacco damaged or burnt in feveral Warehoufes, *without any Amendment: And alfo*,

The Council have agreed to the Bill, *intituled*, An Act[2] for the Eafe and Relief of the People, by paying the Burgeffes Wages in Money for this prefent Seffion of Affembly, *without any Amendment: And alfo*,

The Council have agreed to the Refolve *for erecting a Statue to the Memory of Lord* Botetourt: *And alfo*,

The Council have agreed to the Refolve *for paying the Public Printer for binding the Books of the Acts of laft Seffion: And alfo*,

The Council have agreed to the Refolve *for paying feveral Sums of Money to feveral Infpectors: And alfo*,

The Council have agreed to the Refolve *for paying feveral Sums of Money to the Officers of the General Affembly.*

And then the Meffenger withdrew.

Mr *Dudley Digges* reported, from the Committee appointed to examine the enrolled Bills and Refolves, that the Committee had examined the enrolled Bills and Refolves accordingly, and rectified fuch Miftakes as were found therein; and that they are truly enrolled.

Ordered, That Mr *Dudley Digges* do carry the enrolled Bills and Refolves to the Council, for their Infpection.

A *Meffage* from the Council by Mr *Blair*.

Mr *Speaker*,
The Council have Infpected the enrolled Bills and Refolves and are fatiffied that they are truly enrolled.

And then the Meffenger withdrew.
A *Meffage* from the Prefident by Mr *Blair*:

Mr *Speaker*,
The Prefident commands this Houfe to attend his Honour immediately, in the Council Chamber.

Accordingly Mr *Speaker*, with the Houfe, went up to attend his Honour, in the Council

[1] Hening, VIII, p. 493.   [2] Ibid, VIII, p. 505.

cil Chamber, where his Honour was pleafed to give his Affent to the feveral public and private Bills and Refolves following, *viz.*

An Act[1] *for further continuing the Act intituled an Act for the better regulating and difciplining the Militia.*

An Act[2] *for the Relief of the Sufferers by the Lofs of Tobacco damaged or burnt in feveral Warehoufes.*

An Act[3] *to impower the Inhabitants of the Parifh of* Augufta, *in the County of* Augufta, *to elect a Veftry.*

An Act[4] *for the Eafe and Relief of the People by paying the Burgeffes Wages in Money for this prefent Seffion of Affembly.*

A *Refolve* for erecting a Statue to the Memory of Lord *Botetourt.*

A *Refolve* for paying four hundred and fifty Pounds per Annum to *William Rind,* the Public Printer.

A *Refolve* for paying the Keeper of the Public Gaol his Salary.

A *Refolve* for paying the Public Printer for binding Books of the Acts of laft Seffion.

A *Refolve* for paying feveral Sums of Money to feveral Infpectors.

A *Refolve* for paying feveral Sums of Money to the Officers of the General Affembly.

After which his Honour was pleafed to make a Speech to the Council and this Houfe, as followeth, *viz.*

Gentlemen of the Council, Mr *Speaker, and Gentlemen of the Houfe of Burgeffes,*

I am now to return you my Thanks for the Readinefs with which you have entered upon the Bufinefs I recommended to you, and for your conftant Attention and Application to it.

I am perfuaded that your Conduct, on this Occafion, will be highly approved by your Country in general, and that thofe who will be relieved by the Act that is paffed for that Purpofe, will always think of you with Honour and Gratitude.

Before I part with you let me entreat the Favour of your Affiftance, in your different Departments, to preferve the Peace, Order, and good Government, in your feveral Counties, which, I have the Pleafure to obferve, have fubfifted during my fhort Adminiftration.

I will not detain you longer than to acquaint you that I have thought fit to prorogue this Affembly to the fourth Thurfday *in* October *next; and it is accordingly prorogued to that Time.*

---

[1] Hening, VIII, p. 503.   [2] Ibid, VII, p. 493.   [3] Ibid, VIII, p. 504.   [4] Ibid, VIII, p. 505.

JOURNAL

of the

HOUSE OF BURGESSES

1772

Burgeſſes.

Accomack	Southey Simpſon James Henry	Glouceſter	Thomas Whiting Lewis Burwell
Albemarle	Thomas Walker *Thomas Jefferſon	Goochland	John Woodſon Thomas Mann Randolph
Amelia	John Winn John Tabb	Halifax	*Nathaniel Terry *Iſaac Coles
Amherſt	William Cabell, Jr. Joſeph Cabell	Hampſhire	*James Mercer Alexander White
Auguſta	John Wilſon Samuel McDowell	Hanover	Patrick Henry, Jr. John Smith
Bedford	*John Talbot *Charles Lynch	Henrico	Richard Randolph Richard Adams
Berkeley	Robert Rutherford *Thomas Hite	Iſle of Wight	James Bridger Richard Hardy
Botetourt	Andrew Lewis John Bowyer	James City	Robt. Carter Nicholas Lewis Burwell
Brunſwick	John Jones Thomas Stith	Jameſtown King and Queen	Champion Travis George Brooke
Buckingham	Charles May Henry Bell		John Tayloe Corbin
Caroline	Edmund Pendleton Walker Taliaferro	King George	Joſeph Jones William Fitzhugh
Charles City	William Acrill Benjamin Harriſon	King William	Auguſtine Moore William Aylett
Charlotte	Paul Carrington James Speed	Lancaſter	Richard Mitchell Charles Carter
Cheſterfield	Archibald Cary Benjamin Watkins	Loudoun	Thomſon Maſon Francis Peyton
The College	John Page	Louiſa	*Richard Anderſon Dabney Carr
Culpeper	Henry Pendleton Henry Field, Jr.	Lunenburg	Richard Claiborne Thomas Pettus
Cumberland	William Fleming Alexander Trent	Mecklenburg	Matthew Marrable *Robert Munford
Dinwiddie	Robert Bolling John Baniſter	Middleſex	Edmund Berkeley James Montague
Dunmore	*Francis Slaughter *Joſeph Watſon	Nanſemond	Benjamin Baker Lemuel Riddick
Elizabeth City	Henry King Worlich Weſtwood	New Kent	Burwell Baſſett Bartholomew Dandridge
Eſſex	James Edmondſon William Roane	Norfolk	Thomas Newton, Jr. James Holt
Fairfax	George Waſhington John Weſt	Norfolk Borough Northampton	Joſeph Hutchings Severn Eyre
Fauquier	Thomas Marſhall James Scott		John Burton
Frederick	Robert Rutherford James Wood	Northumberland	Peter Preſley Thornton Spencer Mottrom Ball

*Not ſhown by the Journal to have been preſent during the Aſſembly.

Orange	Zachariah Burnley Thomas Barbour	Spotſylvania	George Stubblefield Mann Page, Jr.
Pittſylvania	*John Donelſon Hugh Innes	Stafford	John Alexander Yelverton Peyton
Prince Edward	Peter Legrand Paſchall Greenhill	Surry	Allen Cocke *Hartwell Cocke
Prince George	Richard Bland Peter Poythreſs	Suſſex	David Maſon Richard Blunt
Prince William	Fouſhee Tebbs Henry Lee	Warwick	William Harwood William Langhorne
Princeſs Anne	Edward Hack Moſeley, Jr. Chriſtopher Wright	Weſtmoreland	Richard Henry Lee Richard Lee
Richmond	Robert Wormeley Carter Francis Lightfoot Lee	Williamſburg	Peyton Randolph
Southampton	Edwin Gray Henry Taylor	York	Dudley Digges Thomas Nelſon, Jr.

*Not ſhown by the Journal to have been preſent during the Aſſembly.

Changes in the Perſonnel, 1772.

Buckingham	Charles May ſucceeded Benjamin Howard
Henrico	Samuel Duval ſucceeded Richard Randolph
King William	Auguſtine Moore ſucceeded Philip Whitehead Claiborne
Lunenburg	Thomas Pettus ſucceeded Henry Blagrave

By his **Excellency**, the Right Honourable **John**, Earl of **Dunmore**, his Majesty's Lieutenant and Governor General of the Colony and Dominion of **Virginia**, and Vice Admiral of the same:

A PROCLAMATION

For diffolving the General Affembly.

Virginia, to wit:

Whereas, the General Affembly ftands prorogued to the fourth *Thurfday* in this Month. And whereas I have thought fit, for divers Confiderations regarding his Majefty's Service, to diffolve the faid Affembly; I have therefore, by and with the Advice and Confent of his Majefty's Council, iffued this Proclamation, declaring the faid Affembly to be diffolved; and it is hereby diffolved accordingly. Of which all his Majefty's Subjects within this Colony are required to take Notice.

Given under my Hand, and the Seal of the Colony, at *Williamfburg*, this 12th Day of *October*, 1771, and in the eleventh Year of his Majefty's Reign.

Dunmore

GOD SAVE THE KING.

By his **Excellency**, the Right Honourable **John**, Earl of **Dunmore**, his Majefty's Lieutenant and Governor General of the Colony and Dominion of **Virginia**, and Vice Admiral of the fame:

A PROCLAMATION.

Virginia, to wit:

Whereas, the General Affembly is fummoned to meet on *Thurfday* the twelfth Day of next Month, and I find no urgent Occafion for the faid Affembly's meeting at that Time: I have therefore thought fit, by and with the Advice of his Majefty's Council, by this Proclamation, in his Majefty's Name, further to prorogue the faid Affembly to the fecond *Thurfday* in *January* next.

Given under my Hand, and the Seal of the Colony, at *Williamfburg*, this 20th Day *November*, 1771, and in the twelfth Year of his Majefty's Reign.

Dunmore.

GOD SAVE THE KING.

By his **Excellency,** the Right Honourable **John,** Earl of **Dunmore,** his Majefty's Lieutenant and Governor General of the Colony and Dominion of **Virginia,** and Vice Admiral of the fame:

A PROCLAMATION.

Virginia, to wit:

Whereas, the General Affembly ftands prorogued to the fecond *Thurfday* in *January* next, and I find no urgent Occafion for the faid Affembly's meeting at that Time: I have therefore thought fit, by and with the Advice and Confent of his Majefty's Council, by this Proclamation, in his Majefty's Name, further to prorogue the faid Affembly to *Thurfday* the 6th Day of *February* next; at which Time their attendance is required at the Capitol, in the City of *Williamfburg*.

Given under my Hand, and the Seal of the Colony, at *Williamfburg* aforefaid, this 12th Day of *December*, 1771, and in the twelfth Year of his Majefty's Reign.

Dunmore.

GOD SAVE THE KING.

A PROCLAMATION.

Virginia, to wit:

His EXCELLENCY, JOHN, Earl of DUNMORE, his Majefty's Lieutenant and Governor General of the Colony and Dominion of VIRGINIA, and Vice Admiral of the fame, to *William Nelfon, Thomas Nelfon, Richard Corbin, William Byrd, Philip Ludwell Lee, John Tayloe, Robert Carter, Robert Burwell, George William Fairfax, John Page,* Efquires, *James Horrocks,* Clerk, and *Ralph Wormeley,* Junior, Efquire. KNOW YE that, by Virtue of the Powers and Authorities to me granted by his Majefty, I do hereby authorize and impower you, the faid *William Nelfon, Thomas Nelfon, Richard Corbin, William Byrd, Philip Ludwell Lee, John Tayloe, Robert Carter, Robert Burwell, George William Fairfax, John Page, James Horrocks,* and *Ralph Wormeley,* Junior, or any two of you, to adminifter the Oaths appointed by Act of Parliament to be taken, inftead of the Oaths of Allegiance and Supremacy, the Oath appointed to be taken by an Act of Parliament made in the fixth Year of the Reign of his prefent Majefty King GEORGE the Third, intituled *An Act for altering the Oath of Abjuration, and the Affurance, and for amending fo much of an Act of the feventh Year of her late Majefty Queen* ANNE, intituled, *An Act for the Improvement of the Union of the two Kingdoms, as after the Time therein limited requires the Delivery of certain Lifts and Copies therein mentioned to Perfons indicted of High Treafon, or Mifprifion of Treafon;* as alfo the Teft, to all fuch Perfons as are or fhall be returned to ferve in this prefent General Affembly, as Burgeffes; as alfo to the Clerk of the Houfe of Burgeffes, or Clerks of any of the Committees of the faid Houfe, that fhall be appointed during this Seffion; and to caufe them to fubfcribe the faid laft mentioned Oath, as alfo the Teft; and to Adminifter the Oath of Clerk to the Clerk of the faid Houfe; and alfo the Clerk or Clerks of Committees.

Given under my Hand, and the Seal of the Colony, at *Williamfburg,* the 4th Day of *February,* 1772, in the twelfth Year of the Reign of our Sovereign Lord King GEORGE the Third.

Dunmore.

A PROCLAMATION.

Thursday, the 6th of February, 12 George III. 1772.

The Right Honourable JOHN Earl of DUNMORE his Majesty's Lieutenant and Governor General of the Colony and Dominion of VIRGINIA, and Vice Admiral of the same, having, by Proclamation hereunto annexed, and Writs of Summons bearing Date of the 31st Day of *October* last, called the General Assembly to meet this Day; and having made a Commission, under his Hand, and the Seal of the Colony, hereunto also annexed, to the Honourable *William Nelson, Thomas Nelson, Richard Corbin, William Byrd, Philip Ludwell Lee, John Tayloe, Robert Carter, Robert Burwell, George William Fairfax, John Page,* Esquires, *James Horrocks,* Clerk, and *Ralph Wormeley,* Junior, Esquire, for administering the Oaths appointed to be taken by the Members of the House of Burgesses; and several of the said Commissioners attending in the Council Chamber, the usual Place for administering the said Oaths to the Members of the House of Burgesses, at the Opening of a General Assembly; and *Benjamin Waller,* Esquire, Clerk of the Secretary's Office, having delivered in a Book of the Names of such Members as had been returned; and *George Wythe,* Clerk of the House of Burgesses, attending, according to his Duty, the said Commissioners administered the said Oaths to such Members of the House of Burgesses as then appeared; and there not being a sufficient Number of them to proceed to Business, upon Information that the General Assembly was to be therefore prorogued, the Members went again to the Council Chamber, where the Proclamation was read for proroguing the General Assembly until To-morrow; which Proclamation is as followeth, *viz.*

Virginia, to wit:

Whereas this Day was by me appointed for the meeting of the General Assembly, but the Badness of the Roads has prevented the Number of Burgesses requisite to make a House from attending; I have therefore thought fit, by and with the Advice and Consent of his Majesty's Council, by this Proclamation, in his Majesty's Name, to prorogue the said Assembly until Tomorrow; at which Time their Attendance is required at the Capitol, in the City of *Williamsburg,* for the Dispatch of public Business.

Given under my Hand, and the Seal of the Colony, at *Williamsburg,* aforesaid, this 6th Day of *February,* 1772, and in the twelfth Year of his Majesty's Reign.

Dunmore.

GOD SAVE THE KING.

A PROCLAMATION.

Friday, the 7th of February, 12 George III. 1772.

Several Members this Day appearing, being informed that the General Affembly was to be again prorogued by Proclamation, they went up to the Council Chamber; where the Proclamation was read, for proroguing the General Affembly until Tomorrow which proclamation is as followeth, *viz.*

Virginia, to wit:

Whereas, this Day was by me appointed for the meeting of the General Affembly, but the Badnefs of the Roads has prevented the Number of Burgeffes requifite to make a Houfe from attending; I have therefore thought fit, by and with the Advice and Confent of his Majefty's Council, by this Proclamation, in his Majefty's Name, to prorogue the faid Affembly until Tomorrow; at which Time their Attendance is required at the Capitol, in the City of *Williamfburg*, for the Difpatch of public Bufinefs.

Given under my Hand, and the Seal of the Colony, at *Williamfburg*, this 7th Day of *February*, 1772, and in the twelfth Year of his Majefty's Reign.

Dunmore.

GOD SAVE THE KING.

A PROCLAMATION.

Saturday, the 8th of February, 12 Geo. III. 1772.

Several Members this Day appearing, being informed that the General Affembly was to be again prorogued by Proclamation, they went up to the Council Chamber; where the Proclamation was read, for proroguing the General Affembly until *Monday* next; which Proclamation is as followeth, *viz.*

Virginia, to wit:

Whereas, this Day was by me appointed for the meeting of the General Affembly, but the Badnefs of the Roads have prevented the Number of Burgeffes requifite to make a Houfe from attending; I have therefore thought fit, by and with the Advice of his Majefty's Council, by this proclamation, in his Majefty's Name, to prorogue the faid Affembly till *Monday* next; at which Time their Attendance is required at the Capitol, in the City of *Williamfburg*, for the Difpatch of public Bufinefs.

Dunmore.

GOD SAVE THE KING.

JOURNAL

of the

HOUSE OF BURGESSES

*G*ENERAL *Affembly, begun and held at the Capitol, in the City of WILLIAMS-BURG, on MONDAY the tenth Day of FEBRUARY in the twelfth Year of the Reign of our Lord GEORGE the Third, by the Grace of GOD, of GREAT-BRITAIN, FRANCE and IRELAND, King, Defender of the Faith, &c. Annoque Domini* 1772.

On which Day, being the firft Day of the meeting of this General Affembly, purfuant to the feveral Proclamations hereunto annexed, and the Writs, which had before iffued for that Purpofe, feveral of the Commiffioners, named in the Commiffion hereunto alfo annexed, attended in the Council Chamber, with the Clerk, and adminiftered the Oaths appointed to be taken by the Members of the Houfe of Burgeffes to fuch of the faid Members as then appeared; which being done, the Members all repaired to their Seats in the Houfe of Burgeffes: After which a Meffage was delivered by *John Blair*, Efquire, Clerk of the General Affembly.

Gentlemen,
The Governor commands this Houfe to attend his Excellency immediately in the Council Chamber.

Accordingly the Houfe went up to attend his Excellency in the Council Chamber, where his Excellency was pleafed to fay to them:

Gentlemen of the Houfe of Burgeffes,
You muft return again to your Houfe, and immediately proceed to the choice of a Speaker.

And the Houfe being returned,
Richard Bland, Efquire, one of the Members for the County of *Prince George*, addreffing himfelf to the Clerk (who, ftanding up, pointed to him, and then fat down) put the Houfe in Mind of the Governor's Commands to proceed to the Choice of a Speaker, and moved, that *Peyton Randolph*, Efq; who had, in feveral former General Affemblies, fhewn himfelf to be every Way qualified for the Office, fhould take the Chair of this Houfe, as Speaker: *And thereupon,*

M*r Randolph* was elected without Oppofition, and was taken out of his Place by two Members, who led him from thence to the Chair, and having afcended the uppermoft Step, and ftanding there, M*r Randolph* returned his Thanks to the Houfe for this recent Inftance of their Approbation, and affured them that he would endeavor to conduct himfelf with Attention, Impartiality, and Steadinefs, in the Difcharge of the important Duties of his Office.

And thereupon he fat down in the Chair; and then the Mace (which before lay under the Table) was laid upon the Table.

Ordered, That a Meffage be fent to the Governor, to acquaint his Excellency, that this Houfe, in Obedience to his Commands, have made Choice of a Speaker, and to know his Pleafure when they fhall attend to prefent him; and that M*r Bland*, M*r Riddick*, and M*r Cary*, do wait upon him with the faid Meffage.

They

They accordingly withdrew, and, being returned, Mr *Bland* reported, that the Governor was pleafed to fay, he would fend an Anfwer by a Meffenger of his own.

A *Meffage* from the Governor by Mr *Blair*:

Mr *Speaker*,

The Governor commands this Houfe to attend his Excellency immediately in the Council Chamber.

Accordingly Mr *Speaker* elect, with the Houfe, went up to attend his Excellency in the Council Chamber; and he was pleafed to declare his Approbation of their Choice.

Then Mr *Speaker* did, in the Name and on Behalf of the Houfe, lay Claim to all their antient Rights and Privileges, particularly a Freedom of Speech and Debate, Exemption from Arrefts, and Protection for their Eftates; and laftly, for himfelf, requefted that his Errors might not be imputed to the Houfe.

The Governor anfwered, that he fhould take Care to defend them in all their juft Rights and Privileges.

The Houfe being returned,

Mr *Speaker* reported, that the Houfe had attended the Governor in the Council Chamber; where his Excellency was pleafed to approve the Choice they had made of him to be their Speaker, and to grant and allow to them, upon Petition of Claim made by him to his Excellency, in the Name and on the Behalf of the Houfe of Burgeffes, all their antient Rights and Privileges; particularly a Freedom of Speech and Debate, Exemption from Arrefts, and Protection for their Eftates.

Mr *Speaker* alfo reported, that the Governor was pleafed to make a Speech to the Council and this Houfe; of which Mr *Speaker* faid, he had, to prevent Miftakes, obtained a Copy; which he read to the Houfe, and is as followeth, *viz.*

> Gentlemen of the Council, Mr Speaker, and
>   Gentlemen of the Houfe of Burgeffes,
>
> I am happy that the Circumftances of the Colony, correfponding with my own Defires, give me an Opportunity, fo foon after my Entrance upon this Government, of procuring your Advice and Affiftance, to enable me to execute the high and arduous Truft, which is repofed in me, in a Manner that may prove fatiffactory to our gracious Sovereign, by being beneficial to his faithful Subjects of this antient Dominion.
>
> It is my ardent Wifh, and fhall be my conftant Endeavor, that my Adminiftration may be marked by ufeful Services to the Colony; to this End, if any Improvements can be introduced, upon wife and practicable Principles, you may depend on my zealous Co-operation; if proper Means can be fallen upon to direct the Skill, and invigorate the Induftry of the People, in making the beft Ufe of the natural Advantages of this Country, to which Providence has been fo eminently bountiful; to regulate and encourage Agriculture, the Object of greateft Concern to every Country, which cannot fail to extend your Commerce, open new Sources of Wealth, and add frefh Motives, of mutual Benefit, ftill to increafe the Dependance of this important Colony and the Parent Country on each other, it will be extremely agreeable to me to labour towards accomplifhing fuch defirable Purpofes.
>
> Mr Speaker, and Gentlemen of the Houfe of Burgeffes,
>
> I have nothing in particular to afk of you at this Time: The Zeal for the public Good, which, I am perfuaded, will actuate all the Proceedings of the Houfe of Burgeffes, renders fuperfluous any Exhortations of mine, to excite you to avoid unneceffary Delays, and thereby an Increafe of Expences to your Conftituents.
>
> Gentlemen of the Council, Mr Speaker, and
>   Gentlemen of the Houfe of Burgeffes,
>
> I have only to add, that you fhall find me ready to concur with you in whatever is for the Intereft and Advantage of your Country, fully confiding in the known Wifdom and Loyalty of this diftinguifhed Affembly, that nothing will be offered me incompatible with

my

my Duty to affent to; and, on all Occafions, I fhall be forward to promote the Welfare of the People of Virginia.

Refolved, That an humble Addrefs be prefented to his Excellency the Governor, returning him the fincere Thanks of this Houfe, for his kind and obliging Speech at the Opening of this Seffion; to congratulate him on his Appointment to this Government, expreffing the great Pleafure we receive in finding his Excellency fo warmly difpofed to
5 promote the Profperity of this Country, and affuring him that we will, upon all Occafions, do every Thing in our Power, confiftent with the Duty we owe our Conftituents, to render his Lordfhip's Adminiftration agreeable; and that we will proceed immediately to the Confideration of the important Bufinefs of the Country, on which we are now affembled, and give it all the Difpatch which the Nature of it will admit.

Ordered, That a Committee be appointed to draw up an Addrefs, to be prefented to the Governor, upon the faid Refolution.

And a *Committee* was appointed of Mᵣ *Treafurer,* and Mᵣ *Nelfon.*

Ordered, That the Governor's Speech to the Council, and this Houfe, be referred to the faid Committee.

Refolved, That the Governor's Speech be taken into Confideration upon *Wednefday* next.

Refolved, That this Houfe will, upon *Wednefday* next, refolve itfelf into a Committee of the whole Houfe, to take into Confideration the Governor's Speech.

Ordered, That the Reverend *Thomas Price,* Clerk, be appointed Chaplain to this Houfe, and that he attend to read Prayers, in the Houfe, every Morning, at nine of the Clock.

Ordered, That Mᵣ *Treafurer* do go to the Council, and acquaint them that Mᵣ *Price* is appointed Chaplain to this Houfe, and that he will attend to read Prayers, in the Houfe, every Morning, at nine of the Clock.

Ordered, That *Robert Hyland, William Hicks,* and *John Creagh,* be appointed Doorkeepers to this Houfe; and that they give their Attendance accordingly.

A *Petition* of *William Jenings,* praying that he may be appointed another Doorkeeper, to this Houfe; *and alfo,*

A *Petition* of *Michael Maccarty* for the fame; *and alfo,*

A *Petition* of *John Jones* for the fame; *and alfo,*

A *Petition* of *William Drinkard* for the fame; *and alfo,*

A *Petition* of *William Page* for the fame; *and alfo,*

A *Petition* of *James Atherton* for the fame,

Were feverally prefented to the Houfe, and read.

Refolved, That the faid Doorkeeper be chofen by Way of balloting.

Ordered, That the Members of this Houfe do immediately prepare Tickets, to be put into a Glafs, with the Name of the Perfon to be the faid Doorkeeper.

The *Glafs* being accordingly brought in;

The *Clerk* went with the fame, on each Side of the Houfe, to receive the faid Tickets:

And the *Members* having put in their Tickets, the Glafs was brought up to the Clerk's Table.

Ordered, That a Committee be appointed to examine the Tickets; and that they do report to the Houfe upon which of the faid Petitioners the Majority falls.

And a *Committee* was appointed of Mᵣ *Bland,* Mᵣ *Riddick,* Mᵣ *Harrifon,* Mᵣ *Treafurer,* Mᵣ *Nelfon,* and Mᵣ *Baffett,* and they are to withdraw immediately.

Mᵣ *Bland* reported from the Committee, that they had examined the Tickets accordingly, and that the Majority falls upon *William Drinkard;* and he read the Report in his Place, and afterwards delivered it in at the Clerk's Table; where the fame was twice read, and is as followeth, *viz.*

William Drinkard,————— 28

Ordered, That the faid *William Drinkard* be appointed Doorkeeper to this Houfe; and that he give his Attendance accordingly.

Ordered

Ordered, That Mr *Treasurer* do provide a decent Suit of Clothes, with a great Coat, for every one of the Doorkeepers attending this House.

And then the House adjourned till Tomorrow Morning eleven of the Clock.

Tuesday, the 11th of February, 12 George III. 1772.

MR *Speaker* acquainted the House that he had received a Letter from the Speaker of the Lower House of Assembly of the Province of *Maryland*, inclosing certain Resolutions of the said Lower House of Assembly, relative to the erecting and supporting a Lighthouse upon *Cape Henry*.

And he delivered the *Letter* and *Resolutions* in at the Clerk's Table.

Ordered, That the said Letter and Resolutions do lie upon the Table, to be perused by the Members of the House.

Mr *Treasurer* reported, from the Committee, appointed to draw up an Address, to be presented to the Governor, that the Committee had drawn up an Address accordingly, which they had directed him to report to the House; and he read the same in his Place, and afterwards delivered it in at the Clerk's Table; where the same was read, and is as followeth, *viz.*

> *My Lord,*
>
> *We his Majesty's most dutiful and loyal Subjects, the Burgesses of* Virginia, *now met in General Assembly, beg Leave to return your Excellency our sincere Thanks for your very kind and obliging Speech at the Opening of this Session.*
>
> *The appointment of a Ruler, of your Lordship's eminent and exalted Station, to preside over this his Majesty's antient Dominion, we cannot but esteem a repeated Instance of the favorable Attention of our most Gracious Sovereign to his faithful Subjects of* Virginia; *and therefore take the earliest Opportunity of congratulating your Excellency on an Event, from which we flatter ourselves much Honour, and many signal Advantages, will be derived to this Colony.*
>
> *We receive, my Lord, with the utmost Satisfaction, those earnest Declarations you are pleased to make of your warm Attachment to the true Interest and Prosperity of our Country, and beg your Lordship will be assured that we shall be ready, on all Occasions, most chearfully to do every Thing in our Power, consistent with the Duty we owe our Constituents, to make your Administration easy and agreeable to you.*
>
> *We will, my Lord, immediately proceed to the important Business of the Country, on which we are now assembled, and give it all the Dispatch which the Variety of Affairs, that may come under our Consideration, will admit of.*

The said *Address* being read a second Time;

Resolved, Nemine Contradicente, That the House doth agree with the Committee in the said Address, to be presented to the Governor.

Resolved, That the said Address be presented to his Excellency by the whole House.

Ordered, That the Gentlemen, who drew up the said Address, do wait upon the Governor to know his Pleasure, when this House shall attend his Excellency, to present their Address.

A *Petition* of sundry Persons, of the Town of *Suffolk*, whose Names are thereunto subscribed, was presented to the House, and read; setting forth, that many Persons residing in the said Town, raise Hogs and Goats, and suffer them to run at Large therein, to the great Damage of the Petitioners and others; and therefore praying that an Act may pass to restrain the Inhabitants of the said Town from permitting Hogs and Goats to go at Large within the same.

Ordered, That Leave be given to bring in a Bill pursuant to the Prayer of the said Petition; and that Mr *Riddick* do prepare and bring in the same.

A *Petition* of the Magistrates of the County of *Surry*, and others, whose Names are

thereunto

thereunto fubfcribed, was prefented to the Houfe, and read; praying that the Court of the faid County may be appointed to be held on the fourth *Tuefday* inftead of the third *Tuefday* in the Month.

7 *Ordered*, That Leave be given to bring in a Bill purfuant to the Prayer of the faid Petition; and that Mr *Bland* do prepare and bring in the fame.

Ordered, That a Committee for Religion be appointed.

And a *Committee* was appointed of Mr *Treafurer*, Mr *Cary*, Mr *Charles Carter*, Mr *Harwood*, Mr *Richard Lee*, Mr *Acrill*, Mr *Patrick Henry*, Mr *Banifter*, Mr *Bland*, Mr *Hutchings*, Mr *Lewis Burwell*, of *James City*, Mr *Carrington*, Mr *Simpfon*, Mr *David Mafon*, Mr *Harrifon*, Mr *Digges*, Mr *Nelfon*, Mr *Innes*, Mr *Bridger*, Mr *Winn*, Mr *Berkeley*, and Mr *Woodfon*. And they are to meet and adjourn from Day to Day, and to take into their Confideration all Matters and Things relating to Religion and Morality, and all fuch as fhall be from Time to Time referred to them, and report their Proceedings, with their Opinions thereupon, to the Houfe; and the faid Committee are to have Power to fend for Perfons, Papers, and Records for their Information.

Ordered, That Mr *Richard Cary* be appointed Clerk to the faid Committee.

Ordered, That a Committee of Privileges and Elections be appointed.

And a *Committee* was appointed of Mr *Edmund Pendleton*, Mr *Treafurer*, Mr *Bland*, Mr *Cary*, Mr *Harrifon*, Mr *Lewis Burwell*, of *James City*, Mr *Digges*, Mr *Patrick Henry*, Mr *Charles Carter*, Mr *Nelfon*, Mr *Carrington*, Mr *Richard Lee*, Mr *Riddick*, Mr *Banifter*, Mr *Whiting*, Mr *Robert Wormeley Carter*, Mr *John Page*, Mr *James Henry*, Mr *Dandridge*, and Mr *Holt*. And they are to meet and adjourn from Day to Day, and to examine, in the firft Place, all Returns of Writs for electing Burgeffes to ferve in this prefent General Affembly, and compare the fame with the Form prefcribed by Law, and to take into their Confideration all fuch Matters as fhall or may come in Queftion, touching Returns, Elections, and Privileges, and to report their Proceedings, with their Opinions thereupon, from Time to Time, to the Houfe; and the faid Committee are to have Power to fend for Perfons, Papers, and Records, for their Information.

Ordered, That Mr *Richard Starke* be appointed Clerk to the faid Committee.

Refolved, That in all Cafes of controverted Elections, to be heard at the Bar of this Houfe, or before the Committee of Privileges and Elections, the Petitioners do, by themfelves, or by their Agents, within a convenient Time, to be appointed, either by the Houfe or the Committee of Privileges and Elections, as the Matter to be heard fhall be before the Houfe, or the faid Committee, deliver to the fitting Members, or their Agents, Lifts of the Perfons intended by the Petitioners to be objected to, who voted for the fitting Members, giving, in the faid Lifts, the feveral Heads of Objections, and diftinguifhing the fame againft the Names of the Voters excepted to; and that the fitting Members do, by themfelves, or their Agents, within the fame Time, deliver the like Lifts, on their Part, to the Petitioners, or their Agents.

Ordered, That a Committee of Propofitions and Grievances be appointed.

And a *Committee* was appointed of Mr *Bland*, Mr *Treafurer*, Mr *Cary*, Mr *Harrifon*, Mr *Lewis Burwell*, of *James City*, Mr *Digges*, Mr *Harwood*, Mr *Nelfon*, Mr *Baffett*, Mr *Charles Carter*, Mr *Riddick*, Mr *Carrington*, Mr *Acrill*, Mr *Patrick Henry*, Mr *Hutchings*, Mr *Newton*, Mr *Richard Lee*, Mr *Adams*, Mr *David Mafon*, Mr *Simpfon*, Mr *Banifter*, Mr *Whiting*, Mr *Trent*, Mr *Poythrofs*, Mr *Woodfon*, Mr *Gray*, Mr *Taylor*, Mr *Bolling*, Mr *John Page*, Mr *Berkeley*, Mr *Burton*, and Mr *Baker*. And they are to meet and adjourn from Day to Day,

8 and to take into their Confideration all Propofitions and Grievances that fhall come legally certified to this Affembly, and to report their Proceedings; with their Opinions thereupon, from Time to Time, to the Houfe; and all fuch Propofitions and Grievances are to be delivered to the Clerk of the Houfe, and by him to the faid Committee of Courfe. And the faid Committee are to have Power to fend for Perfons, Papers, and Records, for their Information.

Ordered, That Mr *Richard Starke* be appointed Clerk to the faid Committee.

Ordered, That a Committee of Public Claims be appointed.

And a *Committee* was appointed of Mr *Cary*, Mr *Richard Lee*, Mr *Newton*, Mr *David Mafon*

Mafon, Mr *Bridger*, Mr *Harwood*, Mr *Simpfon*, Mr *Woodfon*, Mr *Adams*, Mr *Poythrefs*, Mr *Gray*, Mr *Taylor*, Mr *Trent*, Mr *Burton*, Mr *Pettus*, Mr *Watkins*, Mr *Smith*, and Mr *Hardy*. And they are to meet and adjourn from Day to Day, and to take into their Confideration all Public Claims, referred from the laft to this Seffion of Affembly, and alfo all fuch Claims as fhall be regularly certified and prefented to this Seffion, and to report their Proceedings, with their Opinions thereupon, to the Houfe, when they have gone through the faid Claims. And all Perfons that have any Claims are to deliver them to the faid Committee of Courfe; and they are to have Power to fend for Perfons, Papers, and Records, for their Information.

Ordered, That Mr *Hind Ruffell* be appointed Clerk to the faid Committee.

Ordered, That a Committee for Courts of Juftice be appointed.

And a *Committee* was appointed of Mr *Woodfon*, Mr *Gray*, Mr *Taylor*, Mr *Thomas Mann Randolph*, Mr *Pettus*, Mr *Thornton*, Mr *Weftwood*, Mr *King*, Mr*Claiborne*, Mr *Montague*, Mr *Blunt*, Mr *Langhorne*, Mr *James Henry*, Mr *John Jones*, Mr *Speed*, and Mr *Holt*. And they are to meet and adjourn from Day to Day, and to take into their Confideration all Matters relating to Courts of Juftice, and fuch other Matters, as fhall from Time to Time, be referred to them, and report their Proceedings, with their Opinions thereupon, to the Houfe. And the faid Committee are to Infpect the Journal of the laft Seffion, and draw up a State of the Matters then depending and undetermined, and the Progrefs that was made therein, and report the fame to the Houfe; and alfo examine what Laws have expired fince the laft Seffion, and infpect fuch temporary Laws as will expire with the End of this Seffion, or are near expiring, and report the fame to the Houfe with their Opinions, which of them are fit to be revived and continued. And the faid Committee are to have Power to fend for Perfons, Papers, and Records, for their Information.

Ordered, That Mr *Thomas Everard* be appointed Clerk to the faid Committee.

Ordered, That a Committee of Trade be appointed.

And a *Committee* was appointed of Mr *Harrifon*, Mr *Hutchings*, Mr *Newton*, Mr *Adams*, Mr *Whiting*, Mr *Burton*, Mr *Treafurer*, Mr *Innes*, Mr *Baker*, Mr *Winn*, Mr *Travis*, Mr *Pettus*, Mr *Trent*, Mr *Acrill*, Mr *Riddick*, Mr *Bland*, Mr *Smith*, Mr *Bell*, and Mr *Wright*. And they are to meet and adjourn from Day to Day, and to take into their Confideration all Things relating to the Trade of this Colony, and all Matters that fhall be from Time to Time referred to them, and to report their Proceedings, with their Opinions thereupon, to the Houfe. And the faid Committee are to have Power to fend for Perfons, Papers, and Records, for their Information.

Ordered, That Mr *Richard Cary* be appointed Clerk to the faid Committee.

Refolved, That eleven of the Committees for Religion, Privileges and Elections, and Propofitions and Grievances, and five of any other Committee, be a sufficient Number to proceed on Bufinefs.

A *Petition* of Mr *Henry Blagrave* was prefented to the Houfe, and read; fetting forth, that a greater Number of legal Freeholders voted for the Petitioner, at the laft Election of Burgeffes to ferve in the General Affembly, for the County of *Lunenburg*, than for Mr *Thomas Pettus*, who was returned duly elected, and therefore praying the Confideration of the Houfe in the Premifes.

Ordered, That the Confideration of the faid Petition be referred to the Committee of Privileges and Elections, and that they do examine the Matter thereof, and report the fame, with their Opinion thereupon, to the Houfe.

A *Petition* of *Wills Cowper*, was prefented to the Houfe, and read; fetting forth, that a Negro Man Slave of the Petitioner, named *Frank*, who had ran away, having done Mifchief, and committed Thefts in the Neighborhood, whilft he lay out, the Petitioner endeavoured to outlaw him, which he was prevented from doing, by feveral Accidents; and that, in the mean Time, the faid Slave being difcovered by one *James Bates*, and not only refufing to furrender, but attacking the faid *James Bates*, he the faid *James Bates*, in Defence of himfelf, difcharged a loaded Gun at the faid Slave, by which he was irrecoverably wounded in one of his Legs, and foon after died; and therefore praying that the faid Petitioner may be allowed the Value of the faid Slave.

Ordered

Ordered, That the Confideration of the faid Petition be referred to the Committee of Public Claims, and that they do examine the Matter thereof, and report the fame, with their Opinion thereupon, to the Houfe.

And then the Houfe adjourned till Tomorrow Morning eleven of the Clock.

Wednesday, the 12th of February, 12 George III. 1772.

SEVERAL other *Members* having taken the Oaths appointed to be taken by Act of Parliament, and repeated and fubfcribed the Teft, took their Places in the Houfe.

Ordered, That Mr *Edmund Pendleton*, and Mr *Mitchell*, be added to the Committee for Religion.

Ordered, That Mr *Mitchell* be added to the Committee of Trade.

Ordered, That Mr *James Henry*, and Mr *Edmund Pendleton*, be added to the Committee of propofitions and Grievances.

A *Petition* of feveral Perfons of the County of *Nanfemond*, whofe Names are thereunto fubfcribed, was prefented to the Houfe, and read; fetting forth, that a Bridge over the North Fork of the Weftern Branch of *Nanfemond* River, from the Land of *Thomas Milner*, to the Land of *Jacob Darden*, would be very beneficial to many People who carry their Commodities to Market at *Milner's* Warehoufe, in the faid County, as well as to the Merchants trading there; and that the Expence of building a Bridge is propofed to be wholly defrayed by Subfcribers, and therefore praying that an Act may pafs to impower fome perfons to receive Subfcriptions, and, with the Money thereby raifed, erect a Bridge at the Place aforefaid.

Ordered, That the faid Petition be referred to the Confideration of the Committee of propofitions and Grievances, and that they do examine the Matter thereof, and report the fame, with their Opinion thereupon, to the Houfe.

10 *Ordered*, That an Addrefs be made to the Governor, to order a new Writ to iffue for the electing of a Burgefs to ferve in this prefent General Affembly, for the County of *King William*, in the Room of Mr *Philip Whitehead Claiborne*, deceafed, and that Mr *Aylett* do wait upon his Excellency with the faid Addrefs.

Ordered, That an Addrefs be made to the Governor, to order a new Writ to iffue for the electing of a Burgefs to ferve in this prefent General Affembly, for the County of *Buckingham*, in the Room of Mr *Benjamin Howard*, deceafed, and that Mr *Bell* do wait upon his Excellency with the faid Addrefs.

Mr *Treafurer* reported, from the Committee of Privileges and Elections, that the Committee had examined the Returns of feveral Writs for electing Burgeffes to ferve in this prefent General Affembly, and had agreed upon a Report, which they had directed him to make to the Houfe, and he read the Report in his Place, and afterwards delivered it in at the Clerk's Table; where the fame was read, and is as followeth, *viz.*

Your *Committee* beg Leave to report to the Houfe, that no Return hath been made of the Writ for electing Burgeffes to ferve in this prefent General Affembly for the County of *Halifax;* and that the Return of the Writ for electing Burgeffes to ferve in this prefent General Affembly for the County of *Surry,* is made in the following Words, *viz.* "*This is to certify that by Virtue of this Writ, an Election was made for the County of* Surry, *and two Burgeffes chofen, to wit,* Hartwell Cocke, *and* Allen Cocke, *Gentlemen, to ferve the faid County; but* Thomas Bailey, *the then Sheriff, who was taken ill, and died before a proper Certificate of their being elected was made, and figned. Given under my hand this* 12th *Day of* February, 1772. William Bailey, D. S.''

The faid *Report* being read a fecond Time;

A *Member* acquainted the Houfe, that, between the Tefte and Return of the faid Writ for electing Burgeffes to ferve for the County of *Halifax*, there was no Sheriff qualified to execute the fame: *And thereupon,*

Ordered, That an Addrefs be made to the Governor, to order a new Writ to iffue for the

the electing of Burgeffes to ferve in this prefent General Affembly, for the County of *Halifax*, no Members having been returned to ferve for that County by Virtue of the former Writ; and that Mr *Carrington* do wait upon his Excellency with the faid Addrefs.

Ordered, That fo much of the faid Report as relates to the Return of the faid Writ for electing Burgeffes to ferve for the County of *Surry* be re-committed to the faid Committee of Privileges and Elections.

Mr *Bland* prefented to the Houfe, according to Order, a Bill for altering the Court Day of *Surry* County and the fame was received, and read the firft Time.

Refolved, That the Bill be read a fecond Time.

Mr *Treafurer* reported to the Houfe, that the Governor having been waited on, purfuant to the Order of Yefterday, to know his Pleafure when he would be attended by this Houfe, had been pleafed to appoint to be attended Tomorrow, at two of the Clock in the Afternoon, in the Council Chamber.

The *Order* of the Day being read for the Houfe to refolve itfelf into a Committee of the whole Houfe, to take into Confideration the Governor's Speech;

Ordered, That his Excellency's Speech to the Council and this Houfe be referred to the faid Committee.

Then the Houfe refolved itfelf into the faid Committee.

Mr *Speaker* left the Chair.

Mr *Bland* took the Chair of the Committee.

Mr *Speaker* refumed the Chair.   11

Mr *Bland* reported from the Committee, that they had made a Progrefs in the Matter to them referred; and that he was directed by the Committee to move that they may have Leave to fit again.

Refolved, That this Houfe will, upon *Tuefday* next, refolve itfelf into a Committee of the whole Houfe, to take into their further Confideration the Governor's Speech.

Mr *Cary* reported, from the Committee of Public Claims, that the Committee had examined the Matter of the petition of *Wills Cowper*, to them referred, and had come to a Refolution, which they had directed him to report to the Houfe; and he read the Report in his Place, and afterwards delivered it in at the Clerk's Table; where the Refolution of the Committee was read, and is as followeth, *viz.*

Refolved, That it is the Opinion of this Committee, that the faid Petition be rejected.

The faid *Petition* being read a fecond Time;

Ordered, That the faid Report be re-committed to the faid Committee of Public Claims.

A *Petition* of the Mayor, Aldermen, and Common Council, of the Borough of *Norfolk*, and of feveral other Perfons, whofe Names are thereunto fubfcribed, was prefented to the Houfe, and read; fetting forth, that large Quantities of Gunpowder being frequently ftored in Warehoufes, in the faid Borough, not to be retailed there, but to be tranfported to other Places, the Petitioners are juftly apprehenfive their Perfons and property, in Cafe of Fire, are expofed to great Danger, which they cannot effectually guard againft, the Chamber of the Borough being deficient, and the Common Hall having no Power by a Tax to defray the Expence of providing a fafe Repofitory for fo combuftible an Article; and therefore praying that an Act may pafs to empower the Common Hall of the faid Borough to affefs, on the Inhabitants thereof, fo much Money as will be fufficient for buying a Lot of Ground, and building a Magazine, and to compel Perfons bringing Gunpowder to the faid Borough, to ftore the fame in the faid Magazine.

Ordered, That the faid Petition be referred to the Confideration of the Committee of Propofitions and Grievances; and that they do examine the Matter thereof, and report the fame, with their Opinion thereupon, to the Houfe.

A *Petition* of feveral Perfons of the County of *Lunenburg*, whofe Names are thereunto fubfcribed, was prefented to the Houfe, and read; fetting forth, that the Petitioners, being of the Society of Chriftians, called *Baptifts*, find themfelves reftricted in the Exercife of their Religion, their Teachers imprifoned under various Pretences, and the Benefits of the Toleration Act denied them, although they are willing to conform to the

true

true Spirit of that Act, and are loyal and quiet Subjects; and therefore praying that they may be treated with the fame kind Indulgence, in religious Matters, as *Quakers, Prefbyterians*, and other Proteftant Diffenters, enjoy.

Ordered, That the faid Petition be referred to the Confideration of the Committee for Religion, and that they do examine the Matter thereof, and report the fame, with their Opinion thereupon, to the Houfe.

And then the Houfe adjourned till Tomorrow Morning eleven of the Clock.

Thursday, the 13th of February, 12 George III. 1772.

12 SEVERAL other *Members*, having taken the Oaths appointed to be taken by Act of Parliament, and repeated and fubfcribed the Teft, took their places in the Houfe.

A *Petition* of *Nathaniel Weft Dandridge*, was prefented to the Houfe, and read; fetting forth, that by an Act of General Affembly, made in the feventh Year of the Reign of his Prefent Majefty, intituled *An Act[1] to veft certain intailed Lands in* Nathaniel Weft Dandridge, *Efquire, in Fee Simple, and for fettling Slaves in Lieu thereof*, A Tract of Land, on *Turkey* Creek, in the County of *Hanover*, whereof the Petitioner was feized as Tenant in Tail, and the Boundaries of which were by the Act fuppofed to include fourteen Hundred and fixty-fix Acres and a Half, was vefted in him in Fee Simple, and certain Slaves, of greater or equal Value, were fettled in Lieu thereof; and further fetting forth, that the Survey of the faid Land, made before that paffing of the Act, was erroneous, it appearing by a late accurate Refurvey thereof, that within the faid Boundaries are contained no more than eleven Hundred and feventy-feven Acres, and therefore praying that out of the adjacent Lands, whereof the Petitioner is feized as Tenant in Fee Tail, the Deficiency, being two Hundred and eighty-nine Acres, may be vefted in him in Fee Simple.

Ordered, That Leave be given to bring in a Bill purfuant to the Prayer of the faid Petition, and that Mr *Patrick Henry* do prepare and bring in the fame.

Mr *Edmund Pendleton* reported, from the Committee of Privileges and Elections, to whom it was re-committed, the Matter, as it appeared to them, touching the Election, for the County of *Surry*, together with the Refolution of the Committee thereupon; and he read the Report in his Place, and afterwards delivered it in at the Clerk's Table, where the fame was read, and is as followeth, *viz.*

It *appears* to your Committee that the Writ for the faid Election came to the Hands of Mr *John Watkins*, then Sheriff of the faid County, who appointed the Election to be held at the Court-Houfe, on the 25th Day of *November*, and made due Publication of the faid Writ and Appointment; that before the Day of Election, Mr *Thomas Bailey* was appointed, and duly qualified, as Sheriff of the faid County, and on the faid 25th Day of *November*, at the Court-Houfe, proceeded to the making of the Election in a regular Manner; the Polls of which being laid before the Committee, the Numbers of Voters thereupon appear as followeth, *viz.*

For Mr *Hartwell Cocke*....................................176
    Mr *Allen Cocke*.................................... 134
    Mr *Charles Judkins*.............................. 95
    Mr *William Simmonds*........................... 59
    Mr *William Allen*.................................. 16

Upon which Mr *Bailey*, the Sheriff, proclaimed Mr *Hartwell Cocke*, and Mr *Allen Cocke*, duly elected to ferve as Burgeffes in this prefent General Affembly for the faid County; but before a Return was made of the faid Writ, and within a very few Days after the Election, the faid *Thomas Bailey* died, without making fuch Return; and Mr

William

---

[1] Hening, VIII, p. 224.

William Bailey, who was a Deputy of the faid *Thomas Bailey*, and prefent and affifting at the taking of the Poll, made the Certificate annexed to the Writ.

Upon the whole *Matter*, the Committee came to the following Refolution, *viz.*

Refolved, That it is the Opinion of this Committee, that the faid *Hartwell Cocke*, and *Allen Cocke*, ought to be admitted to their Seats in the Houfe, as Members for the faid County, notwithftanding the Return of the faid Writ is not, and from the peculiar Circumftances of the Cafe cannot be, made in the Form prefcribed by Law.

Mʳ *Riddick* prefented to the Houfe, according to Order, a Bill to prevent Hogs and Goats going at Large in the Town of *Suffolk;* and the fame was received, and read the firft Time.

Refolved, That the Bill be read a fecond Time.

Ordered, That Mʳ *Aylett*, and Mʳ *Claiborne*, be added to the Committee for Religion.

Ordered, That Mʳ *Bolling*, Mʳ *Baffett*, and Mʳ *Mofeley*, be added to the Committee of Privileges and Elections.

Ordered, That Mʳ *Aylett*, Mʳ *Holt*, Mʳ *Corbin*, Mʳ *Mann Page*, Mʳ *Brooke*, and Mʳ *Allen Cocke*, be added to the Committee of propofitions and Grievances.

Ordered, That Mʳ *Mofeley* be added to the Committee of Trade.

Ordered, That Mʳ *Corbin*, be added to the Committee of Public Claims.

Refolved, That all have Voices who come to the Committee of Privileges and Elections; and that this be declared a ftanding Order of the Houfe.

Mʳ *Edmund Pendleton* reported, from the Committee of Privileges and Elections, that the Committee had, according to Order, examined the Returns of feveral Writs for electing Burgeffes to ferve in this prefent General Affembly, and compared the fame with the Form prefcribed by Law, and had come to feveral Refolutions, which they had directed him to report to the Houfe; and he read the Report in his Place, and afterwards delivered it in at the Clerk's Table; where the fame was read, and is as followeth, *viz.*

Refolved, That it is the Opinion of this Committee, that the Returns of the feveral Writs for electing Burgeffes to ferve in this prefent General Affembly for the Counties of *Accomack, Albemarle, Caroline, Charles City, Cumberland, Elizabeth City, Fauquier, Gloucefter, Hanover, King & Queen, King William, Lancafter, Lunenburg, Nanfemond, New Kent, Norfolk, Northumberland, Pittfylvania,* and *York,* and for the City of *Williamfburg,* and Borough of *Norfolk,* are made in the Form prefcribed by Law.

Refolved, That it is the Opinion of this Committee, that the Returns of the feveral Writs for electing Burgeffes to ferve in this prefent General Affembly for the Counties of *Amelia, Augufta, Botetourt, Brunfwick, Buckingham, Charlotte, Chefterfield, Dinwiddie, Fairfax, Goochland, Henrico, James City, Ifle of Wight, Louifa, Mecklenburg, Middlefex, Northampton, Prince George, Richmond, Southampton, Spotfylvania, Stafford, Suffex, Warwick,* and *Weftmoreland,* for the College of *William* and *Mary,* and for *Jameftown,* are not made in the Form prefcribed by Law.

The faid *Refolutions* being feverally read a fecond Time, were, upon the Queftion feverally put thereupon, agreed to by the Houfe.

The Houfe being informed that the Sheriff of the County of *Ifle of Wight* attended;

Ordered, That the faid Sheriff do amend his Return of the Writ for electing Burgeffes to ferve in this prefent General Affembly for the County of *Ifle of Wight;* and he amended the faid Return accordingly.

Ordered, That the Returns of the feveral Writs for electing Burgeffes to ferve in this prefent General Affembly for the other Counties in the laft Refolution mentioned, be amended by the Clerk at the Table; and the faid Returns were amended by the Clerk accordingly.

A *Meffage* from the Governor by Mʳ *Blair;*

Mʳ *Speaker,*
The Governor is now ready to receive the Addrefs of your Houfe in the Council Chamber.

Accordingly Mʳ *Speaker,* with the Houfe, went up; and being returned, he reported, that

that the Houfe had attended the Governor with their Addrefs, to which his Excellency was pleafed to give this Anfwer:

Gentlemen,

I am obliged to you for this Addrefs, and for your Congratulations on the high Honour which his Majefty has conferred upon me. I have ever confidered the true Intereft of Government, and of the People, to be infeparable, and make this Principle the Rule of my Conduct; therefore I flatter myfelf that you will never have Caufe to refufe me the Support which you are now pleafed to promife me.

Mr *Edmund Pendleton* reported, from the Committee of Privileges and Elections, that the Committee had partly examined the Matter of the Petition of Mr *Henry Blagrave*, to them referred, complaining of an undue Election and Return of Mr *Thomas Pettus*, to ferve as a Burgefs in this prefent General Affembly for the County of *Lunenburg*, and had come to feveral Refolutions, which they had directed him to report to the Houfe; and he read the Report in his Place, and afterwards delivered it in at the Clerk's Table; where the Refolutions of the Committee were read, and are as followeth, *viz.*

14

Refolved, That it is the Opinion of this Committee, that the Perfons who voted at the faid Election, whofe Freeholds are queftioned either by the Petitioner, or fitting Member, be examined before *Lyddal Bacon, Thomas Wynne, Elifha Betts, Thomas Tabb, William Taylor, Anthony Street, Abraham Maury*, and *Jonathan Patterfon*, Gentlemen, or any five of them, whether they be Freeholders or not, except fuch of them as did fwear to their Freeholds at the faid Elections.

Refolved, That it is the Opinion of this Committee, that the Petitioner and fitting Member be at Liberty to examine Witneffes before the fame perfons, as to the Freeholds or other Qualifications of any Perfon, who voted at the faid Election, although fuch Perfon fwore to his Freehold at the Election, or fhall fwear to the fame at the Examination; and that it be an Inftruction to the Perfons, before whom fuch Examinations are taken, to examine how long fuch Voters have been in Poffeffion of, and paid Quit rents for, the Lands or Tenements, in Right of which they voted at the Election, and that they return the Depofitions they fhall take before the 17th Day of *March* next.

Refolved, That it is the Opinion of this Committee, that the petitioner give the fitting Member ten Days Notice of the Time and Place when and where he intends to examine his Witneffes; alfo a Lift in Writing of the Names of the Voters he intends to except to, diftinguifhing againft each Name the feveral Heads of Exception; and that the fitting Member do the like to the Petitioner.

Refolved, That it is the Opinion of this Committee, that the further Confideration of the faid petition be referred to the faid 17th Day of *March* next.

The faid *Refolutions* being feverally read a fecond Time, were, upon the Queftion feverally put thereupon, agreed to by the Houfe.

And then the Houfe adjourned till Tomorrow Morning eleven of the Clock.

Friday, the 14th of February, 12 George III. 1772.

MR *Bland* reported, from the Committee of Propofitions and Grievances, that the Committee had examined the Matter of feveral Petitions to them referred, and had come to feveral Refolutions; which they had directed him to report to the Houfe; and he read the Report in his Place, and afterwards delivered it in at the Clerk's Table; where the Refolutions of the Committee were read, and are as followeth, *viz.*

Refolved, That it is the Opinion of this Committee, that the Petition of divers Inhabitants of the County of *Southampton*, praying that an Act may pafs to impower them to take a Toll of all Waggons paffing the Bridges over *Nottoway* River, within the faid County, be rejected.

Refolved

Resolved, That it is the Opinion of this Committee, that the Petition of several Persons of the County of *Nansemond*, praying that an Act may pass to impower Persons to receive Subscriptions for building a Bridge over the *North* Fork of the *Western* Branch of *Nansemond* River, is reasonable.

Resolved, That it is the Opinion of this Committee, that the Petition of the Mayor, Aldermen, and Common Council, and other Persons, of the Borough of *Norfolk*, praying that an Act may pass to impower the Common Hall of the said Borough to assess on the Inhabitants thereof so much Money as will be sufficient for buying a Lot of Ground, and building a Magazine, and to compel Persons bringing Gunpowder to the said Borough, to store the same in the said Magazine, is reasonable.

The said *Resolutions*, being severally read a second Time, were, upon the Question severally put thereupon, agreed to by the House.

Ordered, That Bills be brought in upon the second and third Resolutions; and that the Committee of Propositions and Grievances do prepare, and bring in the same.

A *Petition* of several persons of the Parish of *Saint John*, in the County of *King William*, whose Names are thereunto subscribed, was presented to the House, and read; setting forth, that the Vestry of the said Parish are divided among themselves by Party-spirit, which prevents their meetings, and interrupts their proceeding in the Affairs of the Parish, and that they are pursuing Measures detrimental to the Parishioners; and therefore praying that the said Vestry may be dissolved.

Ordered, That the said Petition be referred to the Consideration of the Committee for Religion, and that they do examine the Matter thereof, and report the same, with their Opinion thereupon, to the House.

Mr *Cary* reported, from the Committee of Public Claims, to whom the Petition of *Wills Cowper* had been referred, and to whom the Report of the Matter of the said Petition was re-committed, that the Committee had further considered the Matter of the said petition, and had directed him to report the same, as it appeared to them, together with the Resolution of the Committee thereupon, to the House; and he read the Report in his Place, and afterwards delivered it in at the Clerk's Table; where the same was read, and is as followeth, *viz.*

It appears to your *Committee*, from a Certificate of Mr *Josiah Riddick*, from the County of *Nansemond*, that he was applied to by *Wills Cowper*, on the 10th Day of *February*, 1771, being *Sunday*, for an Outlawry against a Negro of the said *Cowper's*, who was then run away; but as there was to be no Sermon that Day, he did not grant one. The *Sunday* following Mr *Cowper* sent a Message to Mr *Riddick*, to know if his Negro was outlawed, and, if not, desired him to do it that Day. But there being a deep Snow on the Ground, Mr *Riddick* apprehending that there would be Nobody at Church, again neglected to make the Outlawry. That afternoon he was informed, that one *James Bates* had carried the Negro Home to his Master; but in taking him the Negro was so wounded, that he died in a short Time afterwards. Mr *Riddick* certifies, that the said Negro was, in his Opinion, worth seventy-five Pounds.

It further appears to your *Committee*, by the Deposition of *James Bates*, that he (*Bates*) was informed that Mr *Cowper's* Runaway Negro *Frank* had stolen an Ax that Night; and that if he would go after him, the Negro might be taken. That *Bates* prevailed on his Brother to go with him; but being separated in the Woods, the Deponent discovered a Camp, and in it the Slave in the petition mentioned, with a large Knife in one Hand, and a Club in the other. That he (*Bates*) ordered the Negro to surrender, or threatened that he would shoot him. The Negro told him to shoot, and be damned, and advanced upon him almost to the Muzzle of the Gun. *Bates*, thinking his Life in Danger, fired upon the Slave, and wounded him in the right Leg. On which the Negro knocked him down with the Club, and run off. As soon as *Bates* recovered, he called for his Companions, but they not joining him, he pursued the Negro himself, and in a small Distance came up with him, and discovered him whetting his Knife on his Hand. *Bates* then clubbed his Gun, knocked the Fellow down, and wounded him in the Head with the Cock of his Gun, notwithstanding which he would not submit, till a Negro belonging

belonging to *Mills Riddick* came up. *Bates* then carried the Negro to his Mafter, who immediately fent for a Doctor, and the Negro died, as the Deponent was informed, a few Days after, of a Mortification.

It *alfo* appears to your Committee, by the Depofition of Doctor *Colqohoun*, that on the 17th Day of *February*, 1771, he was fent for by Mr *Cowper* to a Negro of his who had been fhot. That he found the Negro wounded in the right Leg, and on the Head. That, notwithftanding all his Care, a Mortification came on in his Leg and Thigh, of which he died in a few Days.

It does not appear to your *Committee*, that the Negro had been Guilty of any Felony, or that his Mafter had made Application to any other Magiftrate but Mr *Riddick*, for an Outlawry.

Whereupon your *Committee* came to the following Refolution.

Refolved, That it is the Opinion of this Committee, that the faid Slave ought not to be paid for by the Public.

The faid *Refolution* being read a fecond Time, was, upon the Queftion put thereupon, agreed to by the Houfe.

A *Petition* of *Peter Pelham*, Keeper of the Public Gaol, was prefented to the Houfe, and read; fetting forth, that the Salary of forty Pounds *per Annum*, granted to the Petitioner by the laft General Affembly, will ceafe at the End of this Seffion of Affembly, unlefs it be continued; and that, from the Scarcity and Dearnefs of Provifions, it is difficult to afford a comfortable Subfiftence to the unhappy Prifoners under his Care, out of the ten Pounds of Tobacco *per* Day, allowed for the Maintenance of each of them; and therefore praying that his Salary may be further continued, and that he may have fuch other Relief as to the Houfe may feem reafonable.

Ordered, That the faid petition be referred to the Confideration of the Committee of propofitions and Grievances, and that they do examine the Matter thereof, and report the fame, with their Opinion thereupon, to the Houfe.

Ordered, That Mr *John Page* be added to the Committee for Religion.

Ordered, That Mr *Riddick* have Leave to be abfent from the Service of this Houfe till *Monday* Sevennight.

Mr *Patrick Henry* prefented to the Houfe, according to Order, a Bill to dock the Intail of certain Lands whereof *Nathaniel Weft Dandridge* is feized; and the fame was received, and read the firft Time.

Refolved, That the Bill be read a fecond Time.

Ordered, That Mr *Thornton* have Leave to be abfent from the Service of this Houfe till *Thurfday* next.

Ordered, That Mr *Langhorne* be added to the Committee of Public Claims.

And then the Houfe adjourned till Tomorrow Morning eleven of the Clock.

Saturday, the 15th of February, 12 George III. 1772.

MR *Woodfon* reported, from the Committee of Courts of Juftice, that the Committee had, according to Order, infpected the Journal of the laft Seffion of Affembly, and drawn up a State of the Matters then depending, and undetermined, and the Progrefs that was made therein, and had directed him to report the fame, as it appeared to them, to the Houfe; and he read the Report in his Place, and afterwards delivered it in at the Clerk's Table; where the fame was read, and is as followeth, *viz.*

It appears to your *Committee*, that at the firft Seffion of the faid Affembly, it was ordered, that the Committee of Propofitions and Grievances, to whom the Petition of feveral Perfons of the County of *Accomack*, praying that the faid County may be divided, and the Petition of feveral other Perfons of the faid County in Oppofition to the faid Divifion, were feverally referred, fhould be difcharged from proceeding upon the faid

petitions

petitions, and the Confideration of the faid Petitions was deferred till the then next Seffion of Affembly.

That the *Petition* of fundry Inhabitants of this Colony, praying that the *Brick-Houfe* Landing, on *Wafhington's* Land, in the County of *Weftmoreland*, may be declared a Public Landing, and a Road opened from thence to the *Weftmoreland* main Road; *Alfo*

The *Petition* of divers of the Inhabitants of the Counties of *Charlotte* and *Halifax*, praying that the Ferry over *Staunton* River, at *Fuqua's*, may be removed to a Ford two Miles above the faid *Fuqua's; Alfo,*

The *Petition* of divers Inhabitants of the County of *Bedford*, praying that an Act may pafs directing Slopes to be made in Mill-Dams, and impowering certain Perfons to prefcribe the Method of making fuch Slopes; *Alfo,*

The *Petition* of divers Inhabitants on *Goofe* Creek, in the County of *Bedford*, praying that *Jeremiah Early* may be compelled to open a Gate in his Mill-Dam, at the Mouth of the faid Creek, for the Admiffion of Fifh; *Alfo,*

The *Petitions* of divers Inhabitants of the Counties of *Stafford, King George*, and *Weftmoreland*, for reforming the Boundaries of the faid Counties refpectively; *And alfo,*

The *Petitions* of divers of the Inhabitants of the Counties of *Richmond* and *Weft-moreland*, in Oppofition thereto, were feverally prefented to the Houfe, and read, and referred to the Committee of Propofitions and Grievances, to examine into the Matter thereof, and to report their Opinion thereupon to the Houfe; that the faid Committee reported that they had had the fame under their Confideration, and were of the Opinion, in which the Houfe agreed, that the Confideration of the faid Petitions fhould be referred to the then next Seffion of Affembly:

That the *Petition* of *Benjamin Grymes*, in Behalf of himfelf and his Creditors, to be allowed a reafonable Satiffaction for the Damage done their Slave, who was committed to Gaol for Hogftealing, and was froftbitten during his Confinement; *Alfo,*

The *Petition* of *John Doncaftle*, fetting forth that he long fince had paid two hundred and fifty nine Pounds eighteen Shillings for the Hire of 2 Waggons 226 Days in the Ser-vice of this Colony, for which he never received Satiffaction, having been prevented from an earlier Application to the Houfe, and praying Relief, were feverally prefented to the Houfe, and read, and referred to the Committee of Public Claims, to examine into the Matter thereof, and to report their Opinion thereupon to the Houfe; that the faid Committee reported that they had had the fame under their Confideration, and were of Opinion, in which the Houfe agreed, that the Confideration of the faid Petitions fhould be referred to the then next Seffion of Affembly.

It alfo appears to this *Committee*, that at the fecond Seffion of the faid Affembly, it was ordered that the Confideration of all fuch Propofitions and Petitions as were deferred from the firft till the fecond Seffion of Affembly, and all fuch Public Claims, Propofitions, and Petitions, as had come, or fhould come, certified to the faid fecond Seffion, fhould be deferred till the next Seffion of the General Affembly:

That feveral *Petitions* of the Inhabitants of the County of *Spotfylvania*, whofe Names are thereunto fubfcribed, were prefented to the Houfe, and read; fetting forth, that the Petitioners have long laboured under many Grievances, from the inconvenient Situation of their County Court Houfe, and praying the Houfe to make Application to the Commanding Officer of the Colony, to iffue his Writ of Adjournment, and appoint the Court to be held at fome Place nearest to the Center of the County; *Alfo,*

Several *Petitions* of the Inhabitants in the Fork of *Rapidan* and *Robinfon* Rivers, in the County of *Culpeper*, whofe Names are thereunto fubfcribed, were prefented to the Houfe, and read; fetting forth, that the Petitioners live much further from the Court-Houfe in their own County, than they do from the Court-Houfe in the County of *Orange*, and praying that fo much of the County of *Culpeper* as is between the *Rapidan* and *Robinfon* Rivers may be added to the County of *Orange*; *Alfo,*

A *Petition* of the Veftrymen of the Parifh of *Hamilton*, in the County of *Fauquier*, whofe Names are thereunto fubfcribed, in Behalf of the Inhabitants of the faid Parifh, was prefented to the Houfe and read; fetting forth, that before the late Divifion of the

faid

faid Parifh, made by Act of General Affembly, a Majority of one hundred Tithables, by Agreement, was to be left therein, but that, by the Line eftablifhed, the faid Parifh hath, inftead of a Majority, fixty Tithables fewer than the other Parifh of *Leeds*, and praying that an Act may pafs for dividing the faid Parifhes, by a Line beginning at the Place mentioned in the faid Act of Affembly, and running from thence, in a direct Courfe, to the Mouth of *Carter's* Run, which will include fuch a Number of Tithables as the Petitioners think themfelves entitled to by the faid Agreement; *Alfo*,

17   A *Petition* of feveral Perfons of the Counties of *Augufta*, *Botetourt*, *Hanover*, and *Albemarle*, whofe Names are thereunto fubfcribed, was prefented to the Houfe, and read; fetting forth, that the *Warm Springs* in the Counties of *Augufta* and *Botetourt* had been found to be very falutary to the Difeafed and Infirm, who had drank of their Waters, but that it is very difficult for the Perfons who moft want that Relief to procure it, there being no good Roads to thofe Places; and that great Advantages would be derived to the Country by opening and clearing fuch Roads thither, and propofing that a Sum of Money, fufficient for the Purpofe, may be allowed by the Public, to open a fafe and good Road from the *Warm Springs* to *Jening's* Gap; that a Turnpike be eftablifhed at the Pafs of the *Warm Springs* Mountains, with a reafonable Toll for keeping the Road in Repair, and that Truftees be appointed to receive Subfcriptions, as well for keeping the Road in Repair, as for building Houfes for the Reception and Security of the poor Sick who refort to the Springs, and to fee the Public and private Money appropriated, for the Purpofes aforefaid, faithfully applied: *Alfo*,

A *Petition* of the Reverend *Alexander Gordon*, Clerk, Rector of the Parifh of *Antrim*, was prefented to the Houfe, and read; fetting forth, that the Law which was propofed laft Seffion of Affembly, for raifing the Price of his Tobacco, or paying it in Kind, but did not receive the Affent of the Governor, was founded in Juftice and Equity; that the Petitioner fuffers more Toil and Fatigue in attending his Cure than moft other Clergymen in the Colony, and that his Salary, as it is now paid, is not adequate to his Expence and Trouble, and praying that the Houfe will grant him fuch Redrefs as fhall appear juft and reafonable; *alfo*,

A *Petition* of *William Wilkinfon*, and *John Pinchback*, Infpectors of Tobacco at *Waddy's* Warehoufes, in the County of *New Kent*, was prefented to the Houfe, and read; fetting forth, that the faid Warehoufes were broken open the 8th Day of *July* laft, and 536 Pounds of Tobacco ftolen out of the fame, for which the petitioners had been obliged to pay, and praying that they may be repaid for the faid Tobacco; *alfo*,

A *Petition* of the Freeholders and Inhabitants of the County of *Lunenburg*, whofe Names are thereunto fubfcribed, was prefented to the Houfe, and read; fetting forth, that large Quantities of Tobacco are annually brought from *North-Carolina* to this Colony, and infpected, and fold here, moftly for Gold and Silver, which is carried out from hence, and paffed at higher Rates than it is here, and that the Owners of fuch Tobacco do not contribute any Thing towards building and fupporting Bridges, and clearing and repairing Roads, and praying that a Duty be laid upon Tobacco imported from *North-Carolina*, and that the value of Gold and Silver Coin be made equal to Sterling, or to what it paffeth for in the neighbouring Colonies; *alfo*,

A *Petition* of *John Young*, of the County of *Dinwiddie*, was prefented to the Houfe, and read; fetting forth that a Slave called *Mofes*, belonging to the Petitioner, having been fome Time abfent from his Mafter's Service, and having committed Thefts and Outrages in the Neighbourhood, and being outlawed in due Form, was apprehended and brought before a Magiftrate, and charged with Felony, and there being ftrong Proofs of his Guilt, was ordered by the Magiftrate to be carried to Prifon, but that the faid Slave, before he could be committed, died through fome Mifmanagement, as is fufpected, in the Perfons who apprehended, and were carrying him to the Court-Houfe, and praying that the Houfe will grant fuch Relief to the Petitioner as fhall feem juft; *alfo*,

A *Petition* of the Freeholders and Inhabitants of the County of *Lunenburg*, whofe Names are thereunto fubfcribed, was prefented to the Houfe, and read; fetting forth, that Part of the Act of General Affembly, intituled an Act for amending the Staple of

Tobacco

Tobacco, and for preventing Frauds in his Majesty's Customs, allowing the Purchasers of Tobacco to have the same reviewed, is unreasonable, and praying that that Part of the said Act may be repealed, or that the Owners of Tobacco, unjustly refused, may have a Review as well as the Purchaser; *also*,

A *Petition* of *Rowland Ward*, was presented to the House, and read; setting forth, that his Negro Man Slave, named *Cæsar*, having been duly outlawed, was killed in an Attempt to apprehend him, and that the said Slave was valued, by the Court of *Amelia* County, to the Sum of one hundred Pounds, and praying that the Value of the said Slave may be paid him by the Public; *also*,

A *Petition* of sundry Inhabitants of the County of *Mecklenburg*, whose Names are thereunto subscribed, was presented to the House, and read; setting forth, that the Importation of Tobacco from *North Carolina* to this Colony is very detrimental to the Trade of the latter, and praying that such Importation may be prohibited, or restrained; *and also*,

A *Petition* of *William Hackney*, and *Rowland Sutton*, Inspectors at *Kemp's* Warehouse, in the County of *Middlesex*, was presented to the House, and read; setting forth, that in the Night of the 9th Day of *July*, 1771, the Doors of the said Warehouse were broke open, and a Hogshead of Tobacco belonging to *Philip Ludwell Grymes*, Esq; weighing 995 Pounds Nett was taken out of the said Warehouse, and all the Tobacco, except a few Bundles, carried away, and that the said Loss did not happen by any Neglect of the Petitioners, who are nevertheless liable to make the said *Grymes* Satiffaction for the same, and praying that the House will afford them such Relief as they shall think just and reasonable. And by the House it was ordered, that the Consideration of the said several Petitions should be deferred till the next Session of General Assembly.

Ordered, That the Petition of several Persons of the County of *Accomack*, praying that the said County may be divided, and a Petition of several other Persons of the said County in Opposition to the said Division; *and also*, the Petition of sundry Inhabitants of this Colony, praying that the *Brick-House* Landing, on *Washington's* Land, in the County of *Westmoreland*, may be declared a Public Landing, and a Road opened from thence to the *Westmoreland* main Road; *and also*, the Petition of divers of the Inhabitants of the Counties of *Charlotte* and *Halifax*, praying that the Ferry over *Staunton* River, at *Fuqua's*, may be removed to a Ford two Miles above the said *Fuqua's*; *and also*, the Petition of divers Inhabitants of the County of *Bedford*, praying that an Act may pass, directing Slopes to be made in Mill-Dams, and impowering certain Persons to prescribe the Method of making such Slopes; *and also*, the Petitions of divers Inhabitants on *Goose* Creek, in the County of *Bedford*, praying that *Jeremiah Early* may be compelled to open a Gate in his Mill-Dam, at the Mouth of the said Creek, for the Admission of Fish; *and also*, the Petitions of divers Inhabitants of the Counties of *Stafford*, *King George*, and *Westmoreland*, for reforming the Boundaries of the said Counties respectively, and the Petitions of divers Inhabitants of the Counties of *Richmond* and *Westmoreland*, in Opposition thereto; *and also*, the several Petitions of the Inhabitants of the County of *Spotsylvania*, praying the House to make Application to the Commanding Officer of the Colony, to issue his Writ of Adjournment, and appoint the Court to be held at some Place nearest to the Center of the County; *and also*, the several Petitions of the Inhabitants in the Fork of *Rapidan* and *Robinson* Rivers, in the County of *Culpeper*, praying that so much of the said County as lies between those two Rivers may be added to the County of *Orange*; *and also*, the Petition of several Persons of the Counties of *Augusta*, *Botetourt*, *Hanover*, and *Albemarle*, proposing that a Sum of Money sufficient for the Purpose may be allowed by the Public to open a safe and good Road from the Warm Springs in the Counties of *Augusta* and *Botetourt* to *Jening's* Gap, that a Turnpike be established at the Pass of the *Warm* Springs Mountains, with a reasonable Toll for keeping the Road in Repair, and that Trustees be appointed, as well for keeping the Road in Repair, as for building Houses for the Reception and Security of the poor Sick, who resort to the Springs, and to fee the Public and Private Money appropriated for those Purposes faithfully applied; and also the Petition of the Free-

holders

holders and Inhabitants of the County of *Lunenburg*, praying that a Duty be laid upon Tobacco imported from *North Carolina*, and that the Value of Gold and Silver Coin be made equal to Sterling, or to what it paffeth for in the Neighbouring Colonies; *and alfo*, the Petition of the Freeholders and Inhabitants of the County of *Lunenburg* praying that fo much of the Act of General Affembly, intituled *An Act[1] for amending the Staple of Tobacco, and for preventing Frauds in his Majefty's Cuftoms*, as allows the Purchafer of Tobacco to have the fame reviewed, may be repealed, or that the Owners of Tobacco, unjuftly refufed, may have a Review, as well as the Purchafer; *and alfo*, the Petition of the Inhabitants of the County of *Mecklenburg*, praying that the Importation of Tobacco from *North Carolina* to this Colony may be prohibited or reftrained; in the faid Report mentioned, be feverally referred to the Confideration of the Committee of Propofitions and Grievances; and that they do examine the Matters thereof, and report the fame, with their Opinions thereupon, to the Houfe.

Ordered, That the Petition of *Benjamin Grymes*, in Behalf of himfelf and his Creditors, to be allowed a reafonable Satiffaction for the Damage done their Slave, who was committed to Gaol for Hogftealing, and was froftbitten during his Confinement; *and alfo*, the Petition of *John Doncaftle*, praying to be reimburfed two hundred and fifty-nine Pounds and eighteen Shillings, paid for the Hire of two Waggons, employed 226 Days in the Service of this Colony; *and alfo*, the Petition of *William Wilkinfon*, and *John Pinchback*, Infpectors of Tobacco at *Waddy's* Warehoufes, in the County of *New-Kent*, praying that they may be repaid for 536 Pounds of Tobacco ftolen out of the faid Warehoufe; *and alfo*, the Petition of *John Young*, of the County of *Dinwiddie*, praying that he may be paid for an outlawed Slave, who having been apprehended, and charged with Felony, died in his Way to Prifon, to which he was ordered to be committed, that he might be tried for the Crime he was accufed of; *and alfo*, the Petition of *Rowland Ward*, praying that the Value of his Slave *Cæfar*, who, having been duly outlawed, was killed in an Attempt to apprehend him, may be paid to him by the Public; *and alfo* the Petition of *William Hackney*, and *Rowland Sutton*, Infpectors at *Kemp's* Warehoufe, in the County of *Middlefex*, praying to be allowed for a Hogfhead of Tobacco taken out of the faid Warehoufe, and carried away, in the faid Report mentioned, be feverally referred to the Confideration of the Committee of Public Claims, and that they do examine the Matter thereof, and report the fame, with their Opinions thereupon, to the Houfe.

Ordered, That the Petition of the Veftrymen of the Parifh of *Hamilton*, in the County of *Fauquier*, praying that an Act may pafs for dividing the faid Parifh, and the Parifh of *Leeds*, fo as to include in the former fome of the Tithables now in the other; *and alfo*, the Petition of the Reverend *Alexander Gordon*, Clerk, Rector of the Parifh of *Antrim*, praying Redrefs, his Salary, as it is now paid, not being adequate to his Expence and Trouble, in the faid Report mentioned, be feverally referred to the Confideration of the Committee for Religion, and that they do examine the Matters thereof, and report the fame, with their Opinions thereupon, to the Houfe.

Several other *Members* having taken the Oaths appointed to be taken by Act of Parliament, and repeated and fubfcribed the Teft, took their Places in the Houfe.

A *Petition* of feveral Perfons, being of the Veftry of the Parifh of *St. John*, in the County of *King William*, whofe Names are thereunto fubfcribed, was prefented to the Houfe, and read; taking Notice of the Petition prefented to this Houfe, for diffolving the faid Veftry, and praying that the Petitioners may have Leave to vindicate their Conduct, and for that Purpofe, that the faid Veftry may be directed to attend, with their Clerk and Records, at fuch Time as the Houfe fhall enter into the Inquiry.

Ordered, That the faid Petition be referred to the Confideration of the Committee for Religion, and that they do examine the Matter thereof, and report the fame, with their Opinions thereupon, to the Houfe.

Ordered, That Mr *Eyre* be added to the Committee for Religion, and to the Committee of Trade.

Ordered

---

[1] Hening, VIII, p. 69.

Ordered, That Mr *Eyre*, Mr *Roane*, and Mr *Joseph Jones* be added to the Committee of Privileges and Elections, and to the Committee of Propositions and Grievances.

Ordered, That Mr *Walker*, and Mr *Legrand* be added to the Committee for Courts of Justice.

And then the House adjourned till Monday Morning next eleven of the Clock.

Monday, the 17th of February, 12 George III. 1772.

SEVERAL other *Members*, having taken the Oaths appointed to be taken by Act of Parliament, and repeated and subscribed the Test, took their Places in the House.

A *Petition* of *Bernard Markham*, Agent for the Estate of *Brett Randolph*, deceased, was presented to the House, and read; setting forth, that *Charles*, a Negro Slave, belonging to the said Estate, having run away, the Petitioner procured a Proclamation of Outlawry to be issued against him, and afterwards the said Slave was so wounded, in an Attempt to apprehend him, that he died, and that he had been valued by the Court of *Cumberland* County; and praying that the said Valuation may be paid by the Public to the said Estate.

Ordered, That the said Petition be referred to the Consideration of the Committee of Public Claims, and that they do examine the Matter thereof, and report the same, with their Opinion thereupon, to the House.

A *Petition* of *James Winfrey* was presented to the House and read; setting forth, that the Petitioner being summoned by the Sheriff of *Chesterfield* County, to guard *Mark Edwards*, a Criminal, sent from that County to the Public Gaol, the Petitioner's Horse died on the Road through the Fatigue of that Journey; and therefore praying, that he may be allowed the Value of the said Horse by the Public.

Ordered, That the said Petition be referred to the Consideration of the Committee of Public Claims; and that they do examine the Matter thereof, and report the same, with their Opinion thereupon, to the House.

Ordered, That Leave be given to bring in a Bill, to impower the Clerks of the County Courts to issue certain Writs of Execution into other Counties; and that Mr *Edmund Pendleton* and Mr *Bland* do prepare, and bring in the same.

Ordered, That Mr *Carr*, Mr *Wright*, Mr *Fleming*, and Mr *Walker* be added to the Committee for Religion.

Ordered, That Mr *William Cabell*, Mr *Carr*, Mr *Fleming*, and Mr *Walker*, be added to the Committee of Privileges and Elections.

Ordered, That Mr *William Cabell*, Mr *Joseph Cabell* and Mr *Robert Wormeley Carter*, be added to the Committee of Propositions and Grievances.

Ordered, That Mr *Andrew Lewis* be added to the Committee of Public Claims.

A *Bill* to dock the Intail of certain Land whereof *Nathaniel West Dandridge* is seized, was read a second Time.

Resolved, That the Bill be committed to Mr *Patrick Henry*, Mr *Smith*, Mr *Edmund Pendleton*, Mr *Bassett*, Mr *Dandridge*, Mr *Carr*, and Mr *Aylett*.

Mr *Cary* reported from the Committee of Public Claims, that the Committee had examined the Matters of several Petitions to them referred, and had come to several Resolutions thereupon; which they had directed him to report to the House; and he read the Report in his Place, and afterwards delivered it in at the Clerk's Table; where the same was read, and is as followeth, *viz.*

Resolved, That it is the Opinion of this Committee, that the Petition of *William Wilkinson*, and *John Pinchback*, Inspectors of Tobacco at *Waddy's* Warehouse, to be reimbursed for 536 Pounds of Tobacco, stolen out of the said Warehouse, for which they have satisfied the Proprietor thereof, is reasonable; and that they ought to be allowed the Sum of four Pounds sixteen Shillings and Sixpence for the same.

On *Consideration* of the Petition of *Rowland Ward* it appears to your Committee, that

that

that the Slave *Cæfar*, in the Petition mentioned, was duly outlawed, and killed in an Attempt to take him; that the Court of the County of *Amelia* valued him to one hundred Pounds; and that he had been thrice tried by the faid Court for Felony, and had once received the Benefit of Clergy.

Refolved, That it is the Opinion of this Committee, that the faid Petition is reafonable; and that the Petitioner ought to be allowed the Sum of one hundred Pounds for the faid Slave.

The faid *Refolutions*, being feverally read a fecond Time, were, upon the Queftion feverally put thereupon, agreed to by the Houfe.

Mr *Treafurer* reported from the Committee for Religion, that the Committee had partly examined the petition of feveral Perfons, of the Parifh of *Saint John*, in the County of *King William*, praying that the Veftry of the faid Parifh may be diffolved; *and alfo*, the Petition of feveral Members of the faid Veftry in Oppofition thereto, and had come to feveral Refolutions, which they had directed him to report to the Houfe; and he read the Report in his Place, and afterwards delivered in at the Clerk's Table; where the Refolutions of the Committee were read, and are as followeth, *viz.*

21

Refolved, That it is the Opinion of this Committee, that the faid Petitions to be heard before the Committee on *Monday* the fecond Day of *March* next.

Refolved, That it is the Opinion of this Committee, that the Veftry of the faid Parifh be ferved with a Copy of the firft mentioned Petition, and have feven Days previous Notice of the Time when the faid Petition is to be heard before the Committee.

Refolved, That it is the Opinion of this Committee, that the Clerk of the faid Veftry do attend the Committee at the Time aforefaid, with the Veftry Books relative to the Subject Matter of the faid Petitions; and that he be ferved with a Copy of this Refolution feven Days previous to the Time appointed for hearing the fame.

The faid *Refolutions* being feverally read a fecond Time, were, upon the Queftion feverally put thereupon, agreed to by the Houfe.

And then the Houfe adjourned till Tomorrow Morning eleven of the Clock.

Tuesday, the 18th of February, 12 George III. 1772.

SEVERAL other *Members* having taken the Oaths appointed to be taken by Act of Parliament, and repeated and fubfcribed the Teft, took their Places in the Houfe.

The *Order* of the Day being read, for the Houfe to refolve itfelf into a Committee of the whole Houfe, to take into their further Confideration the Governor's Speech;

Refolved, That this Houfe will, To-morrow, refolve itfelf into the faid Committee.

Mr *Bland* reported from the Committee of propofitions and Grievances, that the Committee had examined the Matters of feveral Petitions to them referred, and had come to feveral Refolutions thereupon, which they had directed him to report to the Houfe; and he read the Report in his Place, and afterwards delivered it in at the Clerk's Table; where the Refolutions of the Committee were read, and are as followeth, *viz.*

Refolved, That it is the Opinion of this Committee, that fo much of the Petition of *Peter Pelham* as prays a Continuance of his Salary, is reafonable.

Refolved, That it is the Opinion of this Committee, that the Refidue of the faid Petition, praying a further Allowance for the Maintenance of Prifoners, be rejected.

Refolved, That it is the Opinion of this Committee, that the petition of the Inhabitants of *Richmond* County and others, praying that public Warehoufes, for the Infpection of Tobacco, may be by Law re-eftablifhed on *Totufkey* Creek, in the faid County, is reafonable.

The *firft* Refolution of the Committee, being read a fecond Time, was, upon the Queftion put thereupon, agreed to by the Houfe.

Refolved, That the Sum of forty Pounds, *per Annum*, be paid to *Peter Pelham*, Keeper

of

of the Public Gaol, as his Salary, to continue to the End of the next Seffion of General Affembly.

Ordered, That Mr *Nelfon* do carry the faid Refolution to the Council, and defire their Concurrence.

The *fecond* Refolution of the Committee, being read a fecond Time, was, upon the Queftion put thereupon, agreed to by the Houfe.

The *fubfequent* Refolution of the Committee, being read a fecond Time, was, upon the Queftion put thereupon, agreed to by the Houfe.

Ordered, That the faid Refolution do lie upon the Table.

The Houfe was moved, that Part of an Act, made in the twenty-fecond Year of the Reign of his late Majefty King *George* the Second, intituled *An Act¹ for fettling the Titles and Bounds of Lands, and for preventing unlawful hunting and ranging*, might be read.

And the fame being read accordingly;

Ordered, That Leave be given to bring in a Bill to repeal a Claufe of the Act of Affembly, made in the twenty-fecond Year of his late Majefty *George* the Second, intituled *An Act for fettling the Titles and Bounds of Lands, and for preventing unlawful hunting and ranging;* and that Mr *Bland*, Mr *Eyre*, Mr *Richard Henry Lee*, and Mr *Patrick Henry* do prepare and bring in the fame.

Mr *Cary* reported from the Committee of Public Claims, that the Committee had examined the Matters of feveral Petitions to them referred, and had come to feveral Refolutions thereupon, which they had directed him to report to the Houfe; and he read the Report in his Place, and afterwards delivered it in at the Clerk's Table; where the Refolutions of the Committee were read, and are as followeth, *viz.*

Refolved, That it is the Opinion of this Committee, that the Petition of *James Winfrey*, to be allowed for a Horfe, which was impreffed to convey a Guard over a Criminal to the Public Gaol, and died on the Way, is reafonable, and that he ought to be allowed the Sum of twenty-four Pounds for the said Horfe.

Refolved, That it is the Opinion of this Committee, that the Petition of *Bernard Markham*, Agent for the Eftate of *Brett Randolph*, deceafed, for an Allowance for *Charles*, a Negro Slave, belonging to the faid Eftate, who was outlawed, and died of Wounds he received when he was apprehended, is reafonable, and that the faid Eftate ought to be allowed the Sum of eighty Pounds for the faid Slave.

The faid *Refolutions* being feverally read a fecond Time, were, upon the Queftion feverally put thereupon, agreed to by the Houfe.

A *Petition* of *Nathaniel Raines* and *Lewis Brown*, Infpectors of Tobacco at *Boyd's* Warehoufes, was prefented to the Houfe, and read; fetting forth, that, during the laft Year's Infpection, two thoufand four hundred and thirty-four Hogfheads of Tobacco were received at the faid Warehoufes, whereby the Sum of three hundred and feventy-feven Pounds was paid into the Treafury, and that the Petitioners are allowed only fixty Pounds, each, for their Salary, which they conceive is not a Recompence for their Trouble; and further fetting forth, that two thoufand eight hundred and thirty-feven Pounds of Tobacco had been ftolen out of the faid Warehoufes, for which the petitioners had been obliged to pay the owners, at the Rate of twenty Shillings per Hundred Weight; and therefore praying, that they may be allowed ten Pounds each, for their great Trouble the laft Year, with the like yearly Increafe of Salary for the future; and that they may be reimburfed by the Public for the ftolen Tobacco aforefaid.

Ordered, That the faid petition be referred to the Confideration of the Committee of Public Claims; and that they do examine the Matter thereof, and report the fame, with their Opinion thereupon, to the Houfe.

Mr *Edmund Pendleton* prefented to the Houfe, according to Order, a Bill to empower the Clerks of County Courts to iffue certain Writs of Execution into other Counties; and the fame was received, and read the firft Time.

Refolved, That the Bill be read a fecond Time.

Mr *Treafurer* acquainted the Houfe, that he had a Meffage from the Governor to this

---

¹ Hening, V, p. 408.

this Houfe, figned by his Excellency; and he prefented the fame to the Houfe; and it was read by Mr *Speaker*, and is as followeth, *viz.*

Gentlemen,

I have thought proper to lay before you a *Lift of the Fees*, which I found had been *ufually paid to the Clerks of my Predeceffors in this Government, but which has been objected to in one Inftance fince I have taken the Adminiftration upon me. In order, therefore, to give the People over whom I have the Honour to prefide the cleareft Proof of the Upright-nefs of my own Intentions, and to let them fee my Readinefs to remove, as foon as I can difcover it, every Poffibility of a Difpute between me and thofe whofe Affection I would gladly con-ciliate, I defire you will take the faid Lift of Fees under your Confideration; and, as I fuppofe if they appear to be juft and reafonable to you, upon Comparifon of them with what is the Practice in fimilar Cafes, in all other Governments, that you will have no Objections to the eftablifhing of them by Law; fo, on my Part, if you judge otherwife of them, I fhall not Hefitate at confenting to abolifh them all, or in Part, exactly as you fhall think proper to propofe.*

Dunmore.

The Lift mentioned in the faid Meffage is as followeth, *viz.*

FEES ufually paid to the GOVERNOR'S CLERK.

	l.	s.	d.		l.	s.	d.
For County Lieutenant's Com-miffion	2	0	0	Coroner's	0	10	0
Colonel's	1	1	6	Mediterranean Pafs	1	15	0
Lieutenant Colonel's	1	1	6	Quarter Mafter's	1	0	0
Major's	1	1	6	Prefentation to a Parifh	1	10	0
Sheriff's	1	5	0	Efcheat Mafter	1	1	6
Principal Infpector's	0	15	0	Comiffary of Stores	1	1	6
Affiftant Infpector	0	10	0				

28 *Refolved*, That this Houfe will, upon *Thurfday* next, refolve itfelf into a Committee of the whole Houfe, to take into Confideration the Governor's Meffage, and the Lift of Fees therein mentioned.

A *Petition* of feveral Freeholders of the County of *Henrico*, whofe Names are there-unto fubfcribed, was prefented to the Houfe, and read; fetting forth, that when the Writ for electing Burgeffes to ferve in this prefent General Affembly for the faid County, came to the Hands of the then Sheriff, Mr *George Cox*, he appointed a Day for the Election, of which Notice was given in feveral Churches; but Mr *Cox's* Office expiring before the Day, the fucceeding Sheriff, Mr *Nathaniel Wilkinfon*, undertook to appoint another Day, of which Notice was alfo given in the Churches; and in Confequence of fuch different Ap-pointments, but few of the Freeholders attended; and further fetting forth, that the Time between the laft Appointment and the Election did not exceed eighteen Days, which the Petitioners conceive not to be the Notice by Law prefcribed; and that Mr *Wilkinfon*, when he did give Notice, was not qualified to execute his Office; and therefore praying, that the faid Election, which the Petitioners apprehend not to have been a proper one, may be declared void, and that a new Writ may iffue for electing Burgeffes to ferve in this prefent General Affembly for the faid County.

Ordered, That the faid Petition be referred to the Confideration of the Committee of Privileges and Elections; and that they do examine the Matter thereof, and report the fame, with their Opinion thereupon, to the Houfe.

Ordered, That Mr *Richard Henry Lee*, Mr *Francis Lightfoot Lee*, Mr *Rutherford*, Mr *Wood*, and Mr *White* be added to the Committee for Religion.

Ordered, That Mr *Richard Henry Lee*, and Mr *Francis Lightfoot Lee* be added to the Committee of Privileges and Elections.

Ordered

Ordered, That Mr *Wood*, Mr *Rutherford*, Mr *Richard Henry Lee*, and Mr *Francis Lightfoot Lee* be added to the Committee of propofitions and Grievances.

Ordered, That Mr *Richard Henry Lee*, and Mr *White* be added to the Committee for Courts of Juftice.

A *Petition* of *William Hoye* was prefented to the Houfe, and read; fetting forth, that *Limbo*, a Negro Man Slave of one *John Glover*, having run away, a Proclamation of Outlawry iffued againft him, after which the Petitioner purchafed him from the faid *Glover*; and that the faid Slave is dead of a Wound he received in the apprehending of him, and was valued to the Sum of eighty-five Pounds; and praying that the Value of the faid Slave may be paid to the Petitioner by the Public.

Ordered, That the faid Petition be referred to the Confideration of the Committee of Public Claims; and that they do examine the Matter thereof, and report the fame, with their Opinion thereupon, to the Houfe.

Mr *Edmund Pendleton* reported from the Committee of Privileges and Elections, to whom the Petition of feveral Freeholders of the County of *Henrico*, complaining of an undue Election and Return of Members to ferve in this prefent General Affembly for the faid County, was referred, that the Committee had partly examined the Matter of the faid Petition, and had come to a Refolution, which they had directed him to report to the Houfe; and he read the Report in his Place, and afterwards delivered it in at the Clerk's Table; where the Refolution of the Committee was read, and is as followeth, *viz.*

Refolved, That it is the Opinion of this Committee, that the Subject-Matter of the faid Petition be heard before the Committee on *Thurfday*, the 27th Day of this Inftant.

The faid *Refolution*, being read a fecond Time, was, upon the Queftion put thereupon, agreed to by the Houfe.

And then the Houfe adjourned till Tomorrow Morning eleven of the Clock.

Wednesday, the 19th of February, 12 George III. 1772.

*O*RDERED, That Mr *Treafurer* do lay his Accounts before the Houfe.

A *Petition* of *Samuel Sherwin* was prefented to the Houfe, and read; fetting forth, that the Petitioner's Negro Man Slave, named *Peter*, having been duly outlawed, was killed in an Attempt to take him, of which fufficient Proof was made before the Court of the County of *Dinwiddie*, and that the faid Slave was valued, by the faid Court, to the Sum of ninety Pounds; and praying that the Value of the faid Slave may be paid him by the Public.

Ordered, That the faid Petition be referred to the Confideration of the Committee of Public Claims, and that they do examine the Matter thereof, and report the fame, with their Opinion thereupon, to the Houfe.

Mr *Treafurer*, according to Order, laid his Accounts before the Houfe.

Ordered, That the faid Accounts do lie upon the Table, to be perufed by the Members of the Houfe.

A *Bill* for altering the Court Day of *Surry* County was read a fecond Time.

Refolved, That the Bill be committed to the Committee for Courts of Juftice.

Mr *Patrick Henry* reported from the Committee, to whom the Bill to dock the Intail of certain Land whereof *Nathaniel Weft Dandridge* is feized, was committed, that the Committee had examined the Allegations of the Bill, and found the fame to be true, and that the Committee had directed him to report the Bill to the Houfe, without any Amendment; and he delivered the Bill in at the Clerk's Table.

Ordered, That the Bill be engroffed.

Ordered, That it be an Inftruction to the Committee for Courts of Juftice, to whom the Bill for altering the Court Day of *Surry* County, is committed, that they have Power to receive a Claufe, or Claufes, for altering the Court Day of the County of *Princefs Anne*.

A *Bill* to impower the Clerks of County Courts to iffue certain Writs of Execution into other Counties was read a fecond Time.

Refolved

Resolved, That the Bill be committed to Mr *Edmund Pendleton*, and Mr *Bland*.

Mr *Richard Henry Lee* reported, from the Committee for Courts of Justice, that the Committee had further inspected the Journals of the last Assembly, and drawn up a State of another Matter then depending and undetermined, and the Progress that was made therein, and had directed him to report the same, as it appeared to them, to the House; and he read the Report in his Place, and afterwards delivered it in at the Clerk's Table; where the same was read, and is as followeth, *viz.*

It appears to your *Committee*, that a Petition of several Persons of the County of *Augusta*, inhabiting that Part of the South Western Frontier, known by the Name of *Holston* and *New* River, whose Names are thereunto subscribed, was presented to the House, and read; setting forth, that they are very remote from the Court-House of the said County, whereby they suffer many Inconveniences, and praying that the Settlements on the Waters of *Holston* and *New* River may be made a distinct County; and, by Order of the House, the Consideration of the said Petition was deferred till the then next Session of Assembly.

Ordered, That the said Petition be referred to the Consideration of the Committee of Propositions and Grievances; and that they do examine the Matter thereof, and report the same, with their Opinion thereupon, to the House.

A *Petition* of Mr *Samuel DuVal*, of the County of *Henrico*, on behalf of himself, and the Freeholders of the said County, was presented to the House, and read; setting forth, that at the last Election of Burgesses to serve in this Present General Assembly, for the said County, a greater Number of Freeholders voted for the Petitioner, who was one of the Candidates, than for Mr *Richard Randolph*, who was, with Mr *Richard Adams*, returned duly elected; and therefore praying that the Poll taken at the said Election may be examined, and that the Petitioner may be declared duly elected a Burgess for the said County.

Ordered, That the said petition be referred to the Consideration of the Committee of Privileges and Elections; and that they do examine the Matter thereof, and report the same, with their Opinion thereupon, to the House.

A *Petition* of *William Bicknal* was presented to the House, and read; setting forth, that a Horse of the Petitioner was impressed by a Deputy-Sheriff of the County of *Amherst*, in Order to convey to the Public Gaol one *Thomas Welch*, who was charged with Horse stealing, and ordered by the Court of the said County to be tried for the said Offence before the General Court and that the said Sheriff, as he returned, being unable to lead the Horse further than *Richmond* Town, left him there, in the Care of one *Archibald Mackendrix*, from whom the Horse either strayed or was stolen; and therefore praying, that the Petitioner may be allowed the Value of his Horse so lost in the Service of the Public.

Ordered, That the said Petition be referred to the Consideration of the Committee of Public Claims; and that they do examine the Matter thereof, and report the same, with their Opinion thereupon, to the House.

A *Petition* of *John Loving*, Jun. and *Robert Montgomery*, was presented to the House, and read; setting forth, that one *Andrew Lightle* being accused of Felony, and the Court of *Amherst* County, upon his Examination, being of Opinion he ought to be tried for the said Offence before the General Court, the petitioners were bound in a Recognizance to appear and testify on Behalf of the King, against the Prisoner upon his Trial, and did attend according to their Recognizance; but that, for Reasons unknown to them, they were not called upon to be examined, and that their Attendance was not entered; and humbly submitting their Case to the Consideration of this Honourable House, and praying Relief.

Ordered, That the said Petition be referred to the Consideration of the Committee of Public Claims; and that they do examine the Matter thereof, and report the same, with their Opinion thereupon, to the House.

The *Order* of the Day being read, for the House to resolve itself into a Committee of the whole House, to take into their further Consideration the Governor's Speech:

Ordered

Ordered, That the Letter received by Mr *Speaker* from the Speaker of the Lower Houfe of Affembly of the Province of *Maryland*, and the Refolutions of the faid Lower Houfe of Affembly, relative to the erecting and fupporting a Light-Houfe upon *Cape Henry*, which were ordered to lie upon the Table, be referred to the faid Committee.

Then the Houfe refolved itfelf into the faid Committee.

Mr *Speaker* left the Chair.

Mr *Bland* took the Chair of the Committee.

Mr *Speaker* refumed the Chair.

Mr *Bland* reported from the Committee that they had made a further Progrefs in ²⁶ the Matter to them referred; and that he was directed by the Committee to move, that they may have Leave to fit again.

Refolved, That this Houfe will, upon *Tuefday* next, refolve itfelf into a Committee of the whole Houfe, to take into their further Confideration the Governor's Speech.

A *Petition* of *William Booth* and *Elizabeth* his Wife was prefented to the Houfe, and read; fetting forth, that the Petitioners, in Right of the Wife, by Virtue of the Will of her Grandfather, *Henry Afhton*, Gentlemen, deceafed, are feized in Fee Tail, of five hundred Acres of Land, on *Nomony* River, in the County of *Weftmoreland;* and that, if the Intail of the faid Land be docked, the petitioners will be able to make a better Provifion, than they can otherwife do, not only for their younger Children, but for the Heir in Tail; and therefore praying that an Act may pafs for docking the Intail of the faid Land, and empowering Truftees to fell the fame, and lay out the Money raifed by the Sale thereof in the Purchafe of other Lands, of greater Value.

Ordered, That Leave be given to bring in a Bill purfuant to the Prayer of the faid Petition; and that Mr *Richard Henry Lee* do prepare, and bring in the fame.

And then the Houfe adjourned till Tomorrow Morning eleven of the Clock.

Thursday the 20th of February. 12 George III. 1772.

SEVERAL other *Members*, having taken the Oaths appointed to be taken by Act of Parliament, and repeated and fubfcribed the Teft, took their Places in the Houfe.

Ordered, That Leave be given to bring in a Bill to amend an Act, intituled *An Act¹ to prevent malicious maiming and wounding*; and that Mr *Gray*, and Mr *David Mafon* do prepare and bring in the fame.

Mr *Edmund Pendleton* reported from the Committee, to whom the Bill to impower the Clerks of County Courts to iffue certain Writs of Execution into other Counties, was committed, that the Committee had gone through the Bill, and made an Amendment thereunto, which they had directed him to report to the Houfe; and he read the Report in his Place, and afterwards delivered the Bill, with the Amendment, in at the Clerk's Table; where the Amendment was twice read; and upon the Queftion put thereupon, was agreed to by the Houfe.

Ordered, That the Bill, with the Amendment, be engroffed.

Mr *Richard Henry Lee* reported from the Committee of Courts of Juftice, who were appointed to enquire what Laws are expired fince the laft Seffion, or will expire with the End of this Seffion, or are near expiring, and to report their Opinion to the Houfe which of them are fit to be revived or continued, that the Committee had enquired accordingly, and had come to feveral Refolutions, which they had directed him to report to the Houfe; and he read the Report in his Place, and afterwards delivered it in at the Clerk's Table; where the Refolutions of the Committee were read, and are as followeth, *viz.*

Refolved, That it is the Opinion of this Committee, that the Act of Affembly, made in the 10th Year of his prefent Majefty's Reign, intituled *An Act² for giving a Salary to the Speaker of the Houfe of Burgeffes*, which expired at the Meeting of this prefent Affembly, ought to be revived.

Refolved

---

¹ Hening, VI, p. 250.   ² Ibid, VIII, p. 394.

Resolved, That it is the Opinion of this Committee, that the Act of Assembly, made in the 7th Year of his present Majesty's Reign, intituled *An Act[1] for appointing a Treasurer,* which was continued by another Act, made in the 10th Year of his said Majesty's Reign, and which will expire at the End of this present Session of Assembly, ought to be further continued.

Resolved, That it is the Opinion of this Committee, that the Act of Assembly, made in the 19th Year of the Reign of his late Majesty King *George* the Second, intituled *An Act[2] for the better regulating and collecting certain Officers Fees, and for other Purposes therein mentioned,* which hath been continued by several Acts, and amended by four Acts, in the 1st, 3rd, 7th, and 8th, Years of his present Majesty's Reign, and which will expire on the 12th Day of *April* next, ought to be further continued.

Resolved, That it is the Opinion of this Committee, that the Act of Assembly, made in the 10th Year of his present Majesty's Reign, intituled *An Act[3] for destroying Crows and Squirrels in certain Counties, therein mentioned,* which will expire on the 21st Day of *December next,* ought to be continued and amended.

Resolved, That it is the Opinion of this Committee, that the Act of Assembly, made in the 3rd Year of his present Majesty's Reign, intituled *An Act[4] for the more effectual keeping the public Roads and Bridges in Repair,* which was amended and continued by another Act, made in the 7th Year of his said Majesty's Reign, and which expired on the 16th Day of *December* last, ought to be revived.

Resolved, That it is the Opinion of this Committee, that the Act of Assembly, made in the 30th Year of the Reign of his late Majesty King *George* the Second, intituled *An Act[5] for the better regulating and disciplining the Militia,* which was continued by several Acts, and amended by an Act, made in the 7th Year of his present Majesty's Reign, and which will expire on the 20th Day of *July* next, ought to be further continued.

Resolved, That it is the Opinion of this Committee, that the Act of Assembly, made in the 30th Year of the Reign of his late Majesty King *George* the Second, intituled *An Act[6] for reducing the several Acts of Assembly for making Provision against Invasions and Insurrections, into one Act,* which hath been continued by three other Acts, made in the 3rd, 7th, and 10th, Years of his present Majesty's Reign, and which will expire the 8th Day of *June,* 1773, ought to be further continued.

Resolved, That it is the Opinion of this Committee, that the Act of Assembly, made in the 32d Year of the Reign of his late Majesty King *George* the Second, intituled *An Act[7] for reducing the several Acts for laying a Duty upon Liquors into one Act,* which was continued by several Acts, and amended by one Act, made in the 10th Year of his present Majesty's Reign, and which will expire on the 1st Day of *June,* 1773, ought to be further continued.

Resolved, That it is the Opinion of this Committee, that the Act of Assembly, made in the 25th Year of the Reign of his late Majesty King *George* the Second, intituled *An Act[8] for reviving the Duty upon Slaves, to be paid by the Buyers, for the Term therein mentioned;* and one other Act of Assembly, made in the 33rd Year of his said late Majesty's Reign intituled *An Act[9] to oblige Persons bringing Slaves into this Colony from* Maryland, Carolina, *and the* West-Indies, *for their own Use, to pay a Duty,* which have been continued by several other Acts, and which will expire on the 20th Day of *April* 1773, ought to be further continued, and amended.

Resolved, That it is the Opinion of this Committee, that the Act of Assembly, made in the 3rd Year of his present Majesty's Reign, intituled *An Act[10] for establishing Pilots, and regulating their Fees,* which was continued by two other Acts, made in the 7th and 10th Years of his said Majesty's Reign, and which will expire on the 20th Day of *April,* 1773, ought to be further continued.

Resolved, That it is the Opinion of this Committee, that the Act of Assembly, made in the 5th Year of his present Majesty's Reign, intituled *An Act[11] for increasing the Reward for killing Wolves, within certain Counties, to be paid by the respective Counties wherein*

the

---

1 Hening, VIII, p. 211. 2 Ibid, V. p. 326. 3 Ibid, VIII, p. 389. 4 Ibid, VII, p. 577.
5 Ibid, VII, p. 93. 6 Ibid, VII, p. 106. 7 Ibid, VII, p. 265. 8 Ibid, VI, p. 217.
9 Ibid, VII, p. 338. 10 Ibid, VII, p. 580. 11 Ibid, VIII, p. 147.

the Service shall be performed, and which was continued by another Act, made in the 7th Year of his said Majesty's Reign (except as to the Counties of *Buckingham, Fauquier,* and *Loudoun*) and continued and amended by another Act, made in the 10th Year of his said Majesty's Reign, and which will expire on the 1st Day of *June*, 1773, ought to be further continued and amended.

Resolved, That it is the Opinion of this Committee, that the Act of Assembly, made in the 5th Year of the Reign of his present Majesty, intituled *An Act[1] for amending the Staple of Tobacco, and for preventing Frauds in his Majesty's Customs,* which was continued and amended by an Act, made in the 7th Year of his said Majesty's Reign, and further continued by another Act, made in the 8th Year of his said Majesty's Reign, and also continued and amended by another Act, made in the 10th Year of his said Majesty's Reign, and which will expire on the 1st Day of *October*, 1773, ought to be further continued.

Resolved, That it is the Opinion of this Committee, that the Act of Assembly, made in the 10th Year of his present Majesty's Reign, intituled *An Act[2] for reimbursing the Inhabitants of* King William *and* Hanover *Counties the Expence of clearing* Pamunkey *River*, which was amended by another Act made in the same Year, and which will expire the 21st Day of *December*, 1773, ought to be further continued.

The said *Resolutions*, being severally read a second Time, were, upon the Question severally put thereupon, agreed to by the House.

Ordered, That a Bill or Bills be brought in pursuant to the *first, second, third, fourth, eleventh* and *thirteenth* Resolutions of the Committee; and that the Committee for Courts of Justice do prepare, and bring in the same.

Ordered, That a Bill or Bills be brought in pursuant to the *fifth, sixth, seventh,* and *twelfth* Resolutions of the Committee; and that the Committee of Propositions and Grievances do prepare, and bring in the same.

Ordered, That a Bill or Bills be brought in pursuant to the *eighth, ninth,* and *tenth* Resolutions of the Committee; and that the Committee of Trade do prepare, and bring in the same.

Mr *Bland* reported from the Committee of Propositions and Grievances, to whom the Petition of the Inhabitants and Freeholders of *Elizabeth City* County, praying that the Inspection of Tobacco at the Public Warehouse at *Hampton* may be disjoined from that at *Denbigh*, was referred, that the Committee had examined the Matter of the said Petition, and had come to a Resolution thereupon, which they had directed him to report to the House; and he read the Report in his Place; and afterwards delivered it in at the Clerk's Table, where the Resolution of the Committee was read, and is as followeth, *viz.*

Resolved, That it is the Opinion of this Committee, that the said petition is reasonable.

The said *Resolution* being read a second Time, was, upon the Question put thereupon, agreed to by the House.

Ordered, That the said Resolution do lie upon the Table.

Ordered, That a Committee be appointed to examine the Treasurer's Accounts; and that they do state in Account, as well the Balance due from the late Treasurer to the Public, as the several Funds by Law appropriated for the Redemption of the Treasury Notes, together with the Amount of such Notes remaining in Circulation; and that they do also state an Account of the Balances now due from the several Sheriffs for Taxes, and report the same to the House.

And a *Committee* was appointed of Mr *Bland*, Mr *Richard Henry Lee*, Mr *Harrison*, Mr *Charles Carter*, Mr *Eyre*, Mr *Patrick Henry*, Mr *Digges*, and Mr *Fitzhugh*.

The House was moved, that Part of an Act, made in the thirty-second Year of the Reign of King *Charles* the Second, intituled *An Act[3] of free and general Pardon, Indemnity, and Oblivion*, might be read.

And the same being read accordingly;

Ordered, That Leave be given to bring in a Bill to repeal Part of an Act passed in the

thirty

---

1 Hening, VIII, p. 69.   2 Ibid, VIII, p. 407.   3 Ibid, II, p. 458.

thirty-fecond Year of the Reign of King *Charles* the Second, intituled *An Act of free and general Pardon, Indemnity, and Oblivion;* and that Mr *Eyre,* Mr *James Henry,* and Mr *Bland* do prepare, and bring in the fame.

An ingroffed *Bill* to dock the Intail of certain Land whereof *Nathaniel Weft Dandridge* is feized, was read the third Time.

Refolved, That the Bill do pafs; and that the Title be, *An Act*[1] *to dock the Intail of certain Land whereof* Nathaniel Weft Dandridge *is feized.*

Ordered, That Mr *Patrick Henry* do carry the Bill to the Council, and defire their Concurrence.

The *Order* of the Day being read;

Refolved, That this Houfe will, Tomorrow, refolve itfelf into a Committee of the whole Houfe, to take into Confideration the Governor's Meffage, and the Lift of Fees therein mentioned.

Mr *Edmund Pendleton* reported, from the Committee of Privileges and Elections, to whom the Petition of Mr *Samuel DuVal* complaining of an undue Election and Return of Mr *Richard Randolph* to ferve as a Burgefs in this prefent General Affembly for the County of *Henrico,* was committed, that the Committee had partly examined the Matter of the faid *Petition,* and had come to a Refolution, which they had directed him to report to the Houfe; and he read the Report in his Place, and afterwards delivered it in at the Clerk's Table; where the Refolution of the Committee was read, and is as followeth, *viz.*

Refolved, That it is the Opinion of this Committee, that the further Confideration of the faid Petition be deferred till *Friday* the twenty-eighth Inftant.

The faid *Refolution* being read a fecond Time, was, upon the Queftion put thereupon, agreed to by the Houfe.

A *Petition* of *Benjamin Waller* was prefented to the Houfe, and read; fetting forth, that *Nathaniel Walthoe,* late of the City of *Williamfburg,* Efquire, deceafed, being feized of Mefuages, Lands, and Tenements, in this Colony, by his laft Will and Teftament in Writing, among other Things, devifed all his Eftate in *Virginia* to his Sifter *Henrietta,* and his Nieces *Mary Hart,* and *Martha Hart,* all of the Kingdom of *Great Britain,* to be equally divided between them, but declared the Eftate to be chargeable with all his Debts in *Virginia,* and with feveral Legacies; and of his Will appointed *Thomas Waller,* of *London,* Stationer, the petitioner, and *George Davenport,* who is fince deceafed, Executors and afterwards died feized; that the Petitioner having proved the Will, and fold the, Teftator's perfonal Eftate, paid fuch of his *Virginia* Debts as appeared, and the faid Particular Legacies, and remitted confiderable Sums of Money to the faid three Legatees in *Great-Britain;* that the faid *Henrietta, Mary,* and *Martha,* by Letter of Attorney, have appointed the petitioner to fell all the Eftate devifed to them as aforefaid, and he hath actually fold two of the faid Tenements; but the Petitioner hath lately difcovered, that the faid *Henrietta* was married, above twenty Years ago, to one Mr *Marmillod,* a Native of *Switzerland,* or *Sweden,* with whom fhe removed to *France,* where he then refided; and that fhe foon after returned to *England,* and hath lived there ever fince, feparate from her Hufband, who hath continued Abroad, and is now in *Denmark;* that fhe is infirm, and wants Support, and hath, as the Petitioner is informed, Power from her Hufband to tranfact all their Affairs; and that the Hufband, being an Alien, hath not, as the Petitioner is advifed, any Right in her Lands and Tenements; and therefore praying that the faid *Henrietta,* or the Petitioner, as her Attorney, may be enabled to fell and convey the Lands and Tenements devifed to her as aforefaid, in the fame Manner as if fhe were a Feme Sole, fo as to bind her and her Heirs.

Ordered, That Leave be given to bring in a Bill purfuant to the Prayer of the faid Petition; and that Mr *Edmund Pendleton* do prepare, and bring in the fame.

Ordered, That Leave be given to bring in a Bill for appointing an Agent; and that Mr *Harrifon,* Mr *Edmund Pendleton,* and Mr *Patrick Henry* do prepare, and bring in the fame.

A

---

[1] Hening, VIII, p. 638.

A *Petition* of *Thomas Guy*, of the County of *Accomack*, was prefented to the Houfe, and read; fetting forth, that *John Fleharty*, charged with Grand Larceny, having been ordered by the Court of the faid County, held for his Examination, to be tried for the faid Offence before the Juftices of *Oyer* and *Terminer*, in *June*, 1769, the petitioner was bound in a Recognizance to appear as a Witnefs againft the Prifoner, and did attend accordingly, and was examined, but by fome Accident his Attendance was not entered; and praying to be allowed for the fame.

Ordered, That the faid petition be referred to the Confideration of the Committee of Public Claims; and that they do examine the Matter thereof, and report the fame, with their Opinion thereupon, to the Houfe.

A *Petition* of *William Todd*, Gentleman, was prefented to the Houfe, and read; fetting forth, that the petitioner is feifed of a large Eftate in Lands, as Tenant in Tail Male, but hath very few Slaves to work the fame; and that it will be advantageous to himfelf, as well as to thofe who fhall fucceed to the Inheritance, to fell Part of the faid Lands, and, with the Money arifing from the Sale, purchafe Slaves, to be annexed to the remaining Lands; and therefore praying that an Act may pafs for that Purpofe.

Ordered, That Leave be given to bring in a Bill purfuant to the Prayer of the faid Petition; and that Mr *Edmund Pendleton* do prepare, and bring in the fame.

Ordered, That it be an Inftruction to the Gentleman, who is appointed to prepare, and bring in the faid Bill, that he have Power to receive a Claufe or Claufes for afcertaining the Bounds of Part of the intailed Lands whereof the faid *William Todd* is feized.

Ordered, That Mr *Bridger* have Leave to be abfent from the Service of this Houfe till the laft Day of this Month.

Ordered, That Mr *Dandridge* and Mr *Fitzhugh* be added to the Committee of Propofitions and Grievances.

Ordered, That Mr *Dandridge* be added to the Committee for Courts of Juftice.

Ordered, That Mr *Fitzhugh* be added to the Committee of Privileges and Elections.

And then the Houfe adjourned till Tomorrow Morning, eleven of the Clock.

Friday, the 21st of February, 12 George III. 1772.

SEVERAL other *Members* having taken the Oaths appointed to be taken by Act of Parliament, and repeated and fubfcribed the Teft, took their Places in the Houfe.

Mr *Richard Lee* reported from the Committee of Public Claims, to whom the Petitions of feveral Perfons were referred, that the Committee had examined the Matters of the faid petitions, and had come to feveral Refolutions thereupon, which they had directed him to report to the Houfe; and he read the Report in his Place, and afterwards delivered it in at the Clerk's Table; where the Refolutions of the Committee were read, and are as followeth, *viz.*

Refolved, That it is the Opinion of this Committee, that the Petition of *John Loving*, junior, and *Robert Montgomery*, to be allowed for travelling and Attendance as Witneffes for the King on the Trial of *Andrew Lightle*, for Felony in the General Court, is reafonable; and that they ought to be allowed five hundred and feventy Pounds of Tobacco, each, for the fame.

Refolved, That it is the Opinion of this Committee, that the Petition of *Samuel Sherwin*, to be allowed for his Negro Man Slave *Peter*, who was duly outlawed and killed in an Attempt to take him, is reafonable; and that he ought to be allowed the Sum of ninety Pounds for the faid Slave.

Refolved, That it is the Opinion of this Committee, that from the feveral Depofitions hereunto annexed, relative to the Petition of *William Bicknal*, and to which your Committee begs Leave to refer the Houfe, the faid petition is reafonable; and that the Petitioner ought to be allowed the Sum of nine Pounds for the Horfe in the faid Petition mentioned.

Refolved

Refolved, That it is the Opinion of this Committee, that the Petition of *Thomas Guy*, a Witnefs for the King againft *John Fleharty*, a Criminal from *Accomack* County, on Sufpicion of Grand Larceny, for an Allowance for traveling to, and attending the Court of *Oyer* and *Terminer*, with Ferriages, in *June*, 1769, on the Trial of the faid Criminal, is reafonable; and that he ought to be allowed five hundred and ten Pounds of Tobacco for the fame.

The *two* firft Refolutions of the Committee, being feverally read a fecond Time, were, upon the Queftion feverally put thereupon, agreed to by the Houfe.

The *Third* Refolution of the Committee being read a fecond Time;

Ordered, That the faid Refolution be re-committed.

Ordered, That the faid Refolution be re-committed to the fame Committee, to whom the Petition of the faid *William Bicknal* was referred.

The fubfequent *Refolution* of the Committee, being read a fecond Time, was, upon the Queftion put thereupon, agreed to by the Houfe.

An ingroffed *Bill*, to impower the Clerks of the County Courts to iffue certain Writs of Execution into other Counties, was read the third Time.

Refolved, That the Bill do pafs; and that the Title be, *An Act[1] to impower the Clerks of County Courts to iffue certain Writs of Execution into other Counties.*

Ordered, That Mr *Edmund Pendleton* do carry the Bill to the Council, and defire their Concurrence.

Mr *Richard Lee* reported from the Committee of Public Claims, to whom the Petition of *William Hoye* was referred, that the Committee had examined the Matter of the faid Petition; and had directed him to report the fame, as it appeared to them, together with the Refolution of the Committee thereupon, to the Houfe; and he read the Report in his Place, and afterwards delivered it in at the Clerk's Table; where the fame was read, and is as followeth, *viz.*

It appears to your *Committee*, that the Slave in the Petition mentioned, was duly outlawed, and afterwards taken and committed to the Gaol of the County of *Buckingham*; that he broke out of the faid Gaol, and burned it, and afterwards in apprehending him he was wounded, of which Wound he died, as appears by a Coroner's Inqueft taken on the Body of the faid Slave. It alfo appears to your Committee, by a Certificate under the Hand of the faid Coroner, that the faid Slave was of the Value of eighty-five Pounds.

Upon the whole *Matter* the Committee came to the following Refolution,

Refolved, That it is the Opinion of this Committee, that the faid petition is reafonable; and that the Petitioner ought to be allowed the faid Sum of eighty-five Pounds for the faid Slave.

The faid *Refolution*, being read a fecond Time, was, upon the Queftion put thereupon, agreed to by the Houfe.

Mr *Harrifon* prefented to the Houfe, according to Order, a Bill for appointing an Agent; and the fame was received, and read the firft Time.

Refolved, That the Bill be read a fecond Time.

Ordered, That the faid Bill be read a fecond Time upon *Wednefday* the fourth Day of *March* next.

Ordered, That this Houfe be called over upon *Wednefday* the fourth Day of *March* next.

Ordered, That the Letters which have paffed between *Edward Montagu*, Efquire, late Agent for this Colony, and the Committee of Correfpondence, fince the firft Day of *November*, in the Year of our Lord, 1769, be laid before the Houfe.

A *Petition* of *Cornelius Thomas* was prefented to the Houfe, and read; fetting forth, that the Ferry over the *Fluvanna* River, from the Land of the Petitioner, in the County of *Amherft*, to the Land of *Nicholas Davies*, in the County of *Bedford*, is not frequented; and therefore praying, that fo much of the Act of General Affembly, made in the fifth Year of the Reign of his prefent Majefty, as eftablifhed the faid Ferry, may be repealed.

Ordered, That the faid Petition be referred to the Confideration of the Committee of Propofitions and Grievances; and that they do examine the Matter thereof, and report the fame, with their Opinion thereupon, to the Houfe.

Ordered

----

[1] Hening, VIII, p. 516.

Ordered, That Mr *Alexander* and Mr *Ball* be added to the Committee for Religion.

Ordered, That Mr *Alexander* be added to the Committee of Privileges and Elections.

Ordered, That Mr *Ball*, Mr *Marable*, Mr *Edmondfon*, and Mr *Alexander* be added to the Committee of propofitions and Grievances.

Ordered, That Mr *Marable* and Mr *Ball* be added to the Committee of Public Claims.

Ordered, That Mr *Yelverton Peyton*, and Mr *Edmondfon* be added to the Committee for Courts of Juftice.

Ordered, That Mr *Stubblefield* be added to the Committee of Trade.

The *Order* of the Day being read;

The Houfe refolved itfelf into a Committee of the whole Houfe, to take into Confideration the Governor's Meffage, and the Lift of Fees therein mentioned.

Mr *Speaker* left the Chair.

Mr *Bland* took the Chair of the Committee.

Mr *Speaker* refumed the Chair.

Mr *Bland* reported from the Committee, that they had come to a Refolution, which he read in his Place, and afterwards delivered in at the Clerk's Table; where the fame was read, and is as followeth, *viz.*

Refolved, That it is the Opinion of this Committee, that an humble Addrefs be prefented to his Excellency the Governor, returning him our fincere Thanks for his very polite and candid Meffage; expreffing our great Satiffaction in finding his Excellency fo cordially difpofed to cultivate with the Country that agreeable Harmony which is moft likely to conciliate to him the Affections of all his Majefty's loyal Subjects of *Virginia*, and thereby eftablifh their mutual Happinefs upon the moft folid and permanent Foundations; affuring his Lordfhip of the great Refpect we bear to his important and exalted Station amongft us, and the Neceffity we think there is of fupporting the Honour and Dignity of our Governors; but, at the fame Time, humbly reprefenting to his Excellency that we confider the Emoluments of Government, as by Law eftablifhed, adequate and amply fufficient for thofe Purpofes; that the Fees which appear to have been received by the Clerks of his Lordfhip's Predeceffors for iffuing Commiffions for the Appointment of Public Officers, and which we are now, for the firft Time, regularly informed of by his Meffage and the Lift accompanying it, are unknown to our Laws, and that, therefore, we cannot fufficiently applaud his Lordfhip's Wifdom and Goodnefs in embracing fo early an Opportunity of expreffing his Willingnefs, if they fhould be found difagreeable to us, as they really are, to have them totally abolifhed.

The faid *Refolution*, being read a fecond Time, was, upon the Queftion put thereupon, agreed to by the Houfe.

Ordered, That a Committee be appointed to draw up an Addrefs, to be prefented to the Governor, upon the faid Refolution.

And a *Committee* was appointed of Mr *Bland*, Mr *Treafurer*, Mr *Pendleton*, and Mr *Patrick Henry*.

Ordered, That Mr *Wright* have Leave to be abfent from the Service of this Houfe till *Thurfday* next.

And then the Houfe adjourned till Tomorrow Morning eleven of the Clock.

Saturday, the 22d of February, 12 George III. 1772.

MR *Richard Henry Lee* prefented to the Houfe, according to Order, a Bill for further continuing the Act, intituled *An Act¹ for the better regulating and collecting certain Officers Fees, and for other Purpofes therein mentioned;* and the fame was received, and read the firft Time.

Refolved, That the Bill be read a fecond Time.

Ordered, That the faid Bill be read a fecond Time, upon *Thurfday*, the fifth Day of *March* next.

A *Petition* of feveral Perfons of the County of *Mecklenburg*, whofe Names are thereunto

unto fubfcribed, was prefented to the Houfe, and read; fetting forth, that the petitioners, being of the Society of Chriftians, called *Baptifts*, find themfelves reftricted in the Exercife of their Religion, their Teachers imprifoned under various Pretences, and the Benefits of the Toleration Act denied them, although they are willing to conform to the true Spirit of that Act, and are loyal and quiet Subjects; and therefore praying,that they may be treated with the fame kind Indulgence in religious Matters as *Quakers, Prefbyterians*, and other Proteftant Diffenters enjoy.

Ordered, That the faid Petition be referred to the Confideration of the Committee for Religion, and that they do examine the Matter thereof, and report the fame, with their Opinion thereupon, to the Houfe.

Mr *Richard Henry Lee* prefented to the Houfe, according to Order, a Bill for further continuing the Act, intituled *An Act¹ for appointing a Treafurer;* and the fame was received, and read the firft Time.

Refolved, That the Bill be read a fecond Time.

Ordered, That Mr *Patrick Henry* have Leave to be abfent from the Service of this Houfe till *Wednefday* Sevennight.

Mr *Richard Lee* reported from the Committee of Public Claims, to whom the Petition of *William Bicknal* had been referred, and to whom the Refolution of the faid Committee upon the faid Petition was re-committed, that the Committee had examined the Matter of the faid petition, and had directed him to report the fame, as it appeared to them, together with the Refolution of the Committee thereupon, to the Houfe; and he read the Report in his Place, and afterwards delivered it in at the Clerk's Table; where the fame was read, and is as followeth, *viz.*

It appears to your *Committee*, that *Gabriel Penn*, one of the Under Sheriffs of *Amherft* County, in the Month of *September*, 1771, impreffed a Horfe, belonging to the petitioner, to convey *Thomas Welch*, a Criminal, from the faid County to the Public Gaol; that the faid Sheriff, on his Return home, being fo much indifpofed or lamed by a Boil that he could not lead the faid Horfe any further than *Richmond* Town, he left him there with a certain *Archibald Mackendrix*, of that Place, to be taken Care of till he fhould be fent for by the faid *Penn*. It alfo appears to your Committee, that the faid *Penn*, on the third Day after his Return home, difpatched a Meffenger for the faid Horfe; but that he was either ftrayed or ftolen from the Pafture in which he was put by the faid *Mackendrix*, fo that the faid Meffenger did not get him, and he has not fince been heard of. It alfo appears to your Committee, from a Certificate under the Hands of three Perfons, appointed and fworn to value the faid Horfe, that he was worth nine Pounds.

Upon the whole the *Committee* came to the following Refolution:

Refolved, That it is the Opinion of this Committee, that the faid Petition is reafonable; and that the Petitioner ought to be allowed the Sum of nine Pounds for the faid Horfe.

The faid *Refolution*, being read a fecond Time, was, upon the Queftion put thereupon, agreed to by the Houfe.

Ordered, That Mr *Thomas Mann Randolph* have Leave to be abfent from the Service of this Houfe for a Fortnight.

A *Petition* of the Mayor, Recorder, Aldermen, and Common Council of the City of *Williamfburg*, and of feveral other *Perfons*, whofe Names are thereunto fubfcribed, was prefented to the Houfe, and read; fetting forth, that by a Survey made it appears that a Canal or Cut may be carried from *Archer's Hope* Creek, running into *James* River, to *Queen's* Creek, running into *York* River, for the Navigation of Boats and other Veffels with heavy Burthens, whereby an eafy Communication will be made between thofe two Rivers, which the petitioners conceive will be of great Advantage, not only to the faid City, but to the Trade carried on in the faid Rivers, and will probably encourage the like Works in other Parts of the Colony, to the Improvement of its Commerce; and further fetting forth, that the Petitioners apprehend it will be neceffary that proper Tolls or Duties be impofed upon Boats and Veffels paffing in and through the faid Canal, for

the

_____
¹ Hening, VIII, p. 211.

the fupporting and rendering effectual the faid Navigation; and therefore praying, that Leave may be given to bring in a Bill for enabling the Petitioners, at the Expence of themfelves, and of other voluntary Contributors, to make the faid Canal, and continue the fame navigable, in fuch Manner, and with fuch Powers and Authorities, to be vefted in them for that Purpofe, as to the Houfe fhall feem meet.

Ordered, That Leave be given to bring in a Bill purfuant to the Prayer of the faid Petition; and that Mr *Treafurer* and Mr *Richard Henry Lee* do prepare, and bring in the fame.

Mr *Richard Henry Lee* prefented to the Houfe, according to Order, a Bill to revive the Act, intituled *An Act¹ for giving a Salary to the Speaker of the Houfe of Burgeffes;* and the fame was received, and read the firft Time.

Refolved, That the Bill be read a fecond Time.

Ordered, That Mr *John Jones* have Leave to be abfent from the Service of this Houfe till *Monday* Sevennight.

A *Petition* of the Veftry of the Parifh of *Frederick*, in the County of *Frederick*, was prefented to the Houfe, and read; fetting forth, that the late Parifh of *Frederick* was, by an Act made in the tenth Year of the Reign of his prefent Majefty, divided into three Parifhes, called *Frederick*, *Norborne*, and *Beckford*; and that by the faid Act, reciting that there would be a new Church in each of the Parifhes of *Frederick* and *Norborne*, the Charges of which had lately been defrayed by the Inhabitants of *Frederick*, before the Divifion, it was enacted, that the Veftries of the Parifhes of *Frederick* and *Norborne*, when elected, fhould account for the faid Churches, according to their feveral Cofts, and refund to the Veftry of the Parifh of *Beckford* a proportion thereof, according to the Number of Tithables in their Parifhes, refpectively, at the Time the fame fhould take Place; and reprefenting, that the Church mentioned in the Act to be in the Parifh of *Frederick*, is not worth the firft Coft, having been built fo long ago as the Year 1764, and the workmanfhip having been executed infufficiently, fo that it is likely foon to become ruinous; and further reprefenting, that there are two Chapels, of Confiderable Value, in the Parifh of *Beckford*, one of which was built in the Year 1768; and therefore praying, that Commiffioners may be appointed to afcertain the prefent Value of the faid Church and Chapels, as they hope this Honourable Houfe will be of Opinion the Parifh of *Frederick*, ought not to be charged with more than a proportion of the Sum the Church exceeds the two Chapels in Value, and that the Petitioners may have fuch Relief in the Premifes as to the Houfe fhall feem reafonable.

Ordered, That the faid Petition be referred to the Confideration of the Committee for Religion; and that they do examine the Matter thereof, and report the fame, with their Opinion thereupon, to the Houfe.

A *Petition* of *Auftin Hewlett*, furviving Infpector at *Waddy's* Warehoufe, in the County of *New Kent*, was prefented to the Houfe, and read; fetting forth, that in *July* laft, the faid Warehoufe was broke open, whilft the Petitioner and *John Pinchback*, deceafed, the other Infpector, were neceffarily abfent, attending their Duty at *Littlepage's* Warehoufe under the fame Infpection, and four hundred and fifty Pounds of uninfpected Tobacco were ftolen, for which the Owner recovered of the Infpectors, and the Petitioner hath been obliged to pay to him three Pounds and fifteen Shillings, with two Pounds eleven Shillings and ten Pence for the Cofts of Suit; and therefore praying, that the faid Sums of Money may be repaid to the Petitioner by the Public.

Ordered, That the faid Petition be referred to the Confideration of the Committee of Public Claims; and that they do examine the Matter thereof, and report the fame, with their Opinion thereupon, to the Houfe.

A *Petition* of the Infpectors at *Blandford* Warehoufe, in the County of *Prince George*, was prefented to the Houfe, and read; fetting forth, that in *November* laft, the petitioners loft out of the faid Warehoufe two thoufand feven hundred and thirty-two Pounds of Tobacco, for which they have been obliged to pay the Owners at the Rate of twenty Shillings by the Hundred Weight; and therefore praying, that the faid Money may be repaid to the Petitioners by the Public.

Ordered

¹ Hening, VIII, p. 394.

Ordered, That the faid Petition be referred to the Confideration of the Committee of Public Claims; and that they do examine the Matter thereof, and report the fame, with their Opinion thereupon, to the Houfe.

Mr *Edmund Pendleton* prefented to the Houfe, according to Order, a Bill to enable *Henrietta Marmillod* to fell and difpofe of the Eftate devifed to her by her Brother *Nathaniel Walthoe*, Efquire, deceafed, notwithftanding her Coverture; and the fame was received, and read the firft Time.

Refolved, That the Bill be read a fecond Time.

And then the Houfe adjourned till Monday Morning next, eleven of the Clock.

Monday, the 24th of February, 12 George lll. 1772.

SEVERAL other *Members* having taken the Oaths appointed to be taken by Act of Parliament, and repeated and fubfcribed the Teft, took their Places in the Houfe.

Mr *Bland* reported, from the Committee appointed to draw up an Addrefs, to be prefented to the Governor, that they had drawn up an Addrefs accordingly, which they had directed him to report to the Houfe; and he read the fame in his Place, and afterwards delivered it in at the Clerk's Table, where the fame was read, and is as followeth, *viz.*

My Lord,

We, his Majefty's dutiful Subjects, humbly beg Leave to return your Excellency our unfeigned Thanks for your very candid and polite Meffage. It affords us the higheft Pleafure and Satiffaction to find your Excellency fo cordially difpofed to cultivate with the Country that agreeable Harmony which will undoubtedly conciliate to you the Affection of his Majefty's loyal Subjects of Virginia, *and thereby eftablifh our mutual Happinefs upon the moft folid and permanent Foundation.*

We bear the greateft Refpect to your Excellency's important and exalted Station amongft us, and think there is a neceffity for fupporting the Honour and Dignity of our Governors; but, my Lord, give us Leave, on this Occafion, humbly to reprefent to your Excellency, that we confider the Emoluments of Government, as by Law eftablifhed, adequate and amply fufficient for thofe Purpofes. The Fees which appear to have been received by the Clerks of your Excellency's Predeceffors for iffuing Commiffions for the Appointment of Public Officers, and which we are now, for the firft Time, regularly informed of by your Lordfhip's Meffage, are unknown to our Laws; and therefore we cannot fufficiently applaud your Lordfhip's Wifdom and Goodnefs in embracing fo early an Opportunity of expreffing your Willingnefs, if they fhould be found difagreeable to us, as they really are, to have them totally abolifhed.

The faid *Addrefs* being read a fecond Time;

Refolved, That the Houfe doth agree with the Committee in the faid Addrefs, to be prefented to the Governor.

Ordered, That the faid Addrefs be prefented to his Excellency by the whole Houfe.

Ordered, That the Gentlemen who drew up the faid Addrefs, do wait upon the Governor to know his Pleafure, when this Houfe fhall attend his Excellency, to prefent their Addrefs.

A *Bill* for further continuing the Act, intituled *An Act for appointing a Treafurer,* was read a fecond Time.

Ordered, That the Bill be ingroffed.

A *Petition* of feveral Perfons of the County of *Amelia*, whofe Names are thereunto fubfcribed, fetting forth, that the Petitioners, being of the Community of Chriftians who worfhip God under the Denomination of Baptifts, are reftricted in their religious Exercifes; that, if the Act of Toleration does not extend to this Colony, they are expofed to fevere Perfecution; and, if it does extend hither, and the Power of granting Licences to

Teachers

Teachers be lodged, as is suppofed, in the General Court alone, the Petitioners muft fuffer confiderable Inconveniences, not only becaufe that Court fits not oftener than twice in the Year, and then at a Place far remote, but becaufe the faid Court will admit a fingle Meeting-Houfe and no more in one County; and that the Petitioners are loyal and quiet Subjects, whofe Tenets in no wife affect the State: and therefore praying a Redrefs of their Grievances, and that Liberty of Confcience may be fecured to them; *and alfo*

A *Petition* of feveral Perfons of the County of *Suffex*, whofe Names are thereunto fubfcribed, fetting forth, that the Petitioners, being of the Society of Chriftians, called Baptifts, find themfelves reftricted in the Exercife of their Religion, their Teachers imprifoned under various Pretences, and the Benefits of the Toleration Act denied them, although they are willing to conform to the true Spirit of that Act, and are loyal and quiet Subjects; and therefore praying, that they may be treated with the fame kind Indulgence in religious Matters as Quakers, Prefbyterians, and other Proteftant Diffenters enjoy;

Were feverally *prefented* to the Houfe, and read.

Ordered, That the faid Petitions be referred to the Confideration of the Committee for Religion; and that they do examine the Matter thereof, and report the fame, with their Opinion thereupon, to the Houfe.

A *Bill* to revive the Act, intituled *An Act[1] for giving a Salary to the Speaker of the Houfe of Burgeffes*, was read a fecond Time.

Ordered, That the Bill be ingroffed.

A *Memorial* of the Court of Directors of the Public Hofpital for Perfons of infane and difordered Minds was prefented to the Houfe, and read; reprefenting that the Memorialifts, in Compliance with an Act of the late General Affembly, took the earlieft Opportunity of executing the Truft repofed in them; that they purchafed eight Lots of Land in a retired Part of the City of *Williamfburg*, for one hundred and twelve Pounds, and agreed with an Undertaker to build fuch an Houfe as they judged would beft anfwer the Purpofe; a Plan of which, with the Articles, is ready to be laid before this Honourable Houfe; that it is hoped the Work, wherein a confiderable Progrefs is already made, will be finifhed by the Time limited; and further reprefenting, that the Memorialifts, finding that what they fuppofed to be the Defign of the Affembly could not be effected without exceeding the Sum allowed by the Act, at firft inclined to make up the difference by Subfcriptions, but conceiving that might be deemed improper, engaged at all Events that the whole Money requifite fhould be paid, intending to lay their Proceedings before this Honourable Houfe; and further reprefenting, that befides the Coft of the Ground, and of the Building, when finifhed, amounting in the whole to about fixteen hundred Pounds, it will be neceffary to inclofe a Garden and Yards for Patients to walk and take the Air in; and that a Keeper and Matron muft be employed, and other incidental Charges will accrue, which are not provided for by Law; and therefore humbly fubmitting it to the Confideration of the Houfe to make further Provifion and Eftablifhments as they may think proper and neceffary to enable the Court to carry the laudable Intention of the Affembly into complete Execution.

Ordered, That the faid Memorial be referred to the Confideration of a Committee of the whole Houfe.

Refolved, That this Houfe will, upon *Wednefday* next, refolve itfelf into a Committee of the whole Houfe, to confider of the faid Memorial.

The Houfe was moved that the Order, made upon *Saturday*, the fifteenth day of this Inftant, that the Petitions of divers Inhabitants of the Counties of *Stafford*, *King George*, and *Weftmoreland*, for reforming the Boundaries of the faid Counties, refpectively, and the Petitions of divers Inhabitants of the Counties of *Richmond*, and *Weftmoreland*, in Oppofition thereto, be referred to the Confideration of the Committee of Propofitions and Grievances; and that they do examine the Matter thereof, and report the fame, with their Opinion thereupon, to the Houfe, might be read.

And the fame being read accordingly;

Ordered

---

[1] Hening, VIII, p. 394

Ordered, That the faid Order be difcharged.

Several *Petitions* of the Inhabitants of the Parifh of *Beckford*, in the County of *Frederick*, praying, that the faid County may be divided into two Counties; *and alfo*

Several *Petitions* of the Inhabitants of the County of *Frederick*, praying that the faid County may be divided into three Counties; *and alfo*

A *Petition* of the Inhabitants of the Town of *Winchefter*, in the County of *Frederick*, praying that the faid County may be divided into three Counties;

Were feverally prefented to the Houfe, and read.

Ordered, That the faid Petitions be referred to the Confideration of the Committee of Propofitions and Grievances; and that they do examine the Matter thereof, and report the fame, with their Opinion thereupon, to the Houfe.

A *Bill* to enable *Henrietta Marmillod* to fell and difpofe of the Eftate, devifed to her by her Brother *Nathaniel Walthoe*, Efquire, deceafed, notwithftanding her Coverture, was read a fecond Time.

Refolved, That the Bill be committed to Mr *Edmund Pendleton*, Mr *Treafurer*, Mr *Lewis Burwell*, of *James City*, Mr *Digges*, Mr *Nelfon*, Mr *Harwood*, Mr *Langhorne*, Mr *Baffett*, and Mr *Dandridge*.

Mr *Bland* prefented to the Houfe, according to Order, a Bill to repeal one Claufe of the Act of Affembly, intituled *An Act¹ for fettling the Titles and Bounds of Lands, and for preventing unlawful hunting and ranging;* and the fame was received, and read the firft Time.

Refolved, That the Bill be read a fecond Time.

Ordered, That Mr *David Mafon* have Leave to be abfent from the Service of this Houfe, till *Wednefday* Sevennight.

Ordered, That Leave be given to bring in a Bill for the more fpeedy and eafy Adminiftration of Juftice; and that Mr *Edmund Pendleton*, Mr *Bland*, Mr *Henry Lee*, Mr *Harrifon*, Mr *Treafurer*, Mr *Jofeph Jones*, Mr *Fleming*, Mr *Carr*, Mr *Holt*, Mr *Dandridge*, Mr *White*, Mr *Carrington*, and Mr *Digges*, do prepare and bring in the fame.

Ordered, That Mr *Henry Lee*, Mr *Wilfon*, and Mr *Marfhall* be added to the Committee for Religion, and to the Committee of Propofitions and Grievances.

Ordered, That Mr *Henry Lee* be added to the Committee of Privileges and Elections.

Ordered, That Mr *Scott*, Mr *Bowyer*, Mr *Jofeph Cabell*, and Mr *Macdowel* be added to the Committee of Public Claims.

And then the Houfe adjourned till Tomorrow Morning eleven of the Clock.

Tuesday, the 25th of February, 12 George III. 1772.

MR *Treafurer* prefented to the Houfe, according to Order, a Bill for cutting a navigable Canal from *Archer's Hope* Creek to *Queen's* Creek, through the City of *Williamfburg*; and the fame was received, and read the firft Time.

Refolved, That the Bill be read a fecond Time.

Mr *Richard Henry Lee* prefented to the Houfe, according to *Order*, a Bill for further continuing and amending the Act, intituled *An Act² for increafing the Reward for killing Wolves within certain Counties, to be paid by the refpective Counties wherein the Services fhall be performed;* and the fame was received, and read the firft Time.

Refolved, That the Bill be read a fecond Time.

Mr *Richard Henry Lee* prefented to the Houfe, according to Order, a Bill for continuing the Act, intituled *An Act³ for reimburfing the Inhabitants of King William and Hanover Counties the Expence of clearing Pamunkey River;* and the fame was received, and read the firft Time.

Refolved, That the Bill be read a fecond Time.

Ordered, That Mr *William Cabell* have Leave to be abfent from the Service of this Houfe for a Fortnight.

Mr

---

¹ Hening, V. p. 408.   ² Ibid, VIII, p. 147.   ³ Ibid, VIII, p. 407.

Mr *Bland* reported, from the Committee of Propofitions and Grievances, to whom feveral Petitions were referred, that the Committee had examined the Matters of the faid Petitions,and had come to feveral Refolutions thereupon,which they had directed him to report to the Houfe; and he read the Report in his Place, and afterwards delivered it in at the Clerk's Table; where the Refolutions of the Committee were read, and are as followeth, *viz.*

Refolved, That it is the Opinion of this Committee, that the petition of the Inhabit-ants of the County of *Mecklenburg*, praying that the Importation of Tobacco from *North Carolina* to this Colony may be prohibited, or reftrained, be rejected.

Refolved, That it is the Opinion of this Committee, that the petition of divers Free-holders and Inhabitants of *Lunenburg* County, praying that a Duty may be impofed upon Tobacco brought into this Colony from *Carolina*, and that the Value of Gold and Silver may be raifed, be rejected.

Refolved, That it is the Opinion of this Committee, that fo much of the Petition of the Freeholders and Inhabitants of *Lunenburg* County, as prays a Repeal of that Part of the Act for amending the Staple of Tobacco, and for preventing Frauds in his Majefty's Cuftoms,which allows the Purchafers of Tobacco to have the fame reviewed, be rejected.

Refolved, That it is the Opinion of this Committee, that the Refidue of the faid Petition, praying that the Owners of Tobacco, unjuftly, refufed may have a Review, as well as the Purchafer, is reafonable.

The two *firft* Refolutions of the Committee being read a fecond Time, were, upon the Queftion feverally put thereupon, agreed to by the Houfe.

The *third* Refolution of the Committee being read a fecond Time;

And the *Queftion* being put that the Houfe doth agree with the Committee in the faid Refolution;

It paffed in the Negative.

Refolved, That fo much of the Petition of the Freeholders and Inhabitants of *Lunen-burg* County,as prays a Repeal of that Part of the Act for amending the Staple of Tobacco, and for preventing Frauds in his Majefty's Cuftoms, which allows the Purchafers of Tobacco to have the fame reviewed, is reafonable.

Ordered, That the faid Refolution do lie upon the Table.

The fubfequent *Refolution* of the Committee being read a fecond Time;

And the *Queftion* being put that the Houfe doth agree with the Committee in the faid Refolution;

It paffed in the Negative.

Refolved, That the Refidue of the faid Petition, praying that the Owners of Tobacco, unjuftly refufed, may have a Review as well as the Purchafer, be rejected.

Mr *Treafurer* reported, from the Committee for Religion, to whom feveral Petitions were referred, that the Committee had examined the Matters of the faid Petitions, and had come to feveral Refolutions thereupon, which they had directed him to report to the Houfe; and he read the Report in his Place, and afterwards delivered it in at the Clerk's Table; where the Refolutions of the Committee were read, and are as followeth, *viz.*

Refolved, That it is the Opinion of this Committee, that the Petitions of fundry Inhabitants of the Counties of *Lunenburg*, *Mecklenburg*, *Suffex*, and *Amelia*, of the Society of Chriftians called *Baptifts*, praying that they may be treated with the fame kind Indulgence, in religious Matters, as Quakers, Prefbyterians, and other Proteftant Diffenters enjoy, fo far as they relate to allowing the petitioners the fame Toleration, in Matters of Religion, as is enjoyed by his Majefty's diffenting Proteftant Subjects of *Great-Britain*, under different Acts of Parliament, is reafonable.

Refolved, That it is the Opinion of this Committee, that the Petition of the Veftry of *Frederick* Parifh, in the County of *Frederick*, praying that Commiffioners may be appointed to afcertain the prefent Value of a Church and two Chapels in the faid Petition mentioned, and that the faid Parifh of *Frederick* may not be charged with more than a Proportion of the Sum the Church exceeds the two Chapels in Value, is reafonable.

The

The faid *Refolutions* being feverally read a fecond Time, were, upon the Queftion feverally put thereupon, agreed to by the Houfe.

Ordered, That a Bill or Bills be brought in purfuant to the faid Refolutions; and that the Committee for Religion do prepare and bring in the fame.

Mr *Bland* reported, from the Committee of Propofitions and Grievances, to whom the Petition of *Cornelius Thomas*, praying that fo much of the Act of General Affembly, made in the fifth Year of the Reign of his prefent Majefty, as eftablifhed a Ferry over the *Fluvanna* River, from the Land of the Petitioner, in the County of *Amherft*, to the Land of *Nicholas Davies*, in the County of *Bedford*, may be repealed, was referred, that the Committee had examined the Matter of the faid petition, and had come to a Refolution thereupon, which they had directed him to report to the Houfe; and he read the Report in his Place, and afterwards delivered it in at the Clerk's Table; where the Refolution of the Committee was read, and is as followeth, *viz.*

Refolved, That it is the Opinion of this Committee, that the faid Petition is reafonable.

The faid *Refolution* being read a fecond Time, was, upon the Queftion put thereupon, agreed to by the Houfe.

Ordered, That a Bill be brought in purfuant to the faid Refolution; and that the Committee of Propofitions and Grievances do prepare and bring in the fame.

The *Order* of the Day being read;

Refolved, That this Houfe will, Tomorrow, refolve itfelf into a Committee of the whole Houfe, to take into their further Confideration the Governor's Speech.

Ordered, That Leave be given to bring in a Bill for eftablifhing a Town on the Land adjoining to the Court-Houfe of *Botetourt* County; and that Mr *Edmund Pendleton*, and Mr *Bowyer*, do prepare and bring in the fame.

Ordered, That it be an Inftruction to the Committee for Religion, that they do inquire into the State of the eftablifhed Religion in this Colony, and Report the fame, as it fhall appear to them, to the Houfe.

Ordered, That Mr *Bowyer* be added to the Committee for Religion.

Mr *Eyre* prefented to the Houfe, according to Order, a Bill to repeal Part of an Act, paffed in the thirty-fecond Year of the Reign of King *Charles* the Second, intituled *An Act[1] of free and general Pardon, Indemnity, and Oblivion;* and the fame was received, and read the firft Time.

Refolved, That the Bill be read a fecond Time.

Ordered, That Leave be given to bring in a Bill for better regulating the Election of Veftries; and that Mr *Henry Lee*, and Mr *Richard Henry Lee*, do prepare and bring in the fame.

A *Petition* of *Daniel Hamlin* was prefented to the Houfe, and read; fetting forth, that his Negro Man Slave *Parriot*, having attempted to Murder his Miftrefs, and dangeroufly wounded her, ran away, and was outlawed, and afterwards killed himfelf; and praying the Houfe to make him a reafonable Satiffaction for the faid Slave.

Ordered, That the faid petition be referred to the Confideration of the Committee of Public Claims; and that they do examine the Matter thereof, and report the fame, with their Opinion thereupon, to the Houfe.

And then the Houfe adjourned till Tomorrow Morning eleven of the Clock.

Wednesday, the 26th of February, 12 George III. 1772.

MR *Richard Henry Lee* prefented to the Houfe, according to Order, a Bill for vefting in Truftees certain Lands, whereof *William Booth*, Gentleman, and *Elizabeth* his Wife, are feifed in Fee Tail, to be fold, and for laying out the Money arifing from the Sale in purchafing other Lands, to be fettled to the fame Ufes; and the fame was received, and read the firft Time.

Refolved, That the Bill be read a fecond Time.

[1] Hening, II. p. 458.

A

A *Petition* of the Magiftrates and feveral Perfons of the County of *Surry*, and of feveral Perfons of the Town of *Cobham*, and others, whofe Names are thereunto fubfcribed, was prefented to the Houfe, and read; fetting forth, that, in Purfuance of an Act of General Affembly, made in the third Year of the Reign of King *William* and Queen *Mary*, intituled *An Act[1] for Ports*, fifty Acres of Land, on the lower Side of *Gray's* Creek, were purchafed by the faid County, and vefted in Truftees, and laid off into Lots for a Town, called *Cobham*, and that Perfons have bought, and entered for and made Improvements upon many of the faid Lots; but their Titles are difputed, it being doubtful whether the Truftees under whom they Claim, having been appointed by the Court of the faid County to fucceed fuch as removed, or were difabled by Age and Infirmity to execute the Office, had Power to Act; and praying that fuch Titles may be confirmed, upon reimburfing the County due Proportions of the Purchafe Money; that the Lots undifpofed of may be vefted in Truftees for the Purpofes and under the Conditions mentioned in the faid Act; and that fuch Truftees may be empowered to perpetuate their Succeffion, and to make Orders for the regular building the Houfes, and for repairing the Streets of the faid Town; and moreover praying that it may not be lawful to erect or to continue Wooden Chimnies, or to keep Swine going at large in the faid Town, and that a Ferry may be eftablifhed from thence, inftead of *Crouche's* Creek to *Jameftown*.

Ordered, That the faid petition be referred to the Confideration of the Committee of Propofitions and Grievances; and that they do examine the Matter thereof, and report the fame, with their Opinion thereupon, to the Houfe.

M[r] *Edmund Pendleton* reported from the Committee, to whom the Bill, to enable *Henrietta Marmillod* to fell and difpofe of the Eftate devifed to her by her Brother, *Nathaniel Walthoe*, Efquire, deceafed, notwithftanding her Coverture, was committed, that the Committee had examined the Allegations of the Bill and found the fame to be true; and that the Committee had directed him to report the Bill to the Houfe, without any Amendment; and he delivered the Bill in at the Clerk's Table.

Ordered, That the Bill be engroffed.

Ordered, That M[r] *Richard Henry Lee*, M[r] *Francis Lightfoot Lee*, M[r] *Lewis Burwell*, of *James City*, M[r] *Nelfon*, M[r] *Fitzhugh*, and M[r] *Cary* be added to the Gentlemen, who were appointed to prepare, and bring in a Bill, for the more fpeedy and eafy Adminiftration of Juftice.

Ordered, That M[r] *Fitzhugh* and M[r] *Jofeph Jones* be added to the Committee for Religion.

A *Petition* of the Veftrymen of the Parifh of *Saint Martin*, in the Counties of *Hanover* and *Louifa*, whofe Names are thereunto fubfcribed, was prefented to the Houfe, and read; fetting forth, that the Inhabitants of the faid Parifh are defirous of choofing Veftrymen; and therefore praying, that an Act may pafs to empower them to do fo.

Ordered, That Leave be given to bring in a Bill purfuant to the Prayer of the faid Petition; and that M[r] *Carr* do prepare, and bring in the fame.

M[r] *Harrifon* prefented to the Houfe, according to Order, a Bill, to continue an Act, intituled *An Act[2] to continue and amend an Act, intituled An Act for reducing the feveral Acts made for laying a Duty upon Liquors into one Act;* and the fame was received, and read the firft Time.

Refolved, That the Bill be read a fecond Time.

M[r] *Harrifon* prefented to the Houfe, according to Order, a Bill, to continue an Act, intituled *An Act[3] for eftablifhing Pilots, and regulating their Fees;* and the fame was received, and read the firft Time.

Refolved, That the Bill be read a fecond Time.

A *Petition* of *Robert Ruffin* was prefented to the Houfe, and read; fetting forth, that the Petitioner, at great Trouble and Expence, hath reclaimed a large Marfh, through which a Caufey leads to his Ferry; and that he is apprehenfive of confiderable Damage from Hogs, whofe Accefs to his faid Marfh cannot be prevented without expenfive Inclofures; and therefore praying, that he may be permitted to conftruct a Gate on his high Land, contiguous to his faid Marfh, for Travellers to pafs through to the faid Ferry.

Ordered

---

[1] Hening, III, p. 53.   [2] Ibid, VIII, p. 335.   [3] Ibid, VII, p. 580.

Ordered, That the faid Petition be referred to the Confideration of the Committee of propofitions and Grievances; and that they do examine the Matter thereof, and report the fame, with their Opinion thereupon, to the Houfe.

A *Petition* of feveral Perfons of the Parifh of *Southam*, in the County of *Cumberland*, whofe Names are thereunto fubfcribed, was prefented to the Houfe, and read; fetting forth, that the faid Parifh is large, and the Tithables therein numerous; and therefore praying, that the fame may be divided, by a Line, beginning at the Mouth of *Muddy* Creek, on *James* River, and running to *Swan's* Road, at *Roberts's* Race Ground, and along *Swan's* Road to *Buckingham* Road, and from thence to the Mouth of *Swan's* Creek on *Appomattox* River, or by fome other convenient Line, that will leave an equal Number of Tithables in each Parifh.

Ordered, That the faid petition be referred to the Confideration of the Committee for Religion; and that they do examine the Matter thereof, and report the fame, with their Opinion thereupon, to the Houfe.

Refolved, That the Sum of twenty-five Pounds *per Annum* be paid to *Peter Pelham* for his Salary as Organift, to continue till the End of the next Seffion of General Affembly.

Ordered, That Mʳ *Nelfon* do carry the Refolution to the Council, and defire their Concurrence.

A *Petition* of *Jacob Micheaux*, of the County of *Cumberland*, was prefented to the Houfe, and read; fetting forth, that the Petitioner's Fences, by which he made a Lane through his Plantation, in the faid County, to *Micheaux's* Ferry, had been lately carried away by the great Frefh, and that the Petitioner has very little Timber to renew the faid Fences; and therefore praying, that an Act may pafs, empowering him to erect and keep a Gate acrofs the Road to the faid Ferry.

Ordered, That the faid petition be referred to the Confideration of the Committee of Propofitions and Grievances; and that they do examine the Matter thereof, and report the fame, with their Opinion thereupon, to the Houfe.

An engroffed *Bill*, for further continuing the Act, intituled *An Act¹ for appointing a Treafurer*, was read the third Time.

Refolved, That the Bill do pafs; and that the Title be *An Act², for further continuing the Act, intituled An Act for appointing a Treafurer*.

Ordered, That Mʳ *Richard Henry Lee* do carry the Bill to the Council, and defire their Concurrence.

An engroffed *Bill*, to revive the Act, intituled *An Act³ for giving a Salary to the Speaker of the Houfe of Burgeffes*, was read the third Time.

Refolved, That the Bill do pafs; and that the Title be, *An Act⁴, to revive the Act, intituled an Act for giving a Salary to the Speaker of the Houfe of Burgeffes*.

Ordered, That Mʳ *Richard Henry Lee* do carry the Bill to the Council, and defire their Concurrence.

Mʳ *Treafurer* prefented to the Houfe, from the Court of Directors of the Hofpital for the Reception of Ideots, Lunatics, and perfons of infane and difordered minds, a Plan of the faid Hofpital, together with the Articles of Agreement, for building the fame, between *Benjamin Powell*, of the one Part, and the faid Court of Directors, of the other Part.

Ordered, That the faid Plan and Articles of Agreement be referred to the Confideration of the Committee of the whole Houfe, to whom it is referred to confider of the Memorial of the Court of Directors of the Public Hofpital, for Perfons of infane and difordered Minds.

A *Petition* of *John Taliaferro* was prefented to the Houfe, and read; fetting forth, that the Place called *Hackley's*, belonging to the Petitioner, in the County of *King George*, is very convenient for a Ferry; and therefore praying, that the Ferry, which was formerly kept from thence, over *Rappahannock* River, to the Land of the Honourable *Richard Corbin*, Efquire, in the County of *Caroline*, may be re-eftablifhed.

Ordered

¹ Hening, VIII, p. 211.   ² Ibid, VIII, p. 588.   ³ Ibid, VIII. p. 394.   ⁴ Ibid, VIII, p. 587.

Ordered, That the faid Petition be referred to the Confideration of the Committee of Propofitions and Grievances; and that they do examine the Matter thereof, and report the fame, with their Opinion thereupon, to the Houfe.

A *Petition* of *William Bruce*, and *David Bronaugh*, Infpectors of Tobacco at *Morton's* Warehoufes, in the County of *King George*, was prefented to the Houfe, and read; fetting forth, that, in the Year 1770, the Petitioners loft out of the faid Warehoufes, without any Neglect or other Default in them, one thoufand Eight hundred and forty-eight Pounds of Tobacco, for Part of which they have been obliged to pay after the Rate of twenty-five Shillings, and for the Refidue after the Rate of twenty-two Shillings and fix Pence, *per* Hundred; and therefore praying the Houfe to make them fuch Allowance for the fame as fhall appear juft.

Ordered, That the faid Petition be referred to the Confideration of the Committee of Public Claims; and that they do examine the Matter thereof, and report the fame, with their Opinion thereupon, to the Houfe.

A *Petition* of *William Bruce* and *William Harrifon*, Infpectors of Tobacco at *Gibfon's* and *Morton's* Warehoufes, in the County of *King George*, was prefented to the Houfe, and read; fetting forth, that, in the Year 1771, the Petitioners loft out of the faid Warehoufes three thoufand one hundred and forty Pounds of Tobacco, which they believe to have been ftolen; and further fetting forth, that, in the Month of *May* laft, twenty eight Hogfheads of Tobacco, in the Houfes at *Morton's* were fo damaged by heavy Rains, whilft the Petitioners attended at *Gibfon's*, that fifteen hundred and fixty-eight Pounds of Tobacco were deftroyed; and that the Owners of Part of the faid Tobacco have refufed to receive it, and one of them hath brought an Action againft the Petitioners, and therefore praying Relief.

Ordered, That the faid Petition be referred to the Confideration of the Committee of Public Claims; and that they do examine the Matter thereof, and Report the fame, with their Opinion thereupon, to the Houfe.

Ordered, That the Order of the Day, for the Houfe to refolve itfelf into a Committee of the whole Houfe, to take into their further Confideration the Governor's Speech, be now read.

And the faid *Order* being read accordingly;

The Houfe refolved itfelf into the faid Committee.

Mr *Speaker* left the Chair.

Mr *Bland* took the Chair of the Committee.

Mr *Speaker* refumed the Chair.

Mr *Bland* reported from the Committee, that they had gone through the Matters referred to them, and had come to feveral Refolutions thereupon, which he read in his Place, and afterwards delivered in at the Clerk's Table, where the fame were read, and are as followeth, *viz.*

Refolved, That it is the Opinion of this Committee, that a Committee be appointed to view the Lands on both Sides of *James* River from *Weftham*, to the navigable Water below the Falls; and that they make an exact Survey of the faid Lands, and return a Plan thereof, with an Eftimate of the Expence of making a navigable Canal, for the Paffage of Boats, through the fame, to the next General Affembly.

Refolved, That it is the Opinion of this Committee, that to remove the Seat of Government, to a Place more central and convenient to the People, will be a great Eafe and Relief to them, in Point of Expence and Trouble, and be a Means of faving much Labour that may be otherwife ufefully employed, in increafing the Riches and Commerce of the Colony, and therefore will be a Public Benefit.

Refolved, That this Committee doth willingly concur with the Lower Houfe of Affembly of *Maryland* in the Expediency of building a Light-Houfe on *Cape Henry*, in this Colony; and it is the Opinion of this Committee, that Commiffioners be appointed to proceed to erect fuch Light-Houfe as foon as the Affembly of *Maryland* fhall pafs an Act, of the fame Import with the Act to be paffed by the General Affembly of this Colony, for that Purpofe.

Refolved

Refolved, That it is the Opinion of this Committee, that a Sum, not exceeding fix thoufand Pounds, be paid, by the Treafurer of this Colony, to the faid Commiffioners, to enable them to carry on the faid Building; and that a Duty be laid on the Tonnage of all Ships, and other Veffels, coming into this Colony, other than from *Maryland*, to repay fo much as fhall be expended in erecting the faid Light-Houfe, and to provide a proper Fund for lighting and fupporting the fame.

The *firft* Refolution being read a fecond Time, was, upon the Queftion put thereupon, agreed to by the Houfe.

The *fecond* Refolution being read a fecond Time;

And the *Queftion* being put that the Houfe doth agree with the Committee in the faid Refolution;

The Houfe divided.

The *Noes* went forth.

Teller for the *Yeas* M[r] *Nelfon*   34
Teller for the *Noes* M[r] *Edmund Pendleton*   25

So it was refolved in the Affirmative.

The fubfequent *Refolutions* of the Committee being feverally read a fecond Time, were, upon the Queftion feverally put thereupon, agreed to by the Houfe.

Ordered, That a Bill or Bills be brought in purfuant to the *firft* and *fecond* Refolutions; and that the Committee of Propofitions and Grievances do prepare, and bring in the fame.

Ordered, That a Bill or Bills be brought in purfuant to the *third* and *fourth* Refolutions; and that the Committee of Trade do prepare, and bring in the fame.

The other *Order* of the Day being read;

Refolved, That this Houfe will, Tomorrow, refolve itfelf into a Committee of the whole Houfe, to confider of the Memorial of the Court of Directors for the Public Hofpital for Perfons of infane and difordered Minds.

A *Bill* to repeal Part of an Act, paffed in the thirty-fecond Year of the Reign of King *Charles* the Second, intituled *An Act[1] of free and general Pardon, Indemnity, and Oblivion*, was read a fecond Time.

Ordered, That the Bill be engroffed.

A *Petition* of *John Hancock* and *Margaret* his Wife, was prefented to the Houfe, and read; fetting forth, that the faid *John* is feifed, in Fee Tail, of three hundred and feventy Acres of Land in the Parifh of *Dettingen* and County of *Prince William*, called the *Deep Hole Tract*, and is feifed in Fee Simple, in Right of his faid Wife, of four hundred and fifty Acres of Land, in the County of *Amherft*; and that it will be greatly to the Advantage of their Iffue, and more to the Advantage of the Wife, who is confenting thereto, if the faid four hundred and fifty Acres of Land, with certain Slaves, be fettled in Lieu of the faid three hundred and feventy Acres; and therefore praying, that an Act may pafs for that Purpofe, and for vefting the laft mentioned Tract of Land in the faid *John Hancock* in Fee Simple.

Ordered, That Leave be given to bring in a Bill purfuant to the Prayer of the faid Petition; and that M[r] *Henry Lee* do prepare, and bring in the fame.

A *Bill* to repeal one Claufe of the Act of Affembly, intituled *An Act[2] for fettling the Titles and Bounds of Lands, and for preventing unlawful hunting and ranging*, was read a fecond Time.

Ordered, That the Bill be engroffed.

Ordered, That the faid Bill be read the third Time, upon *Wednefday* next.

A *Petition* of feveral Perfons, of the County of *New Kent*, whofe Names are thereunto fubfcribed, was prefented to the Houfe, and read; fetting forth, that the Union of *Littlepage's* and *Waddy's* Infpections is extremely inconvenient; and therefore praying that the fame may be feparated.

Ordered, That the faid Petition be referred to the Confideration of the Committee of Propofitions and Grievances; and that they do examine the Matter thereof, and report

the

---
[1] Hening, II, p.458.   [2] Ibid, V. p. 408.

the fame, with their Opinion thereupon, to the Houfe.

A *Bill* for further continuing and amending the Act, intituled *An Act[1] for increafing the Reward for killing Wolves, within certain Counties, to be paid by the refpective Counties wherein the Services fhall be performed*, was read a fecond Time.

Refolved, That the Bill be committed to the Committee of Propofitions and Grievances.

A *Bill* for continuing the Act, intituled *An Act[2] for reimburfing the Inhabitants of* King William *and* Hanover *Counties the Expence of clearing* Pamunkey *River*, was read a fecond Time.

Refolved, That the Bill be committed to Mr *Edmund Pendleton*, Mr *Patrick Henry*, Mr *Smith*, and Mr *Aylett*.

A *Bill* for cutting a navigable Canal from *Archer's Hope* Creek to *Queen's* Creek, through the City of *Williamfburg*, was read a fecond Time.

Refolved, That the Bill be committed.

Refolved, That the Bill be committed to a Committee of the whole Houfe.

Refolved, That this Houfe will, Tomorrow, refolve itfelf into a Committee of the whole Houfe upon the faid Bill.

And then the Houfe adjourned till Tomorrow Morning, eleven of the Clock.

Thursday, the 27th of February, 12 George III. 1772.

A *Member* returned upon a new Writ, having taken the Oaths appointed to be taken by Act of Parliament, and repeated and fubfcribed the Teft, took his Place in the Houfe.

Mr *Bland* reported to the Houfe, that the Governor, having been waited upon, purfuant to the Order of *Monday* laft, to know his Pleafure, when he would be attended by this Houfe, had been pleafed to appoint to be attended Tomorrow, in the Council Chamber.

Ordered, That Leave be given to bring in a Bill, to amend and explain an Act, intituled *An Act[3] concerning Water Mills;* and that the Committee of Propofitions and Grievances do prepare, and bring in the fame.

Mr *Treafurer* prefented to the Houfe, according to Order, a Bill for extending the Benefit of the feveral Acts of Toleration to his Majefty's Proteftant Subjects, in this Colony, diffenting from the Church of *England*; and the fame was received, and read the firft Time.

Refolved, That the Bill be read a fecond Time.

A *Petition* of feveral Freeholders and Inhabitants of the Parifh of *Dale*, in the County of *Chefterfield*, whofe Names are thereunto fubfcribed, was prefented to the Houfe, and read; fetting forth, that there is no other Parifh in the faid County, and that there are four Churches, and more than three thoufand Tithables in it; and praying that the faid Parifh may be divided into two Parifhes, by *Falling* Creek, from the Mouth thereof to Col. *Cary's* Mill-Dam, thence by the Road to the Bridge over *Swift* Creek, near the Court-Houfe, and thence by the faid Road to the Mouth of *Winterpock* Creek.

Ordered, That the faid Petition be referred to the Confideration of the Committee for Religion; and that they do examine the Matter thereof, and report the fame, with their Opinion thereupon, to the Houfe.

A *Petition* of *William Rind*, Printer, was prefented to the Houfe, and read; fetting forth, that his Salary, as Printer to the Public, will expire at the End of this Seffion of Affembly; and therefore praying, that the fame may be further continued.

Refolved, That the Sum of four hundred and fifty Pounds *per Annum*, be allowed to *William Rind*, Printer, to continue to the End of the next Seffion of General Affembly, as a full Confideration for printing the Journal of the Houfe of Burgeffes, and the Laws of each Seffion, and fending as many Copies of the Laws to the County

Court

---

[1] Hening, VIII, p. 147.　　[2] Ibid, VIII, p. 407.　　[3] Ibid, VI, p. 55.

Court Clerks, as there are acting Justices in the Commission, in each respective County, and one other, which is to be Half Bound, for the Use of the Court, and ten to the Clerks of the Courts of Hustings, in the City of *Williamsburg*, and Borough of *Norfolk*, and printing Inspectors Receipts, and Books, Proclamations, and Public Advertisements.

Ordered, That Mr *Richard Henry Lee* do carry the Resolution to the Council, and desire their Concurrence.

Ordered, That Mr *Riddick* be added to the Gentlemen, who were appointed to prepare, and bring in a Bill for the more speedy and easy Administration of Justice.

Ordered, That Mr *Moore* be added to the Committee of Propositions and Grievances.

Mr *Edmund Pendleton* reported from the Committee of *Privileges and Elections*, to whom the Petition of several Freeholders of the County of *Henrico*, complaining of an undue Election and Return of Members to serve in this present General Assembly for the said County, was referred, that the Committee had further examined the Matter of the said Petition, and had directed him to report the same, together with the Resolution of the Committee thereupon, to the House; and he read the Report in his Place, and afterwards delivered it in at the Clerk's Table; where the same was read, and is as followeth, *viz.*

It appears to your *Committee*, that Mr *George Cox* was appointed Sheriff of the said County by Commission, dated the 28th of *October*, 1769, and was sworn into Office on the 6th of *November* following; that the Writ for the last Election of Burgesses for the said County came to the Hands of the said *George Cox*, on the 4th Day of *November*, 1771, who, on the same Day, appointed the Election to be made on the 29th of the same Month, and sent Copies of the Writ and Appointment to the Readers of the several Churches (the Minister being out of the Parish) who published the same on the *Sunday* following; that there being no Court held for the said County in the said Month of *November*, to qualify the succeeding Sheriff, and it being supposed that the said *Cox* could not make the Election on the Day appointed, as his two Years would expire before that Time, Mr *Cox*, by Advice of others, and Consent of all of the declared Candidates, on the 17th of *November*, altered the Day of Election to the 6th of *December*, with a View that the succeeding Sheriff might, in the mean Time, be qualified, and take the Election, Notice of which Alteration was published in each Church in the County; that on the 2nd Day of *December*, Mr *Wilkinson*, the succeeding Sheriff, was duly sworn into Office, and proceeded to the Election on the 6th, having first procured the Consent of all the Candidates present, that he might so proceed; that Mr *Adams*, and Mr *Randolph*, upon the Poll, taken in a fair and usual Manner, had the greatest Number of Votes, and were returned as duly elected. It appears to the Committee, that many Freeholders were absent on the Day of Election, but that it was more probably occasioned by the Badness of the Weather than the Want of Notice of the Day last appointed.

Whereupon the *Committee* came to the following Resolution:

Resolved, That it is the Opinion of this Committee, that the said Mr *Adams*, and Mr *Randolph*, are not duly elected to serve as Burgesses in this present General Assembly for the said County of *Henrico*.

The said *Resolution*, being read a second Time, was, upon the Question put thereupon, agreed to by the House.

Ordered, That an Address be made to the Governor, to order a new Writ to issue for the electing of Burgesses to serve in this present General Assembly for the County of *Henrico*, in the Room of Mr *Richard Adams* and Mr *Richard Randolph*, whose Election was illegal; and that Mr *Cary* do wait upon his Excellency with the said Address.

Ordered, That the Committee of Privileges and Elections, to whom the Petition of Mr *Samuel DuVal*, praying that the Poll taken at the Election of Burgesses to serve in this present General Assembly for the County of *Henrico*, may be examined, and that the Petitioner may be declared duly elected a Burgess for the said County, was referred, be discharged from proceeding upon the said Petition.

And the said *Petition* was, by Leave of the House, withdrawn.

A

A *Bill* to prevent Hogs and Goats going at large in the Town of *Suffolk* was read a second Time.

Ordered, That the Bill be engroffed.

Ordered, That Mr *Watkins* have Leave to be abfent from the Service of this Houfe till Tomorrow Sevennight.

Ordered, That Mr *Edmund Pendleton* have Leave to be abfent from the Service of this Houfe till *Thurfday* next.

Mr *Cary* reported from the Committee of Public Claims, to whom the petition of *Daniel Hamlin* was referred, that the Committee had examined the Matter of the faid Petition, and had directed him to report the fame, together with the Refolution of the Committee thereupon, to the Houfe, and he read the Report in his Place, and afterwards delivered it in at the Clerk's Table; where the fame was read, and is as followeth, *viz.*

It appears to your *Committee,* by the Depofitions of *Miller Woodfon,* and *Daniel Hamlin,* jun. that they, the faid Deponents, were, about the 6th of *October,* 1770, at the Houfe of *Daniel Hamlin,* the Petitioner, and faw the Wife of the faid Petitioner lying on a Bed, who appeared to be in great Diftrefs, her Head and Arm being much bruifed, and very bloody, who informed them that it was occafioned by a Negro, known by the Name of *Parriot,* the Property of her Hufband; that, from the appearance of the Wound, together with the Defcription fhe gave of the Weapon with which it was made, they, the faid Deponents, fufpected the faid Negro had attempted to murder her; that about the 20th of *February* following, they, the faid Deponents, being again at the Houfe of the Petitioner, were conducted, by one of the Family, to a Place in the Woods, a fmall Diftance from the Houfe, where, it was fuppofed, the faid Negro *Parriot* had hanged himfelf; that they there faw a human Scull, with feveral other Members of the Body, which they fuppofed were the Remains of the faid Negro *Parriot*; that at the place where the Bones were found the faid Deponent *Daniel* faw fome wearing Apparel, which he well knew belonged to the faid Negro *Parriot*; and further, that he difcovered the faid Negro not till after he was duly outlawed, and believed the faid Outlawry was made before he was known by his Mafter's Family to be dead.

It further appears to your *Committee,* by the Depofitions of *Henry Hamlin,* and *Thomas Roberts,* that about the 6th of *October,* 1770, they, the faid Deponents, being fent for, came to the Houfe of the Petitioner, and faw his Wife much wounded on her Head, and one of her Arms broke; that they were informed by the Petitioner, that he faw his Negro *Parriot* wound his faid Wife, and immediately run away; and that he has not fince been heard of but from the Suppofition of his having hanged himfelf.

It further appears to your *Committee,* by the Depofitions of *John Rowlett,* and *Stephen Neal,* that they, the faid Deponents, were, in the Month of *February* laft, fent for by the Petitioner to fee a Negro of his who had hanged himfelf; that at the Place where it was fuppofed he was hanged, they faw the Bones and Cloathing of a Perfon whom, from the faid Cloathing they believed to be the Slave that they heard outlawed at Church, as a Runaway, belonging to the Petitioner.

Whereupon the *Committee* came to the following Refolution:

Refolved, That it is the Opinion of this Committee, that the faid petition be rejected.

The faid *Refolution,* being read a fecond Time, was, upon the Queftion put thereupon, agreed to by the Houfe.

The Houfe, according to Order, refolved itfelf into a Committee of the whole Houfe, to confider of the Memorial of the Court of Directors, for the Public Hofpital, for Perfons of infane and difordered Minds.

Mr *Speaker* left the Chair.

Mr *Bland* took the Chair of the Committee.

Mr *Speaker* refumed the Chair.

Mr *Bland* reported from the Committee, that they had come to a Refolution, which they had directed him to report to the Houfe; and he read the Report in his Place,

and

and afterwards delivered it in at the Clerk's Table; where the Refolution of the Committee was read, and is as followeth, *viz.*

Refolved, That it is the Opinion of this Committee, that a Sum of Money, not exceeding eight hundred Pounds, be paid by the Treafurer, upon the Governor's Warrant, to the Court of Directors of the Hofpital for Ideots, Lunatics, and Perfons of infane and difordered Minds, to be by them laid out in finifhing the faid Hofpital, and making proper Inclofures for the Patients to walk, and take the Air in.

The faid *Refolution,* being read a fecond Time, was, upon the Queftion put thereupon, agreed to by the Houfe.

Ordered, That a Bill be brought in purfuant to the faid Refolution; and that the Committee of Propofitions and Grievances do prepare, and bring in the fame.

An engroffed *Bill,* to enable *Henrietta Marmillod* to fell and difpofe of the Eftate devifed to her by her Brother, *Nathaniel Walthoe,* Efquire, deceafed, notwithftanding her Coverture, was read the third Time.

Refolved, That the Bill do pafs; and that the Title be *An Act*[1] *to enable* Henrietta Marmillod *to fell and difpofe of the Eftate devifed to her by her Brother,* Nathaniel Walthoe, *Efquire, deceafed, notwithftanding her Coverture.*

Ordered, That Mr *Richard Henry Lee* do carry the Bill to the Council, and defire their Concurrence.

A *Bill* for extending the Benefit of the feveral Acts of Toleration to his Majefty's Proteftant Subjects in this Colony, diffenting from the Church of *England,* was read a fecond Time.

Refolved, That the Bill be committed to the Committee for Religion.

A *Bill* to continue an Act, intituled *An Act*[2] *to continue and amend an Act, intituled An Act for reducing the feveral Acts, made for laying a Duty upon Liquors, into one Act,* was read a fecond Time.

Refolved, That the Bill be committed to the Committee of Trade.

The other *Order* of the Day being read;

The Houfe refolved itfelf into a Committee of the whole Houfe, upon the Bill for cutting a navigable Canal from *Archer's Hope* Creek to *Queen's* Creek, through the City of *Williamfburg.*

Mr *Speaker* left the Chair.

Mr *Bland* took the Chair of the Committee.

Mr *Speaker* refumed the Chair.

Mr *Bland* reported from the Committee, that they had gone through the Bill, and made an Amendment thereunto; which they had directed him to report to the Houfe; and he read the Report in his Place, and afterwards delivered the Bill, with the Amendment, in at the Clerk's Table; where the Amendment was twice read, and, upon the Queftion put thereupon, was agreed to by the Houfe.

Ordered, That the Bill, with the Amendment, be engroffed.

Mr *Bland* reported from the Committee of Propofitions and Grievances, that the Committee had examined the Matter of feveral Petitions to them referred, and had come to feveral Refolutions thereupon, which they had directed him to Report to the Houfe; and he read the Report in his Place, and afterwards delivered it in at the Clerk's Table, where the Refolutions of the Committee were read, and are as followeth, *viz.*

Refolved, That it is the Opinion of this Committee, that the petitions of the Inhabitants of the Town of *Winchefter,* and County of *Frederick,* praying that the faid County may be divided into three Counties, are reafonable.

Refolved, That it is the Opinion of this Committee, that the Petitions of the Inhabitants of the Parifh of *Beckford,* in the County of *Frederick,* praying that the faid County may be divided into two Counties, be rejected.

The faid *Refolutions,* being feverally read a fecond Time, were, upon the Queftion feverally put thereupon, agreed to by the Houfe.

Ordered

---

[1] Hening, VIII, p. 627.   [2] Ibid, VIII, p. 335.

Ordered, That a Bill be brought in purfuant to the *firft* Refolution; and that the Committee of Propofitions and Grievances do prepare, and bring in the fame.

And then the Houfe adjourned till Tomorrow Morning eleven of the Clock.

Friday, the 28th of February, 12 George III. 1772.

MR *Bland*, from the Committee of Correfpondence, prefented to the Houfe, purfuant to their Order, the Letters which have paffed between *Edward Montagu*, Efquire, late Agent for this Colony, and the faid Committee, fince the 1ft Day of *November*, in the Year of our Lord 1769.

Ordered, That the faid Letters do lie upon the Table, to be perufed by the Members of the Houfe.

Ordered, That Mr *Le Grand* have Leave to be abfent from the Service of this Houfe for a Fortnight.

Mr *Bland* reported, from the Committee of propofitions and Grievances, that the Committee had examined the Matters of feveral petitions, to them referred, and had come to feveral Refolutions thereupon, which they had directed him to report to the Houfe; and he read the Report in his Place, and afterwards delivered it in at the Clerk's Table, where the Refolutions of the Committee were read, and are as followeth, *viz.*

Refolved, That it is the Opinion of this Committee, that the petition of *Robert Ruffin*, praying that he may be empowered by Law to erect a Gate acrofs the Public Road leading to the faid *Ruffin's* Ferry, is reafonable.

Refolved, That it is the Opinion of this Committee, that the petition of *Jacob Micheaux*, praying that he may be empowered by Law to erect a Gate acrofs the public Road leading to the faid *Micheaux's* Ferry, is reafonable.

The faid *Refolutions*, being feverally read a fecond Time, were, upon the Queftion feverally put thereupon, agreed to by the Houfe.

Ordered, That a Bill or Bills be brought in purfuant to the faid Refolutions, and that the Committee of Propofitions and Grievances do prepare, and bring in the fame.

Ordered, That it be an Inftruction to the faid Committee, that they have Power to receive a Claufe or Claufes, to enable *Richard Bland*, Efq; to erect a Gate or Gates upon the main Road leading through his Land, upon *Bennet's* Creek, in the County of *Nanfemond*.

A *Claim* of *Henry Riddick*, late Sheriff of the County of *Nanfemond*, for three hundred and fixty Pounds of Tobacco, which were levied on *John Arrington*, and *John Stockdale*, but which he never received, the Debtors having removed to *Carolina*, and left no Eftate in this Colony to fatiffy the fame, was prefented to the Houfe, and read.

Ordered, That it be an Inftruction to the Committee of Public Claims, that they do allow the faid Claim in the Book of Public Claims.

Mr *Bland* reported from the Committee to whom the Bill for further continuing and amending the Act, intituled An Act[1] *for increafing the Reward for killing Wolves within certain Counties, to be paid by the refpective Counties wherein the Services fhall be performed*, was committed, that the Committee had directed him to report the Bill to the Houfe, without any Amendment; and he delivered the Bill in at the Clerk's Table,

Ordered, That the Bill be engroffed.

An engroffed *Bill* to repeal Part of an Act, paffed in the thirty-fecond Year, of the Reign of King *Charles* the Second, intituled An Act[2] *of free and general Pardon Indemnity, and Oblivion*, was read the third Time.

Refolved, That the Bill do pafs; and that the Title be, An Act[3] *to repeal Part of an Act, paffed in the thirty-fecond Year of the Reign of King* Charles *the Second*, intituled An Act *of free and general Pardon, Indemnity, and Oblivion*.

Ordered, That Mr *Eyre* do carry the Bill to the Council, and defire their Concurrence.

A

---

[1] Hening, VIII, p. 147   Ibid II, p. 458.   [3] Not recorded as a law.

A *Bill* to continue an Act, intituled *An Act*[1] *for eftablifhing Pilots, and regulating their Fees*, was read a fecond Time.

Ordered, That the Bill be engroffed.

An engroffed *Bill* to prevent Hogs and Goats going at large in the Town of *Suffolk*, was read the third Time.

Refolved, That the Bill do pafs; and that the Title be, *An Act*[2] *to prevent Hogs and Goats going at large in the Town of* Suffolk.

Ordered, That M[r] *Riddick* do carry the Bill to the Council, and defire their Concurrence.

An engroffed Bill for cutting a navigable Canal from *Archer's Hope* Creek to *Queen's* Creek, through the City of *Williamfburg*, was read the third Time.

Refolved, That the Bill do pafs; and that the Title be, *An Act*[3] *for cutting a navigable Canal from* Archer's Hope *Creek to* Queen's *Creek, through the City of* Williamfburg.

Ordered, That M[r] *Treafurer* do carry the Bill to the Council, and defire their Concurrence.

Ordered, That M[r] *Carr* have Leave to be abfent from the Service of this Houfe till *Monday* Sevennight.

A *Petition* of feveral Perfons of the County of *King & Queen*, whofe Names are thereunto fubfcribed, was prefented to the Houfe, and read; fetting forth, that the Petitioners fuffer great Inconvenience by the Difcontinuance of the Tobacco Infpection at *Walkerton*, and humbly propofing that fo much of the Act of General Affembly as difcontinued the faid Infpection may be repealed, and the Infpection revived.

Ordered, That the faid petition be referred to the Confideration of the Committee of Propofitions and Grievances; and that they do examine the Matter thereof, and report the fame, with their Opinion thereupon, to the Houfe.

A *Petition* of feveral Perfons of the County of *King William*, whofe Names are thereunto fubfcribed, was prefented to the Houfe, and read; fetting forth, that the petitioners fuffer great Inconvenience by the Difcontinuance of the Tobacco Infpection at *Waller's*, and humbly propofing that fo much of the Act of General Affembly as difcontinued the faid Infpection may be repealed, and the Infpection revived.

Ordered, That the faid petition be referred to the Confideration of the Committee of propofitions and Grievances; and that they do examine the Matter thereof, and report the fame, with their Opinion thereupon, to the Houfe.

A *Petition* of *Robert King* was prefented to the Houfe, and read; fetting forth, that the Petitioner is proprietor of the Land on which the *Piping Tree* Warehoufe ftands, and Keeper of a Public Ferry at the fame Place, which is very convenient for an Ordinary, and that he is likewife one of the Infpectors of Tobacco at the faid Warehoufe; and further fetting forth, that the Act of General Affembly, prohibiting Infpectors from keeping public Houfes, is very detrimental to him, and therefore humbly praying that this Honourable Houfe will take the particular Circumftances of his uncommon Cafe into their Confideration, and grant him fuch Relief therein as to them fhall feem juft.

Ordered, That the faid Petition be referred to the Confideration of the Committee of propofitions and Grievances; and that they do examine the Matter thereof, and report the fame, with their Opinion thereupon, to the Houfe.

A *Petition* of feveral Perfons of the Parifh of *St. John*, in the County of *King William*, whofe Names are thereunto fubfcribed, was prefented to the Houfe, and read; fetting forth, that the Veftry of the faid Parifh are divided among themfelves by Party Spirit, which prevents their Meetings, and interrupts their proceeding in the Affairs of the Parifh, and that they are purfuing Meafures detrimental to the Parifhioners; and therefore praying that the faid Veftry may be diffolved.

Ordered, That the faid petition be referred to the Confideration of the Committee for Religion; and that they do examine the Matter thereof, and report the fame, with their Opinion thereupon, to the Houfe.

Several *Petitions* of the Freeholders and Inhabitants of the Counties of *King George*
and

---

[1] Hening, VI, p. 490.   [2] Ibid, VIII, p. 620.   [3] Ibid, VIII, p. 556.

and *Stafford* were prefented to the Houfe, and read; fetting forth, that the faid Counties, in their prefent Form, being long and narrow, are very inconvenient, which may be remedied, if the faid Counties be divided by a Line running from *Potowmack* River to *Rappahannock* River; and therefore praying that the faid Counties may be divided accordingly by a Line to be made by Commiffioners. 50

Ordered, That the faid Petitions be referred to the Confideration of the Committee of Propofitions and Grievances; and that they do examine the Matter thereof, and report the fame, with their Opinion thereupon, to the Houfe.

A *Petition* of *Michael Robinfon* and *John Steward*, Infpectors of Tobacco at *Royfton's* Warehoufe, was prefented to the Houfe, and read; fetting forth, that the Petitioners have as much trouble in their Office, and Infpect nearly as much Tobacco, as the Infpectors at *Frederickfburg* Warehoufe, and yet the Salaries of the Petitioners have been reduced ten Pounds; and therefore humbly praying, that they may have the fame Allowance as they had formerly.

Ordered, That the faid Petition be referred to the Confideration of the Committee of Propofitions and Grievances; and that they do examine the Matter thereof, and report the fame, with their Opinion thereupon, to the Houfe.

A *Petition* of *Daniel Kidd* was prefented to the Houfe, and read; fetting forth, that, in the Year 1768, the Petitioner was fummoned by the Sheriff of *Augufta* County, to attend at the Capitol in *Williamfburg*, as one of the Jury, upon the Trial of *Robert Macmahon*, a Criminal, but that the Sheriff having omitted to infert the Petitioner's Name in the Panel returned upon the Venire Facias, although he attended according to the Summons, he was not allowed for it; and therefore praying Relief.

Ordered, That the faid petition be referred to the Confideration of the Committee of Public Claims; and that they do examine the Matter thereof, and report the fame, with their Opinion thereupon, to the Houfe.

Ordered, That Mr *Roane* have Leave to be abfent from the Service of this Houfe till this Day Sevennight.

A *Claim* of *Edward Niblet*, for taking up a Runaway Slave, which had been prefented at the laft General Affembly, but was not allowed, becaufe the Name of the Owner of the Slave was not known, was prefented to the Houfe, and read.

Ordered, That the faid Claim be referred to the Confideration of the Committee of Public Claims; and that they do examine the Matter thereof, and report the fame, with their Opinion thereupon, to the Houfe.

Ordered, That Leave be given to bring in a Bill, to explain and amend an Act, intituled *An Act[1] prefcribing the Method of appointing Sheriffs, and for limiting the Time of their Continuance in Office, and directing their Duty therein;* and that the Committee of Propofitions and Grievances do prepare, and bring in the fame.

Ordered, That Leave be given to bring in a Bill, to amend an Act, intituled *An Act[2] directing the Trial of Slaves committing capital Crimes, and for the more effectual punifhing Confpiracies and Infurrections of them, and for the better Government of Negroes, Mulattoes, and Indians, bond or free;* and that the Committee of propofitions and Grievances do prepare, and bring in the fame.

A *Meffage* from the Governor by Mr *Blair*.

Mr *Speaker*,
The *Governor is now ready to receive the Addrefs of your Houfe in the Council Chamber.*

Accordingly Mr *Speaker*, with the Houfe, went up; and, being returned, he reported, that the Houfe had attended the Governor, with their Addrefs, to which his Excellency was pleafed to give this Anfwer.

Mr *Speaker and Gentlemen of the Houfe of Burgeffes, I am obliged to you for your polite Addrefs; and as you are of Opinion that the Fees received by the Clerks of my Predeceffors* 51

---

[1] Hening, V, p. 515. [2] Ibid, IV, p. 126.

ceffors, for iffuing public Commiffions, were illegal, I will not only take Care that my Clerk fhall not in future receive any, but alfo that he fhall return thofe which he has received fince my Arrival in this Colony.

Refolved, Nemine Contradicente, That the Sincere and grateful Thanks of this Houfe be returned to his Excellency the Governor, for the kind and obliging Anfwer he was pleafed to make to the Addrefs of this Houfe.

Ordered, That Mr *Bland,* Mr *Harrifon,* Mr *Treafurer,* Mr *Edmund Pendleton,* Mr *Cary,* and Mr *Richard Henry Lee,* do wait upon his Excellency with the faid Refolution.

And then the Houfe adjourned till Tomorrow Morning eleven of the Clock.

Saturday. the 29th of February. 12 George lll. 1772.

MR *Cary* reported from the Committee of Public Claims, to whom the Petition of *William Bruce* and *William Harrifon,* Infpectors at *Gibfon's* and *Morton's* Warehoufes, in the County of *King George,* was referred, that the Committee had examined the Matter of the faid Petition, and had directed him to report the fame, as it appeared to them, together with the Refolutions of the Committee thereupon, to the Houfe; and he read the Report in his Place, and afterwards delivered it in at the Clerk's Table; where the fame was read, and is as followeth, *viz.*

It appears to your *Committee,* that the Houfe, in which two of the Hogfheads of Tobacco that were loft had been depofited, were infufficient; that the other Hogfhead was taken out of a fufficient Houfe, with feveral more, for the purpofe of coming at fome particular Tobacco, which was wanted to be fhipped off; that the Petitioners, not being able to replace them immediately, rolled them into an open Houfe, where they remained a few Days, in which Time the faid Hogfhead of Tobacco was loft. It further appears to your Committee, that, by Means of a great Rain that fell in the Month of *May* laft, the Water flowed into one of the faid Warehoufes, and partly damaged thirty-nine Hogfheads of Tobacco, which lay next to the Ground; that the Petitioners uncafed the fame, and feparated the good Tobacco from the bad, and found the bad to be fifteen hundred and fixty-eight Pounds. It further appears to your Committee, that *Robert Gilchrift,* Proprietor of fourteen Hogfheads, and *Thomas Hodge,* of feven Hogfheads, being Part of the thirty-nine Hogfheads of Tobacco damaged as aforefaid, have refufed to receive the fame, and that the faid *Gilchrift* has commenced an Action at Law againft the Petitioners for the Recovery of the faid fourteen Hogfheads, for which he paid at the Rate of twenty Shillings *Per Cent.* and that the faid *Hodge* paid, for the feven Hogfheads aforefaid, at the Rate of fourteen Shillings, Sterling, *per Cent.* and charges the Petitioners the Sums of eighteen Pence *per* Hogfhead, for the Difference of Infpection, and three Shillings and fix Pence, *per* Hogfhead, Freight.

Whereupon the *Committee* came to the following Refolutions;

Refolved, That it is the Opinion of this Committee, that fo much of the faid petition, as relates to the Tobacco ftolen out of the faid Warehoufes, be rejected.

Refolved, That it is the Opinion of this Committee, that fo much of the faid Petition, as relates to the damaged Tobacco, is reafonable; and that the Petitioners ought to be allowed for the fame, at the Rate of eighteen Shillings *per Cent.* and the further Sum of four Pounds feventeen Shillings and fix Pence for their Trouble, in uncafing and trimming the faid thirty nine Hogfheads of Tobacco, and fecuring the good that was faved.

The *firft* Refolution of the Committee, being read a fecond Time, was, upon the Queftion put thereupon, agreed to by the Houfe.

The fubfequent *Refolution* of the Committee, being read a fecond Time;

Ordered, That the faid Refolution be recommitted.

Ordered, That the faid Refolution be recommitted to the faid Committee to whom the Petition of the faid *William Bruce,* and *William Harrifon,* was referred.

Mr

Mr *Bland* prefented to the Houfe, according to Order, a Bill for further continuing the Acts for better regulating and difciplining the Militia; and the fame was received, and read the firft Time.

Refolved, That the Bill be read a fecond Time.

An engroffed *Bill* for further continuing and amending the Act, intituled *An Act[1] for increafing the Reward for killing Wolves within certain Counties, to be paid by the refpect-ive Counties wherein the Services fhall be performed*, was read the third Time.

Refolved, That the Bill do pafs; and that the Title be, *An Act[2] for further continu-ing and amending the Act, intituled An Act for increafing the Reward for killing Wolves within certain Counties, to be paid by the refpective Counties wherein the Services fhall be performed*.

Ordered, That Mr *Richard Henry Lee* do carry the Bill to the Council, and defire their Concurrence.

Ordered, That Mr *Smith*, and Mr *Edmondfon*, have Leave to be abfent from the Service of this Houfe till *Monday* Sevennight.

Mr *Treafurer* reported from the Committee for Religion, to whom feveral Petitions were referred, that the Committee had examined the Matters of the faid Petitions, and had come to feveral Refolutions thereupon, which they had directed him to report to the Houfe; and he read the Report in his Place, and afterwards delivered it in at the Clerk's Table; where the Refolutions of the Committee were read, and are as followeth, *viz.*

Refolved, That it is the Opinion of this Committee, that the petition of fundry In-habitants of the upper End of the Parifh of *Southam*, in the County of *Cumberland*, praying a Divifion thereof, is reafonable.

Refolved, That it is the Opinion of this Committee, that the petition of the Free-holders and Inhabitants of *Dale* Parifh, in the County of *Chefterfield*, praying a Divifion thereof, is reafonable.

The faid *Refolutions* being feverally read a fecond Time, were, upon the Queftion feverally put thereupon, agreed to by the Houfe.

Ordered, That a Bill or Bills be brought in, purfuant to the faid Refolutions; and that the Committee for Religion do prepare, and bring in the fame.

Ordered, That Mr *Eyre* have Leave to be abfent from the Service of this Houfe till *Thurfday* next.

Mr *Bland* reported from the Committee of Propofitions and Grievances, to whom the Petitions of the Inhabitants of the Counties of *King George* and *Stafford*, praying that a new Boundary Line between the faid Counties may be made by Commiffioners, were referred, that the Committee had examined the Matter of the faid Petitions, and had come to a Refolution thereupon, which they had directed him to report to the Houfe; and he read the Report in his Place, and afterwards delivered it in at the Clerk's Table; where the Refolution of the Committee was read, and is as followeth, *viz.*

Refolved, That it is the Opinion of this Committee, that the faid Petitions are rea-fonable.

The faid *Refolution* being read a fecond Time, was, upon the Queftion put thereupon, agreed to by the Houfe.

Ordered, That a Bill be brought in purfuant to the faid Refolution; and that Mr *Alexander*, Mr *Jofeph Jones*, Mr *Fitzhugh*, and Mr *Yelverton Peyton*, do prepare, and bring in the fame.

Mr *Cary* reported from the Committee of Public Claims, to whom the Petition of *William Bruce*, and *David Bronaugh*, Infpectors at *Morton's* Warehoufes, in the County of *King George*, was referred, that the Committee had examined the Matter of the faid Petition, and had directed him to report the fame, as it appeared to them, together with the Refolution of the Committee thereupon, to the Houfe; and he read the Report in his Place, and afterwards delivered it in at the Clerk's Table; where the fame was read, and is as followeth, *viz.*

It appears to your *Committee*, that, at the Time the Tobacco was loft, as fet forth in the faid Petition, the faid Warehoufes were infufficient.

Whereupon

---

[1] Hening, VIII, p. 147.   [2] Ibid, VIII, p. 595.

Whereupon the *Committee* came to the following Refolution;

Refolved, That it is the Opinion of this Committee, that the faid Petition be rejected.

The faid *Refolution,* being read a fecond Time, was, upon the Queftion put thereupon, agreed to by the Houfe.

Mr *Bland* prefented to the Houfe, according to Order, a Bill for further continuing the Act, intituled *An Act*[1] for *reducing the feveral Acts of Affembly for making Provifion againft Invafions and Infurrections, into one Act;* and the fame was received, and read the firft Time.

Refolved, That the Bill be read a fecond Time.

A *Petition* of *Ralph Gibbs, Jofeph Laurence, Robert Laurence, Jofeph Outland, Jofiah Outland,* and *Robert Laurence,* Junior, of the Parifh of *Suffolk,* in the County of *Nanfemond,* was prefented to the Houfe, and read; fetting forth, that the Petitioners refide in, and are the only Inhabitants of a Place, called *Rofcow's Neck,* in an extreme Part of the faid County, and that they are at a great diftance from their County Court-Houfe, and neareft Parifh Church, and have no Paffage to either of thofe Places, or indeed any other public Place, in their own County, without travelling feveral Miles through the County of *Ifle of Wight,* and therefore humbly praying that the faid Neck of Land may be added to the Parifh of *Newport,* and County of *Ifle of Wight,* to which the Petitioners are much more convenient.

Ordered, That Leave be given to bring in a Bill purfuant to the Prayer of the faid Petition; and that Mr *Hardy* and Mr *Riddick* do prepare, and bring in the fame.

Mr *Cary* reported from the Committee of Public Claims, to whom the petitions of feveral Perfons were referred, that the Committee had examined the Matters of the faid petitions, and had come to feveral Refolutions thereupon; which they had directed him to report to the Houfe; and he read the Report in his Place, and afterwards delivered it in at the Clerk's Table; where the Refolutions of the Committee were read, and are as followeth, *viz.*

Refolved, That it is the Opinion of this Committee, that fo much of the Petition of *Auftin Hewlet,* furviving Infpector at *Waddy's* Warehoufe, in *New Kent* County, as relates to the Tobacco ftolen out of the faid Warehoufe, for which the petitioner has paid the Proprietor thereof, is reafonable; and that he ought to be reimburfed the Sum of three Pounds and fifteen Shillings for the fame.

Refolved, That it is the Opinion of this Committee, that fo much of the faid petition, as relates to the Cofts expended by the petitioner, in defending a Suit commenced againft him, for the Recovery of the Value of the faid Tobacco, be rejected.

Refolved, That it is the Opinion of this Committee, that the Petition of *Daniel Kidd,* to be allowed for travelling to, and attending the General Court, as a Venire Man, on the Trial of *Robert Macmahon,* is reafonable; and that he ought to be allowed fix hundred and fifty Pounds of Tobacco, for the fame.

The faid *Refolutions,* being feverally read a fecond Time, were, upon the Queftion feverally put thereupon, agreed to by the Houfe.

Mr *Bland* prefented to the Houfe, according to Order, a Bill, for building a Bridge over the Weftern Branch of *Nanfemond* River, by Subfcription; and the fame was received, and read the firft Time.

Refolved, That the Bill be read a fecond Time.

An engroffed *Bill,* to continue an Act, intituled *An Act*[2] *for eftablifhing Pilots, and regulating their Fees,* was read the third Time.

Refolved, That the Bill do pafs; and that the Title be, *An Act*[3] *to continue an Act, intituled An Act for eftablifhing Pilots, and regulating their Fees.*

Ordered, That Mr *Harrifon* do carry the Bill to the Council, and defire their Concurrence.

And then the Houfe adjourned till Monday Morning next, eleven of the Clock.

𝔐onday

---

[1] Hening, VIII, p. 514.   [2] Ibid, VI, p. 490.   [3] Ibid, VIII, p. 542.

Monday, the 2d of March, 12 George III. 1772.

SEVERAL other *Members* having taken the Oaths appointed to be taken by Act of Parliament, and repeated and fubfcribed the Teft, took their Places in the Houfe.

And then the Houfe adjourned till Tomorrow Morning, eleven of the Clock.

Tuesday, the 3d of March, 12 George III. 1772.

SEVERAL other *Members*, having taken the Oaths, appointed to be taken by Act of Parliament, and repeated and fubfcribed the Teft, took their Places in the Houfe.

A *Petition* of *James Blackwell*, the younger, was prefented to the Houfe, and read; fetting forth, that the Petitioner was feifed, as Tenant in Fee Tail, of a Tract of Land, in *Blackwell's* Neck, in the County of *Hanover*, containing about five hundred Acres, and having no Slaves, hath been obliged to fell and difpofe of the fame for his Lifetime, and hath agreed to exchange the Reverfion with *Carter Braxton*, of the County of *King William*, Efquire, for a Tract of Land, in the laft mentioned County, containing two hundred and fixty Acres, and certain Negro Slaves; and therefore praying that an Act may pafs to veft the Reverfion of the faid five hundred Acres of Land in the faid *Carter Braxton*, and his Heirs, and to fettle, in Lieu thereof, the faid two hundred and fixty Acres, with the Slaves aforefaid, upon the petitioner, in Fee Tail.

Ordered, That Leave be given to bring in a Bill purfuant to the Prayer of the faid Petition; and that Mr *Treafurer* do prepare, and bring in the fame.

A *Petition* of *John Robinfon*, late a Soldier in the *Virginia* Regiment, was prefented to the Houfe, and read; fetting forth, that he had ferved fix years in the faid Regiment, and received feveral Wounds, which difabled him from Maintaining himfelf by his own Labour, and had been captivated by the Enemy; and that he had been prevented from applying to this Houfe, with other Perfons in his Circumftances, to whom their Bounty was extended, and therefore praying Relief.

Ordered, That the faid Petition be referred to the Confideration of a Committee; and that they do examine the Matter thereof, and report the fame, with their Opinion thereupon, to the Houfe;

And it is *referred* to Mr *Wafhington*, Mr *Henry Lee*, and Mr *Lewis*.

Ordered, That Leave be given to bring in a Bill to explain and amend an Act, intituled *An Act*[1] *to oblige the Owners of Mills, Hedges, or Stops, on the Rivers therein mentioned, to make Openings or Slopes therein, for the Paffage of Fifh;* and that Mr *Marfhall* do prepare, and bring in the fame.

Mr *Henry Lee* prefented to the Houfe, according to Order, a Bill for better regulating the Election of Veftries; and the fame was received, and read the firft Time.

Refolved, That the Bill be read a fecond Time.

Mr *Bland* prefented to the Houfe, according to Order, a Bill for further continuing the Acts for the more effectual keeping the public Roads and Bridges in Repair; and the fame was received, and read the firft Time.

Refolved, That the Bill be read a fecond Time.

Ordered, That Mr *Wafhington* and Mr *Francis Peyton* be added to the Committee for Religion.

Ordered, That Mr *Wafhington* be added to the Committee of Privileges and Elections.

Ordered, That Mr *Tabb* and Mr *Wafhington* be added to the Committee of Propofitions and Grievances.

Ordered, That Mr *Henry Pendleton*, Mr *Field*, Mr *Francis Peyton*, Mr *Stith*, Mr *Barbour*, and Mr *Burnley*, be added to the Committee for Courts of Juftice.

Ordered, That Mr *Tabb* be added to the Committee of Trade.

Ordered

[1] Hening, VIII. p. 361.

Ordered, That M*r* *Henry Pendleton*, M*r* *Stith*, M*r* *Field*, M*r* *Barbour*, and M*r* *Burnley*, be added to the Committee of Public Claims.

M*r* *Bland* prefented to the Houfe, according to Order, a Bill for dividing the County of *Frederick* into three diftinct Counties; and the fame was received, and read the firft Time.

Refolved, That the Bill be read a fecond Time.

A *Complaint* being made to the Houfe, that, in Breach of the Privilege of this Houfe, *Roger Gregory*, of the County of *King William*, had caufed one *Holt Richefon* to be arrefted, at the Suit of the faid *Roger Gregory*, whilft the faid *Holt Richefon* was attending, as a Witnefs, in a Matter depending before the Committee for Religion;

Ordered, That it be referred to the Committee of Privileges and Elections, to examine the Matter of the faid Complaint, and report the fame, with their Opinion thereupon, to the Houfe.

A *Petition* of *David Vaughan*, and *William Dews*, Infpectors of Tobacco at *Gloucefter* Town Warehoufe, was prefented to the Houfe, and read; fetting forth, that in the Month of *September*, 1770, the faid Warehoufe was broke open, and four thoufand Pounds Weight of Tobacco were ftolen therefrom, without any Neglect or Default of the Petitioners, for the Value whereof they are anfwerable to the Owners; and therefore praying that that may be allowed for the faid Tobacco by the Public.

Ordered, That the faid petition be referred to the Confideration of the Committee of Public Claims; and that they do examine the Matter thereof, and report the fame, with their Opinion thereupon, to the Houfe.

A *Meffage* from the Council by M*r* *Blair*.

M*r* *Speaker*,

The Council have agreed to the Bill, *intituled*, An Act[1] to revive the Act, intituled An Act for giving a Salary to the Speaker of the Houfe of Burgeffes, *without any Amendment; and alfo*

The Council have agreed to the Bill, *intituled* An Act[2] for further continuing the Act, intituled An Act for appointing a Treafurer, *without any Amendment; and alfo,*

The Council have agreed to the Bill, *intituled* An Act[3] for further continuing and amending the Act, intituled An Act for increafing the Reward for killing Wolves, within certain Counties, to be paid by the refpective Counties, wherein the Services fhall be performed, *without any Amendment; and alfo,*

The Council have agreed to the Bill, *intituled* An Act[4] to enable *Henrietta Marmillod* to fell and difpofe of the Eftate devifed her by her Brother *Nathaniel Walthoe*, Efq; deceafed, notwithftanding her Coverture, *without any Amendment; and alfo,*

The Council have agreed to the Refolve *for paying four hundred and fifty Pounds* per Annum *to* William Rind, *the Public Printer; and alfo,*

The Council have agreed to the Bill, *intituled* An Act[5] to prevent Hogs and Goats going at large in the Town of *Suffolk*, with an Amendment, *to which Amendment the Council defire the Concurrence of this Houfe.*

And then the Meffenger withdrew.

The Houfe proceeded to take the faid Amendment into Confideration.

And the faid Amendment was read, and is as followeth, *viz.*

Line 8, after "*Goat*" infert "*belonging to any of the Inhabitants of the faid Town.*"

The faid *Amendment*, being read a fecond Time, was, upon the Queftion put thereupon, agreed to by the Houfe.

Ordered, That M*r* *Riddick* do carry the Bill to the Council, and acquaint them, that this Houfe hath agreed to the Amendment made by them.

A *Bill* for vefting in Truftees certain Lands, whereof *William Booth*, Gentleman, and *Elizabeth* his Wife, are feized in Fee Tail, to be fold, and for laying out the Money

arifing

---

[1] Hening, VIII, p. 587.   [2] Ibid, VIII, p. 588   [3] Ibid, VIII, p. 595.   [4] Ibid, VIII, p. 627.
[5] Ibid, VIII, p. 620.

arifing from the Sale in purchafing other Lands, to be fettled to the fame Ufes, was read 56
a fecond Time.

Refolved, That the Bill be committed to Mr *Richard Henry Lee*, Mr *Richard Lee*,
Mr *Thornton*, Mr *Ball*, Mr *Robert Wormeley Carter*, Mr *Francis Lightfoot Lee*, Mr *Jofeph
Jones*, and Mr *Fitzhugh*.

Ordered, That Mr *Winn* be added to the Committee of Public Claims.

A *Bill* for building a Bridge over the Weftern Branch of *Nanfemond* River, by Subfcription, was read a fecond Time.

Ordered, That the Bill be engroffed.

A *Bill* for further continuing the Act, for better regulating and difciplining the
Militia, was read a fecond Time.

Refolved, That the Bill be committed to the Committee of Propofitions and Grievances.

A *Bill*, for further continuing the Act intituled, *An Act[1] for reducing the feveral
Acts of Affembly for making Provifion againft Invafions and Infurrections, into one Act*,
was read a fecond Time.

Ordered, That the Bill be engroffed.

Ordered, That Mr *James Henry* be added to the Gentlemen, who were appointed to
prepare, and bring in a Bill, for the more fpeedy and eafy Adminiftration of Juftice.

Ordered, That nine of the faid Committee be a fufficient Number to proceed on
Bufinefs.

A *Petition* of *John Pitt* was prefented to the Houfe, and read; fetting forth, that
the petitioner is feifed of a Tract of Land, containing two thoufand and three hundred
Acres, in the County of *Accomack*, whereon a Public Warehoufe for the Infpection of
Tobacco ftands; and that the faid Tract of Land, on three Sides thereof, is bounded by
Waters, which form a Neck about four Miles long, and one Mile broad, and, by Means
of the Roads leading to the faid Warehoufe, is rendered of little Value to the Petitioner;
and therefore praying that an Act may pafs to empower the Petitioner to erect Gates
acrofs the faid Roads.

Ordered, That the faid Petition be referred to the Confideration of the Committee of
Propofitions and Grievances; and that they do examine the Matter thereof, and report
the fame, with their Opinion thereupon, to the Houfe.

A *Petition* of the Merchants, Traders, and Inhabitants of the Town of *Alexandria*,
and County of *Fairfax*, whofe Names are thereunto fubfcribed, was prefented to
the Houfe, and read; alledging that the Petitioners did, in the laft Seffion of General
Affembly, apply by Petition to this Houfe, fetting forth the bad Condition of the Roads
from the Mountains to the Town of *Alexandria*, and praying the Houfe to devife fome
Method for making the Roads more ufeful; which petition was referred to the Confideration of a Committee, who agreed upon a Report, and alfo came to a Refolution; but the
Relief propofed to be granted by the faid Refolution was not carried into Execution;
and reprefenting to the Houfe, that unlefs fome Provifion be made in this important
Affair, the Country in general, as well as the Petitioners, muft fuffer confiderably; and
therefore praying the Houfe to take the Matter into Confideration, and grant fuch
Relief as fhall feem proper.

Ordered, That the faid Petition be referred to the Confideration of the Committee
of Propofitions and Grievances; and that they do examine the Matter thereof, and report
the fame, with their Opinion thereupon, to the Houfe.

A *Bill*, for further continuing the Act, for the more effectual keeping the Public
Roads and Bridges in repair, was read a fecond Time.

Refolved, That the Bill be committed to the Committee of Propofitions and Grievances.

Mr *Hardy* prefented to the Houfe, according to Order, a Bill for adding Part of the
County of *Nanfemond* to the County of *Ifle of Wight*; and the fame was received, and 57
read the firft Time.

Refolved

---

[1] Hening, VIII, p. 514.

Refolved, That the Bill be read a fecond Time.

Ordered, That Mr *Dandridge* have Leave to be abfent from the Service of this Houfe till *Friday* next.

Several *Petitions* of fundry Inhabitants of the County of *Spotfylvania*, whofe Names are thereunto fubfcribed, was prefented to the Houfe, and read; taking Notice of feveral Petitions of other Inhabitants of the faid County, formerly prefented to the Houfe, fetting forth, that the Petitioners had long laboured under many Grievances from the inconvenient Situation of their Court-Houfe; and praying the Houfe to make Application to the Commanding Officer of the Colony to iffue his Writ of Adjournment, and appoint the Court to be held at fome Place neareft to the Center of the County; and reprefenting, that, if thofe Petitioners fhould be indulged in what they defire, it would be no Relief to them, but rather a greater Inconvenience than the one they complain of, and that the Town of *Frederickfburg*, in which the faid Court-Houfe ftands, is the moft convenient Place for it; and therefore praying that the faid former petitions for appointing the faid Court to be held at another Place, may be rejected.

Ordered, That the faid Petitions be referred to the Confideration of the Committee of Propofitions and Grievances; and that they do examine the Matter thereof, and report the fame, with their Opinion thereupon, to the Houfe.

Mr *Bland* reported from the Committee of Privileges and Elections, to whom the Complaint that, in Breach of the Privilege of this Houfe, *Roger Gregory*, of the County of *King William*, had caufed one *Holt Richefon* to be arrefted, at the Suit of the faid *Roger Gregory*, whilft the faid *Holt Richefon* was attending as a Witnefs before the Committee for Religion, was referred, that the Committee had examined the Matter of the faid Complaint; and had directed him to report the fame, together with the Refolutions of the Committee thereupon, to the Houfe; and he read the Report in his Place, and afterwards delivered it in at the Clerk's Table; where the fame was read, and is as followeth, *viz.*

It appears to your *Committee*, that Mr *Holt Richefon*, being requefted to communicate to the feveral Veftrymen of the Parifh of *Saint John*, in the County of *King William*, the Copy of a petition preferred to the Houfe, for a Diffolution of the faid Veftry, and alfo the Refolutions of the Houfe thereupon, did accordingly communicate them, among others, to Mr *Roger Gregory*, a Member of the faid Veftry, who read the faid Refolutions, and was informed, by the faid *Richefon*, that he, the faid *Richefon*, was fummoned as a Witnefs to attend the Committee of Religion, on the fecond Inftant, having received a Letter from Mr *Aylett*, one of the Reprefentatives for the faid County of *King William*, that he had fent up a fummons for that Purpofe, to which the faid *Gregory* made anfwer, he hoped he fhould be down fooner as a Burgefs for the faid County. That fuch Summons, was accordingly ferved on the faid *Richefon*, and in Obedience thereto he did attend the faid Committee of Religion.

It further appears to your *Committee*, that the faid Mr *Roger Gregory* wrote the following Letter, with the Memorandum at Top, directed to Mr *John Tazewell*.

Roger Gregory	*verfus John Quarles*, fenior, Cafe, Damage,	£ 600
Same	*verfus James Quarles*, Cafe, Damage,	70
Same	*vorfus Holt Richefon*, Cafe, Damage,	600

Mr. Tazewell.

Sir,

If the above Gentlemen fhould be in Williamfburg, *as I expect, fhall be much obliged to you to commence Suit againft them, or either of them, as above, to* York Court; *and as they are weighty Suits, fhall be further oblige to you, to speak to* Mr Richard Starke, *to join you in them for me. As foon as I hear the Suit is commenced, will furnifh you with the Accounts, as well as fend you both your Fees.*

I am,

Sir,

Your very humble Servant,

Roger Gregory.

To Mr *John Tazewell.*

February 29, 1772.

That

That, in Confequence of the faid Letter, the faid Mr *Tazewell* applied to Mr *Everard*, the Clerk of *York*, who iffued a Writ agreeable to the Memorandum at the Head of the faid Letter, againft Mr *Richefon*, which was delivered to Mr *Ruffell*, the Under Sheriff of the faid County, who executed the fame, and detains the faid *Richefon* in Cuftody; but that neither Mr *Everard* nor Mr *Tazewell* knew, that the faid *Richefon* was fummoned to attend the Committee as a Witnefs.

It further appears to your *Committee*, that the faid *Ruffell*, the Under Sheriff, about an Hour after he had arrefted Mr *Richefon*, being informed by the faid *Richefon*, that he was fummoned as a Witnefs, as aforefaid, and could not be legally arrefted, applied to a Member of this Houfe, for his Advice and Directions, who informed the faid *Ruffell* 58 of the ftanding Order of the Houfe, that all Witneffes attending the Committees fhould be privileged from Arrefts, but gave him no particular Advice; whereupon another Member of the Houfe told the faid *Ruffell*, who feemed to be under great Difficulty and Uneafinefs, that he would be anfwerable for Mr *Richefon* till the Determination of the Houfe could be had thereupon; and that the faid *Ruffell*, of his own Accord, attended, in order to be informed of fuch Determination.

Upon the whole *Matter*, your Committee came to the following Refolutions;

Refolved, That it is the Opinion of this Committee, that the faid *Roger Gregory* is guilty of a high Contempt and Breach of the Privileges of the Houfe.

Refolved, That it is the Opinion of this Committee, that Mr *Thomas Everard* and Mr *John Tazewell* are not guilty of a Breach of the Privileges of the Houfe.

Refolved, That it is the Opinion of this Committee, that the faid *William Ruffell* is guilty of a Breach of the privileges of the Houfe, by detaining the faid *Richefon* in his Cuftody, after he was informed, that the faid *Richefon* was under the Protection of the Houfe.

The faid *Refolutions*, being feverally read a fecond Time, were, upon the Queftion feverally put thereupon, agreed to by the Houfe.

Ordered, That the faid *Roger Gregory*, for his faid Contempt and Breach of Privilege, be taken into Cuftody of the Sargeant at Arms, attending this Houfe; and that Mr *Speaker* do iffue his Warrant accordingly.

Ordered, That Mr *William Ruffell* be excufed, inafmuch as his Offence appears to have proceeded from the Difficulties he was under how to act on the Occafion.

Ordered, That the faid *William Ruffell* do forthwith difcharge the faid *Holt Richefon* out of Cuftody, for which this Houfe will indemnify the faid *William Ruffell*.

Ordered, That the faid *William Ruffell* do forthwith difcharge *John Quarles*, the elder, whom, in Breach of the Privilege of this Houfe, the faid *Roger Gregory* had caufed to be arrefted at his Suit, whilft the faid *John Quarles* was attending, as a Witnefs, in a Matter depending before the Committee for Religion, out of Cuftody, for which this Houfe will indemnify the faid *William Ruffell*.

Ordered, That Mr *Carrington* have Leave to be abfent from the Service of this Houfe till the twenty-fifth Day of this Inftant.

And then the Houfe adjourned till Tomorrow Morning eleven of the Clock.

Wednesday, the 4th of March, 12 George III. 1772.

A Petition of *Elizabeth Derrick*, Widow, in Behalf of herfelf, and her Son *Benjamin Goff*, an Infant, was prefented to the Houfe, and read; fetting forth, that in the Month of *January*, 1770, *Jack*, a Negro Man Slave, belonging to the Eftate of the Petitioner's former Hufband, was committed to the Gaol of the County of *Weftmoreland*, charged with Felony, and was found guilty of Hogftealing; and that, during his Confinement, he was fo froftbitten, that in a few Days after his Trial he died; and therefore praying, that the Houfe will allow the Petitioner the Value of the faid Slave.

Ordered, That the faid Petition be referred to the Confideration of the Committee

of

of Public Claims; and that they do examine the Matter thereof, and report the fame, with their Opinion thereupon, to the Houfe.

Mr *Richard Henry Lee* reported from the Committee, to whom the Bill for vefting in Truftees certain Lands, whereof *William Booth*, Gentleman, and *Elizabeth* his Wife are feifed in Fee Tail, to be fold, and for laying out the Money, arifing from the Sale, in purchafing other Lands, to be fettled to the fame Ufes, was committed, that the Committee had examined the Allegations of the Bill, and found the fame to be true; and that the Committee had directed him to report the Bill to the Houfe, without any Amendment; and he delivered the Bill in at the Clerk's Table.

Ordered, That the Bill be engroffed.

Ordered, That Mr *Mofeley* have Leave to be abfent from the Service of this Houfe till *Monday* Sevennight.

Mr *Bland* prefented to the Houfe, according to Order, a Bill to remove the Seat of Government to a Place more convenient to the Inhabitants of this Colony; and the fame was received, and read the firft Time.

And the *Queftion* being put, that the Bill be read a fecond Time;

The Houfe divided.

The *Noes* went forth.

Teller for the *Yeas*, Mr *Charles Carter*,   45
Teller for the *Noes*, Mr *Harrifon*,   32

So it was refolved in the Affirmative.

The *Order* of the Day being read, for the fecond reading of the Bill for appointing an Agent;

The faid *Bill* was read a fecond Time.

Refolved, That the Bill be committed.

Refolved, That the Bill be committed to a Committee of the whole Houfe.

Refolved, That this Houfe will, upon *Friday* next, refolve itfelf into a Committee of the whole Houfe upon the faid Bill.

Ordered, That all the Letters which have paffed between the Committee of Correfpondence and *Edward Montagu*, Efq; late Agent for this Colony, fince his Appointment until the firft Day of *November*, 1769, be laid before the Houfe.

Mr *Bland* prefented to the Houfe, according to Order, a Bill to empower the Corporation of the Borough of *Norfolk* to affefs a Tax on the Inhabitants thereof, for the Purpofe therein mentioned; and the fame was received, and read the firft Time.

Refolved, That the Bill be read a fecond Time.

Mr *Wafhington* reported from the Committee, to whom the Petition of *John Robinfon* late a Soldier in the *Virginia* Regiment, was referred, that the Committee had examined the Matter of the faid Petition; and had come to a Refolution thereupon, which they had directed him to report to the Houfe; and he read the Report in his Place, and afterwards delivered it in at the Clerk's Table, where the Refolution of the Committee was read, and is as followeth, *viz.*

Refolved, That it is the Opinion of this Committee, that the faid petition is reafonable; and that the Petitioner ought to be allowed the Sum of five Pounds, for his prefent Relief, and the further Sum of fix Pounds, *per Annum*, during Life, as a Confideration for the Wounds he received, and the Hardfhips he underwent, in the Service of the Colony.

The faid *Refolution*, being read a fecond Time, was, upon the Queftion put thereupon, agreed to by the Houfe.

Refolved, That the Sum of five Pounds be paid to *John Robinfon*, late a Soldier in the *Virginia* Regiment; and that the Sum of fix Pounds, *per Annum*, be paid to the faid *John Robinfon*, during his Life, as a Recompence for the Wounds he received, and the Hardfhips he underwent, in the Service of his County.

Ordered, That Mr *Wafhington* do carry the Refolution to the Council, and defire their Concurrence.

A *Petition* of feveral perfons, of the County of *Loudoun*, whofe Names are thereunto fubfcribed, was prefented to the Houfe, and read; fetting forth, that a public Ferry over

Potowmack

Potowmack River, from the Land of the Right Honourable the Earl of *Tankerville*, at a Plantation in Poffeffion of *John Furrow* and *Alexander Ream*, would be very convenient; and therefore praying, that an Act may pafs for eftablifhing a Ferry there.

Ordered, That the faid petition be referred to the Confideration of the Committee of Propofitions and Grievances; and that they do examine the Matter thereof, and report the fame, with their Opinion thereupon, to the Houfe.

A *Petition* of *Philip Hand* was prefented to the Houfe, and read; fetting forth, that the petitioner was a Soldier in the *Virginia* Regiment, and whilft he ferved as fuch, received a Wound by a Shot in his left Arm, which hath difabled him from maintaining himfelf by his own Labour; and praying Relief.

Ordered, That the faid Petition be referred to the Confideration of a Committee; and that they do examine the Matter thereof, and report the fame, with their Opinion thereupon, to the Houfe;

And it is *referred* to Mr *Rutherford*, Mr *Wafhington*, Mr *Lewis*, and Mr *Wood*.

A *Petition* of feveral Perfons of the County of *Nanfemond*, whofe Names are thereunto fubfcribed, was prefented to the Houfe, and read; praying that an Act may pafs for defraying the Expence of repairing *Nottoway* Bridge, and of improving the Roads in the Counties of *Brunfwick*, *Southampton*, and *Ifle of Wight*, by a Toll to be laid upon certain loaded Waggons and Carts.

Ordered, That the faid petition be referred to the Confideration of the Committee of Propofitions and Grievances; and that they do examine the Matter thereof, and report the fame, with their Opinion thereupon, to the Houfe.

A *Petition* of feveral Perfons of the County of *Culpeper*, whofe Names are thereunto fubfcribed, was prefented to the Houfe, and read; taking Notice of a petition of feveral other Perfons of the faid County, for adding that Part of the faid County which lies between the *Rapidan* and *Robinfon* Rivers to the County of *Orange*; and fetting forth, that the propofed Alteration would deprive the County of *Culpeper* of a large Proportion of the Tithables thereof, and make the Form of it irregular, and that the Inconvenience complained of is common to fome of the Inhabitants of almoft every County, thofe who refide in the extreme Parts being in many Places nearer to the Court-Houfe of another County than to that of their own; and therefore praying that the petition for the faid Alteration may be rejected.

Ordered, That the faid Petition be referred to the Confideration of the Committee, to whom the Petition of feveral Perfons of the County of *Culpeper*, for adding that Part of the faid County which lies between the *Rapidan* and *Robinfon* Rivers to the County of *Orange* is referred; and that they do examine the Matter of this petition, and report the fame, with their Opinion thereupon, to the Houfe.

A *Petition* of *Robert Hamilton*, of the County of *Loudoun*, was prefented to the Houfe, and read; fetting forth, that the petitioner having been bound by a Recognizance to appear at the Court of *Oyer* and *Terminer*, in the Month of *June*, in the Year 1767, as a Witnefs againft *James Golding*, charged with Felony, attended accordingly, and was examined; but that his allowance for that Service was not levied; and therefore praying that the fame may be levied.

Ordered, That the faid Petition be referred to the Confideration of the Committee of Public Claims; and that they do examine the Matter thereof, and report the fame, with their Opinion thereupon, to the Houfe.

Mr *Cary* reported from the Committee of Public Claims, to whom the petition of *John Young* was referred, that the Committee had examined the Matter of the faid petition, and had directed him to report the fame, together with the Refolution of the Committee thereupon, to the Houfe; and he read the Report in his Place, and afterwards delivered it in at the Clerk's Table; where the fame was read, and is as followeth, viz.

It appears to your *Committee*, that the Slave *Mofes*, in the Petition mentioned, was a Runaway, and was duly outlawed; that during the Time he continued out, he was guilty of Felony and Burglary; that he was apprehended, and carried before a Magiftrate, who

who, upon Examination, committed him to Gaol, in Order that he might be tried for the faid Offence; but that, in a very short Time after the Gaoler received him, he expired, occafioned, as was fuppofed, by the great Fatigue he underwent in endeavoring to efcape his Purfuers. It further appears to your Committee that the faid Slave was worth eighty Pounds.

Whereupon your *Committee* came to the following Refolution;

Refolved, That it is the Opinion of this Committee, that the faid petition is reafonable; and that the Petitioner ought to be allowed the faid Sum of eighty Pounds for the faid Slave.

The faid *Refolution*, being read a fecond Time, was, upon the Queftion put thereupon, agreed to by the Houfe.

Mr *Bland* reported from the Committee of Propofitions and Grievances, to whom feveral petitions were referred, that the Committee had examined the Matters of the faid Petitions, and had come to feveral Refolutions thereupon, which they had directed him to report to the Houfe; and he read the Report in his Place, and afterwards delivered it in at the Clerk's Table, where the Refolutions of the Committee were read, and are as followeth, *viz.*

Refolved, That it is the Opinion of this Committee, that the petition of *John Talia-ferro*, praying that the Ferry acrofs *Rappahannock* River, from the Landing, formerly *Hackley's*, in the County of *King George*, to the Land of *Richard Corbin*, Efq; in the County of *Caroline*, may be re-eftablifhed, be rejected.

Refolved, That it is the Opinion of this Committee, that fo much of the Petition of the Inhabitants of *Augufta* County as prays that a Sum of Money may be granted for opening a new Road over the blue Ridge of Mountains, at a Place called *Craig's Gap*, between *Swift Run* and *Rockfifh Gaps*, is reafonable.

Refolved, That it is the Opinion of this Committee, that fuch other Part of the faid petition, as prays the Aid of the Houfe, towards altering and amending the Roads at *Rockfifh* and *Swift Run Gaps*, be rejected.

Refolved, That it is the Opinion of this Committee, that the Refidue of the faid petition, praying that the Courts of the Counties adjacent to the County of *Augufta*, and through which the Roads from *Rockfifh* and *Swift Run Gaps* are extended, may be obliged to levy Money on their refpective Counties, for keeping the fame in Repair, be rejected.

Refolved, That it is the Opinion of this Committee, that the petition of divers Free-holders of the County of *Augufta*, praying that the Juftices of the faid County may be empowered to levy as much Money on the Inhabitants thereof as fhall be fufficient for repairing the Roads over the blue Ridge of Mountains, at *Swift Run* and *Rockfifh Gaps*, is reafonable.

Refolved, That it is the Opinion of this Committee, that the Petition of divers Inhabitants of the Counties of *Hanover*, *Albemarle*, *Augufta*, and *Botetourt*, praying that a Sum of Money may be granted for opening a fafe and good Road from the Warm Springs to *Jening's Gap*, and that a Turnpike may be eftablifhed, and Truftees appointed to receive Subfcriptions, for keeping the faid Road in Repair, and building Houfes for the Reception of the Sick, is reafonable.

Refolved, That it is the Opinion of this Committee, that the Petition of *John Pitt*, praying that he may be empowered by Law to erect Gates acrofs the Road leading to the Public Warehoufes for the Infpection of Tobacco, on the Land of the faid *John*, is reafonable.

The *firft* Refolution of the Committee, being read a fecond Time, was, upon the Queftion put thereupon, agreed to by the Houfe.

The *fecond* Refolution of the Committee being read a fecond Time;

And the *Queftion* being put, that the Houfe doth agree with the Committee in the faid Refolution;

It paffed in the Negative.

Refolved, That fo much of the Petition of the Inhabitants of *Augufta* County, as

prays

prays that a Sum of Money may be granted, for opening a new Road over the blue Ridge of Mountains, at a Place called *Craig's Gap*, between *Swift Run* and *Rockfish Gaps*, be rejected.

The *third* Refolution of the Committee being read a fecond Time;

Ordered, That the faid Refolution be recommitted to the faid Committee of Propofitions and Grievances.

The *fourth* Refolution of the Committee, being read a fecond Time;

Ordered, That the faid Refolution be recommitted to the faid Committee of Propofition and Grievances.

The *fifth* Refolution of the Committee being read a fecond Time;

Ordered, That the faid Refolution be recommitted to the faid Committee of Propofitions and Grievances.

The fubfequent *Refolutions* of the Committee, being feverally read a fecond Time, were, upon the Queftion feverally put thereupon, agreed to by the Houfe.

Ordered, That the Committee of Propofitions and Grievances do prepare, and bring in a Bill purfuant to the faid fixth Refolution.

Ordered, That it be an Inftruction to the Committee of Propofitions and Grievances, who are appointed to prepare and bring in a Bill or Bills, purfuant to the Refolutions of the faid Committee, which were reported to the Houfe, upon *Friday*, the 28th Day of laft Month, and which were agreed to by the Houfe, that they have Power to receive a Claufe or Claufes purfuant to the feventh Refolution of the faid Committee, which was this Day reported, and agreed to by the Houfe.

A *Meffage* from the Council by Mr *Blair*.

Mr *Speaker*,

The Council have agreed to the Bill, *intituled* An Act[1] to dock the Intail of certain Lands whereof *Nathaniel Weft Dandridge* is feifed, *without any Amendment; and alfo,*

The Council have agreed to the Refolve *for paying a Salary to the Keeper of the Public Gaol; and alfo,*

The Council have agreed to the Refolve *for paying a Salary to* Peter Pelham, *Organift;* and alfo,

The Council have agreed to the Bill, *intituled* An Act[2] for cutting a navigable Canal from *Archer's Hope* Creek to *Queen's* Creek, through the City of *Williamfburg, with fome Amendments, to which Amendments the Council defire the Concurrence of this Houfe.*

And then the Meffenger withdrew.

The Houfe proceeded to take the faid *Amendments* into Confideration.

And the faid *Amendments* were read; and are as followeth, viz.

Line 2, after "*through*" infert "*or near.*"

In the Title, after "*through*" infert "*or near.*"

The faid *Amendments*, being feverally read a fecond Time, were, upon the Queftion feverally put thereupon, agreed to by the Houfe.

Ordered, That Mr *Treafurer* do carry the Bill to the Council, and acquaint them, that this Houfe hath agreed to the Amendments made by them.

The *Order* of the Day being read, for the third reading of the Bill to repeal one Claufe of the Act of Affembly, intituled An Act[3] *for fettling the Titles and Bounds of Lands, and for preventing unlawful hunting and ranging;*

The faid *Bill* was read the third Time.

Refolved, That the Bill do pafs; and that the Title be, An Act[4] *to repeal one Claufe of the Act of Affembly, intituled An Act for fettling the Titles and Bounds of Lands, and for preventing unlawful hunting and ranging.*

Ordered, That Mr *Bland* do carry the Bill to the Council, and defire their Concurrence.

Ordered, That Mr *Marable* have Leave to be abfent from the Service of this Houfe till the fifteenth Day of this Inftant.

Ordered

---

[1] Hening, VIII, p. 638. [2] Ibid, VIII, p. 556. [3] Ibid, V, p. 408. [4] Not recorded as a law.

Ordered, That Mr *Lewis* and Mr *Macdowell* be added to the Committee of Propofitions and Grievances.

The other *Order* of the Day being read;

Ordered, That the Call of the Houfe be adjourned till *Friday* next.

And then the Houfe adjourned till Tomorrow Morning, eleven of the Clock.

Thursday, the 5th of March, 12 George III. 1772.

ANOTHER *Member* having taken the Oaths appointed to be taken by Act of Parliament, and repeated and fubfcribed the Teft, took his Place in the Houfe.

Ordered, That a Committee be appointed to examine the enrolled Bills:

And a *Committee* was appointed of Mr *Digges*, Mr *Lewis Burwell*, of *James City*, Mr *Banifter*, Mr *Henry Lee*, Mr *Jofeph Jones*, Mr *Watkins*, Mr *James Henry*, and Mr *White*.

The *Order* of the Day being read for the fecond reading of the Bill, for further continuing the Act, intituled *An Act[1] for the better regulating and collecting certain Officers Fees, and for other Purpofes therein mentioned;*

The faid *Bill* was read a fecond Time.

Refolved, That the Bill be committed.

Refolved, That the Bill be committed to a Committee of the whole Houfe.

Refolved, That this Houfe will, upon *Wednefday* next, refolve itfelf into a Committee of the whole Houfe upon the faid Bill.

Mr *Bland*, from the Committee of Correfpondence, prefented to the Houfe, purfuant to their Order, the Letters which have paffed between the faid Committee and *Edward Montagu*,[2] Efq; late Agent for this Colony, fince his Appointment, until the firft Day of *November*, in the Year 1769.

Ordered, That the faid Letters, and alfo the Letters which have paffed between the the faid late Agent and Committee, fince the faid firft Day of *November*, and which were ordered to lie upon the Table, be referred to the Committee of the whole Houfe, to whom the Bill for appointing an Agent is committed.

Ordered, That Mr *Greenhill* have Leave to be abfent from the Service of this Houfe until the End of this Seffion.

Ordered, That it be an Inftruction to the Committee of Public Claims, that they do levy upon the tithable Perfons of the Parifh of *Overwharton*, in the County of *Stafford*, four thoufand fix hundred and eighty-fix Pounds of Tobacco, and one Pound eleven Shillings and three Pence, the Expences incurred in the Profecution of certain Petitions, prefented to the laft General Affembly, for diffolving the Veftry of the faid Parifh.

Mr *Bland* reported from the Committee of Propofitions and Grievances, to whom feveral Petitions were referred, that the Committee had examined the Matters of the faid Petitions, and had come to feveral Refolutions thereupon, which they had directed him to report to the Houfe; and he read the Report in his Place, and afterwards delivered it in at the Clerk's Table; where the Refolutions of the Committee were read, and are as followeth, *viz.*

Refolved, That it is the Opinion of this Committee, that the petition of the Inhabitants within the Fork of *Rapidan* and *Robinfon* Rivers, in the County of *Culpeper*, praying to be added to the County of *Orange*, be rejected.

Refolved, That it is the Opinion of this Committee, that the petition of divers Inhabitants of the faid County of *Culpeper*, in Oppofition thereto, is reafonable.

Refolved, That it is the Opinion of this Committee, that the Petition of the Inhabitants of *Fairfax* County, praying that the public Roads may be rendered more ufeful, is reafonable.

Refolved, That it is the Opinion of this Committee, that the Petition of the Traders of *Nanfemond* County, praying that an Act may pafs for defraying the Expence of repairing *Nottoway* Bridge, and of improving the Roads in the Counties of *Brunfwick*, *Southampton*

---

[1] Hening, V, p. 326.   [2] Montagu Correfpondence Virginia State Library.

Southampton, and *Iſle of Wight*, by a Toll to be impoſed on certain loaded Waggons and Carts, is reaſonable.

The ſaid *Reſolutions*, being ſeverally read a ſecond Time, were, upon the Queſtion ſeverally put thereupon, agreed to by the Houſe.

Ordered, That it be an Inſtruction to the Committee of Propoſitions and Grievances to whom the Bill for further continuing the Acts for the more effectual keeping the public Roads and Bridges in Repair, is committed, that they have Power to receive a Clauſe, or Clauſes, purſuant to the third and fourth of the ſaid Reſolutions.

M*r* *Edmund Pendleton* preſented to the Houſe, according to Order, a Bill to dock the Intail of certain Lands whereof *William Todd*, Gentleman, is ſeized, and for other Pur-poſes therein mentioned; and the ſame was received, and read the firſt Time.

Reſolved, That the Bill be read a ſecond Time.

A *Petition* of *Ralph Wormeley* was preſented to the Houſe, and read; ſetting forth, that by an Act, paſſed in the 7th Year of the Reign of his preſent Majeſty, the Intail of a Tract of Land, on *Wormeley's* Creek, in the County of *York*, whereof the Petitioner was ſeiſed as Tenant in Fee Tail, was docked, and, in Lieu thereof, four thouſand Acres of Land, in the County of *Frederick*, were ſettled as an Equivalent; and further ſetting forth, that the Value of the ſaid Land in *Frederick* exceeds the Value of the ſaid Land in *York*, and that the Petitioner intends to leave a great Number of Slaves, with his other entailed Lands, to his eldeſt Son, who is willing and conſents that the ſaid Land in *Frederick* may be veſted in the Petitioner in Fee Simple, that he may be enabled to make Proviſion for his younger Sons; and therefore praying that Leave may be given to bring in a Bill for veſting the ſaid four thouſand Acres of Land in the Petitioner in Fee Simple. 64

Ordered, That Leave be given to bring in a Bill purſuant to the Prayer of the ſaid petition, and that M*r* *Berkeley* do prepare, and bring in the ſame.

M*r* *Alexander* preſented to the Houſe, according to Order, a Bill to appoint Com-miſſioners to ſtrike a dividing Line between the Counties of *Stafford* and *King George;* and the ſame was received, and read the firſt Time.

Reſolved, That the Bill be read a ſecond Time.

A *Petition* of the Freeholders and Inhabitants of the County of *Prince William*, whoſe Names are thereunto ſubſcribed, was preſented to the Houſe, and read; ſetting forth, that the Tobacco Fees of public Officers are exorbitant, oppreſſive, and unequal, and that the Penalties inflicted for charging unwarrantable Fees are too ſmall; and therefore praying the Houſe to take thoſe Matters into Conſideration, and to grant ſuch Relief as ſhall appear juſt.

Ordered, That the ſaid Petition be referred to the Committee of the whole Houſe, to whom the Bill for further continuing the Act, intituled *An Act[1] for the better regulating and collecting certain Officers Fees, and for other Purpoſes therein mentioned*, is committed.

A *Petition* of *Robert Garrett*, and *William Plunket*, late Inſpectors of Tobacco at *Conway's* Warehouſe, in the County of *Caroline*, was preſented to the Houſe, and read; ſetting forth, that in the Year 1770, notwithſtanding the utmoſt Care and Vigilance of the Petitioners, there were ſtolen out of the ſaid Warehouſe fifteen hundred Pounds of Tobacco, for which they have been obliged to make Satiſfaction to the Proprietors thereof, and therefore praying to be reimburſed by the Public.

Ordered, That the ſaid petition be referred to the Conſideration of the Committee of Public Claims; and that they do examine the Matter thereof, and report the ſame, with their Opinion thereupon, to the Houſe.

Ordered, That it be an Inſtruction to the Committee of Propoſitions and Grievances, who are appointed to prepare and bring in a Bill, to continue an Act, intituled *An Act[2] for amending the Staple of Tobacco, and for preventing Frauds in his Majeſty's Cuſtoms*, that they make Proviſion in the ſaid Bill for re-eſtabliſhing an Inſpection of Tobacco on *Totuſkey* Creek, in the County of *Richmond; and alſo*, for disjoining the Inſpections at *Hampton* and *Denbigh;* and alſo for repealing that Part of the ſaid Act which allows the Purchaſers of Tobacco to have the ſame reviewed.

A *Petition* of *John Reynolds* and *William Edmondſon*, Inſpectors of Tobacco at *Hobbs Hole* Warehouſe, in the County of *Eſſex*, was preſented to the Houſe, and read;

fetting

---

[1] Hening, V, p. 326. [2] Ibid, VIII, p. 69.

fetting forth, that, in *January* laft, the faid Warehoufe was broke open, and a Hogf-head of Tobacco was ftolen thereout, for which the Petitioners are liable to make Satif-faction to the Owner; and therefore praying Relief.

Ordered, That the faid Petition be referred to the Confideration of the Committee of Public Claims; and that they do examine the Matter thereof, and report the fame, with their Opinion thereupon, to the Houfe.

Mʳ *Gray* prefented to the Houfe, according to Order, a Bill to amend an Act, inti-tuled *An Act[1] to prevent malicious maiming and wounding;* and the fame was received, and read the firft Time.

Refolved, That the Bill be read a fecond Time.

A *Petition* of *Robert Garrett* and *Henry Ware,* Infpectors of Tobacco at *Conway's* Warehoufe, in the County of *Caroline,* was prefented to the Houfe, and read; fetting forth, that, in the Year 1771, notwithftanding the utmoft Care and Vigilance of the Petitioners, there were ftolen out of the faid Warehoufe three Hogfheads of Tobacco weighing three thoufand and one hundred Pounds, for which they have been obliged to make Satiffaction to the Proprietors thereof; and therefore praying to be reimburfed by the Public.

Ordered, That the faid petition be referred to the Confideration of the Committee of Public Claims; and that they do examine the Matter thereof, and report the fame, with their Opinion thereupon, to the Houfe.

Mʳ *Treafurer* prefented to the Houfe, according to Order, a Bill to dock the Intail of certain Lands whereof *James Blackwell* the younger is feifed, and for other Purpofes therein mentioned; and the fame was received, and read the firft Time.

Refolved, That the Bill be read a fecond Time.

A *Petition* of *Chriftopher Perfect, Jofhua Taylor,* and *John Macginnis,* fetting forth, that the Petitioners, having been bound by Recognizance to appear at the Court of *Oyer* and *Terminer,* in *December,* 1767, as Witneffes againft *James Golding,* a Criminal fent from the County of *Loudoun,* to be tried before the faid Court, appeared accordingly, and were examined; but that their Allowance for Travelling and Attendance was not levied; and therefore praying, that the fame may now be levied; *and alfo,*

A *Petition* of *Thomas Lewis,* Adminiftrator of the Eftate of *Richard Coombs,* deceafed, fetting forth, that *Mary Coombs,* for whofe Appearance at a Court of *Oyer* and *Terminer,* in *December,* 1767, as a Witnefs againft *James Golding,* a Criminal fent from the County of *Loudoun,* to be tried before the faid Court, the faid *Richard Coombs,* her Hufband, was bound by Recognizance, appeared accordingly, and was examined; but that her allowance for Travelling and Attendance was not levied; and therefore praying, that the fame may now be levied for the petitioner, Were feverally prefented to the Houfe, and read.

Ordered, That the faid Petitions be referred to the Confideration of the Committee of Public Claims; and that they do examine the Matter thereof, and report the fame, with their Opinion thereupon, to the Houfe.

And then the Houfe adjourned till Tomorrow Morning, eleven of the Clock.

Friday, the 6th of March, 12 George III. 1772.

ANOTHER *Member* having taken the Oaths appointed to be taken by Act of Parliament, and repeated and fubfcribed the Teft, took his Place in the Houfe.

Mʳ *Cary* reported from the Committee of Public Claims, to whom the Petition of *William Bruce* and *William Harrifon,* Infpectors of Tobacco at *Gibfon's* and *Morton's* Warehoufes, in the County of *King George,* had been referred, and to whom the Report of the Matter of the faid Petition, and the Refolutions of the Committee thereupon, were recommitted, that the Committee had further examined the Matter of the faid Petition, and had directed him to report the fame, together with the Refolutions of the Committee thereupon, to the Houfe; and he read the Report in his Place, and afterwards delivered it in at the Clerk's Table, where the fame was read, and is as followeth, *viz.*

It

---

[1] Hening, VI, p. 250.

It appears to your *Committee*, that the Damage which the Tobacco received was not occafioned by any Neglect of the Infpectors, but by a great Rain that fell in the Month of *May* laft, and flowed into the faid Warehoufes, an Inftance of which does not appear before to have happened there, and damaged the Tobacco that lay next to the Ground, although it was placed on Pieces of Timber to fecure it. It further appears to your Committee, by feveral Certificates, and a Lift produced, that fourteen Hogfheads of the faid Tobacco, weighing Nett 16,123 Pounds, were the property of *Robert Gilchrift*, for which he paid at the Rate of twenty Shillings *per Cent.* feven Hogfheads, Nett 7071 Pounds, were the Property of *Thomas Hodge*, for which he paid at the Rate of fourteen Shillings Sterling *Per Cent.* which faid twenty-one Hogfheads were refufed by the Proprietors thereof, fix Hogfheads, Nett 6157 Pounds, were the Property of Perfons unknown to the Petitioners, and one Hogfhead marked GC, No. 89, was twice entered in the faid Lift; that there were eleven Hogfheads more omitted in the faid Petition, which the Owners received, that loft 389 Pounds; and that by the faid Lift the Marks, Numbers, and Weights, of the whole Tobacco, together with the Quantity damaged in each Hogfhead, appear as followeth:

Marks.	No.	Grofs.	Tare.	Nett.	Damage.	
RB.	133	1168	114	1054		
DG.	158	1160	109	1051	16	
Do.	159	1180	131	1049	153	
HT.	236	1133	106	1027	6	
Do.	238	1225	125	1100	4	
WS.	107	1309	126	1183	17	
SS.	66	1218	121	1097	25	
Do.	72	1299	130	1169	1	Belonging to
Do.	73	1439	132	1307	3	*Robert Gilchrift.*
Do.	205	1294	125	1169	5	
Do.	208	1404	120	1284	1	
Do.	64	1286	123	1163	7	
GC.	94	1310	121	1208	31	
Do.	89	1374	112	1262	20	
				16123		
WS.	50	1250	121	1129	56	
WR.	228	1022	114	908	155	
Do.	289	1160	114	946	86	Belonging to
WS.	111	1222	119	1103·	111	*Thomas Hodge.*
Do.	323	1160	93	1067	55	
RS.	128	1024	114	910	70	
IP.	97	1117	109	1008	115	
				7071		
WR.	124	1096	104	992	44	
WC.	177	1236	107	1129	17	Belonging to
TC.	62	1254	95	1159	40	Perfons un-
WC.	174	1277	104	1173	88	known to the
RP.	279	1173	106	1067	7	Petitioners.
IK.	197	755	118	637	26	
				6157		
GC.	89	1374	112	1264	20 A Duplicate	
EP.	380	1102	105	997	4	
SS.	336	1104	102	1002	52	
IA.	246	1080	104	978	10	
MD.	115	1114	116	998	31	
RS.	262	1271	109	1162	20	
IC.	104	1110	105	1005	5	Received by the
WS.	74	1177	114	1063	23	owners thereof.
MR.	161	1054	104	950	4	
WM.	258	1170	109	1061	133	
HL.	369	1425	122	1303	40	
IG.	330	1139	115	1028	67	

Whereupon

Whereupon the *Committee* came to the following Refolutions:

Refolved, That it is the Opinion of this Committee, that fo much of the faid petition as relates to the damaged Tobacco is reafonable; and that the Petitioners ought to be allowed at the following Rates, for fuch Tobacco as appears by the faid Lift to have loft upwards of twenty-four Pounds in the Hogfhead, that was refufed by the Owners, to wit, for three Hogfheads of the faid *Gilchrift's* Tobacco, weighing Nett 3354 Pounds, at twenty Shillings *per Cent*. for feven Hogfheads, the faid *Hodge's* Property, weighing Nett 7071 Pounds, at fixteen Shillings and ten Pence *per Cent*. and for four Hogfheads, the Property of Perfons unknown to the Petitioners, weighing Nett 3961 Pounds, and 493 pounds, the lofs fuftained in the eleven Hogfheads, which were received, and the other fix Hogsheads that loft lefs than twenty-five Pounds each, at twenty Shillings *per Cent*. and the further Sum of four Pounds feventeen Shillings and fix pence for their Trouble in uncafing and trimming the whole Tobacco, and fecuring the good that was faved.

Refolved, That it is the Opinion of this Committee, that the fourteen Hogfheads of Tobacco, for which the Petitioners are allowed, ought to be fold for the Benefit of the Public.

The faid *Refolutions*, being feverally read a fecond Time, were, upon the Queftion feverally put thereupon, agreed to by the Houfe.

Ordered, That a Bill be brought in purfuant to the fecond Refolution; and that the Committee of Public Claims do prepare, and bring in the fame.

76   Mʳ *Bland* reported from the Committee, who were appointed to examine the Treaf-urer's Accounts, and to ftate in Account as well the Balance due from the late Treafurer to the Public, as the feveral Funds by Law appropriated for the Redemption of the Treafury Notes, together with the Amount of fuch Notes remaining in Circulation, and alfo to ftate an Account of the Balances now due from the feveral Sheriffs, for Taxes, that the Committee had examined and ftated the faid Accounts accordingly, and had directed him to report the fame, as they appeared to them, to the Houfe; and he read the Report in his Place, and afterwards delivered it in at the Clerk's Table, where the fame was read, and is as followeth, *viz*.

The *Committee* have examined the Treafurer's Accounts of the feveral Sums of Money received and iffued at the Public Treafury fince the laft Settlement in General Affembly, and, upon comparing them with the proper Vouchers, find that they are fairly and juftly ftated.

It appears to your *Committee*, that the Balance in the Treafurer's Hands for Cafh received from the feveral Collectors of Taxes appropriated to the Redemption of the old Treafury Notes amounted to 9178 *l*. 6 *s*. 4 *d*. of which they have burned and deftroyed 3550 *l*. 6 *s*. 3 *d*. that of the Taxes impofed for the Redemption of the 10,000 *l*., iffued in the Year 1770, there hath been received in the Whole 11,487 *l*. 9 *s*.8 *d*. Farthing, of which there was formerly burned, by the ftanding Committee, 290 *l*. and your Committee have now burned and deftroyed 113 *l*. fo that there remains in the Treafury on the former Account, a Balance of 5628 *l*. 0 1 *d*. and on the latter, after deducting the Treafurer's Commiffions, a Balance of 10,785 *l*. 2 *s*. 1 *d*. Farthing; which feveral Balances the Treaf-urer produced to us.

Your *Committee* likewife find that there is in the Treafurer's Hands a Balance of 1882 *l*. 6 *s*. 3 *d*.¼ due to the Account of the Public Treafury, which the Treafurer alfo produced.

Your *Committee* have examined the State of the old Treafury Notes, and find that of them there now remains in Circulation 88,189 *l*. 15 *s*. They have alfo examined the late Treafurer's Account, and find a Balance of 72,362 *l*. 19 *s*. 4 *d*. principal Money ftill due from his Eftate to the Public.

It *appears*, that of the old Arrears due from the Collectors of the Land and Poll Tax, and Taxes on Carriages, there is ftill due the Sum of 18,748 *l*. 1 *s*. 3 *d*. a particular Account of which is annexed; that there are feveral arrears due from fome of the Clerks and other Collectors, the amount of which cannot be exactly afcertained, as their Accounts are

not

not made up at the Treaſury; but it is ſuppoſed they cannot be leſs than 2000 *l*. Upon the whole Matter, it appears to your Committee, that the Funds appropriated for the Redemption of the old Treaſury Notes, when the Arrears are paid in, will exceed the Sum in Circulation 10,549 *l*. 6 *s*. 3 *d*. which your Committee are hopeful will be amply ſufficient to make good all Loſſes that may happen in the ſaid Arrears, and all Expences attending the Collection thereof. Add to this the ſeveral Treaſury Notes which have probably been loſt and deſtroyed, which your Committee are of the Opinion will prove a conſiderable Saving to the Country, though they cannot pretend to fix the amount of the ſame. For the better Illuſtration of this Part of their Report, your Committee beg Leave to refer to the annexed Account.

Your *Committee* ſubmit to the Conſideration of the Houſe what Meaſures ought to be purſued to enforce the moſt expeditious Payment of the ſeveral Arrears, and humbly give it as their Opinion that ſome certain Period ought to be fixed for calling in and ſinking all the old Treaſury Notes now in Circulation.

The ſaid *Account*, annexed to the Report, is as followeth, *viz*.

Dr.   The Colony of *Virginia* for the Redemption of the old Treaſury Notes.   Cr.

	l.	*s.*	*d.*		*l.*	*s.*	*d.*
To Balance of Notes in Circulation,	88189	15	0	By the principal Debt due from the late Treaſurer's Eſtate,	72362	19	11
Balance,	10549	6	3	By Balance due from the ſeveral Sheriffs,	18748	1	3
	98739	1	3	By Balance from Inſpectors Clerks, and Sheriffs, for Wheel Carriages, about	2000	0	0
				By Balance now in the Treaſury, in Specie, for the Redemption of the old Notes,	5628	0	1
					98739	1	3

Mr *Bland* from the ſaid Committee alſo delivered in at the Clerk's Table an Account of the Balances now due from the ſeveral Sheriffs for Taxes.

The ſaid *Report* was, upon the Queſtion put thereupon, agreed to by the Houſe.

Reſolved, That the Treaſurer's Accounts do paſs.

Ordered, That Mr *Bland* do carry the Treaſurer's Accounts to the Council, and deſire their Concurrence.

Ordered, That the ſaid Account of the Balances due from the ſeveral Sheriffs for Taxes do lie upon the Table, to be peruſed by the Members of the Houſe.

A *Petition* of *Roger Gregory* was preſented to the Houſe, and read; ſetting forth, that, in Obedience to the Authority of the Houſe, he is attending, in Order to receive ſuch Sentence as the Houſe ſhall be pleaſed to inflict for his Offence; that he is very deeply concerned to have incurred their Diſpleaſure; and that he did not know, that a Witneſs, ſummoned to attend any Committee appointed by the Houſe, was privileged from Arreſts, having never heard of the ſtanding Order of the Houſe for the Protection of ſuch Witneſs; that his ſole Motive for requeſting Suits to be brought againſt Mr *Richeſon* and Mr *Quarles*, in the Court of *York*, was the Certainty of a more ſpeedy Determination there, than he could expect in the Court of the County where they reſide; and that he had deſired the Perſon, who carried the Letter to his Attorney, directing thoſe Suits to be brought, to deliver a Meſſage, not to do anything in the Matter, if the Defendants were entitled to Privilege; and humbly aſking Pardon of the Houſe for his Offence.

Ordered, That the ſaid *Roger Gregory* be diſcharged out of Cuſtody, paying his Fees.

Mr *Bland* preſented to the Houſe, according to Order, a Bill for appointing Commiſſioners to view the Lands on both Sides of *James* River, from *Weſtham*, to the navigable

gable Water, below the Falls of the faid River, and for other Purpofes therein mentioned; and the fame was received, and read the firft Time.

Refolved, That the Bill be read a fecond Time.

A *Memorial* of the Deputy Clerk of the County Court of *Hampfhire* was prefented to the Houfe, and read; fetting forth a great Variety of impertinent and incoherent Matter, upon the Subject of Officers Fees; and not complaining of any Grievance, nor praying for any Relief.

And the *Queftion* being put, that the faid Memorial be referred to the Confideration of a Committee;

It paffed in the Negative.

Refolved, That the faid Memorial be rejected.

Mr *Bland* prefented to the Houfe, according to Order, a Bill for clearing a Road from the Warm Springs, in *Augufta*, and for other Purpofes therein mentioned; and the fame was received, and read the firft Time.

Refolved, That the Bill be read a fecond Time.

Ordered, That Mr *Riddick* and Mr *Yelverton Peyton* have Leave to be abfent from the Service of this Houfe till *Monday* Sevennight.

Ordered, That the Order of the Day for the Houfe to refolve itfelf into a Committee of the whole Houfe upon the Bill for appointing an Agent, be now read.

And the faid *Order* being read accordingly;

The Houfe refolved itfelf into the faid Committee.

Mr *Speaker* left the Chair.

Mr *Bland* took the Chair of the Committee.

Mr *Speaker* refumed the Chair.

Mr *Bland* reported from the Committee, that they had directed him to report the Bill to the Houfe without any Amendment; and he delivered the Bill in at the Clerk's Table.

And the *Queftion* being put, that the Bill be engroffed;

It paffed in the Negative.

Refolved, That the Bill be rejected.

Ordered, That Mr *Burnley* have Leave to be abfent from the Service of this Houfe till *Thurfday* next.

And then the Houfe adjourned till Tomorrow Morning eleven of the Clock.

Saturday, the 7th of March, 12 George III. 1772.

MR *Bland* reported from the Committee of Propofitions and Grievances, to whom feveral Petitions were referred, that the Committee had examined the Matters of the faid Petitions, and had come to feveral Refolutions thereupon, which they had directed him to report to the Houfe; and he read the Report in his Place, and afterwards delivered it in at the Clerk's Table; where the Refolutions of the Committee were read, and are as followeth, *viz.*

Refolved, That it is the Opinion of this Committee, that the petition of divers Inhabitants of the County of *Accomack*, praying that the faid County may be divided into two diftinct Counties, be rejected.

Refolved, That it is the Opinion of this Committee, that the Petition of other Inhabitants of the faid County, in Oppofition thereto, is reafonable.

Refolved, That it is the Opinion of this Committee, that the Petition of fundry Inhabitants of *Loudoun* County, praying that a Ferry may be eftablifhed acrofs *Potowmack* River, from the Land of the Right Honourable the Earl of *Tankerville*, in the Tenure and Occupation of *John Furrow*, and *Alexander Reame*, in the faid County of *Loudoun*, to the Oppofite Shore in *Maryland*, is reafonable.

Refolved, That it is the Opinion of this Committee, that the Petition of divers Inhabitants of *New Kent* County, praying that the Infpections of Tobacco at *Littlepage's* and *Waddy's* Warehoufes, may be difunited, is reafonable.

Refolved

Refolved, That it is the Opinion of this Committee, that the Petition of divers Inhabitants of the County of *King William*, praying that the Infpection of Tobacco at *Waller's* Warehoufe may be revived, is reafonable.

Refolved, That it is the Opinion of this Committee, that the Petition of divers Inhabitants of *King & Queen* County, praying that the Infpection of Tobacco at *Walkerton* may be revived, is reafonable.

Refolved, That it is the Opinion of this Committee, that the Petition of the Infpectors of Tobacco at *Royfton's* Warehoufe, in the County of *Spotfylvania*, praying that their Salaries may be increafed to fixty Pounds *per Annum*, which were formerly allowed them, is reafonable.

Refolved, That it is the Opinion of this Committee, that the Petition of *Robert King*, one of the Infpectors of Tobacco at the *Piping Tree* Warehoufe, praying that he may be permitted to keep an Ordinary at the faid Warehoufe, be rejected.

The faid *Refolutions*, being feverally read a fecond Time, were, upon the Queftion feverally put thereupon, agreed to by the Houfe.

Ordered, That it be an Inftruction to the faid Committee, who are appointed to prepare and bring in a Bill for repealing fo much of the Act made in the fifth Year of the Reign of his prefent Majefty, intituled *An Act[1] for appointing feveral new Ferries, and for other Purpofes therein mentioned*, as eftablifhed a Ferry from the Land of *Cornelius Thomas* over the *Fluvanna* to the Land of *Nicholas Davies*, that they have Power to receive a Claufe or Claufes purfuant to the third Refolution of the faid Committee, this Day reported, and agreed to by the Houfe.

Ordered, That it be an Inftruction to the faid Committee, who are appointed to prepare and bring in a Bill for further continuing the Act made in the fifth Year of the Reign of his prefent Majefty, intituled *An Act[2] for amending the Staple of Tobacco, and for preventing Frauds in his Majefty's Cuftoms*, that they make Provifion in the faid Bill for difuniting the Infpections of Tobacco at *Littlepage's* and *Waddy's* Warehoufes, in the County of *New-Kent;* and alfo for reviving the Infpections of Tobacco at *Waller's* Warehoufe, in the County of *King William*, and at *Walkerton*, in the County of *King & Queen*, and uniting the former with *Quarles's*, and the latter with *Mantapike* Infpections; and alfo for increafing the Salaries of the Infpectors of Tobacco at *Royfton's*, in the County of *Spotfylvania*, to fixty Pounds *per Annum*.

Ordered, That Mr *Tebbs* be added to the Committees of Propofitions and Grievances, and of Public Claims.

Mr *Henry Lee* prefented to the Houfe, acording to Order, a Bill to dock the Intail of certain Lands whereof *John Hancock* is feifed, and for fettling other Lands and Slaves in Lieu thereof; and the fame was received, and read the firft Time.

Refolved, That the Bill be read a fecond Time.

A *Petition* of the Chiefs of the *Nottoway Indians* was prefented to the Houfe, and read; fetting forth, that by an Act, paffed in the eighth Year of the Reign of his late Majefty King *George* the Second, Truftees were appointed to fell the Lands therein mentioned, belonging to that Nation of *Indians*, and fituate on the North Side of *Nottoway* River, fo as no Perfon fhould be allowed to purchafe more than four hundred Acres in one Tract; and that in furveying and laying off the faid Land into fuch Lots, feveral fmall Parcels were left undifpofed of, which are not occupied by the faid *Indians*, all their Lands on the North Side of the faid River, except thofe fmall Parcels, being conveyed to fundry Perfons in Purfuance of the faid recited Act, and other Acts of Affembly; and that it will be for the Advantage of the Petitioners, that the fame fhould be fold; and further reprefenting, that the Petitioners are in Poffeffion of a large quantity of Land on the South Side of the faid River *Nottoway*, moft of which is unoccupied by, and of little Ufe to them; and therefore praying that an Act may pafs empowering Perfons to fell all the remaining Lands of the Petitioners on the North Side of the faid River, and to leafe out for their Benefit Part not exceeding half of their Lands on the South Side.

Ordered

---

[1] Hening, VIII, p. 44.   [2] Ibid, VIII, p. 69.

Ordered. That a Bill be brought in purfuant to the Prayer of the faid Petition; and that Mʳ *Gray*, and Mʳ *Taylor*, do prepare, and bring in the fame.

Ordered, That Mʳ *Stubblefield* have Leave to be abfent from the Service of this Houfe till *Friday* next.

A *Petition* of *John Thornley*, and *William Harrifon*, Infpectors of Tobacco at *Gibfon's* Warehoufes, in the County of *King George*, was prefented to the Houfe, and read; fetting forth, that in the Year 1770, two Hogfheads of Crop, and a Parcel of Tranffer Tobacco, in the Whole amounting to two thoufand three hundred and nineteen Pounds, were ftolen out of the faid Warehoufes; and praying to be allowed for their faid Lofs.

Ordered, That the faid Petition be referred to the Confideration of the Committee of Public Claims; and that they do examine the Matter thereof, and report the fame, with their Opinion thereupon, to the Houfe.

Ordered, That Mʳ *Fitzhugh* have Leave to be abfent from the Service of this Houfe till *Thurfday* Sevennight.

Ordered, That Leave be given to bring in a Bill for calling in and finking the old Treafury Notes now in Circulation; and that Mʳ *Bland*, Mʳ *Richard Henry Lee*, Mʳ *Harrifon*, Mʳ *Charles Carter*, Mʳ *Eyre*, Mʳ *Patrick Henry*, Mʳ *Digges*, and Mʳ *Fitzhugh*, do prepare, and bring in the fame.

A *Bill* for better regulating the Election of Veftries was read a fecond Time.

Refolved, That the Bill be committed to the Committee for Religion.

Ordered, That Leave be given to bring in a Bill to amend an Act, intituled *An Act[1] for clearing* Matapony *River*; and that Mʳ *Edmund Pendleton*, and Mʳ *Berkeley*, do prepare, and bring in the fame.

Ordered, That Mʳ *Patrick Henry*, Mʳ *Banifter*, and Mʳ *Alexander*, be added to the Gentlemen who are appointed to prepare and bring in a Bill for the more fpeedy and eafy Adminiftration of Juftice.

A *Bill* for dividing the County of *Frederick* into three diftinct Counties was read a fecond Time.

Refolved, That the Bill be committed to the Committee of Propofitions and Grievances.

Ordered, That Mʳ *Brooke*, and Mʳ *Berkeley*, have Leave to be abfent from the Service of this Houfe till *Monday* Sevennight.

71 A *Bill* for adding Part of the County of *Nanfemond* to the County of *Ifle of Wight*, was read a fecond Time.

Ordered, That the Bill be engroffed.

A *Bill* to remove the Seat of Government to a Place more convenient to the Inhabitants of this Colony, was read a fecond Time.

Refolved, That the Bill be committed.

Refolved, That the Bill be committed to a Committee of the whole Houfe.

Refolved, That this Houfe will, upon *Tuefday* next, refolve itfelf into a Committee of the whole Houfe upon the faid Bill.

A *Bill* to empower the Corporation of the Borough of *Norfolk* to affefs a Tax on the Inhabitants thereof for the Purpofe therein mentioned, was read a fecond Time.

Ordered, That the Bill be engroffed.

An engroffed *Bill* for further continuing the Act, intituled *An Act[2] for reducing the feveral Acts of Affembly for making Provifion againft Invafions and Infurrections into one Act*, was read the third Time.

Refolved, That the Bill do pafs; and that the Title be, *An Act[3] for further continuing the Act, intituled An Act for reducing the feveral Acts of Affembly for making Provifion againft Invafions and Infurrections into one Act*.

Ordered, That Mʳ *Richard Henry Lee* do carry the Bill to the Council, and defire their Concurrence.

A *Bill* to amend an Act, intituled *An Act[4] to prevent malicious maiming and wounding*, was read a fecond Time.

Refolved

---

[1] Hening, VI, p. 394.   [2] Ibid, VII. p. 106.   [3] Ibid, VIII, p. 514.   [4] Ibid, VI. p. 250.

Refolved, That the Bill be committed to the Committee of Propofitions and Griev-ances,

An engroffed *Bill* for vefting in Truftees certain Lands whereof *William Booth*, Gentleman, and *Elizabeth* his Wife, are feized in Fee Tail, to be fold, and for laying out the Money arifing from the Sale in purchafing other Lands, to be fettled to the fame Ufes, was read the third Time.

Refolved, That the Bill do pafs; and that the Title be, *An Act¹ for vefting in Truftees certain Lands whereof* William Booth, *Gentleman, and* Elizabeth *his Wife, are feifed in Fee Tail, to be fold, and for laying out the Money arifing from the Sale in purchafing other Lands, to be fettled to the fame Ufes.*

Ordered, That Mr *Richard Henry Lee* do carry the Bill to the Council, and defire their Concurrence.

A *Bill* to appoint Commiffioners to ftrike a dividing Line between the Counties of *Stafford* and *King George*, was read a fecond Time.

Ordered, That the Bill be engroffed.

A *Bill* to dock the Intail of certain Lands whereof *William Todd*, Gentleman, is feifed, and for other Purpofes therein mentioned, was read a fecond Time.

Refolved, That the Bill be committed to Mr *Edmund Pendleton*, Mr *Corbin*, Mr *Aylett*, Mr *Moore*, and Mr *Montagu*.

A *Bill* to dock the Intail of certain Lands whereof *James Blackwell*, the younger, is feifed, and for other Purpofes therein mentioned, was read a fecond Time.

Refolved, That the Bill be committed to Mr *Treafurer*, Mr *Patrick Henry*, Mr *Smith*, Mr *Aylett*, Mr *Moore*, Mr *Corbin*, and Mr *Edmund Pendleton*.

A *Bill* for appointing Commiffioners to view the Lands on both Sides of *James* River, from *Weftham*, to the navigable Water below the Falls of the faid River, and for other Purpofes therein mentioned, was read a fecond Time.

Refolved, That the Bill be committed to the Committee of Propofitions and Griev-ances.

A *Bill* for clearing a Road from the Warm Springs, in *Augufta*, and for other Purpofes therein mentioned, was read a fecond Time.

Refolved, That the Bill be committed to the Committee of Propofitions and Griev-ances.

And then the Houfe adjourned till Monday Morning next eleven of the Clock.

Monday, the 9th of March. 12 George III. 1772.

ANOTHER *Member* having taken the Oaths appointed to be taken by Act of Parliament, and repeated and fubfcribed the Teft, took his Place in the Houfe.

Ordered, That Mr *Talbot*, and Mr *Anderfon* be added to the Committees of Propofitions and Grievances, and of Public Claims.

Mr *Richard Lee* reported from the Committee of Public Claims, to whom the Petition of *John Doncaftle* was referred, that the Committee had examined the Matter of the faid Petition, and had directed him to report the fame, together with the Refolution of the Committee thereupon, to the Houfe; and he read the Report in his Place, and afterwards delivered it in at the Clerk's Table; where the fame was read, and is as followeth, *viz.*

It appears to your *Committee* that two of the Petitioner's Waggons were, by Order of *William Byrd*, Efquire, employed one hundred and ninety fix Days, each, in the Ser-vice of the Colony, in the Year 1759, for which it does not appear to your Committee that the Petitioner has received any Satiffaction.

Whereupon the *Committee* came to the following Refolution:

Refolved, That it is the Opinion of this Committee, that the faid Petition is reafon-able; and that the Petitioner ought to be allowed the Sum of two hundred and twenty-five

¹ Hening, VIII, p. 640.

five Pounds and eight Shillings for the Services aforesaid, with Interest on the same, from the ninth Day of *June*, 1770, till paid.

The said *Resolution*, being read a second Time, was, upon the Question put thereupon, agreed to by the House.

Mr *Richard Henry Lee* reported, from the Committee for Courts of Justice, to whom the Bill for altering the Court Day of *Surry* County, was committed, that the Committee had gone through the Bill, and had made several Amendments thereunto, which they had directed him to report to the House; and he read the Report in his Place, and afterwards delivered the Bill, with the Amendments, in at the Clerk's Table; where the Amendments were once read throughout, and then, a second Time, one by one, and, upon the Question severally put thereupon, were agreed to by the House.

Ordered, That the Bill, with the Amendments, be ingrossed.

A *Petition* of *Joseph Turner* was presented to the House, and read; setting forth, that the petitioner had been Inspector of Tobacco at the Warehouses at the College and Capitol Landings for many Years, and hopes he always executed his Office with Integrity and Approbation; and that he is obliged to keep a Negro to assist in the laborious Work at the said Warehouses, for which, and his own Attendance, he used to receive a Salary of thirty-five Pounds, which was reduced the last General Assembly to twenty-five Pounds, a Sum by no Means adequate to his Trouble and Expence; and therefore praying, that his said Salary may be raised to what it formerly was.

Ordered, That the said petition be referred to the Consideration of the Committee of Propositions and Grievances; and that they do examine the Matter thereof, and report the same, with their Opinion thereupon, to the House.

Mr *Richard Lee* reported from the Committee of Public Claims, to whom several petitions were referred, that the Committee had examined the Matters of the said Petitions, and had come to several Resolutions thereupon, which they had directed him to report to the House; and he read the Report in his Place, and afterwards delivered it in at the Clerk's Table; where the Resolutions of the Committee were read, and are as followeth, *viz.*

Resolved, That it is the Opinion of this Committee, that the petition of *Robert Hamilton*, to be allowed for traveling to, and attending the Court of *Oyer* and *Terminer*, in *December*, 1767, as a Witness for the King against *James Golding*, a Criminal from *Loudoun* County, is reasonable; and that the petitioner ought to be allowed six hundred and eighteen Pounds of Tobacco for the same.

Resolved, That it is the Opinion of this Committee, that the petition of *Thomas Lewis*, Administrator of the Estate of *Richard Coombs*, deceased, to be allowed for *Mary*, the Wife of the said *Richard*, her travelling to, and attending the Court of *Oyer* and *Terminer*, in *December*, 1767, as a Witness for the King against *James Golding*, a Criminal from *Loudoun* County, is reasonable; and that the petitioner ought to be allowed six hundred and eighteen Pounds of Tobacco for the same.

Resolved, That it is the Opinion of this Committee, that the Petition of *Christopher Perfect*, *Joshua Taylor*, and *John Macginnis*, to be allowed for traveling to, and attending the Court of *Oyer* and *Terminer*, in *December*, 1767, as Witnesses for the King against *James Golding*, a Criminal from *Loudoun* County, is reasonable; and that the Petitioners ought to be allowed six hundred and eighteen Pounds of Tobacco, each, for the same.

Resolved, That it is the Opinion of this Committee, that the Petition of the Inspectors at *Blandford* Warehouse, in the County of *Prince George*, to be allowed for the Tobacco stolen out of the said Warehouse, be rejected; it appearing, that, at the Time the said Tobacco was lost, the said Warehouse was insufficient.

Resolved, That it is the Opinion of this Committee, that so much of the Petition of *Nathaniel Raines* and *Lewis Brown*, Inspectors at *Boyd's* Warehouses, as relates to the Tobacco stolen out of the said Warehouses, be rejected; it appearing, that, at the Time the said Tobacco was lost, the said Warehouses were insufficient.

Resolved, That it is the Opinion of this Committee, that the Residue of the said Petition is reasonable; and that the Petitioners ought to be allowed the Sum of ten Pounds,

each

each, for their Trouble the laft Year, and the further Allowance of ten Pounds, each, *per Annum*, for the future, as an Increafe of Salary.

The *firft, fecond,* and *third* Refolutions of the Committee, being feverally read a fecond Time, were, upon the Queftion feverally put thereupon, agreed to by the Houfe.

The *fourth* Refolution of the Committee, being read a fecond Time;

Ordered, That the faid Refolution be recommitted to the faid Committee of Public Claims.

The *fifth* Refolution of the Committee, being read a fecond Time;

Ordered, That the faid Refolution be recommitted to the faid Committee of Public Claims.

The fubfequent *Refolution* of the Committee, being read a fecond Time, was, upon the Queftion put thereupon, agreed to by the Houfe.

Ordered, That it be an Inftruction to the Committee of Propofitions and Grievances, who are appointed to prepare and bring in a Bill for further continuing an Act, made in the fifth Year of the Reign of his prefent Majefty, intituled *An Act[1] for amending the Staple of Tobacco, and for preventing Frauds in his Majefty's Cuftoms,* that they make Provifion in the faid Bill for increafing the Salaries of the Infpectors of Tobacco at *Boyd's* Warehoufes, in the County of *Prince George,* ten Pounds *per Annum,* each.

A *Petition* of feveral perfons, of the County of *Fairfax,* whofe Names are thereunto fubfcribed, was prefented to the Houfe, and read; fetting forth, that two Lots in the Town of *Colchefter,* in the faid County, Numbers 6 and 42, on which, with a third Lot, Number 29, an Infpection of Tobacco was eftablifhed in or about the Year 1763, being improper Situations, the Warehoufes were built upon the faid Lot Number 29, and upon an adjoining Lot, Number 7, belonging to the fame Proprietor; and that the Court of the faid County have lately ordered another Warehoufe to be built in the faid Town, the moft convenient Place for which, there not being Room on the faid Lots 7 and 29, is the Lot, Number 8, adjoining one of the others; and further fetting forth, that the Salary allowed to each of the Infpectors at the faid Warehoufes, which has been lately reduced to thirty five Pounds, *per Annum,* is inadequate to their Trouble, lefs than is allowed to other Infpectors whofe Services do not deferve more, and not fufficient to engage Men of Characters to undertake the Office; and therefore praying, that the faid Lots 7 and 8, inftead of 6 and 42, may be eftablifhed as the legal Infpection; and that the Salaries of the faid Infpectors may be made equal with thofe of other Infpectors, who perform no greater Services; and that the Infpectors of the laft Year may have a reafonable Compenfation for their Trouble.

Ordered, That the faid petition be referred to the Confideration of the Committee of Propofitions and Grievances; and that they do examine the Matter thereof, and report the fame, with their Opinion thereupon, to the Houfe.

Ordered, That it be an Inftruction to the Committee of Propofitions and Grievances, who are appointed to prepare and bring in a Bill purfuant to the Refolutions of the faid Committee, which were reported to the Houfe, upon *Friday,* the 28th Day of laft Month, and which were agreed to by the Houfe, that they have Power to receive a Claufe or Claufes, to empower *James Edmondfon* to erect a Gate or Gates upon the main Road leading through his Land, from *Pifcataway* Ferry, in the County of *Effex.*

Mr *Richard Henry Lee* prefented to the Houfe, according to Order, a Bill for continuing and amending the Act, intituled *An Act[2] for deftroying Crows and Squirrels in certain Counties therein mentioned;* and the fame was received, and read the firft Time.

Refolved, That the Bill be read a fecond Time.

A *Petition* of divers of the Inhabitants of the Parifh of *Albemarle,* in the County of *Suffex,* whofe Names are thereunto fubfcribed, was prefented to the Houfe, and read; fetting forth, that the faid Parifh is extenfive, and the Tithables thereof numerous, and that there are four Churches in it; and therefore praying that the faid Parifh may be divided into two Parifhes.

A

---

[1] Hening, VIII, p. 69. [2] Ibid, VIII, p. 389.

A *Motion* was made, and the Queftion being put, that the faid Petition be referred to the Confideration of a Committee;

It paffed in the Negative.

Refolved, That the Petition be rejected.

A *Petition* of *Thomas Coleman* and *Thomas Butler*, Infpectors of Tobacco at *Aylett's* and *Todd's* Warehoufes, in the Counties of *King William* and *King and Queen*, was prefented to the Houfe, and read; praying that their Salaries may be increafed.

Ordered, That the faid Petition be referred to the Confideration of the Committee of Propofitions and Grievances; and that they do examine the Matter thereof, and report the fame, with their Opinion thereupon, to the Houfe.

M'r *Bland* reported from the Committee of Propofitions and Grievances, to whom feveral petitions were referred, that the Committee had examined the Matters of the faid petitions, and had come to feveral Refolutions thereupon, which they had directed him to report to the Houfe; and he read the Report in his Place, and afterwards delivered it in at the Clerk's Table; where the Refolutions of the Committee were read, and are as followeth, *viz.*

Refolved, That it is the Opinion of this Committee, that the petition of divers Inhabitants on *Goofe* Creek, in the County of *Bedford*, praying that *Jeremiah Early* may be compelled to open a Gate in his Mill Dam, at the Mouth of the faid Creek, for admitting Fifh, be rejected.

Refolved, That it is the Opinion of this Committee, that the petition of divers Inhabitants of *Bedford* County, praying that an Act may pafs, directing Slopes to be made in Mill Dams, and impowering certain Perfons to prefcribe the Manner of making the fame, is reafonable.

The faid *Refolutions*, being feverally read a fecond Time, were, upon the Queftion feverally put thereupon, agreed to by the Houfe.

Ordered, That a Bill be brought in purfuant to the fecond Refolution; and that the faid Committee do prepare, and bring in the fame.

And then the Houfe adjourned till Tomorrow Morning, eleven of the Clock.

Tuesday, the 10th of March, 12 George III. 1772.

SEVERAL other *Members* having taken the Oaths appointed to be taken by Act of Parliament, and repeated and fubfcribed the Teft, took their Places in the Houfe.

M'r *Treafurer* reported from the Committee for Religion, to whom the Petitions of the Inhabitants of the Parifh of *Saint John*, in the County of *King William*, praying a Diffolution of the Veftry of the faid Parifh, and alfo the Petition of feveral Veftrymen of the faid Parifh, in Oppofition thereto, were referred, that the Committee had examined the Matter of the faid Petitions, and had directed him to report the fame, together with the Refolutions of the Committee thereupon, to the Houfe; and he read the Report in his Place, and afterwards delivered it in at the Clerk's Table; where the fame was read, and is as followeth, *viz.*

Upon the firft *Article* of Charge, "fuggefting that a Party Spirit fubfifts amongft the Members of the Veftry, whereby the Bufinefs of the Parifh is retarded, and other great Inconveniences fuftained," it appears to your Committee, from the Teftimony of *William Peters Martin*, that he heard M'r *Thomas Claiborne*, one of the Veftry, fay, upon being told the Parifhioners were diffatiffied with the Conduct of the Veftry, and particularly at their not Meeting, that he would never attend as a Veftryman again; that he knows fome of the Parifhioners refufed to receive the Orders of Veftry for Proceffioning, alledging that they had not been made in proper Time; that he heard Col. *Francis Weft*, when in Liquor and in a Paffion, but out of Veftry, declare that he had rather be found at Sheepftealing, than in Veftry again, and that he would never more go to Veftry; that M'r *John Quarles*, another of the Veftry, refenting this Behaviour, fome

Abufe

Abuſe followed on both Sides, and a Struggle enſued; that this happened upwards of a Year ago; that the ſaid *Martin*, upon hearing who were Candidates for Seats in the Veſtry, in Caſe a Diſſolution ſhould take Place, publicly declared, if thoſe Candidates ſhould be elected, ſome of whom he thought ignorant Men, that the Pariſh, in his Opinion, would not be ſo well ſerved as by the preſent Veſtry; and that he therefore hoped the Veſtry would not be diſſolved.

It further appears to your *Committee*, from the Teſtimony of *John Watkins*, that he has frequently attended the Veſtry; but never diſcovered any Party Spirit in the Members.

It alſo *appears* to your *Committee*, from the Teſtimony of *Iſaac Quarles*, that he was at *King William* Court-Houſe, the 27th of *December* laſt, when a Veſtry was appointed to be held for laying the Pariſh Levy; that Col. *Braxton* deſired him to go to Col. *Francis Weſt*, and inform him, that there were ſix Veſtrymen aſſembled; and that he deſired he would come, in Order to make a Veſtry; but if the ſaid *Weſt* was not able, he was deſired to wait on Mr *Roger Gregory*, another Veſtryman, and tell him the ſame; that he accordingly went to Col. *Weſt's* Houſe, and delivered his Meſſage, but the ſaid *Weſt* was unable to attend; that, Mr *Gregory* being preſent, he delivered him the like Meſſage, but the ſaid *Gregory* ſaid, he had been waiting ſome Time there to ſee whether Col. *Bernard* and *Thomas Moore* went up the Road, that it was then too late to do Buſineſs, and he would not go; that the ſaid *Quarles* ſtayed at Col. *Weſt's* about an Hour, when he returned to the Court-Houſe, the Sun being about an Hour high; that the Diſtance from Col. *Weſt's* to the Court-Houſe is about ſeven Miles.

It likewiſe *appears* to your *Committee*, from the Teſtimony of *Thomas Roſe*, that he hath been Clerk of the ſaid Veſtry about four Years; that he never obſerved any Diſputes in the ſaid Veſtry, or anything of a Party Spirit, amongſt the Members, except what is hereafter mentioned; that about eighteen months ago, upon a Queſtion being agitated in Veſtry, whether they ſhould purchaſe Land for a new Glebe, or add to the old one, ſome Warmths and Diſputes aroſe, but the Veſtry came to no Concluſion that Day, upon that particular Buſineſs; that he thinks theſe Diſputes and Warmths might have prevented the Veſtry's coming to a Determination; that, when it was propoſed in Veſtry, that a Piece of Land called *Tuckcoman's* belonging to Mr *Thomas Claiborne*, ſhould be purchaſed for a Glebe, the ſaid *Claiborne* declared he thought the Pariſh not able to buy it, and that he would not vote in the Queſtion; that, though this was propoſed, and talked of in the Veſtry, no Queſtion was put relative to the ſaid Land, the Veſtry agreeing to wait and ſee how much could be raiſed by Subſcription, from an Unwillingneſs to tax the People more than 300 *l.* at that Time; that, to his Knowledge, no Queſtion was ever put at any other Time in Veſtry, concerning the Purchaſe of this Tract of Land; that, during his Clerkſhip, Mr *Thomas Claiborne* has given due Attendance, conducted himſelf, in his Opinion, as well as any Member of the ſaid Veſtry, and, as far as he knows or believes, with Candor and Impartiality.

It further *appears* to your *Committee*, from the Teſtimony of the Reverend *Henry Skyring*, that at a Veſtry held in *October*, 1770, ſome Words paſſed between him and Mr *Braxton*, a Member of the Veſtry, occaſioned, as he believes, by a Miſunderſtanding between them; that the Queſtion then put was, whether they ſhould add to the preſent Glebe, or purchaſe a new one? To which the ſaid *Skyring*, with ſome Warmth, anſwered that, as to adding to the old Glebe, "their Honours were at Stake to do it, ſhould he at any Time call upon them; but that the Situation of the Glebe was then Diſagreeable to him;" that there were other warm Diſputes amongſt the Members of the Veſtry that Day upon the ſame Queſtion; that Mr *Braxton* aſked him, out of Veſtry, whether it would be agreeable to him if the Veſtry ſhould come to a Reſolution of purchaſing a Tract of Land belonging to the ſaid *Braxton*, called *Broad Neck*, which Queſtion he remembers he did not anſwer; that Lands belonging to Mr *Quarles*, Mr *Thomas Claiborne*, and others, had been propoſed for the ſame Purpoſe, though Mr *Claiborne's* Land, he believes, was not mentioned when thoſe Diſputes happened; that Mr *Thomas Claiborne*, ever ſince his being of the Veſtry, has given due Attendance; that he thinks him an uſeful

and

and an impartial Member; that when the said *Claiborne's* Land was proposed to be purchased for a Glebe, he declared he would not give his Vote, as he thought the Parish
unable to make such a Purchase; that, however, the Question was never put; that the
said *Claiborne* attended the Day Mʳ *Gregory* was sent for, and did not come; that he has
not yet received his Salary for the Year 1769, when the said *Claiborne* was Collector,
though he does not blame him, or any of the Vestry, but his Deputy *Thomas Littlepage*,
whom he had so good an Opinion of, at that Time, that he would have preferred him as a
Collector; that he has seen, from under the Hand of said *Littlepage*, a State of his
Accounts as Deputy Collector for the said *Claiborne*, wherein he fully acquits the said
Claiborne from the Payment of the Minister, and the other Parish Creditors; that the
first Time the Vestry was called was, as he thinks, the 18ᵗʰ of *November* last; there were
present Col. *Francis West*, Mess. *John Quarles, Garlick, Braxton*, and *John West;* that
Mʳ *Philip Whitehead Claiborne* was at that Time on his Death Bed; that Col. *Bernard*
76 *Moore* was very ill with the Gout; that Mʳ *Roger Gregory* had lost his Lady not more than
three or four Days before, and that Mʳ *Thomas Claiborne*, as he understood, was attending *Essex* Court; that he cannot particularly say what was the Reason of Col. *Thomas
Moore's* not attending, but believes, at that Time, he was afraid of the Sheriff; that the
next Time, they proposed to hold a Vestry, the same Reasons, in some Measure, prevailed to prevent it; the said *Philip Whitehead Claiborne*, and *Bernard Moore*, could not
possibly attend, and Mʳˢ *Gregory* was not then buried.

It also *appears* to your *Committee*, from the Testimony of *Fendall Southerland*, that
he has often been at Vestries held for *Saint John's* Parish, and has heard many Disputes
among the Vestrymen, which he thinks seemed to look like a Party Spirit in the said
Vestry; that he hath heard Mʳ *Thomas Claiborne*, Mʳ *Gregory*, Col. *Francis West*, and
others, of the said Vestry, say that the Vestry wanted to make Parties to carry Points; that
Mʳ *William Dandridge*, one of the Vestry, has resigned, and he heard the said *Dandridge*
say he did it on Account of some Disputes which happened in Vestry; that several of the
Persons appointed to procession Lands have declared that they would not proceed in
their Business, as the Time for beginning was past before they received the Orders, and
they could not compleat them before the Return Day; that he was at the Court-House the
27ᵗʰ of *December* last, the Day appointed to lay the Parish Levy, and there being only
six Members, a Messenger was dispatched for Col. *West*, as the said *Southerland* understood, or Mʳ *Gregory*, if Col. *West* could not come; that when the Messenger returned, he
informed the Members of the Vestry present, that the said *West* was too much indisposed
to attend, and that the said *Gregory* said he had waited some Time for Col. *Moore* to have
gone up with him, but that it was then too late, and he would not come, or Words to that
Purpose; that upon this being told the said *Braxton*, he declared he never would meet in
that Vestry again, and that it was high Time for a Dissolution; that he would draw a
Petition for the People to sign for that Purpose, which he did, as the said *Braxton* informed him; that he believes the said *Braxton*, with many others, signed the said Petition;
that he hath heard the said *Braxton, Thomas Claiborne, John Quarles, Roger Gregory,*
and *Francis West*, declare that they were willing a Dissolution should take Place, and
would sign a petition; that he heard the said *Thomas Claiborne* in Vestry, some Years ago,
say the Vestry had levied 2000 lbs. of Tobacco for the Minister contrary to Law; and that,
if for no other Reason, the said Vestry ought to be dissolved; that he has heard some
others of the Vestry declare that, as there was not one of the Vestry living who had been
chosen by the People, the said Vestry ought to be dissolved for that Reason.

It further *appears* to your *Committee*, from the Testimony of *Holt Richeson*, that he
was at a Vestry held at the Court House, when a Dispute happened about purchasing
Land for a new Glebe; that Mʳ *Roger Gregory*, some Time before that, desired him to
speak to Mʳ *William Dandridge*, to join their Party; on which he, thinking the said *Dandridge* was not to be influenced, told him he did not chuse to do it, as he thought it would
be using the said *Dandridge very ill*, and that he would have a Right to break his Head;
to which the said *Gregory* replied, if the said *Dandridge* did not join them, they could not
carry their Point in purchasing a Piece of Land, called *Tuckcoman's*; that in Course of

the

the Debate, that Day, about purchafing *Tuckcoman's*, Col. *Weft* infifted it would be cheaper to purchafe that Land than to add to the Glebe; on which feveral Difputes arofe, and the Veftry broke up, without doing any Bufinefs; that the fame Evening he heard Mr *William Dandridge* declare he would not fit in Veftry again, unlefs it was to lay the Parifh Levy, and foon afterwards he refigned; that fome Time laft Fall, being at Mr *Thomas Claiborne's*, in Converfation with him, the faid *Claiborne* mentioned fome Gentlemen, who he thought would be proper to fill up the Vacancies in the Veftry; that Mr *Claiborne* further faid, that he himfelf, and Mr *Gregory*, had pitched upon three as Veftrymen, who, if they were chofen, would join them, and then the lower Gentlemen, would have a ftronger Party than the upper, and they fhould be able to do as they pleafed, or Words to that Effect; that the faid *Richefon* replied, if Col. *Thomas Moore* appeared at Veftry, the upper Members would be on a footing with them, and they could not carry their Point; to which faid *Claiborne* anfwered, if he, *Moore*, would not join them, he would put a Paper into Mr *Rofe*, the Sheriff's Hands, which fhould keep him from attending, by which Means it would be in his Power to have thofe Gentlemen chofen he had pitched upon; that the Perfons the faid *Claiborne* mentioned to have joined him in carrying the Point, of chufing Veftrymen, were Col. *Francis Weft*, Mr *John Weft*, and Mr *Roger Gregory*, and the Perfons propofed to be chofen were Meff. *Ferdinando Leigh*, *William Claiborne*, and *Richard Gregory*; that on his telling Mr *Braxton*, and Mr *William Dandridge*, the Converfation that paffed between Mr *Thomas Claiborne* and him, Mr *Dandridge* anfwered, that before the Parifh fhould be impofed upon, he would qualify, and act himfelf, as he was then re-chofen by the Veftry; that accordingly the faid *Dandridge* went to Court to qualify, but no Court was held that Day; fince which the faid *Dandridge's* Indifpofition has prevented his qualifying; that there are but nine Members qualified to act as Veftrymen in the Parifh, fince the Death of Mr *Philip Whitehead Claiborne*, which happened fome Time about the firft of *December* laft.

It likewife *appears* to your *Committee*, from the Teftimony of Mr *William Dandridge*, Veftryman of the faid Parifh, that the Reafon of his refigning his Seat in Veftry was, that after a Queftion had been argued, and five of the Members, which were a Majority, had agreed to come to a Refolution, and enter an Order thereupon, the other three Members, then prefent, refufed to fign the Orders, and the Veftry were obliged to break up without doing any Bufinefs; that the three Gentlemen who refufed to fign, were Col. *Francis Weft*, Mr *Thomas Claiborne*, and Mr *Roger Gregory;* and that it is cuftomary, in that Veftry, for all the Members prefent to fign the Orders.

It alfo *appears* to your *Committee*, from the Teftimony of Mr *Carter Braxton*, that on the 27th of *December* laft, fix of the Veftry of *Saint John's* Parifh, having met at *King William* Court-Houfe, to do the Bufinefs of the Parifh, they, or fome of them, defired Mr *Claiborne* to write a Letter to Col. *Weft*, and Mr *Roger Gregory*, defiring them, or one of them, to attend, but a Meffenger was difpatched for that Purpofe before Mr *Claiborne*, who had retired to write the Letter, returned with it; that the faid *Claiborne*, apprehenfive that the Veftry might fufpect him of not having wrote what they had defired, requefted the faid *Braxton* to read the Letter, upon Perufal of which he was fully convinced that it only contained the Senfe of the Veftry; that the faid *Claiborne* told the faid *Braxton*, then Sheriff of the faid County, that he had an Execution againft Mr *Thomas Moore*, who was then prefent, and was directed to put the faid Execution into the faid *Braxton's* Hands, but that he would not do it, as the faid *Moore* came up to do the Parifh Bufinefs; that he, the faid *Braxton*, never did difcover any Party Spirit, or Partiality, in the faid *Claiborne*, as a Veftryman; that he had often differed with him in Opinion, but that he did not impute it to any private Views of the faid *Claiborne;* that he thinks the faid *Claiborne* one of the moft able and ferviceable Veftrymen in the Parifh; that he, the faid *Braxton*, with the other Members of the Veftry, did folicit Mr *William Dandridge*, who had refigned, to refume his Seat in the Veftry; that the faid *Dandridge* made fome flight Objections, as to the Propriety of refigning one Day, and refuming the fame Place the next, but defired fome Time to think of it; that the Veftry, however, re-elected the faid *Dandridge*, as they knew him to be a worthy Member; that the faid *Dandridge* has never

yet

yet qualified, but did some Time in *December* last, on being told what Mr *Richeson* asserted, declare he would act rather than the Parish should be imposed upon. The said *Braxton*, being asked whether he did not desire Mr *William Aylett* to meet at the next Court, in Order to qualify the said *Dandridge*, before the meeting of the Vestry, which was appointed to be held on the 27th of *December*, replied, that he did not remember such Conversation, but would admit he had done so; the said *Braxton* being asked by Mr *Samuel Garlick* his Opinion of him, as a Vestryman, replied, that he believed him to be a worthy, honest Man, and a good Vestryman.

It further *appears* to your *Committee*, from the Testimony of *Bernard Powers*, that he was at the Court-House the 27th of *December* last, when a Vestry was appointed to be held to lay the Parish Levy, and understanding that there was not a sufficient Number to hold a Vestry, Col. *Braxton* sent Mr *Isaac Quarles* for Col. *West*, and Mr *Gregory;* that the said *Quarles* returned, and informed the said *Braxton* that Col. *West* was unable to come, and that Mr *Gregory* would not come; that this seemed to displease the said *Braxton*, and he then declared he thought it was high Time to move for a Dissolution, when the Gentlemen of the Vestry would not attend to do Business, and that he would draw a Petition for that Purpose; that Mr *Thomas Claiborne*, another Vestryman, who was then present, likewise said, "do it as soon as you will, and if I don't sign it, it will be because I cannot write"; that soon after a Petition, said to be drawn by the said *Braxton*, was handed about, and the said *Powers* was asked to sign it, which he did, with many others.

With *Respect* to the *second* and *third* Articles of Charge, complaining that the said Vestry had made an Order to petition this House for a Law to enable them to sell their Glebe, and allow the Rector of the Parish fifty Pounds a Year, in Lieu thereof, and suggesting that by the said Vestry's taking such a Step, the Parish had lost about the Sum of four hundred Pounds, subscribed in that, and the neighbouring Parishes, to make Additions to the Glebe, it appears to your Committee, that the Vestry judging their present Glebe insufficient for the Minister, on the 29th Day of *November*, 1768, made an Order, appointing Mr *Philip Whitehead Claiborne, Samuel Garlick, William Dandridge, Thomas Moore,* and *John West*, Gentlemen, or any three of them, to view the Lands of *James Quarles*, and make Report of the Value thereof to the next Vestry; that at another Vestry, held the 30th of *November*, 1770, the said Vestry not having then fixed on a Piece of Land for a Glebe, it was ordered, that *James Quarles, Francis West, Bernard Moore, Philip Whitehead Claiborne, John West, Samuel Garlick* and *Carter Braxton*, Gentlemen, or any three of them, should meet at the Court House, on *Tuesday* the 11th of *December* following, by nine o'Clock, to view the Lands adjacent to the Glebe, and make Report to the Vestry of the Value and Conveniences of the same, that the said Vestry might be informed of the most proper Piece of Land that could be annexed to the Glebe.

It further *appears* to your *Committee*, that on the 25th Day of *August*, 1770, the said Vestry, being apprehensive that the Reverend Mr *Skyring* would leave their Parish, as they understood an advantageous Offer had been made him from another, in Hopes of inducing him to continue with them, set on Foot, and actually entered into Articles of Subscription, in the Words following, to wit: "We the Subscribers, being willing and very desirous of keeping our present Incumbent, the Reverend Mr *Henry Skyring*, in the Parish of *St. John*, and County of *King William;* and whereas we have this Day thought in Vestry, that the Glebe, now appropriated for the Use of the Minister in the said Parish, is insufficient for the Support of him, and, at the same Time, were of Opinion that the Vestrymen of the said Parish could not, with Propriety, tax the People sufficiently to purchase such a Glebe as might or would be agreeable to the present Incumbent, we have fell on the following Method, *viz.* we, and each of us, do hereby agree, and do bind ourselves, our Heirs, Executors, and Administrators, to pay the Sums respectively subscribed to each of our Names, for and towards purchasing such a Piece of Land as shall be agreeable to the said Mr *Skyring*, for the Use of the said *Skyring*, and his Successors, as Ministers of the Parish aforesaid, for and towards enabling the Vestry to purchase a sufficient Glebe for the said Parish; and in Order to render the Collection of the same more certain, we, and each of us, do hereby authorize and empower the Vestry of our

said

said Parish to levy the Sums respectively subscribed to our Names, on our Goods and Chattels, Lands and Tenements to be collected by such Person as shall by the said Vestry be appointed to collect the Parish Levy next to be laid;" that there was subscribed two hundred and forty-two Pounds in all, of which one hundred and seventy Pounds were subscribed by different Members of the Vestry.

It further *appears* to your *Committee*, that, on the 8th Day of *December* following, other Articles of Subscription were set on Foot, which are contained in these Words, to wit, "Whereas on the 25th Day of *August* last, the Vestry of *Saint John's* Parish met at the House of Mr *Richard Banks*, and being very desirous of keeping the present Incumbent, Mr *Henry Skyring*, they then fell upon a Method of raising a Sum of Money by Subscription to purchase Lands for the said Incumbent, and Use of the Parish, but since which it is thought more expedient to lay out Part of the Money so subscribed in purchasing Negroes for the Use of Mr *Henry Skyring*, during his Continuance, as Rector in this Parish, and in Case of the Death or Resignation of the said Mr *Henry Skyring*, the said Negroes shall be vested in the Vestry of the said parish of *Saint John*, and the Profits and Increase arising from such Negroes to be laid out either for the Support of the next Incumbent, or lessening the Parish Levy, as the said Vestry shall think proper; we and each of us do hereby agree, and do bind ourselves, our Heirs, Executors, and Administrators, to pay the Sums respectively subscribed to each of our Names, first, for and towards purchasing four Slaves, two of which to be Females, the Overplus to be applied in purchasing or adding any Lands to the present Glebe that the Vestry shall think proper. It is hereby declared by the said Vestry, that the Subscribers to this shall be discharged from the Payment of the former Subscription of the above Date, and in Order to render the Collection of the same more certain, we, and each of us, do hereby authorize and empower the Vestry of our said parish to levy the Sums, respectively subscribed to our Names, on our Goods, and Chattels, Lands, and Tenements, to be collected by such Person as shall by the said Vestry be appointed to collect the Parish Levy;" which last mentioned Articles were subscribed by Mr *John Roane*, and several others, who had subscribed the former Articles.

It further *appears* to your *Committee*, that the Vestry taking into Consideration the Value of the Land which had been viewed, and which was estimated at 400 *l*. and finding the Repairs of their present Glebe would amount to 200 *l*. at least, they judged it most for the Interest of the Parish to accept a Proposal, made by their Minister, to allow him 50 *l. per Annum* in Lieu of the Glebe, and accordingly, at a Vestry held the 22d of *April*, 1771, it was ordered, that the Churchwardens, for the Time being, should prepare a Petition, to be signed by the Vestry, to apply to the next Session of Assembly, for Leave to sell their present Glebe, it being adjudged in Vestry that the same was insufficient, and to allow the Vestry to comply with a Bargain that Day made with their present Incumbent, the Reverend Mr *Henry Skyring*, which was to allow him 50 *l*. a Year, in Lieu of another Glebe to be bought, during his Residence in the said Parish, and the Parish to receive five *Per Cent*. on the Amount of the Sale of the said Glebe.

It further *appears* to your *Committee*, from the Declarations of several of the Vestry, that the Money proposed to be raised by the Subscription is still left in the Hands of the Subscribers, unappropriated, and is now intended to be laid out in Slaves, for the Use of the present Incumbent, provided he remains in the Parish, and the Contract before mentioned takes Place.

It further *appears* to your *Committee*, from the Testimony of *John Roane*, that he, being at the Upper Church in the said Parish, saw a Paper handed about, to raise a Sum of Money, by Subscription, to purchase a Glebe, in Order to induce the Minister to continue in the Parish; that Mr *William Aylett* and he subscribed 40 *s.* each, and on their way Home, the said *Aylett* expressed some Dissatisfaction at the Smallness of the Sum, and that they agreed to make each of their Subscriptions ten Pounds, but that he thinks his Design in subscribing has not been carried into Execution, and that therefore he does not think himself obliged to pay any Part of the Money, as he has understood the Vestry intends to lay out the Money in Slaves, instead of Land; that

he

he figned the fecond Subfcription, fuppofing it a Copy of the firft, and therefore did not read it; that the faid *Aylett* and *Roane* live in *Saint David's* Parifh.

It alfo *appears* to your *Committee*, from the Teftimony of *Holt Richefon*, that he thought the Defign of the Subfcription was to purchafe a Glebe, to induce Mr *Skyring* to continue in the Parifh, and that otherwife the Subfcription was to be of no Effect, if a Sufficiency could not be procured for that Purpofe.

Upon *inquiring* into the *fourth* and laft Article of Charge, complaining that the faid Veftry in the Years 1766, and 1767, made an Order to Rent out the Glebe, and allow the Minifter 2000 lbs. of Tobacco, and Cafk, a Year, in Lieu thereof, that the Tobacco had been annually levied on the Petitioners, and the Glebe rented out in a very imprudent Manner, for the inconfiderable Sum of 5 *l. per Annum*, and this not regularly accounted for, it appears to your Committee, that at a Veftry, held the 15th of *April*, 1766, it was "refolved, that the Veftry do levy for the Reverend Mr *Skyring* 2000 lbs. of Tobacco, and Cafk, yearly, in Lieu of the Glebe, during his Pleafure;" and that at another Veftry, held the 24th of *November*, in the fame Year, it was "ordered, that the Churchwardens let the repairing of the Glebe, and rented it out for the Ufe of the Parifh," and that, at another Veftry, held the 1ft Day of *December*, 1769, "Col. *Francis Weft* acknowledged himfelf indebted to the Parifh, for the Rent of the Glebe, two Years, ten Pounds."

It further *appears* to your *Committee*, from the Teftimony of Mr *Samuel Garlick*, a Member of the faid Veftry, that he, amongft the reft of the Veftry, confented to let Col. *Francis Weft* live as a Tenant on the Glebe, the firft Year, for putting the Fences and keeping the Houfes in Order, and that he was to pay, for the fecond Year, 10 *l.* Rent; that in his Opinion, it was a very advantageous Bargain for the Parifh, as Col. *Weft* informed him, he had got fourteen thoufand Rails, and made fome little Repairs to the Glebe; that, in the Month of *February* laft, after Notice had been given by public Advertifements, the renting of the Glebe was fet up at public Auction, that no Perfon offered more than 6 *l.* a Year, till he, for the Benefit of the Parifh, bid for the faid Glebe, and raifed the Rent to 10 *l.* 10 *s.* 6 *d.* at which Price it was let to one *Jafon Ifbell*, who gave Bond and Security for the Payment of the fame.

It further *appears* to your *Committee*, from the Teftimony of Mr *Carter Braxton*, upon his being afked why the Veftry rented the Glebe to Col. *Weft*, without fetting it up, to the higheft Bidder that he did not recollect whether he was in Veftry at that Time, or not, but that the Veftrymen told him it was let to Col. *Weft*, becaufe he was to live on the Glebe, make some slight Repairs, and renew the Fences, and that they expected he would take more Care of it than any other Perfon, for which Reafon he was to have it the firft Year Rent free.

It further *appears*, from an Account stated in the Veftry Book, that the Parifh has had Credit for ten Pounds, the Rent due from Col. *Weft*, though on that Account Mr *Claiborne*, the Collector, appears indebted to the Parifh upwards of four Pounds, which the prefent Collector has taken upon himfelf. Several of the Veftrymen declared before your Committee, that they thought it for the intereft of the Parifh to allow their Minifter 2000 lbs. of Tobacco, rather than put the Parifh to the Expence of repairing the Glebe, which they fuppofed would have coft upwards of two hundred Pounds.

It further *appears* to your *Committee*, from the Teftimony of Mr *Thomas Rofe*, that the Parifh Levy this Year is 24 lbs. of Tobacco *per* Poll; that laft Year it was fettled at 40, as the Veftry had in View the repairing of the Churches, but this not having been done, there remained a Quantity of Tobacco in Hand, which occafioned a Reduction of the prefent Year's Levy, and that for several Years preceding the laft, the Levy has not exceeded 30 and 30 odd Pounds of Tobacco *per* Poll.

Upon the whole *Matter*, your Committee came to the following Refolutions, *viz.*

Refolved, That it is the Opinion of this Committee, that fo much of the firft Article of Charge, as alledges fuch a Party Spirit to have fubfifted amongft the Members of the prefent Veftry, as is in the highest Degree prejudicial to the true Intereft of the Parifh, that it created Warmths, retarded Bufinefs, and hath, of late years, prevented

Meetings

Meetings; that feveral of the Veftry have declared they never would meet again in Veftry, and expreffed a Willingnefs for a Diffolution to take Place, hath been proved, and is true.

Refolved, That it is the Opinion of this Committee, that fo much of the faid firft Article, as fuggefts, that the Prevalence of a Party Spirit amongft the Members of the faid Veftry hath prevented the laying of the Parifh Levy for the laft Year, hath not been proved, and is not true.

Refolved, That it is the Opinion of this Committee, that the faid Veftry, with refpect to any Thing laid to their Charge, either in the fecond, or third Article, have not been Guilty of any Breach of their Duty.

Refolved, That it is the Opinion of this Committee, that the faid Veftry, with Refpect to any Charge laid againft them in the fourth, and laft Article, have not been Guilty of any Breach of their Duty.

Refolved, That it is the Opinion of this Committee, that the faid Petitions, praying that a Law may be enacted to diffolve the faid Veftry, be rejected.

The *firft* Refolution of the Committee being read a fecond Time;

The *Amendment* following was propofed to be made thereunto, *viz.*

To add at the End thereof thefe Words, *viz.*

"*As to thofe Members who refufed to confirm the Refolution of the Veftry, by figning their Orders, and neglected to attend the faid Veftry, to do the Parifh Bufinefs, when duly fummoned thereto, but not as to the other Members of the faid Veftry.*"

And the faid *Amendment* was, upon the Queftion put thereupon, agreed to by the Houfe.

Refolved, That the Houfe doth agree with the Committee in the faid Refolution fo amended, that fo much of the firft Article of Charge as alledges fuch a Party Spirit to have fubfifted amongft the Members of the prefent Veftry, as is, in the higheft Degree, prejudicial to the true Intereft of the Parifh; that it created Warmths, retarded Bufinefs, and hath of late Years prevented Meetings; that feveral of the Veftry have declared they never would meet again in the Veftry, and expreffed a Willingnefs for a Diffolution to take Place, hath been proved, and is true, as to thofe Members who refufed to confirm the Refolution of the Veftry, by figning their Orders, and neglected to attend the faid Veftry, to do the Parifh Bufinefs, when duly fummoned thereto, but not as to the other Members of the faid Veftry.

The *fecond, third,* and *fourth* Refolutions of the Committee, being feverally read a fecond Time, were, upon the Queftion feverally put thereupon, agreed to by the Houfe.

The fubfequent *Refolution* of the Committee, being read a fecond Time;

And the Queftion being put, that the Houfe doth agree with the Committee in the faid Refolution;

It paffed in the Negative.

Refolved, That the faid Petitions, praying that a Law may be enacted to diffolve the faid Veftry, are reafonable.

Ordered, That Mr *Aylett* and Mr *Dandridge* be added to the Gentleman, who is appointed to prepare, and bring in a Bill, purfuant to the Prayer of the Petition of the Veftrymen of the Parifh of *Saint Martin,* in the Counties of *Hanover* and *Louifa,* for an Act to diffolve the Veftry of the faid Parifh.

Ordered, That it be an Inftruction to the Gentlemen who are appointed to prepare and bring in the faid Bill, that they do make Provifion in the faid Bill for diffolving the Veftry of the Parifh of *Saint John,* in the County of *King William.*

Mr *Treafurer* prefented to the Houfe, according to Order, a Bill for dividing the Parifhes of *Southam,* in the County of *Cumberland,* and *Dale,* in the County of *Chefterfield;* and the fame was received, and read the firft Time.

Refolved, That the Bill be read a fecond Time.

A *Petition* of feveral Perfons of the County of *Amelia,* whofe Names are thereunto fubfcribed, praying that a Public Warehoufe, for the Reception of Wheat, may be eftablifhed, under proper Regulations, at *Gateffield,* on *James* River; *and alfo,*

A

A *Petition* of several Persons of the County of *Chesterfield*, whose Names are thereunto subscribed, praying that Public Warehouses, for the Reception of Wheat, may be established, under proper Regulations, at some convenient Place or Places, Upon *James* River; *and also*,

A *Petition* of several Persons of the County of *Cumberland*, whose Names are thereunto subscribed, praying that a Public Warehouse, for the Reception of Wheat, may be established, under proper Regulations, at *Rocky Ridge*, or *Chester*, on *James* River,

80   Were severally *presented* to the House, and read.

Ordered, That the said Petitions be referred to the Consideration of the Committee of Propositions and Grievances; and that they do examine the Matter thereof, and report the same, with their Opinion thereupon, to the House.

The *Order* of the Day being read;

Resolved, That this House will, upon *Friday* next, resolve itself into a Committee of the whole House upon the Bill to remove the Seat of Government to a Place more convenient to the Inhabitants of this Colony.

Mr *Bland* reported from the Committee of Propositions and Grievances, to whom the Petition of the Magistrates, and several Persons of the County of *Surry*, and of several Persons of the Town of *Cobham*, and others, was referred, that the Committee had examined the Matter of the said petition, and had come to several Resolutions thereupon, which they had directed him to report to the House; and he read the Report in his Place, and afterwards delivered it in at the Clerk's Table; where the Resolutions of the Committee were read, and are as followeth, *viz.*

Resolved, That it is the Opinion of this Committee, that so much of the said petition, as prays that the Titles to the Lots, purchased of former Trustees for the said Town of *Cobham*, may be confirmed, and new Trustees for the said Town appointed, is reasonable.

Resolved, That it is the Opinion of this Committee, that such other Part of the said Petition, as prays that Swine may be prohibited from going at large in the said Town, be rejected.

Resolved, That it is the Opinion of this Committee, that the Residue of the said petition, praying that the Ferry from *Crouche's* Creek to *Jamestown* may be discontinued, and a Ferry from *Gray's* Creek to *Jamestown* be established, is reasonable.

The said *Resolutions*, being severally read a second time, were, upon the Question severally put thereupon, agreed to by the House.

Ordered, That a Bill be brought in pursuant to the first Resolution; and that the said Committee do prepare, and bring in the same.

Ordered, That it be an Instruction to the said Committee, who are appointed to prepare, and bring in a Bill for repealing so much of the Act made in the fifth Year of the Reign of his present Majesty, intituled *An Act*[1] *for appointing several new Ferries, and for other Purposes therein mentioned*, as established a Ferry from the Land of *Cornelius Thomas*, over the *Fluvanna*, to the Land of *Nicholas Davies*, that they have Power to receive a Clause or Clauses pursuant to the third Resolution.

A *Petition* of several Persons of the County of *Botetourt*, whose Names are thereunto subscribed, was presented to the House, and read; setting forth, that the Distance which the Petitioners go to Market, with their Commodities, the chief of which is Hemp, would be lessened sixty Miles, by a Road over the South Mountain, the Cost of making which, it is apprehended, would not exceed three hundred Pounds; and therefore praying that such Road may be opened at the Expence of the Public.

Ordered, That the said Petition be referred to the Consideration of the Committee of Trade; and that they do examine the Matter thereof, and report the same, with their Opinion thereupon, to the House.

A *Petition* of several Persons of the County of *Elizabeth City*, whose Names are thereunto subscribed, was presented to the House, and read; setting forth, that the Pond of a Water Grist Mill in the said County, belonging to the infant Heir of *Booth Armistead*, deceased, is not only injurious to the Health of those who live in the neighbourhood

---

[1] Hening, VIII, p. 44.

bourhood thereof, but renders large Quantities of fruitful Land, which might eafily be drained, unprofitable, and hinders the carrying of a great deal of valuable Timber to Market, that the faid Mill does not grind more than half the Year, and is of little Advantage to the Cuftomers; and therefore praying that an Act may pafs to difcontinue the faid Mill, or that the Petitioners may have fuch other Redrefs as fhall feem juft.

Ordered, That the faid Petition be referred to the Confideration of the Committee of Propofitions and Grievances; and that they do examine the Matter thereof, and report the fame, with their Opinion thereupon, to the Houfe. 81

And then the Houfe adjourned till Tomorrow Morning eleven of the Clock.

Wednesday, the 11th of March, 12 George III. 1772.

MR *Marfhall* prefented to the Houfe, according to Order, a Bill to explain and amend an Act, intituled An Act[1] *to oblige the Owners of Mills, Hedges, or Stops, on the Rivers therein mentioned, to make Openings or Slopes therein for the Paffage of Fifh;* and the fame was received, and read the firft Time.

Refolved, That the Bill be read a fecond Time.

A *Meffage* from the Council by Mr *Blair:*

Mr *Speaker,*

The Council have agreed to the Bill, *intituled* An Act[2] for further continuing the Act, intituled an Act for reducing the feveral Acts of Affembly for making Provifion againft Invafions and Infurrections into one Act, *without any Amendment; and alfo,*

The Council have agreed to the Bill, intituled an Act[3] to empower the Clerks of County Courts to iffue certain Writs of Execution into other Counties, *without any Amendment; and alfo,*

The Council have agreed to the Bill, *intituled* An Act[4] to continue an Act, intituled an Act for eftablifhing Pilots, and regulating their Fees, *without any Amendment; and alfo,*

The Council have agreed to the Bill, *intituled* An Act[5] for vefting in Truftees certain Lands, whereof *William Booth* and *Elizabeth* his Wife are feifed in Fee Tail, to be fold, and for laying out the Money, arifing from the Sale, in purchafing other Lands, to be fettled to the fame Ufes, *without any Amendment; and alfo,*

The Council have agreed to the Refolve *for paying a Sum of Money, and an Annuity to* John Robinfon.

And then the Meffenger withdrew.

Mr *Cary* reported from the Committee of Public Claims, to whom the Petition of Infpectors of Tobacco at *Blandford* Warehoufes, in the County of *Prince George*, had been referred, and to whom the Refolution of the Committee thereupon was recommitted, that the Committee had further examined the Matter of the faid Petition, and had directed him to report the fame, together with the Refolution of the Committee thereupon, to the Houfe; and he read the Report in his Place, and afterwards delivered it in at the Clerk's Table; where the fame was read, and is as followeth, *viz.*

It appears to your *Committee*, that there are two Warehoufes at the Infpection at *Blandford*, one of which is open on one Side, and the other on both; that the faid Houfes are inclofed in a Yard by a Wall about feven Feet high, made with Pofts fet in the Ground, and Inch Planks laid clofe together, and nailed thereon with twenty Penny Nails; that the back Side of one, and the Ends of both the faid Houfes, ferve as Part of the Inclofure, and are ftrong and fecure; and that the Gates to the faid Wall are fupplied with ftrong Locks and Chains.

Whereupon your *Committee* came to the following Refolution:

Refolved, That it is the Opinion of this Committee, that the faid Petition of the Infpectors at *Blandford* be rejected.

The

---

[1] Hening, VIII, p. 361.   [2] Ibid, VIII, p. 514.   [3] Ibid, VIII, p. 516.   [4] Ibid, VIII, p. 542.
[5] Ibid, VIII, p. 640

The said *Resolution*, being read a second Time, was, upon the Question put thereupon, agreed to by the House.

Ordered, That it be an Instruction to the Committee of Propositions and Grievances, who are appointed to prepare and bring in a Bill pursuant to the Resolutions of the said Committee, which were reported to the House upon *Friday*, the 28th Day of last Month, and which were agreed to by the House, that they have Power to receive a Clause or Clauses to empower *George Washington*, Esquire, to erect and Keep a Gate or Gates, on his Land, across the Road leading to *Posey's* Ferry, on *Potowmack* River; and also to empower *Joseph Cabell*, Esquire, to erect and keep a Gate or Gates, on his Land, across the Road leading to his Ferry on *James* River; and also to empower *Burwell Basset*, Esquire, to erect and keep a Gate or Gates, on his Land, across the Road, leading to the Brick House Ferry, on *York* River.

Mr *Cary* reported from the Committee of Public Claims, to whom the Petition of *Nathaniel Raines* and *Lewis Brown*, Inspectors of Tobacco at *Boyd's* Warehouses, in the County of *Prince George*, had been referred, and to whom one of the Resolutions of the Committee thereupon was recommitted, that the Committee had further examined the Matter of the said Petition, and had directed him to report the same, together with the Resolution of the Committee thereupon, to the House; and he read the Report in his Place, and afterwards delivered it in at the Clerk's Table; where the same was read, and is as followeth, *viz.*

It appears to your *Committee*, that there are two Warehouses at the Inspection at *Boyd's*, which by a Wall made with Posts set in the Ground, and inch Planks laid close together, and nailed thereon with twenty Penny Nails, and running from the Ends of one of the said Houses to the Ends of the other, inclose a Yard; that the Outsides and Ends of the said Houses serve as part of the said Enclosure, and are strong and secure, but that the Insides fronting the Yard are open, and that the Gates to the said Wall are supplied with strong Locks and Chains.

Whereupon your *Committee* came to the following Resolution:

Resolved, That it is the Opinion of this Committee, that that Part of the said Petition of the Inspectors at *Boyd's* Warehouses, which relates to the stolen Tobacco, be rejected.

The said *Resolution*, being read a second Time, was, upon the Question put thereupon, agreed to by the House.

Mr *Harrison* reported from the Committee of Trade, to whom the petition of several Persons of the County of *Botetourt*, inhabiting the Place called the *Cow Pasture*, and on *Craig's* Creek and *James* River, praying that a Road may be made over the South Mountain, at the Expence of the Public, was referred, that the Committee had examined the Matter of the said Petition, and had come to several Resolutions thereupon, which they had directed him to report to the House; and he read the Report in his Place, and afterwards delivered it in at the Clerk's Table; where the Resolutions of the Committee were read, and are as followeth, *viz.*

Resolved, That it is the Opinion of this Committee, that the further Consideration of the said petition be deferred till the next Session of General Assembly.

Resolved, That it is the Opinion of this Committee, that Commissioners be appointed to examine the Place proposed for the said Road, and that they report the Conveniences and Inconveniences thereof to the next Session of General Assembly.

The said *Resolutions*, being severally read a second Time, were, upon the Question severally put thereupon, agreed to by the House.

Ordered, That a Bill be brought in pursuant to the last Resolution; and that the Committee of Trade do prepare, and bring in the same.

A *Claim* of *Benjamin Powell* for repairing the Magazine; *and also,*

A *Claim* of *Joseph Kidd* for repairing the Magazine,

Were severally *presented* to the House, and read.

Ordered, That the said Claims be referred to the Consideration of the Committee of Public Claims; and that they do examine the Matter thereof, and report the same, with their Opinion thereupon, to the House.

Mr

Mr *Gray* prefented to the Houfe, according to Order, a Bill to enable the *Nottoway Indians* to leafe certain Lands, and for other Purpofes therein mentioned; and the fame was received, and read the firft Time.

Refolved, That the Bill be read a fecond Time.

A *Petition* of *Thomas Garth* was prefented to the Houfe, and read; fetting forth, that a few Days before the Flood, which happened in *May* of the laft Year, the Infpectors at *Shockoe* having opened a Hogfhead of the Petitioner's Tobacco, and finding it in too high Cafe at that Time, had it laid by for further Infpection; that in the mean Time the Flood came and damaged the Tobacco; and that the Commiffioners appointed by the Act of General Affembly, made for the Relief of thofe who fuffered by that Calamity, allowed the petitioner for his faid Hogfhead of Tobacco no more than four Pounds three Shillings and four Pence, the Sum at which by the faid Act a refufed Hogfhead of Tobacco was eftimated; whereas the petitioner conceives his faid Hogfhead of Tobacco ought to have been confidered, not as a refufed, but as an uninfpected Hogfhead, for which he was intitled by the faid Act to receive nine Pounds; and therefore praying that he may be allowed the further Sum of four Pounds fixteen Shillings and eight Pence.

A *Motion* was made, and the Queftion being put, that the faid petition be referred to the Confideration of a Committee;

It paffed in the Negative.

Refolved, That the petition be rejected.

Mr *Bland* reported from the Committee of Propofitions and Grievances, to whom feveral Petitions were referred, that the Committee had examined the Matters of the faid Petitions, and had come to feveral Refolutions thereupon, which they had directed him to report to the Houfe; and he read the Report in his Place, and afterwards delivered it in at the Clerk's Table; where the Refolutions of the Committee were read, and are as followeth, *viz.*

Refolved, That it is the Opinion of this Committee, that the Petitions of the Inhabitants of the Counties of *Amelia, Chefterfield,* and *Cumberland,* praying that public Warehoufes may be eftablifhed for the Reception of Wheat, are reafonable.

Refolved, That it is the Opinion of this Committee, that fo much of the Petition of divers Inhabitants of the County of *Fairfax,* as prays that the Lots, numbered 7 and 8 in the Plan of the Town of *Colchefter,* may be added to the Lot, numbered 29, whereon to eftablifh Warehoufes for the Reception of Tobacco, is reafonable.

Refolved, That it is the Opinion of this Committee, that fuch other Part of the faid Petition, as prays that the Infpectors Salaries at the faid Town of *Colchefter* may be encreafed, is reafonable, and that they ought to be allowed, each, the Sum of 45 *l. per Annum.*

Refolved, That it is the Opinion of this Committee, that the Refidue of the faid Petition, praying that the faid Infpectors at *Colchefter* may be allowed a Compenfation for their laft Year's extraordinary Trouble and Services, is reafonable, and that they ought to be allowed, each, the Sum of 10 *l.*

Refolved, That it is the Opinion of this Committee, that the petition of *Jofeph Turner,* one of the Infpectors at the College and Capitol Landings, praying that his Salary may be encreafed to 35 *l. per Annum* as formerly, be rejected.

Refolved, That it is the Opinion of this Committee, that the petition of *Thomas Coleman,* and *Thomas Butler,* Infpectors of Tobacco at *Aylett's* and *Todd's* Warehoufes, in the Counties of *King William* and *King & Queen,* praying an Encreafe of their Salaries, be rejected.

Refolved, That it is the Opinion of this Committee, that the petition of divers Inhabitants of the County of *Elizabeth City,* praying that an Act may pafs to difcontinue a Water Mill, in the faid County, belonging to the infant Heir of *Booth Armiftead,* deceafed, be rejected.

The faid *Refolutions,* being feverally read a fecond Time, were, upon the Queftion feverally put thereupon, agreed to by the Houfe.

Ordered

Ordered, That a Bill be brought in purfuant to the firft Refolution; and that the Committee of Trade do prepare, and bring in the fame.

Ordered, That it be an Inftruction to the Committee of Propofitions and Grievances, who are appointed to prepare and bring in a Bill, for further continuing an Act made in the fifth Year of the Reign of his prefent Majefty, intituled *An Act[1] for amending the Staple of Tobacco, and for preventing Frauds in his Majefty's Cuftoms*, that they do make Provifion in the faid Bill, purfuant to the fecond and third Refolutions of the faid Committee, this Day reported, and agreed to by the Houfe.

Ordered, That the Committee of Public Claims do make an Allowance, in the Book of Public Claims, purfuant to the fourth Refolution of the Committee of Propofitions and Grievances, this Day reported, and agreed to by the Houfe.

A *Petition* of *Robert Goodwin* was prefented to the Houfe, and read; fetting forth, that a fhort Time before the Infpection at *Falmouth* was difcontinued, the Petitioner had repaired, at very confiderable Expence, the Warehoufes, of which he is Proprietor, and which are now become ufelefs to him; and therefore humbly praying the Confideration of the Houfe whether he ought not to be allowed a reafonable Satiffaction for the fame.

Ordered, That the faid Petition be referred to the Confideration of the Committee of Public Claims; and that they do examine the Matter thereof, and report the fame, with their Opinion thereupon, to the Houfe.

A *Petition* of Freeholders, Houfekeepers, and other Inhabitants of the County of *Bedford*, whofe Names are thereunto fubfcribed, fetting forth, that there is but one Parifh in the faid County, called *Ruffell*, which is near ninety Miles in length, and that there is a fufficient Number of Tithables in the fame to bear the Expences of two Parifhes; and therefore praying that the faid Parifh may be divided by a ftraight Line, from the Mouth of *Goofe* Creek, on *Staunton* River, to the upper End of *Fleming's* Mountain, on *James* River; *and alfo*,

Several *Petitions* of fundry Freeholders and Inhabitants of the Parifh of *Ruffell*, in the County of *Bedford*, whofe Names are thereunto fubfcribed, taking Notice of an Application intended to be made to this Houfe for dividing the faid Parifh, and fetting forth, that the faid Divifion will be inconvenient, and that the Number of Tithables in the faid Parifh is little more than two thoufand, of whom many are infolvent, and that five Churches have lately been built in it, which, if it be divided, will be rendered Ufelefs; and fubmitting it to the Confideration of the Houfe, whether the faid Parifh ought to be divided.

Ordered, That the faid Petitions be referred to the Confideration of the Committee for Religion; and that they do examine the Matter thereof, and report the fame, with their Opinion thereupon, to the Houfe.

A *Petition* of *William Garrard* and *Thomas Mountjoy*, Infpectors of Tobacco at *Cave's* Warehoufe, in the County of *Stafford*, was prefented to the Houfe, and read; fetting forth, that the Quantity of Tobacco brought to the faid Infpection is confiderably greater than it was formerly; and therefore praying that their Salaries may be encreafed.

Ordered, That the faid petition be referred to the Confideration of the Committee of Propofitions and Grievances; and that they do examine the Matter thereof, and report the fame, with their Opinion thereupon, to the Houfe.

A *Petition* of *Laurence Afhton*, of the County of *King George*, was prefented to the Houfe, and read; fetting forth, that in the Year 1771, *Aaron*, a Negro Man Slave of the Petitioner, who had run away and concealed himfelf in the County of *Weftmoreland*, and againft whom, in Order to reclaim him, the Petitioner had caufed a Proclamation of Outlawry to be duly publifhed, being purfued, and refufing to furrender himfelf, was fhot at, and flain; and therefore praying that the Petitioner may be paid for his faid Slave by the Public.

Ordered, That the faid Petition be referred to the Confideration of the Committee

of

---

[1] Hening, VIII, p. 69.

of Public Claims; and that they do examine the Matter thereof, and report the fame, with their Opinion thereupon, to the Houfe.

A *Petition* of *William Aylett*, Proprietor of the Public Warehoufes for the Infpection of Tobacco, at *Aylett's*, in the County of *King William*, was prefented to the Houfe, and read; fetting forth, that hitherto the Petitioner hath kept the faid Warehoufes in Repair, at very great Expence, but that the Court of the faid County hath lately ordered the faid Warehoufes to be repaired, in fuch a Manner that the Petitioner cannot afford to do it for the Rent by Law allowed, and that the Petitioner is willing to deliver up the faid Warehoufes to the Public, upon being paid the Value of them; and therefore praying, that proper Perfons may be appointed to afcertain the faid Value, to be paid to the Petitioner, or that he may be otherwife relieved, as this Honourable Houfe fhall think juft.

Ordered, That the faid Petition be referred to the Confideration of the Committee of Propofitions and Grievances; and that they do examine the Matter thereof, and report the fame, with their Opinion thereupon, to the Houfe.

The *Order* of the Day being read;

Refolved, That this Houfe will, Tomorrow, refolve itfelf into a Committee of the whole Houfe, upon the Bill for further continuing the Act, intituled *An Act*[1] *for the better regulating and collecting certain Officers Fees, and for other Purpofes therein mentioned.*

A *Petition* of *John Meredith* and *John Timberlake*, Infpectors of Tobacco, at the Brick Houfe Warehoufe, in the County of *New-Kent*, was prefented to the Houfe, and read; fetting forth, that by the Difcontinuance of the Infpection at *Hog Neck* the Trouble of the Infpectors at the Brick Houfe being much increafed, their Wages were raifed from twenty-five to thirty Pounds *per Annum*, but in the Year 1769, were again reduced to twenty-five Pounds, which the Petitioners humbly conceive is not an adequate Satiffaction for their conftant Attendance and great Trouble; and therefore praying that their Salaries may be fettled at thirty Pounds *per Annum*.

Ordered, That the faid Petition be referred to the Confideration of the Committee of Propofitions and Grievances; and that they do examine the Matter thereof, and report the fame, with their Opinion thereupon, to the Houfe.

An engroffed *Bill* for building a Bridge over the Weftern Branch of *Nanfemond* River, by Subfcription, was read the third Time.

Refolved, That the Bill do pafs; and that the Title be, *An Act*[2] *for building a Bridge over the Weftern Branch of* Nanfemond *River, by Subfcription.*

Ordered, That Mr *Bland* do carry the Bill to the Council, and defire their Concurrence.

Mr *Cary* reported from the Committee of Public Claims, to whom the Petition of *John Reynolds* and *William Edmondfon*, Infpectors of Tobacco, at *Hobb's Hole* Warehoufes, in the County of *Effex*, was referred, that the Committee had examined the Matter of the faid Petition, and had directed him to report the fame, together with the Refolution of the Committee thereupon, to the Houfe, and he read the Report in his Place, and afterwards delivered it in at the Clerk's Table; where the fame was read, and is as followeth, *viz.*

It appears to your *Committee*, by a Certificate of the Teftimony of the faid *John Reynolds*, and *William Edmondfon*, that on the Night of the 25th or 26th of *January* laft, fome Perfon or Perfons (by drawing the Staples which confined the Bolt) broke open one of the Doors of the faid Warehoufe; that the Snow, which fell at that Time, prevented the faid Infpectors, for feveral Days, from attending their Bufinefs, but as foon as the Weather permitted, they went to the faid Warehoufe, and difcovered that a Hogfhead of Tobacco, weighing Nett 1101 Pounds, was ftolen, which faid Tobacco they fufpected was taken, and carried on Board a Ship, that failed from *Tappahannock* on the 3rd of *February* laft, for that fome Time after, on a Marfh below the Town, an empty Hogfhead was found, on which were the Mark, Number, and Weight of the faid Tobacco, together with the Stamp of the faid Warehoufe. It further appears to your Committee, by

other

---

[1] Hening, V, p. 326.   [2] Ibid, VIII, p. 552.

other Teftimony, that the faid Infpectors are very careful Perfons; and that at the Time the faid Tobacco was loft, the faid Warehoufe was in good repair.

Whereupon your *Committee* came to the following Refolution:

Refolved, That it is the Opinion of this Committee, that the faid Petition is reafonable, and that the Petitioners ought to be allowed at the Rate of twenty Shillings *per* Hundred, for the Hogfhead of Tobacco in the faid Petition mentioned.

86   The faid *Refolution*, being read a fecond Time, was, upon the Queftion put thereupon, agreed to by the Houfe.

The Houfe being informed that Mr *John Madifon*, Clerk of the Court of the County of *Augufta*, Mr *Thomas Ruffin*, Clerk of the Court of the County of *Dinwiddie*, Mr *Robert Munford*, Clerk of the Court of the County of *Halifax*, and Mr *Fortunatus Sydnor*, Deputy Clerk of the Court of the County of *Henrico*, had not, purfuant to the Order of this Houfe, fent Copies of the Lifts of Tithables in their refpective Counties, to the Clerk of this Houfe, before or fince the Meeting of this General Affembly;

Ordered, That the Serjeant at Arms, attending this Houfe, do fend to the faid Clerks for fuch Lifts; and that the Expences thereof be levied upon the faid Clerks refpectively.

Mr *Cary* reported from the Committee of Public Claims, to whom the Petition of *John Thornley* and *William Harrifon*, Infpectors of Tobacco at *Gibfon's* Warehoufes, in the County of *King George*, was referred, that the Committee had examined the Matter of the faid Petition, and had directed him to report the fame, together with the Refolution of the Committee thereupon, to the Houfe; and he read the Report in his Place, and afterwards delivered it in at the Clerk's Table; where the fame was read, and is as followeth, *viz.*

It appears to your *Committee*, by the Depofitions of fundry Perfons, that at the Time the Tobacco in the faid Petition mentioned was loft, the faid Warehoufes were in good Repair; that the faid Infpectors, as was their conftant Cuftom, faw that the Doors of the faid Warehoufes were all well fecured, when they left them, but on their Return, the next Morning, found the Lock broke, and one of the Doors forced off the Hinges; that upon Examination, they difcovered that two Hogfheads of Crop, weighing Nett 2000 Pounds, and 319 Pounds of Tranffer Tobacco, were ftolen; and that they immediately fearched for the fame, but their Endeavors proved ineffectual.

Whereupon your *Committee* came to the following Refolution:

Refolved, That it is the Opinion of this Committee, that the faid petition is reafonable; and that the Petitioners ought to be allowed for the 2000 Pounds of Crop Tobacco, at the Rate of twenty Shillings *per* Hundred, and for the 319 Pounds of Tranffer, at Two pence *per* Pound.

The faid *Refolution*, being read a fecond Time, was, upon the Queftion put thereupon, agreed to by the Houfe.

An engroffed *Bill*, to empower the Corporation of the Borough of *Norfolk* to affefs a Tax on the Inhabitants thereof, for the Purpofe therein mentioned, was read the third Time.

Refolved, That the Bill do pafs; and that the Title be, *An Act*[1] *to empower the Corporation of the Borough of* Norfolk *to affefs a Tax on the Inhabitants thereof, for the Purpofe therein mentioned.*

Ordered, That Mr *Bland* do carry the Bill to the Council, and defire their Concurrence.

Ordered, That Mr *Lewis Burwell*, of *Gloucefter*, be added to the Committee for Religion, the Committee of Propofitions and Grievances, and the Committee for Courts of Juftice.

And then the Houfe adjourned till Tomorrow Morning eleven of the Clock.

𝕿hursday

---

1 Hening, VIII, p. 611.

Thursday, the 12th of March, 12 George III. 1772.

THE *Order* of the Day being read;

The Houfe refolved itfelf into a Committee of the whole Houfe, upon the Bill for further continuing the Act, intituled *An Act[1] for the better regulating and collecting certain Officers Fees, and for other Purpofes therein mentioned.*

Mʳ *Speaker* left the Chair.

Mʳ *Bland* took the Chair of the Committee.

Mʳ *Speaker* refumed the Chair.

Mʳ *Bland* reported from the Committee, that they had gone through the Bill, and made feveral Amendments thereunto, which they had directed him to report, when the Houfe will pleafe to receive the fame.

Ordered, That the Report be now received.

Mʳ *Bland* accordingly reported from the faid Committee, the Amendments which the Committee had made to the Bill, and which they had directed him to report to the Houfe; and he read the Report in his Place; and afterwards delivered the Bill, with the Amendments, in at the Clerk's Table; where the Amendments were read once throughout, and then a fecond Time, one by one, and, upon the Queftion feverally put thereupon, were agreed to by the Houfe.

Ordered, That the Bill, with the Amendments, be engroffed.

And then the Houfe adjourned till Tomorrow Morning, eleven of the Clock.

Friday, the 13th of March, 12 George III. 1772.

Mʳ *Bland* prefented to the Houfe, according to Order, a Bill to continue and amend the Act, intituled *An Act[2] to continue and amend the Act intituled An Act for amending the Staple of Tobacco, and for preventing Frauds in his Majefty's Cuftoms*; and the fame was received, and read the firft Time.

Refolved, That the Bill be read a fecond Time.

Mʳ *Harrifon* prefented to the Houfe, according to Order, a Bill to continue and amend an Act, intituled *An Act[3] for reviving the Duty upon Slaves, to be paid by the Buyers;* alfo to continue and amend an Act, intituled *An Act to oblige Perfons bringing Slaves into this Colony from* Maryland, Carolina, *and the* Weft-Indies, *for their own Ufe, to pay a Duty;* and the fame was received, and read the firft Time.

Refolved, That the Bill be read a fecond Time.

A *Memorial* of *Andrew Eftave* was prefented to the Houfe, and read; fetting forth, that in Purfuance of the Act of General Affembly, made in the tenth Year of the Reign of his prefent Majefty, intituled *An Act[4] for encouraging the making Wine*, the petitioner hath been for fome Time cultivating a Vineyard, which he hath diligently attended to, but that he cannot, without endangering its Succefs, employ the Labourers therein, fo as to make Crops of Corn, and other Things neceffary for his and their Subfiftence; that he hath been obliged, with the Confent of the Truftees, to fell one of the Servants, who was unprofitable, upon twelve Months Credit; that his Vines are now in a thriving State, and that he is convinced of the Practicability of the Scheme, and is willing to provide for the Profecution of it in Cafe of his Death; and that he is ready and defirous to inftruct any Apprentices that the faid Truftees may put under him; and praying the Confideration of the Houfe, and that they will be pleafed to grant him fuch Affiftance and Relief as to them fhall feem meet.

Ordered, That the faid Memorial be referred to the Confideration of the Committee of Trade, and that they do examine the Matter thereof, and report the fame, with their Opinion thereupon, to the Houfe.

Mʳ

---

[1] Hening, V, p. 326.   [2] Ibid, VIII, p, 318.   [3] Ibid, VIII, p. 530. (Original Acts, IV, p. 317; VII, p. 338.)   [4] Ibid, VIII, p. 364.

Mr *Edmund Pendleton* reported from the Committee, to whom the Bill for continuing the Act, intituled *An Act¹ for reimburfing the Inhabitants of* King William, *and* Hanover *Counties, the Expence of clearing* Pamunkey *River*, was committed, that the Committee had directed him to report the Bill to the Houfe, without any Amendment; and he delivered the Bill in at the Clerk's Table.

Ordered, That the Bill be engroffed.

Mr *Bland* reported from the Committee of Propofitions and Grievances, to whom feveral petitions were referred, that the Committee had examined the Matters of the faid Petitions, and had come to feveral Refolutions thereupon, which they had directed him to report to the Houfe; and he read the Report in his Place, and afterwards delivered it in at the Clerk's Table; where the Refolutions of the Committee were read, and are as followeth, *viz.*

Refolved, That it is the Opinion of this Committee, that the petition of the Infpectors at *Cave's* Warehoufes, in the County of *Stafford*, praying that their Salaries may be increafed, is reafonable, and that they ought to be allowed the additional Sum of five Pounds *per Annum* each.

Refolved, That it is the Opinion of this Committee, that the Petition of divers Inhabitants of this Colony, praying that the Brick Houfe Landing, upon the River *Potowmack*, may be eftablifhed as a public Landing, and that a Road may be opened, from the faid Landing, to the main Road of the County of *Weftmoreland*, be rejected.

The faid *Refolutions*, being feverally read a fecond Time, were, upon the Queftion feverally put thereupon, agreed to by the Houfe.

Ordered, That the faid Report do lie upon the Table until the fecond reading of the Bill to continue and amend the Act, intituled *An Act² to continue and amend the Act, intituled An Act for amending the Staple of Tobacco, and for preventing Frauds in his Majefty's Cuftoms.*

Mr *Edmund Pendleton* prefented to the Houfe, according to Order, a Bill for eftablifh-ing a Town on the Lands adjoining the Court-Houfe of *Botetourt* County; and the fame was received, and read the firft Time.

Refolved, That the Bill be read a fecond Time.

A *Bill* to dock the Intail of certain Lands whereof *John Hancock* is feifed, and for fettling other Lands and Slaves, in Lieu thereof, was read a fecond Time.

Refolved, That the Bill be committed to Mr *Henry Lee*, Mr *Tebbs*, Mr *Jofeph Cabell*, Mr *Bell*, and Mr *Wafhington*.

A *Petition* of the Truftees of the Town of *Alexandria*, whofe Names are thereunto fubfcribed, was prefented to the Houfe, and read; fetting forth, that certain Lots in the faid Town, being low Marfhy Ground, the Proprietors whereof refufe or neglect to drain and improve the fame, are injurious to the Health of the Inhabitants of the faid Town; and therefore praying, that the faid Proprietors may be obliged to drain the faid Lots, within a limited Time, at their own Expence.

Ordered, That the faid petition be referred to the Confideration of the Committee of Propofitions and Grievances, and that they do examine the Matter thereof, and report the fame, with their Opinion thereupon, to the Houfe.

Refolved, That this Houfe will receive no Petitions or Claims after the twenty-third Day of this Month.

Mr *Treafurer* reported from the Committee for Religion, to whom the Bill for better regulating the Election of Veftries was committed, that the Committee had gone through the Bill, and made feveral Amendments thereunto, which they had directed him to report to the Houfe; and he read the Report in his Place, and afterwards delivered the Bill, with the Amendments, in at the Clerk's Table; where the Amendments were once read throughout, and then a fecond Time, one by one, and upon the Queftion feverally put thereupon, were, with Amendments to feveral of them, agreed to by the Houfe.

Ordered, That the Bill, with the Amendments, be engroffed.

An

---

¹ Hening, VIII, p. 407.   ² Ibid, VIII, p. 232.

An engroffed *Bill* to appoint Commiffioners to ftrike a dividing Line between the Counties of *Stafford* and *King George*, was read the third Time.

Refolved, That the Bill do pafs; and that the Title be, *An Act[1] to appoint Commiffioners to ftrike a dividing Line between the Counties* of Stafford *and* King George.

Ordered, That Mr *Alexander* do carry the Bill to the Council, and defire their Concurrence.

Mr *Cary* reported from the Committee of Public Claims, to whom the Petition of *David Vaughan* and *William Dews*, Infpectors of Tobacco at *Gloucefter* Town Warehoufes, was referred, that the Committee had examined the Matter of the faid Petition, and had directed him to report the fame, together with the Refolution of the Committee thereupon, to the Houfe, and he read the Report in his Place, and afterwards delivered it in at the Clerk's Table; where the fame was read, and is as followeth, *viz.*

It appears to your *Committee*, that in the Month of *September*, 1770, the faid Warehoufes were broke open twice, and 2989 Pounds of Crop, and 1000 Pounds of Tranffer Tobacco ftolen out of the fame, for which the Petitioners have paid at the Rates of twenty-two Shillings and fix Pence *per* hundred for the Crop Tobacco, and twenty Shillings per hundred for the Tranffer; and that the faid Warehoufes, each Time, on the Evening before the Tobacco was loft, were well fecured with good Locks and Bolts, and that they were then in good Repair.

Whereupon your *Committee* came to the following Refolution:

Refolved, That it is the Opinion of this Committee, that the faid Petition is reafonable; and that the Petitioners ought to be allowed, for the Crop Tobacco, at the Rate of twenty-two Shillings and fix Pence *per* hundred, and for the Tranffer, at twenty Shillings *per* hundred, amounting in the whole to the Sum of forty-three Pounds twelve Shillings and fix Pence.

The faid *Refolution*, being read a fecond Time, was, upon the Queftion put thereupon, agreed to by the Houfe.

A *Petition* of the Truftees of the Town of *Alexandria*, whofe Names are thereunto fubfcribed, was prefented to the Houfe, and read; fetting forth, that the Wharf at *Point Weft* in the faid Town, originally built by the Public, and afterwards rebuilt and enlarged by the Petitioners, at the Expence of one hundred Pounds, is now in a ruinous Condition, occafioned chiefly by Ships heaving down by, and mooring at the faid Wharf; and praying that the faid Wharf may be vefted in the Petitioners, and that fuch a Tax may be impofed upon Veffels heaving down by, and mooring at it, except thofe which take Tobacco from the public Warehoufes in the faid Town, as will enable the petitioners to repair and extend the faid Wharf.

Ordered, That the faid petition be referred to the Confideration of the Committee of Trade; and that they do examine the Matter thereof, and report the fame, with their Opinion thereupon, to the Houfe.

Mr *Carr* prefented to the Houfe, according to Order, a Bill for diffolving the Veftries of the Parifhes of *Saint Martin*, in the Counties of *Hanover* and *Louifa*, and of *Saint John*, in the County of *King William*; and the fame was received, and read the firft Time.

Refolved, That the Bill be read a fecond Time.

A *Petition* of the Merchants and Traders in the Town of *Alexandria* was prefented to the Houfe, and read; fetting forth, that the heavy Duty impofed upon the Importers of Rum is injurious to the Trade of the faid Town, and hath a manifeft Tendency to give great Advantage to their Neighbours of *Maryland*, who are not fubject to any fuch Duty; and praying Relief.

Ordered, That the faid Petition be referred to the Confideration of the Committee of Trade, to whom the Bill to continue an Act, intituled *An Act[2] to continue and amend an Act, intituled an Act for reducing the feveral Acts, made for laying a Duty upon Liquors, into one Act*, is committed.

Ordered, That Leave be given to bring in a Bill to amend an Act, intituled *An Act[3]*
concerning

1 Hening, VIII, p. 601.   2 Ibid, VIII, p. 335.   3 Ibid, VI. p. 24.

concerning Seamen; and that Mr *Hutchings* and Mr *Banifter* do prepare, and bring in the fame.

The *Order* of the Day being read;

Refolved, That this Houfe will, upon *Tuefday* next, refolve itfelf into a Committee of the whole Houfe upon the Bill to remove the Seat of Government to a Place more convenient to the Inhabitants of this Colony.

Ordered, That Leave be given to bring in a Bill to amend the Act for the better Prefervation of the Breed of Deer, and preventing unlawful hunting; and that Mr *Cary* do prepare, and bring in the fame.

A *Petition* of fundry Inhabitants of the County of *Bedford,* whofe Names are thereunto fubfcribed, was prefented to the Houfe, and read; fetting forth, that an Infpection of Tobacco in the faid County would be convenient and beneficial to the Petitioners, who are willing to fuftain the Expence thereof; and praying that fuch an Infpection may be eftablifhed at the Town of *New London,* in the faid County.

Ordered, That the faid petition be referred to the Confideration of the Committee of Propofitions and Grievances; and that they do examine the Matter thereof, and report the fame, with their Opinion thereupon, to the Houfe.

Mr *Edmund Pendleton* prefented to the Houfe, according to Order, a Bill to amend an Act, intituled *An Act¹ for clearing* Mattapony *River;* and the fame was received, and read the firft Time.

Refolved, That the Bill be read a fecond Time.

Ordered, That Mr *Aylett* have Leave to be abfent from the Service of this Houfe till this Day Sevennight.

An engroffed *Bill* for adding Part of the County of *Nanfemond* to the County of *Ifle of Wight,* was read the third Time.

Refolved, That the Bill do pafs; and that the Title be, *An Act² for adding Part of the County of* Nanfemond *to the County of* Ifle of Wight.

Ordered, That Mr *Hardy* do carry the Bill to the Council, and defire their Concurrence.

An engroffed *Bill,* for altering the Court Day of *Surry* County, was read the third Time.

Refolved, That the Bill do pafs; and that the Title be, *An Act³ for altering the Court Days of the Counties of* Surry *and* Princefs Anne.

Ordered, That Mr *Bland* do carry the Bill to the Council, and defire their Concurrence.

A *Bill* for continuing and amending the Act, intituled *An Act⁴ for deftroying Crows and Squirrels, in certain Counties therein mentioned,* was read a fecond Time.

Refolved, That the Bill be committed to Mr *Richard Henry Lee,* Mr *Lewis,* and Mr *Wright.*

Ordered, That Leave be given to bring in a Bill, to compel Ships, importing Convicts, Servants, and Slaves, infected with the Gaol Fever or Small-Pox, to perform Quarantine; and that Mr *Richard Henry Lee,* and Mr *Treafurer,* do prepare, and bring in the fame.

A *Bill* for dividing the Parifhes of *Southam,* in the County of *Cumberland,* and *Dale,* in the County of *Chefterfield,* was read a fecond Time.

Refolved, That the Bill be committed to the Committee for Religion.

A *Bill* to enable the *Nottoway Indians* to leafe certain Lands, and for other Purpofes therein mentioned, was read a fecond Time.

Refolved, That the Bill be committed to Mr *Gray,* Mr *Taylor,* Mr *Baker,* Mr *Riddick,* Mr *Bridger,* and Mr *Hardy.*

A *Bill* to explain and amend an Act, intituled *An Act⁵ to oblige the Owners of Mills, Hedges, or Stops on the Rivers therein mentioned, to make Openings or Slopes therein, for the Paffage of Fifh,* was read a fecond Time.

Refolved, That the Bill be committed to Mr *Marfhall,* and Mr *John Jones.*

An engroffed *Bill* for further continuing the Act, intituled *An Act⁶ for the better regulating*

---

¹ Hening, VI, p. 394. ² Ibid, VIII, p. 602. ³ Ibid, VIII, p. 519. ⁴ Ibid, VIII, p. 389.
⁵ Ibid, VIII, p. 361. ⁶ Ibid, V, p. 326.

regulating and collecting certain Officers Fees, and for other Purposes therein mentioned, was read the third Time.

Resolved, That the Bill do pass; and that the Title be, *An Act[1] for further continuing and amending the Act, intituled an Act for the better regulating and collecting certain Officers Fees, and for other Purposes therein mentioned.*

Ordered, That Mr *Richard Henry Lee* do carry the Bill to the Council, and desire their Concurrence.

And then the House adjourned till Tomorrow Morning eleven of the Clock.

Saturday, the 14th of March, 12 George III. 1772.

SEVERAL other *Members,* returned upon new Writs, having taken the Oaths appointed to be taken by Act of Parliament, and repeated and subscribed the Test, took their Places in the House.

Ordered, That Mr *Baker* have Leave to be absent from the Service of this House till the End of this Session.

Mr *Richard Henry Lee* reported from the Committee, to whom the Bill for continuing and amending the Act, intituled *An Act[2] for destroying Crows and Squirrels in certain Counties, therein mentioned,* was committed, that the Committee had gone through the Bill, and made several Amendments thereunto, which they had directed him to report to the House; and he read the Report in his Place, and afterwards delivered the Bill, with the Amendments, in at the Clerk's Table; where the Amendments were once read throughout; and then a second Time, one by one, and, upon the Question severally put thereupon, were agreed to by the House.

Ordered, That the Bill, with the Amendments, be engrossed.

A *Petition* of *Richard Sanford* and *John Rhodes,* Inspectors of Tobacco at *Hunting* Creek Warehouses, was presented to the House, and read; setting forth, that the Quantity of Tobacco brought to the said Warehouses, since the late Reduction of the Petitioners Salaries, is considerably greater than it had been for several Years before; and therefore praying that their Salaries may be increased so as to be adequate to their Trouble, and that they may be allowed a reasonable Compensation for the Loss they have sustained by the said Reduction.

Ordered, That the said petition be referred to the Consideration of the Committee of Propositions and Grievances; and that they do examine the Matter thereof, and report the same, with their Opinion thereupon, to the House.

Mr *Richard Henry Lee* presented to the House, according to Order, a Bill to compel Ships, importing Convicts, Servants, or Slaves, infected with the Gaol Fever, or Small-Pox, to perform Quarantine; and the same was received, and read the first Time.

Resolved, That the Bill be read a second Time.

Mr *Cary* reported from the Committee of Public Claims, to whom the Petition of *Robert Goodwin,* to be allowed for repairing the Warehouses in *Falmouth,* the Inspection at which was discontinued last General Assembly, was referred, that the Committee had examined the Matter of the said petition, and had come to a Resolution thereupon, which they had directed him to report to the House; and he read the Report in his Place, and afterwards delivered it in at the Clerk's Table; where the Resolution of the Committee was read, and is as followeth, *viz.*

Resolved, That it is the Opinion of this Committee, that the said Petition be rejected.

The said *Resolution,* being read a second Time, was, upon the Question put thereupon, agreed to by the House.

Mr *Bland* presented to the House, according to Order, a Bill for making further provision for the Support and Maintenance of Ideots, Lunatics, and other Persons of unsound Minds; and the same was received, and read the first Time.

Resolved, That the Bill be read a second Time.

M^r

---

[1] Hening, VIII, p. 515.   [2] Ibid, VIII, p. 389.

Mr *Cary* reported from the Committee of Public Claims, to whom the Petition of *Laurence Afhton* was referred, that the Committee had examined the Matter of the faid Petition, and had directed him to report the fame, together with the Refolution of the Committee thereupon, to the Houfe; and he read the Report in his Place, and afterwards delivered it in at the Clerk's Table; where the fame was read, and is as followeth, *viz.*

It appears to your *Committee*, that *Aaron*, a Negro Man Slave, was a Runaway, and duly outlawed; that during the Time he was out he killed feveral Hogs, and did other Mifchief; that he refufed to furrender himfelf, when difcovered, and, with a Knife, wounded a Negro, who attempted to take him, in feveral Places; that he was immediately fhot at and wounded by a certain *Elliot Monroe*, the Perfon who apprehended him, of which Wound he died; and that the faid *Aaron* was a very likely Slave, and worth at leaft eighty Pounds.

Whereupon your *Committee* came to the following Refolution:

Refolved, That it is the Opinion of this Committee, that the faid petition is reafonable; and that the petitioner ought to be allowed the faid Sum of eighty Pounds for the faid Slave.

The faid *Refolution*, being read a fecond Time, was, upon the Queftion put thereupon, agreed to by the Houfe.

Mr *Bland* prefented to the Houfe, according to Order, a Bill for keeping in Repair feveral Roads and Bridges, and for other Purpofes therein mentioned; and the fame was received, and read the firft Time.

Refolved, That the Bill be read a fecond Time.

A *Petition* of feveral Perfons of the County of *Caroline*, whofe Names are thereunto fubfcribed, was prefented to the Houfe, and read; fetting forth, that the petitioners, being of the Society of Chriftians, called Baptifts, are not indulged with the free Exercife of their Religion; that they are deprived of the Benefits of the Toleration Act, although they are willing to conform to the Spirit of it, and are loyal and quiet Subjects; and that their Teachers are perfecuted, whilft Liberty of Confcience is permitted to diffenting Proteftants of other Perfuafions; and therefore praying that the petitioners may meet with the fame kind Indulgence in Religious Matters as the Quakers, Prefbyterians, and other diffenting Proteftants do enjoy.

Ordered, That the faid petition do lie upon the Table.

Mr *Bland* reported from the Committee of propofitions and Grievances, to whom the Bill for dividing the County of *Frederick* into three diftinct Counties, was committed, that the Committee had gone through the Bill, and made feveral Amendments thereunto, which they had directed him to report to the Houfe; and he read the Report in his Place, and afterwards delivered the Bill, with the Amendments, in at the Clerk's Table; where the Amendments were once read throughout, and then a fecond Time one by one, and, upon the Queftion feverally put thereupon, were, with Amendments to feveral of them, agreed to by the Houfe.

Ordered, That the Bill, with the Amendments, be engroffed.

A *Petition* of the Inhabitants of the Upper Part of the Parifh of *Dryfdale*, in the County of *Caroline*, fetting forth, that the petitioners refide at a great Diftance from their Parifh Church, and cannot be relieved either by a Divifion of the Parifh, which, although it be long, is fo narrow that the Tithables thereof are not numerous enough for two Parifhes, or by building a third Church, whereby Divine Service at each would be lefs frequently performed; and further fetting forth, that a new Parifh may be conveniently formed out of *Dryfdale* and the adjoining Parifh of *Saint Margaret*, by an Union of the upper Ends thereof; and therefore praying that an Act may pafs for that Purpofe; *and alfo*,

Several *Petitions* of the Inhabitants of the Parifh of *Saint Margaret*, in the County of *Caroline*, taking Notice of an Application intended to be made to this Houfe for adding Part of the faid Parifh to the upper End of the Parifh of *Dryfdale*, in Order to form another Parifh; and, fetting forth, that the Figure of *Saint Margaret's* Parifh is nearly fquare, and the Churches built therein, at very confiderable Expence, are fo difpofed

as

as to be convenient to all the parifhioners; and that, by the Model propofed, the Parochial Affeffments upon the petitioners will be encreafed, as they conceive, unjuftly; and therefore praying, that the faid Parifh of *Saint Margaret* may remain as it is,

Were feverally *prefented* to the Houfe, and read.

Ordered, That the faid petitions be referred to the Confideration of the Committee for Religion; and that they do examine the Matter thereof, and report the fame, with their Opinion thereupon, to the Houfe.

Mr *Bland* reported from the Committee of Propofitions and Grievances, to whom the Bill to amend an Act, intituled *An Act¹ to prevent malicious maiming and wounding*, was committed, that the Committee had gone through the Bill, and made feveral Amendments thereunto, which they had directed him to report to the Houfe; and he read the Report in his Place, and afterwards delivered the Bill, with the Amendments, in at the Clerk's Table; where the Amendments were once read throughout, and then a fecond Time, one by one, and, upon the Queftion feverally put thereupon, were agreed to by the Houfe.

Ordered, That the Bill, with the Amendments, be engroffed.

Ordered, That Mr *Thomas Mann Randolph* be added to the Committee of Privileges and Elections, and the Committee of Propofitions and Grievances.

Ordered, That the Committee of Public Claims do levy, in the Book of Public Claims, the Tobacco to be paid to the Witneffes, who attended the Committee of Privileges and Elections, upon the hearing of the petition of feveral Freeholders of the County of *Henrico*, complaining of an undue Election and Return of Mr *Richard Adams* and Mr *Richard Randolph* to ferve as Burgeffes in this prefent General Affembly for the faid County, at the Rate by Law allowed to Witneffes travelling to and attending at the General Court.

Ordered, That Mr *Adams* be added to the Committee of Propofitions and Grievances, the Committee of Public Claims, and the Committee of Trade.

Ordered, That Leave be given to bring in a Bill, to amend an Act, intituled *An Act² directing the Duty of Surveyors of Land*; and that Mr *John Page*, Mr *Marfhall* and Mr *Bland* do prepare, and bring in the fame.

A *Bill* for diffolving the Veftries of the Parifhes of *Saint Martin*, in the Counties of *Hanover* and *Louifa*, and of *Saint John*, in the County of *King William*, was read a fecond Time.

Refolved, That the Bill be committed to the Committee for Religion.

A *Bill* to continue and amend an Act, intituled *An Act³ for reviving the Duty upon Slaves, to be paid by the Buyers*; alfo to continue and amend an Act, intituled *An Act⁴ to oblige Perfons bringing Slaves into this Colony from* Maryland, Carolina, *and the* Weft-Indies, *for their own Ufe, to pay a Duty*, was read a fecond Time.

Refolved, That the Bill be committed.

Refolved, That the Bill be committed to a Committee of the whole Houfe.

Refolved, That this Houfe will, upon *Monday* next, refolve itfelf into a Committee of the whole Houfe upon the faid Bill.

A *Bill* for eftablifhing a Town on the Lands adjoining the Court-Houfe of *Botetourt* County, was read a fecond Time.

Ordered, That the Bill be engroffed.

A *Bill* to amend an Act, intituled *An Act⁵ for clearing* Mattapony *River*, was read a fecond Time.

Refolved, That the Bill be committed to Mr *Edmund Pendleton*, Mr *Aylett*, Mr *Moore*, Mr *Brooke*, and Mr *Corbin*.

Mr *Hutchings* prefented to the Houfe, according to Order, a Bill to amend an Act, intituled *An Act⁶ concerning Seamen;* and the fame was received, and read the firft Time.

Refolved, That the Bill be read a fecond Time.

An

---

¹ Hening, VI, p. 250. ² Ibid, VI, p. 33. ³ Ibid, VIII, p. 530. ⁴ Ibid, VII, p. 338.
⁵ Ibid, VI, p. 394. ⁶ Ibid, VI, p. 24.

94 An engroffed *Bill* for continuing the Act, intituled *An Act[1] for reimburfing the Inhabitants of* King William *and* Hanover *Counties the Expence of clearing* Pamunkey *River*, was read the third Time.

Refolved, That the Bill do pafs; and that the Title be, *An Act[2] for continuing the Act, intituled an Act for reimburfing the Inhabitants of* King William *and* Hanover *Counties the Expence of clearing* Pamunkey *River.*

Ordered, That Mr *Richard Henry Lee* do carry the Bill to the Council, and defire their Concurrence.

A *Bill* to continue and amend the Act, intituled *An Act[3] to continue and amend the Act, intituled an Act for amending the Staple of Tobacco, and for preventing Frauds in his Majefty's Cuftoms*, was read a fecond Time.

Refolved, That the Bill be committed to the Committee of Propofitions and Grievances.

Ordered, That Mr *Holt* have Leave to be abfent from the Service of this Houfe till *Thurfday* Sevennight.

And the Houfe adjourned till Monday Morning next, eleven of the Clock.

Monday. the 16th of March, 12 George III. 1772.

ORDERED, That Leave be given to bring in a Bill to amend an Act, intituled *An Act[4] for regulating the Practice of Attornies;* and that Mr *Hutchings* and Mr *Gray* do prepare, and bring in the fame.

A *Petition* of feveral perfons of the Counties of *Henrico* and *Hanover*, whofe Names are thereunto fubfcribed, was prefented to the Houfe, and read; fetting forth, that the prefent Ferry over *James* River from the Hemp Landing to *Shockoe*, is become very inconvenient, the Water at one of the Landings being made too shoal by the late great Frefh; and therefore praying, that a public Ferry may be eftablifhed from *Rocket's*, on the Land of *Charles Lewis*, over the faid River, to the Land of the Honourable *William Byrd*, Efquire, where there are good Landings.

Ordered, That the faid Petition be referred to the Confideration of the Committee of propofitions and Grievances; and that they do examine the Matter thereof, and report the fame, with their Opinion thereupon, to the Houfe.

An engroffed *Bill* for better regulating the Election of Veftries, was read the third Time.

Refolved, That the Bill do pafs; and that the Title be, *An Act[5] for better regulating the Election of Veftries.*

Ordered, That Mr *Henry Lee* do carry the Bill to the Council, and defire their Concurrence.

An engroffed *Bill* for continuing and amending the Act, intituled *An Act[6] for deftroying Crows and Squirrels in certain Counties therein mentioned*, was read the third Time.

Refolved, That the Bill do pafs; and that the Title be, *An Act[7] for continuing and amending the Act, intituled an Act for deftroying Crows and Squirrels in certain Counties therein mentioned*

Ordered, That Mr *Richard Henry Lee* do carry the Bill to the Council, and defire their Concurrence.

An engroffed *Bill* to amend an Act, intituled *An Act[8] to prevent malicious maiming and wounding*, was read the third Time.

Refolved, That the Bill do pafs; and that the Title be, *An Act[9] to amend an Act, intituled an Act to prevent malicious maiming and wounding.*

Ordered, That Mr *Gray* do carry the Bill to the Council, and defire their Concurrence.

An

---

[1] Hening, VIII, p. 407. [2] Ibid, VIII, p, 623. [3] Ibid, VIII, p. 318. [4] Ibid, VII, p. 397.
[5] Not recorded as a law. [6] Hening, VIII, p. 389. [7] Ibid, VIII, p. 596. [8] Ibid, VI, p. 250.
[9] Ibid, VIII, p. 520.

An engroffed *Bill* for eftablifhing a Town on the Lands adjoining the Court-Houfe of *Botetourt* County, was read the third Time.

Refolved, That the Bill do pafs; and that the Title be, *An Act[1] for eftablifhing the Town of* Fincaftle, *in the County of* Botetourt.

Ordered, That Mr *Edmund Pendleton* do carry the Bill to the Council, and defire their Concurrence.

A *Bill* to amend an Act, intituled *An Act[2] concerning Seamen*, was read a fecond Time.

Refolved, That the Bill be committed to Mr *Edmund Pendleton*, and Mr *Hutchings*.

A *Bill* to compel Ships importing Convicts, Servants, or Slaves, infected with the Gaol-Fever, or Small-Pox, to perform Quarantine, was read a fecond Time.

Refolved, That the Bill be committed to the Committee of Propofitions and Grievances.

A *Bill* for making farther Provifion for the Support and Maintenance of Ideots, Lunatics, and Perfons of unfound Minds, was read a fecond Time.

Ordered, That the Bill be engroffed.

A *Bill* for keeping in Repair feveral Roads and Bridges, and for other Purpofes therein mentioned, was read a fecond Time.

Refolved, That the Bill be committed to the Committee of Propofitions and Grievances

The *Order* of the Day being read;

The Houfe refolved itfelf into a Committee of the whole Houfe upon the Bill to continue and amend an Act, intituled *An Act[3] for reviving the Duty upon Slaves, to be paid by the Buyers*; alfo to continue and amend an Act, intituled *An Act to oblige Perfons bringing Slaves into this Colony from* Maryland, Carolina, *and the* Weft-Indies, *for their own Ufe, to pay a Duty*.

Mr *Speaker* left the Chair.

Mr *Bland* took the Chair of the Committee.

Mr *Speaker* refumed the Chair.

Mr *Bland* reported from the Committee, that they had gone through the Bill, and made feveral Amendments thereunto, which they had directed him to report to the Houfe; and he read the Report in his Place, and afterwards delivered the Bill, with the Amendments, in at the Clerk's Table; where the Amendments were once read throughout, and then a fecond Time, one by one, and, upon the Queftion feverally put thereupon, were, with an Amendment to one of them, agreed to by the Houfe.

Ordered, That the Bill, with the Amendments, be engroffed.

And then the Houfe adjourned till Tomorrow Morning, eleven of the Clock.

Tuesday, the 17th of March, 12 George III. 1772.

ANOTHER *Member* having taken the Oaths appointed to be taken by Act of Parliament, and repeated and fubfcribed the Teft, took his Place in the Houfe.

Mr *Hutchings* reported from the Committee, to whom the Bill to amend an Act, intituled *An Act[4] concerning Seamen*, was committed, that the Committee had gone through the Bill, and made an Amendment thereunto, which they had directed him to report to the Houfe; and he read the Report in his Place, and afterwards delivered the Bill, with the Amendment, in at the Clerk's Table; where the Amendment was twice read, and, upon the Queftion put thereupon, was agreed to by the Houfe.

Ordered, That the Bill, with the Amendment, be engroffed.

Mr *Cary* reported from the Committee of Public Claims, that the Committee having, according to the Order of the Houfe, infpected the Report of the Committee of Claims

laft

---

[1] Hening, VIII, p. 616. [2] Ibid, VI, p. 24. [3] Ibid, VIII, p. 530. (Original Acts, IV, p. 317; VII, p. 338.) [4] Ibid, VI. p. 24.

laft Seffion, and alfo read, confidered, and regulated the Claims prefented to this Seffion of Affembly, had entered fuch of the faid Claims as were allowed in a Book; and had directed him to report the fame to the Houfe; and he read the Report in his Place; and afterwards delivered the Book in at the Clerk's Table.

Ordered, That the Book of Public Claims do lie upon the Table, to be perufed by the Members of the Houfe.

M[r] *Bland* prefented to the Houfe, according to Order, a Bill for appointing Truftees to regulate the making of Slopes for the Paffage of Fifh in the Mill Dams within the County of *Bedford*; and the fame was received, and read the firft Time.

Refolved, That the Bill be read a fecond Time.

A *Petition of* fundry Inhabitants of the County of *Nanfemond*, whofe Names are thereunto fubfcribed, was prefented to the Houfe, and read; fetting forth, that the Petitioners refiding in that Part of the faid County, which is on the South Side of the River *Nottoway*, are about thirty Miles diftant from the Court-Houfe of their County, but not more than thirteen Miles from the Court of the County of *Southampton;* and therefore praying that an Act may pafs for adding the aforefaid Part of the County of *Nanfemond* to the faid County of *Southampton.*

Ordered, That the Confideration of the faid Petition be deferred till the next Seffion of General Affembly.

M[r] *Treafurer* reported from the Committee for Religion, to whom the Bill for extending the Benefit of the feveral Acts of Toleration to his Majefty's Proteftant Subjects in this Colony, diffenting from the Church of *England*, was committed, that the Committee had gone through the Bill, and made an Amendment thereunto, which they had directed him to report to the Houfe; and he read the Report in his Place, and afterwards delivered the Bill, with the Amendment, in at the Clerk's Table; where the Amendment was twice read, and, upon the Queftion put thereupon, was agreed to by the Houfe.

Ordered, That the Bill, with the Amendment, be engroffed.

Ordered, That the Bill, when engroffed, be printed.

Ordered, That the Bill be read the third Time upon the firft Day of *July* next.

M[r] *Bland* reported from the Committee of Propofitions and Grievances, to whom feveral Petitions were referred, that the Committee had examined the Matters of the faid Petitions, and had come to feveral Refolutions thereupon, which they had directed him to report to the Houfe; and he read the Report in his Place, and afterwards delivered it in at the Clerk's Table; where the Refolutions of the Committee were read, and are as followeth, *viz.*

Refolved, That it is the Opinion of this Committee, that the petition of divers Inhabitants of the County of *Bedford*, praying that an Infpection of Tobacco may be eftablifhed at *New-London*, in the faid County, be rejected.

Refolved, That it is the Opinion of this Committee, that the petition of *John Meredith* and *John Timberlake*, Infpectors of Tobacco at the Brick Houfe, in *New-Kent* County, praying that their Salaries may be raifed to thirty Pounds *per Annum*, each, is reafonable.

Refolved, That it is the Opinion of this Committee, that the Petition of *John Rhodes* and *Richard Sandford*, Infpectors of Tobacco at *Hunting* Creek, praying that their Salaries may be increafed; and an Allowance made them for their extraordinary Trouble the two laft Years, is reafonable; and that they ought to be allowed five Pounds, each, additional Salary, *per Annum*, and ten Pounds, each, for their extraordinary Trouble the two laft Years.

The faid *Refolutions*, being feverally read a fecond Time, were, upon the Queftion feverally put thereupon, agreed to by the Houfe.

Ordered, That it be an Inftruction to the Committee of Propofitions and Grievances, to whom the Bill to continue and amend the Act, intituled *An Act[1] to continue and amend the Act, intituled An Act for amending the Staple of Tobacco, and for preventing Frauds in his Majefty's Cuftoms*, is committed, that they have Power to receive a Claufe or

Claufes

---

[1] Hening. VIII, p. 318.

Claufes, for increafing the Salaries of the Infpectors of Tobacco, at *Cave's* Warehoufes, in the County of *Stafford*, five Pounds *per Annum* each; and alfo for increafing the Salaries of the Infpectors of Tobacco at the *Brick* Houfe, in the County of *New Kent*, to thirty Pounds *per Annum* each; and alfo for increafing the Salaries of the Infpectors of Tobacco at *Hunting* Creek, five Pounds *per Annum* each.

Ordered, that the Allowance of ten Pounds to *John Rhodes* and *Richard Sandford*, Infpectors of Tobacco at *Hunting* Creek, each, for their extraordinary Trouble the two laft Years, be entered in the Book of Public Claims by the Clerk.

And the faid *Allowance* was entered accordingly.

A *Meffage* from the Council by Mr *Blair:*

Mr *Speaker*,

The Council have agreed to the Bill, *intituled* An Act[1] for building a Bridge over the *Weftern Branch* of *Nanfemond* River by Subfcription, *without any Amendment; and alfo,*

The Council have agreed to the Bill, *intituled* An Act[2] for continuing the Act, intituled an Act for reimburfing the Inhabitants of *King William* and *Hanover Counties* the Expence of clearing *Pamunkey* River, *without any Amendment; and alfo,*

The Council have agreed to the Bill, *intituled* An Act[3] for adding Part of the County of *Nanfemond* to the County of *Ifle of Wight, without any Amendment; and alfo,*

The Council have agreed to the Bill, *intituled* An Act[4] to empower the Corporation of the Borough of *Norfolk* to affefs a Tax on the Inhabitants thereof, for the Purpofes therein mentioned, *without any Amendments; and alfo,*

The Council have agreed to the Bill, *intituled* An Act[5] to appoint Commiffioners to ftrike a dividing Line between the Counties of *Stafford* and *King George*, with *an Amendment, to which Amendment the Council defire the Concurrence of this Houfe; and alfo,*

The Council have agreed to the Bill, *intituled* An Act[6] for altering the Court Days of the Counties of *Surry* and *Princefs Anne, with fome Amendments to which Amendments the Council defire the Concurrence of this Houfe; and alfo,*

The Council have agreed to the Treafurer's *Accounts.*

And he prefented the faid *Accounts* at the Bar.

And then the Meffenger withdrew.

Ordered, That Mr *Bland* do carry the Treafurer's Accounts to his Excellency the Governor, and defire his Affent thereunto.

Ordered, That the Order of the Day for the Houfe to refolve itfelf into a Committee of the whole Houfe upon the Bill to remove the Seat of Government to a Place more convenient to the Inhabitants of this Colony, be now read.

And the faid *Order* being read accordingly;

The Houfe refolved itfelf into the faid Committee.

Mr *Speaker* left the Chair.

Mr *Bland* took the Chair of the Committee.

Mr *Speaker* refumed the Chair.

Mr *Bland* reported from the Committee, that they had made a Progrefs in the Bill, and that he was directed by the Committee to move that they may have Leave to fit again.

Refolved, That this Houfe will, Tomorrow, refolve itfelf into a Committee of the whole Houfe, to confider further of the faid Bill.

Ordered, That Mr *White*, Mr *Macdowell*, and Mr *Simpfon* have Leave to be abfent from the Service of this Houfe till the End of this Seffion.

Mr *Edmund Pendleton* prefented to the Houfe, according to Order, a Bill to dock the Intail of certain Lands, whereof *Ralph Wormeley*, Efq; is feifed; and the fame was received, and read the firft Time.

Refolved, That the Bill be read a fecond Time.

And then the Houfe adjourned till Tomorrow Morning, eleven of the Clock.

𝔚𝔢𝔡𝔫𝔢𝔰𝔡𝔞𝔶

---

[1] Hening, VIII, p. 552.   [2] Ibid, VIII, p. 623.   [3] Ibid, VIII, p. 602.   [4] Ibid, VIII, p. 611.

[5] Ibid, VIII, p. 601.   [6] Ibid, VIII, p. 519.

Wednesday, the 18th of March, 12 George III. 1772.

A Member returned upon a new Writ having taken the Oaths Appointed to be taken by Act of Parliament, and repeated and subscribed the Test, took his Place in the House.

A *Bill* to dock the Intail of certain Lands whereof *Ralph Wormeley*, Esquire, is seised, was read a second Time.

Resolved, That the Bill be committed to Mr *Richard Henry Lee*, Mr *Wood*, Mr *Rutherford*, Mr *Marshall*, Mr *Scott*, and Mr *Francis Peyton*.

A *Message* from the *Governor* by Mr *Blair*:

Mr *Speaker*,
I am Commanded by the Governor to deliver to this House a Letter received by his Excellency from the Earl of Hillsborough; upon the Subject of a Copper Coinage.

And he *presented* the said Letter at the Bar.
And then the Messenger withdrew.
And the said *Letter* was read.
Ordered, That the said Letter be referred to the Consideration of a Committee of the whole House.

Resolved, That this House will, upon *Wednesday* next, resolve itself into a Committee of the whole House to consider of the said Letter.

Mr *Harrison* presented to the House, according to Order, a Bill for erecting a Lighthouse on *Cape Henry*; and the same was received, and read the first Time.

Resolved, That the Bill be read a second Time.

Mr *Edmund Pendleton* reported from the Committee of Privileges and Elections, to whom the Petition of Mr *Henry Blagrave*, complaining of an undue Election and Return of Mr *Thomas Pettus* to serve as a Burgess in this present General Assembly for the County of *Lunenburg*, was referred, that the Committee had examined the Merits of the said Election, and had directed him to report the same, together with the Resolutions of the Committee thereupon, to the House; and he read the Report in his Place, and afterwards delivered it in at the Clerk's Table; where the same was read, and is as followeth, *viz.*

It appears to your *Committee*, that *Francis Degraffenreidt*, who voted for Mr *Pettus* at the said Election, was put into Possession by his Father of about four hundred Acres of Land, above a Year before the Election, who made him a Deed for the same in *October*, 1771; that the greatest Part of the Land lies, as he believes, in *Charlotte* County, but does not know how much; that he never voted in *Charlotte* under the same Freehold, nor hath paid any Quitrents, but believes his Father hath always paid the same in *Lunenburg* County.

Resolved, That it is the Opinion of this Committee, that the said *Francis Degraffenreidt* had a Right to vote for Burgesses at the said Election.

It appears to your *Committee*, that *Charles Parish*, who also voted for Mr *Pettus* at the said Election, was possessed of an undivided fourth Part of six hundred and fifteen Acres, which he holds under his father's Will; that by the said Will he was to have Possession at his Age of twenty-one Years, which Possession he obtained since the fifth Day of *November*, 1770; and says he believes he is of Age, but would not swear it.

Resolved, That it is the Opinion of this Committee, that the said *Charles Parish* had a Right to vote for Burgesses at the said Election.

It further appears to your *Committee*, that *Zachariah Davis*, who likewise voted for Mr *Pettus*, the sitting Member, held seventy odd Acres of unimproved Land, devised to him by the Will of one *John Blackston*, who died above two Years ago; that the same fell into his Possession immediately on the Death of the said *Blackston*, and that he hath enjoyed it ever since; that the said Will was proved in the Year 1771, before the Election; that he has never conveyed away the said Land, and that he improved it in *January*, 1771, and has paid one Year's Quitrents for the same.

Resolved

Refolved, That it is the Opinion of this Committee, that the faid *Zachariah Davis* had no Right to vote for Burgeffes at the faid Election.

It appears to your *Committee*, that twenty-five other Perfons, who voted for Mr *Pettus* at the faid Election, had no Right to give fuch Votes; and their particular Cafes were not defired by either Party to be fpecially reported.

It appears to your *Committee*, that *David Garland*, the Sheriff of the County, who held the Election, and made the Return, was entered upon the Poll as a Voter for Mr *Pettus*.

Refolved, That it is the Opinion of this Committee, that the Vote of the faid *David Garland*, ought not to ftand upon the faid Poll.

It appears to your *Committee*, that fifteen Perfons who voted at the faid Election for the petitioner had no Right to vote; and their Cafes were not defired to be reported.

The *Committee* then proceeded to confider how the Poll would ftand upon the Refolutions aforefaid.

Upon cafting up the faid Poll it appeared there were

For Mr *Pettus*. 192
From which deduct the Voters difqualified as aforefaid 27
_____
Remains 165
_____
For Mr *Blagrave* 179
From which deduct the bad Votes 15
_____
164

And add the Votes of *Nathaniel Lafoon*, and *Hugh Wallace*, who appear to have
    voted for the Petitioner, but their Names not entered upon the Poll. 2
_____
166

The *Petitioner* appears to have a Majority of 1

Refolved, Therefore, that it is the Opinion of this Committee, that Mr *Thomas Pettus* is not duly elected to ferve as a Burgefs in this prefent General Affembly for the County of *Lunenburg*.

Refolved, That it is the Opinion of this Committee, that Mr *Henry Blagrave* is duly elected to ferve as a Burgefs in this prefent General Affembly for the faid County.

The faid *Refolutions*, being feverally read a fecond Time, were, upon the Queftion feverally put thereupon, agreed to by the Houfe.

Ordered, That the Clerk do amend the Return for the County of *Lunenburg*, by rafing out the Name of *Thomas Pettus*, and inferting the Name of *Henry Blagrave*, inftead thereof. And he amended the Return accordingly.

Mr *Henry Lee* reported from the Committee, to whom the Bill to dock the Intail of certain Lands whereof *John Hancock* is feifed, and for fettling other Lands and Slaves, in Lieu thereof, was committed, that the Committee had examined the Allegations of the Bill, and found the fame to be true; and that the Committee had directed him to report the Bill to the Houfe, without any Amendment; and he delivered the Bill in at the Clerk's Table.

Ordered, That the Bill be engroffed.

Mr *Harrifon* prefented to the Houfe, according to Order, a Bill to appoint Commiffioners to view a Place propofed for a Road through the *South* Mountain; and the fame was received, and read the firft Time.

Refolved, That the Bill be read a fecond Time.

A *Petition* of the Inhabitants and Freeholders of the County of *Frederick*, whofe Names are thereunto fubfcribed, was prefented to the Houfe, and read; fetting forth, that the Navigation of the River *Potowmack* from Tide-Water to Fort *Cumberland*, if properly improved, would be productive of great Advantage, not only to thofe who are fettled upon the adjacent Lands, but to the whole Colony, by introducing a moft extenfive Trade; and therefore praying, that an Act may pafs for opening the Naviga-

tion

tion of the faid River, at the Expence of the Public, to be reimburfed by reafonable Tolls upon the Commodities which fhall be carried in the faid River; or for granting the like Tolls to fuch Adventurers as fhall be willing to undertake the Work, at their own Expence; or for impowering Truftees to receive and lay out the Money, which Sub-fcribers may voluntarily contribute, for that Purpofe.

100   *Ordered*, That the faid Petition be referred to the Confideration of the Committee of Propofitions and Grievances; and that they do examine the Matter thereof, and report the fame, with their Opinion thereupon, to the Houfe.

The *Order* of the Day being read;

Refolved, That this Houfe will, Tomorrow, refolve itfelf into a Committee of the whole Houfe to confider further of the Bill to remove the Seat of Government to a Place more convenient to the Inhabitants of this Colony.

Mr *Harrifon* reported from the Committee of Trade, to whom the Bill to continue an Act, intituled *An Act*[1] *to continue and amend an Act, intituled an Act for reducing the feveral Acts made for laying a Duty upon Liquors into one Act*, was committed, that the Committee had directed him to report the Bill to the Houfe, without any Amendment; and he delivered the Bill in at the Clerk's Table.

Ordered, That the faid Bill be recommitted.

Ordered, That the faid Bill be recommitted to a committee of the whole Houfe.

Refolved, That this Houfe will, upon *Friday* next, refolve itfelf into a Committee of the whole Houfe upon the faid Bill.

A *Petition* of *Richard Hewitt* and *Elias Hore*, Infpectors of Tobacco at *Aquia* Ware-houfes, in the County of *Stafford*, was prefented to the Houfe, and read; fetting forth, that, by Means of heavy Rains in the laft Summer, a large Quantity of Tobacco in the faid Warehoufes was damaged, which it was not in the Power of the Petitioners to pre-vent; and further fetting forth, that the petitioners receive only forty Pounds *per Annum*, for their Salary, which is not equal to what is paid to other Infpectors, whofe Trouble is lefs; and therefore praying, that they may be allowed for the faid damaged Tobacco, and have fuch Salary as the Houfe fhall think juft.

Ordered, That the faid Petition be referred to the Confideration of the Committee of Public Claims; and that they do examine the Matter thereof, and report the fame, with their Opinion thereupon, to the Houfe.

Ordered, That Mr *Bolling*, Mr *William Cabell*, Mr *Jofeph Cabell*, and Mr *Gray*, be added to the Committee for Religion.

Mr *Harrifon* reported from the Committee of Trade, to whom the petition of the Truftees of the Town of *Alexandria*, praying that the Wharf at *Point Weft*, in the faid Town, may be vefted in the Petitioners, and that fuch a Tax may be impofed upon Veffels heaving down by, and mooring at it, except thofe which bring Tobacco to or take it from the public Warehoufes in the faid Town, as will enable the Petitioners to repair and extend the faid Wharf, was referred, that the Committee had examined the Matter of the faid Petition, and had come to a Refolution thereupon, which they had directed him to report to the Houfe; and he read the Report in his Place, and afterwards delivered it in at the Clerk's Table; where the Refolution of the Committee was read, and is as followeth, *viz.*

Refolved, That it is the Opinion of this Committee, that the faid petition is reafonable.

The faid *Refolution*, being read a fecond Time, was, upon the Queftion put thereupon, agreed to by the Houfe.

Ordered, That a Bill be brought in purfuant to the faid Refolution; and that the faid Committee do prepare and bring in the fame.

A *Petition* of feveral Perfons, whofe Names are thereunto fubfcribed, was prefented to the Houfe, and read; fetting forth, that the Water in the Creek, at *Cave's* Infpection, is fo fhallow, that a Boat, with four Hogfheads of Tobacco, cannot eafily go down it, and it is daily growing worfe; and that the Expences of the faid Infpection confiderably exceeds the Money it brings into the Treafury; and that the building of a Warehoufe,

by

---
[1] Hening, VIII, p. 335.

by Virtue of an Order of the County Court of *Stafford*, at the faid Infpection, was lately [101]
undertaken by *Thomas Mountjoy*, one of the Infpectors there, in a private, unfair, and
illegal Manner, and for a much larger Sum than the Work is really worth; and therefore
praying, that the faid Infpection may be difcontinued; and that the Houfe will take the
whole Matter into their Confideration, and do therein what fhall feem beft.

Ordered, That the faid Petition be referred to the Confideration of the Committee
of Propofitions and Grievances; and that they do examine the Matter thereof, and
report the fame, with their Opinion thereupon, to the Houfe.

And then the Houfe adjourned till Tomorrow Morning, eleven of the Clock.

Thursday, the 19th of March, 12 George III. 1772.

ANOTHER *Member* having taken the Oaths appointed to be taken by Act of
Parliament, and repeated and fubfcribed the Teft, took his Place in the Houfe.
A *Meffage* from the Council by Mr *Blair:*

Mr *Speaker*,
   The Council have agreed to the Bill, *intituled* An Act[1] for continuing and
amending the Act, intituled An Act for deftroying Crows and Squirrels, in certain
Counties therein mentioned, *without any Amendment; and alfo,*
   The Council have agreed to the Bill *intituled* An Act[2] for further continuing and
amending the Act, intituled An Act for the better regulating and collecting certain
Officers Fees, and for other Purpofes therein mentioned, *with an Amendment, to which
Amendment, the Council defire the Concurrence of this Houfe; and alfo,*
   The Council have agreed to the Bill, *intituled* An Act[3] to amend an Act, intituled An
Act to prevent malicious maiming and wounding, *with fome Amendments, to which
Amendments the Council defire the Concurrence of this Houfe.*

And then the Meffenger withdrew.
   The Houfe proceeded to take into Confideration the Amendment made by the
Council to the Bill intituled *An Act[4] for further continuing and amending the Act*, intituled
*An Act for the better regulating and collecting certain Officers Fees, and for other Purpofes
therein mentioned.*
   And the faid *Amendment* was read, and is as followeth, *viz.*
   Line 15, Leave out '*ten Shillings,*' and infert '*thirteen Shillings and four Pence,*'
inftead thereof.
   The faid *Amendment*, being read a fecond Time, was, upon the Queftion put thereupon, difagreed to by the Houfe.
   Ordered, That a Meffage be fent to the Council to inform them that this Houfe
cannot agree to the Amendment by them propofed to the faid Bill, and to defire that
they will pafs the fame without the Amendment; and that Mr *Patrick Henry* do carry
the faid Meffage.
   A *Petition* of Mr *Thomas Pettus* was prefented to the Houfe, and read; fetting forth,
that at the Election of Burgeffes to ferve in this prefent General Affembly, for the County
of *Lunenburg*, Mr *Richard Claiborne*, and Mr *Henry Blagrave*, with the Petitioner, were
Candidates, when the faid Mr *Claiborne*, and the petitioner, were returned duly elected,
fince which this Honourable Houfe hath determined that the Petitioner was not duly [102]
elected, and that the faid Mr *Blagrave* was duly elected; and further fetting forth, that the
Election of the faid Mr *Blagrave* was illegal, he having appointed feveral Perfons to treat
in his Favour, as well after the Publication of the Writ, as on the Day of Election; and
the Perfons fo appointed having actually treated many Freeholders accordingly with
Liquor in the Morning of the Day of Election, and before the Poll began; and therefore
praying the Confideration of the Houfe in the Premiffes.

Ordered

---

[1] Hening, VIII, p. 596.   [2] Ibid, VIII, p. 515.   [3] Ibid, VIII, p. 520.   [4] Ibid, VIII, p. 515.

Ordered, That the faid petition be referred to the Confideration of the Committee of Privileges and Elections; and that they do examine the Matter thereof, and report the fame, with their Opinion thereupon, to the Houfe.

Mr *Treafurer* reported from the Committee for Religion, to whom the Petition of feveral Inhabitants of the Parifh of *Dryfdale*, in the County of *Caroline*, praying that a new Parifh may be formed out of the faid Parifh of *Dryfdale*, and the adjoining Parifh of *Saint Margaret*, by an Union of the upper Ends thereof, *and alfo*, the feveral Petitions of the Inhabitants of the faid Parifh of *Saint Margaret*, in Oppofition thereto, were referred, that the Committee had come to a Refolution, which they had directed him to report to the Houfe; and he read the Report in his Place, and afterwards delivered it in at the Clerk's Table, where the Refolution of the Committee was read, and is as followeth, *viz.*

Refolved, That it is the Opinion of this Committee, that the further Confideration of the faid Petitions be deferred till the next Seffion of General Affembly.

The faid *Refolution*, being read a fecond Time, was, upon the Queftion put thereupon, agreed to by the Houfe.

Mr *Richard Henry Lee* reported from the Committee, to whom the Bill to dock the Intail of certain Lands whereof *Ralph Wormeley*, Efquire, is feifed, was committed, that the Committee had examined the Allegations of the Bill, and found the fame to be true, and that the Committee had directed him to report the Bill to the Houfe, without any Amendment; and he delivered the Bill in at the Clerk's Table.

Ordered, That the Bill be engroffed.

Ordered, That Mr *Tabb* have Leave to be abfent from the Service of this Houfe till the End of this Seffion of General Affembly.

A *Memorial* of the Veftrymen of the Parifh of *Leeds*, in the Counties of *Fauquier* and *Prince William*, was prefented to the Houfe, and read; taking Notice of an Application of the Veftrymen of the Parifh of *Hamilton*, in the faid Counties, to this Houfe, for another Divifion of the faid Parifhes, in Confequence of a pretended Agreement previous to the former Divifion, that the faid Parifh of *Hamilton* fhould have a Majority of one hundred Tithables left in it, and denying fuch Agreement ever to have been made by any Perfons who had Power to contract for the Inhabitants of *Leeds;* and fetting forth, that there is now a greater Number of Tithables in the faid Parifh of *Hamilton*, than in the faid Parifh of *Leeds*, and that before they were divided, two large Churches, one of Brick, and the other of Wood, were built, both which are in the prefent Parifh of *Hamilton*, and that the Petitioners have been obliged to build four Churches in their own Parifh, at a very confiderable Expence; and therefore praying that the faid Petition, for another Divifion of the faid Parifhes, may be rejected, and that the Parifhioners of *Hamilton* may be obliged to refund, to thofe of *Leeds*, a reafonable proportion of the Tobacco paid for building the faid Brick Church.

Ordered, That the faid petition be referred to the Confideration of the Committee for Religion, to whom the faid Petition of the Veftrymen of the Parifh of *Hamilton* is referred; and that they do examine the Matter of this Petition, and report the fame, with their Opinion thereupon, to the Houfe.

A *Petition* of the Inhabitants of the County of *King George*, and others, whofe Names are thereunto fubfcribed, was prefented to the Houfe, and read; fetting forth, that the Petitioners futter many Inconveniences, and meet with frequent Difappointments, by the Union of *Gibfon's* and *Morton's* Infpections, and therefore praying Relief.

Ordered, That the faid Petition be referred to the Confideration of the Committee of Propofitions and Grievances; and that they do examine the Matter thereof, and report the fame, with their Opinion thereupon, to the Houfe.

The *Order* of the Day being read;

Refolved, That this Houfe will, Tomorrow, refolve itfelf into a Committee of the whole Houfe, to confider further of the Bill to remove the Seat of Government to a Place more convenient to the Inhabitants of this Colony.

And then the Houfe adjourned till Tomorrow Morning, eleven of the Clock.

𝔉𝔯𝔦𝔡𝔞𝔶

Friday. the 20th of March. 12 George III. 1772.

A *Petition* of *Caldwell Pettypoole* was prefented to the Houfe, and read; fetting forth that the petitioner is feifed, in Right of *Mary* his Wife, in Fee Tail, of a Tract of Land, containing two hundred and eighty-one Acres, lying in the Parifh of *Henrico*, in the County of *Henrico*, a great Diftance from the Place of his Refidence, which he might fell for a high Price, much to the Advantage of his Wife and Family, if he was enabled fo to do; and therefore praying that an Act may pafs for that Purpofe, upon making an equivalent Settlement, to which his Wife is confenting.

Ordered, That Leave be given to bring in a Bill purfuant to the Prayer of the faid Petition; and that Mr *Adams* and M^r *DuVal* do prepare, and bring in the fame.

Mr *Cary* prefented to the Houfe, according to Order, a Bill for appointing Commiffioners for fettling the Tobacco damaged in the public Warehoufes at *Morton's;* and the fame was received, and read the firft Time.

Refolved, That the Bill be read a fecond Time.

The *Order* of the Day being read;

The Houfe refolved itfelf into a Committee of the whole Houfe to confider further of the Bill to remove the Seat of Government to a Place more convenient to the Inhabitants of this Colony.

Mr *Speaker* left the Chair.

Mr *Bland* took the Chair of the Committee.

Mr *Speaker* refumed the Chair.

Mr *Bland* reported from the Committee, that they had gone through the Bill, and made feveral Amendments thereunto, which they had directed him to report, when the Houfe will pleafe to receive the fame.

Ordered, That the Report be now received.

Mr *Bland* accordingly reported from the faid Committee the Amendments which the Committee had made to the Bill, and which they had directed him to report to the Houfe; and he read the Report in his Place, and afterwards delivered the Bill, with the Amendments, in at the Clerk's Table; where the Amendments were once read throughout, and then a fecond Time, one by one, and upon the Queftion feverally put thereupon, were agreed to by the Houfe.

Ordered, That the Bill, with the Amendments, be engroffed.

A *Petition* of the Inhabitants of the Parifh of *Stratton Major*, in the County of *King and Queen*, was prefented to the Houfe, and read; fetting forth, that the Petitioners, for feveral Years paft, have been oppreffed and grieved by the arbitrary, illegal, and unwarrantable Proceedings of the faid Veftry; that the faid Veftry unneceffarily built a very coftly Church in the faid Parifh, and fuffered others more conveniently fituated to become ruinous; and that the faid Veftry have chofen one of their Members Clerk of the Veftry, and continue him in Office, contrary to Law, and have not obferved and fulfilled the Directions of the Act of General Affembly, in the Appointment of Proceffioners, and regiftering their Proceedings; and therefore praying that the faid Veftry may be diffolved.

Ordered, That the Confideration of the faid Petition be deferred till the next Seffion of General Affembly.

The other *Order* of the Day being read;

Refolved, That this Houfe will, Tomorrow, refolve itfelf into a Committee of the whole Houfe upon the Bill to continue an Act, intituled *An Act¹ to continue and amend an Act, intituled an Act for reducing the feveral Acts made for laying a Duty upon Liquors into one Act.*

Refolved, That an humble Addrefs be prepared to be prefented to his Majefty to exprefs the high Opinion we entertain of his benevolent Intentions towards his Subjects in the Colonies, and that we are thereby induced to afk his paternal Affiftance in averting

ing

---

¹ Hening, VIII, p. 335.

ing a Calamity of a moft alarming Nature; that the Importation of Negroes from *Africa* has long been confidered as a Trade of great Inhumanity, and, under its prefent Encouragement, may endanger the Exiftence of his *American* Dominions; that Self-Prefervation therefore urges us to implore him to remove all Reftraints on his Governors from paffing Acts of Affembly, which are intended to check this pernicious Commerce; and that we prefume to hope the Interefts of a few of his Subjects in *Great-Britain* will be difregarded, when fuch a Number of his People look up to him for Protection in a Point fo effential; that, when our Duty calls upon us to make Application for his Attention to the Welfare of this his antient Colony, we cannot refrain from renewing thofe Proffeffions of Loyalty and Affection we have fo often, with great Sincerity, made, or from affuring him, that we regard his Wifdom and Virtue as the fureft Pledges of the Happinefs of his People.

Ordered, That a Committee be appointed to draw up an Addrefs to be prefented to his Majefty upon the faid Refolution.

And a *Committee* was appointed of Mr *Harrifon*, Mr *Cary*, Mr *Edmund Pendleton*, Mr *Richard Henry Lee*, Mr *Treafurer*, and Mr *Bland*.

A *Petition* of feveral Perfons, of the Parifh of *Overwharton*, in the County of *Stafford*, whofe Names are thereunto fubfcribed, was prefented to the Houfe, and read; fetting forth, that the Election of Veftrymen for the faid parifh, by Virtue of a late Act of the General Affembly, was made in an unfair, irregular and illegal Manner; and therefore praying that the prefent Veftry of the faid Parifh may be diffolved.

Ordered, That the faid petition be referred to the Confideration of the Committee for Religion; and that they do examine the Matter thereof, and report the fame, with their Opinion thereupon, to the Houfe.

Mr *Bland* reported from the Committee of Propofitions and Grievances, to whom feveral Petitions were referred, that the Committee had examined the Matter of the faid Petitions, and had come to feveral Refolutions thereupon, which they had directed him to report to the Houfe; and he read the Report in his Place, and afterwards delivered it in at the Clerk's Table; where the Refolutions of the Committee were read, and are as followeth, *viz.*

Refolved, That it is the Opinion of this Committee, that the Petition of divers Inhabitants of the County of *Spotfylvania*, praying that the Houfe will apply to the Governor, for his Majefty's Writ, to adjourn the Court of the faid County, from the Town of *Frederickfburg*, to a Place more convenient to the Inhabitants of the faid County, is reafonable.

Refolved, That it is the Opinion of this Committee, that the Petition of divers Inhabitants of the faid County, in Oppofition thereto, be rejected.

The faid *Refolutions*, being feverally read a fecond Time, were, upon the Queftion feverally put thereupon, agreed to by the Houfe.

Ordered, That a Committee be appointed to draw up an Addrefs, to be prefented to the Governor, upon the firft of the faid Refolutions.

And a *Committee* was appointed of Mr *Bland*, Mr *Edmund Pendleton*, Mr *Richard Henry Lee*, Mr *Treafurer*, Mr *Harrifon*, Mr *Cary*, Mr *Stubblefield*, and Mr *Mann Page*.

Mr *Edmund Pendleton* reported from the Committee, to whom the Bill to amend an Act, intituled *An Act[1] for clearing* Mattapony *River*, was committed, that the Committee had directed him to report the Bill to the Houfe without any Amendment; and he delivered the Bill in at the Clerk's Table.

Ordered, That the Bill be engroffed.

Ordered, That Mr *David Mafon* be added to the Committee of Privileges and Elections.

A *Petition* of fundry Inhabitants of the Parifh of *Saint James*, in the County of *Mecklenburg*, whofe Names are thereunto fubfcribed, was prefented to the Houfe, and read, fetting forth that the Veftry of the faid Parifh, having caufed three large Churches and a Chapel to be built, confulted as to the Situations thereof, the Conveniency of the Veftrymen themfelves, rather than that of the Petitioners; and that the faid Veftry having agreed to receive into the Parifh a Minifter, who was approved of by the Parifhioners

---

[1] Hening, VI, p. 394.

ioners, afterwards suddenly received another Minister, who was a Stranger to them; and that the said Vestry, in Order to enable one *Rogers*, a notorious Gamester, of infamous Character, to obtain Holy Orders, gave him a Recommendation to a Benefice, but took a Bond from him, with Security, in the Penalty of one thousand Pounds, that he should not claim under that Title; and therefore praying that the said Vestry may be dissolved.

Ordered, That the said petition be referred to the Consideration of the Committee for Religion; and that they do examine the Matter thereof, and report the same, with their Opinion thereupon, to the House.

Mr *Bland* reported from the Committee of propositions and Grievances, to whom several Petitions were referred, that the Committee had examined the Matters of the said Petitions, and had come to several Resolutions thereupon, which they had directed him to report to the House; and he read the Report in his Place, and afterwards delivered it in at the Clerk's Table; where the Resolutions of the Committee were read, and are as followeth, *viz.*

Resolved, That it is the Opinion of this Committee, that the Petition of the Inhabitants of *Henrico* and *Hanover* Counties, praying that a Ferry may be established across *James* River, from a Place called *Rocket's* Landing, in the said County of *Henrico*, to the Land of the Honourable *William Byrd*, Esq; in the County of *Chesterfield*, be rejected.

Resolved, That it is the Opinion of this Committee, that the Petition of divers Inhabitants of the County of *King George*, praying that the Inspections of Tobacco at *Gibson's* and *Morton's* Warehouses may be disunited, is reasonable.

Resolved, That it is the Opinion of this Committee, that the petition of divers Inhabitants of the County of *Stafford*, praying that the Inspection of Tobacco at *Cave's* Warehouses may be discontinued, be rejected.

Resolved, That it is the Opinion of this Committee, that so much of the Petition of divers Inhabitants of the County of *Frederick*, as prays that the Navigation of the River *Potowmack*, from Tide Water to Fort *Cumberland*, may be improved at the Expence of the Public, be rejected.

Resolved, That it is the Opinion of this Committee, that the Residue of the said Petition, praying that the said Navigation may be improved by Subscription, or Lottery, is reasonable.

The said *Resolutions*, being severally read a second Time, were, upon the Question severally put thereupon, agreed to by the House.

Ordered, That it be an Instruction to the said Committee, to whom the Bill to continue and amend the Act, intituled *An Act*[1] *to continue and amend the Act, intituled* 106 *an Act for amending the Staple of Tobacco, and for preventing Frauds in his Majesty's Customs*, is committed, that they have Power to receive a Clause or Clauses pursuant to the second of the said Resolutions.

Ordered, That a Bill be brought in pursuant to the last of the said Resolutions; and that the said Committee do prepare, and bring in the same.

Mr *Cary* reported from the Committee of Public Claims, to whom the Petitions of *Robert Garrett* and *William Plunket*, late Inspectors, and of the said *Robert Garrett* and *Henry Ware*, present Inspectors, at *Conway's* Warehouse, in the County of *Caroline*, were referred, that the Committee had examined the Matter of the said Petitions, and had directed him to report the same, together with the Resolutions of the Committee thereupon, to the House; and he read the Report in his Place, and afterwards delivered it in at the Clerk's Table; where the same was read, and is as followeth, *viz.*

It appears to your *Committee*, that, at the Times the Tobacco mentioned in the said Petitions was stolen, the said Warehouses were insufficient; that previous thereto the said Inspectors had often applied to the Court of the County of *Caroline*, to put the said Warehouses in proper Repair; and that the said Court, in the Month of *October*, 1770, appointed Persons to let the same, but before the Repairs were made, the said Tobacco was stolen.

Whereupon the *Committee* came to the following Resolutions:

Resolved

---

1 Hening, VIII, p. 318.

Refolved, That it is the Opinion of this Committee, that the faid Petition of *Robert Garrett* and *William Plunket* is reafonable, and that they ought to be allowed the Sum of thirteen Pounds and ten Shillings, for the Tobacco in the faid Petition mentioned.

Refolved, That it is the Opinion of this Committee, that the faid Petition of *Robert Garrett* and *Henry Ware* is reafonable; and that they ought to be allowed the Sum of thirty-one Pounds, for the Tobacco in the faid Petition mentioned.

The faid *Refolutions*, being feverally read a fecond Time, were, upon the Queftion feverally put thereupon, agreed to by the Houfe.

A *Petition* of *John Rictor*, of the County of *Fauquier*, was prefented to the Houfe, and read; fetting forth, that the Land of the petitioner, whereon he lives, in the faid County, is conveniently fituated for a Town; and that feveral Tradefmen have already fettled at that Place, and others are willing to fettle there, in Cafe a Town be eftablifhed, and therefore praying that an Act may pafs for laying off fifty Acres of the faid Land into Lots for that Purpofe.

Ordered, That Leave be given to bring in a Bill purfuant to the Prayer of the faid petition, and that Mr *Marfhall*, and Mr *Scott*, do prepare, and bring in the fame.

Ordered, That Mr *May* be added to the Committee for Religion, and the Committee of Propofitions and Grievances.

Mr *Cary* reported from the Committee of Public Claims, to whom the Petition of *Elizabeth Derrick* was referred, that the Committee had examined the Matter of the faid Petition, and had directed him to report the fame, together with the Refolution of the Committee thereupon, to the Houfe; and he read the Report in his Place, and afterwards delivered it in at the Clerk's Table; where the fame was read, and is as followeth, *viz.*

It appears to your *Committee*, that the Negro Man Slave *Jack*, mentioned in the faid Petition, was committed to Gaol for hogftealing, and that during his Confinement he was froftbitten, by which Means he died in a few Days after his Trial.

Whereupon your *Committee* came to the following Refolution:

Refolved, That it is the Opinion of this Committee, that the faid Petition is reafonable, and that the faid *Elizabeth Derrick* ought to be allowed the Sum of feventy-five Pounds for the faid Slave.

The faid *Refolution*, being read a fecond Time, was, upon the Queftion put thereupon, agreed to by the Houfe.

Ordered, That the feveral Allowances of thirteen Pounds and ten Shillings to *Robert Garrett*, and *William Plunket*, and of thirty-one Pounds to the faid *Robert Garrett*, and *Henry Ware*, for Tobacco ftolen out of *Conway's* Warehoufe; *and alfo* the Allowance of feventy-five Pounds to *Elizabeth Derrick*, for a Slave, who having been froftbitten during his Imprifonment as a Felon, died a few Days after his Trial, be entered in the Book of Public Claims by the Clerk.

And the faid *Allowances* were feverally entered accordingly.

A *Petition* of *Benjamin Lankford*, and *Richard Booker*, was prefented to the Houfe, and read; fetting forth, that the Petitioners are Proprietors of a public Ferry over *Staunton* River, from the Land of *Edward Booker*, deceafed, in the County of *Halifax*, to the Land of *John Fuqua*, deceafed, and that the Rate of the faid Ferry, which was formerly fettled at two Pence *per* Man, was afterwards raifed to three Pence; but that the Act, by which the Ferriage was raifed, contained a fufpending Claufe, and it is uncertain whether the faid Act hath been approved of by his Majefty, and therefore praying that the Rate of the faid Ferry may be made equal to that of other Ferries over the fame River.

Ordered, That it be an Inftruction to the Committee of Propofitions and Grievances, who are appointed to prepare and bring in a Bill for repealing fo much of the Act, made in the fifth Year of the Reign of his prefent Majefty, intituled *An Act*[1] *for appointing feveral*

---
1 Hening, VIII, p. 44.

several new Ferries, and for other Purpofes therein mentioned, as eftablifhed a Ferry from the Land of *Cornelius Thomas,* over the *Fluvanna,* to the Land of *Nicholas Davies,* that they do make Provifion in the faid Bill for fettling the Ferriage from the Land of *Edward Booker,* deceafed, over *Staunton* River, to the Land of *John Fuqua,* deceafed.

Ordered, That Mr *Duval* be added to the Committee for Religion.

And then the Houfe adjourned till Tomorrow Morning, eleven of the Clock.

Saturday, the 21st of March, 12 George III. 1772.

ANOTHER *Member* having taken the Oaths appointed to be taken by Act of Parliament, and repeated and fubfcribed the Teft, took his Place in the Houfe.

A *Petition* of *Benjamin Winflow* was prefented to the Houfe, and read; fetting forth, that in the Year 1760, the Petitioner, having received a recruiting Commiffion, from Lieutenant Governor *Fauquier,* to enlift Men for the *Cherokee* Expedition, and being particularly directed by his Inftructions not to regard the Size of the Soldiers, if they were young and healthy, and had good Legs, recruited one *John Bromley,* about eighteen Years of Age, and in every other refpect, except his Stature, unexceptionable, to whom the Petitioner advanced the ten Pounds Bounty Money, and who was fupported by the Petitioner in a March from the Neighbourhood of *Frederickf-burg* to *Bryant's* Camp, on *Roanoke,* where the faid *John Bromley* was objected to and refufed, becaufe he was under Size, by the Commanding Officer; and further fetting forth, that the Petitioner, underftanding that the General Affembly had repaid to Officers in the like Circumftances their enlifting Money and Expences, defired Mr *Benjamin Grymes,* then a Member for the County of *Spotfylvania,* to lay the Cafe before the Houfe of Burgeffes, and put into his Hands the Vouchers to juftify his Claim, but, it feems, the Matter was never confidered by that Honourable Houfe; and therefore praying that fuch Satiffaction may now be made to him as fhall feem juft.

Ordered, That the faid Petition be referred to the Confideration of the Committee of Public Claims; and that they do examine the Matter thereof, and report the fame, with their Opinion thereupon, to the Houfe.

The Houfe proceeded to take into Confideration the Amendment made by the Council to the Bill, intituled *An Act[1] to Appoint Commiffioners to ftrike a dividing Line between the Counties of* Stafford *and* King George. [108]

And the faid *Amendment* was read, and is as followeth, *viz.*

Line 17, leave out "*fucceeding General,*" and infert "*Seffion of*" inftead thereof.

The faid *Amendment,* being read a fecond Time, was, upon the Queftion put thereupon, agreed to by the Houfe.

Ordered, That Mr *Alexander* do carry the Bill to the Council, and acquaint them, that this Houfe hath agreed to the Amendment made by them.

A *Petition* of *Jofeph Byrn,* of the County of *Frederick,* was prefented to the Houfe, and read; fetting forth, that a Tract of Land on *Shanando* River, in the faid County, whereof the Petitioner is feifed, in Right of his Wife, is a very convenient Place for a public Ferry; and therefore praying that fuch Ferry may be eftablifhed from thence, over the faid River, to the oppofite Bank.

Ordered, That the faid petition be referred to the Confideration of the Committee of Propofitions and Grievances; and that they do examine the Matter thereof and report the fame, with their Opinion thereupon, to the Houfe.

The Houfe proceeded to take into Confideration the Amendments made by the Council to the Bill intituled *An Act[2] to amend an Act,* intituled *An Act to prevent malicious maiming and wounding;* and the faid Amendments were read, and are as followeth, *viz.*

Line 11, after "*gouging,*" infert "*plucking or putting out an Eye;*" leave out "*or,*" and after "*biting,*" infert "*kicking, or ftamping upon.*"

The

---

[1] Hening, VIII, p. 601. [2] Ibid, VIII, p. 520.

The faid *Amendments*, being feverally read a fecond Time, were, upon the Queftion feverally put thereupon, agreed to by the Houfe.

Ordered, That Mr *Gray* do carry the Bill to the Council, and acquaint them that this Houfe hath agreed to the Amendments made by them.

A *Petition* of *Fielding Lewis*, and others, Veftrymen of the Parifh of *Saint George*, in the County of *Spotfylvania*, was prefented to the Houfe, and read; fetting forth, that the Church Yard of the faid Parifh, in the Town of *Frederickfburg*, lying, for the moft Part, on the Side of a Hill, is not a proper Situation for a new Church, which it will foon be neceffary to build, and befides, is not large enough, nor fit, for a burying Ground; and therefore praying that the Petitioners may be impowered to fell fo much of the faid Church Yard as hath not been ufed for Interment, and to lay out the Money arifing from the Sale, or fo much of it as fhall be fufficient, in purchafing other Land in the faid Town more convenient for the Purpofes aforefaid.

Ordered, That Leave be given to bring in a Bill purfuant to the Prayer of the faid Petition; and that Mr *Mann Page* do prepare, and bring in the fame.

The Houfe proceeded to take into Confideration the Amendments made by the Council to the Bill intituled *An Act for altering the Court Days of the Counties of* Surry, *and* Princefs Anne.

And the faid *Amendments* were read, and are as followeth, *viz.*

Line 2, after "*Surry*" infert "*Bedford.*"

Line 8, after "*Month,*" infert "*and the Court of the faid County of* Bedford *fhall be held on the fourth* Monday *in every Month.*"

In the *Title* of the Bill after "*Surry*" infert "*Bedford.*"

The faid *Amendments*, being feverally read a fecond Time, were, upon the Queftion feverally put thereupon, agreed to by the Houfe.

Ordered, That Mr *Bland* do carry the Bill to the Council, and acquaint them that this Houfe hath agreed to the Amendments made by them.

A *Petition* of *William Roane*, Gentleman, was prefented to the Houfe, and read; fetting forth that the petitioner had agreed to purchafe a Tract of fifteen hundred Acres of Land, in the County of *King and Queen*, from *John Randolph Grymes*, to whom the faid Land was devifed by the Will of his Father, the Honourable *Philip Grymes*, Efquire, deceafed, for feven hundred and fifty Pounds, but that it hath been fince difcovered that the faid Land, by fome Anceftor of the Family, had been entailed, and was not fubject to the faid Will; and further fetting forth, that *Philip Ludwell Grymes*, Efquire, the eldeft Son and Heir of the Body of the faid *Philip Grymes*, the Teftator, having been amply provided for by his Father, is willing and defirous that his faid Brother fhould have all the Benefit intended for him by the faid Devife; and therefore praying that Leave may be given to bring in a Bill for vefting the Fee Simple Eftate of the faid fifteen hundred Acres of Land in the Petitioner, upon Payment of the Confideration Money aforefaid to the faid *John Randolph Grymes*.

Ordered, That Leave be given to bring in a Bill purfuant to the Prayer of the faid Petition; and that Mr *Edmund Pendleton* and Mr *Nelfon* do prepare, and bring in the fame.

Ordered, That Mr *Weft*, Mr *Mann Page*, and Mr *Taliaferro* be added to the Committee for Religion.

Ordered, That Mr *Weft* be added to the Committee of Privileges and Elections.

Ordered, That Mr *Taliaferro*, Mr *Bowyer*, and Mr *Weft* be added to the Committee of Propofitions and Grievances.

A *Petition* of *John Pollard* and *Thomas Sharpe*, Infpectors of Tobacco at *Dixon's* Warehoufes, in the Town of *Falmouth*, and County of *King George*, was prefented to the Houfe, and read; fetting forth that the Salaries of the Petitioners, for feveral years before the late Act of General Affembly, which reduced them to forth-five Pounds *per Annum* each, had been equal to thofe of the Infpectors at *Falmouth* Warehoufes, who are ftill allowed fifty Pounds each, and who do not Infpect more Tobacco than the Petitioners, the Quantity brought annually to each Infpection being from twelve to

fifteen

fifteen hundred Hogfheads; and therefore praying that this Houfe will encreafe their Salaries for the future, and make them Amends for the faid Reduction.

Ordered, That the faid Petition be referred to the Confideration of the Committee of Propofitions and Grievances; and that they do examine the Matter thereof, and report the fame, with their Opinion thereupon, to the Houfe.

Several *Petitions* of fundry Inhabitants of the Counties of *Suffex* and *Dinwiddie*, whofe Names are thereunto fubfcribed, were prefented to the Houfe and read; taking Notice of an Application intended to be made to this Houfe, for obliging the Owners of Mills, on *Nottoway* River, to make in their Dams Slopes, of a new and extraordinary Kind; and reprefenting, that the Slopes propofed would render the Mills unprofitable, and probably carry them away, by which the People in that Part of the Country, watered by very few conftant Streams, would fuffer greater Inconvenience than the free Paffage of Fifh would compenfate; and therefore praying that no Alteration may be made in the Law relating to Slopes in Mill Dams.

Ordered, That the faid Petition be referred to the Confideration of the Committee of Propofitions and Grievances; and that they do examine the Matter thereof, and report the fame, with their Opinion thereupon, to the Houfe.

Ordered, That Mr *Montagu* have Leave to be abfent from the Service of this Houfe till *Wednefday* next.

A *Petition* of feveral Inhabitants of the Parifh of *Dryfdale*, in the County of *Caroline*, whofe Names are thereunto fubfcribed, was prefented to the Houfe, and read; taking Notice of an Application intended to be made to this Houfe for a Divifion of the faid Parifh; and fetting forth that the Petitioners think the Divifion unreafonable; and reprefenting that it would not relieve thofe who wifh for it, without deferting both the prefent Churches in the Parifh, and building others; and therefore praying that the faid Parifh may not be divided.

Ordered, That the Confideration of the faid Petition be deferred till the next Seffion of General Affembly.

An engroffed *Bill* for dividing the County of *Frederick* into three diftinct Counties was read the third Time.

Refolved, That the Bill do pafs; and that the Title be, *An Act¹ for dividing the County of* Frederick *into three diftinct Counties.*

Ordered, That Mr *Bland* do carry the Bill to the Council, and defire their Concurrence.

Several *Petitions* of the Inhabitants of the County of *Caroline*, whofe Names are thereunto fubfcribed, were prefented to the Houfe, and read; fetting forth that the Rivers *Mattapony* and *Pamunkey* are capable of an extenfive Navigation, which might confiderably leffen the Expence of carrying Commodities to Market; that all Rivers, as the Petitioners Conceive, ought to remain open, not only for the Purpofes of Commerce, but that the Paffage for Fifh being free, all Men may equally partake of that natural Supply of Provifions; and that the General Affembly, with a View to fuch defirable Ends, have empowered Truftees to receive Subfcriptions for clearing *Mattapony* and *Pamunkey*, in Confequence of which feveral Sums of Money were raifed and laid out, but the good Intention of the Legiflature hath been wholly defeated by the erecting Mill Dams, and fetting Fifh Hedges and Stops acrofs the faid Rivers; and therefore humbly fubmitting it to the Wifdom of the Houfe to provide an effectual Remedy to remove all prefent Obftructions, and prevent them for the future.

Ordered, That the Confideration of the faid Petitions be deferred till the next Seffion of General Affembly.

Mr *Treafurer* reported from the Committee for Religion, to whom the Petition of fundry Inhabitants of the Parifh of *Overwharton*, in the County of *Stafford*, praying that the Veftry of the faid Parifh may be diffolved, was referred, that the Committee had come to a Refolution, which they had directed him to report to the Houfe; and he read the Report in his Place, and afterwards delivered it in at the Clerk's Table; where the Refolution of the Committee was read, and is as followeth, *viz.*

Refolved

---

¹ Hening, VIII, p. 597.

Refolved, That it is the Opinion of this Committee, that the Confideration of the faid Petition be deferred till the next Seffion of General Affembly.

The faid *Refolution*, being read a fecond Time, was, upon the Queftion put thereupon, agreed to by the Houfe.

A *Petition* of *Martha Lavie*, Widow, was prefented to the Houfe, and read; fetting forth that the Petitioner's late Hufband *James Lavie*, who attended the Committee of Correfpondence, as their Meffenger and Door-keeper, for which this Houfe made him an Allowance in *November*, 1769, had received nothing for his faid Services from that Time until he died; and therefore praying that the Petitioner, who is left in indigent Circumftances, may be allowed by this Honourable Houfe whatever they may think the faid *James Lavie* deferved.

Refolved, That the Sum of ten Pounds be paid to the faid *Martha Lavie*.

Ordered, That the faid Allowance be entered in the Book of Public Claims.

And the fame was entered accordingly.

111

Mr *Treafurer* reported from the Committee for Religion, to whom the Petition of fundry Inhabitants of the Parifh of *Saint James*, in the County of *Mecklenburg*, praying that the Veftry of the faid Parifh may be diffolved, was referred, that the Committee had come to a Refolution, which they had directed him to report to the Houfe; and he read the Report in his Place, and afterwards delivered it in at the Clerk's Table; where the Refolution of the Committee was read, and is as followeth, *viz.*

Refolved, That it is the Opinion of this Committee, that the Confideration of the faid Petition be deferred till the next Seffion of General Affembly.

The faid *Refolution*, being read a fecond Time, was, upon the Queftion put thereupon, agreed to by the Houfe.

An engroffed *Bill* to continue and amend an Act, intituled *An Act[1] for reviving the Duty upon Slaves to be paid by the Buyers;* alfo to continue and amend an Act, intituled *An Act[2] to oblige Perfons, bringing Slaves into this Colony from* Maryland, Carolina, *and the* Weft-Indies, *for their own Ufe, to pay a Duty*, was read the third Time.

Refolved, That the Bill do pafs; and that the Title be, *An Act[3] for continuing and amending feveral Acts, and reviving one Act, for laying Duties upon Slaves imported*.

Ordered, That Mr *Harrifon* do carry the Bill to the Council, and defire their Concurrence.

Mr *Marfhall* reported from the Committee, to whom the Bill to explain and amend an Act, intituled *An Act[4] to oblige the Owners of Mills, Hedges, or Stops, on the Rivers therein mentioned, to make Openings or Slopes therein for the Paffage of Fifh*, was committed that the Committee had gone through the Bill, and made feveral Amendments thereunto, which they had directed him to report to the Houfe; and he read the Report in his Place; and afterwards delivered the Bill, with the Amendments in at the Clerk's Table; where the Amendments were once read throughout, and then a fecond Time, one by one, and, upon the Queftion feverally put thereupon, were agreed to by the Houfe.

Ordered, That the Bill, with the Amendments, be engroffed.

Mr *Edmund Pendleton* reported from the Committee of Privileges and Elections, to whom the Petition of Mr *Thomas Pettus*, complaining of an undue Election of Mr *Henry Blagrave* to ferve as a Burgefs in this prefent General Affembly for the County of *Lunenburg*, was referred, that the Committee had come to feveral Refolutions, which they had directed him to report to the Houfe; and he read the Report in his Place, and afterwards delivered it in at the Clerk's Table; where the Refolutions of the Committee were read, and are as followeth, *viz.*

Refolved, That it is the Opinion of this Committee, that the petitioner and fitting Member be at Liberty to examine Witneffes before *Lyddal Bacon, Thomas Wynne, Elifha Betts, Thomas Tabb, Jonathan Patterfon, Anthony Street, William Taylor*, and *Abraham Maury*, or any three of them, at the Court-Houfe of the faid County, on *Friday*, the 27th Inftant, if fair, if not, the next fair Day, touching any Treats or Entertainments, given by the fitting Member, or his Agents, to the Freeholders of the faid

County

---

[1] Hening, VIII, p. 530.   [2] Ibid, VII, p. 338.   [3] Ibid, VIII, p. 530.   [4] Ibid VIII, p. 361.

County, after the Writ for electing Burgeffes for the faid County was iffued, or on the Day of Election before the Poll was concluded; and that the faid Commiffioners do return the Depofitions before the firft Day of *April* next.

Refolved, That it is the Opinion of this Committee, that the Confideration of the faid Petition be deferred till the faid firft Day of *April* next.

The faid *Refolutions*, being feverally read a fecond Time, were, upon the Queftion feverally put thereupon, agreed to by the Houfe.

Mr *Marfhall* prefented to the Houfe, according to Order, a Bill to eftablifh a Town on the Land of *John Rictor*, in the County of *Fauquier*; and the fame was received, and read the firft Time.

Refolved, That the Bill be read a fecond Time.

The *Order* of the Day being read;

Refolved, That this Houfe will, upon *Tuefday* next, refolve itfelf into a Committee of the whole Houfe upon the Bill to continue an Act, intituled *An Act[1] to continue and amend an Act, intituled an Act for reducing the feveral Acts made for laying a Duty upon Liquors into one Act.* [112]

Ordered, That Leave be given to bring in a Bill to amend an Act intituled *An Act[2] to amend the Act, intituled an Act to oblige the Owners of Mills, Hedges, or Stone Stops, on fundry Rivers therein mentioned, to make Openings or Slopes therein for the Paffage of Fifh, and for other Purpofes therein mentioned;* and that Mr *John Jones*, and Mr *Stith*, do prepare and bring in the fame.

And then the Houfe adjourned till Monday *Morning next, eleven of the Clock.*

Monday, the 23d of March, 12 George III. 1772.

SEVERAL *Petitions* of the Inhabitants of the Parifh of *Dale*, in the County of *Chefterfield*, whofe Names are thereunto fubfcribed, were prefented to the Houfe, and read; taking Notice of an Application made to this Houfe by a few Perfons for dividing the faid Parifh; and fetting forth that much the greater Number of the Parifhioners do not defire the faid Divifion; and therefore praying that the faid Parifh may not be divided.

Ordered, That the faid Petition be referred to the Confideration of the Committee for Religion, to whom the Bill for dividing the Parifhes of *Southam*, in the County of *Cumberland*, and *Dale*, in the County of *Chefterfield*, is committed.

Mr *Bland* prefented to the Houfe, according to Order, a Bill for appointing Truftees for the Town of *Cobham*, and for other Purpofes therein mentioned; and the fame was received, and read the firft Time.

Refolved, That the Bill be read a fecond Time.

A *Petition* of the Mayor, Recorder, Aldermen, and Common Council of the City of *Williamfburg* was prefented to the Houfe, and read; fetting forth that the Bill which hath paffed this Houfe, and hath been agreed to by the Council, intituled *An Act[3] for cutting a navigable Canal from* Archer's Hope Creek *to* Queen's *Creek, through or near the City of* Williamfburg, may not be carried into Execution, fome of the Perfons through whofe Lands the faid Canal muft pafs, being Infants, who cannot confent to, and others having it in their Power to hinder the cutting thereof; and therefore praying that Leave may be given to bring in a Bill for enabling the Truftees and Directors of the faid Work to cut or dig through the Lands of any Perfon or Perfons, under fuch Reftrictions and Regulations as the Houfe fhall think juft and reafonable.

Ordered, That Leave be given to bring in a Bill purfuant to the Prayer of the faid petition; and that Mr *Bland* and Mr *Alexander* do prepare, and bring in the fame.

Mr *Bland* prefented to the Houfe, according to Order, a Bill to permit certain Perfons therein mentioned to erect Gates acrofs the public Roads leading through their Lands; and the fame was received, and read the firft Time.

Refolved

---

[1] Hening, VIII, p. 335. [2] Ibid, VII, p. 590. [3] Ibid, VIII, p. 556.

Refolved, That the Bill be read a fecond Time.

Mr *Treafurer* reported from the Committee for Religion, to whom the Bill for diffolving the Veftries of the Parifhes of *Saint Martin*, in the Counties of *Hanover* and *Louifa*, and of *Saint John*, in the County of *King William*, was committed, that the Committee had gone through the Bill, and made an Amendment thereunto, which they had directed him to report to the Houfe; and he read the Report in his Place, and afterwards delivered the Bill, with the Amendment, in at the Clerk's Table; where the Amendment was twice read, and, upon the Queftion put thereupon, was agreed to by the Houfe.

Ordered, That the Bill, with the Amendment, be engroffed.

A *Petition* of feveral Perfons of the County of *Charlotte*, whofe Names are thereunto fubfcribed, was prefented to the Houfe, and read; fetting forth, that the Place, at which the Ferry over *Staunton* River, called *Fuqua's*, is kept, is not fo proper for that Purpofe as another Place about a Mile and a half above, and therefore praying that the faid Ferry may be difcontinued, and another appointed at the laft mentioned Place, from the Land of *Walter Coles* to the Land of *Jofeph Fuqua*.

Ordered, That the faid Petition be referred to the Confideration of the Committee of Propofitions and Grievances; and that they do examine the Matter thereof, and report the fame, with their Opinion thereupon, to the Houfe.

A *Petition* of *William Rind* was prefented to the Houfe, and read; fetting forth, that the Treafurer was directed by this Houfe to pay to the Petitioner for printing Bills of Credit for the thirty thoufand Pounds emitted in Purfuance of an Act of the laft General Affembly, the Sum of one hundred Pounds, which was not a fufficient Compenfation; and therefore praying fuch further Allowance as fhall feem juft and reafonable.

Ordered, That the faid Petition be referred to the Confideration of the Committee of Public Claims; and that they do examine the Matter thereof, and report the fame, with their Opinion thereupon, to the Houfe.

Mr *Harrifon* reported from the Committee of Trade, to whom the Memorial of *Andrew Eftave* was referred, that the Committee had examined the Matter of the faid Memorial, and had come to feveral Refolutions thereupon, which they had directed him to report to the Houfe; and he read the Report in his Place, and afterwards delivered it in at the Clerk's Table; where the Refolutions of the Committee were read, and are as followeth, *viz.*

Refolved, That it is the Opinion of this Committee, that the Treafurer of this Colony pay to the Truftees, in the faid Memorial mentioned, the Sum of fifty-three Pounds and ten Shillings, to be by them laid out in purchafing another Slave in Lieu of the one fold by the faid *Eftave*, with their Confent, for twelve Months Credit, upon their delivering the Bond given for Payment thereof to the faid Treafurer, who is to receive the fame, and thereby to reimburfe the Public the Sum aforefaid.

Refolved, That it is the Opinion of this Committee, that the Sum of forty-two Pounds and fifteen Shillings ought to be allowed and paid by the Public to the faid *Andrew Eftave* for fo much neceffarily expended by him in carrying on the Works of the Vineyard in the faid Memorial mentioned.

Refolved, That it is the Opinion of this Committee, that the faid *Andrew Eftave* ought to be further allowed by the Public the Sum of fifty Pounds *per Annum*, for two Years, to be paid to him quarterly.

The faid *Refolutions*, being feverally read a fecond Time, were, upon the Queftion feverally put thereupon, agreed to by the Houfe.

Ordered, That the Allowance of fifty-three Pounds and ten Shillings to the Truftees appointed by the Act of General Affembly, for encouraging the making Wine, and alfo the Allowance of forty-two Pounds and fifteen Shillings to *Andrew Eftave*, be entered in the Book of Public Claims by the Clerk.

And the fame were entered accordingly.

Refolved, That the Sum of fifty Pounds *per Annum* be paid to *Andrew Eftave* during the Term of two Years, by quarterly Payments.

Ordered

Ordered, That M[r] *Harrifon* do carry the Refolution to the Council, and defire their Concurrence.

Ordered, That M[r] *Patrick Henry* have Leave to be abfent from the Service of this Houfe till the End of this Seffion of General Affembly.

Refolved, That the Sum of thirty-fix Pounds and fourteen Shillings be paid to *Benjamin Powell*, for the Balance of his Account, for building a Dwelling Houfe at the public Vineyard, and furnifhing Materials for the fame. 114

Ordered, That M[r] *Harrifon* do carry the Refolution to the Council, and defire their Concurrence.

A *Petition* of *Jacob Strickley* and *Henry Funk*, in Behalf of themfelves, and their Chriftian Brethren, of the Sect, called Menonifts, was prefented to the Houfe, and read; fetting forth that the Petitioners and their Friends are comfortably fettled on the Frontiers of this Colony, where they can fupport themfelves and their Families, if they may be relieved from the Payment of Fines for not performing military Duty, which their religious Tenets forbid them to exercife; and therefore praying that they may be exempt from fuch Penalties.

Ordered, That the faid Petition be referred to the Confideration of the Committee of Propofitions and Grievances; and that they do examine the Matter thereof, and report the fame, with their Opinion thereupon, to the Houfe.

A *Meffage* from the Council by M[r] *Blair*.

M[r] *Speaker*,

The Council have agreed to the Bill, *intituled* An Act[1] for eftablifhing the Town of *Fincaftle*, in the County of *Botetourt*, *without any Amendment; and alfo,*

The Council do infift upon the Amendment *made by them to the Bill, intituled* An Act[2] for further continuing and amending the Act, intituled an Act for the better regulating and collecting certain Officers Fees, and for other Purpofes therein mentioned, *difagreed to by this Houfe, and do defire the Houfe will recede from their Difagreement thereunto.*

And then the Meffenger withdrew.

The faid *Amendment* being again read;

The *Amendment* following was propofed to be made thereunto, *viz.*

Leave out "*thirteen Shillings and four Pence*," and infert "*twelve Shillings and fix Pence*," inftead thereof.

And the faid *Amendment* to the Amendment was, upon the Queftion put thereupon, agreed to by the Houfe.

Then the *Queftion* being put, that the Houfe doth agree to the Amendment made by the Council, with the faid Amendment thereunto;

It was refolved in the Affirmative.

Ordered, That M[r] *Richard Henry Lee* do carry the Bill to the Council, and acquaint them, that this Houfe hath agreed to the Amendment made by them, with an Amendment, to which Amendment to the Amendment this Houfe doth defire the Concurrence of the Council.

M[r] *Edmund Pendleton* prefented to the Houfe, according to Order, a Bill for the more eafy and fpeedy Adminiftration of Juftice; and the fame was received, and read the firft Time.

Refolved, That the Bill be read a fecond Time.

A *Petition* of *John Burton*, late a Soldier in the *Virginia* Regiment, was prefented to the Houfe, and read; fetting forth that the Petitioner, whilft he was in that Service, was fo wounded in an Engagement by two Mufket Balls, one of which, lodged in the Small of his Back, could never be extracted, that he is unable by his own Labour, and hath no other Means to maintain himfelf, and that he fuffers continual Pain, and is in great Diftrefs; and therefore humbly praying Relief.

Ordered, That the faid Petition be referred to the Confideration of the Committee of Public Claims; and that they do examine the Matter thereof, and report the fame, with their Opinion thereupon, to the Houfe.

M[r]

---

[1] Hening, VIII, p. 616.   [2] Ibid, VIII, p. 515.

Mr *Treafurer* prefented to the Houfe, according to Order, a Bill for appointing Commiffioners to afcertain the Value of certain Churches and Chapels in the Parifhes of
115 *Frederick, Norborne,* and *Beckford,* and for other Purpofes therein mentioned; and the
fame was received.

Ordered, That the Bill do lie upon the Table.

A *Petition* of *William Ayres,* of the County of *King George,* was prefented to the
Houfe, and read; fetting forth that the Petitioner hath, for many Years, adminiftered
a Medicine to Perfons afflicted with the Flux, with such Succefs that not one of his
Patients, who followed his Directions, ever died of that Difeafe; and therefore praying
that the Houfe will make him an Allowance for communicating fo ufeful a Remedy
to the public, which he is willing to do, upon receiving a reafonable Satiffaction.

Ordered, That the faid petition be referred to the Confideration of a Committee;
and that they do examine the Matter thereof, and report the fame, with their Opinion
thereupon, to the Houfe.

And it is *referred* to Mr *Roane,* Mr *Simpfon,* Mr *Edmondfon,* Mr *Jofeph Jones,* and
Mr *Fitzhugh.*

Several *Petitions* of fundry Freeholders and Inhabitants of the Counties of *Prince
George, Dinwiddie, Brunfwick, Amelia, Mecklenburg, Lunenburg,* and *Suffex,* whofe
Names are thereunto fubfcribed, were prefented to the Houfe, and read; fetting forth,
that the Warehoufes for Infpection of Tobacco, upon *Appamattox* River, are not fufficient to contain the Quantities of that Commodity brought thither, neither are the
prefent Infpectors able to difpatch fo much Bufinefs, which moreover will probably
increafe; and therefore praying that another Infpection may be eftablifhed upon the
Lots of Col. *Robert Bolling,* in the Town of *Blandford,* in the County of *Prince George.*

Ordered, That the faid Petition be referred to the Confideration of the Committee
of Propofitions and Grievances; and that they do examine the Matter thereof, and report
the fame, with their Opinion thereupon, to the Houfe.

A *Petition* of fundry Inhabitants of the County of *Dinwiddie,* whofe Names are
thereunto fubfcribed, was prefented to the Houfe, and read; fetting forth, that it is
neceffary to eftablifh another Warehoufe for the Reception of Tobacco brought to
Peterfburg; and therefore praying that another Infpection may be eftablifhed on the
Land of Col. *Robert Bolling,* at *Cedar Point, Bolling's Point* and *Bollingbrooke* Warehoufes.

Ordered, That the faid Petition be referred to the Confideration of the Committee
of Propofitions and Grievances; and that they do examine the Matter thereof, and report
the fame, with their Opinion thereupon, to the Houfe.

A *Petition* of *William Robinfon,* of the County of *King George,* was prefented to the
Houfe, and read; fetting forth that a Negro Man Slave, named *Edinburg,* belonging to
the Petitioner, ran away from his Quarter, at a great Diftance from him, and that the
Petitioner did all in his Power to procure the faid Slave to be outlawed, but before that
was done, the faid Slave, having been apprehended and confined, was let loofe by another
Slave, and running into the River was drowned; and therefore praying that he may
be allowed the Value of his faid Slave by the Public.

A *Motion* was made, and the Queftion being put, that the faid Petition be referred
to the Confideration of a Committee;

It paffed in the Negative.

And then the Houfe adjourned till Tomorrow Morning, eleven of the Clock.

Tuesday. the 24th of March, 12 George III. 1772.

116 MR *Bland* reported from the Committee of Propofitions and Grievances, to
whom the Bill for keeping in Repair feveral Roads and Bridges, and for
other purpofes therein mentioned, was committed, that the Committee had
gone through the Bill, and made feveral Amendments thereunto, which
they had directed him to report to the Houfe; and he read the Report in his Place, and
afterwards delivered the Bill, with the Amendments, in at the Clerk's Table; where the
Amendments

Amendments were once read throughout, and then a fecond Time, one by one, and, upon the Queftion feverally put thereupon, were agreed to by the Houfe.

Ordered, That the Bill, with the Amendments, be engroffed.

Mʳ *Bland* reported from the Committee of Propofitions and Grievances, to whom the Bill for further continuing the Acts for better regulating and difciplining the Militia, was committed, that the Committee had gone through the Bill, and made feveral Amendments thereunto, which they had directed him to report to the Houfe; and he read the Report in his Place, and afterwards delivered the Bill, with the Amendments, in at the Clerk's Table; where the Amendments were once read throughout, and then a fecond Time, one by one, and, upon the Queftion feverally put thereupon, were, with fome Amendments to one of them, agreed to by the Houfe.

Ordered, That the Bill, with the Amendments, be engroffed.

An engroffed *Bill* to remove the Seat of Government to a Place more convenient to the Inhabitants of this Colony was read the third Time.

And the *Queftion* being put that the Bill do pafs;

The Houfe divided.

The *Noes* went forth.

Tellers for the *Yeas,*	{ Mʳ *Treafurer,* { Mʳ *Riddick,*	48
Tellers for the *Noes,*	{ Mʳ *Edmund Pendleton,* { Mʳ *Cary,*	32

So it was *refolved* in the Affirmative;

And that the *Title* of the Bill be, *An Act[1] to remove the Seat of Government to a Place more convenient to the Inhabitants of this Colony.*

Ordered, That Mʳ *Bland* do carry the Bill to the Council, and defire their Concurrence.

A *Meffage* from the Council by Mʳ *Blair:*

Mʳ *Speaker,*

The Council have agreed to the Amendment *made by this Houfe to the Amendment made by the Council to the Bill, intituled* An Act[2] for further continuing and amending the Act, intituled an Act for the better regulating and collecting certain Officers Fees, and for other Purpofes therein mentioned; *and alfo,*

The Council have agreed to the Bill, *intituled* An Act[3] for dividing the County of *Frederick* into three diftinct Counties, *without any Amendment.*

And then the Meffenger withdrew.

Mʳ *Speaker* acquainted the Houfe, that he had received a Letter from the Speaker of the Affembly of *North Carolina,* upon the Subject Matter of a Sollicitation, by Agents, to obtain Permiffion to import Salt to the *Britifh* Dominions in *America,* from *Spain* and *Portugal.*

And he delivered the *Letter* in at the Clerk's Table.

Ordered, That the faid Letter do lie upon the Table, to be perufed by the Members of the Houfe.

Mʳ *Bland* reported from the Committee of Propofitions and Grievances, to whom the Bill for clearing a Road from the Warm Springs in *Augufta,* and for other Purpofes therein mentioned, was committed, that the Committee had gone through the Bill, and made feveral Amendments thereunto, which they had directed him to report to the Houfe; and he read the Report in his Place, and afterwards delivered the Bill, with the Amendments, in at the Clerk's Table;

And the Houfe being informed, that fome other Amendments are neceffary to be made to the faid Bill;

Ordered, That the faid Bill be recommitted.

Ordered, That the faid Bill be recommitted to the Committee, to whom the fame was committed.

A

---

[1] Not recorded as a law.　[2] Hening, VIII. p. 515.　[3] Ibid, VIII. p. 597.

A *Bill* for the more eafy and fpeedy Adminiftration of Juftice was read a fecond Time.

Refolved, That the Bill be committed.

Refolved, That the Bill be committed to a Committee of the whole Houfe.

Refolved, That this Houfe will, Tomorrow, refolve itfelf into a Committee of the whole Houfe upon the faid Bill.

Mr *Bland* prefented to the Houfe, according to Order, a Bill to enlarge the Power of the Truftees appointed to carry into Execution an Act paffed this prefent Seffion of Affembly, intituled *An Act[1] for cutting a navigable Canal from* Archer's Hope *Creek to* Queen's *Creek, through or near the City of* Williamfburg; and the fame was received, and read the firft Time.

Refolved, That the Bill be read a fecond Time.

Ordered, That the Bill be now read a fecond Time.

The *Bill* was accordingly read a fecond Time.

Refolved, That the Bill be committed.

Refolved, That the Bill be committed to a Committee of the whole Houfe.

Refolved, That this Houfe will, upon *Thurfday* next, refolve itfelf into a Committee of the whole Houfe upon the faid Bill.

Ordered, That Leave be given to bring in a Bill for the Eafe and Relief of the People by paying the Burgeffes Wages in Money for this prefent Seffion of Affembly; and that Mr *Henry Lee* do prepare, and bring in the fame.

The *Order* of the Day being read;

Refolved, That this Houfe will, upon *Thurfday* next, refolve itfelf into a Committee of the whole Houfe upon the Bill to continue an Act, intituled *An Act[2] to continue and amend an Act, intituled an Act for reducing the feveral Acts made for laying a Duty upon Liquors into one Act.*

Mr *Treafurer* reported from the Committee for Religion, to whom feveral Petitions and Memorials were referred, that the Committee had examined the Matters of the faid Petitions and Memorials, and had come to feveral Refolutions thereupon, which they had directed him to report to the Houfe; and he read the Report in his Place, and afterwards delivered it in at the Clerk's Table; where the Refolutions of the Committee were read, and are as followeth, *viz*.

Refolved, That it is the Opinion of this Committee, that the further Confideration of the Petition of fundry Inhabitants of the Parifh of *Ruffell*, in the County of *Bedford*, praying that the faid Parifh may be divided, and alfo of the feveral Petitions in Oppofition thereto, be deferred till the next Seffion of Affembly.

Refolved, That it is the Opinion of this Committee, that the Memorial of the Reverend *Alexander Gordon*, Rector of *Antrim*, in the County of *Halifax*, fetting forth that his Salary, as it is now paid, is not adequate to his Expence and Trouble, and praying Redrefs, is reafonable; and that he ought to be allowed the fame Salary as other Minifters are intitled to receive under an Act of Affembly, paffed in the 22^d Year of his late Majefty's Reign, intituled *An Act[3] for the Support of the Clergy, and for the regular collecting and paying the Parifh Levies.*

Refolved, That it is the Opinion of this Committee, that the Petition of the Veftrymen of the Parifh of *Hamilton*, in the County of *Fauquier*, praying that the faid Parifh and the Parifh of *Leeds* may be divided by a new Line, be rejected.

Refolved, That it is the Opinion of this Committee, that the Memorial of the Veftrymen of the faid Parifh of *Leeds*, in Oppofition to the Petition for another Divifion thereof, and praying that the faid Parifh of *Hamilton* may be obliged to refund to the Parifh of *Leeds*, a Proportion of the Tobacco paid for building a Brick Church, in the Memorial mentioned, is reafonable.

The

118

---

[1] Hening, VIII, p. 556.   [2] Ibid, VIII, p. 335.   [3] Ibid, VI, p. 88.

The faid *Refolutions*, being feverally read a fecond Time, were, upon the Queftion feverally put thereupon, agreed to by the Houfe.

Ordered, That a Bill or Bills be brought in purfuant to the fecond and laft Refolutions and that the faid Committee do prepare, and bring in the fame.

And then the Houfe adjourned till Tomorrow Morning, eleven of the Clock.

Wednesday, the 25th of March, 12 George III. 1772.

MR *Cary* reported from the Committee of Public Claims, to whom feveral Petitions were referred, that the Committee had examined the Matters of the faid Petitions, and had come to feveral Refolutions thereupon, which they had directed him to report to the Houfe; and he read the Report in his Place, and afterwards delivered it in at the Clerk's Table; where the Refolutions of the Committee were read, and are as followeth, *viz.*

Refolved, That it is the Opinion of this Committee, that the petition of *John Burton*, late a Soldier in the *Virginia* Regiment, is reafonable; and that he ought to be allowed the Sum of ten Pounds for his prefent Relief, and the further Sum of five Pounds *per Annum* during his Life, in Confideration of the Wounds he received and the Hardfhips he fuffered in the Service, and of his being thereby rendered incapable of getting a neceffary Subfiftence.

Refolved, That it is the Opinion of this Committee, that the petition of *William Rind*, praying that a further Allowance may be made him for printing Bills of Credit to the Amount of thirty thoufand Pounds, emitted in Purfuance of an Act of the laft General Affembly, is reafonable; and that he ought to be paid the Sum of fixty Pounds for the fame.

Refolved, That it is the Opinion of this Committee, that the Petition of *Benjamin Winflow* is reafonable; and that he ought to be allowed, by the Public, the Sum of ten Pounds and ten Shillings, for the Bounty Money, and fubfifting the Recruit, in the Petition mentioned.

Refolved, That it is the Opinion of this Committee, that the Petition of *William Hackney* and *Rowland Sutton*, Infpectors of Tobacco at *Kemp's* Warehoufe, in the County of *Middlefex*, is reafonable; and that the Petitioners ought to be allowed the Sum of eight Pounds nineteen Shillings and one Penny; it appearing that the faid Warehoufes at the Time the Tobacco, in the Petition mentioned, was ftolen, were in good Repair, and well fecured with good Locks and Bolts, and that the Lofs was not occafioned by any Neglect of the Petitioners.

Refolved, That it is the Opinion of this Committee, that the Confideration of the Petition of *Benjamin Grymes*, in Behalf of himfelf and of his Creditors, to be allowed a reafonable Satiffaction for the Damage done their Slave, who was committed to Gaol for Hogftealing, and was froftbitten, during his Confinement, be deferred till the next Seffion of General Affembly.

The faid *Refolutions*, being feverally read a fecond Time, were, upon the Queftion feverally put thereupon, agreed to by the Houfe.

Ordered, That the feveral Allowances of ten Pounds to *John Burton, and alfo* of fixty Pounds to *William Rind, and alfo* of ten Pounds and ten Shillings to *Benjamin Winflow, and alfo* of eight Pounds nineteen Shillings and one Penny to *William Hackney* and *Rowland Sutton*, be entered in the Book of Public Claims by the Clerk.

And the faid *Allowances* were entered accordingly.

Refolved, That the Sum of five Pounds *per Annum* be paid to *John Burton*, a poor wounded Soldier, during his Life.

Ordered, That Mr *Cary* do carry the Refolution to the Council, and defire their Concurrence.

The *Order* of the Day being read, for the Houfe to refolve itfelf into a Committee of the whole Houfe upon the Bill for the more eafy and fpeedy Adminiftration of Juftice;

The

The Houfe refolved itfelf into the faid Committee.

Mᵣ *Speaker* left the Chair.

Mᵣ *Bland* took the Chair of the Committee.

Mᵣ *Speaker* refumed the Chair.

Mᵣ *Bland* reported from the Committee, that they had made a Progrefs in the Bill; and that he was directed by the Committee to move, that they may have Leave to fit again.

Refolved, That this Houfe will, Tomorrow, refolve itfelf into a Committee of the whole Houfe to confider further of the faid Bill.

119 The other *Order* of the Day being read.

Refolved, That this Houfe will, Tomorrow, refolve itfelf into a Committee of the whole Houfe, to confider of the Letter from the Earl of *Hillfborough* to the Governor, upon the Subject of a Copper Coinage.

And then the Houfe adjourned till Tomorrow Morning, eleven of the Clock.

Thursday, the 26th of March, 12 George III. 1772.

AN engroffed *Bill* to dock the Intail of certain Lands whereof *Ralph Wormeley*, Efquire, is feifed, was read the third Time.

Refolved, That the Bill do pafs; and that the Title be, *An Act*[1] *to dock the Intail of certain Lands whereof* Ralph Wormeley, *Efquire, is feifed.*

Ordered, That Mᵣ *Berkeley* do carry the Bill to the Council, and defire their Concurrence.

Ordered, That the Chaplain do attend to read Prayers, every Morning, at eight of the Clock.

Ordered, That Mᵣ *Bland* do go to the Council, and acquaint them, that the Chaplain will attend to read Prayers, at eight of the Clock, every Morning, in the Houfe.

An engroffed *Bill* for keeping in Repair feveral Roads and Bridges, and for other Purpofes therein mentioned, was read the third Time.

Refolved, That the Bill do pafs; and that the Title be, *An Act*[2] *for keeping in Repair feveral Roads, and for other Purpofes therein mentioned.*

Ordered, That Mᵣ *Riddick* do carry the Bill to the Council, and defire their Concurrence.

Ordered, That Mᵣ *James Henry* have Leave to be abfent from the Service of this Houfe till the End of this Seffion of General Affembly.

Ordered, That Leave be given to bring in a Bill to exempt certain Counties from the Regulations of an Act for continuing and amending the Act, intituled *An Act*[3] *for the better regulating and collecting certain Officers Fees, and for other Purpofes therein mentioned;* and that Mᵣ *William Cabell*, Mᵣ *Edmund Pendleton*, Mᵣ *Dandridge*, and Mᵣ *Marable*, do prepare, and bring in the fame.

Mᵣ *Bland* reported from the Committee of Propofitions and Grievances, to whom the Petition of the Settlers on the Waters of *Holfton* and *New River*, formerly in the County of *Augufta*, but now in the County of *Botetourt*, praying that a new County may be eftablifhed on the faid Waters, was referred, that the Committee had examined the Matter of the faid Petition, and had come to a Refolution thereupon, which they had directed him to Report to the Houfe; and he read the Report in his Place, and afterwards delivered it in at the Clerk's Table; where the Refolution of the Committee was read, and is as followeth, *viz.*

Refolved, That it is the Opinion of this Committee, that the faid Petition is reafonable.

The faid *Refolution*, being read a fecond Time, was, upon the Queftion put thereupon, agreed to by the Houfe.

Ordered, That a Bill be brought in purfuant to the faid Refolution; and that the faid Committee do prepare, and bring in the fame.

Mᵣ

---

[1] Hening, VIII, p. 637.   [2] Ibid, VIII, p. 543.   [3] Ibid, V. p. 38.

Mr *Hutchings* prefented to the Houfe, according to Order, a Bill to amend an Act, intituled *An Act*[1] *for regulating the Practice of Attornies;* and the fame was received, and read the firft Time.

And the *Queftion* being put, that the Bill be read a fecond Time;

It paffed in the Negative.

Mr *John Page* prefented to the Houfe, according to Order, a Bill to amend an Act, intituled *An Act*[2] *directing the Duty of Surveyors of Land;* and the fame was received, and read the firft Time.

Refolved, That the Bill be read a fecond Time.

Ordered, That Mr *Carrington* be added to the Gentlemen, who are appointed to prepare and bring in a Bill purfuant to the Prayer of the Petition of *Caldwell Pettypoole.* 120

A *Meffage* from the Council by Mr *Blair:*

Mr *Speaker,*

The Council have agreed to the Bill, *intituled* An Act[3] for continuing and amending feveral Acts, and reviving one Act for laying Duties upon Slaves imported, *without any Amendment; and alfo,*

The Council have agreed to the Bill, *intituled* An Act[4] to dock the Intail of certain Lands whereof *Ralph Wormeley,* Efquire, is feifed, *without any Amendment; and alfo,*

The Council have agreed to the Refolve *for paying feveral Sums of Money to* Andrew Eftave; *and alfo,*

The Council have agreed to the Refolve *for paying a Sum of Money to* Benjamin Powell.

And then the Meffenger withdrew.

Mr *Treafurer* prefented to the Houfe, according to Order, a Bill to allow the Minifter of the Parifh of *Antrim,* in the County of *Halifax,* the fame Salary as other Minifters are intitled to receive under an Act of Affembly paffed in the twenty-fecond Year of his late Majefty's Reign, intituled *An Act*[5] *for the Support of the Clergy, and for the regular collecting the Parifh Levies;* and the fame was received, and read the firft Time.

Refolved, That the Bill be read a fecond Time.

The *Order* of the Day being read, for the Houfe to refolve itfelf into a Committee of the whole Houfe, to confider further of the Bill for the more eafy and fpeedy Adminif-tration of Juftice;

The Houfe refolved itfelf into the faid Committee.

Mr *Speaker* left the Chair.

Mr *Bland* took the Chair of the Committee.

Mr *Speaker* refumed the Chair.

Mr *Bland* reported from the Committee, that they had gone through the Bill, and made feveral Amendments thereunto, which they had directed him to report to the Houfe; and he read the Report in his Place, and afterwards delivered the Bill, with the Amendments, in at the Clerk's Table.

Ordered, That the faid Bill be recommitted.

Ordered, That the faid Bill be recommitted to a Committee of the whole Houfe.

Refolved, That this Houfe will, Tomorrow, refolve itfelf into a Committee of the whole Houfe to confider further of the faid Bill.

Mr *Mann Page* prefented to the Houfe, according to Order, a Bill to empower the Veftry of the Parifh of *Saint George,* in *Spotfylvania* County, to fell Part of the Church Yard within the Town of *Frederickfburg;* and the fame was received, and read the firft Time.

Refolved, That the Bill be read a fecond Time.

Mr *William Cabell* prefented to the Houfe, according to Order, a Bill to exempt certain Counties from the Regulations of an Act for continuing and amending the Act,

intituled

[1] Hening, VII, p. 397. [2] Ibid, VI, p. 33. [3] Ibid, VIII, p. 530. [4] Ibid, VIII, p. 637.
[5] Ibid, VI, p. 88.

intituled *An Act[1] for the better regulating and collecting certain Officers Fees, and for other Purpofes therein mentioned;* and the fame was received, and read the firft Time.

Refolved, That the Bill be read a fecond Time.

Ordered, That the Bill be now read a fecond Time.

The *Bill* was accordingly read a fecond Time.

Ordered, That the Bill be engroffed.

M[r] *Cary* reported from the Committee of Public Claims, to whom the Petition of *Richard Hewitt* and *Elias Hore*, Infpectors of Tobacco at *Aquia* Warehoufes, in the County of *Stafford*, was referred, that the Committee had examined the Matter of the faid Petition, and had come to feveral Refolutions thereupon, which they had directed him to Report to the Houfe; and he read the Report in his Place, and afterwards delivered it in at the Clerk's Table; where the Refolutions of the Committee were read, and are as followeth, *viz.*

Refolved, That it is the Opinion of this Committee, that Commiffioners be appointed to ftate an Account of the Tobacco damaged in the faid Warehoufes, and enquire by what Means fuch Damage happened, and report the fame to the next Seffion of Affembly.

Refolved, That it is the Opinion of this Committee, that fo much of the faid Petition, as prays that the Salaries of the faid Infpectors may be encreafed, is reafonable; and that they ought to be allowed, each, an additional Salary of ten Pounds *per Annum.*

The faid *Refolutions*, being feverally read a fecond Time, were, upon the Queftion feverally put thereupon, agreed to by the Houfe.

Ordered, That the firft Refolution do lie upon the Table until the fecond reading of the Bill for appointing Commiffioners for felling the Tobacco damaged in the public Warehoufe at *Morton's.*

Ordered, That it be an Inftruction to the Committee of Propofitions and Grievances, to whom the Bill to continue and amend the Act, intituled *An Act[2] to continue and amend the Act, intituled an Act for amending the Staple of Tobacco, and for preventing Frauds in his Majefty's Cuftoms,* is committed, that they have Power to receive a Claufe or Claufes purfuant to the fecond Refolution.

M[r] *Edmund Pendleton* reported from the Committee, to whom the Bill to dock the Intail of certain Lands whereof *William Todd*, Gentleman, is feifed, and for other Purpofes therein mentioned, was committed, that the Committee had examined the Allegations of the Bill, and found the fame to be true; and that the Committee had directed him to report the Bill to the Houfe, without any Amendment; and he delivered the Bill in at the Clerk's Table.

Ordered, That the Bill be engroffed.

M[r] *Harrifon* prefented to the Houfe, according to Order, a Bill to veft the Wharf at *Point Weft*, in the Town of *Alexandria*, in the Truftees of the faid Town for the Purpofes therein mentioned; and the fame was received, and read the firft Time.

Refolved, That the Bill be read a fecond Time.

M[r] *John Jones* prefented to the Houfe, according to Order, a Bill to amend an Act, intituled *An Act[3] to amend an Act intituled an Act to oblige the Owners of Mills, Hedges, or Stone Stops, on fundry Rivers therein mentioned, to make Openings or Slopes therein for the Paffage of Fifh, and for other Purpofes therein mentioned;* and the fame was received, and read the firft Time.

Refolved, That the Bill be read a fecond Time.

Ordered, That the Bill be now read a fecond Time.

The *Bill* was accordingly read a fecond Time.

Refolved, That the Bill be committed to the Committee of Propofitions and Grievances.

The other *Orders* of the Day being read;

Refolved, That this Houfe will, upon *Monday* next, refolve itfelf into a Committee of the whole Houfe, upon the Bill to continue an Act, intituled *An Act[4] to continue and amend*

[1] Hening, V, p. 38. [2] Ibid, VIII, p. 318. [3] Ibid, VII, p. 590. [4] Ibid, VIII, p. 335.

amend an Act, intituled an Act for reducing the feveral Acts for laying a Duty upon Liquors into one Act.

Refolved, That this Houfe will, upon *Monday* next, refolve itfelf into a Committee of the whole Houfe to confider of the Letter from the Earl of *Hillfborough* to the Governor upon the Subject of a Copper Coinage.

Refolved, That this Houfe will, Tomorrow, refolve itfelf into a Committee of the whole Houfe, upon the Bill to enlarge the Power of the Truftees appointed to carry into Execution an Act paffed this prefent Seffion of Affembly, intituled *An Act*[1] *for cutting a navigable Canal from* Archer's Hope *Creek to* Queen's *Creek, through or near the City of* Williamfburg.

Mr *Cary* prefented to the Houfe, according to Order, a Bill to amend the Act, intituled *An Act*[2] *for the better Prefervation of the Breed of Deer, and preventing unlawful hunting;* and the fame was received, and read the firft Time.

Refolved, That the Bill be read a fecond Time.

The Houfe was moved, that the *Order* made upon *Tuefday* laft, that the Committee for Religion do prepare, and bring in a Bill or Bills purfuant to the fecond and laft Refolutions of the faid Committee, which were upon that Day reported, and agreed to by the Houfe, might be read.

And the fame being read accordingly;

Ordered, That the faid Order, as to preparing and bringing in a Bill upon the faid laft Refolution, be difcharged.

Mr *Treafurer* reported from the Committee for Religion, to whom the feveral petitions of fundry Inhabitants of the Parifh of *Dale,* in the County of *Chefterfield,* praying that the faid Parifh may not be divided, was referred, that the Committee had examined the Matter of the faid Petitions, and had come to a Refolution thereupon, which they had directed him to report to the Houfe; and he read the Report in his Place, and afterwards delivered it in at the Clerk's Table; where the Refolution of the Committee was read, and is as followeth, *viz.*

Refolved, That it is the Opinion of this Committee, that the faid Petitions be rejected.

The faid *Refolution,* being read a fecond Time, was, upon the Queftion put thereupon, agreed to by the Houfe.

Mr *Henry Lee* prefented to the Houfe, according to Order, a Bill for the Eafe and Relief of the People by paying the Burgeffes Wages in Money for the prefent Seffion of Affembly; and the fame was received, and read the firft Time.

Refolved, That the Bill be read a fecond Time.

A *Bill* for appointing Commiffioners to afcertain the Value of certain Churches and Chapels in the Parifhes of *Frederick, Norborne,* and *Beckford,* and for other Purpofes therein mentioned, which, upon *Monday* laft was prefented to the Houfe, was read the firft Time.

Refolved, That the Bill be read a fecond Time.

Ordered, That the Bill be now read a fecond Time.

The *Bill* was accordingly read a fecond Time.

Refolved, That the Bill be committed to Mr *Henry Lee,* Mr *Francis Peyton,* Mr *Marfhall,* and Mr *Scott.*

Ordered, That it be an Inftruction to the faid Committee, that they have Power to receive a Claufe or Claufes purfuant to the laft of the Refolutions of the Committee for Religion, which, upon *Tuefday* laft, were reported, and agreed to by the Houfe.

An engroffed *Bill* for making further Provifion for the Support and Maintenance of Ideots, Lunatics, and other Perfons of unfound Minds, was read the third Time.

Refolved, That the Bill do pafs; and that the Title be, *An Act*[3] *for making further Provifion for the Support and Maintenance of Ideots, Lunatics, and other Perfons of unfound Minds.*

Ordered, That Mr *Bland* do carry the Bill to the Council, and defire their Concurrence.

And then the Houfe adjourned till Tomorrow Morning, eleven of the Clock.

Friday

---

[1] Hening, VIII, p. 556.   [2] Ibid, V, p. 60.   [3] Hening, VIII, p. 594.

Friday, the 27th of March, 12 George III. 1772.

AN engroffed *Bill* to amend an Act, intituled *An Act*[1] *concerning Seamen*, was read the third Time.

Refolved, That the Bill do pafs; and that the Title be, *An Act*[2] *to amend an Act, intituled an Act concerning Seamen.*

Ordered, That Mr *Hutchings* do carry the Bill to the Council, and defire their Concurrence.

Mr *Treafurer* reported from the Committee for Religion, who were appointed to enquire into the State of the eftablifhed Religion in this Colony, that the Committee had enquired accordingly, and had come to a Refolution, which they had directed him to report to the Houfe; and he read the Report in his Place, and afterwards delivered it in at the Clerk's Table; where the fame was read, and the Refolution of the faid Committee is as followeth, *viz.*

Refolved, That it is the Opinion of this Committee, that for fuperintending the Conduct of the Clergy a Jurifdiction confifting of Laymen and Clergymen be eftablifhed.

The faid *Refolution* being read a fecond Time;

Ordered, That the faid Report be referred to the Confideration of a Committee of the whole Houfe.

Refolved, That this Houfe will now refolve itfelf into a Committee of the whole Houfe to confider of the faid Report.

The Houfe accordingly refolved itfelf into the faid Committee.

Mr *Speaker* left the Chair.

Mr *Harrifon* took the Chair of the Committee.

Mr *Speaker* refumed the Chair.

Mr *Harrifon* reported from the Committee, that they had come to a Refolution, which they had directed him to report, when the Houfe will pleafe to receive the fame.

Ordered, That the Report be now received.

Mr *Harrifon* accordingly reported the Refolution which the Committee had directed him to report to the Houfe, which he read in his Place, and afterwards delivered it in at the Clerk's Table; where the fame was read, and is as followeth, *viz.*

Refolved, That it is the Opinion of this Committee, that the Houfe be moved, that Leave may be given to bring in a Bill to eftablifh a Jurifdiction for fuperintending the Conduct of the Clergy, to be exercifed by Clergymen, with an Appeal to a Court of Delegates.

Ordered, That Leave be given to bring in a Bill to eftablifh a Jurifdiction for fuperintending the Conduct of the Clergy, to be exercifed by Clergymen, with an Appeal to a Court of Delegates; and that Mr *Harrifon*, Mr *Treafurer*, and Mr *Bland*, do prepare and bring in the fame.

Ordered, That Mr *Riddick*, Mr *Richard Henry Lee*, Mr *Barbour*, Mr *Francis Lightfoot Lee*, and Mr *Stith*, have Leave to be abfent from the Service of this Houfe till the End of this Seffion of General Affembly.

The *Orders* of the Day being read;

Refolved, That this Houfe will, Tomorrow, refolve itfelf into a Committee of the whole Houfe, to confider further of the Bill for the more eafy and speedy Adminiftration of Juftice.

Refolved, That this Houfe will, upon *Tuefday* next, refolve itfelf into a Committee of the whole Houfe, upon the Bill to enlarge the Power of the Truftees appointed to carry into Execution an Act paffed this prefent Seffion of Affembly, intituled *An Act*[3] *for cutting a navigable Canal from* Archer's Hope *Creek to* Queen's *Creek, through or near the City of* Williamfburg.

Mr *Bland* reported, from the Committee appointed upon *Friday* laft, to draw up an Addrefs, to be prefented to the Governor, that the Committee had drawn up an Addrefs

accordingly

---

[1]   Hening, VI. p. 24.   [2]   Ibid, VIII, p. 523.   [3]   Ibid, VIII, p. 556.

accordingly, which they had directed him to report to the House; and he read the same in his Place, and afterwards delivered it in at the Clerk's Table; where the same was read, and is as followeth, *viz.*

My Lord,

The Burgeffes of Virginia, *now met in General Affembly, beg Leave humbly to repre-fent, that they have received a Petition from a confiderable Number of the Inhabitants of the County of* Spotfylvania, *fetting forth that the Petitioners have for many Years fuffered great Hardfhips and unneceffary Expences from the inconvenient Situation of the Court-Houfe in the Town of* Frederickfburg, *near one Corner of the County; and that they have been difappointed in feveral Applications to former Governors, for Relief, by adjourning the Court to a Place more convenient to the Inhabitants.*

Without meaning to draw into Queftion any juft Prerogative of the Crown, which it is their Inclination, as well as Intereft, ever to fupport, but thinking it their indifpenfable Duty to communicate to your Excellency any Grievance the People they reprefent may fuftain, from the Exercife of the Powers of Government, in Inftances where their Cafes may not have been fully explained, the Burgeffes have taken into their mature Confideration, as well the faid Petition, as one, in Oppofition thereto, from fundry Inhabitants in and near the faid Town of Frederickfburg, *and are of Opinion, that fuch Removal would be juft and proper, for the following, among other, Reafons.*

Firft, That Court-Houfes, being defigned for the Adminiftration of Juftice, built at the Expence of the whole People of the County, and the ufual Place for the Exercife of the Militia of General Mufters, they conceive, fhould be fo placed, as that a Majority may refort to them, with equal Eafe and Convenience, as far as may be, which can only happen by holding the Court in the Centre.

Secondly, That though the Encouragement of Towns may be ufeful to Trade and Commerce, Objects worthy of the Public Attention, yet they are of Opinion, that fuch Encouragement ought to be given by other Means than that of facrificing the Eafe and Convenience of the People in the Adminiftration of Juftice.

Thirdly, By holding the Court in one Corner of the County, many poor People muft be obliged, as has happened in this Cafe, to travel double the Diftance they need go, and under the Neceffity of neglecting their Families and Bufinefs, by ftaying all Night from Home, at Expences very injurious to them, when, from the Centre, every Perfon might be able to return Home the fame Day.

Thefe Reafons, with fuch others as may occur, the Burgeffes humbly fubmit to your Lordfhip's Confideration, and cannot avoid intreating your Excellency to relieve the People, by ordering the faid County Court to be adjourned to, and held at, fome Place in or near the Centre of the County.

The faid *Addrefs*, being read a fecond Time;

Refolved, That the Houfe doth agree with the Committee in the faid Addrefs, to be prefented to the Governor.

Ordered, That the faid Addrefs be prefented to his Excellency by the Gentlemen who drew up the fame.

Mr *Treafurer* reported from the Committee, to whom the Bill to dock the Intail of certain Lands whereof *James Blackwell*, the younger, is feifed, and for other Purpofes therein mentioned, was committed, that the Committee had examined the Allegations of the Bill, and found the fame to be true; and that the Committee had gone through the Bill, and made feveral Amendments thereunto, which they had directed him to report to the Houfe; and he read the Report in his Place, and afterwards delivered the Bill, with the Amendments, in at the Clerk's Table; where the Amendments were once read throughout, and then a fecond Time, one by one, and, upon the Queftion feverally put thereupon, were agreed to by the Houfe.

Ordered, That the Bill, with the Amendments, be engroffed.

The Houfe was moved, that the Order, made upon *Wednefday* the 11th Day of this

Inftant

Inftant, that the Committee of Trade do prepare and bring in a Bill purfuant to the firft Refolution of the Committee of Propofitions and Grievances, which was, upon that Day, reported, and agreed to by the Houfe, might be read.

And the fame being read accordingly;

Ordered, That the faid Order be difcharged.

And then the Houfe adjourned till Tomorrow Morning eleven of the Clock.

Saturday, the 28th of March, 12 George lll. 1772.

THE Houfe, according to Order, refolved itfelf into a Committee of the whole Houfe, to confider further of the Bill for the more eafy and fpeedy Adminiftration of Juftice.

M⁣r *Speaker* left the Chair.

M⁣r *Bland* took the Chair of the Committee.

M⁣r *Speaker* refumed the Chair.

M⁣r *Bland* reported from the Committee, that they had made feveral other Amendments to the Bill, which they had directed him to report to the Houfe; and he read the Report in his Place, and afterwards delivered the Bill, with the Amendments, in at the Clerk's Table.

Ordered, That the Bill, with the Amendments, be printed.

A *Meffage* from the Council by M⁣r *Blair*:

M⁣r *Speaker*,

The Council have agreed to the Bill, *intituled* An Act[1] for keeping in repair feveral Roads, and for other Purpofes therein mentioned, *with an Amendment, to which Amendment the Council defire the Concurrence of this Houfe.*

And then the Meffenger withdrew.

The Houfe proceeded to take the faid Amendment into Confideration.

And the faid *Amendment* was read, and is as followeth, *viz.*

Line 38, after '*Drivers*' infert '*and Owners.*'

The faid *Amendment*, being read a fecond Time, was, upon the Queftion put thereupon, agreed to by the Houfe.

Ordered, That M⁣r *Bland* do carry the Bill to the Council, and acquaint them, that this Houfe hath agreed to the Amendment made by them.

Ordered, That M⁣r *Jofeph Cabell*, M⁣r *Edmund Pendleton*, M⁣r *Bowyer*, M⁣r *Burton*, and M⁣r *Edmondfon*, have Leave to be abfent from the Service of this Houfe until the End of this Seffion of General Affembly.

Ordered, That a Committee be appointed to enquire into the Circumftances of the Affairs of the late Treafurer, and that they report the State thereof, with their Opinion by what Means the Money due from him to the Public may be fecured, to the Houfe.

And a *Committee* was appointed of M⁣r *Bland*, M⁣r *Eyre*, M⁣r *Treafurer*, M⁣r *Harrifon*, M⁣r *Jofeph Jones*, M⁣r *Charles Carter*, M⁣r *Digges*, M⁣r *Fitzhugh*, and M⁣r *Banifter*.

Ordered, That Leave be given to bring in a Bill to regulate the Allowances to the Keeper of the Public Prifon for the Maintenance of poor Prifoners and Runaways; and that M⁣r *Nelfon*, M⁣r *Bland*, and M⁣r *Treafurer*, do prepare and bring in the fame.

Ordered, That Leave be given to bring in a Bill for further regulating the Practice of Attorneys; and that M⁣r *Bland*, M⁣r *Cary*, and M⁣r *Treafurer*, do prepare and bring in the fame.

And then the Houfe adjourned till Monday Morning next, eleven of the Clock.

Monday

---

[1] Hening, VIII, p. 543.

Monday, the 30th of March, 12 George III. 1772.

ANOTHER *Member* having taken the Oaths appointed to be taken by Act of Parliament, and repeated and subscribed the Test, took his Place in the House.

Ordered, That the Order of the Day, for the House to resolve itself into a Committee of the whole House, upon the Bill to continue an Act, intituled *An Act*[1] *to continue and amend an Act, intituled an Act for reducing the several Acts, made for laying a Duty upon Liquors into one Act, be now read.*

And the same being read accordingly;

Ordered, That the said Order be discharged.

Ordered, That the Bill be engroffed.

Ordered, That Mr *Thomson Mason* be added to the Committee for Religion, the Committee of Privileges and Elections, and the Committee of Propositions and Grievances.

The other *Order* of the Day being read;

Resolved, That this House will, Tomorrow, resolve itself into a Committee of the whole House, to consider of the Letter from the Earl of *Hillsborough* to the Governor, upon the Subject of a Copper Coinage.

Mr *Gray* reported from the Committee, to whom the Bill to enable the *Nottoway* Indians to lease certain Lands, and for other Purposes therein mentioned, was committed, that the Committee had examined the Allegations of the Bill, and found the same to be true; and that the Committee had gone through the Bill, and made an Amendment thereunto, which they had directed him to report to the House; and he read the Report in his Place, and afterwards delivered the Bill, with the Amendment, in at the Clerk's Table; where the Amendment was twice read, and, upon the Question put thereupon, was agreed to by the House.

Ordered, That the Bill, with the Amendment, be engroffed.

A *Bill* for erecting a Lighthouse on Cape *Henry* was read a second Time.

Resolved, That the Bill be committed to Mr *Harrison*, Mr *Eyre*, Mr *Bland*, Mr *Newton*, Mr *Hutchings* and Mr *Holt*.

Ordered, That it be an Instruction to the Committee of Propositions and Grievances, who are appointed to prepare and bring in a Bill, for repealing so much of the Act made in the fifth Year of the Reign of his present Majesty, intituled *An Act*[2] *for appointing several new Ferries, and for other Purposes therein mentioned,* as established a Ferry from the Land of *Cornelius Thomas,* over the *Fluvanna,* to the Land of *Nicholas Davies,* that they have Power to receive a Clause or Clauses, for establishing a Ferry, over *James* River, from the Land of *William Crow,* to the Land of *Andrew Boyd,* in the County of *Botetourt.*

Mr *Bland* presented to the House, according to Order, a Bill for dividing the County of *Botetourt* into two distinct Counties; and the same was received, and read the first Time.

Resolved, That the Bill be read a second Time.

Mr *Roane* reported from the Committee, to whom the Petition of *William Eyres* was referred, that the Committee had examined the Matter of the said Petition, and had directed him to report the same, as it appeared to them, together with the Resolution of the Committee thereupon, to the House; and he read the Report in his Place, and afterwards delivered it in at the Clerk's Table; where the same was read, and is as followeth, *viz.*

It appears to the *Committee,* from a Certificate subscribed by a great Number of Persons, whose Veracity is well known to the Committee, that the Petitioner has, for several Years past, been employed by sundry Persons in curing and stopping the Flux, in their Families, and has had general Success therein, having never lost a Patient, who followed his Directions. It further appears to the Committee, by a Certificate from one *Thomas Turner,* Esquire, that the Petitioner has lately cured, of that Disease,

several

---

[1] Hening, VIII, p. 529. [2] Ibid, VIII, p. 44.

feveral of his, the faid *Turner's* Family, many of whom, it was thought, would die of it. It further *appears* to the Committee, by a Certificate from one *George Turnbull*, that, notwithftanding he had the Affiftance of a Phyfician, he lay fourteen Days ill of that Difeafe, and his Life, the whole Time, was much defpaired of; that in an Hour after the Petitioner had adminiftered to him, he found great Eafe, and, in a fhort Time, was perfectly cured, and by following his Directions the Diforder ftopped.

Whereupon the *Committee* came to the following Refolution:

Refolved, That it is the Opinion of this Committee, that the Publication of his Remedy, and Manner of treating that Difeafe, may be of public Utility.

The faid *Refolution* being read a fecond Time;

And the *Queftion* being put, that the Houfe doth agree with the Committee in the faid Refolution;

It paffed in the Negative.

Ordered, That Mʳ *Treafurer* do caufe the Names of all the Sheriffs, who have failed to collect and account for the public Taxes, together with the Balances due from them refpectively, to be published in the *Virginia Gazette*, at fuch Times as he fhall think proper, before the 10ᵗʰ Day of *November* next.

Mʳ *Bland* reported from the Committee of Propofitions and Grievances, to whom feveral Petitions were referred, that the Committee had examined the Matters of the faid Petitions, and had come to feveral Refolutions thereupon; which they had directed him to report to the Houfe; and he read the Report in his Place, and afterwards delivered it in at the Clerk's Table; where the Refolutions of the Committee were read, and are as followeth, *viz.*

Refolved, That it is the Opinion of this Committee, that the Petition of *William Aylett*, Proprietor of the public Warehoufes on his Land, in the County of *King William*, praying that he may deliver up the faid Warehoufes to the Public, and that their Value may be afcertained by Perfons, to be appointed for that Purpofe, be rejected.

Refolved, That it is the Opinion of this Committee, that fo much of the Petition of *John Pollard* and *Thomas Sharpe*, Infpectors at *Dixon's* Warehoufe, in the County of *King George*, as prays that their Salaries may be increafed, is reafonable; and that they ought to be allowed the Sum of fifty Pounds *per Annum*, each.

Refolved, That it is the Opinion of this Committee, that the Refidue of the faid petition, praying fome Compenfation for Lofs by the Reduction of their Salaries, in the Year 1769, is reafonable; and that they ought to be allowed ten Pounds, each, for the two laft Years.

Refolved, That it is the Opinion of this Committee, that the Confideration of the Petition of *Jofeph Byrn*, praying that a Ferry may be eftablifhed, over *Shenandoah* River, from his Land, in the County of *Frederick*, to the Land of *Bryan Martin*, Efquire, oppofite thereto, ought to be deferred till the next Seffion of Affembly.

Refolved, That it is the Opinion of this Committee, that fo much of the petition of the Inhabitants of the Counties of *Halifax* and *Charlotte*, as prays that the Ferry, over *Staunton* River, from the Land of *William Fuqua*, deceafed, to the Land of *Walter Coles*, oppofite thereto, may be difcontinued, is reafonable.

Refolved, That it is the Opinion of this Committee, that the Refidue of the faid Petition, praying that a Ferry may be eftablifhed, over the faid River, from the Land of *Walter Coles*, in *Halifax* County, to the Land of *Joseph Fuqua*, in the County of *Charlotte*, is reafonable.

The *firft* Refolution of the Committee being read a fecond Time;

Ordered, That the faid Refolution be recommitted.

Ordered, That the faid Refolution be recommitted to the faid Committee, to whom the petition of the faid *William Aylett* was referred.

The fubfequent *Refolutions* of the Committee, being feverally read a fecond Time, were, upon the Queftion feverally put thereupon, agreed to by the Houfe.

Ordered, That it be an Inftruction to the faid Committee, to whom the Bill to con-

tinue

tinue and amend the Act, intituled *An Act*[1] *to continue and amend the Act, intituled an Act for amending the Staple of Tobacco, and for preventing Frauds in his Majefty's Cuftoms*, was committed, that they have Power to receive a Claufe or Claufes, purfuant to the fecond Refolution of the faid Committee, this Day reported, and agreed to by the Houfe.

Ordered, That it be an Inftruction to the faid Committee, who are appointed to prepare and bring in a Bill, for repealing fo much of the Act, made in the fifth Year of the Reign of his prefent Majefty, intituled *An Act*[2] *for appointing feveral new Ferries, and for other Purpofes therein mentioned*, as eftablifhed a Ferry from the Land of *Cornelius Thomas*, over the *Fluvanna*, to the Land of *Nicholas Davies*, that they have Power to receive a Claufe or Claufes, purfuant to the fifth and fixth Refolutions of the faid Committee, this Day reported, and agreed to by the Houfe.

Ordered, That the Allowance of ten Pounds to *John Pollard* and *Thomas Sharpe*, Infpectors of Tobacco at *Dixon's* Warehoufe, in the County of *King George*, each, be entered in the Book of Public Claims by the Clerk.

And the faid *Allowance* was entered accordingly.

M[r] *Bland* prefented to the Houfe, according to Order, a Bill to encourage the further Settlement of the Town of *Alexandria*, in the County of *Fairfax;* and the fame was received, and read the firft Time.

Refolved, That the Bill be read a fecond Time.

Ordered, That M[r] *Thomas Mann Randolph*, M[r] *Jofeph Jones*, M[r] *Speed*, and M[r] *May*, have Leave to be abfent from the Service of this Houfe till the End of this Seffion of General Affembly.

A *Bill* to permit certain Perfons therein mentioned to erect Gates acrofs the public Roads, leading through their Lands, was read a fecond Time.

Refolved, That the Bill be committed to the Committee of Trade.

M[r] *Bland* reported from the Committee of Propofitions and Grievances, to whom the Petition of the Diffenters, called Menonifts, praying that they may be exempt from the Penalties inflicted for not attending Mufters, was referred, that the Committee had examined the Matter of the faid Petition, and had come to a Refolution thereupon, which they had directed him to report to the Houfe; and he read the Report in his Place, and afterwards delivered it in at the Clerk's Table, where the Refolution of the Committee was read, and is as followeth, *viz.*

Refolved, That it is the Opinion of this Committee, that the faid Petition is reafonable.

Ordered, That the faid Report do lie upon the Table.

The Houfe proceeded to take into Confideration the Book of Public Claims.

And the faid *Book* was partly read.

Ordered, That the further Confideration of the faid Book be adjourned till Tomorrow.

Ordered, That the Committee of Public Claims do ftate an Account of the Allowances to be made to the Witneffes, who attended the Commiffioners, to be examined touching the Matter of the Petition of M[r] *Henry Blagrave*, complaining of an undue Election and Return of M[r] *Thomas Pettus* to ferve as a Burgefs in this prefent General Affembly, for the County of *Lunenburg*, and report the fame to the Houfe.

Ordered, That the Committee of Public Claims do ftate an Account of the Allowances to be made to the Witneffes, who attended the Committee for Religion, upon the hearing of the Petitions of feveral Perfons of the Parifh of *Saint John*, in the County of *King William*, for diffolving the Veftry of the faid Parifh, and the Petition of the Veftrymen of the faid Parifh, in Oppofition thereto, and report the fame to the Houfe.

A *Bill* for appointing Truftees to regulate the making of Slopes for the Paffage of Fifh, in the Mill Dams within the County of *Bedford*, was read a fecond Time.

Refolved, That the Bill be committed to the Committee of Propofitions and Grievances.

An engroffed *Bill* to dock the Intail of certain Lands whereof *John Hancock* is feifed, and for fettling other Lands and Slaves, in Lieu thereof, was read the third Time.

Refolved, That the Bill do pafs; and that the Title be, *An Act*[3] *to dock the Intail of certain*

_____
[1] Hening, VIII, p. 318   [2] Ibid, VIII, p. 44.   [3] Ibid, VIII, p. 635.

certain Lands whereof John Hancock *is feifed, and for fettling other Lands and Slaves, in Lieu thereof.*

Ordered, That M*ʳ* *Henry Lee* do carry the Bill to the Council, and defire their Concurrence.

An engroffed *Bill* to dock the Intail of certain Lands whereof *James Blackwell*, the younger, is feifed, and for other Purpofes therein mentioned, was read the third Time.

Refolved, That the Bill do pafs; and that the Title be, *An Act[1] to dock the Intail of certain Lands whereof* James Blackwell, *the younger, is feifed, and for other Purpofes therein mentioned.*

Ordered, That M*ʳ* *Treafurer* do carry the Bill to the Council, and defire their Concurrence.

And then the Houfe adjourned till Tomorrow Morning, eleven of the Clock.

Tuesday, the 31st of March, 12 George III. 1772.

A Bill to appoint Commiffioners to view a Place propofed for a Road through the South Mountain was read a fecond Time.

Ordered, That the Bill be engroffed.

The *Order* of the Day being read, for the Houfe to refolve itfelf into a Committee of the whole Houfe, to confider of the Letter from the Earl of *Hillfborough* to the Governor upon the Subject of a Copper Coinage;

Ordered, That the Extracts of Letters which have paffed between M*ʳ* *Treafurer*, and M*ʳ* *John Norton*, of *London*, Merchant, upon the fame Subject, and which were this Day laid before the Houfe by M*ʳ* *Treafurer*, be referred to the faid Committee.

Then the Houfe refolved itfelf into the faid Committee.

M*ʳ* *Speaker* left the Chair.

M*ʳ* *Bland* took the Chair of the Committee.

M*ʳ* *Speaker* refumed the Chair.

M*ʳ* *Bland* reported from the Committee, that they had come to feveral Refolutions, which they had directed him to report, when the Houfe will pleafe to receive the fame.

Ordered, That the Report be now received.

M*ʳ* *Bland* accordingly reported the Refolutions, which the Committee had directed him to report to the Houfe; which he read in his Place, and afterwards delivered in at the Clerk's Table; where the fame were read, and are as followeth, *viz.*

Refolved, That it is the Opinion of this Committee, that an humble Addrefs be prefented to his Excellency the Governor, returning him the Thanks of the Houfe for communicating the Earl of *Hillfborough's* Letter on the Subject of Copper Money; expreffing the Satiffaction we have received, on finding the Propofal, formerly made, for the Introduction of fuch Coin into this Colony, is likely to be carried into Execution, and the Obligations we are under to his Majefty's Minifter for giving fuch earneft Attention to the Views of the Colony in this Refpect; affuring his Lordfhip that we entirely approve the Scheme, which the Earl of *Hillfborough* hath been pleafed to recommend, and that we wish to adopt it, in every Part.

Refolved, That it is the Opinion of this Committee, that fo much of the feveral Acts of Affembly, made in the firft Year of the Reign of his late Majefty, and in the tenth Year of the Reign of his prefent Majefty, as refpects Copper Coin, ought to be amended, and adapted to the Terms now propofed, for iffuing and circulating Copper Money in this Colony.

The faid *Refolutions*, being feverally read a fecond Time, were, upon the Queftion feverally put thereupon, agreed to by the Houfe.

Ordered, That M*ʳ* *Treafurer* and M*ʳ* *John Page* do wait upon his Excellency with the firft Refolution.

Ordered

---

1 Hening, VIII, p. 641.

Ordered, That a Bill be brought in purfuant to the fecond Refolution; and that Mr *Treafurer* and Mr *John Page* do prepare, and bring in the fame.

Mr *Bland* prefented to the Houfe, according to Order, a Bill to amend the Act, intituled *An Act[1] directing the Trial of Slaves committing capital Offences, and for the more effectual punifhing Confpiracies and Infurrections of them, and for the better Government of Negroes, Mulattoes, and Indians, bond or free;* and the fame was received, and read the firft Time.

Refolved, That the Bill be read a fecond Time.

Ordered, That the Bill be now read a fecond Time.

The *Bill* was accordingly read a fecond Time.

Refolved, That the Bill be committed.

Refolved, That the Bill be committed to a Committee of the whole Houfe.

Refolved, That this Houfe will, upon *Thurfday* next, refolve itfelf into a Committee of the whole Houfe upon the faid Bill.

Mr *Harrifon* reported from the Committee of Trade, to whom the Bill to permit certain Perfons, therein mentioned, to erect Gates, acrofs the public Roads, leading through their Lands, was committed, that the Committee had examined the Allegations of the Bill, and found the fame to be true; and that the Committee had gone through the Bill, and made feveral Amendments thereunto, which they had directed him to report to the Houfe; and he read the Report in his Place, and afterwards delivered the Bill, with the Amendments, in at the Clerk's Table; where the Amendments were once read throughout, and then a fecond Time, one by one, and, upon the Queftion feverally put thereupon, were agreed to by the Houfe. 180

Ordered, That the Bill, with the Amendments, be engroffed.

The other *Orders* of the Day being read;

Refolved, That this Houfe will, Tomorrow, refolve itfelf into a Committee of the whole Houfe, upon the Bill to enlarge the Power of the Truftees, appointed to carry into Execution an Act paffed this prefent Seffion of Affembly, intituled *An Act[2] for cutting a navigable Canal from* Archer's Hope *Creek to* Queen's *Creek, through or near the City of* Williamfburg.

Ordered, That the further Confideration of the Book of Public Claims be further adjourned till Tomorrow.

Mr *Bland* prefented to the Houfe, according to Order, a Bill for further regulating the Practice of Attornies; and the fame was received, and read the firft Time.

And the *Queftion* being put, that the Bill be read a fecond Time;

It paffed in the Negative.

An engroffed *Bill* to amend an Act, intituled *An Act[3] for clearing* Mattapony *River*, was read the third Time.

Refolved, That the Bill do pafs; and that the Title be, *An Act[4] to amend an Act, intituled an Act for clearing* Mattapony *River*.

Ordered, That Mr *Aylett* do carry the Bill to the Council, and defire their Concurrence.

Mr *Bland* reported from the Committee of Propofitions and Grievances, to whom the Bill to compel Ships importing Convicts, Servants, or Slaves infected with the Gaol Fever, or Small-Pox, to perform Quarantine, was committed, that the Committee had gone through the Bill, and made feveral Amendments thereunto, which they had directed him to Report to the Houfe; and he read the Report in his Place, and afterwards delivered the Bill, with the Amendments, in at the Clerk's Table; where the Amendments were once read throughout, and then a fecond Time, one by one, and, upon the Queftion feverally put thereupon, were agreed to by the Houfe.

Ordered, That the Bill, with the Amendments, be engroffed.

Mr *Nelfon* prefented to the Houfe, according to Order, a Bill for regulating the Allowances to the Keeper of the public Prifon, for the Maintenance of poor Prifoners for Debt, and Runaways; and the fame was received, and read the firft Time.

Refolved, That the Bill be read a fecond Time.

And then the Houfe adjourned till Tomorrow Morning, eleven of the Clock.

Wednesday

---

[1] Hening, VI, p, 104. [2] Ibid, VIII, p. 556. [3] Ibid, VI, p. 394. [4] Ibid, VIII, p. 579.

Wednesday, the 1st of April, 12 George. III. 1772.

MR *Bland* reported from the Committee, who were appointed to enquire into the Circumftances of the Affairs of the late Treafurer, and to report the State thereof, with their Opinion by what Means the Money due from him to the Public may be fecured, that the Committee had confidered the Matter referred to them, and had directed him to report the fame, as it appeared to them, to the Houfe; and he read the Report in his Place, and afterwards delivered it in at the Clerk's Table; where the fame was read, and is as followeth, *viz.*

It appears to your *Committee*, from a Lift of Debts laid before them by the Adminif-trators of the late Treafurer, that there is due, at this Time, to his Eftate, from different Perfons, the Sum of one hundred and nine thoufand and fixty-three Pounds twelve Shillings and three pence, of which your Committee believe the Sum of twenty-two thoufand one hundred and feventy Pounds eight Shillings and nine Pence will be entirely loft, but, from the beft Information they could receive, they are of Opinion, that the Refidue of the Debts, amounting to eighty-fix thoufand eight hundred and ninety-three Pounds three Shillings and fix pence, will prove good, though it is uncertain in what Time the Adminiftrators will be able to collect the fame.

It further appears to your *Committee*, that many Suits have been commenced, and Judgments obtained, for different Balances; that feveral Perfons Eftates have been fold, and Bonds taken, fome of which remain unpaid. Upon the whole, it appears to your Committee, that the Adminiftrators, confidering the complicated and perplexed Situation of their Inteftate's Affairs, have ufed every prudent Meafure to fecure and get in the Debts due to the Eftate, and your Committee are of Opinion, that they ought to continue their Endeavors to have all the Accounts finally clofed, and enforce the moft expeditious Payments of the feveral Balances, which are ftill due.

Ordered, That the Report do lie upon the Table;

Mr *Bland* reported from the Committee of Propofitions and Grievances, to whom the Bill to amend an Act, intituled *An Act*[1] *to amend an Act, intituled an Act to oblige the Owners of Mills, Hedges, or Stone Stops on fundry Rivers, therein mentioned, to make Openings or Slopes therein for the Paffage of Fifh, and for other Purpofes therein mentioned,* was committed, that the Committee had gone through the Bill, and made feveral Amendments thereunto, which they had directed him to report to the Houfe; and he read the Report in his Place, and afterwards delivered the Bill, with the Amendments, in at the Clerk's Table; where the Amendments were once read throughout, and then a fecond Time, one by one; and, upon the Queftion feverally put thereupon, were agreed to by the Houfe.

Ordered, That the Bill, with the Amendments, be engroffed.

A *Bill* for appointing Commiffioners for felling the Tobacco damaged in the public Warehoufes at *Morton's,* was read a fecond Time.

Refolved, That the Bill be committed to Mr *Alexander* and Mr *Yelverton Peyton.*

Ordered, That it be an Inftruction to the faid Committee, that they have Power to receive a Claufe or Claufes purfuant to the firft Refolution of the Committee of Public Claims, which, upon *Thurfday* laft, was reported, and agreed to by the Houfe.

Mr *Harrifon* reported from the Committee appointed upon *Friday,* the twentieth Day of laft Month, to draw up an Addrefs to be prefented to his Majefty, that the Committee had drawn up an Addrefs accordingly, which they had directed him to report to the Houfe; and he read the fame in his Place, and afterwards delivered it in at the Clerk's Table; where the fame was read, and is as followeth, *viz.*

Moft Gracious Sovereign,

We, your Majefty's dutiful and loyal Subjects, the Burgeffes of Virginia, *now met in General Affembly, beg Leave, with all Humility, to approach your Royal Prefence.*

The many Inftances of your Majefty's benevolent Intentions and moft gracious Dif-

pofition

---

[1] Hening, VII, p. 590.

pofition to promote the *Profperity* and *Happinefs* of your *Subjects* in the Colonies, *encourage us to look up to the Throne, and implore your Majefty's paternal Affiftance in averting a Calamity of a moft alarming Nature.*

The *Importation of Slaves into the Colonies from the Coaft of* Africa *hath long been confidered as a Trade of great Inhumanity, and, under its prefent Encouragement, we have too much Reafon to fear will endanger the very Exiftance of your Majefty's* American *Dominions.*

We *are fenfible that fome of your Majefty's Subjects in* Great-Britain *may reap Emoluments from this Sort of Traffic, but when we confider that it greatly retards the Settlement of the Colonies, with more ufeful Inhabitants, and may, in Time, have the moft deftructive Influence, we prefume to hope that the Intereft of a few will be difregarded when placed in Competition with the Security and Happinefs of fuch Numbers of your Majefty's dutiful and loyal Subjects.*

Deeply impreffed with thefe Sentiments, we moft humbly befeech your Majefty to remove all thofe Reftraints on your Majefty's Governors of this Colony, which inhibit their affenting to fuch Laws as might check fo very pernicious a Commerce.

Your *Majefty's antient Colony and Dominion of* Virginia *hath, at all Times, and upon every Occafion, been entirely devoted to your Majefty's facred Perfon and Government, and we cannot forego this Opportunity of renewing thofe Affurances of the trueft Loyalty, and warmeft Affection, which we have fo often, with the greateft Sincerity, given to the beft of Kings, whofe Wifdom and Goodnefs we efteem the fureft Pledges of the Happinefs of all his People.*

The faid *Addrefs* being read a fecond Time;

Refolved, Nemine contradicente, That the Houfe doth agree with the Committee in the faid Addrefs, to be prefented to his Majefty.

Refolved, That an Addrefs be prefented to his Excellency the Governor, to defire that he will be pleafed to tranfmit the Addrefs to his Majefty, and to fupport it in fuch Manner as he fhall think moft likely to promote the defirable End propofed.

Ordered, That the faid Addrefs be prefented to the Governor by the Gentlemen who drew up the Addrefs to his Majefty.

Mr *Treafurer* prefented to the Houfe, according to Order, a Bill to amend the feveral Acts of Affembly, refpecting the Currency of Copper Money, in this Colony; and the fame was received, and read the firft Time.

Refolved, That the Bill be read a fecond Time.

An engroffed *Bill,* to explain and amend an Act, intituled *An Act*[1] *to oblige the Owners of Mills, Hedges, or Stops, on the Rivers therein mentioned, to make Openings or Slopes therein, for the Paffage of Fifh,* was read the third Time.

Refolved, That the Bill do pafs; and that the Title be, *An Act*[2] *to explain and amend an Act, intituled an Act to oblige the Owners of Mills, Hedges, or Stops, on the Rivers therein mentioned, to make Openings or Slopes therein, for the Paffage of Fifh.*

Ordered, That Mr *Marfhall* do carry the Bill to the Council, and defire their Concurrence.

Ordered, That Mr *Carr,* Mr *Banifter,* Mr *Watkins,* Mr *Mitchell,* and Mr *Henry Pendleton,* have Leave to be abfent from the Service of this Houfe till the End of this Seffion of General Affembly.

Mr *Bland* reported from the Committee of Propofitions and Grievances, to whom feveral Petitions were referred, that the Committee had examined the Matters of the faid Petitions, and had come to feveral Refolutions thereupon, which they had directed him to report to the Houfe; and he read the Report in his Place, and afterwards delivered it in at the Clerk's Table; where the Refolutions of the Committee were read, and are as followeth, *viz.*

Refolved, That it is the Opinion of this Committee, that the petitions of divers Inhabitants of the County of *Prince George,* and others, praying that new Warehoufes,

for

132

---

1   Hening, VIII, p. 361.   2 Ibid, VIII, p. 581.

for the Infpection of Tobacco, may be eftablifhed on the Lots of *Robert Bolling*, adjoining *Davis's* Landing, in the Town of *Blandford*, is reafonable.

Refolved, That it is the Opinion of this Committee, that the petition of divers Inhabitants of the County of *Dinwiddie*, and others, praying that new Warehoufes, for the Infpection of Tobacco, may be eftablifhed on the Land of *Robert Bolling*, at *Cedar Point*, is reafonable.

The faid *Refolutions*, being feverally read a fecond Time, were, upon the Queftion feverally put thereupon, agreed to by the Houfe.

Ordered, That it be an Inftruction to the Committee of Propofitions and Grievances, to whom the Bill to continue and amend the Act, intituled *An Act*[1] *to continue and amend the Act, intituled An Act for amending the Staple of Tobacco, and for preventing Frauds in his Majefty's Cuftoms*, is committed, that they have Power to receive a Claufe or Claufes purfuant to the faid Refolutions.

Ordered, That it be an Inftruction to the faid Committee, that they have Power to receive a Claufe or Claufes for reducing the Salaries of the Infpectors of Tobacco at *Robert Bolling's, Bollingbrooke, Blandford*, and *Boyd's* Warehoufes, ten Pounds each.

M[r] *Bland* prefented to the Houfe, according to Order, a Bill to repeal fo much of the Act, made in the fifth Year of his prefent Majefty's Reign, as eftablifhes a Ferry from the Land of *Cornelius Thomas*, in the County of *Amherft*, over the *Fluvanna* River, to the Land of *Nicholas Davies*, oppofite thereto, in the County of *Bedford;* and the fame was received, and read the firft Time.

Refolved, That the Bill be read a fecond Time.

A *Bill* to eftablifh a Town on the Land of *John Rictor*, in the County of *Fauquier*, was read a fecond Time.

Refolved, That the Bill be committed to M[r] *Thomfon Mafon*, and M[r] *Francis Peyton*.

Ordered, That it be an Inftruction to the faid Committee, that they have Power to receive a Claufe or Claufes for reftraining Hogs from going at Large in the Town of *Leefburg*, in the County of *Loudoun*.

A *Bill* for appointing Truftees for the Town of *Cobham*, and for other Purpofes therein mentioned, was read a fecond Time.

Ordered, That the Bill be engroffed.

An engroffed *Bill* for diffolving the Veftries of the Parifhes of *Saint Martin*, in the Counties of *Hanover* and *Louifa*, and of *Saint John*, in the County of *King William*, was read the third Time.

Refolved, That the Bill do pafs; and that the Title be, *An Act*[2] *for diffolving the Veftries of the Parifhes of* Saint Martin, *in the Counties of* Hanover *and* Louifa, *and of* Saint John, *in the County of* King William.

Ordered, That M[r] *Aylett* do carry the Bill to the Council, and defire their Concurrence.

Ordered, That Leave be given to bring in a Bill for regulating the Method of fuing out Writs of *Alias Capias*, in the County Courts, for altering *Loudoun* Court Day, and for other Purpofes; and that M[r] *Thomfon Mafon*, M[r] *Francis Peyton*, and M[r] *Henry Lee*, do prepare, and bring in the fame.

Ordered, That this Houfe be called over Tomorrow.

The *Order* of the Day being read for the Houfe to refolve itfelf into a Committee of the whole Houfe, upon the Bill to enlarge the Power of the Truftees, appointed to carry into Execution an Act paffed this prefent Seffion of Affembly, intituled *An Act*[3] *for cutting a navigable Canal from* Archer's Hope *Creek to* Queen's *Creek, through or near the City of* Williamfburg;

The Houfe refolved itfelf into the faid Committee.

M[r] *Speaker* left the Chair.

M[r] *Bland* took the Chair of the Committee.

M[r] *Speaker* refumed the Chair.

M[r] *Bland* reported from the Committee, that they had gone through the Bill, and
made

[1] Hening, VIII, p. 318.   [2] Ibid, VIII, p. 607.   [3] Ibid, p. 556.

made feveral Amendments thereunto, which they had directed him to report when the Houfe will pleafe to receive the fame.

Ordered, That the Report be now received.

Mr *Bland* accordingly reported from the faid Committee the Amendments which the Committee had made to the Bill, and which they had directed him to report to the Houfe; and he read the Report in his Place, and afterwards delivered the Bill, with the Amendments, in at the Clerk's Table; where the Amendments were once read throughout, and then a fecond Time, one by one, and, upon the Queftion feverally put thereupon, were agreed to by the Houfe.

Ordered, That the Bill, with the Amendments, be engroffed.

The other *Order* of the Day being read;

Ordered, That the further Confideration of the Book of Public Claims be further adjourned till Tomorrow.

And then the Houfe adjourned till Tomorrow Morning eleven of the Clock.

Thursday, the 2nd of April, 12 George III. 1772.

MR *Marfhall* reported from the Committee, to whom the Bill for appointing Commiffioners to afcertain the Value of certain Churches and Chapels in the Parifhes of *Frederick, Norborne,* and *Beckford,* and for other Purpofes therein mentioned, was committed, that the Committee had gone through the Bill, and made feveral Amendments thereunto, which they had directed him to report to the Houfe; and he read the Report in his Place, and afterwards delivered the Bill, with the Amendments, in at the Clerk's Table; where the Amendments were once read throughout, and then a fecond Time, one by one, and, upon the Queftion feverally put thereupon, were agreed to by the Houfe.

Ordered, That the Bill, with the Amendments, be engroffed.

Mr *Bland* prefented to the Houfe, according to Order, a Bill to amend the Act, intituled *An Act[1] prefcribing the Method of appointing Sheriffs, and for limiting the Time of their Continuance in Office, and directing their Duty therein;* and the fame was received, and read the firft Time.

Refolved, That the Bill be read a fecond Time.

Ordered, That the Bill be now read a fecond Time.

The *Bill* was accordingly read a fecond Time.

Refolved, That the Bill be committed.

Refolved, That the Bill be committed to a Committee of the whole Houfe.

Refolved, That this Houfe will, Tomorrow, refolve itfelf into a Committee of the whole Houfe upon the faid Bill.

Mr *Cary* reported from the Committee of Public Claims, to whom it was referred to ftate an Account of the Allowances, to be made to the Witneffes who attended the Commiffioners, to be examined touching the Matter of the Petition of Mr *Henry Blagrave,* complaining of an undue Election and Return of Mr *Thomas Pettus,* to ferve as Burgefs, in this prefent General Affembly, for the County of *Lunenburg,* that the Committee had ftated an Account accordingly; and had directed him to report the fame to the Houfe; and he read the Report in his Place; and afterwards delivered it in at the Clerk's Table, where the Account was read, and is as followeth, *viz.*

	Pounds of Nett Tobacco.
To *David Garland,* Sheriff of *Lunenburg* County, for fummoning feventy Witneffes on Behalf of the faid *Blagrave.*	490
To the faid *Garland,* for fummoning thirty-eight Witneffes, on Behalf of the faid *Pettus,*	266
To *Sion Spencer,* Sheriff of *Charlotte* County, for fummoning five Witneffes, on Behalf of the faid *Pettus.*	35

Ordered

---

1 Hening, V, p. 515.

Ordered, That the faid feveral Allowances be entered in the Book of Public Claims, by the Clerk.

And the faid *Allowances* were entered accordingly.

A *Motion* was made, and the Queftion being put, that two hundred and eighty feven Pounds of Tobacco, the Sheriff's Fees for fummoning forty-one Witneffes, on Behalf of Mr *Henry Blagrave*, be levied upon him, it appearing that he admitted the Voters, with refpect to whofe Freeholds the faid Witneffes were examined, to be duly qualified;

It was refolved in the Affirmative.

Ordered, That the Allowance of the faid two hundred and eighty-feven Pounds of Tobacco to the County of *Lunenburg*, to be levied upon the faid *Henry Blagrave*, be entered in the Book of Public Claims, by the Clerk.

And the faid *Allowance* was entered accordingly.

A *Motion* was made, and the Queftion being put, that one hundred and nineteen Pounds of Tobacco, the Sheriff's Fees for fummoning feventeen Witneffes, on Behalf of Mr *Thomas Pettus*, be levied upon him, it appearing that he admitted the Voters, with refpect to whofe Freeholds the faid Witneffes were examined, to be duly qualified;

It was refolved in the Affirmative.

135 *Ordered*, That the Allowance of the faid one hundred and nineteen Pounds of Tobacco, to the County of *Lunenburg*, to be levied upon the faid *Thomas Pettus*, be entered in the Book of Public Claims, by the Clerk.

And the faid *Allowance* was entered accordingly.

Mr *Cary* reported from the Committee of Public Claims, to whom it was referred to ftate an Account of the Allowances to be made to the Witneffes, who attended the Committee for Religion, upon the hearing of the Petitions of feveral Perfons of the Parifh of *Saint John*, in the County of *King William*, for diffolving the Veftry of the faid Parifh, and the Petition of the Veftrymen of the faid Parifh, in Oppofition thereto, that the Committee had ftated an Account accordingly, and had directed him to report the fame to the Houfe; and he read the Report in his Place, and afterwards delivered it in at the Clerk's Table; where the Account was read, and is as followeth, *viz.*

Witneffes.	Attendance.	Diftance.	Pounds of Nett Tobacco.
John Watkins,	2 Days,	40 Miles	252
Bernard Powers,	2	40	252
Holt Richefon,	4	30	342
William Peters Martin,	3		182
Ifaac Quarles,	4	40	372
John Roane,	5	45	447
			1847

Ordered, That the faid feveral Allowances be entered in the Book of Public Claims, by the Clerk.

And the faid *Allowances* were entered accordingly.

A *Motion* was made, and the Queftion being put, that the faid one thoufand eight hundred and forty-feven Pounds of Tobacco be levied on the Inhabitants of the Parifh of *Saint John*, in the County of *King William;*

It was refolved in the Affirmative.

Ordered, That the Allowance of the faid one thoufand eight hundred and forty-feven Pounds of Tobacco to the faid County of *King William*, to be levied upon the Inhabitants of the faid Parifh of *Saint John*, be entered in the Book of Public Claims, by the Clerk.

And the faid *Allowance* was entered accordingly.

A *Meffage* from the Council by Mr *Blair:*

Mr

Mr Speaker,

The Council have agreed to the Bill, *intituled* An Act[1] for diffolving the Veftries of the Parifhes of *Saint Martin,* in the Counties of *Hanover,* and *Louifa,* and of *Saint John,* in the County of *King William, without any Amendment; and alfo,*

The Council have agreed to the Bill, *intituled* An Act[2] for making further Provifion for the Support and Maintenance of Ideots, Lunatics, and other Perfons of unfound Minds, *without any Amendment; and alfo,*

The Council have agreed to the Bill, *intituled* An Act[3] to amend an Act, intituled an Act for clearing *Mattapony* River, *without any Amendment; and alfo,*

The Council have agreed to the Bill, *intituled* An Act[4] to dock the Intail of certain Lands whereof *James Blackwell,* the younger, is feifed, and for other Purpofes therein mentioned, *without any Amendment; and alfo,*

The Council have agreed to the Bill, *intituled* An Act[5] to dock the Intail of certain Lands whereof *John Hancock* is feifed, and for fettling other Lands, and Slaves, in Lieu thereof, *without any Amendment; and alfo,*

The Council have agreed to the Bill, *intituled* An Act[6] to amend an Act intituled An Act concerning Seamen, *with an Amendment, to which Amendment the Council defire the Concurrence of this Houfe.*

And then the Meffenger withdrew.

The Houfe proceeded to take the faid *Amendment* into Confideration.

And the faid *Amendment* was read, and is as followeth, *viz.*

Line 14, after *"Churchwardens"* infert *"or either of them."*

The faid *Amendment,* being read a fecond Time, was, upon the Queftion put there-upon, agreed to by the Houfe.

Ordered, That Mr *Hutchings* do carry the Bill to the Council, and acquaint them that this Houfe hath agreed to the Amendment made by them.

Mr *Nelfon* prefented to the Houfe, according to Order, a Bill to veft certain intailed Lands, whereof *Philip Ludwell Grymes,* Gentleman, is feifed, in *William Roane,* Gentleman, in Fee Simple; and the fame was received, and read the firft Time.

Refolved, That the Bill be read a fecond Time.

Ordered, That Mr *Hardy* have Leave to be abfent from the Service of this Houfe till *Monday* next.

Ordered, That Mr *Thornton,* and Mr *Taliaferro,* have Leave to be abfent from the Service of this Houfe till the End of this Seffion of General Affembly.

The *Order* of the Day being read, for the Houfe to refolve itfelf into a Committee of the whole Houfe, upon the Bill to amend the Act, intituled *An Act[7] directing the Trial of Slaves committing capital Offences, and for the more effectual punifhing Confpiracies and Infurrections of them, and for the better Government of Negroes, Mulattoes, and* Indians, *bond or free.*

Refolved, That this Houfe will, Tomorrow, refolve itfelf into a Committee of the whole Houfe upon the faid Bill.

The *Order* of the Day being read, for the Houfe to take into their further Confidera-tion the Book of Public Claims;

Ordered, That the further Confideration of the faid Book be further adjourned till Tomorrow.

Mr *Bland* reported from the Committee of Privileges and Elections, to whom the Petition of Mr *Thomas Pettus,* complaining of an undue Election and Return of Mr *Henry Blagrave,* to ferve as a Burgefs in this prefent General Affembly, for the County of *Lunenburg,* was referred, that the Committee had examined the Matter of the faid Petition, and had directed him to report the fame, together with the Refolutions of the Committee thereupon, to the Houfe; and he read the Report in his Place, and afterwards delivered it in at the Clerk's Table; where the fame was read, and is as followeth, *viz.*

Your

1   Hening, VIII, p. 607.   2 Ibid, VIII, p. 594.   3 Ibid, VIII, p. 579.   4 Ibid, VIII, p. 641.
5 Ibid, VIII, p. 635.   6 Ibid, VIII, p. 523.   7 Ibid, VI, p. 104.

Your *Committee* take Leave to obferve, in the firft Place, that the fitting Member did not appear before them, either in Perfon, or by his Counfel; whereupon your Committee proceeded to confider the material Depofitions taken and returned, purfuant to the Order of the Houfe, from whence it appears, by the Evidence of one *James Johnfon*, an Ordinary Keeper, in the County of *Lunenburg*, that on the Day of the laft Election of Burgeffes for the faid County, before the Poll was opened, Mr *Blagrave* applied to him, and told him if any Perfons wanted Drams to let them have them, which he accordingly did, to the Value of twenty Shillings, or thereabouts, and for which he expects to receive Satiffaction; but that Mr *Blagrave* did not folicit his Vote or Intereft; that he heard one *Jofeph Smith*, alfo an Ordinary Keeper, in the faid County, fay that he treated for Mr *Blagrave* on the Day of the faid Election, but he did not declare whether by Mr *Blagrave's* Directions or not. It alfo appears, from the Evidence of *Thomas Garrett*, that about a Fortnight before the laft Election for the faid County of *Lunenburg*, he loft his Pocket Book, and one *Chriftopher Maconico* engaged to give him another, of the Value of five Shillings, provided he would vote for Mr *Blagrave* at the enfuing Election; in Confideration whereof he did vote for Mr *Blagrave*, and has fince received the Book; that he thinks he fhould not have voted for him without fuch Promife, and that on the Morning of the Day of Election, and before the Poll was opened, Mr *Blagrave* came to him, and carried him to the Ordinary Door, into which he entered, and there drank plentifully of Wine, and was told by one *Jofeph Smith*, the Ordinary Keeper, that he was partaking of Mr *Blagrave's* Treat. *It alfo* appears to your Committee, by the Evidence of the faid *Chriftopher Maconico*, that fome Time before the laft Election of Burgeffes for *Lunenburg* County, he being at the Houfe of Mr *Thomas Garrett*, complaining of the Lofs of his Pocket Book, he told him if he would vote for Mr *Blagrave* he would give him another, to which *Garrett* agreed, and at the Election performed his Promife; that fome Time after the faid *Garrett* applied for the Pocket Book, and *Maconico* gave him an old *Scotch* Almanack, of lefs than four pence Value, as it was not agreed that the Book fhould be of any particular Value; that he never expects any Satiffaction for it; that in Conference with the faid *Garrett*, at the Courthoufe, the faid *Garrett* informed him there were two Things he had fworn before Mr *Abraham Maury*, which were wrong, *viz.* the faying the Pocket Book was to be of five Shillings Value, and that he did not vote for Mr *Blagrave* in Confideration thereof. It further appears to your Committee, by the Evidence of one *John White*, that on the Day of the laft Election of Burgeffes for the County of *Lunenburg*, the faid *White* meeting Mr *Blagrave*

187 between *James Johnfon's* Ordinary and *Smith's* Ordinary, after the ufual Compliments of Salutation had paffed, Mr *Blagrave* faid to him, "You don't drink Toddy; come along with me, and we will try to get a Dram"; whereupon they went together into the faid *Smith's* Ordinary, and Mr *Blagrave* called to the faid *Smith*, who produced fome Rum in a Tumbler, but that he was in no Wife induced thereby to vote for Mr *Blagrave*.

Whereupon your *Committee* came to the following Refolution.

Refolved, That it is the Opinion of this Committee, that the faid Mr *Thomas Pettus* has fully made good his charge againft the faid Mr *Henry Blagrave*.

Refolved, That it is the Opinion of this Committee, that faid Mr *Henry Blagrave* is not duly elected to ferve as a Burgefs, in this prefent General Affembly, for the County of *Lunenburg*.

The faid *Refolutions*, being feverally read a fecond Time, were, upon the Queftion feverally put thereupon, agreed to by the Houfe.

Ordered, That an Addrefs be made to the Governor, to Order a new Writ to Iffue, for the electing of a Burgefs, to ferve in this prefent General Affembly, for the County of *Lunenburg*, in the Room of Mr *Henry Blagrave*, whofe Election is declared void; and that Mr *Claiborne* do wait upon his Excellency with the faid Addrefs.

A *Bill* to encourage the further Settlement of the Town of *Alexandria*, in the County of *Fairfax*, was read a fecond Time.

Refolved, That the Bill be committed to the Committee of Trade.

M^r

Mr *Bland* reported from the Committee of Propofitions and Grievances, to whom the Bill for appointing Truftees to regulate the making of Slopes, for the Paffage of Fifh, in the Mill Dams, within the County of *Bedford*, was committed, that the Committee had gone through the Bill, and made feveral Amendments thereunto, which they had directed him to report to the Houfe; and he read the Report in his Place, and afterwards delivered the Bill, with the Amendments, in at the Clerk's Table.

And the Houfe being informed, that fome other Amendments are neceffary to be made to the faid Bill;

Ordered, That the faid Bill be recommitted to the Committee of Propofitions and Grievances.

Mr *Alexander* reported from the Committee, to whom the Bill for appointing Com-miffioners, for felling the Tobacco damaged in the public Warehoufe at *Morton's* was committed, that the Committee had gone through the Bill, and made an Amendment thereunto, which they had directed him to report to the Houfe; and he read the Report in his Place, and afterwards delivered the Bill, with the Amendment, in at the Clerk's Table; where the Amendment was twice read, and, upon the Queftion put thereupon, was agreed to by the Houfe.

Ordered, That the Bill, with the Amendment, be engroffed.

Mr *Bland* reported from the Committee of Propofitions and Grievances, to whom the Bill for clearing a Road from the Warm Springs, in *Augufta*, and for other Purpofes therein mentioned, was recommitted, that the Committee had made feveral other Amendments to the Bill, which they had directed him to report to the Houfe; and he read the Report in his Place, and afterwards delivered the Bill, with the Amendments, in at the Clerk's Table; where the Amendments were once read throughout, and then a fecond Time, one by one, and, upon the Queftion feverally put thereupon, were, with feveral Amendments to one of them, agreed to by the Houfe.

Ordered, That the Bill, with the Amendments, be engroffed.

Mr *Rutherford* reported from the Committee, to whom the Petition of *Philip Hand* was referred, that the Committee had examined the Matter of the faid Petition, and had directed him to report the fame, together with the Refolution of the Committee there-upon, to the Houfe; and he read the Report in his Place, and afterwards delivered it in at the Clerk's Table; where the fame was read, and is as followeth, *viz.*

It appears to your *Committee*, by the Information of Mr *Rutherford* (a Member of the Houfe) and others (the Petitioner himfelf being unable to attend) that the faid *Philip Hand* is very aged and infirm; that he has been in the Service of the Country, as fet forth in his Petition, and that one of his Arms is greatly difabled, and much fcarified, which he affirms was occafioned by a Wound he received in the Service; that by his extreme Poverty, and enfeebled State, it was very difficult for him to get a proper cer-tificate of his Cafe, from the late Surgeon of the Regiment, in which he ferved; and, in the mean Time, muft fuffer the Miferies incident to his diftreffed Circumftances.

Whereupon your *Committee* came to the following Refolution.

Refolved, That it is the Opinion of this Committee, that the faid Petition is reafonable.

The faid *Refolution*, being read a fecond Time, was, upon the Queftion put there-upon, agreed to by the Houfe.

Refolved, That the Sum of fix Pounds be paid to *Philip Hand*, for his prefent Relief, and the Sum of five Pounds, *per Annum*, during his Life.

Ordered, That Mr *Rutherford* do carry the Refolution to the Council, and defire their Concurrence.

Ordered, That Mr *Carrington* be added to the Gentlemen, who are appointed to prepare and bring in a Bill, for regulating the Method of fuing out Writs of *Alias Capias*, in the County Courts, for altering *Loudoun* Court Day, and for other Purpofes.

Ordered, That it be an Inftruction to the Gentlemen who are appointed to prepare and bring in the faid Bill, that they do make Provifion therein for altering the Court Day of the County of *Pittfylvania*.

An

An engroſſed *Bill*, for further continuing the Acts, for better regulating and diſciplining the Militia, was read the third Time.

An engroſſed *Clauſe* was offered to be added to the ſaid Bill, by Way of Ryder, for exempting the diſſenting Proteſtants, called *Menoniſts*, from performing Military Duty.

And the ſaid *Clauſe* was thrice read, and, upon the Queſtion put thereupon, agreed to by the Houſe, to be made Part of the Bill by Way of Ryder.

Reſolved, That the Bill do paſs; and that the Title be, *An Act[1] for further continuing and amending the Acts, for better regulating and diſciplining the Militia.*

Ordered, That Mr *Bland* do carry the Bill to the Council, and deſire their Concurrence.

A *Bill* to amend an Act, intituled *An Act[2] directing the Duty of Surveyors of Land*, was read a ſecond Time.

Reſolved, That the Bill be committed to the Committee of Propoſitions and Grievances.

A *Bill* to amend an Act, intituled *An Act[3] for the better Preſervation of the Breed of Deer, and preventing unlawful hunting*, was read a ſecond Time.

Reſolved, That the Bill be committed to Mr *Cary*, Mr *Waſhington*, and Mr *Henry Lee*.

A *Bill* to impower the Veſtry of the Pariſh of *Saint George*, in *Spotſylvania* County, to ſell Part of the Church Yard within the Town of *Frederickſburg*, was read a ſecond Time.

Ordered, That the Bill be engroſſed.

And then the Houſe adjourned till Tomorrow Morning, eleven of the Clock.

Friday, the 3rd of April. 12 George III. 1772.

MR *Harriſon* reported from the Committee, to whom the Bill for erecting a Lighthouſe on Cape *Henry*, was committed, that the Committee had gone through the Bill, and made ſeveral Amendments thereunto, which they had directed him to report to the Houſe; and he read the Report in his Place, and afterwards delivered the Bill, with the Amendments, in at the Clerk's Table; where the Amendments were once read throughout, and then a ſecond Time, one by one, and, upon the Queſtion ſeverally put thereupon, were agreed to by the Houſe.

Ordered, That the Bill, with the Amendments, be engroſſed.

Mr *Adams* preſented to the Houſe, according to Order, a Bill to dock the Intail of certain Lands whereof *Calwell Pettypool* and *Mary* his Wife are ſeiſed in Fee Tail, for Purpoſes therein mentioned; and the ſame was received, and read the firſt Time.

Reſolved, That the Bill be read a ſecond Time.

Ordered, That the Bill be now read a ſecond Time.

The *Bill* was accordingly read a ſecond Time.

Reſolved, That the Bill be committed to Mr *Adams*, Mr *Cary*, Mr *DuVal*, Mr *Carrington*, and Mr *Claiborne*.

Mr *Bland* reported to the Houſe, that their Addreſs, of *Friday* the 27th of laſt Month (that the Governor will be pleaſed to order the Court of the County of *Spotſylvania* to be adjourned to, and held at, ſome Place in or near the Centre of the County) had been preſented to his Excellency, who was pleaſed to ſay, that the Addreſs relates to a Queſtion of pure Prerogative, and that he would conſider of it, and ſend an Anſwer to the Houſe.

An engroſſed *Bill* to exempt certain Counties from the Regulations of an Act, for continuing and amending the Act, intituled *An Act[4] for the better regulating and collecting certain Officers Fees, and for other Purpoſes therein mentioned*, was read the third Time.

An engroſſed *Clauſe* was offered to be added to the ſaid Bill, by Way of Ryder, relating to Officers Fees which were due before the 20th Day of *January* laſt.

And the ſaid *Clauſe* was thrice read, and, upon the Queſtion put thereupon, agreed to by the Houſe, to be made Part of the Bill, by Way of Ryder.

Reſolved

---

[1] Not recorded as a law.　　[2] Hening, VI, p. 33.　　[3] Ibid, V, p. 60.　　[4] Ibid V, p. 38.

Refolved, That the Bill do pafs; and that the Title be, *An Act*[1] *to except certain Counties out of an Act, for continuing and amending the Act, intituled an Act for the better regulating and collecting certain Officers Fees, and for other Purpofes therein mentioned.*

Ordered, That M[r] *William Cabell* do carry the Bill to the Council, and defire their Concurrence.

The Houfe was moved, that the Order made upon *Friday* the 20th Day of laft Month, that the Committee of Propofitions and Grievances do prepare, and bring in a Bill, purfuant to the laft Refolution of the faid Committee, which was upon that Day reported, and agreed to by the Houfe, might be read.

And the fame being read accordingly;

Ordered, That the faid Order be difcharged.

M[r] *Bland* reported from the Committee of Propofitions and Grievances, to whom the Bill for appointing Commiffioners to view the Lands, on both Sides of *James* River, from *Weftham* to the navigable Water, below the Falls of the faid River, and for other Purpofes therein mentioned, was committed, that the Committee had gone through the Bill, and made an Amendment thereunto, which they had directed him to report to the Houfe; and he read the report in his Place, and afterwards delivered the Bill, with the Amendment, in at the Clerk's Table; where the Amendment was twice read, and, upon the Queftion put thereupon, was agreed to by the Houfe.

Ordered, That the Bill, with the Amendment, be engroffed.

Ordered, That Leave be given to bring in a Bill for opening and extending the Navigation of the River *Potowmack,* from Fort *Cumberland,* to Tide Water; and that M[r] *Thompfon Mafon,* M[r] *Wafhington,* M[r] *Weft,* M[r] *Francis Peyton,* M[r] *Tebbs,* M[r] *Marfhall,* M[r] *Scott,* M[r] *Henry Lee,* M[r] *Alexander,* and M[r] *Yelverton Peyton,* do prepare and bring in the fame.

M[r] *Treafurer* reported to the Houfe, that their Addrefs of *Tuefday* laft, concerning the Earl of *Hillfborough's* Letter on the Subject of Copper Money, had been prefented to his Excellency the Governor, who was pleafed to fay, that he would tranfmit the Addrefs to Lord *Hillfborough,* and endeavor to forward the Wifhes of the Houfe therein expreffed.

Ordered, That Leave be given to bring in a Bill to amend fo much of an Act of Affembly, intituled *An Act*[2] *for the Infpection of Pork, Beef, Flour, Tar, Pitch, and Turpentine,* as relates to the Infpection of Flour; and that M[r] *Cary,* M[r] *Wafhington,* M[r] *Harrifon,* M[r] *Banifter,* M[r] *Bolling,* and M[r] *Eyre,* do prepare and bring in the fame.

An engroffed *Bill* to dock the Intail of certain Lands whereof *William Todd,* Gentleman, is feifed, and for other Purpofes therein mentioned, was read the third Time.

Refolved, That the Bill do pafs; and that the Title be, *An Act*[3] *to dock the Intail of certain Lands whereof* William Todd, *Gentleman, is feifed, and for other Purpofes therein mentioned.*

Ordered, That M[r] *Carrington* do carry the Bill to the Council, and defire their Concurrence.

A *Bill* for the Eafe and Relief of the People, by paying the Burgeffes Wages in Money, for the prefent Seffion of Affembly, was read a fecond Time.

Ordered, That the Bill be engroffed.

M[r] *Treafurer* reported from the Committee for Religion, to whom the Bill for dividing the Parifhes of *Southam,* in the County of *Cumberland,* and *Dale,* in the County of *Chefterfield,* was committed, that the Committee had gone through the Bill, and made feveral Amendments thereunto, which they had directed him to report to the Houfe; and he read the Report in his Place, and afterwards delivered the Bill, with the Amendments, in at the Clerk's Table; where the Amendments were once read throughout, and then a fecond Time, one by one, and, upon the Queftion feverally put thereupon, were agreed to by the Houfe.

Ordered, That the Bill, with the Amendments, be engroffed.

M[r] *Cary* prefented to the Houfe, according to Order, a Bill to amend fo much of an Act of Affembly, intituled *An Act*[4] *for the Infpection of Pork, Beef, Flour, Tar, Pitch, and*

[1] Not recorded as a law.   [2] Hening, VII, p. 570.   [3] Ibid, VIII, p. 631.   [4] Ibid, VII, p. 570.

and Turpentine, as relates to the Infpection of Flour; and the fame was received, and read the firft Time.

Refolved, That the Bill be read a fecond Time.

A *Bill* to repeal fo much of the Act, made in the fifth Year of his prefent Majefty's Reign, as eftablifhes a Ferry from the Land of *Cornelius Thomas*, in the County of *Amherft*, over the *Fluvanna* River, to the Land of *Nicholas Davies*, oppofite thereto, in the County of *Bedford*, was read a fecond Time.

Refolved, That the Bill be committed to Mr *Carrington*, and Mr *Bowyer*.

A *Bill* to allow the Minifter of the Parifh of *Antrim*, in the County of *Halifax*, the fame Salary as other Minifters are intitled to receive, under an Act of Affembly, paffed in the 22^d Year of his late Majefty's Reign, intituled *An Act[1] for the Support of the Clergy, and for the regular collecting the Parifh Levies*, was read a fecond Time.

Ordered, That the Bill be engroffed.

An engroffed *Bill* to continue an Act, intituled *An Act[2] to continue and amend an Act, intituled an Act for reducing the feveral Acts made for laying a Duty upon Liquors, into one Act*, was read the third Time.

141   *Refolved*, That the Bill do pafs; and that the Title be, *An Act[3] to continue an Act, intituled an Act to continue and amend an Act, intituled an Act for reducing the feveral Acts, made for laying a Duty upon Liquors, into one Act.*

Ordered, That Mr *Harrifon* do carry the Bill to the Council, and defire their Concurrence.

A *Bill* for dividing the County of *Botetourt* into two diftinct Counties, was read a fecond Time.

Ordered, That the Bill be engroffed.

The *Orders* of the Day being read;

Refolved, That this Houfe will, Tomorrow, refolve itfelf into a Committee of the whole Houfe, upon the Bill to amend the Act, intituled, *An Act[4] directing the Trial of Slaves committing capital Offences, and for the more effectual punifhing Confpiracies and Infurrections of them, and for the better Government of Negroes, Mulattoes, and Indians, bond or free.*

Refolved, That this Houfe will, Tomorrow, refolve itfelf into a Committee of the whole Houfe, upon the Bill to amend the Act, intituled, *An Act[5] prefcribing the Method of appointing Sheriffs, and for limiting the Time of their Continuance in Office, and directing their Duty therein.*

Ordered, That the further Confideration of the Book of Public Claims be further adjourned till Tomorrow.

An engroffed *Bill* to enable the *Nottoway* Indians to leafe certain Lands, and for other Purpofes therein mentioned, was read the third Time.

Refolved, That the Bill do pafs; and that the Title be, *An Act[6] to enable the* Nottoway *Indians to leafe certain Lands, and for other Purpofes therein mentioned.*

Ordered, That Mr *Gray* do carry the Bill to the Council, and defire their Concurrence.

A *Bill* for regulating the Allowances to the Keeper of the public Prifon, for the Maintenance of poor Prifoners for Debt, and Runaways, was read a fecond Time.

Refolved, That the Bill be committed to Mr *Bland*, Mr *Nelfon*, Mr *Cary*, Mr *Carrington*, and Mr *Bowyer*.

An engroffed *Bill* to appoint Commiffioners to view a Place propofed for a Road through the *South* Mountains, was read the third Time.

Refolved, That the Bill do pafs; and that the Title be, *An Act[7] to appoint Commiffioners to view a Place propofed for a Road through the* South *Mountain.*

Ordered, That Mr *Lewis* do carry the Bill to the Council, and defire their Concurrence.

A *Bill* to amend the feveral Acts of Affembly refpecting the Currency of Copper Money, in this Colony, was read a fecond Time.

Ordered, That the Bill be engroffed.

An

---

[1] Hening, VI, p. 88.   [2] Ibid, VIII, p. 335.   [3] Ibid, VIII, p. 529.   [4] Ibid, VI. p. 104.
[5] Ibid, V, p. 515.   [6] Ibid, VIII, p. 588.   [7] Ibid, VIII, p. 552.

An engroffed *Bill* to permit certain Perfons, therein mentioned, to erect Gates acrofs the public Roads, leading through their Lands, was read the third Time.

Refolved, That the Bill do pafs; and that the Title be, *An Act[1] to permit certain Perfons, therein mentioned, to erect Gates acrofs the public Roads, leading through their Lands.*

Ordered, That Mr *Bland* do carry the Bill to the Council, and defire their Concurrence,

Mr *Cary* reported from the Committee, to whom the Bill to amend an Act, intituled. *An Act[2] for the better Prefervation of the Breed of Deer, and preventing unlawful Hunting*, was committed, that the Committee had gone through the Bill, and made an Amendment thereunto, which they had directed him to report to the Houfe; and he read the Report in his Place, and afterwards delivered the Bill, with the Amendment, in at the Clerk's Table; where the Amendment was twice read, and, upon the Queftion put thereupon, agreed to by the Houfe.

Ordered, That the Bill, with the Amendment, be engroffed.

An engroffed *Bill* to compel Ships, importing Convicts, Servants, or Slaves, infected with the Gaol Fever, or Small Pox, to perform Quarantine, was read the third Time.

Refolved, That the Bill do pafs; and that the Title be, *An Act[3] to compel Ships, importing Convicts, Servants, or Slaves, infected with the Gaol Fever, or Small Pox, to perform Quarantine.*

Ordered, That Mr *Treafurer* do carry the Bill to the Council, and defire their Concurrence.

A *Bill* to veft certain entailed Lands, whereof *Philip Ludwell Grymes*, Gentleman, is feifed, in *William Roane*, Gentleman, in Fee Simple, was read a fecond Time.

Refolved, That the Bill be committed to Mr *Nelfon*, Mr *Brooke*, Mr *Corbin*, Mr *Aylett*, Mr *Moore*, Mr *Berkeley*, and Mr *Montague*.

An engroffed *Bill* to enlarge the Power of the Truftees, appointed to carry into Execution an Act, paffed in this prefent Seffion of Affembly, intituled, *An Act[4] for cutting a navigable Canal from Archer's Hope Creek to Queen's Creek, through or near the City of Williamfburg*, was read the third Time.

An engroffed *Claufe* was offered to be added to the faid Bill, by Way of Ryder, for exempting certain Perfons from contributing towards the Expence of erecting Bridges over the faid Canal.

And the faid *Claufe* was thrice read, and, upon the Queftion put thereupon, agreed to by the Houfe to be made part of the Bill, by Way of Ryder.

Refolved, That the Bill do pafs; and that the Title be, *An Act[5] to enlarge the Power of the Truftees, appointed to carry into Execution an Act, paffed this prefent Seffion of Affembly, intituled An Act for cutting a navigable Canal from Archer's Hope Creek to Queen's Creek, through or near the City of Williamfburg.*

Ordered, That Mr *Nelfon* do carry the Bill to the Council, and defire their Concurrence.

Mr *Carrington* reported from the Committee, to whom the Bill to repeal fo much of the Act, made in the fifth Year of his prefent Majefty's Reign, as eftablifhes a Ferry from the Land of *Cornelius Thomas*, in the County of *Amherft*, over the *Fluvanna* River, to the Land of *Nicholas Davies*, oppofite thereto, in the County of *Bedford*, was committed, that the Committee had gone through the Bill, and made feveral Amendments thereunto; which they had directed him to report to the Houfe; and he read the Report in his Place, and afterwards delivered the Bill, with the Amendments, in at the Clerk's Table; where the Amendments were once read throughout, and then a fecond Time, one by one, and, upon the Queftion feverally put thereupon, were agreed to by the Houfe.

Ordered, That the Bill, with the Amendments, be engroffed.

An engroffed *Bill* to amend an Act, intituled *An Act[6] to amend an Act, intituled an Act to oblige the Owners of Mills, Hedges, or Stone Stops, on fundry Rivers therein mentioned, to make Openings or Slopes therein, for the Paffage of Fifh, and for other Purpofes therein mentioned*, was read the third Time.

Refolved

---

[1] Not recorded as a law.   [2] Hening, V, p. 60.   [3] Ibid, VIII, p. 537.   [4] Ibid, VIII, p. 556.
[5] Ibid, VIII, p. 562.   [6] Ibid, VII, p. 590.

Refolved, That the Bill do pafs; and that the Title be; *An Act¹ to amend an Act, intituled an Act to amend an Act, intituled an Act to oblige the Owners of Mills, Hedges, or Stone Stops, on fundry Rivers therein mentioned, to make Openings or Slopes therein, for the Paffage of Fifh, and for other Purpofes therein mentioned.*

148 *Ordered*, That Mr *John Jones* do carry the Bill to the Council, and defire their Concurrence.

An engroffed *Bill* for appointing Truftees for the Town of *Cobham*, and for other Purpofes therein mentioned, was read the third Time.

Refolved, That the Bill do pafs; and that the Title be, *An Act² for appointing Truftees for the Town of* Cobham, *and for other Purpofes therein mentioned.*

Ordered, That Mr *Bland* do carry the Bill to the Council, and defire their Concurrence.

An engroffed *Bill* for appointing Commiffioners to afcertain the Value of certain Churches and Chapels, in the Parifhes of *Frederick, Norborne,* and *Beckford,* and for other Purpofes therein mentioned, was read the third Time.

Refolved, That the Bill do pafs; and that the Title be, *An Act³ for appointing Commiffioners to afcertain the Value of certain Churches and Chapels, in the Parifhes of* Frederick, Norborne, *and* Beckford, *and for other Purpofes therein mentioned.*

Ordered, That Mr *Treafurer* do carry the Bill to the Council, and defire their Concurrence.

An engroffed *Bill* for appointing Commiffioners for felling the Tobacco, damaged in the public Warehoufe at *Morton's*, was read the third Time.

Refolved, That the Bill do pafs; and that the Title be, *An Act⁴ for appointing Commiffioners for felling the Tobacco damaged in the public Warehoufe, for the Infpection of Tobacco, at* Morton's, *and for other Purpofes therein mentioned.*

Ordered, That Mr *Alexander* do carry the Bill to the Council, and defire their Concurrence.

And then the Houfe adjourned till Tomorrow Morning, eleven of the Clock.

Saturday, the 4th of April, 12 George III. 1772.

AN engroffed *Bill* for appointing Commiffioners to view the Lands on both Sides of *James* River, from *Weftham* to the navigable Water, below the Falls of the faid River, and for other Purpofes therein mentioned, was read the third Time.

Refolved, That the Bill do pafs; and that the Title be, *An Act⁵ for opening the Falls of* James *River by Subfcription, and for other Purpofes.*

Ordered, That Mr *Bland* do carry the Bill to the Council, and defire their Concurrence.

Mr *Eyre* reported from the Committee of Trade, to whom the Bill to encourage the further Settlement of the Town of *Alexandria*, in the County of *Fairfax*, was committed, that the Committee had gone through the Bill, and made an Amendment thereunto, which they had directed him to report to the Houfe; and he read the Report in his Place, and afterwards delivered the Bill, with the Amendment, in at the Clerk's Table; where the Amendment was twice read, and, upon the Queftion put thereupon, was agreed to by the Houfe.

Ordered, That the Bill, with the Amendment, be engroffed.

Mr *Thomfon Mafon* prefented to the Houfe, according to Order, a Bill for regulating the Method of fuing out Writs of *Alias Capias*, in the County Courts, for altering *Loudoun* Court Day, and for other Purpofes; and the fame was received, and read the firft Time.

Refolved, That the Bill be read a fecond Time.

144 *Ordered*, That the Bill be now read a fecond Time.

The *Bill* was accordingly read a fecond Time.

Refolved

¹ Hening, VIII, p. 583.   ² Ibid, VIII, p. 617.   ³ Ibid, VIII, p. 623.   ⁴ Ibid, VIII, p. 626.
⁵ Ibid, VIII, p, 564.

Refolved, That the Bill be committed to Mᵣ *Thomfon Mafon*, Mᵣ *Francis Peyton*, and Mᵣ *Carrington*.

Mᵣ *Bland* reported from the Committee of Propofitions and Grievances, to whom the Petition of *William Aylett* had been referred, and to whom the Report of the faid Committee thereupon was recommitted, that the Committee had examined the Matter of the faid petition, and had come to feveral Refolutions thereupon, which they had directed him to report to the Houfe; and he read the Report in his Place, and afterwards delivered it in at the Clerk's Table; where the Refolutions of the Committee were read, and are as followeth, *viz.*

Refolved, That it is the Opinion of this Committee, that fo much of the Petition, as prays that the Petitioner may be at Liberty to give up the Warehoufes in *King William* County, of which he is Proprietor, to the Public, and that he may be paid for the fame by the Public, be rejected.

Refolved, That it is the Opinion of this Committee, that the Refidue of the faid Petition, praying fuch other Relief as the Houfe fhall think fit to grant, is reafonable.

The faid *Refolutions*, being feverally read a fecond Time, were, upon the Queftion feverally put thereupon, agreed to by the Houfe.

Ordered, That the faid Report do lie upon the Table.

Mᵣ *Nelfon* reported from the Committee, to whom the Bill to veft certain intailed Lands, whereof *Philip Ludwell Grymes*, Gentleman, is feifed, in *William Roane*, Gentleman, in Fee Simple, was committed, that the Committee had examined the Allegations of the Bill, and found the fame to be true; and that the Committee had gone through the Bill, and made an Amendment thereunto, which they had directed him to report to the Houfe; and he read the Report in his Place, and afterwards delivered the Bill, with the Amendment, in at the Clerk's Table; where the Amendment was twice read, and, upon the Queftion put thereupon, was agreed to by the Houfe.

Ordered, That the Bill, with the Amendment, be engroffed.

Mᵣ *Bland* reported from the Committee of Propofitions and Grievances, to whom the Bill to continue and amend the Act, intituled *An Act¹ to continue and amend the Act intituled An Act for amending the Staple of Tobacco, and for preventing Frauds in his Majefty's Cuftoms*, was committed, that the Committee had gone through the Bill, and made an Amendment thereunto, which they had directed him to report to the Houfe; and he read the Report in his Place, and afterwards delivered the Bill, with the Amendment, in at the Clerk's Table; where the Amendment was twice read, and, upon the Queftion put thereupon, was agreed to by the Houfe.

Ordered, That the Bill, with the Amendment, be engroffed.

The *Orders* of the Day being read;

Refolved, That this Houfe will, upon *Monday* next, refolve itfelf into a Committee of the whole Houfe upon the Bill, to amend the Act, intituled *An Act² directing the Trial of Slaves, committing capital Offences, and for the more effectual punifhing Confpiracies and Infurrections of them, and for the better Government of Negroes, Mulattoes, and Indians, bond or free.*

Refolved, That this Houfe will, upon *Monday* next, refolve itfelf into a Committee of the whole Houfe upon the Bill to amend the Act, intituled, *An Act³ prefcribing the Method of appointing Sheriffs, and for limiting the Time of their Continuance in Office, and directing their Duty therein.*

Ordered, That the further Confideration of the Book of Public Claims be further adjourned till *Monday* next.

Refolved, That feventy-feven Pounds of Tobacco be allowed to *David Garland*, Sheriff of the County of *Lunenburg*, for fummoning eleven Witneffes, to be examined before Commiffioners, touching the Matter of the Petition of Mᵣ *Thomas Pettus*, complaining of an undue Election of Mᵣ*Henry Blagrave*, to ferve as a Burgefs, in this prefent General Affembly, for the faid County, on Behalf of Mᵣ *Blagrave*.

Ordered

ᵣ Hening, VIII, p, 318,   ² Ibid, VI, p, 104,   ³ Ibid, V, p, 515.

Ordered, That the faid Allowance be entered in the Book of Public Claims, by the Clerk.

And the faid *Allowance* was entered accordingly.

A *Motion* was made, and the Queftion being put, that the faid feventy-feven Pounds of Tobacco be levied upon the faid *Henry Blagrave;*

It was refolved in the Affirmative.

Ordered, That the Allowance of the faid feventy-feven Pounds of Tobacco to the County of *Lunenburg,* to be levied upon the faid *Henry Blagrave,* be entered in the Book of Public Claims by the Clerk.

And the faid *Allowance* was entered accordingly.

And then the Houfe adjourned till Monday Morning next, eleven of the Clock.

𝔐onday, the 6th of April, George III. 1772.

ORDERED, That Mr *Carrington,* Mr *Brooke,* and Mr *Holt,* be added to the Committee, who are appointed to examine the enrolled Bills.

Mr *Bland* reported from the Committee of Propofitions and Grievances, to whom the Bill for further continuing the Acts for the more effectual keeping the public Roads and Bridges in Repair, was committed, that the Committee had gone through the Bill, and made an Amendment thereunto, which they had directed him to report to the Houfe, and he read the Report in his Place, and afterwards delivered the Bill, with the Amendment, in at the Clerk's Table; where the Amendment was twice read, and, upon the Queftion put thereupon, was agreed to by the Houfe.

Ordered, That the Bill, with the Amendment, be engroffed.

The Houfe, according to Order, refumed the adjourned Confideration of the Book of Public Claims.

And the *Refidue* of the faid Book was read.

And feveral *Claims* were added to the Book, by the Houfe.

Refolved, That the Book of Public Claims do pafs.

Ordered, That Mr *Cary* do carry the Book of Public Claims to the Council, and defire their Concurrence.

An engroffed *Bill* to repeal fo much of the Act made in the fifth Year of his prefent Majefty's Reign as eftablifhes a Ferry from the Land of *Cornelius Thomas,* in the County of *Amherft,* over the *Fluvanna* River, to the Land of *Nicholas Davies,* oppofite thereto, in the County of *Bedford,* was read the third Time.

Refolved, That the Bill do pafs; and that the Title be, *An Act*[1] *for appointing feveral Ferries, and difcontinuing others, and for other Purpofes.*

Ordered, That Mr *Bland* do carry the Bill to the Council, and defire their Concurrence.

Mr *Thomfon Mafon* prefented to the Houfe, according to Order, a Bill for opening and extending the Navigation of the River *Potowmack,* from Fort *Cumberland* to Tide Water; and the fame was received, and read the firft Time.

Refolved, That the Bill be read a fecond Time.

Ordered, That the Bill be now read a fecond Time.

The *Bill* was accordingly read a fecond Time.

Ordered, That the Bill be engroffed.

Mr *Bland* reported from the Committee of Propofitions and Grievances, to whom the Bill for regulating the Allowances to the Keeper of the public Prifon for the Maintenance of poor Prifoners, for Debt, and Runaways, was committed, that the Committee had gone through the Bill, and made feveral Amendments thereunto, which they had directed him to report to the Houfe; and he read the Report in his Place, and afterwards delivered the Bill, with the Amendments, in at the Clerk's Table; where the Amendments

were

---

[1] *See* Hening, VIII, p. 554.

were once read throughout, and then a second Time, one by one, and, upon the Question severally put thereupon, were agreed to by the House.

Ordered, That the Bill, with the Amendments, be engroffed.

A *Meffage* from the Governor, by M*r Blair:*

M*r Speaker,*

I am commanded by his Excellency the Governor, to deliver to this House a written Meffage, in Answer to their Address, that he would be pleafed to order the Court of the County of Spotfylvania *to be adjourned to, and held at, fome Place in or near the Centre of the County.*

The faid *Meffage* was read, and is as followeth, *viz.*

M*r Speaker, and Gentlemen of the House of Burgeffes,*

I have maturely confidered your Address, and from every Information, which I have been able to procure, it does not appear to me, that the Removal of the Court-House of Spotfylvania *County would be attended with any Benefit, but, on the contrary, that it is for the moft general Advantage of the Inhabitants that it remain where it is at prefent.*

M*r Thomfon Mafon* reported from the Committee, to whom the Bill for regulating the Method of fuing out Writs of *Alias Capias,* in the County Courts, for altering *Loudoun* Court Day, and for other Purpofes, was committed, that the Committee had directed him to report the Bill to the House, without any Amendment; and he delivered the Bill in at the Clerk's Table.

Ordered, That the Bill be engroffed.

A *Meffage* from the Council by M*r Blair:*

M*r Speaker,*

The *Council have agreed to the* Bill, *intituled* An Act[1] to continue an Act, intituled an Act to continue and amend an Act, intituled an Act for reducing the feveral Acts, made for laying a Duty upon Liquors, into one Act, *without any Amendment; and alfo,*

The *Council have agreed to the* Bill, *intituled* An Act[2] to compel Ships, importing Convicts, Servants, or Slaves, infected with the Gaol Fever, or Small Pox, to perform Quarantine, *without any Amendment; and alfo,*

The *Council have agreed to the* Bill, *intituled* An Act[3] to appoint Commiffioners to view a Place propofed for a Road through the South Mountain, *without any Amendment; and alfo,*

The *Council have agreed to the* Bill, *intituled* An Act[4] to dock the Intail of certain Lands, whereof *William Todd,* Gentleman, is feifed, and for other Purpofes therein mentioned, *without any Amendment; and alfo,*

The *Council have agreed to the* Bill, *intituled* An Act[5] to explain and amend an Act, intituled an Act to oblige the Owners of Mills, Hedges, or Stops, on the Rivers therein mentioned, to make Openings or Slopes therein, for the Paffage of Fifh, *without any Amendment; and alfo,*

The *Council have agreed to the* Bill, *intituled* An Act[6] for appointing Truftees for the Town of *Cobham,* and for other Purpofes therein mentioned, *without any Amendment; and alfo,*

The *Council have agreed to the* Bill, *intituled* An Act[7] for appointing Commiffioners, for felling the Tobacco damaged in the public Warehouse, for Infpection of Tobacco, at *Morton's,* and for other Purpofes therein mentioned, *without any Amendment; and alfo,*

The *Council have agreed to the* Bill, *intituled* An Act[8] for appointing Commiffioners to afcertain the Value of certain Churches and Chapels, in the Parifhes of *Frederick, Norborne,* and *Beckford,* and for other Purpofes therein mentioned, *without any Amendment; and alfo,*

The

---

[1] Hening, VIII, p. 529. [2] Ibid, VIII, p. 537. [3] Ibid, VIII, p. 552. [4] Ibid, VIII, p. 631.
[5] Ibid, VIII, p. 581. [6] Ibid, VIII, p. 617. [7] Ibid, VIII, p. 626. [8] Ibid, VIII, p. 623.

147   *The Council have agreed to the* Refolve *for paying an Annuity to* John Burton; *and alfo,*

The Council have agreed to the Bill, *intituled* An Act[1] to enable the *Nottoway* Indians to leafe certain lands, and for other Purpofes therein mentioned, *with fome Amendments, to which Amendments the Council defire the Concurrence of this Houfe.*

And then the Meffenger withdrew.

The Houfe proceeded to take the faid Amendments into Confideration.

And the faid *Amendments* were read, and are as followeth, *viz.*

Line 24, after "*Lie*" infert "*fhall be.*"

Line 42, after "*Plant*" infert "*inclofe with good Fences, and cultivate.*"

The faid *Amendments*, being feverally read a fecond Time, were, upon the Queftion feverally put thereupon, agreed to by the Houfe.

Ordered, That Mr *Gray* do carry the Bill to the Council, and acquaint them that this Houfe hath agreed to the Amendments made by them.

Mr *Thomfon Mafon* reported from the Committee, to whom the Bill to eftablifh a Town on the Land of *John Rictor*, in the County of *Fauquier*, was committed, that the Committee had gone through the Bill, and made an Amendment thereunto, which they had directed him to report to the Houfe; and he read the Report in his Place, and afterwards delivered the Bill, with the Amendment, in at the Clerk's Table; where the Amendment was twice read, and, upon the Queftion put thereupon, was agreed to by the Houfe.

Ordered, That the Bill, with the Amendments, be engroffed.

An engroffed *Bill* for clearing a Road from the Warm Springs, in *Augufta*, and for other Purpofes therein mentioned, was read the third Time.

Refolved, That the Bill do pafs; and that the Title be, *An Act[2] for clearing a Road from the Warm Springs, in* Augufta, *and for other Purpofes therein mentioned.*

Ordered, That Mr *Bland* do carry the Bill to the Council, and defire their Concurrence.

Refolved, That the Sum of fifty Pounds be paid, by the Treafurer of this Colony, out of the Public Money in his Hands, to each of the Members of the Committee appointed by Law for examining the Treafurer's Accounts, and burning the Treafury Notes.

Ordered, That Mr *Bland* do carry the Refolution to the Council, and defire their Concurrence.

An engroffed *Bill* for dividing the Parifhes of *Southam*, in the County of *Cumberland*, and *Dale*, in the County of *Chefterfield*, was read the third Time.

Refolved, That the Bill do pafs; and that the Title be, *An Act[3] for dividing the Parifhes of* Southam, *in the County of* Cumberland, *and* Dale, *in the County of* Chefterfield.

Ordered, That Mr *Treafurer* do carry the Bill to the Council, and defire their Concurrence.

Mr *Bland* prefented to the Houfe, according to Order, a Bill for calling in and finking the old Treafury Notes, now in Circulation; and the fame was received, and read the firft Time.

Refolved, That the Bill be read a fecond Time.

The other *Orders* of the Day being read;

Refolved, That this Houfe will, Tomorrow, refolve itfelf into a Committee of the whole Houfe, upon the Bill to amend the Act, intituled *An Act[4] directing the Trial of Slaves, committing capital Offences, and for the more effectual punifhing Confpiracies and Infurrections of them, and for the better Government of Negroes, Mulattoes, and Indians, bond or free.*

148   *Refolved*, That this Houfe will, Tomorrow, refolve itfelf into a Committee of the whole Houfe upon the Bill to amend the Act, intituled *An Act[5] prefcribing the Method of*

---

[1] Hening, VIII, p. 588.   [2] Ibid, VIII, p. 546.   [3] Ibid, VIII, p. 603.   [4] Ibid, VI, p. 104.
[5] Ibid, V, p. 515.

of appointing Sheriffs, and for limiting the Time of their Continuance in Office, and directing their Duty therein.

An engroffed *Bill* to empower the Veftry of the Parifh of *Saint George,* in *Spotfylvania* County, to fell Part of the Church Yard, within the Town of *Frederickfburg,* was read the third Time.

Refolved, That the Bill do pafs; and that the Title be, *An Act¹ to empower the Veftry of the Parifh of* Saint George, *in* Spotfylvania, *to fell Part of the Church Yard.*

Ordered, That Mʳ *Mann Page* do carry the Bill to the Council, and defire their Concurrence.

An engroffed *Bill* for the Eafe and Relief of the People, by paying the Burgeffes Wages, in Money, for the prefent Seffion of Affembly, was read the third Time.

Refolved, That the Bill do pafs; and that the Title be, *An Act² for the Eafe and Relief of the People, by paying the Burgeffes Wages in Money, for the prefent Seffion of Affembly.*

Ordered, That Mʳ *Henry Lee* do carry the Bill to the Council, and defire their Concurrence.

And then the Houfe adjourned till Tomorrow Morning eleven of the Clock.

Tuesday, the 7th of April, 12 George III. 1772.

ANOTHER *Member* having taken the Oaths appointed to be taken by Act of Parliament, and repeated and fubfcribed the Teft, took his Place in the Houfe.

Mʳ *Carrington* reported from the Committee, to whom the Bill to dock the Intail of certain Lands, whereof *Colwell Pettypool* and *Mary* his Wife are feifed in Fee Tail, for Purpofes therein mentioned, was committed, that the Committee had examined the Allegations of the Bill, and found the fame to be true; and that the Committee had gone through the Bill, and made feveral Amendments thereunto, which they had directed him to report to the Houfe; and he read the Report in his Place, and afterwards delivered the Bill, with the Amendments, in at the Clerk's Table; where the Amendments were once read throughout, and then a fecond Time, one by one, and, upon the Queftion feverally put thereupon, were agreed to by the Houfe.

Ordered, That the Bill, with the Amendments, be engroffed.

An engroffed *Bill* for erecting a Lighthoufe on Cape *Henry* was read the third Time.

Refolved, That the Bill do pafs; and that the Title be, *An Act³ for erecting a Lighthoufe on Cape* Henry.

Ordered, That Mʳ *Harrifon* do carry the Bill to the Council, and defire their Concurrence.

Mʳ *Harrifon* prefented to the Houfe, according to Order, a Bill to eftablifh a Jurifdiction for fuperintending the Conduct of the Clergy; and the fame was received, and read the firft Time.

Refolved, That the Bill be read a fecond Time.

A *Meffage* from the Council by Mʳ *Blair:*

Mʳ *Speaker,*
The Council have agreed to the Bill, *intituled* An Act⁴ to empower the Veftry of the Parifh of *Saint George,* in *Spotfylvania,* to fell part of the Church Yard, *without any Amendment; and alfo,*

The Council have agreed to the Bill, *intituled* An Act⁵ for further continuing and amending the Acts, for better regulating and difciplining the Militia, *with fome Amendments, to which Amendments the Council defire the Concurrence of this Houfe; and alfo,*

The Council have agreed to the Book of Public Claims.

And then the Meffenger withdrew.

Ordered

¹ Hening, VIII, p. 609. ² Ibid, VIII, p. 536. ³ Ibid, VIII, p. 539. ⁴ Ibid, VIII, p. 609.
⁵ Not recorded as a law.

Ordered, That Mr *Cary* do carry the Book of Public Claims to the Governor and defire his Excellency's Affent thereunto.

Mr *Bland* reported from the Committee of Propofitions and Grievances, to whom the Bill to amend an Act, intituled *An Act*[1] *directing the Duty of Surveyors of Land*, was committed, that the Committee had gone through the Bill, and made feveral Amendments thereunto, which they had directed him to report to the Houfe; and he read the Report in his Place, and afterwards delivered the Bill, with the Amendments, in at the Clerk's Table; where the Amendments were once read throughout, and then a fecond Time, one by one, and, upon the Queftion feverally put thereupon, were, with an Amendment to one of them, agreed to by the Houfe.

Ordered, That the Bill, with the Amendments, be engroffed.

Ordered, That Mr *Eyre* have Leave to be abfent from the Service of this Houfe till the End of this Seffion of General Affembly.

The Houfe, according to Order, refolved itfelf into a Committee of the whole Houfe, upon the Bill to amend the Act, intituled *An Act*[2] *directing the Trial of Slaves, committing capital Offences, and for the more effectual punifhing Confpiracies and Infurrections of them, and for the better Government of Negroes, Mulattoes, and Indians, bond or free.*

Mr *Speaker* left the Chair.

Mr *Bland* took the Chair of the Committee.

Mr *Speaker* refumed the Chair.

Mr *Bland* reported from the Committee, that they had gone through the Bill, and made feveral Amendments thereunto, which they had directed him to report, when the Houfe will pleafe to receive the fame.

Ordered, That the Report be now received.

Mr *Bland* accordingly reported from the faid Committee the Amendments which the Committee had made to the Bill, and which they had directed him to report to the Houfe; and he read the Report in his Place, and afterwards delivered the Bill, with the Amendments, in at the Clerk's Table; where the Amendments were once read throughout, and then a fecond Time, one by one, and, upon the Queftion feverally put thereupon, were, with an Amendment to one of them, agreed to by the Houfe.

Ordered, That the Bill, with the Amendments, be engroffed.

The other *Order* of the Day being read;

Refolved, That this Houfe will, Tomorrow, refolve itfelf into a Committee of the whole Houfe, upon the Bill to amend the Act, intituled *An Act*[3] *prefcribing the Method of appointing Sheriffs, and for limiting the Time of their Continuance in Office, and directing their Duty therein.*

The Houfe proceeded to take into Confideration the Amendments made by the Council to the Bill, intituled *An Act*[4] *for further continuing and amending the Acts, for better regulating and difciplining the Militia.*

And the faid *Amendments* were read, and are as followeth, *viz.*

Line 14, after 'notwithftanding,' infert 'and whereas, in the faid firft recited Act, it is enacted, that the Commanding Officer, prefiding at any Court Martial, fhall adminifter the Oath to the other Members of the Court; but no provifion is therein made, and Directions given, for fwearing the prefiding Officer: Be it therefore enacted by the Authority aforefaid, that any Field Officer, then prefent, fhall firft adminifter the Oath to the Commanding Officer, who fhall afterwards adminifter the Oath to the reft of the Officers of the Court. And whereas, by the Act made in the third Year of his prefent Majefty's Reign, intituled An Act*[5] *for amending, and further continuing the Act, for the better regulating and difciplining the Militia, all his Majefty's Juftices of the Peace, within this Colony, who have qualified themfelves for their Offices, by taking the Oaths by Law appointed to be taken by Juftices of the Peace, and who are really and* bona fide *acting Juftices of their refpective Counties, are to be free and exempt from appearing or muftering, either at the private, or General* 150 *Mufters, which Exemption is found, by Experience, to be extremely injurious and detrimental*

1 Hening, VI, p. 33.   2 Ibid, VI, p. 104.   3 Ibid, V, p. 515.   4 Ibid, VIII, p. 503.
5 Ibid, VII, p. 534.

mental to the forming a regular and useful Militia, by withdrawing from the Service a Body of Men, who are best qualified to execute the Commands of Captain, Lieutenant, or Ensign: Be it therefore enacted, by the Authority aforesaid, that so much of the said last recited Act, *as relates to the Exemption of the Justices of the Peace from mustering, be, and the same is hereby declared to be repealed, and made void.*'

Line 26 after '*Amherst*,' insert '*Culpeper*.'

Line 35, leave out '*Menonists*,' and insert '*Mennonites*,' instead thereof.

Line 40, leave out '*Menonists*,' and insert '*Mennonites*,' instead thereof.

The first of the said *Amendments* being read a second Time;

The following *Amendments* were proposed to be made thereunto:

After the Words '*Field Officer*,' to insert the Words '*or Captain*.'

To Leave out the Words, '*And whereas, by the Act made in the third Year of his present Majesty's Reign, intituled* An Act[1] *for amending, and further continuing the Act, for the better regulating and disciplining the Militia, all his Majesty's Justices of the Peace, within this Colony, who have qualified themselves for their Offices, by taking the Oaths by Law appointed to be taken by Justices of the Peace, and who are really and bona fide acting Justices of their respective Counties, are to be free and exempt from appearing or mustering, either at the private, or General Musters; which Exemption is found, by Experience, to be extremely injurious and detrimental to the forming a regular and useful Militia, by withdrawing from the Service a Body of Men, who are best qualified to execute the Commands of Captain, Lieutenant, or Ensign: Be it therefore enacted, by the Authority aforesaid, that so much of the said last recited Act, as relates to the Exemption of Justices of the Peace from mustering, be, and the same is hereby declared to be repealed, and made void.*'

And the same were, upon the Question severally put thereupon, agreed to by the House.

Then the said *Amendment*, thus amended, was, upon the Question put thereupon, agreed to by the House.

The next *Amendment*, being read a second Time, was, upon the Question put thereupon, disagreed to by the House.

The rest of the *Amendments*, being severally read a second Time, were, upon the Question severally put thereupon, agreed to by the House.

Ordered, That Mr *Bland* do carry the Bill to the Council, and acquaint them that this House doth agree to the first of the said Amendments by them proposed to the said Bill, with some Amendments to the said first Amendment, to which Amendments to the Amendment this House doth desire the Concurrence of the Council; and that this House doth disagree to the second of the said Amendments, and hath agreed to the rest of them.

A *Bill* to amend so much of an Act of Assembly, intituled *An Act*[2] *for the Inspection of Pork, Beef, Flour, Tar, Pitch, and Turpentine, as relates to the Inspection of Flour*, was read a second Time.

Resolved, That the Bill be committed to Mr *Cary*, Mr *Harrison*, Mr *Washington*, and Mr *Bolling*.

And then the House adjourned till Tomorrow Morning, eleven of the Clock.

Wednesday, the 8th of April, 12 George III. 1772.

MR *Harrison* reported to the House, that their Address, of *Wednesday* last, that the Governor would be pleased to transmit the Address of this House to his Majesty, and to support it in such Manner as he should think most likely to promote the desirable End proposed, had been presented to his Excellency, who was pleased to say, that he would transmit the Address to his Majesty, and use his Endeavours that the Wishes of the House should be accomplished.

An engrossed *Bill* to amend the several Acts of Assembly respecting the Currency of Copper Money in this Colony, was read the third Time.

Resolved

---

[1] Hening, VII, p. 534.   [2] Ibid, VIII, p. 511.

Refolved, That the Bill do pafs; and that the Title be *An Act[1] to amend the feveral Acts of Affembly refpecting the Currency of Copper Money in this Colony.*

151 *Ordered*, That Mr *Treafurer* do carry the Bill to the Council, and defire their Concurrence.

Ordered, That a Committee be appointed to proportion the Public Levy.

And a *Committee* was appointed of Mr *Cary*, Mr *Gray*, Mr *Taylor* and Mr *Hardy*.

A *Meffage* from the Council by Mr *Blair:*

Mr *Speaker*,

The Council have agreed to the Bill, *intituled* An Act[2] for the Eafe and Relief of the People, by paying the Burgeffes Wages in Money, for the prefent Seffion of Affembly, *without any Amendment; and alfo,*

The Council have agreed to the Bill, *intituled* An Act[3] for clearing a Road from the Warm Springs,in *Augufta*,and for other Purpofes therein mentioned, *without any Amendment; and alfo,*

The Council have agreed to the Bill, *intituled* An Act[4] for dividing the Parifhes of *Southam*, in the County of *Cumberland*, and *Dale*, in the County of *Chefterfield*, *without any Amendment; and alfo,*

The Council have agreed to the Bill, *intituled* An Act[5] for opening the Falls of *James* River, by Subfcription, and for other Purpofes, *with fome Amendments, to which Amendments the Council defire the Concurrence of this Houfe; and alfo,*

The Council have agreed to the Bill, *intituled* An Act[6] for appointing feveral Ferries, and difcontinuing others, and for other Purpofes, *with an Amendment, to which Amendment the Council defire the Concurrence of this Houfe; and alfo,*

The Council have agreed to the Refolve *for paying feveral Sums of Money to the Committee for examining the Treafurer's Accounts, and burning the Treafury Notes; and alfo,*

The Council have agreed to the Refolve *for paying feveral Sums of Money to* Philip Hand.

And then the Meffenger withdrew.

The Houfe proceeded to take into Confideration the Amendments made by the Council to the Bill, intituled *An Act[7] for opening the Falls of* James *River, by Subfcription, and for other Purpofes.*

And the faid *Amendments* were read, and are as followeth, *viz.*

Page 2, Line 43, leave out "*two Shillings,*" and infert "*one Shilling,*" inftead thereof.

Line 45, leave out "*half Penny.*"

Page 3, Line 28, after "*Affigns*" infert '*provided neverthelefs, that every Veffel, returning up the faid Canal, after having delivered her Load below, fhall be exempt from paying any Toll, except for Goods or Merchandizes fuch Veffel fhall then have on Board.*'

Page 4, Line 3, after '*River*' infert '*fo far as they may be damaged by the Canal.*'

Line 4, after '*valued*' infert '*and the Bounds thereof defcribed and afcertained.*'

Line 7, after '*erected*' infert '*provided always, that if it fhould appear, that the Damage done to any Perfon's Land, through which the faid Canal fhall be cut, was not confidered in fuch Valuation, the Owner of fuch Lands may, by applying to the faid Court, procure the fame to be reviewed, and fuch damage to be eftimated, in the fame Manner as is herein before prefcribed, and fhall be entitled to receive and recover fuch new Valuation from the faid Truftees, and fhall, in the fame Manner, have the like further Remedy, as often as any new Damage fhall arife, not before confidered and valued.*'

The faid *Amendments* being feverally read a fecond Time, were, upon the Queftion feverally put thereupon, agreed to by the Houfe.

Ordered, That Mr *Bland* do carry the Bill to the Council, and acquaint them that this Houfe hath agreed to the Amendments made by them.

The Houfe proceeded to take into Confideration the Amendment made by the Council

[1] Hening, VIII, p. 534.   [2] Ibid, VIII, p. 536.   [3] Ibid, VIII, p. 546.   [4] Ibid, VIII, p. 603.
[5] Ibid, VIII, p. 564.   [6] Ibid, VIII, p. 554.   [7] Ibid, VIII, p. 564.

cil to the Bill, intituled *An Act¹ for appointing several Ferries, and discontinuing others, and for other Purposes.*

And the said *Amendment* was read, and is as followeth, *viz.*

Page 2, Line 22, leave out from '*expedient*' to the End of the Bill.

The said *Amendment*, being read a second Time, was, upon the Question put thereupon, disagreed to by the House.

Ordered, That a Message be sent to the Council, to acquaint them that this House doth disagree to the Amendment by them proposed to the said Bill, and doth desire that they will pass the same, without the said Amendment; and that Mᵣ *Bland* do carry the said Message.

An engrossed *Bill* to allow the Minister of the Parish of *Antrim*, in the County of *Halifax*, the same Salary as other Ministers are intitled to receive, under an Act of Assembly, passed in the 22ᵈ Year of his late Majesty's Reign, intituled *An Act² for the Support of the Clergy, and for the regular collecting the Parish Levies*, was read the third Time.

Resolved, That the Bill do pass; and that the Title be, *An Act³ to allow the Minister of the Parish of* Antrim, *in the County of* Halifax, *the same Salary as other Ministers are intitled to receive.*

Ordered, That Mᵣ Treasurer do carry the Bill to the Council, and desire their Concurrence.

An engrossed *Bill* for dividing the County of *Botetourt* into two distinct Counties, was read the third Time.

Resolved, That the Bill do pass; and that the Title be, *An Act⁴ for dividing the County of* Botetourt *into two distinct Counties.*

Ordered, That Mᵣ *Bland* do carry the Bill to the Council, and desire their Concurrence.

An engrossed *Bill* to vest certain intailed Lands, whereof *Philip Ludwell Grymes*, Gentleman, is seised, in *William Roane*, Gentleman, in Fee Simple, was read the third Time.

Resolved, That the Bill do pass; and that the Title be, *An Act⁵ to vest certain intailed Lands, whereof* Philip Ludwell Grymes, *Gentleman, is seised, in* William Roane, *Gentleman, in Fee Simple.*

Ordered, That Mᵣ *Nelson* do carry the Bill to the Council, and desire their Concurrence.

An engrossed *Bill* to amend an Act, intituled *An Act⁶ for the better preservation of the Breed of Deer, and preventing unlawful hunting*, was read the third Time.

Resolved, That the Bill do pass; and that the Title be, *An Act⁷ to amend an Act, intituled an Act for the better preservation of the Breed of Deer, and preventing unlawful hunting.*

Ordered, That Mᵣ *Cary* do carry the Bill to the Council, and desire their Concurrence.

An engrossed *Bill* to continue and amend the Act, intituled *An Act⁸ to continue and amend the Act, intituled an Act for amending the Staple of Tobacco, and for preventing Frauds in his Majesty's Customs*, was read the third Time.

Resolved, That the Bill do pass; and that the Title be, *An Act⁹ to continue and amend the Act, intituled an Act to continue and amend the Act, intituled an Act for amending the Staple of Tobacco, and for preventing Frauds in his Majesty's Customs.*

Ordered, That Mᵣ *Bland* do carry the Bill to the Council, and desire their Concurrence.

An engrossed *Bill* to encourage the further Settlement of the Town of *Alexandria*, in the County of *Fairfax*, was read the third Time.

Resolved, That the Bill do pass; and that the Title be, *An Act¹⁰ to encourage the further Settlement of the Town of* Alexandria, *in the County of* Fairfax.

Ordered, That Mᵣ *Bland* do carry the Bill to the Council, and desire their Concurrence.

An engrossed *Bill* for opening and extending the Navigation of the River *Potowmack*, from Fort *Cumberland* to Tide Water, was read the third Time.

Resolved

¹ Hening, VIII, p. 554.   ² Ibid, VI, p. 88.   ³ Ibid, VIII, p. 610.   ⁴ Ibid, VIII, p. 600.
⁵ Ibid, VIII, p. 630.   ⁶ Ibid, V, p. 60.   ⁷ Ibid, VIII, p. 591.   ⁸ Ibid, VIII, p. 318.
⁹ Ibid, VIII, p. 507.   ¹⁰ Ibid, VIII, p. 613.

Refolved, That the Bill do pafs; and that the Title be, *An Act¹ for opening and extending the Navigation of the River* Potowmack, *from Fort* Cumberland *to Tide Water*.

158 *Ordered*, That Mr *Thomfon Mafon* do carry the Bill to the Council, and defire their Concurrence.

A *Meffage* from the Council by Mr *Blair:*

Mr *Speaker*,
The Council do agree to the *firft* Amendment, *propofed by this Houfe*, *to the Council's firft Amendment*, *to the Bill*, *intituled* An Act² for further continuing and amending the Acts, for better regulating and difciplining the Militia; *but they do infift on the latter Part of their faid firft Amendment*, *difagreed to by the Houfe*, *and defire the Houfe will recede from their Difagreement thereunto; and · alfo the Council do recede from their next Amendment to the faid Bill*, *difagreed to by this Houfe; and alfo*,

The Council do adhere to the Amendment, *by them propofed to the Bill*, *intituled* An Act³ for appointing feveral Ferries, and difcontinuing others, and for other Purpofes, *which hath been difagreed to by this Houfe; and the Council do defire the Houfe will recede from their Difagreement thereunto*.

And then the Meffenger withdrew.

Refolved, That this Houfe doth adhere to the fecond Amendment, made by the Houfe, to the firft Amendment, propofed by the Council, to the Bill intituled *An Act⁴ for further continuing and amending the Acts*, *for better regulating and difciplining the Militia*.

Ordered, That a Meffage be fent to the Council, to acquaint them that this Houfe doth adhere to their faid Amendment to the Amendment; and that Mr *Bland* do carry the faid Meffage.

Refolved, That this Houfe doth adhere to their difagreement to the Amendment, propofed by the Council, to the Bill, intituled *An Act⁵ for appointing feveral Ferries, and difcontinuing others, and for other Purpofes*.

An engroffed *Bill* for regulating the Allowances to the Keeper of the public Prifon, for the Maintenance of poor Prifoners for Debt, and Runaways, was read the third Time.

Refolved, That the Bill do pafs; and that the Title be, *An Act⁶ for regulating the Allowances to the Keeper of the public Prifon*, *for the Maintenance of poor Prifoners for Debt*, *and for other Purpofes therein mentioned*.

Ordered, That Mr *Nelfon* do carry the Bill to the Council, and defire their Concurrence.

Ordered, That Leave be given to bring in a Bill, for eftablifhing feveral new Ferries, and difcontinuing others; and that Mr *Carrington*, and Mr *Bland*, do prepare and bring in the fame.

An engroffed *Bill* to eftablifh a Town on the Land of *John Rictor*, in the County of *Fauquier*, was read the third Time.

An engroffed *Claufe*, was offered to be added to the Bill, by Way of Ryder, for eftablifhing a Town at the Falls of *Potowmack*, in the County of *Fairfax*.

And the faid *Claufe* was thrice read, and, upon the Queftion put thereupon, agreed to by the Houfe, to be made Part of the Bill, by Way of Ryder.

Refolved, That the Bill do pafs; and that the Title be, *An Act⁷ to eftablifh a Town on the Land of* John Rictor, *in the County of* Fauquier, *and for other Purpofes*.

Ordered, That Mr *Marfhall* do carry the Bill to the Council, and defire their Concurrence.

An engroffed *Bill* for further continuing the Acts, for the more effectual keeping the public Roads and Bridges in Repair, was read the third Time.

154 *Refolved*, That the Bill do pafs; and that the Title be, *An Act⁸ to revive and continue the Acts for the more effectual keeping the public Roads and Bridges in Repair*.

Ordered

---

¹ Hening, VIII, p. 570. ² Ibid, VII, p. 534. ³ Ibid, VIII, p. 554. ⁴ Ibid, VII, p. 534.
⁵ Ibid, VIII, p. 554. ⁶ Ibid, VIII, p. 527. ⁷ Ibid, VIII, p. 621. ⁸ Ibid, VIII, p. 542.

Ordered, That Mr *Bland* do carry the Bill to the Council, and defire their Concurrence.

The *Order* of the Day being read;

Refolved, That this Houfe will, Tomorrow, refolve itfelf into a Committee of the whole Houfe, upon the Bill to amend the Act, intituled *An Act*[1] *prefcribing the Method of appointing Sheriffs, and for limiting the Time of their Continuance in Office, and directing their Duty therein.*

An engroffed *Bill* for regulating the Method of fuing out Writs of *Alias Capias*, in the County Courts, for altering *Loudoun* Court Day, and for other Purpofes, was read the third Time.

Refolved, That theBill do pafs; and that the Title be, *An Act*[2] *for altering the Method of fuing out Writs of* Alias Capias, *and other Procefs, in the County Courts, for regulating certain Expences on Attachments, and Writs of Execution, and for altering the Court Days of certain Counties.*

Ordered, That Mr *Thomfon Mafon* do carry the Bill to the Council, and defire their Concurrence.

A *Bill* for calling in and finking the old Treafury Notes now in Circulation, was read a fecond Time.

Refolved, That the Bill be committed.

Refolved, That the Bill be committed to a Committee of the whole Houfe.

Refolved, That this Houfe will, Tomorrow, refolve itfelf into a Committee of the whole Houfe, upon the faid Bill.

A *Meffage* from the Council by Mr *Blair:*

Mr *Speaker,*

The Council have agreed to the Bill, *intituled* An Act[3] for erecting a Lighthoufe on Cape *Henry*, *without any Amendment; and alfo,*

The Council have agreed to the Bill, *intituled* An Act[4] to amend the feveral Acts of Affembly, refpecting the Currency of Copper Money, in this Colony, *without any Amendment; and alfo,*

The Council have agreed to the Bill, *intituled* An Act[5] to veft certain intailed Lands, whereof *Philip Ludwell Grymes*, Gentleman, is feifed, in *William Roane*, Gentleman, in Fee Simple, *without any Amendment; and alfo,*

The Council have agreed to the Bill, *intituled* An Act[6] for dividing the County of *Botetourt* into two diftinct Counties, *without any Amendment; and alfo,*

The Council have agreed to the Bill, *intituled* An Act[7] to amend an Act, intituled an Act to amend an Act, intituled an Act to oblige the Owners of Mills, Hedges, or Stone Stops, on fundry Rivers therein mentioned, to make Openings or Slopes therein, for the Paffage of Fifh, and for other Purpofes therein mentioned, *with fome Amendments, to which Amendments the Council defire the Concurrence of this Houfe; and alfo,*

The Council have agreed to the Bill, *intituled* An Act[8] to enlarge the Power of the Truftees appointed to carry into Execution an Act paffed this prefent Seffion of Affembly, intituled an Act for cutting a navigable Canal, from *Archer's Hope* Creek to *Queen's* Creek, through or near the City of *Williamfburg, with an Amendment, to which Amendment the Council defire the Concurrence of this Houfe.*

The Houfe proceeded to take into Confideration the Amendments, made by the Council, to the Bill, intituled *An Act*[9] *to amend an Act, intituled an Act to amend an Act, intituled an Act to oblige the Owners of Mills, Hedges, or Stone Stops, on fundry Rivers, therein mentioned, to make Openings or Slopes therein, for the Paffage of Fifh, and for other Purpofes therein mentioned.*

And the faid *Amendments* were read, and are as followeth, *viz.*

Page 1, Line 10, after '*Fork*' infert '*and Nottoway.*'

Line 32, leave out '*River*' and infert '*Rivers, and alfo in the River* Nomony' inftead thereof.

Line

---

[1] Hening, V, p. 515.   [2] Ibid, VIII, p. 517.   [3] Ibid, VIII, p. 539.   [4] Ibid, VIII, p. 534.
[5] Ibid, VIII, p. 630.   [6] Ibid, VIII, p. 600.   [7] Ibid, VIII, p. 583.   [8] Ibid, VIII, p. 562.
[9] Ibid, VIII, p. 583.

Line 35, leave out '*River*' and infert '*Rivers*' inftead thereof.

Line 38, leave out '*River*' and infert '*Rivers, or either of them*' inftead thereof.

Line 42, leave out '*River*' and infert '*Rivers or either of them*' inftead thereof.

Page 2, Line 6, leave out '*the faid River*' and infert '*either of the faid Rivers*' inftead thereof.

Line 9, after '*manner*' infert " *And whereas it would be highly reafonable to give the Proprietor of the Land a Remedy, for what he may fuffer, either in the Charge of putting down fuch Fifh Dams, Hedges, or other Stops, or in the Penalty for not doing it, againft the Perfons who have erected, or fhall erect them, without the Confent of fuch Proprietors: Be it therefore further enacted by the Authority aforefaid, that where any Proprietor of Land, fhall, agreeably to the Directions of this Act, pull down any fuch Fifh Dam, Hedge, or Stops put into either of the faid Rivers by any other Perfon or Perfons, without the Confent, in Writing, of fuch Proprietor, or fhall be compelled to pay the Penalty hereby impofed for neglecting to put the fame down, it fhall be lawful for fuch Proprietor, by Action on the Cafe, to be commenced againft fuch other Perfon or Perfons, in any Court of Record, to recover, with Cofts of Suit, all the Charge he or fhe may have been put to in removing fuch Obftructions, or, as the Cafe may be, the Penalty aforefaid, and the Cofts, which fhall be adjudged againft fuch Proprietor, upon any Profecution againft him, or her, for the fame: And if any Defendant or Defendants, in fuch Suit, upon Recovery, fhall not pay down the Amount of the Judgment, or give Security for the Payment thereof, with Intereft, at the End of three Months, every fuch Defendant fhall receive, on his bare Back, fo many Lafhes as the Court fhall think proper to order, not exceeding thirty nine.   And upon any fuch Bond the Obligee, his Executors, or Adminiftrators, fhall be entitled to the fame Remedy on Failure of Payment, as is provided in the Cafe of Bonds given to replevy Eftates, taken by Execution.*"

The faid *Amendments*, being feverally read a fecond Time, were, upon the Queftion feverally put thereupon, difagreed to by the Houfe.

Ordered, That a Meffage be fent to the Council, to acquaint them that this Houfe doth difagree to the Amendments, by them propofed, to the faid Bill, and doth defire, that they will pafs the fame without the faid Amendments; and that Mr *Bland* do carry the faid Meffage.

The *Houfe* proceeded to take into Confideration the Amendment, made by the Council, to the Bill, intituled An Act[1] *to enlarge the Power of the Truftees, appointed to carry into Execution an Act paffed this prefent Seffion of Affembly intituled an Act for cutting a navigable Canal, from* Archer's Hope *Creek, to* Queen's *Creek, through or near the City* of Williamfburg.

And the faid *Amendment* was read, and is as followeth, *viz.*

Line 44, *after* '*Truftees*' *infert,* '*and fo as often as any new Damage fhall arife to any Proprietor, not before confidered, and valued, fuch Proprietor fhall have the like Remedy, for recovering fuch further Damage, from the faid Truftees.*"

The faid *Amendment*, being read a fecond Time, was, upon the Queftion put thereupon, agreed to by the Houfe.

Ordered, That Mr *Nelfon* do carry the Bill to the Council, and acquaint them, that this Houfe hath agreed to the Amendment made by them.

Mr *Carrington* prefented to the Houfe, according to Order, a Bill for eftablifhing feveral new Ferries, and difcontinuing others; and the fame was received, and read the firft Time.

Refolved, That the Bill be read a fecond Time.

Ordered, That the Bill be now read a fecond Time.

The *Bill* was accordingly read a fecond Time.

Ordered, That the Bill be engroffed.

An engroffed *Bill* to amend the Act, intituled An Act[2] *directing the Trial of Slaves, committing capital Offences, and for the more effectual punifhing Confpiracies and Infurrections of them, and for the better Government of Negroes, Mulattoes, and* Indians, *bond or free,* was read the third Time.

Refolved

---

[1] Hening, VIII, p. 562.   [2] Ibid, VI, p. 104.

Refolved, That the Bill do pafs; and that the Title be, *An Act¹ for amending the Acts concerning the Trials and Outlawries of Slaves.*

Ordered, That Mʳ *Bland* do carry the Bill to the Council, and defire their Concurrence.

Ordered, That Mʳ *Speaker* do defire the Governor to order new Writs to iffue for the electing of Burgeffes, to ferve in the General Affembly, for the new Counties, fo foon as they fhall take Place.

An engroffed *Bill* to amend an Act, intituled *An Act² directing the Duty of Surveyors* **156** *of Land*, was read the third Time.

Refolved, That the Bill do pafs; and that the Title be, *An Act³ to amend an Act, intituled an Act directing the Duty of Surveyors of Land.*

Ordered, That Mʳ *John Page* do carry the Bill to the Council, and defire their Concurrence.

An engroffed *Bill* to dock the Intail of certain Lands, whereof *Colwell Pettypool* and *Mary* his Wife are feifed in Fee Tail, for Purpofes therein mentioned, was read the third Time.

Refolved, That the Bill do pafs; and that the Title be, *An Act⁴ to veft certain Lands, whereof* Colwell Pettypool *and* Mary *his Wife are feifed in Fee Tail, in* Jofeph Mayo, *and for fettling other Land and Slaves, to be purchafed, in Lieu thereof.*

Ordered, That Mʳ *Carrington* do carry the Bill to the Council, and defire their Concurrence.

And then the Houfe adjourned till Tomorrow Morning eleven of the Clock.

Thursday, the 9th of April, 12 George III, 1772.

Mʳ *Bland* reported from the Committee of Propofitions and Grievances, to whom the Bill for appointing Truftees to regulate the making of Slopes for the Paffage of Fifh, in the Mill Dams, within the County of *Bedford*, was committed, that the Committee had made feveral other Amendments to the Bill, which they had directed him to report to the Houfe; and he read the Report in his Place, and afterwards delivered the Bill, with the Amendments, in at the Clerk's Table; where the Amendments were once read throughout, and then a fecond Time, one by one, and, upon the Queftion feverally put thereupon, were agreed to by the Houfe.

Ordered, That the Bill, with the Amendments, be engroffed.

A *Bill* to eftablifh a Jurifdiction for fuperintending the Conduct of the Clergy, was read a fecond Time.

Ordered, That the Bill be engroffed.

Ordered, That the Bill be read the third Time, upon the firft Day of *May* next.

An engroffed *Bill* for eftablifhing feveral Ferries, and difcontinuing others, was read the third Time.

Refolved, That the Bill do pafs; and that the Title be, *An Act⁵ for eftablifhing feveral Ferries, and for other Purpofes.*

Ordered, That Mʳ *Carrington* do carry the Bill to the Council, and defire their Concurrence.

Mʳ *Cary* reported, from the Committee appointed to proportion the Public Levy, that the Committee had proportioned the Public Levy accordingly, and ftated the fame in a Book, which they had directed him to report to the Houfe; and he delivered the Book in at the Clerk's Table.

Ordered, That the faid Book do lie upon the Table, to be perufed by the Members of the Houfe.

The *Order* of the Day being read, for the Houfe to refolve itfelf into a Committee of the whole Houfe, upon the Bill to amend the Act, intituled *An Act⁶ prefcribing the*
Method

---

¹ Hening, VIII, p. 522.   ² Ibid, VI, p. 33.   ³ Ibid, VIII, p. 526.   ⁴ Ibid, VIII, p. 643.
⁵ Ibid, VIII, p. 554.   ⁶ Ibid, V, p. 515.

Method of appointing Sheriffs, and for limiting the Time of their Continuance in Office, and directing their Duty therein;

The Houfe refolved itfelf into the faid Committee.

Mr *Speaker* left the Chair.

Mr *Bland* took the Chair of the Committee.

Mr *Speaker* refumed the Chair.

157 Mr *Bland* reported from the Committee, that they had gone through the Bill, and made feveral Amendments thereunto, which they had directed him to report, when the Houfe will pleafe to receive the fame.

Ordered, That the Report be now received.

Mr *Bland* accordingly reported, from the faid Committee, the Amendments which the Committee had made to the Bill, and which they had directed him to report to the Houfe; and he read the Report in his Place, and afterwards delivered the Bill, with the Amendments, in at the Clerk's Table; where the Amendments were once read throughout, and then a fecond Time, one by one, and, upon the Queftion feverally put thereupon, fome of them were difagreed to, and the reft were agreed to by the Houfe; and an Amendment was made by the Houfe to the Bill.

Ordered, That the Bill, with the Amendments, be engroffed.

Mr *Bland* reported from the Committee of Privileges and Elections, that the Committee had, according to Order, examined the Returns of the feveral other Writs, for electing Burgeffes to ferve in this prefent General Affembly, and compared the fame with the Form prefcribed by Law, and had come to feveral Refolutions, which they had directed him to report to the Houfe; and he read the Report in his Place, and afterwards delivered it in at the Clerk's Table; where the Refolutions of the Committee were read, and are as followeth, *viz.*

Refolved, That it is the Opinion of this Committee, that the Returns of the Writs, for electing Burgeffes to ferve in this prefent General Affembly, for the Counties of *Amherft, Buckingham, Effex, Hampfhire*, and *King William*, are made in the Form prefcribed by Law.

Refolved, That it is the Opinion of this Committee, that the Returns of the Writs, for electing Burgeffes to ferve in this prefent General Affembly, for the Counties of *Bedford, Culpeper, Frederick, Henrico, Halifax, King George, Loudoun, Orange, Prince Edward, Prince William*, and *Princefs Anne*, are not made in the Form prefcribed by Law.

The faid *Refolutions* being feverally read a fecond Time, were, upon the Queftion feverally put thereupon, agreed to by the Houfe.

Ordered, That the feveral Returns of the Writs, for electing Burgeffes to ferve in this prefent General Affembly, for the Counties in the laft Refolution mentioned, be amended by the Clerk at the Table.

And the faid *Returns* were amended by the Clerk accordingly.

The other *Order* of the Day being read;

The Houfe refolved itfelf into a Committee of the whole Houfe, upon the Bill for calling in and finking the old Treafury Notes, now in Circulation.

Mr *Speaker* left the Chair.

Mr *Bland* took the Chair of the Committee.

Mr *Speaker* refumed the Chair.

Mr *Bland* reported from the Committee, that the Committee had directed him to report the Bill to the Houfe, without any Amendment; and he delivered the Bill in at the Clerk's Table.

And the *Queftion* being put that the Bill be engroffed;

It paffed in the Negative.

A *Meffage* from the Council by Mr *Blair:*

Mr *Speaker,*

The Council have agreed to the Bill, *intituled* An Act[1] to allow the Minifter of the

Parifh

---

[1] Hening, VIII, p. 610.

Parifh of *Antrim*, in the County of *Halifax*, the fame Salary as other Minifters are intitled to receive, *without any Amendment; and alfo,*

The Council have agreed to the Bill, *intituled* An Act[1] for regulating the Allowances to the Keeper of the Public Prifon, for the Maintenance of poor Prifoners for Debt, and for other Purpofes therein mentioned, *without any Amendment; and alfo,*

The Council have agreed to the Bill, *intituled* An Act[2] for opening and extending the Navigation of the River *Potowmack*, from Fort *Cumberland* to Tide Water, *with an Amendment, to which Amendment the Council defire the Concurrence of this Houfe; and alfo,* 158

The Council have agreed to the Bill, *intituled* An Act[3] to encourage the further Settlement of the Town of *Alexandria*, in the County of *Fairfax*, *with an Amendment, to which Amendment the Council defire the Concurrence of this Houfe.*

And then the Meffenger withdrew.

Ordered, That Leave be given to bring in a Bill for laying a Public Levy; and that Mr *Cary*, Mr *Gray*, Mr *Taylor*, and Mr *Hardy*, do prepare and bring in the fame.

The Houfe proceeded to take into Confideration the Amendment made by the Council to the Bill, intituled *An Act[4] for opening and extending the Navigation of the River* Potowmack, *from Fort* Cumberland *to Tide Water.*

And the faid *Amendment* was read, and is as followeth, *viz.*

Page 5, Line 7, after 'ever' infert '*Provided neverthelefs, that if any further Damage fhould arife to any Proprietor of Land, in Confequence of the opening of fuch Canal, than had been before confidered and valued, it fhall be lawful for fuch Proprietor, as often as any fuch new Damage fhall happen, by Application to the Court of the County where the Land fhall lie, to have fuch further Damages valued by a Jury, in like Manner, and to receive and recover the fame of the faid Truftees; and upon every fuch Valuation, the Jury is hereby directed to defcribe and afcertain the Bounds of the Lands fo valued.*"

The faid *Amendment* being read a fecond Time, was, upon the Queftion put thereupon, agreed to by the Houfe.

Ordered, That Mr *Thomfon Mafon* do carry the Bill to the Council, and acquaint them that this Houfe hath agreed to the Amendment made by them.

An engroffed *Bill* for appointing Truftees to regulate the making of Slopes, for the Paffage of Fifh, in the Mill Dams, within the County of *Bedford*, was read the third Time.

Refolved, That the Bill do pafs; and that the Title be, *An Act[5] for appointing Truftees to regulate the making of Slopes, for the Paffage of Fifh, in the Mill Dams, within the County of* Bedford.

Ordered, That Mr *Talbot* do carry the Bill to the Council, and defire their Concurrence.

The Houfe proceeded to take into Confideration the Amendment made by the Council to the Bill, intituled *An Act[6] to encourage the further Settlement of the Town of* Alexandria, *in the County of* Fairfax.

And the faid *Amendment* was read, and is as followeth, *viz.*

Line 32, after '*proper*' infert "*Provided neverthelefs, that no Forfeiture of any fuch Marfh Lots, as belong to Infants, or Perfons out of the Country, fhall be incurred for want of fuch Draining; but the Truftees fhall be at Liberty to do the fame, and the Guardian of fuch Infants, or the Attorney of fuch Perfons not refident in the Country, fhall be obliged to repay to the Truftees the Expence thereof, if fo much they fhall or may have in their Hands of the Eftate and Effects of fuch Proprietors of the faid Lots.*"

The faid *Amendment*, being read a fecond Time, was, upon the Queftion put thereupon, agreed to by the Houfe.

Ordered, That Mr *Bland* do carry the Bill to the Council, and acquaint them that this Houfe hath agreed to the Amendment made by them.

Mr *Cary* prefented to the Houfe, according to Order, a Bill for laying a Public Levy; and the fame was received and read the firft Time.

Refolved, That the Bill be read a fecond Time.

Ordered, That the Bill be now read a fecond Time.

The

---

[1] Hening, VIII, p. 527. [2] Ibid, VIII, p. 570. [3] Ibid, VIII, p. 613. [4] Ibid, VIII, p. 570.
[5] Ibid, VIII, p. 585. [6] Ibid, VIII, p. 613.

The *Bill* was accordingly read a fecond Time.

Ordered, That the Bill be engroffed.

An engroffed *Bill* to amend the Act, intituled *An Act*[1] *prefcribing the Method of appointing Sheriffs, and for limiting the Time of their Continuance in Office, and directing their Duty therein*, was read the third Time.

Refolved, That the Bill do pafs; and that the Title be, *An Act*[2] *to amend an Act intituled an Act prefcribing the Method of appointing Sheriffs, and for limiting the Time of their Continuance in Office, and directing their Duty therein, and for other purpofes.*

Ordered, That Mr *Bland* do carry the Bill to the Council, and defire their Concurrence.

Mr *Cary* reported from the Committee, to whom the Bill to amend fo much of an Act of Affembly, intituled *An Act*[3] *for the Infpection of Pork, Beef, Flour, Tar, Pitch, and Turpentine, as relates to the Infpection of Flour*, was committed, that the Committee had gone through the Bill, and made feveral Amendments thereunto, which they had directed him to report to the Houfe; and he read the Report in his Place, and afterwards delivered the Bill, with the Amendments, in at the Clerk's Table; where the Amendments were once read throughout, and then a fecond Time, one by one, and, upon the Queftion feverally put thereupon, were agreed to by the Houfe.

Ordered, That the Bill, with the Amendments, be engroffed.

And then the Houfe adjourned till Tomorrow Morning eleven of the Clock.

Friday, the 10th of April, 12 George III. 1772.

ANOTHER *Member* having taken the Oaths appointed to be taken by Act of Parliament, and repeated and fubfcribed the Teft, took his Place in the Houfe.

The *Book* of Public Proportions, which was Yefterday ordered to lie upon the Table, was read, and, upon the Queftion put thereupon, agreed to by the Houfe.

An engroffed *Bill* for laying a Public Levy, was read the third Time.

Refolved, That the Bill do pafs; and that the Title be, *An Act*[4] *for laying a Public Levy.*

Ordered, That Mr *Cary* do carry the Bill to the Council, and defire their Concurrence.

An engroffed *Bill* to amend fo much of an Act of Affembly, intituled *An Act for the Infpection of Pork, Beef, Flour, Tar, Pitch, and Turpentine, as relates to the Infpection of Flour*, was read the third Time.

Refolved, That the Bill do pafs; and that the Title be, *An Act*[5] *to amend fo much of an Act of Affembly intituled an Act for the Infpection of Pork, Beef, Flour, Tar, Pitch, and Turpentine, as relates to the Infpection of Flour.*

Ordered, That Mr *Cary* do carry the Bill to the Council, and defire their Concurrence.

A *Meffage* from the Council by Mr *Blair:*

Mr *Speaker*,

The Council have agreed to the Bill, *intituled* An Act[6] to amend an Act, intituled an Act directing the Duty of Surveyors of Land, *without any Amendment; and alfo,*

The Council have agreed to the Bill, *intituled* An Act[7] for eftablifhing feveral new Ferries, and for other Purpofes, *without any Amendment; and alfo,*

The Council have agreed to the Bill, *intituled* An Act[8] to revive and continue the Acts for the more effectual keeping the public Roads and Bridges in Repair, *without any Amendment; and alfo,*

The Council have agreed to the Bill, *intituled* An Act[9] for altering the Method of fuing out Writs of *Alias Capias*, and other Procefs, in the County Courts, for regulating certain Expences on Attachments, and Writs of Execution, and for altering the Court Days of certain Counties, *without any Amendment; and alfo,*

The

---

[1] Hening, V, p. 515.   [2] Ibid, VIII, p. 524.   [3] Ibid, VIII, p. 511.   [4] Ibid, VIII. p. 533.
[5] Ibid, VIII, p. 511.   [6] Ibid, VIII, p. 526.   [7] Ibid, VIII. p. 554.   [8] Ibid, VIII, p. 542.
[9] Ibid, VIII, p. 517.

The Council have agreed to the Bill, *intituled* An Act[1] to vest certain Lands, whereof *Colwell Pettypool* and *Mary* his Wife are seifed in Fee Tail, in *Jofeph Mayo*, and for fettling other Land and Slaves, to be purchased, in lieu thereof, *without any Amendment; and alfo,*

The Council have agreed to the Bill, *intituled* An Act[2] to eftablifh a Town on the Land of *John Rictor*, in the County of *Fauquier*, and for other Purpofes, *without any Amendments; and alfo,* 160

The Council do not infift upon their firft Amendment *to the Bill, intituled,* An Act[3] to amend An Act intituled An Act to amend An Act intituled An Act to oblige the Owners of Mills, Hedges, or Stone Stops, on fundry Rivers therein mentioned, to make Openings therein, for the Paffage of Fifh, and for other Purpofes therein mentioned, *difagreed to by this Houfe, but they do infift upon the fubfequent Amendments to the faid Bill, difagreed to by this Houfe, and defire the Houfe will recede from their Difagreement thereunto.*

And then the Meffenger withdrew.

Refolved, That this House doth recede from their Difagreement to the faid Amendments.

Ordered, That Mr *Bland* do carry the Bill to the Council, and acquaint them that this Houfe hath receded from their Difagreement to the faid Amendments.

Ordered, That Mr *Speaker* do tranfmit to the Speaker of the Lower Houfe of Affembly, of the Province of *Maryland,* a Copy of the Act for erecting a Lighthoufe on Cape *Henry, and alfo* a Copy of the Act for opening and extending the Navigation of the River *Potowmack,* from Fort *Cumberland,* to Tide Water, and defire the Affembly of the faid Province to enact Laws of the like Import.

A *Meffage* from the Council by Mr *Blair:*

Mr *Speaker,*

The Council have agreed to the Bill, *intituled,* An Act[4] to continue and amend the Act intituled An Act to continue and amend the Act intituled An Act for amending the Staple of Tobacco, and for preventing Frauds in his Majefty's Cuftoms, *with an Amendment, to which Amendment the Council defire the Concurrence of this Houfe; and alfo,*

The Council have agreed to the Bill, *intituled* An Act[5] to amend an Act, intituled An Act for the better Prefervation of the Breed of Deer, and preventing unlawful hunting, *with an Amendment, to which Amendment the Council defire the Concurrence of this Houfe.*

And then the Meffenger withdrew.

The Houfe proceeded to take into Confideration the Amendment, made by the Council, to the Bill, intituled *An Act[6] to continue and amend the Act intituled An Act to continue and amend the Act intituled an Act for amending the Staple of Tobacco, and for preventing Frauds in his Majefty's Cuftoms.*

And the faid *Amendment* was read, and is as followeth, *viz.*

Page 2, Line 11, leave out from '*refpectively,*' to '*and*' in Line 13, and infert, '*and that the Receipts of the Warehoufes, on the Lots of* Robert Bolling, *adjoining* Davis's *Landing, in the Town of* Blandford, *and on the faid* Bolling's *Land, at* Cedar *Point, in the County of* Dinwiddie, *fhall pafs in all Payments where the Receipts of the Warehoufes at* Blandford *and* Bolling's *Point are payable*' inftead thereof.

The faid *Amendment* being read a fecond Time, was, upon the Queftion put thereupon, agreed to by the Houfe.

Ordered, That Mr *Bland* do carry the Bill to the Council, and acquaint them that this Houfe hath agreed to the Amendment made by them.

The Houfe proceeded to take into Confideration the Amendment, made by the Council, to the Bill, intituled *An Act[7] to amend an Act intituled An Act for the better Prefervation of the Breed of Deer, and preventing unlawful Hunting.*

And the faid *Amendment* was read, and is as followeth, *viz.*

Line

[1] Hening, VIII, p. 643. [2] Ibid, VIII, p. 621. [3] Ibid, VIII, p. 583. [4] Ibid, VIII, p. 318.
[5] Ibid, VIII, p. 591. [6] Ibid, VIII, p. 507. [7] Ibid, VIII, p. 591.

Line 32, leave out '*four*' and infert '*fix*' inftead thereof.

The faid *Amendment* being read a fecond Time, was, upon the Queftion put thereupon, agreed to by the Houfe.

161 *Ordered*, That Mr *Cary* do carry the Bill to the Council, and acquaint them that this Houfe hath agreed to the Amendment made by them.

Refolved, That the Sum of eighty Pounds be paid, by the Treafurer of this Colony, to *George Booth*, of *Gloucefter* County, for his Negro Slave *Will*, and the further Sum of ninety Pounds to *Richard Allen*, of *Warwick* County, for his Negro Slave *Jack*, which faid Slaves were, by the Court of the faid County of *Warwick*, condemned for Felony, on their producing to the faid Treafurer Certificates of the Execution of the faid Slaves refpectively.

Ordered, That Mr *Cary* do carry the Refolution to the Council, and defire their Concurrence.

A *Meffage* from the Council by Mr *Blair:*

Mr *Speaker*,

The Council have agreed to the Bill, *intituled* An Act[1] for laying a Public Levy, *without any Amendment; and alfo,*

The Council have agreed to the Bill, *intituled* An Act[2] to amend fo much of an Act of Affembly, intituled An Act for the Infpection of Pork, Beef, Flour, Tar, Pitch, and Turpentine, as relates to the Infpection of Flour, *without any Amendment; and alfo,*

The Council have agreed to the Bill, *intituled* An Act[3] for appointing Truftees, to regulate the making of Slopes, for the Paffage of Fifh, in the Mill Dams within the County of *Bedford, without any Amendment; and alfo,*

The Council have agreed to the Bill, *intituled* An Act[4] to amend an Act intituled An Act prefcribing the Method of appointing Sheriffs, and for limiting the Time of their Contiuance in Office, and directing their Duty therein, and for other Purpofes, *with an Amendment, to which Amendment the Council defire the Concurrence of this Houfe; and alfo,*

The Council have agreed to the Bill, *intituled* An Act[5] for amending the Acts concerning the Trials and Outlawries of Slaves, *with fome Amendments, to which Amendments the Council defire the Concurrence of this Houfe; and alfo,*

The Council have agreed to the Refolve *for paying feveral Sums of Money to* George Booth *and* Richard Allen.

And then the Meffenger withdrew.

The Houfe proceeded to take into Confideration the Amendment, made by the Council, to the Bill, intituled *An Act[6] to amend An Act intituled an Act prefcribing the Method of appointing Sheriffs, and for limiting the Time of their Continuance in Office, and directing their Duty therein, and for other Purpofes.*

And the faid *Amendment* was read, and is as followeth, *viz.*

Line 18, after '*Commiffion*,' infert '*And whereas the Inhabitants of this Colony are liable to be, and in many Inftances have been, impofed upon by the Sheriffs or Collectors of the feveral Counties, for want of an Account ftated, feparately and diftinctly, of the feveral Fees by them collected, for different Officers, and alfo a clear Account of the Quitrents, Public, County, or Parifh Levies, which the faid Sheriffs, or their Deputies, often refufe to give, and often do make Diftrefs, if immediate Payment be not made of a Sum demanded by them in Grofs; which Practices are productive of great Inconveniences: For Remedy whereof, Be it further enacted, by the Authority aforefaid, that every Sheriff, Deputy Sheriff, or Collector, who fhall hereafter receive from any Perfon or Perfons any Officers Fees, Quitrents, Public, County, or Parifh Levies, fhall deliver to the Perfon fo paying a fair and diftinct Account of the feveral Articles, for which he fhall receive the fame, and alfo a Receipt for what fhall be fo paid him; and every Sheriff, Deputy Sheriff, or Collector, failing herein, fhall forfeit and pay, to the Perfon by whom fuch Payment fhall be made, the Sum of twenty*
Shillings

[1] Hening, VIII, p. 533.   [2] Ibid, VIII, p. 511.   [3] Ibid, VIII p. 585.   [4] Ibid, VIII, p. 524.
[5] Ibid, VIII, p. 522.   [6] Ibid, VIII, p. 524.

Shillings, for each Offence, to be recovered, with Cofts, before any Juftice of the Peace of the County, where fuch Sheriff, Deputy Sheriff, or Collector fhall refide, and fuch Sheriff, or other Officer, fhall moreover be liable, to the Party grieved, for all Damages he may fuftain, by Means of fuch Officers demanding and receiving a greater Sum than fhall be really due, to be recovered, by Action of Trefpafs on the Cafe, before any Court of Record within this Colony, in which Action, where the Plaintiff fhall recover, he fhall alfo recover his full Cofts.'

The faid *Amendment*, being read a fecond Time, was, upon the Queftion put thereupon, agreed to by the Houfe.

Ordered, That Mʳ *Carrington* do carry the Bill to the Council, and, acquaint them that this Houfe hath agreed to the Amendment made by them.

The *Houfe* proceeded to take into Confideration the Amendments, made by the Council, to the Bill, intituled An *Act*[1] *for Amending the Acts concerning the Trials and Outlawries of Slaves.*

And the faid *Amendments* were read, and are as followeth, *viz.*

Line 6, leave out from '*Clergy,*' to '*unlefs,*' in the next Line.

Line 19, leave out '*be firft proved,*' and infert '*fhall appear,*' inftead thereof.

Line 20, leave out, '*by the Oath of one or more credible Witnefs or Witneffes.*'

Line 21, after '*Mifchief,*' infert '*or hath been outlying for the Space of ten Days.*'

The three firft *Amendments*, being feverally read a fecond Time, were, upon the Queftion feverally put thereupon, agreed to by the Houfe.

The laft *Amendment*, being read a fecond Time, was, upon the Queftion put thereupon, difagreed to by the Houfe.

Ordered, That a Meffage be fent to the Council, to acquaint them that this Houfe doth difagree to the laft of the faid Amendments, by them propofed to the faid Bill, and doth defire that they will pafs the fame, without the faid laft Amendment; and that Mʳ *Bland* do carry the faid Meffage.

And then the Houfe adjourned till Tomorrow Morning, eleven of the Clock.

Saturday, the 11th of April, 12 George III. 1772.

A *Meffage* from the Council, by Mʳ *Blair:*

Mʳ *Speaker,*
The Council do not infift upon the laft of the Amendments, *made by them, to the Bill, intituled* An act[2] for amending the Acts concerning the Trials and outlawries of Slaves, *to which this Houfe hath difagreed.*

And then the Meffenger withdrew.

Mʳ *Digges* reported from the Committee appointed to examine the enrolled Bills, that the Committee had examined the enrolled Bills, and rectified fuch Miftakes as were found therein, and that they are truly enrolled.

Ordered, That Mʳ*Digges* do carry the enrolled Bills to the Council, for their Infpection.
A *Meffage* from the Council by Mʳ *Blair:*

Mʳ *Speaker,*
The Council have infpected the enrolled Bills, and are fatiffied they are truly enrolled.

And then the Meffenger withdrew.
A *Meffage* from the Governor by Mʳ *Blair:*

Mʳ *Speaker,*
The Governor commands this Houfe to attend his Excellency immediately, in the Council Chamber,

Accordingly Mʳ *Speaker*, with the Houfe, went up to attend his Excellency, in the
Council

1 Hening, VIII, p. 522.   2 Ibid, VIII, p. 522.

Council Chamber, where his Excellency was pleaſed to give his Aſſent to the ſeveral public and private Bills, and Reſolves following, *viz.*

An Act[1] to continue and amend an act, intituled an act to continue and amend the act, intituled an act for amending the ſtaple of tobacco, and for preventing frauds in his Majeſty's cuſtoms.

An act[2] to amend ſo much of an act of Aſſembly, intituled an act for the inſpection of pork, beef, flour, tar, pitch, and turpentine, as relates to the inſpection of flour.

An act[3] for further continuing the act, intituled an act for reducing the ſeveral acts of Aſſembly, for making proviſion againſt invaſions and inſurrections, into one act.

An act[4] for further continuing and amending the act, intituled an act for the better regulating and collecting certain Officers fees, and for other purpoſes therein mentioned.

An act[5] to empower the clerks of county courts to iſſue certain writs of execution into other counties.

An act[6] for altering the method of ſuing out writs of alias capias, and other proceſs in the county courts, for regulating certain expences and attachments, and writs of execution, and for altering the court days of certain counties.

An act[7] for altering the court days of the counties of Surry, Bedford, and Princeſs Anne.

An act[8] to amend an act, intituled an act to prevent malicious maiming and wounding.

An act[9] for amending the acts concerning the trials and outlawries of Slaves.

An act[10] to amend an act, intituled an act concerning ſeamen.

An act[11] to amend the act, intituled an act preſcribing the method of appointing ſheriffs, and for limiting the time of their continuance in office, and directing their duty therein, and for other purpoſes.

An act[12] to amend an act, intituled an act directing the duty of ſurveyors of land.

An act[13] for regulating the allowances to the keeper of the public priſon, for the maintenance of poor priſoners for debt, and for other purpoſes therein mentioned.

An act[14] to continue an Act, intituled an act to continue and amend an act, intituled an act for reducing the ſeveral acts, made for laying a duty upon liquors, into one act.

An act[15] for continuing and amending ſeveral acts, and reviving one act for laying duties upon ſlaves imported.

An act[16] for laying a public levy.

An act[17] to amend the ſeveral acts of Aſſembly reſpecting the currency of copper money in this colony.

An act[18] for the eaſe and relief of the people, by paying the Burgeſſes wages in money, for the preſent ſeſſion of Aſſembly.

An act[19] to compel ſhips, importing convicts, ſervants, or ſlaves, infected with the gaol fever, or ſmallpox, to perform quarantine.

An act[20] for erecting a lighthouſe on Cape Henry.

An act[21] to continue an act, intituled an act for eſtabliſhing pilots, and regulating their fees.

An act[22] to revive and continue the acts for the more effectual keeping the public roads and bridges in repair.

An act[23] for keeping in repair ſeveral roads, and for other purpoſes therein mentioned.

An act[24] for clearing a road from the Warm Springs, in Auguſta, and for other purpoſes therein mentioned.

An act[25] to appoint commiſſioners to view a place propoſed for a road through the South mountain.

An act[26] for building a bridge over the weſtern branch of Nanſemond river by ſubſcription.

An act[27] for eſtabliſhing ſeveral new ferries, and for other purpoſes.

An

1 Hening, VIII, p. 507.　2 Ibid, VIII, p. 511.　3 Ibid, VIII, p. 514.　4 Ibid, VIII, p. 515.
5 Ibid, VIII, p. 516.　6 Ibid, VIII, p. 517.　7 Ibid, VIII, p. 519.　8 Ibid, VIII, p. 520.
9 Ibid, VIII, p. 522.　10 Ibid, VIII, p. 523.　11 Ibid, VIII, p. 524.　12 Ibid, VIII, p. 526.
13 Ibid, VIII, p. 527.　14 Ibid, VIII, p. 529.　15 Ibid, VIII, p. 530.　16 Ibid, VIII, p. 533.
17 Ibid, VIII, p. 534.　18 Ibid, VIII, p. 536.　19 Ibid, VIII, p. 537.　20 Ibid, VIII, p. 539.
21 Ibid, VIII, p. 542.　22 Ibid, VIII, p. 542.　23 Ibid, VIII, p. 543.　24 Ibid, VIII, p. 546.
25 Ibid, VIII, p. 552.　26 Ibid, VIII, p. 552.　27 Ibid, VIII, p. 545.

An act[1] for cutting a navigable canal from Archer's Hope creek to Queen's creek, through or near the city of Williamsburg.

An act[2] to enlarge the power of the trustees appointed to carry into execution an act, passed this present session of Assembly, intituled an act for cutting a navigable canal from Archer's Hope creek to Queen's creek, through or near the city of Williamsburg.

An act[3] for opening the falls of James river, by subscription, and for other purposes.

An act[4] for opening and extending the navigation of the river Potowmack, from Fort Cumberland, to tide water.

An act[5] to amend an act, intituled an act for clearing Mattapony river.

An act[6] to explain and amend an act, intituled an act to oblige the owners of mills, hedges, or stops, on the rivers therein mentioned, to make openings or slopes therein for the passage of fish.

An act[7] to amend an act, intituled an act to amend an act, intituled an act to oblige the owners of mills, hedges, or stone stops, on sundry rivers therein mentioned, to make openings or slopes therein for the passage of fish, and for other purposes therein mentioned.

An act[8] for appointing trustees to regulate the making of slopes for the passage of fish, in the mill dams within the county of Bedford.

An act[9] to revive the act, intituled an act for giving a salary to the Speaker of the House of Burgesses.

An act[10] for further continuing the act, intituled an act for appointing a Treasurer.

An act[11] to enable the Nottoway Indians to lease certain Lands, and for other purposes therein mentioned.

An act[12] to amend an act, intituled an act for the better preservation of the breed of deer, and preventing unlawful hunting.

An act[13] for making further provision for the support and maintenance of Ideots, lunatics, and other persons of unsound minds.

An act[14] for further continuing and amending the act, intituled an act for encreasing the reward for killing wolves, within certain counties, to be paid by the respective counties wherein the services shall be performed.

An act[15] for continuing and amending the act, intituled an act for destroying crows and squirrels in certain counties therein mentioned.

An act[16] for dividing the county of Frederick into three distinct counties.

An act[17] for dividing the county of Botetourt into two distinct counties.

An act[18] to appoint commissioners to strike a dividing line between the counties of Stafford and King George.

An act[19] for adding part of the county of Nansemond to the county of Isle of Wright.

An act[20] for dividing the parishes of Southam, in the county of Cumberland, and Dale, in the county of Chesterfield.

An act[21] for dissolving the vestries of the parish of Saint Martin, in the counties of Hanover and Louisa, and of Saint John, in the county of King William.

An act[22] to empower the vestry of the parish of Saint George, in Spotsylvania, to sell part of the church yard.

An act[23] to allow the Minister of the parish of Antrim, in the county of Halifax, the same salary as other Ministers are intitled to receive.

An act[24] to empower the corporation of the borough of Norfolk to assess a tax on the inhabitants thereof, for the purpose therein mentioned.

An act[25] to encourage the further settlement of the town of Alexandria, in the county of Fairfax.

An act[26] for establishing the town of Fincastle, in the county of Botetourt.

An act[27] for appointing trustees for the town of Cobham, and for other purposes therein mentioned.

An

---

1 Hening, VIII, p. 556. 2 Ibid, VIII, p. 562. 3 Ibid, VIII, p. 564. 4 Ibid, VIII, p. 570.
5 Ibid, VIII, p. 579. 6 Ibid, VIII, p. 581. 7 Ibid, VIII, p. 583. 8 Ibid, VIII, p. 585.
9 Ibid, VIII, p. 587. 10 Ibid, VIII, p. 588. 11 Ibid, VIII, p. 588. 12 Ibid, VIII, p. 591.
13 Ibid, VIII, p. 594. 14 Ibid, VIII, p. 595. 15 Ibid, VIII, p. 596. 16 Ibid, VIII, p. 597.
17 Ibid, VIII, p. 600. 18 Ibid, VIII, p. 601. 19 Ibid, VIII, p. 602. 20 Ibid, VIII, p. 603.
21 Ibid, VIII. p. 607. 22 Ibid, VIII, p. 609. 23 Ibid, VIII, p. 610. 24 Ibid, VIII, p. 611.
25 Ibid, VIII, p. 613. 26 Ibid, VIII, p. 616. 27 Ibid, VIII, p. 617.

164   *An act*[1] *to prevent hogs and goats going at large in the town of Suffolk.*

An act[2] *to establish a town on the land of John Rictor, in the county of Fauquier, and for other purposes.*

An act[3] *for continuing the act, intituled an act, for reimbursing the inhabitants of King William and Hanover counties for the expence of clearing Pamunkey river.*

An act[4] *for appointing commissioners to ascertain the value of certain churches and chapels, in the parishes of Frederick, Norborne, and Beckford, and for other purposes therein mentioned.*

An act[5] *for appointing commissioners for selling the tobacco damaged in the public warehouse, for inspection of tobacco, at Morton's, and for other purposes therein mentioned.*

An act[6] *to enable Henrietta Marmillod to sell and dispose of the estate devised to her by her brother Nathaniel Walthoe, Esq; deceased, notwithstanding her coverture.*

An act[7] *to vest certain intailed lands, whereof Philip Ludwell Grymes, Gentleman, is seised, in William Roane, Gentleman, in fee simple.*

An act[8] *to dock the intail of certain lands, whereof William Todd, Gentleman, is seised, and for other purposes therein mentioned.*

An act[9] *to dock the intail of certain lands, whereof John Hancock is seised, and for settling other lands and slaves in lieu thereof.*

An act[10] *to dock the intail of certain lands, whereof Ralph Wormeley, Esq; is seised.*

An act[11] *to dock the intail of certain land, whereof Nathaniel West Dandridge is seised.*

An act[12] *for vesting in trustees certain lands, whereof William Booth, Gentleman, and Elizabeth his wife, are seised in fee tail, to be sold, and for laying out the money, arising from the sale, in purchasing other lands, to be settled to the same uses.*

An act[13] *to dock the intail of certain lands, whereof James Blackwell, the younger, is seised, and for other purposes therein mentioned.*

An act[14] *to vest certain lands, whereof Colwell Pettypool, and Mary his wife, are seised in fee tail, in Joseph Mayo, and for settling other land and slaves, to be purchased, in lieu thereof.*

A *resolve* for paying four hundred and fifty pounds per annum to *William Rind,* the public printer.

A *resolve* for paying a salary to the keeper of the public gaol.

A *resolve* for paying a salary to *Peter Pelham,* organist.

A *resolve* for paying a sum of money, and an annuity, to *John Robinson.*

A *resolve* for paying a sum of money to *Benjamin Powell.*

A *resolve* for paying several sums of money to *Andrew Estave.*

A *resolve* for paying an annuity to *John Burton.*

A *resolve* for paying several sums of money to *Philip Hand.*

A *resolve* for paying several sums of money to the committee for examining the Treasurer's accounts, and burning the treasury notes.

A *resolve* for paying several sums of money to *George Booth,* and *Richard Allen.*

After which his *Excellency* was pleased to make a Speech to the Council, and this House, as followeth, *viz.*

*Gentlemen of the Council, M*ʳ *Speaker, and Gentlemen of the House of Burgesses,*

The public Business being concluded, it becomes necessary to put an End to this Session of Assembly; and I recommend to you to use your best Endeavours, in your several Counties, to infuse that Spirit of Industry, which alone can make a Country flourish, and to promote a strict Observance of that Order and Regularity, which are equally necessary to the Security of all good Government, as well as to the real Welfare of the People. On my Part, I shall stedfastly watch over the Preservation of your Laws, and ever be ready to administer them for the Protection of all your just Rights and Privileges.

I do prorogue you to Thursday *the twenty-fifth of* June*; you are accordingly prorogued to* Thursday *the twenty-fifth Day of* June *next.*

1 Hening, VIII, p. 620.   2 Ibid, VIII, p. 621.   3 Ibid, VIII, p. 623.   4 Ibid, VIII, p. 623.
5 Ibid, VIII, p. 626.   6 Ibid, VIII, p. 627.   7 Ibid, VIII, p. 630.   8 Ibid, VIII, p. 631.
9 Ibid, VIII, p. 635.   10 Ibid, VIII, p. 637.   11 Ibid, VIII, p. 638.   12 Ibid, VIII, p. 640.
13 Ibid, VIII, p. 641.   14 Ibid, VIII, p. 643.

INDEX

Index

A

Accomac County, Burgesses, 3, 113, 143; Election, 162; Gingoteague, 70; Guilford Inspection, 48; Guy Petition, 180; Mentioned, 181; Petitions, 20, 30, 34, 333; Petition to Divide, 20, 168, 219; Pitt Petition, 206; Pungoteague Warehouse, 43.

Ackiss, John, Burgess, 4, 114.

Acrill, William, Burgess, 3, 113, 143, 157, 158; Signer of Association, xxix.

Acts, of Assembly, Mentioned, xxxi.

Adams, Richard, Burgess, 3, 17, 87, 113, 123, 143, 158, 246, 256, 291; Election, 175, 195; Signer of Association, xxix.

Adams, Thomas, Signer of Association, xxx.

Adie, William, Mentioned, 78.

Africa, Importation of Slaves from, 257, 284.

Agriculture encouraged, 154.

Albemarle County, 54; Burgesses, 3, 113, 143; Election, 162; Petitions, 14, 126, 167; Petition to open road, 168, 211; Road, 32, 37; Saint Anne's Parish, 76; Parish Petition, 224.

Ale, Mentioned, xxviii.

Alexander, John, Burgess, 4, 69, 80, 114, 123, 144, 182, 202, 214, 221, 242, 264, 283, 290, 292, 295; Signer of Association, xxix.

Alexandria, 6, 49, 273; Act to encourage settlement, 310, 316; Bill to encourage settlement, 280, 289, 295, 304; Petitions, 206, 241, 242; Settled, 280.

Alias Capias, writs of, 306, 311, 315.

Alleghany Mountains, Mentioned, xix, xx, xxi, xxii, xxxv.

Alleghany River, Mentioned, xix.

Allen, Richard, Resolve concerning, 313, 317.

Allen, William, Candidate for House of Burgesses, 161.

Alley, Nicholas, Petitioner, 35, 49.

Amelia County, Burgesses, 3, 4, 113, 143; Court, 134, 171; Election, 162; Mentioned, 80; Petitions, 5, 20, 36, 236, 267; For Public Warehouse, 232; Baptists, 185, 188.

America, viii, xviii, xxvi, xxvii, xxviii, 83, 85, 102, 268; Affairs in, xx; British Empire in, xxxii; Episcopal Churches in America, opposed to Episcopate, xxxii; Rights of, xxxii.

American Bishopric, Mentioned, xxxii.

American Dominions, Mentioned, 257.

American State Papers, xxxiv.

American Subjects, Mentioned, xxxii.

Amherst County, Burgesses, 3, 19, 113, 143; Court, 175; Election of Burgesses, 309; Ferry, 293, 294, 297; Fluvanna River, 181; Hancock Petition, 193; Mentioned, 175, 189, 285, 302; Petitions, 14, 124, 127, 131; Sheriff mentioned, 183.

Anconastotah, Indian Chief, xvi.

Anderson, Matthew, Claim, 84; Petition, 16.

Anderson, Richard, Burgess, 3, 90, 113, 143, 222.

Andrews, Robert, Signer of Association, xxxi.

Anne, Queen, Mentioned, 148.

Antrim Parish, 269; Minister's Salary, 272, 293, 304, 310; Minister's Salary Increased, 316; Petition of Rector, 130, 167, 169.

Appomattox River, 5, 20; Ferry, 8; Mentioned, 42, 191, 267.

Aquia Warehouses, Petition of Inspectors, 253, 273.

Archdeacon, James, Signer of Association, xxx.

Archer's Hope Creek, xxxv, 183, 187, 194, 197, 199, 212, 264, 274; Canal, 269, 275, 282, 285, 294, 306, 307, 316.

Armistead, Booth, Deceased, 233, 236.

Armistead, John, 55, 62, 66, 68, 71, 82, 109; Petition, 53.

Armistead, William, 55, 62, 66, 68, 71, 82, 109; Petition, 53.

Arrington, John, Mentioned, 198.

Ashton, Henry, Will, 176.

Ashton, Laurence, Petitioner, 237, 245.

Assembly of 1770, Mentioned, xxv; of 1772, Convened, xxxiii, Mentioned, xxxv; Dissolved, 145; Prorogued, 317. *See* Council, *also* House of Burgesses.

Association of 1770, xxvi, xxvii, xxxi; Signers of, xxix, xxx, xxxi.

Atherton, James, Petition, 155.

Atken, Robert, Mariner, 47, 91.

Atkinson, Roger, Signer of Association, xxxi.

Atlantic, Mentioned, xxxiv.

Attahkullakullah, Indian Chief, xvi.

Attorneys, 12; Petition 9; Practice Regulated, 247, 272.

Atwell, Thomas, Petitioner, 130, 135, 136.

Augusta County, 10, 66, 99; Augusta Parish, 45, 62, 125, 130, 132, 134, 137, 140; Burgesses, 3, 113, 143; Clerk, 239; Election, 162; Holston and New River, 271; Payne's Run, 54; Petitions, 42, 59, 126, 167, 175, 211; Roads, 32, 36, 168, 211, 222, 268, 290, 299, 303, 315; Sheriff, 200, Parish, 130, 132; (Motion to dissolve 45;) Vestry, 62, 125, 134, 137, 140.

Aylett, William, 230; Burgess, 143, 159, 162, 170, 194, 207, 222, 232, 243, 246, 282, 285, 294; Petition 50, 238, 279, 296.

Aylett's Warehouse, 50, 238; Petition of Inspectors, 225, 236.

Ayres, William, Petition, 267.

Ayscough, Christopher, Door-keeper, 101.

B.

Bacon, Lyddal, 263; Member of Committee to Examine Freeholds, 163.

Bailey, Thomas, Burgess, 4, 114, 125; Sheriff of Surry County, 159, 161; Deceased, 162; Signer of Association, xxx.

Bailey, William, 159; Deputy, 162.

Baine, Alexander, Signer of Association, xxx.

Baird, James, Signer of Association, xxxi.

Baker, Benjamin, Burgess, 3, 13, 143, 157, 158, 243, 244; Election of, 40; Mentioned, 121; Signer of Association, xxx.

Baker, Jerman, Signer of Association, xxx.

Baker, Richard, Burgess, 3, 13, 14, 16, 51, 54, 55, 62, 72, 92, 99, 113; Signer of Association, xxix.

Balfour, James, Signer of Association, xxx.

Ball, Spencer Mottrom, Burgess, 3, 113, 123, 143, 182, 206; Signer of Association, xxix.

Ballantine, John, Petitioner, 6.

Bancroft Transcripts, vii, viii, xi, xiii.

Banister, John, Burgess, 3, 94, 113, 125, 127, 143, 157, 213, 221, 243, 277, 284, 292; Signer of Association, xxx.

Banks, Alexander, Signer of Association, xxx.

Banks, Richard, Mentioned, 230.

Baptists, 40, 160, 245; Dissenters, 20.

Barbour, Thomas, Burgess, 3, 113, 125, 144, 204, 205, 275; Signer of Association, xxix.

Barksdale, Nathaniel, Mentioned, 24.

Barraud, Daniel, Signer of Association, xxx.

Barton, Burr, Mentioned, 91.

Barton, David, Petitioner, 54, 76.

Bassett, Burwell, Burgess, 3, 113, 123, 137, 143, 155, 162, 170, 187; Empowered to Erect a Gate, 235; Signer of Association, xxix.

Bates, James, Mentioned, 22, 23, 24, 29, 164, 165; Slave Wounded by, 158; Testimony, 21, 22, 23, 24, 29.

Beckford Parish, Churches, 267, 274, 286, 295, 317; Mentioned, 184; Petition, 197.

Bedford County, Burgesses, 3, 113, 143; Court, 91, 315; Election, 309; Goose Creek, 61, 70, 166, 225; Mentioned, 181, 189, 285, 293, 294, 297; Mill Dams, 290, 308, 310, 313, 316; Petitions, 61, 69, 166, 168, 237, 243, 249; Russell Parish, 269; Trustees Appointed, 280.

Beds, xxviii.

Beef, xxviii, 51, 58, 107, 292, 302, 311, 314; Inspected, 13.

Beer, xxviii.

Bell, Henry, Burgess, 143, 158, 159, 241.

Bell, James, Burgess, 4, 5, 114.

Bell, John, Signer of Association, xxx.

Bennett's Creek, 198.

Berkeley County, Burgesses, 143.

Berkeley, Edmund, Burgess, 113, 121, 143, 157, 214, 221, 271, 294.

Berkeley, Norborne, Baron de Botetourt, Governor of Virginia, 115. *See* Botetourt, Baron de, Governor of Virginia.

Bermuda Hundred, Eppes Petition, 41; Petition, 32; Warehouse Tobacco Stolen out, 43.